LAW AND ECONO
WITH CHINESE CHARA

THE INITIATIVE FOR POLICY DIALOGUE SERIES

The Initiative for Policy Dialogue (IPD) brings together the top voices in development to address some of the most pressing and controversial debates in economic policy today. The IPD book series approaches topics such as capital market liberalization, macroeconomics, environmental economics, and trade policy from a balanced perspective, presenting alternatives, and analyzing their consequences on the basis of the best available research. Written in a language accessible to policymakers and civil society, this series will rekindle the debate on economic policy and facilitate a more democratic discussion of development around the world.

OTHER TITLES PUBLISHED BY OXFORD UNIVERSITY PRESS IN THIS SERIES

Fair Trade for All
Joseph E. Stiglitz and Andrew Charlton

Economic Development and Environmental Sustainability
Edited by Ramón López and Michael A. Toman

Stability with Growth
Joseph E. Stiglitz, José Antonio Ocampo, Shari Spiegel, Ricardo Ffrench-Davis, and Deepak Nayyar

The Washington Consensus Reconsidered
Narcis Serra and Joseph E. Stiglitz

Capital Market Liberalization and Development
Edited by José Antonio Ocampo and Joseph E. Stiglitz

Industrial Policy and Development
Edited by Mario Cimoli, Giovanni Dosi, and Joseph E. Stiglitz

Time for a Visible Hand
Edited by Stephany Griffith-Jones, José Antonio Ocampo, and Joseph E. Stiglitz

Debates in the Measurement of Global Poverty
Edited by Sudhir Anand, Paul Segal, and Joseph E. Stiglitz

Overcoming Developing Country Debt Crises
Edited by Barry Herman, José Antonio Ocampo, and Shari Spiegel

Good Growth and Governance in Africa
Edited by Akbar Noman, Kwesi Botchwey, Howard Stein, and Joseph E. Stiglitz

The Economic Development of Latin America since Independence
Luis Bértola and José Antonio Ocampo

Law and Economics with Chinese Characteristics
Edited by David Kennedy and Joseph E. Stiglitz

Law and Economics with Chinese Characteristics

Institutions for Promoting Development in the Twenty-First Century

Edited by
DAVID KENNEDY AND JOSEPH E. STIGLITZ

OXFORD
UNIVERSITY PRESS

OXFORD
UNIVERSITY PRESS

Great Clarendon Street, Oxford, OX2 6DP,
United Kingdom

Oxford University Press is a department of the University of Oxford.
It furthers the University's objective of excellence in research, scholarship,
and education by publishing worldwide. Oxford is a registered trade mark of
Oxford University Press in the UK and in certain other countries

First Edition published in 2013

Impression: 1

British Library Cataloguing in Publication Data
Data available

ISBN 978–0–19–969854–7 (Hbk)
978–0–19–969855–4 (Pbk)

Printed in Great Britain by
MPG Printgroup, UK

Contents

List of Figures

List of Tables

Notes on Contributors

Kenneth Ayotte is a Professor of Law at Northwestern University School of Law. His areas of interest are bankruptcy, corporate finance, and law and economics. He is the coeditor of the *Research Handbook on the Economics of Property Law* with Henry E. Smith (Edward Elgar Press, 2011) and coauthor of "Optimal Property Rights in Financial Contracting" with Patrick Bolton (*Review of Financial Studies*, forthcoming).

Patrick Bolton is the Barbara and David Zalaznick Professor of Business and member of the Committee on Global Thought at Columbia University. He is also Codirector of the Center for Contracts and Economic Organization at Columbia Law School. His areas of interest are in corporate finance, banking, sovereign debt, political economy, and law and economics. He recently published *Contract Theory* with Mathias Dewatripont (MIT Press, 2005) and coedited *Credit Markets for the Poor* with Howard Rosenthal (Russell Sage Foundation, 2005).

Heping Cao is Professor in the School of Economics at Peking University. His research currently focuses on the study of PIPEs and Chinese financial markets. He has published books and papers both in Chinese and English. He received his PhD from The Ohio State University.

Cai Fang is Professor and Director of the Institute of Population and Labor Economics, Chinese Academy of Social Science (CASS). His research covers economic reform and development, labor migration, and employment in China. He graduated from Renmin University of China in 1982 and received his PhD in economics from Graduate School of the Chinese Academy of Social Sciences in 1989.

Jean-Paul Fitoussi is Professor Emeritus at the Institut d'Études Politiques de Paris and the LUISS, Roma. He is Research Director at the Observatoire Français des Conjonctures Economiques, an institute dedicated to economic research and forecasting of which he was the President from 1990 to 2010. In 1996, he was appointed member of the Economic Commission of the Nation. He was an expert at the European Parliament, Commission of Monetary and Economic Affairs from 2000 to 2010. His research centers on macroeconomics, inequalities and social policies.

Qin Gao is Associate Professor at Fordham University and Research Associate at the Columbia Population Research Center. Her research centers on social policies and their impact on poverty, income inequality, and family economic and subjective well-being. Her most recent work examines the Chinese welfare system in transition and the effectiveness of China's primary anti-poverty program—Dibao.

Antara Haldar is University Lecturer in Law at the University of Cambridge. She was a Research Fellow at the Committee on Global Thought at Columbia University and a Jean Monnet Fellow at the European University Institute. She received her PhD in Law from Trinity College, University of Cambridge, and holds degrees in both economics and law. Her research focuses mostly on issues of law and development.

She is the recipient of numerous academic grants and awards, including the University of Cambridge's prestigious Yorke Prize.

David Kennedy is Manley O. Hudson Professor of Law and Faculty Director of the Institute for Global Law and Policy at Harvard Law School. He teaches international law, international economic policy, legal theory, law and development, and European law. He joined the Harvard Law Faculty in 1981 and holds a PhD from the Fletcher School at Tufts University and a JD from Harvard. He is the author of numerous articles on international law and global governance.

James Kai-sing Kung is Chair Professor and a Senior Fellow of the Institute of Advanced Studies at the Hong Kong University of Science and Technology. He has published widely in the areas of economic development, economic history, and political economy of China in journals including *American Journal of Political Science*, *Review of Economics and Statistics*, and *Explorations in Economic History*.

Zheng Liang is Associate Professor at the School of Public Policy and Management at Tsinghua University and is a Research Fellow of the China Institute for Science and Technology Policy. His current research focuses on science and technology policy, IPR management, and the globalization of R & D. He has published nearly thirty papers in academic journals and co-authored five books.

Benjamin L. Liebman is Professor of Law and the Director of the Center for Chinese Legal Studies at Columbia Law School. His current research focuses on the role of the media in the Chinese legal system, on Chinese tort law, and on the evolution of China's courts and legal profession. Prior to joining the Columbia faculty in 2002, Professor Liebman was an associate in the London and Beijing offices of Sullivan & Cromwell. He also previously served as a law clerk to Justice David Souter and to Judge Sandra Lynch of the First Circuit.

Justin Yifu Lin is Professor and honorary dean, National School of Development at Peking University. He was Senior Vice President and Chief Economist of the World Bank in 2008–12. He received his PhD in Economics from the University of Chicago in 1986 and was the Founding Director and Professor of the China Centre for Economic Research (CCER) at Peking University (1994–2008).

Mingxing Liu is Associate Professor at the China Institute for Educational Finance Research at Peking University. He works on China's economic transition, growth, and local governance. He has published numerous academic articles in international and Chinese journals such as the *Journal of Comparative Economics*, *Urban Studies*, *Political Studies*, and *China Quarterly*.

Curtis J. Milhaupt is Parker Professor of Comparative Corporate Law and Fuyo Professor of Japanese Law at Columbia Law School. His research focuses on the interaction between legal systems and economic organizations and development in comparative perspective. His most recent books include *Law and Capitalism* (with Katharina Pistor) and the edited volume *Transforming Corporate Governance in East Asia*.

Katharina Pistor is Michael I. Sovern Professor of Law at Columbia Law School where she teaches corporate law, comparative law, and law and development. Her research focuses on the legal and institutional underpinnings of economic growth and development and the transformation of law in light of globalization.

Roy Prosterman is Founder and Chairman Emeritus of Landesa (formerly the Rural Development Institute) and Professor Emeritus of Law at the University of Washington in Seattle. Landesa partners with governments to secure land rights for the world's poorest, having worked in over fifty countries, including work in rural China that began in 1987. Professor Prosterman has written extensively on land tenure reform issues.

Carl Riskin is Distinguished Professor of Economics at Queens College, City University of New York, and Senior Research Scholar at Columbia University's Weatherhead East Asian Institute. His research has focused recently on aspects of social development in China, especially the changing faces of poverty and inequality.

Francesco Saraceno is Senior Economist at OFCE-Sciences Po. His main research interests include the relationship between inequality and macroeconomic performance, European macroeconomic policies, and interaction between structural reforms and fiscal and monetary policies. In 2000 he became a member of the Council of Economic Advisors for the Italian Prime Minister's Office. He received his PhDs in Economics from Columbia University and La Sapienza University of Rome.

Joseph E. Stiglitz is University Professor at Columbia University, winner of the 2001 Nobel Memorial Prize in Economics, and a lead author of the 1995 report of the IPCC, which shared the 2007 Nobel Peace Prize. He was chairman of the US Council of Economic Advisors under President Clinton and Chief Economist and Senior Vice President of the World Bank for 1997–2000. Prior to Columbia he held the Drummond Professorship at All Souls College Oxford, and professorships at Yale, Stanford, and Princeton. He is the author of the best-selling *Globalization and Its Discontents*, *Making Globalization Work*, *Fair Trade For All*, and most recently *The Price of Inequality: How Today's Divided Society Endangers Our Future.* He has presented invited lectures on many occasions at the China Development Forum and other events in China.

Ran Tao is Professor in the School of Economics and Director of the China Center for Public Economics and Governance at Renmin University in Beijing. A specialist in the Chinese economy, he has published on the political economy of China's economic transition, land and household registration reform in China's urbanization, local governance, and public finance in rural China. His research has appeared most recently in the Journal of Comparative Economics, Journal of Development Studies, Land Economics, Urban Studies, Political Studies, China Quarterly, and *Land Use Policy.*

Tim Wu is Professor at Columbia Law School and currently serving as Senior Advisor to the Federal Trade Commission. He is the author of *The Master Switch* (Alfred A. Knopf, 2010) which won the Shields Prize as Best Business Book of the year. His best-known work is the development of Net Neutrality theory, but he has also written about copyright and international trade. He was recognized as one of

Harvard's 100 most influential graduates by 02138 magazine, and graduated from McGill University (BSc), and Harvard Law School.

Chenggang Xu is Quoin Professor in the Economic Development at the University of Hong Kong. He has taught and worked at the London School of Economics, Harvard, the IMF, Tsinghua University, and the Chinese Academy of Social Sciences. He has been President of the Asian Law and Economics Association since 2010. He has been involved in Chinese reform debates since the 1980s. He holds a PhD from Harvard.

Lan Xue is a Professor and Dean of the School of Public Policy and Management at Tsinghua University. His teaching and research interests include innovation policy and crisis management. He is also a Nonresident Senior Fellow at the Brookings Institution, a member of the Visiting Committee for Harvard Kennedy School, and a member of the Board of Governors of the International Development Research Center (IDRC). He has a PhD in Engineering and Public Policy from Carnegie Mellon University.

Zhong Zhang is a Lecturer at the School of East Asian Studies at the University of Sheffield. He studied and practiced law in China prior to moving to the UK to pursue a PhD in Law at the University of Manchester. His research interests include Chinese corporate law, securities law, and corporate governance.

Feizhou Zhou is Associate Professor in the Department of Sociology at Peking University. His research focuses primarily on China's rural development and government behavior. He has a PhD in social science from Hong Kong University of Science and Technology.

Introduction

David Kennedy and Joseph E. Stiglitz

As the link between law and economic development has been increasingly recognized, it has become commonplace to assert that development is not possible without a "rule of law" and good property rights. Today, these ideas are promoted in the academy, in the development policy community, and by leading international financial institutions, intergovernmental and nongovernmental organizations. There is even a special unit within the UNDP devoted to the promotion of these ideas.[1] Law is certainly crucial for economic development. But what *kind* of "rule of law" is desirable? What constitutes "good" property rights?

These questions are of particular importance to China as it continues the march toward a market economy "with Chinese characteristics" that it began in 1979, a little more than thirty years ago. China's Eleventh Five-Year Plan recognized that one of the key challenges going forward is to create the institutional infrastructure to facilitate the development of such a market, including an appropriate legal framework of institutions, rules, and regulations. The papers collected here illuminate today's debates about just what legal arrangements are, in fact, appropriate for a market "with Chinese characteristics."

We focus on two broad questions. How might one define and regulate property and other legal rights in a market economy "with Chinese characteristics?" And how should we understand China's experience with significant questions of constitutional design, particularly with respect to centralization and decentralization, and the role of the judiciary? We hope to make visible the range of experimentation and the diversity of experience with legal and institutional design in China, while also offering a range of perspectives on the relevance of Western experience and Western ideas about the links between legal arrangements and economic performance.

We stress throughout the significance—and breadth—of the choices available for China as it establishes the ground rules and institutional structures for an expanding market economy. A key set of issues, discussed below, concerns property rights. A major strand of work in law and development has argued that establishing well-defined property rights is the *central* problem in development. We challenge that presumption. Indeed, we should probably place terms such as "property rights" in quotations, for it is not at all clear what such terms should mean. That is one of the questions under discussion here. Some of the papers in this volume even question the widespread assumption that a better legal system involves a more precise definition of property rights.

These choices are often discussed in the shadow of quite specific ideas about what has and has not worked in the West. While most policymakers know that China could not and should not simply "borrow" legal and institutional frameworks from the United States or some other advanced industrial country, there is no shortage of proposals to import this or that supposedly "best practice" legal arrangement from the West. On the whole, we are skeptical about this kind of importation. This book, in contrast, focuses on what China might indeed learn from the history of the quite different choices that various Western nations have made, and the various ways their choices have played out.

Contemporary discussions of economic development policy, as well as of the legal and institutional arrangements most conducive to sound policy, continue to be influenced by the neoliberal intellectual framework that dominated thinking among economists and jurists in the later years of the last century, especially those informed by the Chicago School tradition.[2] In our view, this orthodoxy, which remains prominent in much of both the legal and the economic academy, is a poor guide to the legal and institutional choices facing China today. This book draws on other traditions within economic and legal thought to highlight the range of choices available to China as it lays the foundations for its own market economy.

The orthodoxy is correct, however, in its insistence that background entitlements are absolutely central to the operation of markets. Legal arrangements matter. How entitlements are allocated and defined can make all the difference over time. They could determine, for instance, whether there emerges a large class of landless peasants, or a small elite group dominating the economy. As a result, it is absolutely critical to focus on the allocation of property and other background entitlements as China sets up the framework for its own distinctive market economy. These background rules—to which we should add corporate law, bankruptcy law, and rules about finance—structure the players who will participate in markets, and how they will interact, settling their respective powers and obligations while establishing an initial allocation of resources, income streams, and risk.

The fact that we dwell so long on issues pertaining to property rights may seem strange in a book about contemporary Chinese economic policy. Economic policy seems far more a matter of institutional arrangements and the details of regulation than of property rights. Private law—contracts, property, the law of obligations—is generally considered part of the *background* for economic policy-making. We are convinced, however, that at this juncture, a rigorous assessment of the nature of property rights is warranted.

We do not intend to provide detailed prescriptions for reforming the legal and institutional structures in any country. Rather, we hope to contribute to debates within academia and within policymaking circles by expanding and informing the intellectual frameworks through which choices among legal and institutional possibilities are made, both in the developing world and in the advanced industrial societies. The fact that China is in the midst of designing its legal and regulatory framework—making decisions that will affect the shape of its economy for decades to come—gives, of course, particular salience to this debate. China provides a concrete setting within which these issues can be discussed.

This book is the result of a series of dialogues among academics and policy-makers from China and around the world, held at the Brooks World Poverty Institute at the University of Manchester, at Columbia University (under the auspices of the Initiative for Policy Dialogue and the Committee on Global Thought), and in Beijing (at Peking University, with the joint sponsorship of the Initiative for Policy Dialogue, the Committee on Global Thought, Columbia Global Centers Beijing, Peking University, Tsinghua University, China Development Research Foundation, The Institute for Global Law and Policy at Harvard Law School, and Brooks World Poverty Institute).[3]

Our authors straddle ongoing intellectual debates in a variety of ways. Some are more familiar with the Chinese economic experience and reflect here on the institutional and legal elements that have been—and ought to be—enshrined within it by focusing on specific policy areas and challenges, from decentralization to health care and urban policy. Individual papers within this volume examine the details of specific development policies and institutional characteristics of the emerging Chinese market economy, assessing the record of the last years and highlighting elements that have—and have not—been successful. Other authors are more familiar with Western debates about the relationship between legal forms and economic performance. They reflect here on the lessons for and from the Chinese experience for our understanding of the links between economics and law. Our authors are not at all of one mind about the nature of the Chinese market economy, nor about the relationship between legal arrangements and economic performance. The authors do share the conviction that China is now entering a critical phase in its economic development and its move to a market economy with Chinese characteristics and that law and institutions are crucial components in the development equation. Each has something important to contribute to our understanding of the potential significance of diverse legal forms for the future of Chinese market capitalism.

TOWARDS A MARKET ECONOMY WITH CHINESE CHARACTERISTICS

China, as we have noted, is now entering a critical phase in its move to a market economy. There are, of course, a variety of types of market economies—the Scandinavian model differs from the Anglo-American, the Japanese, or the Continental European models. Every market economy has distinctive legal and institutional arrangements that reflect its own political, social, and cultural history. History and culture continue to matter, if only because they affect norms and beliefs, which in turn affect how legal and institutional arrangements work in practice. China has committed itself to developing a market economy with its own distinctive characteristics. Those distinctive features are now becoming visible and have increasingly become subjects of debate, both within and outside China, particularly where they diverge from what is understood in one or another place to be "best practice." Our authors offer a number of perspectives on what has and has not worked to this point.

A distinguishing feature of China's evolution, however, is that the economy continues to change rapidly, changing the institutional forms through which economic life proceeds. At one stage, township and village enterprises (so-called "TVEs") dominated China's development strategy. At another, joint ventures dominated. There is no reason to believe that the structures that have dominated in the past decade will do so in the next. Indeed, China has committed itself to deep structural change: for instance, by seeking to become less dependent on exports and to reduce adverse environmental impacts. Organizational forms and regulatory incentives will also need to be able to change. A commitment to economic change and flexibility demands legal and institutional arrangements that are themselves both robust and flexible.

Legal and institutional regimes are constantly evolving through administrative, judicial, and regulatory processes. In every society, the people who participate are affected by political and intellectual currents whether they are elected or appointed. Moreover, institutional and legal structures create vested interests and help form coalitions that shape these processes. We have seen how, in America, they helped shape a process that led to financial market deregulation and bank bailouts; those same processes are helping to shape the post-crisis regulatory debate. The relationship between political choices and institutional forms is itself dynamic and iterative. This will also be true for China.

Nevertheless, starting points matter. Early decisions must be taken with a view toward their dynamic impact on the operation of an evolving market. Discussions over the next few years will have a major effect in determining the kind of market economy into which China will evolve. That evolution will condition—and be conditioned by—the legal and institutional arrangements that are now being put in place. Legal arrangements entrench interests, conditioning the dynamic evolution of market forms. Legal frameworks governing property rights, competition, corporate governance, intellectual property, bankruptcy, contracts, and more will influence what it will mean a generation from now to say the market economy is one with "Chinese characteristics." As a result, this is a particularly important moment to assess differences in institutional arrangements and their consequences. What would normally be an academic exercise could turn out to have an enormous impact on a quarter of the world's population. This volume aims to clarify choices now available to China as it establishes what will become the long-term framework for its own distinctive market economy.

THE RELEVANCE OF LEGAL TRANSPLANTS FOR CHINA

Early on, China recognized that it needed to have a distinctive form of market economy, appropriate to its distinctive circumstances and history. Even with clarity about the kind of economy and society China would like to create going forward, it is not clear now precisely what kinds of legal and institutional arrangements are necessary to achieve those goals. China faces debates about regulation, property rights, and institutional forms that are familiar among economists in the West. Just how relevant are their answers? It is easy to imagine that one might learn what China needs to do to achieve success by studying the legal and institutional arrangements of development success stories—perhaps particularly the advanced industrial economies of North America and Western Europe.

As it turns out, however, these societies have a wide range of distinctive legal and institutional features. Some of their differences are accidents of history and others reflect deeply held cultural views and political choices. Whether these arrangements, transported elsewhere, would be equally successful—or would even embody the same values and political choices—is far from clear. In our experience, those living in a given market economy often overestimate the importance of their own distinctive national arrangements to their own economic success. They may even come to feel their own institutions are required for the success of any market economy. Remarkably, people may feel this way even about institutional arrangements that have resulted from historical accidents or cultural developments far from economic policy—and where other nations have experienced superior economic performance with alternative arrangements. As a result, it is wise to exercise care in looking for successful legal arrangements to import.

Accordingly, we bring a deep skepticism about the desirability of extending popular, if largely mistaken, pieties about the legal prerequisites for strong economic performance in a market economy. Indeed, our discussions over the last three years have left us ever more hesitant to extrapolate from what we think we know about the relationship between law and economics in the West to what ought to characterize the institutional and legal framework for further development in China.

In good part, our hesitance arises from the realization that much "common sense" about the relationship between law and economics in the West itself is incorrect. While it is widely accepted that developing countries need to adopt "good" legal frameworks, there is no agreement today about what that means. If this could be said before the global financial crisis, it is even more so today, as even those in the West are questioning the assumptions underlying the policy frameworks and legal structures that govern economic affairs.

The crisis has destroyed a large number of prevailing myths and shibboleths. It has even thrown into doubt our ability to recognize "bad" frameworks. For instance, independent central banks were supposed to be the "best practice" institutional arrangement for governing financial markets. As it was, more independent central banks, such as those in the US and Europe, performed less well than did less independent central banks, such as those of India, China, and Brazil. The independent central banks were evidently more easily captured by the financial sector that they were supposed to be regulating.

Similarly, before the crisis, most would have thought of America's financial regulatory structure as exemplary. The international financial institutions had urged countries around the world to aspire to that as a "model." The crisis exposed the US regulatory system as having been "captured" (intellectually, if not financially) by those it was supposed to regulate. A system of "revolving doors" on the part of those who wrote and implemented regulations created distorted incentives. And the problems weren't limited to America's financial regulatory structure: defects in corporate governance help explain why bank executives may have done so well, even as shareholders and bondholders lost so much.

Intellectual property provides another example, which we discuss below. While there is widespread support for the notion that there should be some form of intellectual property protection, details matter. America held up its intellectual property regime as "best practice" and tried to extend it to the rest of the world. Within the United States, meanwhile, dissatisfaction with the intellectual property regime has grown. For example, many in the software industry worry that it stifles innovation, while many health advocates believe it impairs access to life-saving medicines. The social, political, and economic choices embedded in the intellectual property regime have been reopened for debate.

This book begins where confidence in the right answers and model practices fades.

THE UNFORTUNATE IMPORTANCE OF NEOLIBERAL POLICY ORTHODOXY

Even as China works to create its own distinctive legal and institutional framework, it will inevitably look to "models" abroad. It will strive to incorporate at least the best ideas, if not the best practices. Moreover, China's success over the past three decades is in no small measure a result of globalization. It will, at the very least, need to harmonize, to some extent, its policy frameworks with those of the rest of the world. As it seeks to attract investment, it will inevitably be sensitive to others' perspectives on its own legal and institutional framework. Much of the debate within the papers in this volume centers around the economic significance of particular regulatory arrangements and forms of property often associated with the Anglo-American economic tradition.[4] The question is, to what extent are these appropriate for China today?

In recent years, as we commented earlier, ideas about the role of law in development have been greatly influenced by attitudes about law held by Chicago School economists responsible for the neoliberal consensus about what constitutes good national economic policy. At the same time, many economists and legal scholars in the United States—and in the international financial institutions—have developed theories and launched empirical studies suggesting the superiority of specific legal and institutional arrangements they regard as characteristic of the Anglo-American model of market economy and which they see as expressing the unvarying demands of market efficiency. One result of this intellectual work has been the emergence, starting in the mid-1980s, of a powerful orthodoxy about the "best practice" legal and institutional arrangements for market efficiency and growth. This legal orthodoxy has run parallel to—and often been linked with—neoliberal economic policy orthodoxy. Like their neoliberal economic cousins, neoliberal proponents of "best practice" legal arrangements have been active in global debates about the institutional framework for national development. They have also been active in discussions about Chinese economic policy, promoting these "best practice" legal and institutional forms as integral to China's transition to a market economy.

In broad terms, the neoliberal orthodoxy, both legal and economic, has been hostile to economic regulation and supportive only of those specific rules thought necessary to "support" markets. The list of legal rules necessary to support a market can seem quite limited: a clear assignment of property rights, strong and independent judiciary to enforce those entitlements, the institutional framework for an independent monetary policy, an effective criminal justice system, particularly with respect to corruption. Other rules are broadly viewed as "distorting" the work of market forces, however important they may be as expressions of political or moral commitment. Underlying this set of policy preferences is a strong presumption that markets are competitive, that the pricing mechanism operates effectively, that markets can handle externalities and public goods on their own, that individuals should bear responsibility for protecting themselves (*caveat emptor*), and that an economic policy oriented to growth ought to distinguish what is necessary for efficiency from what might be desirable for other reasons. There is little attention in this framework to the conditions that might transform efficiency into growth, or to the availability of alternative development paths and alternative equilibria with different distributional effects.

Interestingly, just as these ideas were gaining currency in development policy discussions, the Chicago tradition was itself coming under attack both by economists and legal scholars. In both legal and economic circles, the challenges have been empirical and historical as well as analytic and theoretical.

The historical/empirical critique

Economists and legal scholars have challenged the association of the policies associated with neoliberal economic and legal orthodoxy with economic growth and efficient market organization. They have questioned whether these legal arrangements can be reliably linked, theoretically or empirically, either to market efficiency or to growth, let alone both. East Asia's success—the most rapid growth in the history of the world—based on other premises provides evidence that the neoliberal model (both the economic and legal doctrines) is not necessary for growth. The failure of so many Latin American countries that attempted to follow neoliberal dictates provides evidence that the model is not sufficient for growth. And the repeated crises confronting economies that have adopted that model—of which the current crisis is the most recent and most devastating—shows that whatever growth is produced may not be sustainable and that the "model" is subject to high levels of instability, imposing costs that few developing countries can afford.

Critics of the neoliberal legal movement have gone further, even questioning whether the paradigmatic "best practice" legal forms actually do characterize the American economy. The global financial crisis has shown, for instance, real weaknesses in America's ability to address the legal issues posed as so many debtors are unable or unwilling to meet their obligations. The legal and economic system allowed conflicts of interest to arise between holders of first and second mortgages, and between service providers—conflicts that impaired efficient restructurings of the mortgages.

But even if America's "best practice" legal structures worked well for America at one time, there is no presumption that they will be well designed for another. Questions have also been raised about whether these legal forms can really be made universal, rooted as they are in quite specific cultural and political commitments. Notions such as "best practices" and the ability to transplant legal frameworks from one society—where it might indeed have worked well—to another have all come to be questioned.

All of this raises questions about whether neoliberal legal orthodoxy is at all appropriate for China today—or even provides an appropriate point of departure. To answer that question, it is important to grasp the extent to which the intellectual underpinnings of the neoliberal orthodoxy have also been theoretically and analytically eroded.

The economic critique

The most straightforward and well-known theoretical critique of the neoliberal policy orthodoxy came from within economics. The foundation for the policy prescriptions of the neoliberal tradition was a set of hypotheses about how markets work. The most important of these is the presumption that they are (Pareto)-efficient. The *economic model* was shown to be badly flawed and its conclusions dependent on highly unrealistic assumptions. Slight changes in those assumptions, especially in the direction of increased realism, lead to markedly different results. Even slight frictions could, for instance, lead to highly noncompetitive outcomes. Advances in economics (theoretical and empirical), including the development of game theory and theories of asymmetric information, have provided alternative frameworks, with strikingly different conclusions and markedly different policy implications.

The broad resistance to regulation associated with neoliberal orthodoxy has been criticized by economists as the underlying economic presumptions have been undermined by research over the past three decades. If markets are not in general efficient (which they are not), then there is a role for the state, in addition to *supporting* the market—a market-"correcting" role. Contrary to the neoliberal view, "market failures" are pervasive.

Moreover, while the neoliberal orthodoxy focuses on efficiency, standard economic theory never provided any presumption that market outcomes were "socially acceptable," consistent with any principle of social justice or solidarity. Nor was there any presumption that a Pareto-efficient equilibrium would generate development or lead to growth. The underlying theoretical separation of efficiency from other considerations has been undermined by critiques of the neoclassical model stretching back more than thirty years. It is now clear that in establishing the institutional structure for a market economy, more than efficiency is of concern. Today, almost all societies understand that markets by themselves lead to unacceptable environmental degradation. There is a need for environmental regulation—something that China too has recognized. The neoliberal legal model was not only based on a flawed economic model—its tenets did not necessarily lead to overall economic efficiency—but even more importantly, it left out critical issues of equity and social justice, that we believe need to be at the heart of a country's legal system.

Not surprisingly, given the lack of robustness of the model, the policy conclusions—including for the design of legal and institutional frameworks—were also shown not to be robust. Chicago School reasoning had, for instance, led to skepticism about whether predatory pricing could occur, with the result that the US Supreme Court imposed a heavy burden on anyone attempting to bring a predatory pricing case under the competition laws. Anyone schooled in the new and more robust theories would have come to quite different conclusions. Not only did the newer theories show that markets are not in general (Pareto)-efficient, but they also explained why one cannot separate out issues of equity and efficiency.[5] Choices still need to be made.

The Chicago School ideas about economics have come under particular criticism in the aftermath of the Great Recession of 2008, with leading policymakers (such as Alan Greenspan) and leading thinkers (such as Richard Posner) engaging in what appears to be at least a partial recantation.[6] After all, the neoliberal orthodoxy had helped shape not only the legal framework, but also the behavior of regulators and regulatory policy—and even affected the behavior of investors and banks.

The legal critique

Within the legal academy, the attack was complementary and, in some ways, deeper. To start, it is critical to understand that the background rules structuring market arrangements are not natural entitlements—they are social arrangements designed to promote social objectives. This is most obvious in the case of newer legal innovations such as "intellectual property" or "limited liability corporations." These are social constructions, the merits and designs of which have to be constantly evaluated and reevaluated. But it is no less true of "property" and "contract." In every market economy, each is a complex legal regime reflecting a history of social, political, and economic conflict and debate.

In practice, the legal and institutional structures provide some of the most important "social protections" in modern societies. In every market economy, the particular form of these structures reflects social as well as economic considerations. This is also the case in China. Inattention to the relationship between economic opportunities and social outcomes can have terrible consequences that are difficult or impossible to correct through the political process. The regulatory failures of the financial system in America have resulted in wiping out a significant fraction of the wealth of America's poorest families, unlikely to be made up for by redistributions. The institutional framework has, simultaneously, played an important role in the creation of large inequalities—again, not typically offset by political action. Laws allowing financial firms to engage in predatory lending, combined with new bankruptcy laws, have created a new class of partially indentured servants—people who may have to give as much as 25 percent of what they earn for the rest of their lives to the banks.

In many societies, the place of social responsibilities in the legal architecture for the economy is being rethought. In some nations this has occurred at the constitutional level. South Africa's Constitution incorporated new social and economic rights, including rights relating to housing which have been given new meanings and importance by the judiciary. India's Supreme Court has expanded rights to include environmental protection and access to food. American courts have long supported certain rights to education. Many countries recognize rights to health care. What is entailed by these social and economic rights—how expansive they are—has been a major source of debate. These debates are visible when they play out at the constitutional or legislative level, but they are equally significant in the elaboration of background norms structuring the market itself. Where, as in China, those foundational legal arrangements are being established or altered, the same social considerations come into play.

The legal structure of property and contract, like that of corporate authority and finance, everywhere reflects a complex series of trade-offs among social interests. There is no particular set of rules that is Pareto-optimal—best for all stakeholders—as many economic policymakers influenced by the Chicago School sometimes seem to suggest. Even if there were such a set of rules, there is no assurance they would be Pareto-optimal at another time or in another place. Sometimes rights conflict—unfettered property rights exercised by one individual may conflict with others' right to the environment. Legal frameworks specify how these rights are to be balanced. Establishing a regime of background rules distributes power and resources among various potential market players. There are winners and losers. Background rules often institutionalize these initial gains and losses in ways that compound differences over time. Different institutional designs can lead to quite different outcomes.

In a deeper sense, neoliberal policy orthodoxy ignores a set of basic truths about transforming economic ideas into legal institutions and about the nature of legal reasoning itself. The central distinctions upon which the neoliberal orthodoxy rests turn out to be extremely difficult to maintain when translated into legal terms. The boundary between "market-supporting" and "market-distorting" legal arrangements is notoriously hard to draw. The more you look at it, the harder it is to distinguish private entitlements enforced by the state from regulations imposed by legislation or administrative action. Moreover, distributional choices are built into all these legal rules and institutions that affect both efficiency and equity. More broadly, legal frameworks are both conceptually and sociologically more complex, with more room for choice among alternative legal arrangements than was appreciated by many Chicago School economists who became interested in law as a development tool.

Indeed, a "law and economics" tradition has long existed in the American legal academy, which begins with the necessity to attend to precisely these choices and complexities. Within the legal academy, even those who find the neo-classical economics of the Chicago School largely compelling recognize that when turned into a vernacular for policy, the Chicago School has carried with it unwarranted assumptions about the legal rules that structure a market. Economic actors bargain in the shadow of background rules that distribute bargaining power amongst them. Those initial distributions matter to both efficiency as well as equity, given the transaction costs associated with reallocation.

In the simplistic economic models underlying the Chicago School approach, as we have seen, issues of equity and efficiency are neatly separated. The crude implication for policy is often to assume that distribution can wait—the first objective ought to be efficiency. For development, of course, distribution often cannot wait—efficiency may be less a sure recipe for growth than a ticket to another low-level equilibrium. Focusing on the legal regime, however, brings distribution back into the story right from the start. The background rules of property and contract that undergird market transactions reflect distributional choices that cannot be divided, either sociologically or conceptually, between those which concern efficiency and equity. After all, prices emerge from bargains among people with different entitlements—the structure of those entitlements will affect those bargains.[7]

This might matter less if entitlements could be costlessly rearranged by the market. Indeed, one often finds reference to this idea in the neoliberal economic literature, attributed to Ronald Coase.[8] Unfortunately, things are not this simple. First, as Coase himself recognized, transaction costs are ubiquitous and matter for the assignment of property rights. A long tradition of legal analysis has focused on the implications of this recognition for policy—the ways in which the assignment of property rights might affect the size and impact of transaction costs.[9] Second, the market through which these entitlements might be rearranged must itself also be legally constituted. The power of actors, whether individuals or firms, must be established, their authority with respect to various entitlements specified, the conditions for the enforcement of contracts to rearrange entitlements spelled out, and so forth. In short, from a legal perspective there must be entitlements before there is a market for entitlements, allocating bargaining power and affecting transaction costs in ways that may matter for efficiency as well as equity.

Interestingly, on the "economics" side of neoliberal orthodoxy about development policy, these legal qualifications have often gone unnoticed. The importance of transaction costs has often been ignored or relegated to a footnote, with the implication that, to a first-order approximation, the assignment of property rights made no difference. The importance of background norms to bargaining power and the centrality of distribution to the legal structure of a market have been downplayed. Ironically, this has occurred at the same time advances in economics recognized the importance of these frictions, especially those associated with information costs and asymmetries.[10]

Among economists, there was often an oversimplification of "property rights," a failure to note the responsibilities that might be associated with these rights (an owner of property may be responsible for making sure his property is not used to dump toxic wastes); a failure to note the multiple dimensions of property (in many countries, the owner of a property does not have the rights to the mineral resources below the ground—these remain properties of the state); or a failure to note restrictions (e.g., reservations about rights of way) and the variety of possible "bundles of rights" compatible with a legal regime protecting property. These qualifications become even more important as property rights get extended from real estate to intellectual property: should the owner of these property rights have the right of exclusion, or only the right to collect fair rents from those who "trespass" on his property?

The book aims to bring together the strands of criticism and qualification that have developed among both economists and legal scholars in the wake of the neoliberal orthodoxy's ascendance for development policymakers late in the last century. Our discussions have sought to develop an alliance between increasingly well-known criticisms of neoliberal economic orthodoxy—from which China has been an important dissenting voice and alternative model—and less well-known criticisms of neoliberal *legal orthodoxy,* which has had a far more successful run of late in Chinese policy circles. By bringing those two discussions together, we hope to foster a discussion between alternative economic and legal analytics, set in the context of Chinese experience. By doing so, we hope to contribute to our understanding of fundamental issues about the relationship between economic life and the rule of law. The task going forward is to develop the concrete implications of this alternative view for the design of legal and institutional arrangements in the Chinese context.

OUTLINE OF THIS BOOK

As a general matter, this volume leans against the view that "neoliberal" legal or economic orthodoxy ought to guide Chinese reform. Our project began before the Great Recession, and until the global economic crisis, a number of variants of "market fundamentalism" held sway among some economic and financial "experts" in China, and there appeared to be a risk that these ideas would become embedded into the legal and regulatory framework. We enter the examination of current Chinese development policy and regulatory practice informed by the history of these debates about the relevance of North American and Western European models and the legacy of criticism among economists and lawyers about the usefulness of neoliberal policy prescriptions.

The book is divided into three sections. In the first, we develop the conceptual foundations for our discussions by reviewing debates about both the nature of Chinese economic policy in light of the Eleventh and Twelfth Five-Year Plans, and the potential for a productive engagement between economic and legal criticisms of neoliberal orthodoxy. The third chapter illustrates some of the general themes by looking at two alternative approaches to supporting credit to the poor—the formal "property rights" approach associated with De Soto and the more informal microcredit approach associated with Yunus and his Grameen Bank. There have been many contexts in which the latter approach has been far more successful than the former in promoting development, and especially the well-being of the poorest. The chapter explains why that is so, and the circumstances under which one or the other is more likely to be more effective.

The second part focuses on selected elements in current Chinese economic policy, exploring the relationship between institutional forms and patterns of economic life and development within the emerging Chinese market economy. In thinking about "economic policy" it is conventional to focus on areas that are—or might be—subject to one or another type of *regulation* or administrative action. At the same time, we need to recognize that the legal/institutional framework includes not just regulations, but the laws that relate to property, contracts, tort (liabilities), competition, corporate governance—indeed almost every aspect of a modern economy. We open this section, therefore, with reflections on debates within the West about the nature and desirability of property rights and regulation and, more broadly, governmental engagement in a market economy.

The contributions that follow assess the role of various regimes of "rights" in the Chinese economic transition. We start with the role of property rights, primarily in land, in the economic development of both agricultural and urban areas during the transition. We then expand the focus to intellectual property rights as a component in the Chinese innovation system, and to the rights of corporations (including the internal entitlements of various stakeholders in their governance) and of labor, particularly in the context of the Hukou system. All rights regimes entail social compromise and have social consequences. We foreground the significance of social considerations in the Chinese context through examination of the minimum livelihood guarantee policy and the intergenerational content of social spending. Our objective in this part, taken as a whole, is to heighten awareness of the interactions and parallels among institutional and legal arrangements that seem to concern different areas of economic life or express different overall commitments. Development policy is every bit as complex and significant in the establishment of property rights as in social spending for health care—and they are related.

The interactions among seemingly divergent fields of regulation and entitlement make the institutional framework for considering and reconsidering development policy particularly important.

In the third part, we focus on two issues that have been central to discussions of the appropriate form for the Chinese state in light of the nation's development challenges: the relationship between central and local authority and the relationship between judicial and other modes of legal interpretation, legislation, and enforcement.

CONCLUDING REMARKS

We are convinced that political, social, and cultural values—including concerns about social harmony and the harmony between humans and nature—must drive economic strategy and shape the form of the market economy that China builds for itself in the coming decades. The appropriate legal question is what regulatory and institutional forms are appropriate for China's own evolving economic and political strategy.

We hope that this volume will be of help to those in China as they strive to continue their move to a market economy within a harmonious society, to those in developing countries trying to create an institutional framework consistent with equitable and sustainable development, and to those within the advanced industrial countries trying to reform their institutional and regulatory systems about which the global financial crisis has raised such fundamental questions. As those responsible for making decisions about these institutional arrangements make their choices, and consider the consequences of those choices for their societies, we hope that they will consider the available alternatives to the "neoliberal orthodoxy," alternatives that hold out the promise of higher and more sustainable growth and greater equity.

NOTES

1. After the UN Commission on Legal Empowerment of the Poor, headed by former US Secretary of State Madeleine Albright and Hernando de Soto, issued its report "Making the Law Work for Everyone: Volume I" in June 2008, the UNDP established its Initiative for Legal Empowerment of the Poor. To view all reports and documents published by the Commission see <http://http://www.undp.org/LegalEmpowerment/reports/concept2action.html>.
2. We use the terms "Chicago School" or "neoliberal orthodoxy" as shorthand for the related economic and legal orthodoxies that arose with neoliberalism and continue to preoccupy much debate about development policy. This legal orthodoxy has not been reflected in the best "law and economics" work in the legal field that emerged from the seminal contributions of Coase and his legal followers. That work has often focused precisely on the complexities and ambiguities that are inherent in any legal system but which seem strangely absent among those who now prescribe one or another caricatured "rule of law" best practice as a route to development. For an analysis of the various vernacular ideas about the "rule of law" that have animated development thinking, see Santos (2006). Within economics, the Chicago or neoliberal tradition has often been closely associated with the emphasis on institutions in development, exemplified by the important work of Douglass C. North (see Davis and North 1971; North 1981 and 1990), for which he received the Nobel Prize along with Robert William Fogel in 1993. Of course, North was far from the first to emphasize the importance of institutions. Indeed, a major battle of ideas in mid-twentieth-century economics was between the old institutionalists (such as John R. Commons) and analytic neoclassical economics. Hardly had neoclassical economics won that battle when former disciples of that school began once again emphasizing the importance of institutions, exemplified by Stiglitz's work on sharecropping (1974). There was a heated debate between Stiglitz and the Chicago School economist Steven N. S. Cheung, where the latter claimed that sharecropping made no difference to the equilibrium (see Cheung 1969a and 1969b). Income and output would be exactly the same with or without sharecropping. Stiglitz explained how incomplete contracts and markets, and asymmetries of information gave rise to the institution of sharecropping and that Cheung's conclusions were valid only under assumptions of perfect information and perfect markets—assumptions in which the institution itself would not have existed. It is interesting to note that these ideas have had a very different uptake in legal scholarship.
3. Financial support from the Brooks World Poverty Institute for the first set of meetings was especially critical. The dialogues were organized by the Initiative for Policy Dialogue at Columbia University, with financial support from the Hewlett and Ford Foundations and from the Rockefeller Brothers Fund. Financial support from Columbia University and its Committee on Global Thought is also gratefully acknowledged. Logistical support for meetings in China was provided by the China Development Research Council Foundation, and financial support for the 2009 meeting of the China Task Force at Peking University by the Research Center for Property Exchange at Peking University is also gratefully acknowledged.
4. There is a large literature—mainly from Americans—arguing for the economic superiority of the American legal model. While this empirical literature has been widely debunked, one need only note that correlation is not causation. Moreover, apparently paradoxical examples abound. For instance, one of the most successful countries in Africa—one of the few without extractible natural resources—has been Mauritius,

which lies within the French legal tradition. East Asia has been the most successful region in the world, with few countries adhering to the Anglo-American tradition.

5. For instance, when land is inequitably distributed, some form of tenancy evolves—most commonly sharecropping. Sharecropping greatly attenuates work incentives. Standard (old) theory assumed that lump sum redistributions were possible, but in fact all redistributions entail distortionary taxes. See, for instance, Stiglitz (1994).
6. See, in particular, Posner's recent books (2009, 2010) and Greenspan's *mea culpa* before Congress (cited in Stiglitz 2010: 149).
7. Perhaps one of the reasons that the neoliberal Chicago School placed so little emphasis on these issues is that they focused on a model in which there were so many players in every market that *no one* had bargaining power. But even if there are many firms in the economy and many workers, particular workers bargain with particular firms over wages and working conditions. Transactions costs (including those associated with information imperfections) mean that different firms and workers are not perfect substitutes for each other. At the micro-level, bargaining power matters.
8. See Coase (1937 and 1960).
9. See, for instance, Calabresi and Melamed (1972), reprinted with commentary and a brief history of the "law and economics" movement within the legal academy in Kennedy and Fisher (2006: 401–45).
10. For instance, standard exposition highlighted how assignments of property rights could even resolve problems of externalities. If smokers exerted a negative externality on nonsmokers, an efficient solution could be obtained by assigning property rights either to smokers or to nonsmokers. In one case, the smokers would attempt to bribe the nonsmokers; in the other, the nonsmokers would bribe the smokers. If the sums of the consumer surpluses enjoyed by the smokers as a result of smoking exceeded the losses to the nonsmokers, the equilibrium would entail smoking. But implementing such a scheme required knowledge of the smokers' consumer surpluses, something that could not be easily observed. If the smokers had to actually compensate the nonsmokers, each had an incentive to pretend that his own consumer surplus was low, to free ride on the compensation provided by others. See Farrell (1987).

REFERENCES

Calabresi, Guido and Douglas Melamed (1972), "Property Rules, Liability Rules, and Inalienability: One View of the Cathedral," *Harvard Law Review*, 85/6: 1089–128.

Cheung, Steven N. S. (1969a), *The Theory of Share Tenancy* (Chicago: University of Chicago Press).

——(1969b), "Transaction Costs, Risk Aversion, and the Choice of Contractual Arrangements," *Journal of Law and Economics*, 12/1: 23–42.

Coase, Ronald H. (1937), "The Nature of the Firm," *Economica*, 4/16 (November): 386–405.

——(1960), "The Problem of Social Cost," *Journal of Law and Economics*, 3 (October): 1–44.

Davis, Lance E. and Douglass C. North (1971), *Institutional Change and American Economic Growth* (Cambridge: Cambridge University Press).

Farrell, Joseph (1987), "Information and the Coase Theorem," *Journal of Economic Perspectives*, 1/2: 113–29.

Kennedy, David and William W. Fisher III (2006), *The Canon of American Legal Thought* (Princeton, NJ: Princeton University Press).

North, Douglass C. (1981), *Structure and Change in Economic History* (New York: W. W. Norton).

——(1990), *Institutions, Institutional Change, and Economic Performance* (New York: Cambridge University Press).

Posner, Richard (2009), *A Failure of Capitalism: The Crisis of '08 and the Descent into Depression* (Cambridge, MA: Harvard University Press).

——(2010), *The Crisis of Capitalist Democracy* (Cambridge, MA: Harvard University Press).

Santos, Alvaro (2006), "The World Bank's Uses of the 'Rule of Law' Promise in Economic Development," in David M. Trubek and Alvaro Santos (eds), *The New Law and Economic Development: A Critical Appraisal* (Cambridge: Cambridge University Press), 253–300.

Stiglitz, J. E. (1974), "Incentives and Risk in Sharecropping," *Review of Economic Studies*, 41/2: 219–55.

——(1994), *Whither Socialism?* (Cambridge, MA: MIT Press).

——(2010), *Freefall: America, Free Markets, and the Sinking of the World Economy* (New York: W. W. Norton).

Part I

Conceptual Foundations

1

Law and Development Economics: Toward a New Alliance

David Kennedy[1]

INTRODUCTION: LAW EMBEDDED IN DEVELOPMENT POLICY

Over the last decade or more, experts in economic development policy have lost confidence in the neoliberal package of policy ideas once promoted with enthusiasm across the globe. The results of those policy prescriptions differed widely and were, on the whole, not as salutary as had been expected. Many regions and countries that followed alternative paths did well—often better than those that followed the neoliberal prescriptions to the letter. Over the same period, economists, sociologists, and others launched important intellectual criticisms of the economic ideas that underlay the neoliberal policy set. These criticisms opened new paths for thinking about development policy, often focused on institutions and modes of regulation and administrative action. They also brought with them a new vernacular for arguing about development policy—how extensive are market failures, where are the binding constraints or bottlenecks and how can they be softened, how important are public goods, and so forth. Much of this volume is devoted to elaborating those once heterogeneous, now ever more mainstream, economic ideas and assessing their significance for policymaking in the Chinese context.

Our economic and sociological ideas about development routinely have ideas about law embedded within them. Economists share a set of background ideas about what law is, what it can do, and how it might be used. Often these ideas about law lie hidden in assumptions about the state and the appropriate instruments for policymaking. These assumptions can be difficult to see when economists share a strong consensus about what development is and how to bring it about, as they did in the postwar period and again during the heyday of neoliberalism. When the unity and self-confidence of development economics ebbs, as occurred in the 1970s and is again the case today, and the details and context for policy seem more salient, ideas about law and institutions often lie closer to the surface in discussions of development policy.

Indeed, it is quite striking that, as confidence in the once dominant neoliberal economic prescriptions has faltered, attention has turned ever more to the importance of getting the institutions and legal arrangements right as a precondition for successful economic policymaking. As a result, development economists and policymakers now speak about law all the time, and arguments about law—how it works, what it can and cannot do—have become part of the common repertoire of development practitioners. Reforming the legal system itself has become an important development policy prescription, and policymakers routinely call for a relatively standard set of law reforms to strengthen property and contract rights, ensure transparency or good governance, and build the "rule of law." Something similar took place in the 1960s and 1970s as confidence in the set of economic policies associated with the first phases of import substitution industrialization waned among economists and sociologists. They began talking about legal reforms, both domestically and at the international level.

The turn to law is important. Capital is, after all, a legal institution—a set of entitlements to use, risk, and profit from resources of various kinds. Law defines what it means to "own" something and how one can successfully contract to buy or sell. Financial flows are also flows of legal rights. Labor is also a legal institution—a set of legal rights and privileges to bargain, to work under these but not those conditions, to quit, to migrate, to strike, to retire, and more. Buying and selling are legal institutions—rooted in what it means to own or to sell in a given legal culture, in the background legal arrangements in whose shadow people bargain with one another over price. Markets are built upon a foundation of legal arrangements and stabilized by a regulatory framework. Each of these many institutions and relationships can be defined in different ways, empowering different people and interests. Legal rules and institutions defining what it means to "contract" for the "sale" of "property" might be built to express quite different distributional choices and ideological commitments. One might, for example, give those in possession of land more rights—or one might treat those who would use land productively more favorably.

The particular legal arrangements in a society are terribly important for the success of economic policy. They influence the routine distribution of consequences from changes in policy or other economic adjustments. They can make policies possible—or completely ineffective. They can establish incentives and set bargaining powers in ways conducive to economic exchange and growth—or inimical to it. More importantly, legal arrangements can influence the *path* for economic development. Among many possible paths to growth or stable equilibriums, the one to be found in a given society will be a function of the legal arrangements in place.

For all these reasons, it is important to understand how ideas about law have been and might be brought to bear in development thinking. This would be easier if the best ideas about law could simply be added to economic wisdom about development. Unfortunately, it is not that simple; first, because the best economic thinking about development already has assumptions about law and institutions embedded within it, and they are often not the best legal ideas. Second, legal experts, like economists, disagree about what the "best" ideas are. They are rarely of one mind about what law is, how it works, and what it can be expected to do, let alone about the details of institutional design. In this respect, legal science is no different from economics or sociology—there are schools of thought, mainstream ideas, and more heterogeneous tendencies. As in economics, ideas about law travel in packs. There have been moments of broad consensus and moments of greater doubt and uncertainty about just how law functions in society. Within the range of available professional arguments, individual jurists or whole sections of the profession may have preferences and intellectual habits.

Moreover, these disagreements are unlikely to be cleanly resolved by empirical study or more precise theoretical reflection. Indeed, legal expertise is better understood as a framework of opposed arguments about legal design than as a set of recipes or best practices. The kinds of choices that must be made in designing and operating a legal system return us repeatedly to social and political choices, which may be discussed in the more professional-sounding vernacular of the legal profession, but are rarely resolved by decisive legal argument one way or the other.

Over the last twenty or more years, thinking about development issues in the field of legal science has in some ways paralleled that in economics and sociology. There was a set of dominant ideas about law during the neoliberal period, even as policymakers focused more insistently on macroeconomic stability, privatization, shocks to world prices, and the rest of the now classic neoliberal development program. Among other things, this set of ideas downplayed the potential for public law and regulation while foregrounding private law. It extolled the benefits of legal formality and stigmatized as "corruption" many economic activities that occur in the borderlands of formal law. In this set of ideas, "property rights" had pride of place and were understood in rather formal and absolutist terms.

In more recent years, a range of heterogeneous ideas long present in the legal field have become more significant for thinking about development issues. In methodological terms, these ideas share a great deal with heterogeneous thinking in the social sciences during the same period. They focus on context, on informality, unpredictability, on institutions other than private arm's-length contract, and so on. Among other things, public law and regulation have become more salient, ideas about corruption have become more precise, while the benefits and inevitability of informal economic and legal arrangements have come to be more fully recognized. The significance of choices among various possible background private law regimes and corporate governance regimes has come to be discussed more prominently. In this view, "property rights" are far more nuanced. There are many forms of property entitlement that may be bundled and parceled out in numerous ways, all of which permit some uncompensated injury to the property holder for one or another social purpose.

These heterogeneous ideas about law have not penetrated the world of development policy as firmly as their methodological allies from economics or sociology. In this chapter, we argue for an alliance between the new strands of economic thinking found throughout this volume and the long legal tradition of skepticism about legal formality, about the autonomy and absolute nature of private law, and about other legal ideas closely associated with neoliberal policy reforms. There are two reasons for thinking such an alliance may be helpful. First, as a practical matter, once the specific structure of regulatory arrangements and institutions are foregrounded by economic thought, it will be important to benefit from the most nuanced contemporary thinking about the choices available in arranging institutions and regulations in particular contexts.

The second basis is more a matter of rhetorical and political affinity. Development expertise, however it presents itself, has never been a simple matter of theories, from economics or elsewhere, "applied" in a national context. Expertise about development is more akin to a constellation of associated commitments, favorite ideas, typical strategies, and ideological associations. The work of development policymaking is often argument—generating reasons to push political initiatives in one or another direction or to favor one type of intervention over another. As in other rhetorical domains, styles of argument clump together and can support one another by loose analogy. As economists argue more vigorously for modes of analysis that endogenize social arrangements and matters of political economy, they will find in legal science a parallel set of arguments for endogenizing factors of this type into our understanding of legal arrangements themselves. On the field of rhetorical battle, it can often be useful to have your homolog from an adjacent discipline near at hand.

This article addresses two puzzles. How do—and how should—legal and economic expertise relate to one another in development policy planning? And how might we improve our policymaking in the post-neoliberal period by harnessing related heterogeneous traditions in economics and legal science? The answers to these questions require some history. The policy debates about Chinese development policy that are the subject of this volume contrast doubts and hesitations about what had been neoliberal orthodoxies in development policy circles in the West with the experience and choices available to policymakers in China today. It is precisely in moments such as this, when a powerful global policy orthodoxy unravels, that the range of choice and debate about the links between institutional context and economic theory becomes visible. This is easily apparent if we contrast two moments in which dominant global orthodoxies about development policy began to erode: the postwar orthodoxy of "modernization" through import substitution industrialization (ISI) and the more recent neoliberal orthodoxy that characterized thinking about the transition from socialism at the end of the last century.

THE POSTWAR DEVELOPMENT STATE: LEGAL INSTRUMENTALISM AND ITS DISCONTENTS 1950–70

The potential significance of such an intellectual alliance is perhaps easier to see with the wisdom of hindsight. A brief return to the dominant development ideas and policies of the 1950s and 1960s illustrates the presence of ideas about law beneath a dominant policy set—here, that of import substitution industrialization and modernization. As confidence in import substitution faltered, in part under critical pressure from within the fields of economics, political science, and sociology, confidence in the legal paradigm buttressing the postwar approach to policy remained high within the development field. Looking back, we can see ways in which dominant ideas about law and institutional structure may have hampered efforts to render import substitution policies as flexible, context-specific, and effective as they might have been. Meanwhile, however, within the legal field, heterogeneous criticisms of these dominant legal ideas emerged that could have been useful, but were by and large not engaged.

At the same time, we can see that the prevailing wisdom of neither the economic nor legal professions provided compelling scientific analytics for making the detailed institutional choices necessary to build an effective import substitution development state. Doing so required choices, political ones, taken on the basis of argument and debate—all the more so as confidence in postwar growth and modernization theories ebbed. In arguing for choices that departed from the import substitution orthodoxy of the postwar period, policymakers might well have drawn on arguments rooted in heterogeneous thinking about law as well as economics, sociology, or political science. As it happened, however, the opportunity for a productive interdisciplinary alliance between critical strands of thinking in both fields was lost. Lawyers with heterogeneous sensibilities left the field in what two leading scholars famously termed "self-estrangement."[2]

Legal ideas embedded in postwar economic ideas

Postwar development texts focused on the relationship between economic theories about development and policy objectives. They had far less to say about the *instruments* through which policy choices were to be made effective and even less about the legal and institutional context within which those instruments would operate. Often, the instrument and the objective were used interchangeably, as if the objective to "restrict imports" and the instrument "tariff" were synonymous. A tariff, of course, is a legal rule, and law is generally the medium through which policy instruments are—or are not—made effective. The idea that a tariff will, in fact, restrict imports relies upon assumptions about, among other things, the effectiveness of law in a particular context. In their focus on economic theories and objectives, rather than the design and effectiveness of legal instruments, postwar development experts were not unique. Throughout the development field, we are used to considering the relationship between economic theories—of growth or development or efficiency—and policy objectives. The point of applied economic analysis is to translate economic models into objectives to be pursued by those with (usually public) power to make policy for an economy.

Were we to add legal instruments and ideas to the story, we might imagine the relationship among economic theory, policy, and law as a series of translations of this kind. Economic theories are translated into objectives for policymakers, and translated in turn into legal instruments whose selection might be informed by implied or explicit ideas about law. In both fields, the translation of ideas into action relies on some broad or narrow sense for the specificity of the context for which these policy objectives are appropriate or in which these legal instruments will operate. I use the word "translation" to highlight the gaps that must be overcome to apply legal or economic ideas; it aptly evokes a sense in which the application of such ideas is a matter of argument and persuasion, making an analogy between the context to be addressed and the theoretical framework within which the ideas were developed and refined. Like all such matters of language and disputation, the argumentative links that experts forge as they move among the columns in Figure 1.1 can be far less stable than experts are prone to assert.

In the event, a great deal of law was required to translate the leading postwar economic theories of development into policy. Import substitution industrialization drew on every element of the legal regime. The structure of public finance and budgeting, the authority and structure of institutions, whether public or private,

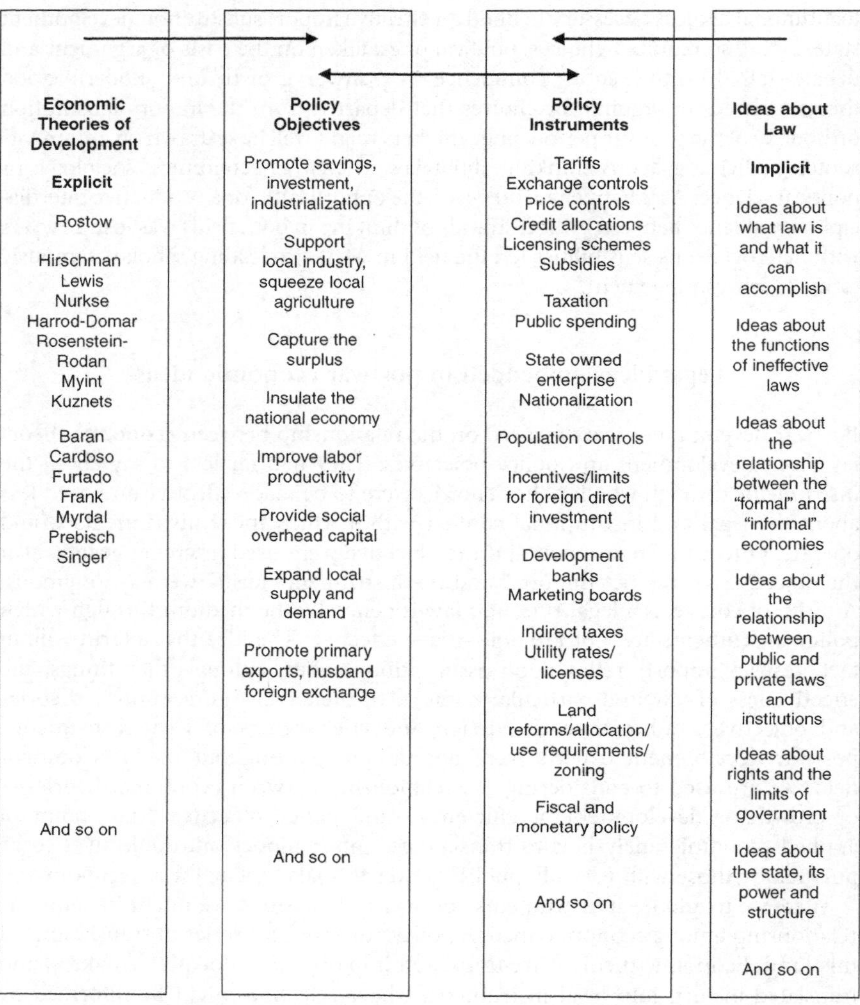

Economic Theories of Development
Explicit
Rostow
Hirschman
Lewis
Nurkse
Harrod-Domar
Rosenstein-Rodan
Myint
Kuznets
Baran
Cardoso
Furtado
Frank
Myrdal
Prebisch
Singer
And so on
Policy Objectives
Promote savings, investment, industrialization
Support local industry, squeeze local agriculture
Capture the surplus
Insulate the national economy
Improve labor productivity
Provide social overhead capital
Expand local supply and demand
Promote primary exports, husband foreign exchange
And so on
Policy Instruments
Tariffs
Exchange controls
Price controls
Credit allocations
Licensing schemes
Subsidies
Taxation
Public spending
State owned enterprise
Nationalization
Population controls
Incentives/limits for foreign direct investment
Development banks
Marketing boards
Indirect taxes
Utility rates/ licenses
Land reforms/allocation/ use requirements/ zoning
Fiscal and monetary policy
And so on
Ideas about Law
Implicit
Ideas about what law is and what it can accomplish
Ideas about the functions of ineffective laws
Ideas about the relationship between the "formal" and "informal" economies
Ideas about the relationship between public and private laws and institutions
Ideas about rights and the limits of government
Ideas about the state, its power and structure
And so on

Figure 1.1. Theories, objectives, instruments, and law, 1950–70

possible modes for regulation, the military and criminal justice system all came into play. Import substitution industrialization demanded the creation of numerous public law institutions, established by statute and implemented by public law bureaucracies: exchange controls, credit licensing schemes, tariffs, subsidy programs, tax incentives, price controls, national commodity monopolies, and so forth. There needed to be a revenue service, a mode of assessment and of payment. Borders needed to be controlled, requiring a customs service, itself mandated and organized. Legislation was necessary to establish exchange controls, marketing boards, and all the other elements of the system. A vastly expanded administrative apparatus, with rule-making, licensing, and other legal authority would need to be set up.

Looking back, we can reconstruct the legal theory implicit in development expertise of the period. Although postwar development experts rarely placed their ideas about law front and center, they did have ideas about law. The relative invisibility of law reflected the common assumption that law had little potential as an independent variable for generating development. Law was a tool for development policymakers, and as the instrument of economic policy, law was assumed to work more or less as advertised.

At the international level, the predominant legal idea was an absolute and formal state sovereignty shielding national political autonomy to pursue the development strategy of choice. The significance of private legal arrangements at the international level was largely overlooked, while the symbolism of legal sovereignty often led to an overestimation of state capacity and autonomy. These economic assumptions about the legal context had their correlatives in legal thought: international legal positivism and formalism.

Two significant ideas were taken for granted about the international legal order: the local nature of public law and the global validity of private law arrangements. Sovereignty seemed to imply that every national state could have whatever public institutional arrangements it desired and could manage its "own" economy in whatever way seemed sensible. This was the meaning of self-determination, and the focus of thought on the public international law status of the newly independent nations of the colonial world. At the same time, it was equally clear that if you took something you owned from one place to another, you still owned it. You would be subject to the law of the place when it came to remedies and obligations, but the global economy was possible because the property and contract relationships entered into in one place would, in one way or another, hold elsewhere. These two principles could certainly come into conflict—a local government could expropriate, for example. In the early years, this was regarded as a political rather than a legal problem. In that sense, speaking quite generally, sovereignty trumped property as a matter of law.

It is now apparent, of course, that neither of these ideas was fully accurate. Private rights are both qualified—and enforced—by sovereign power, not only in their place of origin, but in their transnational exercise. At the same time, sovereign powers to insulate and manage the national economy are everywhere compromised by the juridical and practical effects of transnational economic flows. Moreover, international law restrictions on sovereign policy autonomy are commonplace in the global trading regime, the system of bilateral investment treaties, and, more recently, through the globalization of human rights norms and standards. The interpenetration of international public and private arrangements and the qualification of national sovereignty have both grown in recent decades.

But it is just as important that *awareness* of these limitations and interpenetrations has also grown among development experts. Expectations, about both national public authority and the transnational stability of private rights, have changed. These changes have been strengthened by a tacit confluence of legal ideas critical of an absolutist conception of sovereignty and of a formal separation of public and private authority at the international level, as well as by heterogonous strands of economic and political thought that unbundled the state, strengthened the analogies and overlaps between public and private actors, and stressed the significance of public regulatory capacity whether exercised globally or nationally for the stability of transnational economic flows.

The national legal regime in most newly independent states expanded dramatically as national development plans for ISI were implemented. Colonial law was replaced, customary law overturned or ignored, and a large public law framework was erected to mobilize the nation for economic development. This expansion also came with a set of implicit and explicit legal ideas. Postwar development professionals were optimistic about public law and the capacity of complex administrative systems to translate policy objectives into action—to control borders, implement tariff schedules, suppress black markets, control prices, and collect taxes. When they designed legal institutions, they thought of public entities, linked to the state apparatus, whether the state-owned enterprise or the licensing or marketing board. Law was understood to be an instrument of sovereign power, the means to accomplish a policy objective. In short, law was about enabling the state.

As a result, public law was more salient than private law in the imagination of development experts. The key actors were legislatures and administrative bureaucracies as the creators, consumers, and interpreters of law. When people thought of legal instruments, they thought first about *legislation* and administrative decrees: the pronouncements of the legislature or executive, rather than the pronouncements of judges and customary, contract, or property law. A wide range of previously settled fields of law were opened to new legislation and interpretation in furtherance of the social objectives of national solidarity and national economic development.

This instrumental or pragmatic approach to law stressed the importance of purposive reasoning to link legal arrangements with social needs and objectives. The purposes came from elsewhere—from the society, from government, from the legislature. Law was subordinate to social purposes—implementing the objectives of the society—rather than expressing a priori limits, historic commitments to be respected, or purposes of its own to be achieved. Indeed, the purpose of the legal order itself was the consolidation of national economic and political authority—often associated with national self-determination and decolonization—rather than, say, integrating local economic life into a global economy or facilitating private exchange and private ordering through supplemental regulatory interventions.

Once legal arrangements were understood to have a social purpose, law was to be interpreted strictly or flexibly so as to achieve that developmental purpose. Where purposes were not express, they could be derived from analysis of the social and economic needs of the society, given its stage of economic development. Legal arrangements would need to remain flexible and open to reinterpretation in light of a changing policy objective. Legal norms were imagined to be quite context-specific and in need of careful elaboration in particular cases, rather than fitting together in a tight logical structure. At the same time, individual norms were often constructed so as to maximize the possibility for discretion in implementation—as a principle, for example, rather than a tight rule. Here, the correlative idea in legal science was an instrumental strand of antiformalism.

Of course, all these new legal arrangements were unsettling to existing legal entitlements—think of land reform and the property rights of large landowners. Yet, the law was understood to place few limits on development policy. Distribution was understood to be central to the work of law, allocating resources among social and economic groups—from agriculture to industry, from foreign to local financial institutions—to implement national economic policy objectives. The legal vocabulary of "rights" has often been used to slow the emergence of new economic policies. During this period, however, this was infrequent. The state was thought able to regulate as it pleased, altering private rights without judicial review. Neither constitutional rights nor private law seemed to act as important restraints on the state. Constitutional law was about the organization of executive and legislative power. Judicial review was rare. Both public order and private arrangements were to be coordinated with national policy objectives. Judicial bodies were specialized by subject matter and often internal to administrative structures, or in any event, subordinated to the national policy and political apparatus—their job was less to check the state than to ensure the implementation of policy. The legal difference between military command structures and state apparatuses committed to development was often inconsiderable—both were public administrations, often responsive to presidential authority. These assumptions also had their correlatives within the legal science of the day: functionalism, positivism, and legislative or executive supremacy.

In this general vision, context or culture was viewed predominantly as a potential barrier to effective policy implementation. The idea that context offered resistance or friction to the smooth translation of policy into practice led to the emergence of ideas within legal theory about how policy could be rendered more effective by narrowing the "gap between law in the books and law in action." In this sense, the sociological study of law was harnessed to legal instrumentalism, rather than offering an alternative perspective qualifying legal instrumentalism or encouraging a more dynamic analysis of the interactions between policy instruments and the context of their deployment.

This tendency may have been reinforced by the fact that with national independence and sovereignty came amnesia about the formal and customary law of the colonial regime. The new regimes in Asia and Africa marked their break with the past by foregrounding their commitment to national development and the new legal regimes required to that end and by downplaying any continuity with the legacy of colonial law, which was associated with exploitation. In Latin America, import-substitution-oriented administrative and legislative regimes had already been put in place before the War—in the 1920s in Mexico, the 1930s in Brazil—both informal and indigenous legal arrangements long having been disregarded. Development planners from the North arriving in the South tended to imagine a national legal culture similar to the one they had left behind at home, if, in some way "more primitive." Legal arrangements were simpler, perhaps more formal, and often seemed to run parallel to a separate world of custom and informal practice. In the North, at the time, the informal world of business dealings was coming to be understood as worthy of emulation and support by the law—legal rules should honor business judgment and reflect commercial practice. In the South, the legal environment was imagined otherwise—the goal was to assimilate the informal to the formal, eventually bringing the traditional sector into "modern" modes of legalization. This was not yet a development priority, but it seemed natural to expect that with industrialization and modernization, more births would come to be registered, more property transactions recorded, more income reported, and so forth. And with the subordination of the customary world would come more effective development policy.

By and large, traditional and customary law seemed irrelevant, or at most an obstacle, for development policy. Those who studied the local legal culture of developing societies—largely legal anthropologists from the North—were not particularly interested in law as a development tool. Legal anthropologists and sociologists studying traditional or primitive societies tended to search for functional equivalents to the legal institutions familiar in the developed world—legislation, dispute resolution, contract, and so forth. If anything, their work supported the background notion that traditional societies were functionally similar to, if more primitive than, modern societies, suggesting that there was no inherent reason why they could not come to function along modern lines.

Many of these widely shared legal ideas were not confined to import substitution development regimes. During the first half of the twentieth century, many of these ideas had become widespread among legal elites in the developed world, starting in Europe and spreading to the United States during the Roosevelt New Deal. Expressed differently within different national traditions, the emphasis on public law and administration and on the need to temper nineteenth-century private law with more "social" elements reflecting national interdependence and solidarity was widespread.[3] Development economists influenced by New Deal style welfare states in the United States and Europe doubtless brought these ideas with them to the development context. These ideas seemed modern—a workable substitute in many places for the more rigid-seeming thought associated with the colonial legacy of the Commonwealth. They had been enthusiastically adopted by the international institutions most associated with development in the pre-war period, the International Labor Organization and the League of the Mandates Commission or the Bruce Report. In Latin America, they had entered legal consciousness from France, often through the emerging fields of both labor law and international law, and were often understood to reflect a particularly "American" or national revolutionary identity.

Nevertheless, social, purposive, pragmatic, and antiformal legal ideas resonated differently in the development context. Some antiformal ideas about the structure of legal rules—an openness to or even preference for standards—and an embrace of social custom and informal private ordering by the official legal order advanced more slowly in the South, coming into their own only in the 1960s and 1970s, as they were also absorbed by mainstream public international law. More often, instrumentalism was linked to a more formal tradition, rooted in a public law positivism, which ensured legislative and executive supremacy.

Where antiformalism had seemed essential in the North, and particularly in the United States, in order to unravel the limits thought to have been placed on the emergence of a welfare state by a formalist private law, in the absence of judicial review, such a critical antiformalism was not necessary. In the United Statesian tradition, antiformal and sociologically inspired legal ideas are generally associated with criticism of necessitarian styles of legal argument and interpretation, whether rooted in rights or social purposes. In this critical form, these ideas have always had a heterogeneous feeling about them, even when they have been mainstream. In the developmental context during this period, this was simply far less often the case, perhaps because strong assumptions about legislative and administrative positivism and the absence of judicial review made American traditions of interpretive criticism an unnecessary import. Formalism was already operating in the service of the development state.

As a result, where antiformal ideas did have purchase in the South, they were mobilized less to question than to reinforce the top-down authority of the national developmental state, less to highlight the jurisgenerative dimensions of local culture and private arrangements than to assist the state in penetrating the legal and cultural context more effectively. Private law ideas and elements of the consciousness of classical legal thought would be mobilized only later to resist mainstream development policy.

Thus, the problem was not that critical strands of legal science were unavailable. It was that they did not seem to penetrate the world of development expertise sufficiently to be mobilized to check the excesses or fine-tune the machinery of the postwar development state. The most promising legal ideas for criticizing the excesses and rigidities of the postwar development state—critical of legal formalism, positivism, and instrumentalism—were already well known in the North, having been developed over two generations by sociologically oriented jurists, those associated with the American "legal realists" and their progeny in the legal process school after the war. Unfortunately, these ideas joined the development discussion only much later. Even as confidence in the dominant economic paradigm receded, heterogeneous ideas about law remained marginal. Even those who tried to bring sociologically informed legal ideas to the field through the "law and development" movement of the 1960s and 1970s found themselves harnessed to the project of perfecting the operations of the instrumental development state.

This was all the more true for legal ideas lying further to the left or right, all of which would enter the development field over the coming decades. From the right, legal scholars were already elaborating the ideas that would animate the neoliberal period—priority of private law, international rights, and commitments as a check on the state and legal institutions tested by a standard of market efficiency, supporting rather than regulating markets or distorting prices. But these ideas were not prominent in the development literature of the period. Legal scholars associated with one or another strand of Marxism did focus on the political and social role of law and on the dynamic interaction between social and institutional context and policy. For these thinkers, Polanyi was particularly significant. In this view, development was rooted in a political process, through which the changes necessary for modernization needed to be rendered politically and socially sustainable. Law might serve as an antidote to rapid economic change, allowing disruption to be metabolized by the society. From this perspective, much that seemed like friction or resistance could be reimagined as productive, calibrating the degree of acceptable change. For these ideas to be turned into policy would have required an agent—a legislature, a court, a president—who could stand against the implementation of the plan in the name of its long-term sustainability. In the postwar period, thinking of this kind was rare. It would only be later, under the influence of economic institutionalism, that such heterodox thinking about law would gain purchase.

How legal ideas influence economic policy design

We know that development policymaking is never the mechanical translation of an economic theory into action. There are disagreements among economists about how to proceed, questions of emphasis, of the relative importance of various development objectives, and of how to allocate costs and benefits over time. Even if there were no differences of opinion among economists, however, development policymaking still would not be simple. Unanticipated consequences are ubiquitous. General analytics, as one might expect, are better at generating broad propositions about policy direction than specific institutional recipes. They have more to say about objectives than instruments, still less about the appropriateness of instruments in particular institutional, legal, and cultural contexts. And, of course, it turns out that there are lots of ways to skin a cat, and once these choices are acknowledged, ideas from outside the field of economics begin to crowd into the discussion.

In principle, it is easy to see that there would often be reason to turn to experts in matters of legal and institutional design. Although every elementary course in the economics of trade teaches analytics for determining when to use tariffs or subsidies to protect markets, translating this wisdom into institutional recipes for particular contexts raises questions unanswerable by these analytic models. What seem to be the simplest policy tools—taxes or tariffs or subsidies or licenses—require legal and institutional arrangements that must be embedded in already-existing institutional, social, and political contexts. We need to know about that context to understand the effect—and particularly the dynamic effect—of specific changes in the legal regime.

Moreover, many questions of institutional design that are raised in constructing the apparatus to implement policy fall outside the obvious ambit of economic expertise. New bureaucracies require a legal mandate and a permissible margin of discretion. Policy instruments require methods for enforcement, prescribed penalties, and modes of adjudicating infractions and collecting penalties. A tariff schedule must be adopted; should it be done by legislation or administrative decree? Someone must be authorized to set the tariff, revise it, approve exemptions, collect or fail to collect, prosecute, penalize, and so on. How much discretion ought they to be given at each point to maximize the chances of achieving the policy objective?

In making choices about these questions, development experts then, as now, were prone to speak as if the economic policy objective determined the way forward—and as if the matter was less one for argument than science. In making these assertions, policymakers often restated the overall objective as a reason to pick one institutional design rather than another. We want an effective tariff policy to restrict imports, raise revenues, and protect domestic industry—let us therefore have the most draconian penalties, the most rigid and mechanical customs service, the most powerful legislative act or presidential decree. Or, to ensure the effective policy implementation, we should give local administrative agents the power to adjust terms as conditions change, even tolerating noncompliance when this serves a developmental objective—as when black markets in currency function as tariffs.

It quickly becomes apparent, however, that one can only rarely deduce the optimal legal and institutional arrangements from broad policy objectives. When there were multiple policy objectives, the conflicts among them could be continued into the details of policy design. Even agreement on the objective rarely determines precisely how it ought to be achieved—precisely *how* to encourage savings, *how* to support domestic industry, *how to* capture the returns from primary exports. Which instrument shall we use—tariffs or subsidies? What *kind* of licensing structure or tariff administration best expresses a policy objective? How should we design the instrument—with larger or smaller exemptions, for example? On such questions, economics tends to offer rules of thumb, taxonomies of factors to consider, or values to maximize—which are useful in arguing for one rather than another legal tool, but rarely decisive when it comes to institutional design. Context and the rest of the legal order are too important.

Legal ideas are important when they influence these choices. They can do this by short-circuiting analyses of alternative legal instruments with received wisdom, offering an alternative professional analytic for designing policy tools, suggesting alternative tools or focal points, or by contributing to the repertoire of useful arguments about whether to use this or that policy instrument. In the postwar period, unfortunately, among development experts, the most significant and widely shared legal ideas remained below the surface, ensuring that their influence would predominantly be of the first type. It was only after the economic policy consensus began to break down and previously heterogeneous economic and legal ideas entered the conversation that the field of law was able to play a more constructive role.

Of course, legal experts in a given period may imagine that there is a "most effective" or "best practice" way to set up a legal regime. Given the prevailing ideas about law, for example, it may simply be obvious that some things *are* best understood and addressed as crimes, while other things ought to be addressed using civil liability, incentives, or other arrangements. Moreover, legal experts also share broad-brush maxims or rules of thumb about what works. For example, experts might share the belief that discretion at low levels improves compliance and fine-tunes policy or that strict rules render policy more precise while harsh penalties ensure compliance.

The ideas legal experts bring to the table will rarely be specific to the development context. They have a sense for how rules and legal institutions function, how they are best assembled, how and when the integrity of the legal system itself is at stake in particular arrangements. Their preferences will be influenced by widely shared professional ideas regarding, for example, the relative roles of public and private law, the institutional strong suits of various administrative arrangements, the appropriate relationship between tight rules and broader standards in drafting statutes, decrees or judgments, or the best allocation of discretion among actors in and outside public authority. Indeed, choices among policy instruments often present classic issues of constitutional structure that legal experts will reflect on in very general terms. What are the *appropriate* roles for courts, legislatures, or administrative agencies? An expert's own sense for the strategic value of different legal arrangements, both in the pursuit of development policy objectives and on behalf of the legal process itself, may also play a role.

Like development theories or favorite policy instruments, ideas about legal structure also go in and out of fashion and often spread from more to less developed contexts, often without regard to whether the same answers are appropriate in the developing world. In this sense, the existing array of legal ideas may well cut short careful instrumental calculations about the effectiveness of one or another approach to development policy—just as economic ideas about development may short-circuit analysis of the institutional alternatives available in a particular context. In the postwar period, the result was often a familiar one—policy decisions taken on the basis of very poor assessments of the alternative institutional and legal choices available. The priority accorded public law meant that private ordering was rarely thought of as an instrument of development policy. The disconnect between national and international legal arrangements wrought by the priority given to *sovereignty* in the legal assumptions of policymakers made a variety of transnational cooperative policy arrangements more difficult to imagine or pursue.

Moreover, so long as the background assumptions about how legal systems might be put together remained unexamined, it was not surprising that the links between broad policy objectives and specific institutional arrangements often came to feel more necessary or inevitable than they actually were. For example, it seemed obvious that judges should be institutionally subordinate to the national development plan. The whole point of interpretation and enforcement was to implement the plan. Independent judicial actors deciding how to interpret things based on a different set of values was undesirable to say the least. Indeed, the later campaign to build an "independent judiciary" across the developing world was fueled by the desire to place exogenous limits on the developmental state's policymaking capacity in the name of "rights." In many places, however, the integration of administrative decision-makers into the substantive chain of command led to *less* effective implementation, precisely because an opportunity was lost for an independent control mechanism to check administrative decisions, which began to gather path-dependent momentum. So long as these considerations are not brought above ground for articulation, decisions about the structure of the policy instrument will be made in ways loosely guided by intuitions about what works, as well as by the political and ideological pull of various interests committed to one or another legal form.

There seem two obvious ways out of this difficulty. Either one brings the legal analysis to the surface where it can be made more theoretically satisfying and empirically verified or one returns to economics, rendering economic analytics precise enough to assess the choice of legal instrument in a more satisfyingly determinative fashion. Certainly, given the chance, legal science can sometimes guide the choice of policy instrument. More often, however, legal science also turns out to be underdeterminative, primarily because it contains ideas and arguments that cut in different directions. Although legal experts often do share a consensus about the right answers to questions of constitutional or institutional design, more often, the "best legal practice" is disputed. At its most robust, legal expertise is composed of arguments and counterarguments for particular approaches to institutional design and interpretation.

On the economic side, in principle, we could translate legal preferences—criminalization or civil liability, judicial or administrative control—into alternative methods of taxation, credit, or subsidy allocation, with different winners and losers and different static and dynamic effects on growth or efficiency, and then select among them on the basis of an improved economic analytic, bypassing the stubborn prejudices of legal and institutional experts and improving the effectiveness of development policy. It would often be helpful to develop a more nuanced analysis of the likely distributional impact of institutional designs in a particular context and feed these back into the economic development theory. It is hard to say exactly why, but this kind of analysis is rarely undertaken, particularly during periods in which the legal arrangements and ideas implicated by a given development strategy remain beneath the surface. It is as if standard ideas about appropriate legal institutions substitute for or stymie this kind of analysis.

More importantly, however, it is not at all clear that one could get to the bottom of things this way. There is a tendency, as the analysis becomes ever more contextually precise, for economists to differ more among themselves and for the implications of their analytic models to become less decisive. What you get from both professions are precisely rules of thumb and stock arguments—reduce the length of agency chains, place decisions close to those with information, and so forth. Indeed, the maxims about institutional design extracted from economic analysis are often similar to those found in legal theory, although lawyers may be more familiar with the ubiquity of countermaxims. At the same time, not everything in the legal context is, in fact, plastic. There remain questions of legal and institutional structure that may be determined, or thought to be determined, by the overall institutional and legal context, and are therefore not amenable to rearrangement in the name of an economic policy objective. Just where these limits lie will usually be a matter for dispute among economic, legal, or political experts.

Once it becomes clear that the choice among policy instruments is underdetermined by economic and legal theory, the door is open to debate in other terms. Alternative institutional arrangements may come to stand in for competing economic policy objectives or alternative constitutional ideals, reopening differences of opinion about which way to go. They may also seem freighted with political significance, either because different groups will benefit from setting things up one way rather than another or because they echo larger ideological commitments. Local institutional history, imitation, and the influence of foreign models also played a role. Indeed, the legal materials of the day were far more a set of polarized arguments for more and less discretion, more and less severe penalties, more and less reliance on private initiative, and so on.

Within the developing South, debates about the structure of policy instruments were generally carried on in a political or ideological vernacular, as implicating in some way the *nature* of the state. Given the complexity of the policy apparatus necessary to implement ISI, it is odd that there was so little professional debate about these matters of design. Moreover, at a time in which development policy was understood to be all about distribution, it is surprising that more attention was not paid to the distributive effects of various policy instruments, constructed in different ways. It is as if there is something in the instrumental idea about law that foregoes these assessments of its instrumental potential.

In consequence, it is difficult to imagine that a more precise economic or legal analytic will offer an escape from the terrain of argument about how to pursue development policy. It is in this context—when both economists and legal experts are engaged in arguments about what to do—that the possibility for a productive alliance between heterogeneous (or mainstream) approaches to law and economics arises.

The parallel worlds of legal and economic argument: the examples of discretion, penalties, and the significance of context

In arguments about institutional design, it is surprising how often tendencies in economic and legal thinking run parallel to one another. For example, by the 1950s, legal experts had developed standardized debates about the appropriate level of official discretion to build into a policy instrument, the role of penalties in maximizing compliance with policy instruments, and the desirability of interrupting versus harnessing ongoing social patterns when designing legal instruments. These issues are of significance in the design of import-substitution-style policies and economists also had things to say about each. It should not be surprising that there would be a parallel between the stock arguments made in the two fields about such issues. Nevertheless, in the postwar period, all the possible arguments were not made. In most import substitution regimes, for one reason or another, there seemed to be a default preference for relatively strict rules, strong penalties, and a disinclination to develop a dynamic understanding of the role of context when designing policy instruments. It was with the advent of more heterogeneous inclinations in economics, which emphasized the instability and importance of context and institutions, that more nuanced legal arguments found an ally.

The issue of discretion comes up in a variety of ways, but is probably best known to lawyers as the choice faced by those who establish norms between using relatively strict rules and broader standards to achieve a given legislative objective. Ought the statute to set objectives to be achieved, leaving the means to those who must implement; or ought it to spell things out with more precision? Should the legislator express the substantive objective in vague terms—"reasonable," "proportional," "productive"—or be more precise about what is intended? The more precisely things are spelled out, of course, the less discretion administrative agents or judges will seem to have. Lawyers have generated a number of conventional arguments for and against the use of rules or standards, as well as for and against endowing legal agents with discretion. Indeed, it is also conventional to argue that firm rules may sometimes lead to unpredictable discretion when agents jump the rails of a framework that has lost all links to changing circumstances, and that standards can, in a climate of social consensus, often be more constraining than rules.

The question of how great a penalty or how easily obtainable a remedy will best ensure compliance has also generated a range of conventional arguments in legal science. The death penalty for smuggling—will this reduce smuggling or drive smuggling out of the prosecutorial system altogether? A private right of action with punitive damages—will this generate the socially desirable level of compliance or hold people to obligations from which they should better be allowed free? Whether compliance is enhanced by punitive sanctions, and whether agents will respond to rules with discretion and standards with obedience, will depend upon the context, the agents, the expectations, and strategies of those outside and inside the legal system, as will the question of whether any level of violation might, over time, actually be optimal to the social purpose. To determine whether we ought to interrupt or reinforce existing social practices, harness custom to our policy objective, or break the back of custom, requires a strategic sense about the responses officials and others working in the rule system will make. Will the workaround be more or less effective in mobilizing savings or generating development than compliance with the rule itself would have been?

Once one begins to think about the strategic significance of the context, it will also be clear that, whatever strategy is adopted, there will always be some slippage. The rule will seem too tight, and officials will look the other way at its violation. Or discretion will be exercised wisely, but conditions will have changed. Those outside the legal machinery may game or evade the system. As a result, we will also face a set of choices about when and how to tolerate a residuum of noncompliance. We will need tools with which to argue about the dynamic interaction of actors making strategic use and nonuse of the legal order and the efforts of state actors to implement policy.

Legal experts then and now know that both issues are matters of degree. Legal arrangements can usually be designed to be more or less rule-like and combined with a more or less forceful remedy. Between any two proposed norms or enforcement mechanisms, moreover, legal experts are trained to deploy the full range of arguments one way or the other—by definition, one alternative will involve "less" enforcement or "less" discretion, the other more. They also know that legal science has no one-size-fits-all answer to these questions. Instead, we have a range of repeating arguments that seem both scientific and vaguely ideological, rooted in context-specific sociological data and reflective of professional attitudes about what generally makes a legal system effective or just. Arguments for stricter rules, less discretion, stricter penalties, and less deference to context all seem to hang together with politically conservative, ethically individualistic, and professionally positivist and formalist preferences. Throughout the twentieth century, arguments on the other side, for standards, more discretion, softer penalties, and more sensitivity to the reactions of context, have all seemed heterogeneous by comparison—even when they have been hegemonic within the legal field.

In designing specific policy instruments, it seems sensible to work across the entire spectrum of available arguments to be as nuanced and precise as possible in matching legal instruments to policy objectives and the conditions of context. Although laymen often think first of criminal sanctions, professionals should understand that there are many other ways to enforce a legal entitlement, as well as objectives that might be served by allowing violations. It may be that those who trade currency outside the national bank are committing a crime and come under the authority of the police, prosecutorial authorities, and ultimately the penal or other sanctioning system. But there are other ways to structure the restriction on currency trading. The bank's monopoly authority in a fixed exchange rate regime may be enforced through private remedies instead, through torts or property or other civil regulatory machinery. Various private rights of action may be created for those harmed by the illegal trade, with various penalties, including the payment of damages measured in various ways. Credit or other services may be denied those who cannot show that their funds have been procured through the appropriate channels. Moreover, whatever system is devised, penalties may be more or less—death penalty for black market trading? Punitive damages? Fines? Reeducation? A sharp warning and surveillance? Or perhaps amnesty and recruitment to the state apparatus.

The severity of the punishment and the degree of prosecutorial or judicial discretion ought to be matters of development strategy. Prosecutorial discretion, in the right hands, may mobilize the population to national objectives more effectively than strictly enforced criminal rules. This is particularly true where baseline rules capture an enormous number of potential violators in their net. If everyone in the society is always already in violation of tax rules, selective prosecution, or the threat of selective prosecution, can be an instrument of mobilization, of creating incentives to engage in the development plan.

Similarly, the tolerated level of noncompliance presents opportunities for strategy, rather than simply lamentation about "resistance" or a "failure to penetrate." As economists understand, a tolerated black market may be an effective and administratively simple way to maintain a dual exchange rate. Those who change money on the black market are, in effect, paying a tariff on their imports—the tariff revenues go not to the state, but to the moneychanger. Informal fee structures for administrative services may be more effective than other taxing schemes to harness earnings for investment. In political terms, slippage between the regulation and its implementation can allow the room necessary to permit politically significant constituencies to accept development policies that might otherwise be so adverse to their interests that they could not be implemented. If the upper-middle class can bribe the customs official once in a while to bring consumer goods from abroad, or change money on the black market to purchase luxury imports, they might well tolerate a quite restrictive regime; and the price they pay, if not as high as the tariff wall, will still go to the state employees managing the border. Moreover, between the death penalty for black market trade and tolerated noncompliance lies a range of middle positions. Some moneychangers could be given a privilege to violate the normal rule. These privileges might be formalized through a licensing process, managed as a discretionary grant or by auction, and so forth.

The interesting thing about the postwar period is how rarely the full range of legal possibilities was exploited in import substitution regimes. Development planners often simply assumed that the most "effective" policy instrument would be the one that minimized discretion and heightened penalties so as to maximize compliance. Nor were most import substitution regimes designed with a fine-tuned sense of strategy about the dynamic significance of context for the operation of policy. Development planners and economists seemed to share a favorable attitude toward more precise rules and a disinterest in context that was at odds with much of the contemporary legal theory in the North, if consistent with professional attitudes among lawyers in many developing societies.

It would be the heterogeneous traditions of structuralist and institutionalist economics, from dependency theory through to public choice theory, with their focus on the context of international and national political economy and the dynamic interaction of policy with the strategic behavior of agents both inside and outside the state, which would sharpen attention to alternative possibilities. Argumentative tools to support these tendencies were available within legal science at the time—but were not heard.

One explanation is that a top-down legal order of precise rules simply seemed to "fit" with favorable economic attitudes toward Fordist mass production, just as an inattention to context seemed to "fit" with images of underdeveloped societies as "primitive." The equation of industrialization with development and modernization arose from the observation that productivity gains came from the specialization and routinization of work made possible in modern factories. Although it was certainly possible to imagine substituting labor for capital in the industrialization process, this was generally thought to be a dead end—the point was to make a small number of workers more productive, slowly drawing down the surplus labor stock as they could be absorbed into industry. As a result, discretionary models of organization were stigmatized as "traditional," filled with slack, unable to translate the policy objectives faithfully into practice. With less discretion and more automaticity in the process, resources could be mobilized more effectively for social objectives. It was common, moreover, for economists to remark on the cultural obstacles to disciplined rule-following, which seemed an obstacle to industrialization. Attitudes would need to become more rational, consequentialist, if people were to have the discipline to step up to the productivity levels made possible by the modern factory. Traditional culture would have to give way to new habits of mind and behavior. It seemed natural to apply this set of ideas by analogy to administrative bureaucracy. In factories, there must be an assembly line; in the bureaucracy, there must be rules. In order to transform local culture, one would not think about first harnessing traditional cultural expectations and behavior to policy management.

Hirschman was the most prominent development economist to speculate about the impact of the organization of work on cultural attitudes. He famously argued that one should not wait for traditional attitudes to change; one should implement modes of organization that allowed as little "latitude in performance standards" as possible, with catastrophic consequences for failure, to ensure people had strong incentives to discipline themselves into having the right attitudes. To this end, developing economies should "skip steps" to import more advanced industrial processes in which the process itself left less room to tolerate deviation without provoking the kind of failures that would be noticed and opposed by everyone else in the system.

> . . . the greater or smaller extent of latitude in standards of performance (or tolerance for poor performance) [is] a characteristic inherent in all production tasks. When this latitude is narrow the corresponding task has to be performed *just right;* otherwise, it cannot be performed at all or is exposed to an unacceptable level of risk (for example, high probability of crash in the case of poorly maintained or poorly operated airplanes). Lack of latitude therefore brings powerful pressures for efficiency, quality performance, good maintenance habits, and so on. It thus substitutes for inadequately formed motivations and attitudes, which will be *induced* and generated by the narrow-latitude task instead of presiding over it. . . . According to my way of thinking, the very attitudes alleged to be preconditions of industrialization could be generated on the job and "on the way," by certain characteristics of the industrialization process.[4]

According to Hirschman, just as one should not expect attitudes to precede their usefulness, it would be a mistake to imagine that a well-functioning public administration could emerge before the habits of bureaucratic regularity had had the opportunity to be learned in industry. Looking back, of course, it is easier to see how this might have been translated into a preference for a quite authoritarian administrative style. It is possible to communicate and instill administrative discipline by routinely lining up those who miss their targets before a firing squad. This general preference for tight rules and severe penalties was often shared, however, by legal professionals in the developing world, who were often trained to think of their work in formal and instrumental terms.

Once confidence in the economic theories supporting postwar development policy began to wane, opening the field to heterogeneous strands of thought, legal science had arguments to offer. Jurists had already developed critical perspectives on legal theories that seemed to overvalue formal rules and restraints on discretion or ignored the potential significance of social customs, legal privileges to injure others, and tolerated noncompliance. Arguments for the productive exploitation of economic disequilibrium had analogies in legal arguments for policy instruments that broke with custom or strategized about the dynamic reactions of economic actors inside and outside the state. Of course, these were only analogies—it might well turn out that a more flexible instrument would be more effective in bringing about a rupture or exploiting a disequilibrium. Nevertheless, as economic ideas became more diffuse, there may have been an opportunity to open the legal fabric to include more nuanced tools, while training legal elites in the arts of pragmatic policymaking. Indeed, this was the program of the "law and development movement" from the North that sought to bring heterogeneous strands of legal analysis to development policymaking in the South, and that lost heart (and funding) precisely as the range of economic ideas was about to open up.

The moment of reckoning: chastening postwar economic ideas

We all know that the economic ideas of the postwar period, with their focus on stages of growth and modernization, came under increasing criticism in the 1960s and 1970s from both the left and the right. Economic growth and growth through industrialization came under fire as exclusive development objectives. The number of possible development models increased—much depended upon the specifics of local political and social arrangements, resources, and position in the world economic order. The international context for development seemed newly important. Sociologists and economists substantiated the intuition that modes of insertion in the global economy differ and are significant; that there are structural limits to national economic development imposed by world political and economic structures; and that the most important questions of development policy reside in identifying and using wisely the room within these structural limits to maneuver at the national level. At the same time, local political economy mattered. Development seemed a function of a dynamic interaction with local political and institutional forms. Monopoly interests, foreign investors, and local elites, might all become entrenched by development in ways that came to blunt the potential for further development. At the same time, states might also be an obstacle to development, particularly where they stifled entrepreneurial potential or locked in static relationships between foreign and local interests antagonistic to industrialization. States might be captured by rent-seekers, at home and abroad.

Under the impact of these analyses, policymakers were terrifically inventive, ushering in a range of "second-stage" import substitution approaches to development. Constructive engagement with the trading system would need to be managed. It might be necessary to limit the state or bust up congealed local interests protective of enclave economies or inimical to an appropriately dynamic insertion into the world economy. A larger regulatory framework would be necessary to prevent dynamic relations between leading and lagging sectors, advancing and declining regions, or states from accelerating the decline of the less developed areas. At the global level, development also required new public policy, in the form of a New International Economic Order (NIEO), new development initiatives across the UN system, and new focal points (such as "basic needs" and poverty reduction) on the part of the international financial institutions.

In legal or institutional terms, however, these new policy initiatives were far less inventive. The key remained an instrumental conception of law, top-down regulation, and public administration, all now turned to somewhat different objectives. This was particularly pronounced at the international level, where the NIEO project sought to recapitulate for the world the policy instruments of the national welfare state.

Meanwhile, within the legal field, sociologists and lawyers were working together to criticize the positivist and instrumentalist legal ideas associated with the early developmental state. As in economics, this critical work came from a variety of political and methodological points of view. Critical strands in pragmatist and antiformal legal thought made their way from North to South. Legal process scholars focused on the indeterminate potential in substantive regulation and legislation, stressing the importance of private ordering and institutional process. Private ordering was often more important than public law and could fulfill or frustrate public functions. The legal and quasi-legal process for adjustment and settlement might be more important than the substantive norms purporting to govern the result. Legal sociologists emphasized the extent to which law rarely operates as a straightforward instrumental translation of legislative intention into social practice. The gap between law-in-the-books and law-in-action was not only a failure to penetrate the economic or cultural terrain. People related to the law strategically by using or avoiding legal institutions in their economic and social life. They bargained in the shadow of the law and also about what law to use and how. An appreciation for legal pluralism made decisive top-down policy implementation seem less likely and less virtuous, even totalitarian. The informal arrangements outside the official legal framework ought to be seen as part of the legal fabric itself. Moreover, law might serve not only as an instrument of state power, but also as an important restraint on executive and administrative authority.

At the international level, formal and absolute sovereignty came under attack. State power was itself a legal arrangement; states were part of an international legal community with duties and responsibilities, as well as rights. The new conditions of international economic and social life called for a more interdependent and social conception of international law. The vocabulary of international human rights placed limits on national sovereignty. The new rhetoric of economic and social rights pushed against growth-based definitions of development. At the same time, the top-down welfare state model no longer seemed a useful model for the international legal regime—the General Assembly as legislature or the Specialized Agencies as proto-welfare state agencies.

Common assumptions about the internal structure of law were also questioned. The failures of instrumentalism often resulted from the presence of competing goals within the normative materials. Interpretation would be required to balance considerations in specific cases not only to achieve a predetermined objective, but also to determine the objective to be pursued. Legal scholars focused on the range of purposes and principles immanent in legal materials and on the significance of private as well as public processes for the resolution of conflicts. More attention was paid to the role of exceptions in the legal fabric and to the role of noncompliance, as in the obvious case of prosecutorial discretion. The decision not to enforce a rule could also be a policy tool. Legal procedures and institutions seemed more important than substantive rules. Familiar legal categories—public and private, criminal law and contract—began to blur into one another. Thinking instrumentally, there seemed ever more ways to arrange legal duties and permissions so as to achieve given results. As legal professionals worked with legal materials they increasingly understood to be uncertain, they brought all manner of policy arguments and slogans drawn loosely from other fields, including economics, into the legal realm. Unsurprisingly, these ideas often meant something rather different when ripped from their original scientific context for deployment by lawyers. At the international level, sovereignty was unbundled into a range of powers and capacities to be shared with international institutions—just as new legal forms for public–private partnerships sprang up at the national level.

Figure 1.2 contrasts the mainstream, if implicit, ideas about law in the development profession of the period with these emerging heterogeneous strands of thinking about what law is and what it can achieve.

In the emerging heterodox economic development literatures of the 1960s and 1970s, however, there was little reference to these various strands of heterodox thinking about law. This is unfortunate—an opportunity for alliance was missed. Critical traditions within the field of law that might have been useful in qualifying or fine-tuning professional expectations about what legal tools could accomplish were largely ignored. For example, recent studies have identified nuanced administrative control mechanisms as among the most important factors in the success of those economies that pursued second-stage policies to best effect.[5] Structured neither to ensure the top-down penetration of government objectives into the social context nor to limit the state in the name of private interests, these control mechanisms aimed to provide a technically competent mechanism for ensuring a sensitive back-and-forth between private action and public objective through the calibrated use of incentives, permissions, and regulations. Neither the instrumental positivism of the 1950s and 1960s nor the valorization of private rights characteristic of the neoliberal period offered a useful theorization of such mechanisms. The heterogeneous legal thinking of the post-ISI and post-neoliberal periods, by contrast, focused precisely on this kind of interactive state machinery, which has recently come into vogue under the terms "new governance" or the "new developmental state."[6]

At the international level, a bit more skepticism about the international legal order might have turned the political energy devoted to the NIEO project in more useful directions. The infatuation with sovereignty that understandably followed decolonization led development experts to underestimate the significance of transnational institutions and private ordering. The legal dream of an international social welfare state, centered on the institutional machinery of the United Nations, distracted attention from the rising significance of the international financial institutions. In the debt crisis, the extraterritorial legal significance of First World central banks—and of private banks—would come as a surprise. At the national level, faith in an instrumental law may have contributed to the sclerosis of the developmental state. Attention to the interactions between public and private or formal and informal modes of legal organization would have made

Ideas and assumptions about law: 1950–1980

Mainstream Ideas and Assumptions	**Heterogeneous Ideas and Assumptions (from the left and right)**
Legal pragmatism Law as the instrument of power Functionalism	Legal sociology Gap between law in the books and law in action
Administrative law/bureaucracy Priority of public law Focus on formal regulation	Criticism of legal instrumentalism
Positivism Sovereign authority Legislative or executive supremacy	Legal pluralism More than one legal order More than one function or purpose More than one applicable rule
Little judicial review Judges as administrative agents of sovereign purpose	Significance of informal arrangements, private ordering, customary practices, and norms Importance of exceptions and noncompliance Strategic use of non-enforcement, noncompliance, legal permissions and privileges
Interpretive discretion Antiformalism Standards and principles more significant than rules Expertise	Loss of faith in expert discretion A more emphatic antiformalism
Law as policy	Grasp of the significance of private ordering and dynamics of private reaction to legal rules and institutions Strategic uses of law by social actors
Economic and social rights	Importance of restraints on public power Rise of legal rights as restraints on the state International human rights
International law formalism National sovereignty and self-determination	Pessimism about law as an instrument of social and economic change
United Nations	Judicial review and autonomy
	Public choice theory—rent-seeking Irrationality of the state

Figure 1.2. Ideas and assumptions about law, 1950–80

a more nuanced policy possible, while strengthening understanding of the structure of local political economy.

Inattention to the limits of legal instrumentalism made it more difficult to correct course when policies did not operate as intended. By thinking of law as a relatively transparent instrument for policy, it is more difficult to see policy instruments and legal regimes as the product of social and political struggle or as an independent variable in the policy process. You may not notice the ways parties use and ignore legal arrangements, changing their impact. Or to strategize about the way rules may function, not only as top-down regulations, restraints, or incentives, but also as background entitlements in private and public bargaining. By failing to notice these things, policymakers often responded to disappointment over one initiative by adding another, rather than diagnosing the ways in which the disappointment may have been functional to the array of political and social forces responsible for the initiative. Rather than understanding and harnessing these social forces, experts tended to refine and amend their policy apparatus, multiplying rules and administrative agencies.

The impact of implicit legal ideas is extremely difficult to identify. The implicit legal theory of postwar development professionals may have encouraged policy-makers to overestimate the ease with which social purposes could, in fact, be realized through law—how easily public law initiatives could be implemented, how effective state bureaucracies were. These implicit legal ideas may have made it more difficult to imagine alternative development strategies. The focus on public law may have made it more difficult to imagine how private arrangements might have been harnessed to development objectives. The belief that the price system would not work effectively became something of a self-fulfilling prophecy. Faith in the effectiveness of public administrative intention made it seem unreasonable to think that the amount of investment and the place for its application could be better managed by disaggregated private decisions. It seemed obvious that one needed to jumpstart the market, drawing the private actors to the table, in effect. Using incentives meant using public licenses, tax credits, subsidies, and the like. The sheer scale of infrastructure investment reinforced the sense that only public expenditure and management could do what was necessary. The tendency to lean toward more formal legal instruments, and to focus on their effective penetration of the social context, may have made it more difficult to imagine strategizing about the use of legal permissions and privileges or mobilizing noncompliance in the informal sector toward development objectives. Legal pluralism—the existence of more than one overlapping legal order or rule—can have strategic possibilities that may have been overlooked. The plasticity and usefulness of the background rules of private law and the informal arrangements of ongoing commercial life may also have been undervalued. And perhaps most strikingly, the significance of legal arrangements as limits on state action, whether as individual rights or as a safety valve for social opposition and a pacing mechanism for social change, were all underestimated.

Taken as a whole, the heterogeneous strands within postwar economic and legal thinking are worth revisiting. In the economic field, these are the strands associated with institutionalism, structuralism, and dependency theory. In the legal field, they are the strands associated with the critiques of legal instrumentalism. Although their work was not central in development thinking, legal sociologists were already focused on the gap between legal enactments and legal results. Legal theorists had long since understood the potential significance of informal arrangements, the strategic possibilities opened up by the toleration of noncompliance, and the uses for legal pluralism. We might group these heterogeneous ideas under the diverse banners of pragmatism, realism, sociological study of law, or antiformalism and see them as the legal analog to economic institutionalism, structuralism, or dependency theory. Conspicuously absent were ideas about the priority of private law and individual rights, which would emerge as heterogeneous alternatives in the 1970s and become dominant by the 1980s.

THE LAW OF NEOLIBERALISM: PRIVATE "RULE-OF-LAW" FORMALISM AND ITS DISCONTENTS 1980–2000

With hindsight, we can see that a more successful mobilization of heterogeneous ideas about law might have both helped to fine-tune the postwar development state and contributed to our understanding of the institutional and contextual weaknesses of the postwar import substitution program. It is with that lesson in mind that I turn to the current moment, in which the neoliberal program, once dominant among development experts, has been widely criticized in economic and political terms. This time around, ideas about law have been closer to the surface. Yet it remains true that as heterogeneous economic thinking has edged the neoliberal consensus offstage, little use has been made of insights from critical thinking in the legal field that may have been helpful in understanding the weaknesses of the neoliberal vision and fine-tuning post-Washington Consensus policymaking. Moreover, many of the legal ideas and law reform projects of the neoliberal era continue to be promoted, long after skepticism about the broader economic and political program of which they were a part has become widespread.

The legal program and legal theory of neoliberalism

After a decade or more of drift, contestation, and invention, a broad consensus returned to field of development study in the 1980s and 1990s. The neoliberal program, at the national and international levels, began as an effort to unbuild the postwar developmental state, constraining its policy autonomy, disciplining its economic management, and transferring its economic functions to the private sector and embedding it in the global trade and financial system. The goal was not an improved exercise of state power but rather to disentangle the state from the market and establish more effective restraints on government rent-seeking and public choice bickering. All this was to be accomplished by law. As the instrument of neoliberal policy, national legislation and administrative action would be used to build down the import substitution regime. At the international level, structural adjustment, conditionality, the General Agreement on Tariffs and Trade (GATT), and the global banking system were all legal regimes for which a country could sign up, tying its economic policy arms to the mast.

At the same time, new legal regimes were also necessary, domestically and internationally, to support markets—financial regimes, intellectual property regimes, regimes of commercial law. New statutes and administrative rules were required to structure the privatization of state-owned enterprises, to establish financial institutions, to support new capital markets. Banking and payments systems and insurance schemes all required a new legal framework. Investment laws, corporate laws, and insurance and securities laws were needed, and they were promoted across the developing world through legal reform programs. At the international level, neoliberalism shifted attention away from the United Nations to the GATT and to what would soon become a dense regime of bilateral investment treaties. These treaty regimes were intended to harness a political process of bargaining—through either multilateral "rounds" of tariff reduction or more dispersed bilateral efforts by leading economies to force compliance with standard "best practice" investment treaties—toward the progressive elimination of national regulatory barriers to trade and the liberation of the global market from political interference. This international project required both formally binding treaty commitments and an apparatus—at the national and international levels—for interpreting their central commitments in the spirit of market liberalization.

Managing the neoliberal regime in all these dimensions required enormous skill and precision in rule-making and interpretation. National trade regimes would need to identify and sanction foreign unfair or corrupt practices, by private and public entities alike, without descending into protectionism or rent-seeking or becoming captive to the interests of local exporters. Throughout the Third World, government agencies responsible for industrial policy would need to support commerce and trade, while avoiding price-distorting interventions and rent-seeking. National and international agencies would need to offer technical assistance to explain privatization, as they had once explained marketing boards. Buffer stocks were out, but commodity futures markets were in, and programs were implemented to train farmers across India in the use of the Internet to check prices on the Chicago exchanges. Private arbitrators would need to distinguish contractually intended obligations from fraudulent, self-dealing, coercive arrangements of disguised rent-seeking. Judges would need to rework private law to eliminate the effects of distortive "social" objectives, shrink opportunities for discretion that could be used by national officials to discriminate, and generally orient private law to encourage or mimic the Pareto-optimal arrangements private parties would arrive at were they able to transact without costs. All this would require a new style of legal reasoning.

During the neoliberal period, many millions were spent by the development community on projects to promote what was routinely referred to as "the rule of law" in developing societies and to train national elites for participation in the international institutions and legal arrangements of the new global market. The specific national legal reforms promoted under this banner varied over time. In the first phases of neoliberal enthusiasm, becoming a "normal" developed country meant having familiar market institutions—a stock exchange, a banking system, a corporate law regime—interoperable with global market institutions. Later, the favored legal institutions shifted to elections, courts, judicial review, local human rights commissions, and the legal framework for a robust "civil society." Those promoting the rule of law have supported criminal prosecutors, built administrative capacity to operate new corporate and financial regulatory institutions, and trained local officials to participate in global trade negotiations and institutions. By the end of the neoliberal era, it was common to say that the rule of law defines the good developed state, just as compliance with "international human rights" defines human freedom and human flourishing.

The important point is that throughout the period, the term *rule of law* was routinely used to refer to a specific set of reforms. Sometimes the point was to introduce a legal institution (the stock market, the corporation) familiar in the developed West. At other times, the laws promoted for developing societies under this rubric were quite different from those prevailing in the industrialized West—by turns more formal, more constraining of public authority over the economy, less open to institutional variation, and less well embedded in the local institutional, social, and economic context. Across the period, rule-of-law enthusiasm promoted stereotypes about what law is and how it works in the developed West, occluding points at which developed societies themselves differ or have managed to combine a variety of rules and institutional forms pulling in different directions. It was difficult to remember that the legal order in every developed nation reflects that nation's history of struggle and compromises over questions of political economy and distribution, rather than any one recipe for establishing and regulating a market.

The legal theory implicit in these reform efforts was, in some ways, quite familiar from the postwar period of import substitution industrialization. In many respects, the neoliberal program was as *instrumentalist* and *positivist* about law as the postwar development state had been. National import substitution regimes were to be *unbuilt* by treaty, by statute, by administrative decree. Particularly in the first phase, the statutes proposed to accomplish these goals were quite standardized—offered to one country after another as a kind of global "best practice." The foreign experts bringing new statutes for securities regulation, corporate law, insurance, banking or commercial law, and more, were every bit as dependent upon legislative positivism and as unconcerned about the relationship between law-by-the-books and law-in-action as their modest interventionist predecessors in the immediate postwar years.

Nor were they interested in the dynamic play between contextual interests and legal change. Particularly in states making the "transition" from socialism to the market, the entire point was to disestablish the prior institutional and economic arrangements. With the right political, economic, and legal framework, a new set of interests and actors would emerge, responding to the possibilities opened up by participation in a global and national market. Neoliberal reformers tended to assume that potential market actors were waiting for the right rules—once in place, they would be made use of. If that didn't happen, they were not the right rules. One didn't need to worry too much about the gap or the implementation. The result was a kind of *literalism* about law and legal reform.

Like their postwar predecessors, moreover, neoliberal development experts were drawn to relatively formal ideas about law. They tended to imagine clear rules as the antidote to official discretion run amok in the development state. And like their predecessors, they realized that discretion would sometimes be necessary. At those moments, everything would depend upon the spirit with which officials approached the task of interpretation. They would need to be trained to share a commitment to the technical and broader political or economic axioms of the neoliberal vision. They would then be able to see that neoliberal institutional arrangements were, in the final analysis, compelled by the facts of global economic life, the requirements of markets, and the significance of undistorted prices for the efficient allocation of resources. Where there was discretion, it could be exercised by reference to these broader social facts and needs. Although the content is different, this approach to expert discretion is similar to that of the ISI period. At that time, it was widely imagined that the requirements of interdependence, industrialization, national mobilization, and solidarity could guide the exercise of expert discretion.

The legal theory of the neoliberal development policy also introduced new elements and points of emphasis. The focus shifted from public to private law.

Law emerged as a *limit* on the state—on the discretion of administrators and the mandate of legislators. Private rights, constitutional procedures, judicial review, international obligations—all were intended to constrain the neoliberal state. The focus shifted from sovereignty and administrative or legislative positivism to private rights and private ordering, both nationally and transnationally. In thinking about the legal profession, attention shifted from those who would operate the developmental state to those who would represent private interests in the international corporate bar. The goal was less to ensure that state functionaries understood the needs of national development, than that both public and private experts understood the needs of (largely foreign) capital and were able to formulate rules to "open markets" and encourage its arrival. Where there was formalism, it was a formalism about rights and the limits of public law. Where there was antiformalism about social needs, it was the needs of a(n international) market of undistorted prices.

Within the legal field, both strands of this approach to interpretation had been strongly criticized for some time. The reliance on formal rules stemmed from an overestimation of both their ability to restrain interpretive discretion and the predictability with which they could be expected to translate into results on the ground. The antiformal reliance on social needs and functions had also been criticized for underestimating the difficulty of conjuring an *ought* from an *is* by deduction rather than choice. Social arrangements are notoriously multiple and contradictory and are themselves a reflection of prior legal choices. Arguing from the nature of markets is, in this sense, analogous to arguing from social solidarity or the needs of national development. Markets have many needs and their nature will depend upon the legal arrangements one chooses to put in place. As a result, jurists schooled in this critical tradition are apt to see arguments from social need as opportunities for ideology to displace analysis or for the unacknowledged introduction of diverse subjective preferences into the work of legal analysis.

In the North, these critical strands of legal thinking had helped to chasten agents of the welfare state, opening legal interpretation to engagement with economic, social, and ethical analytics, while focusing legal attention on the legitimacy of legal procedures and institutional arrangements rather than the substantive enthusiasms of the interpretive elite. A century of criticism had undermined confidence that private right could be unfolded as logic against the state. More often, what presented itself as the assertion of private right represented a choice for one rather than another policy, one rather than another approach to governmental engagement with conflicting private interests. (This argument is developed in more detail in this volume's essay on property rights as a recipe for development.)

This tradition might have been helpful to those suspicious of neoliberal enthusiasm for limiting state policy autonomy and discretion in the name of supposedly univocal market needs and private entitlements. Indeed, it must have been an ironic moment for those who had participated in the "law and development movement" in the 1960s and 1970s. Ideas about law that would have been useful in making developmental states more responsive and effective were again being set to one side by those who sought to disestablish those states precisely because they had become rigid and ineffective. Another vast program of legal reform would be mounted in the developing world without the benefit of a sociologically informed, critical, and antiformal legal science.

Over the last decade or more, economists and other development experts have criticized neoliberal ideas about development in a variety of ways. In broad terms, these criticisms have often focused on the need for context-specific policies, for fine-tuning, sequencing, and careful attention to local institutional arrangements, as well as the structures of social, political, and economic power. In part, development policymaking has been rendered more nuanced, attentive to the details of local market failures, public goods problems, agency costs. At the same time, it has also become more attentive to the dynamics of interaction between social or political forces and economic change—focused on structures influencing bargaining power in the international trade system, the impact of political economy on the sequencing of reforms, and the ability to harness or dismantle monopoly capacity to extract rents and mobilize resources. Experts have stressed the availability of alternative development paths—different institutional and distributional arrangements that may be compatible with equivalent levels of growth. In all these ways, as the neoliberal consensus has eroded, experts have stressed that development policy is not a matter of one-size-fits-all, and that what might be termed the politics of development policy cannot be replaced by careful analytics.

These broad themes have been echoed in the criticisms levied within the legal field against prominent elements in the neoliberal law reform program. Three short examples will suffice to illustrate the intellectual affinities between legal and economic styles of critique. Scholars working in critical and sociologically oriented traditions of legal science have criticized the neoliberal preoccupation with stronger judicial power, with private law formalization, and with a campaign against corruption.

Example: judicial review and judicial reform

The most important and visible institutional object of neoliberal reform energy has been the judiciary. More reliable courts with enhanced powers to review legislative and administrative decisions seem like a good idea for lots of reasons, and it often seems that there is little to be said to the contrary. Developed countries often have, or at least are thought to have, reliable judicial systems. They seem promising agents for enforcing private arrangements, supporting criminal prosecution, fighting administrative corruption, and ensuring government respect for human rights, including the right to property.

In the neoliberal picture, courts seemed central to the enforcement of market transactions and the limitation of public discretion. Court enforcement of private law was thought necessary to enable market actors to make use of the new rule systems being put in place. The focus on courts also accompanied a retreat from the legislative and administrative positivism of the modest interventionist period. With powers of *judicial review*, courts could enforce property rights against the executive, restraining its ability to mobilize resources for development and encouraging a retreat from interventionism. Indeed, by strictly enforcing contracts and property rights, it seemed that courts could both support market transactions and resist encroachment by the state. As a result, if the administrative failures of the postwar development state suggested deregulation, adjudicative weakness called for judicial reform. Millions of aid dollars were devoted to judicial training, upgrading judicial infrastructure, and reforming public law arrangements to encourage judicial review. Once reformed and rendered independent of executive and legislative interference, national courts promised to stand behind the new limits of state authority and enforce private ordering arrangements.

Of course, even if improved judges could do all these things—and if judicial reform programs could create judges able and willing to take this on—the connection to economic growth is less obvious. Although there was some empirical evidence that a reputation for good judging correlated with investment and economic performance, it was hardly compelling; as we might imagine, investment and economic performance correlate with many things. In assuming that private market actors would need reliable courts before they would invest or transact, neoliberal development experts ignored a lengthy tradition of sociological study drawing this assumption into question. That tradition had demonstrated that private parties use the legal system strategically, shopping for modes of dispute resolution suitable for their needs. More importantly, their needs differ—for everyone who calls on the state to enforce his contract, there is someone else who hopes the state will be unavailable or unwilling to comply.

Moreover, sociological legal study had long demonstrated that markets do work in the absence of judicial enforcement. This is not only true of black markets and informal markets, but also of most functioning markets in developed economies where litigation is, in fact, quite rare. Indeed, in many places one also hears that overactive judges and overly litigious market actors pose a *threat* to efficiency and growth. As comparative legal study quickly confirms, nations have developed with different allocations of power between administrative, legislative, and judicial authorities. Moreover, developed economies vary in the degree to which economic life is embedded in formal legal institutions. Administrative agencies may also be tasked with responsibility for enforcing commercial arrangements or implementing neoliberal reforms. Private actors often prefer to make their own way, enforcing their reciprocal rights extra-legally, through reputation or informal private sanctions. Or they may be willing to lump their losses rather than seek court enforcement.

Nevertheless, strong courts loomed large in the neoliberal picture of what foreign capital required. Development professionals became convinced that the reputation of national judges was an important element in the investment decisions of foreign investors. If true, this is a puzzling criterion on which to base investment decisions. We know that there is extensive foreign investment in places without functioning judiciaries—even in war zones. As one international oil executive told me when I asked about the legal arrangements his company preferred, "it's all a matter of rate of return." After all, it is not clear that foreign investors in fact use courts at home that often—or that they expect to when investing abroad. Indeed, there is little reason to imagine a priori that courts would be any less subject to local prejudices, incompetence, or rent-seeking than administrators—or any easier to reform. International investors are generally careful to locate dispute resolution in privately organized arbitration schemes or in judicial systems with which they are familiar. Nevertheless, for a period at the turn of the century, having a "reformed" judiciary with powers of judicial review came to signify national willingness to respect investors' rights and allow profit repatriation.

As I remember speaking with development experts and financiers in the South during this period, there was always something oddly disconnected about the way they would frame their interest in judges. After lengthy discussions about economic strategy, in which government had hardly figured, let alone judges, when I asked if there were any legal or institutional changes that would strengthen their strategic hand, they would often say "reform the judiciary." Yet it was hard to avoid the thought that this was a kind of free-floating ideological commitment, a ready answer to questions about law reform, but not something they could link in any way to their own economic strategy. Although potential foreign investors often *said* they wanted better courts during this period, a view reinforced by international financial institutions, private consultants, and the international corporate bar, it would take more study to understand whether this was accompanied by actual use of courts by these actors, either abroad or at home in the industrialized North. It would take still more to discover whether this was a significant factor for other market actors or if it was rather a collective prejudice held by potential foreign investors of the day.

At the time, part of the appeal of courts was the promise that, unlike national executives or legislatures, they would be relatively independent of ideological predilections. They would enforce rights and contracts and statutes in ways that would be predictable because they would track what was *written*, rather than introducing the ideologically driven purposes of the government's development strategy or the subjective preferences of the judge or administrator. In part, this appeal depends upon the clarity of the written law. For a century, it has been a common, if often heterogeneous or critical, observation within the legal field that doctrinal materials have far more gaps, conflicts, and ambiguities than this image of relatively mechanical judicial application suggests. Texts are often intentionally vague, circumstances change, various rules and rule systems may be applicable to a single problem, unanticipated applications present themselves. Moreover, the purposes and principles that might be thought to stand behind the texts, guiding their interpretation, are themselves quite general and often in conflict with one another.

As a result, the image of the judiciary as an escape from ideology also depends on ideas about how judges *reason* under these conditions. Which rights do they choose to enforce, what meanings do they give them, what arguments do they find persuasive? This might be a matter of simply relying upon judges to share a neoliberal—or, a generation earlier, a developmentalist—sensibility. But the image of a nonideological, and yet reliable, judiciary also suggests that judges might share a method of reasoning capable of figuring out how to deal with gaps and conflicts and judgment calls within the legal fabric without relying overtly on the kind of ideological commitment more appropriate for a legislature or executive.

The types of questions that call for such reasoning in the neoliberal program are easy to identify. Take judicial review of legislative acts in the name of preexisting rights. This could easily be a two-edged sword. After all, the modest interventionist regime had also generated a wide range of entitlements—to quotas, subsidies, special licensing, and welfare arrangements, which were to be undone by neoliberal reforms. For judicial review to support the neoliberal reform process, courts would have to distinguish inappropriate price-distorting entitlement claims of the past regime from "real" property rights. To entrust judges with this task required both a faith in the formal distinctiveness and clarity of market-supporting entitlements, as well as confidence that judges, on the whole, could be relied upon to distinguish between property rights that preexist the interventionist state and entitlements that are the product of interventionist action by the state. Legal scholars have puzzled over this distinction for decades, and many feel that they have, in different ways, resolved it. But there remains a strand of legal thought that has generated a variety of internal and external analytic criticisms of these proposed resolutions, undermining confidence in the ability of judges to make these distinctions confidently if they do not come to the problem as committed neoliberals.

The basic problem here is that development experts are turning to law, and judges in particular, to make distinctions for which there is no decisive or compelling economic analytic. After neoliberalism, mainstream economic wisdom instructs us to support, but not to distort, private ordering—and to supplant or regulate private ordering where markets fail, unless the market imperfection, disequilibrium, or monopoly power can be harnessed for developmental purposes. These distinctions are terribly hard to model and to measure. They are no easier to sort out when transformed into legal standards for judges to apply.

This is true whether the rights to be enforced come from conventional private law or from internal corporate administrative regimes, private standard setting, and corporate codes of conduct. As globally uniform and "consensual" substitutes for both national regulation and international standards, private codes were often applied first in global manufacturing as a quality-control device, ratified by global standards-setting bodies, and managed by professional inspectors and complaints procedures. At whatever level they are enforced, all these schemes require interpretive talent to align their terms as applied in practice with market imperatives and avoid entrenching anticompetitive advantages or compounding public goods and agency problems. Doing so requires a mode of legal reasoning that had come under increasing pressure from heterogeneous strands of legal thought over many decades.

This is easily seen at the international level, where the legal regime was also being rethought. Take the GATT: It combines a set of rather vague core legal obligations ("national treatment" and "most-favored nation") with a broad range of vague exceptions (such as "national security"). A great deal depends upon the spirit with which it is implemented—and on the political/legal process through which that implementation takes place. A large legal literature sprang up demonstrating the room for maneuver left open by these texts and the dramatic ways in which the normal practices of developed industrial economies departed from the formulaic "best practice" recipes advocated for the developing world. But this literature did not translate into a marked relaxation in the neoliberal common sense about what these treaty obligations required of developing countries.

Moreover, these international regulatory regimes were notoriously ambivalent in their core requirements and posed stark choices among alternative economic models. Transposing these choices into questions of routine legal interpretation meant leaning heavily on background political and economic assumptions about what is normal or appropriate—on ideologies of one or another sort. This drift from legal analysis to ideology as the need for political choice became apparent had long been a theme in heterogeneous writing about international law, but was rarely part of the discussion among those critical of neoliberal trade policy prescriptions.

For example, most free trade arrangements discourage or prohibit regulatory arrangements that are *equivalent* to tariff barriers or subsidies in the name of free trade. As tariffs came down in the postwar era, industrial nations began to contest elements of one another's background legal regime by asserting that the regulatory environment of their trading partner constituted unfair "nontariff barriers to trade." National trade law regimes are always tempted to interpret any foreign impediment to their imports as an unfair barrier to trade—they would need a vocabulary of self-restraint. For the broad GATT provisions, defining "nontariff barrier" to serve as such a vocabulary requires more than the formal application of the treaty. It also requires interpretive facility with the distinction between an unfair barrier to trade and a normal national background regulation, and neoliberal development professionals were enthusiastic about turning this task over to the new adjudicative machinery of the WTO.

It turns out, however, that it is extremely difficult to identify "unfair" trade practices in legal terms, or to distinguish, say, between "subsidies" and "nontariff barriers" with any logical precision. It is an old legal realist insight that the reciprocal nature of a comparison between two legal rules—or legal regimes—makes it impossible to say which *causes* the harm—or which is "discriminatory." Is Mexico's low minimum wage—or failure to implement its own minimum wage scheme—a prohibited "subsidy" or an "unreasonable" extraterritorial extension of its employment law into the American economy? Are Mexican manufacturers who benefit from nonenforcement of local law "dumping" when they export to American markets? Or, on the other hand, were the United States to impose a compensatory tariff or block imports of Mexican goods that did not comply with American or Mexican regulatory provisions, would Mexico face an unfair "nontariff barrier" or an unreasonable extraterritorial reach of US law? What seemed a technical question of legal interpretation quickly becomes a question of political economy about the sustainability of a low-wage development strategy and about American sovereignty to demand and protect high labor standards for production of goods to be imported to its market.

Legal analysts might, at least in the first instance, draw the distinction in formal terms—if the foreign rule takes the form of a tariff or subsidy, it is an unfair barrier to trade, if not, not. But early on it was recognized that national regulators could use "nontariff barriers" to equally market-restrictive effect. One might be tempted to preclude all *public* regulatory price distortions, while using antitrust to attack parallel private market-distorting arrangements—but too many neoliberal regulatory initiatives might also fall under this ax. What is required is a mode of distinction that analyzes regulations for their actual market-restricting or -enabling potential. In the early stages, background ideas about what is "normal" served the purpose—if farmers *normally* grow wheat, a new railroad may appear to impose the cost; if the difference between American and Mexican wages is "normal," American efforts to raise Mexican standards will seem an abnormal nontariff barrier. As ever more national regulations were contested for their compatibility with national and global trade standards, such default ideas seemed ever less plausible.

Within the legal field, scholars are divided in their response to this difficulty. For some, the answer is a more precise analytic model or empirical assessment, perhaps imported from economics. Others understand these interpretive problems to be beyond the reach of an intellectually satisfying resolution. Here there are two tendencies. For some, the goal is to muddle through, tacking this way and that, to provide a workable interface between national regimes with different ideas about an appropriate level for regulation, guided by the spirit of trade liberalization. For others, the absence of a satisfying interpretive resolution opens up the possibility for political choice, for assessment of alternative economic and social trajectories, and different distributive outcomes. In different ways, each of these responses ought to be useful to post-neoliberal development economists seeking to fine-tune neoliberal recipes in specific situations and open development policy to social and political choice.

In fact, the result was not a more nuanced mode of legal reasoning, still less one rooted in careful economic analytics or case-specific empirical study. Instead, the focus on courts, on private law enforcement, and on judicial review to protect property entitlements from interventionist rent-seeking gave way to a new mode of legal *argument* about policy. This was not the formalism of judicial passivity or deference to plain textual meaning—the spread of judicial review placed courts in a far more central role. To distinguish property entitlements whose enforcement supported the market from entitlements whose enforcement would extend the distorting effects of modest interventionism required a more robust mode of reasoning. A sharp formal distinction between private rights and publicly created entitlements seemed a good place to start, but it would not be the end of the story. Judges would need to determine *which* property rights to enforce in cases of conflict, and how extensively to interpret exceptions. *Some* administratively created rights—concessions to foreign investors exploiting natural resources, tax incentives, exemptions from zoning or local regulation, eminent domain powers—were also part of the neoliberal order. Judges would need to be able to distinguish between rights that must be enforced for the market to succeed and rent-seeking or corrupt entitlement claims that needed to be rejected. In making these distinctions, judges would need to align their interpretation of property rights with good policy sense—participating in the new discourse about the existence, extent, and prognosis for market failures and the justifications for regulation and intervention.

In specific cases, professionals would argue for upholding or overturning a rule by framing it using a new legal vernacular. This new mode of legal reasoning borrowed its language and general spirit from contemporary economic theory. However, instead of a subtle second-best welfare economic analytics, for example, we find a curious amalgam of welfare economic slogans, informal ideas about the type and extent of possible market failures, default ideas about likely governance failures, sporadic empiricism correlating national legal institutions and legal rules with economic performance to identify rule-of-thumb "best practices," informal deference to the attitudes of the foreign investor community, a literalism about law's instrumental potential, and professional conventions of interpretive restraint. The image of a perfectly competitive Kaldor–Hicks-efficient end state provides a kind of loose reference point and target against which to compare various judicial approaches. Legislative or administrative actions are understood to be "more" or "less" interventionist, and then judged by whether market failures or public goods problems or agency problems or transaction costs seem relatively large or small.

The extent to which confidence in the judiciary as an economic manager has outlived confidence in neoliberal economic management is surprising. Economists during and after the neoliberal moment seem to share an overestimation of the judicial capacity both to adopt economic analytics and to remain detached from ideological commitment. It is certainly true that a modern judiciary can adopt the language of post-neoliberal economic analysis. But adjudication remains an interpretive activity. For economists interested in opening development planning either to more fine-grained empirical and theoretical analytics or to more locally informed political choice, it would seen that heterogeneous strands of legal thinking developed to unravel this kind of policy vernacular, revealing elements of ideology and opportunities for political choice within the "rule of law" as practiced by the modern judiciary, would be useful.

Example: formalization

During the neoliberal period, the conviction grew among development professionals that economic performance in the Third World required a formalization of private legal rights. As the evolving neoliberal policy vocabulary became ever more hazy and multifaceted, this idea continued to resonate, in part because it, like judicial reform, promised a way to make policy choices congenial for economic development without making the sort of overtly political choices about distribution of resources which characterized both modest interventionism and the international proposals of the NIEO.

Although the policy vocabulary of neoliberal interpretation was extremely flexible—and has become more so in the last decade—there is no question that the focus on formalization narrowed the range for interpretive maneuver from the more open-ended socially oriented discourse of the preceding periods. The implicit—and sometimes explicit—legal theory of neoliberalism seemed to forget much of what had been commonplace within the domain of legal theory for more than a century about both the limits of law as an instrument of social change and the plasticity of legal rules and standards. To observers who remained committed to the legal theories of prior periods, it often seemed that neoliberalism asked the legal order to perform feats it was unlikely to accomplish and to remain neutral in making distinctions in ways it seemed unlikely to sustain.

One might say that neoliberals promoting formalization seemed to deny the necessity for interpretation and the difficulty of making precisely the sorts of distinctions between market-ordering and market-distorting made salient by their economic ideas. Indeed, the focus on formalization as a *legal* strategy for development seemed to substitute both for the subtle exercises of welfare economic analytics and for the more open-ended juridical policy analysis that emerged from efforts to link identification of market failures with broader empirical hunches and default assumptions.

Theorists had long toyed with the idea that there might be a connection between legal formality and industrial capitalism. The precise economic justifications for legal formality remained vague—it had something to do with improving the rationality and effectiveness of bureaucratic instrumentalism, with ensuring reliability and predictability, with openness and transparency and price signaling, with the reduction of transaction costs; and it carried some of the moral fervor of individualism and responsibility. It emerged as a strategy for opposing acts of administrative discretion associated with import substitution—in calls for the judicial annulment of relevant legislation or administrative decrees in the name of private rights—at first to property or freedom of contract and then to other human rights.

Formalism meant many things. On the instrumental side, neoliberal development policymakers sought to replace regulatory standards with rules so as to restrain bureaucratic discretion, to implement schemes for clear registered titles, to simplify contracts and strengthen enforcement, to eliminate judicial discretion in the interpretation of statutes—and to encourage judicial review of agency discretion. When it came to rights, formalism meant strict enforcement of property and contract, the priority in general of private over public law, and the formalization of existing informal rights (e.g., squatters to receive title). In one strand, associated with parts of the North American "law and economics movement," a formal approach to private law rules was thought most likely to unleash the productivity gains of movement toward a Pareto-optimal allocation of resources.

At the international level, formalism meant strict construction of free trade commitments, the harmonization of private law so as to eliminate "social" exceptions susceptible to differential judicial application, the insulation of the international private law regime from national judiciaries (often through the conclusion of bilateral investment treaties restricting the regulatory capacity of developing nations when they could be seen to alter the settled expectations of foreign private rights holders), the simplification and harmonization of national regulations, the substitution of privately adopted rules for public law standards, the development of a reliable system of bills of lading and insurance to permit contracts "for the delivery of documents" rather than goods—eliminating rejection for nonconformity, and the formalization and standardization of international payments systems and banking regulations.

Since at least Weber, people have asserted that "formalization" of legal entitlements, in one or another sense, is necessary for development. Necessary for transparency, for information and price signaling, to facilitate alienation of property, to reduce transaction costs, to assure security of title and economic return, or to inspire the confidence and trust needed for investment. From the start, legal formalization has meant a wide variety of different things: a scheme of clear and registered titles, of contractual simplicity and reliable enforcement; a legal system of clear rules rather than vague standards; a scheme of legal doctrine whose internal structure was logical and whose interpretation could be mechanical; a system of institutions and courts whose internal hierarchy was mechanically enforced, in which the discretion of judges and administrators was reduced to a minimum; a public order of passive rule following a priority for private over public law; and more. These ideas are all associated with the reduction of discretion and political choice in the legal system, and are defended as instantiations of the old maxim "not under the rule of man but of god and the law."

It is easy to imagine, from the point of view of a particular economic actor, that legal formalization in any of these ways might well enhance the chances for successful economic activity. A clear title may make it easier for me to sell my land and cheaper for my neighbor to buy it. A clear set of nondiscretionary rules about property, credit, or contract might make a foreign legal culture more transparent to a potential foreign investor. The reliable enforcement of contracts might make the investor more likely to trust someone enough to enter into a contract. Indeed, it seems hard to imagine "capital" except as a set of enforceable legal entitlements—a first lesson of law school is that property is less a relation between a person and an object than a relation between people with differing entitlements to use, sell, possess, or enjoy an object. The developing world is full of potential assets—but they have not been harnessed to productive use. Why? Because no one has clear title to them, nor are there predictable rules enforcing expectations about the return on their productive use.

The association of legal formalization with development, however, has always seemed more problematic than this, also since at least Weber. It is from this intuition that a parallel heterogeneous tradition in legal thought has emerged. For starters, it has also been easy to imagine, from the point of view of *other* economic actors, that formalization in each of these ways might well eliminate the chance for productive economic activity. A clear title may help me to sell or defend my claims to land—but it may impede the productive opportunities for squatters now living there or neighbors whose uses would interfere with my quiet enjoyment. A great deal will depend on what we *mean* by clear title—which of the numerous possible entitlements that might go with "title to property" we choose to enforce. Clear rules about investment may make it easy for foreign investors, but by reducing the wealth now in the hands of those with local knowledge about how credit is allocated or how the government will behave. An enforceable contract would be great for the person who wants the promise enforced, but not for the person who has to pay up. As every first-year contracts student learns, it is one thing to say that stable expectations need to be respected and quite another to say whose expectations need to be respected and what those expectations should legitimately or reasonably be. To say anything about the relationship between legal formalization and *development* we would need a theory about how assets in the hands of the title holder *rather than* the squatter, the foreign *rather than* the local investor, will lead to growth, and then to the sort of growth we associate with "development."

Moreover, the urge to formalize law downplays the role of standards and discretion in the legal orders of developed economies. We might think here of the American effort to codify the Uniform Commercial Code to reflect the needs of businesspeople—an effort that returned again and again to the standard of "reasonableness" as a measure for understanding and enforcing contractual terms. We might remember Weber's account of the "English exception"—the puzzle that industrial development seemed to come first to the nation with the most confusing and least formal system of property law and judicial procedure. Or we might think of Polyani's famous argument that rapid industrialization was rendered sustainable, politically, socially, and ultimately economically, in Britain precisely because law slowed the process down.

The focus on legal formalization downplays the role in economic life of the informal sector—the sector governed by norms other than those enforced by the state or that emerges in the gaps among official institutions. It is not only in the post-transition economies of Eastern and Central Europe that the informal sector provided a vibrant source of entrepreneurial energy. The same can be said for many developing and developed economies. Think of the mafia or of the economic life of diasporic and ethnic communities. But think also of the "old boys' network," the striking demonstrations in early law and society literature about the disregard businessmen in developed economies often had for the requirements of form or the enforceability of contracts. One need only visit a contemporary "free trade zone" to experience the economic vibrancy that can emerge from the relaxation of formal regulatory requirements. At the same time, it has become routine within legal science to reflect upon the potential economic efficiency of breaching contracts and the need to not set penalties in ways that will discourage the movement of assets away from arrangements that seemed likely to be profitable some time back, but no longer are. Or think for a moment about the usefulness of incomplete and vague contracts—the room for maneuver left by unstated, unclear, or ambiguous terms. In the field of property law, similar ideas guide thinking about the economic efficiency of trespass, adverse possession, and the privilege to use adjoining properties in economically productive ways even when they injure a neighbor's quiet enjoyment of his property. In short, the informal sector is often an economically productive one. There is also often security, transparency, and reliability in these informal or extralegal sectors—the question is rather security for whom, transparency to whom? And it is difficult for judges, even when focusing on the holy grail of economic efficiency, to avoid exercising discretion in adjudicating between conflicting ways to protect property or alternative modes for interpreting and enforcing contracts.

The story of development through formalization downplays the range of possible legal formalizations, each with its own winners and losers. In a world with multiple potential stable and efficient equilibriums, a great deal will depend upon the path one takes, and much of this will be determined by the choices one makes in constructing the system of background legal norms. Does "being" a corporation mean having an institutional, administrative, or contractual relationship with one's employees? With their children's daycare provider? And so forth. Looking at the legal regime from the inside, we encounter a series of choices, between formality and informality, between different legal formalizations—each of which will make resources available to different people. What is missing from the enthusiasm for the formalization-as-a-development-strategy is both an awareness of the range of choices available and an economic theory about the developmental consequences of taking one path rather than another.

In a particular developing society, for example, it might be that the existing—discretionary, political, informal, or extralegal—system for allocating licenses or credit is entirely predictable and reliable for some local players even if it is not done in accordance with published legal rules. At the same time it might not be transparent to or reliable for foreign investors. This might encourage local, and discourage foreign, participation in this economic sector. We might well have a political theory of development that suggests that one simply cannot have access to a range of other resources necessary to develop without pleasing foreign direct investors. Or we might have an economic theory suggesting that equal access to knowledge favors investment by the most efficient user and that this user will in turn use the profits from that investment in ways more likely to bring about "development," perhaps based on a projection of how foreign, as opposed to local, investors will invest their returns. But the need for such theories—which would themselves be quite open to contestation—is obscured by the simpler idea that development requires a "formal" rule of law.

Indeed, formalization is not only a substitute for subtle neoliberal policy analysis, it also replaces more conventional questions of development policy and planning that demand decisions about distribution. Traditional questions revolve around who will do what with the returns they receive from work or investment, how gains might best be captured and reinvested, or capital flight eliminated. Or about how one might best take spillover effects into account and exploit forward or backward linkages. Or questions about the politics of tolerable growth and social change, about the social face of development itself, about the relative fate of men and women, rural and urban, in different stable equilibriums, along different policy paths.

It is surprising how complete disinterest in the distributional choices one must make in designing a rule of law suitable for a policy of legal formalization drove these heterogeneous legal considerations off the table during the neoliberal era. Hernando de Soto's famous discussion of the benefits of legal formalization in his book *The Mystery of Capital* provides a good illustration. In discussing land reform, he is adamant that squatters be given formal title to the land on which they have settled. Doing so, he claims, will create useful capital by permitting them to eject trespassers, have the confidence to improve the land, or offer it for sale to more productive users. Of course, it will also destroy the capital of the current land owners—and, if the squatter's new rights are enforced, reduce economic opportunities for trespassers and future squatters. Formalization of title will also distribute authority *among* squatters; where families squat together, for example, formalization may move economic discretion from women to men. The implicit assumption that squatters will make more productive use of the land than the current nominal owners may well often be correct. But de Soto provides no reason for supposing that the squatters will be more productive than the trespassers, nor for concluding that exclusive use by one group is preferable to some customary arrangement of mixed use by squatters and trespassers in the shadow of an ambiguous law.

None of these observations is new. Development planners and practitioners have long struggled with precisely these problems. The puzzle is how easily one loses sight of these traditional issues of political and economic theory when the words "rule of law" come into play. There is something mesmerizing about the idea that a formal rule of law could somehow substitute for struggle over these issues and choices, could replace contestable arguments about the consequences of different distributions with the apparent neutrality of legal best practice.

Example: the anticorruption campaign

A third theme running through neoliberal ideas about the potential for using law as a development strategy focuses on eliminating corruption. There is no doubt that enthusiasm for anticorruption measures was strengthened by the widespread sense for the prevalence of "governance failure" in the Third World. But this sociological and political generalization was not the only reason a strong anti-corruption campaign caught on among development professionals in the neo-liberal era.

Like legal formalization, the elimination of corruption was linked to development in a variety of ways. It was promoted to avoid squandered resources, to promote security and predictability, to inspire confidence, eliminate price distortions, and promote an efficient distribution of resources. It seemed self-evident that these things would lead in some way to economic development. Many of the advantages of eliminating corruption run parallel to those of legal formalization—eliminating corruption can seem much like eliminating judicial and administrative discretion. Indeed, sometimes "corruption" is simply a code word for public discretion—the state acts corruptly when it acts by discretion rather than mechanically, by rule.

Eliminating corruption may well enhance the chances for some economic actors to make productive use of their entitlements. The state's discretion, including the discretion to tax, and even the discretion to levy taxes higher than those authorized by formal law, may spur some and retard other economic activities. As with legal formalization more generally, however, it is not difficult to imagine that other actors—including those who are collecting "corrupt" payments—will in turn be less productive once corruption is eliminated. As with the replacement of discretion by legal form, one must link the elimination of corruption to an idea about the likely developmental consequences of one rather than another set of economic incentives. A simple example would be: Who is more likely to reinvest profits productively, the marginal foreign investor brought in as corruption declines, or the marginal administrator whose take on transactions is eliminated? In my experience, such questions are rarely asked, and yet their answer is not at all obvious. We are back to the need for a political and economic theory about which allocation will best spur development.

Enthusiasm for eliminating corruption as a development strategy arises from the broader idea that corruption somehow drains resources from the system as a whole—its costs are costs of transactions, not costs of the product or service purchased. Elimination of such costs lifts all boats. And such costs might as easily be quite formal and predictable as variable and discretionary. Here the desire to eliminate corruption goes beyond the desire for legal form—embracing the desire to eliminate all costs *imposed* on transactions that are not properly costs *of* the transaction. There are at least two difficulties here. First, the connection between eliminating corruption and "development" remains obscure. Even if the move from a "corrupt" legal regime to a "not corrupt" regime produces a one-time efficiency gain, there is no good economic theory predicting that this will lead to growth or development, rather than simply another stable low-level equilibrium. More troubling is the difficulty of distinguishing clearly between the "normal" or "undistorted" price of a commodity and the "costs" associated with a "corrupt" or distortive process for purchasing the commodity or service. These were precisely the sorts of distinctions first addressed by the analytics of welfare economics, then by the looser policy vocabulary of neoliberalism, for which anticorruption and formalization emerged as default substitutes.

Economic transactions rely on various institutions for support, institutions that lend a hand sometimes by form and sometimes by discretion. But the tools these institutions, including the state, use to support transactions are difficult to separate from those that seem to impose costs on the transaction. The difference is often simply one of perspective—if the cost is imposed on you it seems like a cost, if it is imposed on someone else for your benefit it seems like support for your productive transaction. Here the desire to eliminate corruption bleeds off in a variety of directions. But the boundary between "normal" and "distorted" regulation is the stuff of political contestation and intensely disputed economic theory. When the anticorruption project suggests that the rule of law always already knows how to draw this line, it fades into a stigmatizing moralism, akin to the presentiment against the informal sector.

Hernando De Soto again provides a good illustration. He repeatedly asserts that the numerous bureaucratic steps now involved in formalizing legal entitlements are mud in the gears of capital formation and commerce, retarding development. During the neoliberal era, he was a central voice urging simplification of bureaucratic procedures as a development strategy—every minute and every dollar spent going to the state to pay a fee or get a stamp is a resource lost to development. This seems intuitively plausible. But there is a difficulty—when is the state supporting a transaction by formalizing it and when is the state burdening the transaction by adding unnecessary steps or costs? The aspiration seems to be an economic life without friction, each economic act mechanically supported without costs. But legal forms, like acts of discretion, are not simply friction—they are choices, defenses of some entitlements against others. Each bureaucratic step necessary to enforce a formal title is a subsidy for the economic activity of informal users. Indeed, everything that seems like friction to one economic actor will seem like an entitlement, an advantage, an opportunity to another. The point is to develop a theory for choosing among them.

Let us say we begin by defining corruption as the economic crimes of public figures—stealing tax revenues, accepting bribes for legally mandated services. Even here the connection to development is easier to assume than to demonstrate—are these figures more or less likely to place their gains unproductively in foreign bank accounts than foreign investors, say? Even if we define the problem narrowly as one of theft or conversion it is still difficult to be confident that the result will be slower growth. Sometimes, as every first-year property instructor is at pains to explain, it is a good idea to rearrange entitlements in this way, the doctrine of "adverse possession" being the most dramatic example. Practices one could label as "corrupt" may sometimes be more efficient means of capital accumulation, mobilizing savings for local investment. Moreover, rather few economic transactions are best understood as arm's-length bargains—it turns out, for example, that an enormous share of international trade is conducted by through barter, internal administratively priced transactions, or relational contracts between repeat players. The line between tolerable and intolerable differences in bargaining power—between consent and duress—is famously a site for political contestation. And, just as what sometimes look like market-distorting interventions can also be seen to compensate for one or another market failure, so what look like corrupt local preferences can turn out to be efficient forms of price discrimination.

But those promoting anticorruption as a development strategy generally have something more in mind—a pattern of economic crimes that erodes faith in a government of laws in general or actions by public (or private) actors that artificially distort prices, such as unreasonable finder's fees and patterns of police enforcement that protect mafia monopolies. Here, the focus moves from the image of public officials taking bribes to actions that distort free-market prices or are not equally transparent to local and foreign, private and public, interests. Corruption becomes a code word for rent-seeking—for using power to extract a higher price than that which would be possible in an arm's-length or freely competitive bargain—and for practices that privilege locals. At this point, the anticorruption campaign gets mixed up with a broader program of privatization, deregulation, free trade (dismantling government subsidies and trade barriers, requiring national treatment for foreign products and enterprises), and with background assumptions about the distortive nature of costs exacted by public, as opposed to private, actors.

Here the anticorruption project enters arenas of deep contestation. It has been famously difficult to distinguish administrative discretion that prejudices the rule of law from judicial and administrative discretion that characterizes routine practice of the rule of law. It has been equally difficult to distinguish legal rules and government practices that distort a price from the background rules in whose shadow parties are thought to bargain. And there is no a priori reason for identifying public impositions on the transaction as distortions—transaction costs—and private impositions as costs of the good or service acquired. These matters can be disputed in political or economic terms, but the effort to treat corruption reduction as a development strategy substitutes a vague sense of the technical necessity and moral imperative for a "normal" arrangement of entitlements.

It is easy to interpret the arrangement of entitlements normalized in this way in ideological terms. When the government official uses his discretionary authority to ask a foreign investor to contribute to this or that fund before approving a license to invest, that is corruption. When the investor uses his discretionary authority to authorize investment to force a government to dismantle this or that regulation, that is not corruption. When the government distributes import licenses to allocate scarce foreign exchange, it is an opportunity for unproductive rent-seeking by those waiting in line for the license. When property rights allocate scarce national resources to unproductive users waiting for estates to pass by succession, it is *not* rent-seeking. When pharmaceutical companies exploit their intellectual property rights to make AIDS drugs largely unavailable in Africa, while using the profits to buy sports teams, it is not corruption; but when governments tax imports to build palaces, it is.

Perhaps the most telling problem is the difficulty of differentiating some prices and transactions as "normal" and others as "distorted" by improper exercises of power when every transaction is bargained in the shadow of rules and discretionary decisions, both legal and nonlegal, imposed by private and public actors, which could be changed by political contestation. This old American legal realist observation renders incoherent the idea that transactions, national or international, should be allowed to proceed undistorted by "intervention" or rent-seeking. There is simply no substitute for asking whether the particular intervention is a desirable one, both politically and economically. In this sense, seeking to promote development by eliminating "corruption" replaces economic and political choice with a stigmatizing ideology.

Neoliberal law and development economics: a political alliance

Looking back, it is probably more sensible to think of the campaigns for judicial reform, the formalization of rights, and eliminating corruption as political, rather than economic, projects. They were oriented far more explicitly to the perception of governance failure than to economic performance per se. They responded to the widely shared sense among development professionals that Third World governments simply could not be trusted with policymaking, regardless of the approach taken. If the energy of neoliberalism had come, in part, from its enthusiasm for a *small* state, campaigns for formalism and against corruption were also driven by the desire for a *strong* state, capable of enforcing public order and private rights, without messing in the economy. If we think in distributional terms, there is no question that neoliberal legal theory accepted ideas about law more common in the foreign investor community than in most developing nations. Many ideas about the law needed for development turned out to be about the law foreign investors wanted to see. In ex-socialist countries, as elsewhere, there is no doubt that some local players were better situated to play in this new legal world and to deploy this new legal vocabulary than others.

In ideological terms, these ideas about law are difficult to characterize politically. Instrumentalism, positivism, literalism about the economic consequences of legal initiatives—these have characterized all manner of ideological projects. Although a commitment to formalism was long associated in the United States with laissez-faire recollections of the nineteenth-century period of classical legal thought, it has certainly also served other masters. So also, of course, has judicial review. Development projects formalizing small-scale rights to "empower" those in the informal sector as participants in the formal economy were extremely popular across the ideological spectrum, at least in the North. Likewise judicial reform and anticorruption campaigns. Moreover, the mode of legal reasoning about policy that developed—welfare economics, empirical observations, sociological hunches—to determine which state rules were market-supporting and which were not, was used during this period by development professionals on the left, center, and right.

It did seem, however, that at least broadly speaking, the more market failures you thought there were, the more often you thought government initiatives might well correct them, the less certain you were about defaulting to laissez-faire, the more faith you had in Third World government initiatives, the less significant a problem you felt corruption was, the slower you felt the transition to market should proceed, the more skeptical you were about the large-scale benefits of small-scale formalization, the more likely you were to be a center-left or left-wing analyst.

The legal vocabulary of neoliberalism, however capacious ideologically, had its blind spots and biases as well. It was surprising how completely "social" ideas about solidarity and national economic mobilization disappeared from the legal vocabulary on the left—as well, of course, for the center and right. As a policy analytic, the legal vernacular of the neoliberal period had little room for distributional concerns, particularly efforts to see first-order distribution as a tool for development planning. It pushed issues of redistribution, of fairness in allocation and in bargaining, off the table and focused attention on the nature of the local public and private legal order, rather than on the international legal, political, and economic systems. Development policies rooted in distributional analysis were more difficult to imagine and propose. Moreover, as time went on, the world-wide campaigns of legal reform—judicial reform, formalization, anticorruption—had the effect of pushing even neoliberal economic analytics to one side, at least in the legal vernacular for policymaking. The legal projects necessary to create a small economic state with a strengthened public order state reemphasized distinctions between public and private legal orders and institutions that had everywhere been eroded during the same period in the North in favor of more flexible "soft law" styles of governance or public–private partnerships. This certainly responded to the stigma associated with Third World governance, but it also undoubtedly reinforced it.

Legal ideas and assumptions: 1980–2000

Mainstream—neoliberal ideas and assumptions

Instrumentalism and faith in legislative effectiveness continued

Private law > public law
Law as a limit on administrative and legislative discretion
Private rights and constitutional process
Judicial review
Neo-formalism about public law limits

Property rights, yes; price distorting entitlements, no

Private standard-setting and codes of conduct
Government failure

GATT/TRIPS
Formalism about international obligations
Bilateral investment treaties

Formalization of private law and of entrenched rights

Anticorruption campaigns
Transparency

Kaldor–Hicks for judges
Efficiency as adjudicative target

Corporate law reform
Investor protection and guarantees

International human rights as a development strategy

Heterogeneous ideas and assumptions

Legal sociology/limits to legislative effectiveness

Private rent-seeking
Failures of private decision making and management

Legal pluralism

Critiques of formalization and anticorruption as coherent strategies for legal implementation

Significance of background norms for private bargaining power
Market prices a function of background legal entitlements

Critiques of informality and private dispute settlement—ubiquity of unequal bargaining power, information asymmetries, and agency problems

Distributional and cultural significance of alternative corporate governance models

Instability of distinctions between private law and regulation, subsidies and non-tariff barriers, costs of the transaction, and costs of the product
Need for discretion
Distributive significance of interpretive choices

Arguments for regulation:
compensation for market failures, for transaction costs, for information problems, for the irrationality of markets, for protection and allocation of public goods

Reinterpretation of private law arrangements as regulatory

Distributional significance of choices among regulatory forms—disclosure, mandates, private liability, criminal sanction, taxation

Interactions of regulatory machinery, institutional forms, and private rights

Critique of human rights as a recipe for development rather than a vernacular for distributive choice

Figure 1.3. Legal ideas and assumptions, 1980–2000

Within the legal field, however, experts were not all of one mind during the neoliberal period. If we were to simplify the story, we could divide the available intellectual traditions and ideas about law into two broad groups—those associated with the mainstream neoliberal consensus, and those that in one way or another were understood to qualify or critique that consensus. Figure 1.3 provides a summary list of these different groups of ideas.

Lined up in this way, it is clear that there is more than a loose or accidental relationship between the various heterogeneous strands of thinking that have emerged in economics and in law as the neoliberal consensus has faded. Sometimes the association is quite direct—legal reasoning has simply imported ideas about transaction costs and information problems into the repertoire of legal arguments in favor of regulatory or administrative restrictions on the exercise of rights. This kind of importation can run into difficulties, of course—parallel to those that accompanied the effort to transform a nuanced welfare economic analysis into the kind of formula judges could easily apply during the neoliberal enthusiasm for Kaldor–Hicks efficiency analysis as a mode for interpreting and allocating private rights. Indeed, often what the heterogeneous traditions within law have to offer is caution about our ability to translate economic theories about "transaction costs" or "public goods" directly into legal and institutional forms. There often turns out to be more than one way to do this, a fair amount of incoherence in the distinctions themselves when trying to apply them as legal categories, and a real need for economic and political choices about who will bear the costs of making these distinctions in one way rather than another. It is precisely for this reason that an alliance among critical or heterogeneous traditions from law and other disciplines seems promising in our current post-neoliberal age.

OPPORTUNITIES FOR A POST-NEOLIBERAL ALLIANCE: CRITICAL AND HETEROGENEOUS IDEAS FROM LAW AND DEVELOPMENT ECONOMICS

Development experts today do not share the kind of consensus, about either economics or law, which characterized the postwar and neoliberal periods. The situation now is far more chaotic. The field is only just beginning to theorize China's own astonishing recent development. The intuition that China did not play by any known book over the last decades is visible in the widespread use of the word "heterogeneous" to describe Chinese development policy—a catch-all phrase for a combination of policies that seem difficult to categorize as developmentalist or neoliberal, or to unscramble using the common policy vernaculars of the post-neoliberal period.

Of course, there are favorite policy ideas in the field today. Macroeconomic stability, strategic engagement with the international trade system, the pursuit of human rights as a development strategy—all remain popular. Anticorruption and transparency remain common prescriptions for governmental reform, as does the privatization of governance through private standard setting and corporate "social responsibility." New modes of regulation and soft governance dispersing regulatory capacity into the private sector are fashionable in many places. At the international level, there is widespread enthusiasm for forms of "integration," often inspired by the model of the European Union.

Like other currently popular recipes for development, each of these combines intuitions about economics and law. At the same time, development policy today is made everywhere against the background of many generations of previous policy efforts. Arguments about what works and what doesn't from each of those previous moments survive and are often resurrected. Ideas about law, both mainstream and heterogeneous, from the postwar and neoliberal periods survive. Law remains instrumental, purposive—the agent of development policy. It has remained a site and vehicle for complex policy analysis—for weighing and balancing and conducting nuanced market failure analysis. Law has also remained the repository of ontological limits to state policy. Just as neoliberalism had contested dirigiste initiatives as violations of individual—often property—rights, so neoliberalism has been contested from the start by assertions of rights acquired from modest interventionist administrative and legislative arrangements.

Neoliberal reforms to build down modest interventionist regimes have continued, as have efforts to reform corporate law, commercial, securities, and bankruptcy law. Development planners have remained, by and large, enthusiastic about the spread of formal property rights and the formalization of the informal economy, particularly where formalization could facilitate the spread of small-scale credit arrangements—so-called microlending schemes, often targeting women in local communities. But with increased attention to the positive functions of the state, attention has also gone into development of law enforcement, security and military bureaucracies, and into capacity building for participation in global trade, investment, and currency stabilization arrangements.

This enhanced policy role for law, legal institutions, and legal analysis, coupled with a more robust role for judges in weighing acquired rights against justifications for development policies, have all placed the legal system as a whole more centrally in the development story.

Law continues to be seen as the primary vehicle for managing the relationship among public and private institutions—checking against rent-seeking or capture by special interests, and ensuring that administrative agencies, courts, and legislatures keep their focus on legitimate regulation stabilizing markets and supporting market transactions by remedying market failures or compensating for public goods and transaction cost problems, rather than distorting prices or disrupting markets in the name of other development objectives.

The focus on institution and state building in recent development thinking has also relied on law as a vehicle for democratic transformation—law reform, elections, checks and balances, judicial review. *Constitutions* have become development vehicles. Only through democratic checks and balances, according to some public choice theory, can the tendency to capture by special interests be blunted. The ability of national regimes to legitimate the often painful adjustment to global market conditions without succumbing to rent-seeking protectionism will depend, it is often asserted, on their constitutional character. There is much disagreement, of course, about precisely *what* constitution is required—a strong state, an open state, a limited state—but the role of law as a constitutional vocabulary of legitimacy and self-limitation for necessary economic choices is widely accepted.

At the international level, we see a similar range of legal ideas—promotion of human rights as a development strategy, democratization, and legal reform as the vehicle for strengthening national economic performance, the emergence of "soft law" methods of rule-making for social legal fields in Europe, and internationally, the expansion of civil society networks as discussion partners for regulatory conversation. Indeed, the international regime is itself increasingly conceptualized in liberal constitutional terms. The World Trade Organization (WTO) has transformed political negotiations over the appropriate national regulatory scheme—you drop this law and I'll drop that one—into a quasi-judicial legal process of interpretation. Commentators have promoted the WTO as a "world constitution" to facilitate the adjustment of national regulatory regimes to one another. International organizations have come to address development almost exclusively in terms of legal rights—social and economic rights, democratic rights, as well as commercial and property rights.

After more than twenty years, the most significant role played by law in current development thinking is as a *vocabulary for policymaking*. Arguments that would once have been conducted in the vernacular of economics are now made in legal terms. This reflects two tendencies: the diffusion of economic analytics into broad rules of thumb, default preferences, and conflicting considerations; and the simultaneous development within law of modes of reasoning suitable for arguing about such matters. Purposive interpretation implicates legal reasoning in argument about the appropriate pathway to broad social goals like "development."

Although one might think these questions might be better answered with a tight economic analysis, or on the basis of careful empirical study, in fact neither is usually available or decisive enough to avoid the need for a policy vocabulary more open to sociological and ideological hunches and default positions. Law, rather than economics, has become the rhetorical domain for identifying market failures and transaction costs, and attending to their elimination, for weighing and balancing institutional prerogatives, for assessing the proportionality and necessity of regulatory initiatives. Development professionals have harnessed the law to the task of perfecting the market through self-limitation—a development paralleled in the United States legal academy by the "liberal law and economics" movement.

As a vernacular for development policy analysis, law retains elements from each of the preceding periods. It puts a wide variety of different analytic frameworks at the disposal of the development professional. The education of women, for example, might be discussed in the vocabulary of anti-discrimination, perhaps to compensate for the inefficient irrationality of market actors that would otherwise distort the price of women's labor and disrupt the efficient allocation of resources. Or it might be discussed in the vocabulary of human capital investment and capacity building, either to compensate administratively for the collective action problems and transactions costs confronting women seeking to invest in their own skills, or as a component in a national strategy of improving comparative advantage, or mobilizing an underutilized national asset. Women's education might be discussed in a humanitarian or human rights vocabulary, as an element of human freedom, or a responsibility of human solidarity, or simply as the right thing to do. Traces of neoliberalism, modest interventionism, and post-neoliberal thinking, and of right–center–left ideological preferences, have all been sedimented into the legal vocabulary for discussing development.

These are all also technical issues. Will this educational initiative in fact respond to discrimination or be a further distorting affirmative action measure? Will the human capital investment be recouped—how does it compare to other investment opportunities for the society? What do human rights commitments require in the way of women's education? How do you compare this "right thing to do" with other basic needs? What about backlash, the social and political viability of the educational reform, the costs to other development initiatives? And so on. Nevertheless, as a framework for debating such issues, law has increasingly replaced economics and politics.

The legal vernacular is not more decisive or analytically rigorous, but it does seem to be more capacious. Moreover, economic analysis often requires baseline determinations it is not suited to make and law provides a vocabulary for debating them, rather than relying on default assumptions. In the trade context, for example, to determine whether a regulation is a nontariff barrier to trade or part of the "normal" regulatory background on which market prices are set requires a decision exogenous to the economic analysis. Is Mexico subsidizing when it lowers its minimum wage or fails to enforce its own labor legislation, or is the United States imposing a nontariff barrier when it requires Mexico to meet minimum labor standards? The WTO's policy machinery offers an institutional and rhetorical interface between different conceptions of the appropriate answer to such questions—perhaps different national ideas about the "normal" level of wage protection. The development policy vernacular has a similar effect on issues such as women's education—providing a loose argumentative vocabulary which transforms absolute questions—women's education, yes or no—into shades of gray: "Maybe here, to the extent it compensates for discrimination, but not there, where markets work," and so forth.

The legal vocabulary used in discussions is not infinitely plastic, of course. It emphasizes some things and leaves others behind. The appearance of a technical and "balanced" solution to the question whether a living wage is a "normal" or "abnormal" regulatory imposition on the market, or whether we should fear "private rent-seeking" or "public rent-seeking" obscures the sense in which these issues present mutually exclusive political choices. There is no technical way to figure out what level of wage support—or women's education—is normal or nondistortive or market-correcting—or "required by human rights commitments." In the trade context, to decide which regulations are barriers to trade and which are "normal" complements to the market, we should ask whether a regulation is part of a nation's legitimate strategic or comparative advantage—whether we might think of a regulatory arrangement, like plentiful labor, as a factor endowment, rather than a distortion of world prices. Once we go down this road, the door is open for analysis of the distributional consequences of regulation, which would take us to a more overtly political frame for debate.

In this situation, it seems useful to recover and reinterpret the heterogeneous economic, political, and social ideas about development that accompanied the emergence of each phase in the history of development policy. The modern development practitioner will want to be well versed in the broad institutionalist economic tradition, for example, understanding the struggle to endogenize social and institutional factors into economic models of growth and to qualify images of market efficiency by reference to arguments about information costs, public goods, path dependence, and so forth. We will want to remember that one size does not fit all, that everyone lives in a microclimate and a very specific market, most of which are not competitive and are plagued by bargaining power problems of various sorts. We will want to remember that power is socially and institutionally disaggregated, an insight rooted in traditions as diverse as Foucaultian social thought and public choice theory. Development experts with heterogeneous instincts will want to attend to the structures of economic life more broadly, whether expressed through the dynamic relationship between leading and lagging regions or sectors, through world systems ideas about the relationship between centers and peripheries, within national and world economies, or through ideas about dependent development, focusing on modes of intervention in the global economy and the significance of bargaining power, monopoly rights, and access to rents of various kinds.

These heterogeneous strands of economic and political thinking about development reinforce the focus on law. It is difficult to imagine how one might resurrect an interest in economic ideas about dependent development or the interactive dynamics of rising and falling sectors or national economies in a global market without reference to the legal institutions structuring the allocation of rents, bargaining power, and monopoly power in the global marketplace. Similarly, economic criticisms of restraining the regulatory power of developing countries can only be strengthened by legal analysis of the incoherence of the doctrinal categories through which efforts to constrain regulatory capacity are transformed into binding obligations—"regulatory taking," "subsidy," "nontariff barrier," and the like.

At the same time, there are many valuable heterogeneous traditions within law that may also be drawn upon by those with the ambition to unsettle conventional wisdom about the institutional arrangements necessary for development. They begin with the sociological criticism of law as a purposive and instrumental apparatus for bending social behavior to the will of the state—or to the will of the holder of private right. There is a gap between law and social life; informal arrangements and strategic behavior does matter. Public and private entities operate in the shadow of legal arrangements and share loose background assumptions about what those arrangements mean and require. The operations of routine legal arrangements depend heavily upon the social context within which they are embedded—including the other legal and institutional arrangements in place. Law and the top and bottom of an economic or social order are rarely the same.

Legal formalism, in all its various meanings, is not all it has been cracked up to be. There seems an irreducible element of contradiction, incompleteness, and ambiguity in legal arrangements. Legal reasoning and interpretation—and the procedures through which that interpretation occurs, including private reactions to and internalization of legal norms—is more significant than it seems in many neoliberal accounts. More tellingly, perhaps, the styles of legal interpretation proposed during the neoliberal heyday were rarely as robust as they may have seemed. Rather, they relied heavily on stock arguments and shared ideological commitments to slide across the conflicts and ambiguities of even the most formal regimes.

From top to bottom, moreover, legal interpretation and implementation is all about choice and strategy—it is not a substitute for them. Noncompliance often ought to be tolerated, just as contracts often ought to be breached. Permissions to use resources nominally "owned" by others run through our private law, as does the entitlement to use one's property in ways which will damage the value of a neighbor's holdings. Moreover, the legal regime is an amalgam of overlapping and often conflicting arrangements that are not susceptible to resolution into a single coherent scheme, even were there time and resources to pursue all disputes to a single court. It is a notorious error to imagine that legal regimes affecting the environment, for example, will all have the word environmental law in the title. People soil and cleanse the environment in the shadow of numerous legal regimes. One might change our ecology by pulling levers in legal regimes of sovereignty, property, finance, credit, criminal law, corporate governance, torts, and more. Indeed, legal pluralism is an inevitable and often salutary part of modern law—many productive economic activities take place along the vague fault lines

An alliance of heterogeneities

Political and Economic Thought	Legal Thought
Institutionalism in Economics Endogeneity of social and institutional factors Focus on information costs, public goods, path dependence, ubiquity of micro-markets, bargaining power problems, agency problems, monopoly and anticompetitive behavior, transactions costs, arguments for regulation —Stiglitz Social disaggregated powers Public choice theory Power/knowledge—identity constitution —Foucault Social structures and dynamics Dualism—Myrdal Leading and lagging sectors World systems analysis Center and periphery Dependency theory Dependent development Modes of insertion in the global economy Significance of bargaining power; opportunities to capture rents Decisionism—foregrounding the political and ethical choices inherent in policy The experience of deciding/ubiquity of unknowing critiques of expertise Critiques of human rights as universal ethical or economic models	Legal sociology Gap between law in the books and law in action Internal critiques of formalism Conflicts, gaps, and ambiguities in the law Critiques of analytic and formal legal reasoning, whether ethical or instrumental Significance of privileges and competing rights American legal realism Criticism of legal instrumentalism, pragmatism, deduction from social form and purpose Dualing principles and purposes Legal pluralism Overlapping legal regimes The semiotics of legal reasoning The importance of stylized argument fragments and background conceptions of the normal Legal consciousness and the ideological component of legal reasoning Internal and external criticisms of rules and of standards Criticism of modern liberal modes of adjudication rooted in economic analytics, ethical theory, or political philosophy Criticism of expertise, blind spots, and biases The institutional and normative fetishism of best practice Attention to distributive choices Politics and economics of legal science Critiques of human rights

Figure 1.4. An alliance of heterogeneities

between legal regimes and in the space between clear areas of regulation and legal clarity.

Doubtless contemporary scholars working in these many traditions would describe themselves differently and would assemble different lists from those I have sketched here. The point is only to suggest an alliance, not to define its terms or limit its components. Figure 1.4 illustrates the range of heterogeneous ideas put in play over the last decades in law that might correspond to heterogeneous thinking in the fields of economics and politics.

An alliance between these traditions might have at least two different advantages. First, it might offer a more robust policy analytic. A more nuanced and contextual legal analysis of institutional and doctrinal arrangements might improve our analysis of policy prescriptions that explicitly demand more of law and legal institutions. More importantly, perhaps, the critical traditions within the legal and economic fields may help to dislodge the formulaic and sloppy policy sloganeering that has so often come to replace careful analysis. Doing so will require reliance on the critical traditions from both disciplines.

At the same time, there are limits to what a more robust legal vernacular for development policymaking can achieve. All too often, law offers the opportunity to make policy decisions without confronting them as naked political alternatives, while nevertheless accepting that no economic or interpretive analytic is available to determine which way to proceed. It is this combination—escape from the choices of politics and the unsatisfying analytics of economics—which has revitalized the law and development field. But this move to law also has a politics. Legal determinations present themselves as operations of logic, policy analysis, procedural necessity, economic insight, or constitutional commitment. In the background lie a set of choices that are difficult to identify and contest. Although legal norms and institutions define every significant entity and relationship in an economy—money, security, risk, corporate form, employment, insurance—it is difficult to remember that each may be arranged in a variety of ways.

A common theme among these heterogeneous and critical traditions is the impulse to recover the experience of political choice in the making of development policy. One goal of contextualization in each tradition is to disrupt the claims to universal value or function that accompany efforts to theorize a best practice for development policy and open a space for local political choice. The goal for internal critiques of the theories themselves, be they legal or economic, is to identify the gaps and conflicts that require interpretation, and contest as ideological the terms through which that interpretation has often been rendered routine. The aim of all these theoretical innovations is to expand the potential for institutional, doctrinal, and policy experimentation—to embolden the policy class to accept the need for economic, political, and ethical choice and improve the tools by which they can come to that challenge free of unhelpful professional habits and deformations.

Although some minimum level of national institutional functionality seems necessary for economic activity of any sort, this tells us very little. For development, we need to strategize about the choices that go into making one "rule of law" rather than another. Attention to the rule of law offers an opportunity to focus on the political choices and economic assumptions embedded in development policymaking. Unfortunately, however, those most enthusiastic about the rule of law as a development strategy have treated it as a recipe or ready-made rather than as a terrain for contestation and strategy. They have treated its policy vernacular of "balancing" as more analytically decisive than it is. As a result, the politics of law in the neo-institutionalist era has so far largely been the politics of politics denied.

NOTES

1. This essay is part of a larger historical study of the relationship between the expertise of legal and economic development professionals. Portions of the study have been published as "The 'Rule of Law,' Political Choices and Development Common Sense," in D. Trubek and A. Santos (eds), *The New Law and Economic Development* (Cambridge: Cambridge University Press, 2006), 95–173; "Laws and Developments," in A. Perry-Kessaris and J. Hatchard (eds), *Law and Development: Facing Complexity in the 21st Century* (London: Cavendish Publishing, 2003); and "The International Anticorruption Campaign," *University of Connecticut Journal of International Law*, 14/2 (1999). The full study will be published by Princeton Press under the title *Economic Development: An Intellectual History*.
2. Trubek and Galanter (1974). See also Unger (1976).
3. Kennedy (2006).
4. Hirschman (1958: 227).
5. Amsden (2003).
6. Trubek (2009); Sabel (2007); D. M. Trubek and L. Trubek (2007).

REFERENCES

Amsden, A. (2003), *The Rise of "The Rest": Challenges to the West from Late-Industrializing Economies* (New York: Oxford University Press).

Hirschman, A. O. (1958), *The Strategy of Economic Development* (New Haven: Yale University Press).

Kennedy, D. (2006), "Three Globalizations of Law and Legal Thought: 1850–2000," in D. Trubek and A. Santos (eds), *The New Law and Economic Development: A Critical Appraisal* (New York: Cambridge University Press).

Sabel, C. (2007), "Bootstrapping Development: Rethinking the Role of Public Intervention in Promoting Growth," in V. Lee and R. Swedberg (eds), *On Capitalism* (Palo Alto: Stanford University Press), 305–41.

Trubek, D. M. (2009), "Developmental States and the Legal Order: Toward a New Political Economy of Development and Law," *University of Wisconsin Legal Studies Research Paper No. 1075*, Madison.

——and Galanter, M. (1974), "Scholars in Self-Estrangement: Some Reflections on the Crisis in Law and Development," *Wisconsin Law Review*, 4: 1062–101.

——and Trubek, L. (2007), "New Governance and Legal Regulation: Complementarity, Rivalry or Transformation," *Columbia Journal of European Law*, 13: 542.

Unger, R. (1976), *Law in Modern Society* (New York: The Free Press).

2

Creating the Institutional Foundations for a Market Economy

Joseph E. Stiglitz[1]

China's growth over the past thirty years, since it began its march to a market economy, has been truly impressive. Never before has the world seen such sustained growth on a scale remotely as large, one that has improved the well-being of almost a quarter of the world's population. For the past quarter century, China has been growing at a rate in excess of 9 percent, and over thirty years, per capita income has increased fifteen-fold (from $220 to $3590).[2] The only growth experience that is comparable is that of the so-called East Asian miracle economies, with eight of the highest performing economies averaging a growth of per capita income of 5.5 percent during 1965–90; but those successes were both somewhat slower and on a much smaller scale. Previous economic revolutions—such as the Industrial Revolution of the nineteenth century—had seen growth rates peak at around 2 to 3 percent.[3] The golden age of growth in America during the 1950s and 1960s saw growth rates in the same vicinity. China's growth has been three times these numbers.[4] And never before has there been poverty reduction on such a scale. The fraction of the Chinese population living on less than $1 a day has fallen from 63.8 percent in 1981 to 15.3 percent thirty years later.[5]

Part of the key to China's long-run success has been its exceptional combination of pragmatism and vision, constantly adapting to changing needs and circumstances, but keeping a view of the road ahead—a vision of the evolving nature of the economy and of the role of government.

This chapter (and more broadly, this book) focuses on one aspect of China's transition—the creation of the institutions that underlie a market economy. It focuses more narrowly on one set of institutions, the legal frameworks, which provide the rules of the game. How those rules are set will have an enormous impact on how China will evolve in coming decades. If it sets the wrong rules, creates the wrong legal frameworks, establishes "flawed" institutional arrangements, it may be able, at least for a while, to maintain growth; but it could also see a more divided society, marked with greater inequality. It is even possible that growth—correctly measured—will not be sustained. Much depends on the decisions that China makes in the next few years.

As we argued in the Introduction, there is a battle of ideas concerning alternative frameworks. This chapter sets the stage by looking at some of the key challenges facing China at this point in its transition to a market economy.

This chapter is divided into nine sections. First, we discuss the objectives that China should be pursuing in the context of the multiple transitions in which it is engaged. Next, we look at one of the critical institutions, "the plan," which has served to guide China's development over the past fifty-five years. In the following sections, I discuss the critical "transitions"—from export-led growth to domestic-led growth, to an innovative economy, toward an environmentally sustainable economy, to an urban society with livable cities. Finally, we discuss some of the broader institutional innovations that will be required.

OBJECTIVES AND VISION IN AN ECONOMY FACING MULTIPLE TRANSITIONS

China is in the process of making a transition toward a market economy—but all market economies are in transition. Western economies went through the transition from agriculture to manufacturing in the early to mid twentieth century, and then from manufacturing to a service economy and an information/innovation economy in the latter part of that century. In China these transitions are accelerated and occurring at the same time. It is moving simultaneously from an export-led economy to an economy more driven by domestic demand. The nature of China's growth in recent decades has placed a huge toll on the environment, and like many other countries around the world, it is embarking on a transition to an economy that is more sensitive to the environment and to the utilization of depletable natural resources.

There are a series of concurrent demographic transitions taking place, as the consequences of the one-child policy play out and as greater longevity leads to an increasingly aging population.[6] At the same time, there is transition from a largely rural population to a more urban population.

As China thinks about how to shape these transitions, it must have a vision of where it wants to go, a vision that may in fact change over time. As China realized in the beginning of its transition, the world is too complex to articulate a full path between where it is today and where it ultimately wants to be.[7] But unless it has a vision of where it wants to go (even if that vision is somewhat imprecise), and some awareness of the potential bumps in the road, it risks setting off in the wrong direction and winding up in a place where it would rather not be.

The vision of a future economy should be informed by a vision of society, one that sees success not only as an increase in GDP, but also in broader terms. Indeed, there is growing recognition that GDP provides a poor measure of societal well-being. It does not tell whether growth is sustainable or whether the fruits of the growth that does occur are being equitably shared.[8] For instance, there are countries—such as the US—where GDP is increasing, but so too is poverty; real median family annual income is actually declining,[9] so *most* individuals are worse off year after year. Some of the natural-resource-rich countries are increasingly becoming wealthy countries with poor people.

While much of the rest of the developing world, following the Washington Consensus, has directed efforts toward the quixotic quest for higher GDP—with misconceived policies and poor results[10]—China has once again affirmed that it seeks sustainable and *more* equitable increases in real living standards. As China goes about assessing success, it should use metrics that reflect this broad vision.

China's rapid economic growth provides the resources that will enable it to address these broader social objectives.

Inequality

China's success in reducing poverty as it moved to a market economy is commendable; but there has been a concern about the weakening of social safety nets, particularly in the rural sector, with consequences for living standards, reflected, for instance, in life expectancy. Not everyone benefited equally from the rapid growth of the early decades; and though there was enormous success in reducing poverty,[11] inequality grew significantly.[12] The greater reliance on markets meant that in some dimensions, such as health and education, living standards in some rural areas probably deteriorated. (Amartya Sen has pointed out[13] that, while in 1979, the life expectancies in China and India's state of Kerala were roughly the same, today, Kerala has a life expectancy four to five years longer than that of China. Kerala's GDP per capita growth has been less, but it has placed greater priority on improving health.)[14]

These adverse developments in education and health are of concern in their own right; but they also can have far-reaching impacts on future growth.[15] As the 2006 World Bank *World Development Report* emphasizes, inequality is a concern in itself;[16] it affects the nature of our societies, including the nature of political processes—where those with wealth use that wealth, in one way or another, to perpetuate their favored position. As China moves to a market economy, almost surely the influences of such inegalitarian forces (e.g., corporate interests) will grow—a theme to which I will return later.

While most in China have benefited from its rapid growth, such an outcome is not inevitable. Even rapid growth may not lead to increases in living standards for *most* individuals in society.[17] To ensure that that is the case requires appropriate policies and institutions.

China should be concerned too about socioeconomic mobility. What matters is not just inequality at a moment in time, but also equality of opportunity—whether those at the bottom have a fair chance of making it to the middle or top. No society without such opportunities can be considered truly harmonious. Institutions and policies affect opportunity, especially those relating to access to health, education, and economic competitiveness. Some societies, such as those in Europe, have succeeded in markedly increasing equality of opportunity over the past fifty years, while in other societies, such as the United States, in spite of lip service paid to this ideal, changes in the economy and society have led to marked decreases in equality of opportunity.

One of the reasons that many developing countries have faced growing inequality, especially in the aftermath of the Great Recession, is a lack of jobs. It is necessary, of course, to continue rapid growth if China is to provide jobs for the burgeoning population, and if it is to have the resources required to meet vast social needs of its vast population. But other countries have shown that even rapid growth may not lead to a growth of jobs; there can only be job growth if output grows more rapidly than productivity.

The environment

China's rapid growth has also put enormous strains on the environment, and it is clear that such growth is not sustainable over the long run. The path that was being taken prior to the Eleventh Five-Year Plan was not consistent with its articulated social objectives of a harmonious society, and a new direction was needed. Often-quoted statistics bring home the magnitude of the concerns: while China's GDP accounted for only 4 percent of global GDP in 2004, its share of global energy usage was three times larger, and it consumed 28 percent of the world's rolled steel and 50 percent of its cement. The Eleventh Five-Year Plan set forth ambitious goals—for example, a 20 percent reduction in carbon dioxide emissions per unit of GDP from the 2005 level. In order to achieve this 20 percent target, Chinas spent over RMB 1 trillion in the same period, according to media reports, but the target has not really been met.[18]

Some implications

There are some direct implications of this analysis for China. It should look askance at GDP, focusing more on several other measures: (i) *green net national product,* taking into account the depletion of natural resources and the degradation of the environment (even if, say, environmental degradation is imperfectly measured, it is better to attempt to measure it than to ignore it—we know that "zero" is not an accurate number); (ii) *median income,* not mean; (iii) *measures of inequality,* such as the Gini coefficient; and (iv) social indicators, such as life expectancy and educational attainment, *and the distribution of these variables.*

In this arena, as in others, institutions matter: an independent statistical agency lends credence to statistics, giving confidence to both citizens and foreign and domestic investors that various economic statistics can be relied upon. One of the objectives of the National Bureau of Statistics should be the creation of broader metrics of well-being—of economic performance and social progress—such as those I have alluded to.[19]

This is especially important because what we measure affects what we do: if China uses the wrong metrics, it will be tempted to maximize the wrong things.

A market economy with Chinese characteristics

At the onset of China's march to a market economy, it was made clear that the country sought a distinctive form of market economy. It had recognized what some naïve advocates of market economics had not: that there was not one form of market economy but many. The Scandinavian form of market economy is different from that of America or much of the rest of Europe. It has a high level of social protection, a high level of taxation, a high level of social services, a large government role in helping workers move from one job to another. And, to go back to the broader measures of success to which I referred, it is the most successful version of the market economy. The region's performance on many of the United Nations Development Program's Human Development Index is better than that of the United States.[20] Even in the area of narrow economic performance, while Norway's GDP per capita annual growth rate over the period 1970–2008 has been robust (2.6 percent;[21] for the United States in the same period it was 1.9 percent), poverty is low and those in the middle are doing well.

Also, the particular form of market economy in a specific country changes over time as circumstances evolve. The post-World War II social democracies of Europe are markedly different from their nineteenth-century antecedents. The economic system envisaged by the Roosevelt administration's New Deal, which helped to get the country out of the Great Depression, was markedly different from that of a decade earlier. The debate about the appropriate economic role of government remains heated both in the United States and Europe—there is no consensus. (Later, we shall discuss the role that economic science, as well as ideology and interests, play in this debate.)

There are other metrics of societal development for which the particular form of the market economy matters, as evidenced by the many other dimensions in which the Scandinavian region also excels: greater transparency of government, better protection of individual rights, and a much, much smaller fraction of its population in prison (this is an area in which, unfortunately, the United States does increasingly differ from other advanced industrial countries, with a prison population rate many times higher—about ten times higher than Scandinavia[22]).

For many years now, China has emphasized the creation of a "harmonious society," which reflects an emphasis on "balance," such that: (i) disparities be limited between urban and rural areas, between the advanced and less advanced regions, between the rich and poor within any region; (ii) there be a balance between the government and the other parts of the society; and (iii) there be a balance among the sectors of the economy. There needs to be harmony too between "man and nature": the environment has to be treated with respect. And today's growth cannot come at the expense of future growth; growth has to be sustainable. There has to be harmony between today's generation and future generations.

Such a balancing act is necessary both for social and political stability and for economic progress, as I have defined it broadly above. I should add three points.

Balance between the state and the market

First, modern economic theory has emphasized the need for a balanced approach, as we have come to understand the limitations of the market. Too often, Adam Smith's invisible hand, which is supposed to result in individuals' and firms' drive for profits leading to overall societal well-being, is invisible because it's not there: in general, when information and competition are imperfect and markets are incomplete—that is, always—markets are not (Pareto)-efficient. Government can play an important role. Often some combination of ideology and special interests get in the way of recognizing the policy implications of the case for an appropriate balance between the state and markets. But as we look across societies, problems arise as often from too little government as from too much government; frequently, though, the problem is that government does less of what it should do and more of what it should not do. Even if the problem in the past in China has been that government took too active a role in the economy, one must still guard against the danger that in order to compensate, the government will undertake too small a role.

Beyond the state and the market

Second, today, we are increasingly recognizing a tripartite division, among government, the profit-oriented private sector, and civil society, which includes cooperatives, the not-for-profit sector (universities, hospitals), and NGOs. Even in America, traditionally thought of as a quintessentially "capitalist" economy, cooperatives play a vital role, even in business. They are particularly important in the rural/agricultural sector—for instance, the most important producers of products as diverse as butter and raisins are cooperatives. In education, while the for-profit firms have been marked by fraud and scandal, and a few of our top universities are in the public sector, most of the world-class universities lie in the not-for-profit sector.

Countervailing forces

Third, maintaining this balance will not be easy. There are strong underlying forces that are leading to increases in inequality. Some of these are related to the normal functioning of the ordinary laws of supply and demand working their way through the competitive market place. Globalization and technology have worked together to increase the demand for certain types of skills that are in short supply, and wages of individuals with those skills naturally increase in response. Standard economic theory had predicted that globalization would bring with it an increase in inequality in the advanced developed countries, but a decrease in inequality in the developing world, as wages of unskilled workers got bid up. In practice, however, globalization has been accompanied by an increase in inequality in both developed *and* less developed countries. This is probably partly because the very poor—subsistence workers—are being left behind; but it is partly because globalization has been asymmetric, with liberalization of capital increasing at a pace faster than liberalization of labor, leading to unbalanced changes in bargaining positions. A related asymmetry that has also contributed to increasing inequality within developing countries is that the liberalization of trade in goods and services has favored those items in which the rich countries have an advantage as compared to the labor-intensive goods and services that would benefit the poorer countries; and in spite of all the free-market rhetoric, the advanced industrial countries continue with huge subsidies to agriculture, which lowers the incomes of those in the rural sector, who typically (as in China) have incomes far less than those in the urban sector.

More generally, there are strong reasons to believe that the extremes of inequality observed in some of the advanced industrial countries—an inequality that has grown markedly in the past fifteen years—have little to do with the normal workings of an idealized competitive market place, but in fact reflect a set of *market failures*, exemplified by the abuses so evident in the financial scandals that have marked some of the advanced industrial countries over the past two decades,[23] as well as *public policies*, including regressive tax and expenditure policies with tax cuts or bailouts for the rich being paid for in substantial measure by a rollback of the social safety net. Other government policies (such as inadequate enforcement of antitrust laws, poorly designed bankruptcy and corporate governance laws, and poorly designed and implemented privatization programs) have also contributed greatly to inequality. It is important that, as China moves to *its* form of a market economy, it guards itself against this possibility—which would result in a *less* efficient economy and a *less* harmonious society.

The challenges facing China

Institutions have to be designed not for the world of the past, or even of today, but to help China help create the kind of economy and society that it strives to achieve. Maintaining a balance between the public and private sectors, ensuring that the fruits of growth are equitably shared, and preserving the environment are three of the major challenges facing China going ahead, but they are not the only ones.

The structure of China's economy worked well—even as it changed repeatedly—in managing the transition over the past thirty years. China has gone a long way, but the structure that has worked in the past may not work well in the future. In particular, as we explain further, China will have to move away from its reliance on manufacturing to a more balanced economy, in which services will play a more important role; it will have to move away from an export-led growth model to one that is more focused on domestic demand. Sustaining the growth rate of the previous decade into the next will be difficult, if not impossible. China will have to find other engines of growth and adjust to a lower rate of growth.

For instance, in the past decade, exports grew at 23 percent per annum, property development at 20 percent per annum, and the labor force at 1.4 percent per annum. In the next decade, exports are expected to grow at 12 percent, real-estate construction at 10 percent, and the labor force at close to zero.

The move away from export-led growth will mean that the share of exports and private investment in GDP is likely to decrease. What will fill the hole? If China follows the profligate consumption patterns of some Western countries, the future of the entire planet will be in jeopardy. China must focus on improving quality of life: there are huge demands for services, such as health and education. These are not resource-intensive, but in most countries, these types of services are provided (i.e., financed) by the government, and for good reason: these are sectors that are rife with market failures—America's private health care system delivers lower quality care at higher costs than any of the European systems. And the provision of health care is extraordinarily inequitable, with standards of care among the poor at levels below those of some developing countries. China cannot afford to go down that route. But public provision will require public funds, so China may have to look for new sources of tax revenue. Maintaining increases in standards of living will require productivity increases—China will have to move toward an *innovation economy*, which we will describe further.

As China's population continues its urban-oriented migration, ensuring that the cities are livable will be increasingly important and increasingly difficult. This too will require significant government intervention, both in zoning and in the provision of infrastructure. Even as old-fashioned planning has gotten a bad name, cities that have tried to grow without planning have been a disaster.

Running any modern, complex economy requires a vast array of institutions: laws regulating property rights (including intellectual property), protecting the environment, governing the behavior of corporations, institutions for research and learning, town-planning boards. Some of the institutions and arrangements that worked well for China in the past may not be well suited for the future. The rest of this paper sketches some of the key transitions and transformations for China going forward and the institutional reforms that may help China achieve the dynamic harmonious society for which it strives.

PLANNING

China's development has been guided by a series of five-year plans. (As this book went to press, the Twelfth Five-Year plan was being implemented.) In the past, planning entailed specifying not only macroeconomic objectives, but sectoral allocations that would "add up" to ensure the fulfillment of those objectives. With its Eleventh Five-Year Plan, unveiled in March 2005, China changed the nature of what is meant by planning. The Eleventh Five-Year Plan was not a *plan*, as the term was understood in the days of central planning; rather, it recognized that, as China moves to a market economy, a plan should not center around material balances or instructions regarding how much of each commodity should be produced. Instead, it concerns a vision of the evolving nature of the economy and of the role of government; it indicates the priorities for both public expenditures and institutional and policy development; and it provides a framework for coordinating economic activities.

There should be another change in planning as the country moves into its Twelfth Five-Year Plan. In the past, following the traditional planning model, the government has set goals—e.g., for inflation or growth—and many throughout the government have felt strong pressure to meet them. Sometimes, this may have meant fudging the data; but at other times, it has meant pushing hard on the accelerator or brake when there is a risk that the target won't be met. Realism requires that, as the country moves away from a controlled economy, the levers by which government manipulates the economy become more restricted; and in an open market economy, there is inevitably a high level of uncertainty. The government should be setting goals in terms of ranges, and as part of the planning process, make provisions in the event of significant shortfalls.

As China continues its move to a market economy, government will still play a number of important roles. One, the subject of this book, is providing the basic "rules of the game"—the institutional infrastructure underlying the private sector, the laws governing property rights, bankruptcy, corporate governance; the regulations affecting the environment—food and workplace safety, working conditions, and the financial sector; and the tax laws that provide incentives or disincentives for various kinds of activities. But government will continue to play a more direct role in a number of areas, including social protection, education, promoting technology, and the provision of infrastructure. Governments might prefer to avoid difficult choices on how to spend money or what rules (laws, regulations) to adopt, but they cannot. Deciding not to investment in technology or railroads is, after all, a decision. The choices the government makes in these arenas shape the entire economy and society. A decision not to invest in public transportation will lead to an economy more dependent on the automobile, with a host of attendant consequences. That is why it is so important that such decisions be guided by a vision of the society and economy that a country is striving to create, as well as a broad perspective on how the various pieces interact.

A distinctive aspect of the plan has been its comprehensiveness. One of the development lessons to emerge in the late 1990s was that successful strategies are comprehensive. Some complained that a comprehensive strategy lacks focus. But the experiences of earlier development efforts were telling: without a comprehensive vision, one risked failures, for instance, as policymakers improved price incentives for agricultural output without paying attention to the supply of inputs or credit or marketing and physical infrastructure; as they opened up new trade opportunities without the infrastructure or finance to take advantage of these new opportunities; or as they privatized rapidly without attention to the regulatory mechanisms required to prevent exploitation of market power.

A comprehensive approach is important for another reason: the pieces of an economy fit together like interlocking parts. One typically can't replace one part without causing impacts on the others. There was an "old model" of economic growth, largely supply-driven, in which firms reinvested large retained earnings. This created rapid increases in capacity and expansion of employment, and the gap between supply and demand was made up by exports. But, for reasons explained below, this model will be changing in coming years, necessitating many changes in the economic framework. One can't, for instance, just change the exchange rate adjustment mechanism.

The process by which the plan is formulated has also changed over the years, reflecting changes in the economy. Recent plans are not just top-down documents, but are arrived at after extensive consultation.

China's success over the past thirty years, since it began its transition to a market economy, has been based in no small measure on the adaptability of its strategies and policies. As each set of problems was solved, new problems presented themselves, for which new policies and strategies had to be devised. It has also been based on *social innovation*. Because the problems confronting China were different from those that confronted other countries, new solutions had to be found.[24] And it recognized that it could not simply transfer economic institutions (even when they had worked well in other countries); at the very least, they had to be adapted. Not only did the circumstances and history of China differ, but so, to a large extent, did its objectives. These were among the reasons that China talked of a market economy *with Chinese characteristics*.

Even successful Chinese institutions have to be modified and adapted as times change. The Township and Village Enterprises (TVEs), itself a social innovation so central to the successes of the 1980s and early 1990s, could not meet all the challenges that China faced as it became an increasingly important player in the global economy.

The next three sections describe China's transition away from export-led growth, toward an innovation economy and environmental sustainability. The following section focuses more narrowly on the institutional reforms that will be required.

THE TRANSITION AWAY FROM EXPORT-LED GROWTH

China's success, like that of most other East Asian countries, was based on export-led growth. By the middle of the first decade of the twenty-first century, it was clear that China needed to move away from this model, to one based *more* on domestic consumption and investment. (Of course, exports will continue to play an important role. The question is a rebalancing of its growth model.)

Globally, its exporting successes were not well received elsewhere by many who saw their jobs being threatened. It was one thing to talk about the virtues of competition and the market, it was quite another thing for those countries to lose in the market game; and in many quarters, shrill protectionist sentiments began to be expressed. The excess of exports over imports helped stimulate China's economy, but had exactly the opposite effect on other economies.

The trade surplus allowed China to accumulate large amounts of reserves, which could help protect China against the volatility of the global marketplace. Other countries had learned the hard way (in the East Asia crisis) the risks of not having sufficient reserves, and China did not want to follow suit. Still, when China began discussing a move away from export-led growth, it had already accumulated more than US$2 trillion in reserves, more than ample to meet any crisis. (As this book goes to press, reserves exceed US$3 trillion.)

Why export-oriented growth?

It is natural to ask why export-led growth worked for China and for so many of the other East Asian countries. Will the move away from export-led growth adversely affect its overall growth? Are there other ways to meet the needs it satisfied? Export-led growth was important for three reasons. First, it provided the basis of innovation. What separates developing and developed countries is not just a gap in resources, but also a gap in knowledge. As Greenwald and Stiglitz[25] point out, for a variety of reasons, the larger the size of the industrial sector, the more transmission of knowledge is enhanced. The skills learned in that sector then gradually spread to the rest of the economy. Moreover, some of the institutional development required for a successful industrial sector, e.g., of financial markets and education systems, are of enormous benefit to other sectors.

Second, there is intense competition in exports, and competition spurs efficiency and innovation. Success requires meeting international standards, again a benefit that eventually extends throughout the economy.

Third, in the early stages of development, the capacity to produce may outstrip the capacity to consume, or more accurately, the expansion of the demand for the particular goods that are being produced. While there may be latent demands by many households and firms, these are translated into effective demands only if households and firms can get access to credit. But in the earlier stages of development, financial institutions (and the underlying legal infrastructure) that can discriminate between those who are creditworthy and those who are not, as well as enforcing credit contracts, have often not developed.[26] It is easier to lend abroad to finance foreigners' consumption than to lend at home. (More accurately, China has lent money to governments, which it assumed represented low risk of default. Even in more developed countries, the financial markets' record in judging creditworthiness is not particularly stellar.)

Indeed, in recent years, China can be viewed as having been engaged in vendor finance: it has lent much of the money that has enabled those elsewhere to buy its goods. But there is something peculiar about China helping the richest country in the world to live beyond its means,[27] especially when there are so many pressing needs at home.

Why China today can move away from export-led growth

Today, the functions that export-led growth has served can be accomplished in other ways. China is establishing a broad innovation system (see below); it has "learned how to learn"; it does not need to rely on exports for learning. China has created vibrant internal competition, e.g., among TVEs and other establishments. To be sure, there is a need for strong competition laws to ensure that domestic competition remains strong, and China should be wary of those arguing for the establishment of large "national champions," at least when their establishment threatens domestic competition.[28]

Finally, China has made great strides in creating a strong domestic financial system. It would be easy, at this stage, to expand domestic credit, especially for housing and collateralized debt.[29] (Of course, it is imperative, if this is done, that the investment projects be carefully chosen, that the funds for purchases of housing or consumer durables are provided at levels commensurate with individuals' ability to repay, that there is a legal framework and a credit culture that ensure that lent money is repaid, and that China not follow the United States in allowing predatory lending and abusive credit card practices.[30])

Stimulating consumption

In spite of the talk about moving away from export-led growth, China's trade surplus almost tripled from US$102 billion in 2005 to US$290 billion in 2008. It then dropped to US$196 billion in 2009, recording the first annual fall since

2003.[31] Consumption has increased significantly, according to at least some data sources, at a pace faster than GDP,[32] though from a low base (with the share of consumption in GDP half that of the US).[33] Expanding consumption would not only help China move away from its dependence on exports, it would also contribute to rising living standards—the *objective* of development. (As we will discuss further, it will be imperative for the pattern of consumption to be markedly different from that in, say, the US, or the planet cannot survive.)

The question is, why has China had "excessive" savings? There are five hypotheses and each plays a role, though some may be more important than others. And each suggests a set of actions that are likely to increase consumption.

(i) The first is growing inequality. With (marginal) consumption propensities among the rich typically lower than among the poor, an increase in inequality will result in a lower ratio of consumption to GDP. Policies that reduce the degree of inequality would, accordingly, be expected to increase consumption.

(ii) The second is capital market imperfections, especially those facing small- and medium-sized enterprises (SMEs). In the absence of access to funds, those who aspire to be small-business holders—or those already in small businesses—must save at a very high rate to have the funds they need to expand. Hence, improving access to credit would help lower the overall savings rate. Because large banks prefer lending to large businesses, encouraging small regional and community banks may enhance SME access to credit, as would an explicit government program focused on SME lending. In the United States, there is a government program through the Small Business Administration that encourages lending to small businesses by absorbing of some of the risk. There are significant consequences of the lack of available credit. It may have contributed to low growth, suggested by some data, in the number of small businesses in urban areas. This is of particular concern because small businesses are normally associated with job growth and are especially important in providing opportunities for those who, in the past, had none. Many contend that small businesses are the heart of a dynamic economy—while large businesses bring products to market, they depend on a host of small businesses for the real innovations.

(iii) A major barrier to increasing consumption—one that has received extensive discussion—is the lack of an effective social safety net, a strong public health system,[34] an effective social security system, and good publicly provided education. Combined with inadequate private insurance, the lack of social insurance induces a high level of what is called "precautionary" savings. Parents who have to pay for the education of their children also save for these "targeted" needs. Both depress consumption. Social reforms would thus yield a double benefit, reducing China's dependence on exports (and the vagaries of international markets) as they improve standards of living.

(iv) China's one-child policy has been associated with large gender imbalances. Competition for spouses results in an "arms race"—young males accumulate wealth to make themselves more attractive. Loosening the policy and enforcing policies that reduce gender imbalances may help mitigate this problem.[35]

(v) But household savings rates in China are only slightly higher than those of other Asian economies. What is distinctive about China is the low ratio of household income to GDP.[36] Part of the reason for this is the high level of retained earnings, which constitutes part of China's distinctive economic model: the retained earnings are invested to create more jobs and increase supply, but without necessarily a concomitant increase in demand. Globalization makes this possible: international markets absorb the gap between supply and demand. But, as we have suggested, this model is not sustainable.

(vi) The final reason for a high ratio of savings to GDP[37] is the high current account surplus, reflected in the large additions to reserves, and to which the strong fiscal position of the government (in contrast to that elsewhere in the world) contributes. In 2009, the current account surplus amounted to 4.2 percent of GDP. China's fiscal revenue as a percentage of GDP has gone up tremendously from 9.2 percent in 2005 to 19.9 percent in 2009. And during the same period, China's foreign reserves as a percentage of GDP went up from 15.9 percent in 2005 to 46.6 percent in 2009. As we noted before, China has accumulated enough reserves to meet any plausible marketplace variability. Given the high social needs for health and education—and its high private savings rate—China could well afford to have a modest fiscal deficit.[38]

Each of the reasons for low consumption has an associated policy response, many of them of an institutional nature, which we discuss further.

Stimulating investment

Less reliance on exports could, of course, be achieved by expanded investment; but with China's investment rate as high as it is, the issue is not so much the level of investment but its allocation. The worry is that there are a perverse set of incentives at play—with local communities rushing to encourage investment, both to generate jobs and revenues for themselves. Especially in real estate, there is a concern that short-sighted investors are focusing on short-term capital gains rather than long-term returns.

There is a worry too that the high level of retained earnings referred to earlier is part of a system, a supply-side-driven model, rather than a demand-side model: firms invest the retained earnings to create jobs for the millions entering the urban labor force. The result is that there may be excessive investment in some sectors, with small margins, which, in turn, can contribute to risk and fragility.

Still, China has some major investment opportunities going forward. Indeed, it will have to make large investments to facilitate the large transitions described earlier. It must retrofit its economy to reflect the realities of global warming and, more generally, to create a more environmentally sensitive economy. It has to construct housing and new cities to accommodate the millions who will be moving to cities from rural areas. It has to make large investments in the service sector to meet the rising consumption demands of China's increasingly well-off population. If domestic consumption is increased—both by increasing the share of household income in GDP and by decreasing household savings rates—domestic investment will simultaneously increase.

Why China should move away from export-led growth

While China has been discussing moving away from export-led growth for years, progress has been slow. The issue, though, is becoming imperative. With many of the advanced industrial countries facing the possibility of an extended period of slow growth, it will be difficult for China to maintain the rapid pace of export-led growth that has been an important driver for the economy. Moreover, China needs to have stable growth, and some export markets are highly variable. And even if China's export markets were growing more rapidly (and more stably), in many areas, they are reaching saturation: China's growth was rapid as it displaced other vendors. Now that they have been largely displaced, growth is limited to growth in the export markets themselves. Growth through increasing market share from others will be limited.

China will, in addition, be under severe political pressure to reduce its trade imbalances, particularly through letting its exchange rate increase. This will especially be the case if unemployment in the West remains high: monetary policy has reached the limits of its effectiveness, and expansionary fiscal policy looks increasingly politically constrained. That means that attention will center on protectionist policies. To many, China's rapid growth will be seen as occurring at their expense.

It should be clear to China that exchange rate appreciation is unlikely to adequately address the problem of global imbalances. Trade deficits represent macroeconomic imbalances, an excess of domestic investment over domestic savings. America's huge trade deficit today largely reflects its paltry savings (before the Great Recession, its household savings were negative) and its huge fiscal deficit. Nothing that China does, at least with respect to its exchange rate, will affect in a significant way America's national savings or investment; hence, nothing that it does will affect its trade deficit. When China allowed its exchange rate to appreciate by some 25 percent between 2005 and 2009, the trade surplus actually increased, and America's multilateral trade deficit was little affected. (Standard economic theory explains why, at least in the short run, this can be expected, as America has to pay more, in dollars, for the goods it imports. The real beneficiary of exchange rate appreciation may be other developing countries. America is not likely to start producing its own apparel and textiles; rather, it will simply shift its purchases to other countries.[39])

As unjustified as claims that China is engaged in unfair trade policies may be, the realpolitik, however, is that China will continue to come under pressure,[40] and it would be wise to rely more strongly on domestic demand.

China must, of course, be sensitive to the risks associated with exchange rate appreciation. An increase in the exchange rate would still have an adverse effect on the rural sector, potentially increasing rural–urban income disparities. If China appreciates the currency, and subsidizes its farmers—in effect, countervailing the subsidies provided by the US and the EU—it would take away scarce money needed for other developmental objectives, including investments in education and health.

While the world economy remains weak, there can also be adverse effects on the manufacturing export sector. Many firms have small margins, which can sustain them so long as there is strong demand. If many firms were to be forced into bankruptcy, it would increase unemployment and slow China's growth—which would not be good for global recovery.

In effect, China is already embarking on a "real" appreciation as wages rise, putting upward pressure on prices. More important than adjusting exchange rates are the broader strategies discussed earlier in this section, to increase consumption and domestic investment. Whether China engages in a real or nominal exchange rate, it should not expect global imbalances to disappear nor political pressures to be much diminished, at least so long as unemployment in the West remains high.

But there are other reasons for China to adjust its exchange rate. First, slow, gradual adjustments are far better than large episodic adjustments. Second, the current exchange rate may impede the transition of China's economy to its next stage of development. It enables the continuation of the current supply-side model of development, which is not sustainable over the long run. A higher exchange rate would facilitate the transformation of China's economy. It would, of course, be easier for China to adjust its exchange rate if Western countries expanded their economies; exchange rate adjustments can be more easily undertaken in the context of faster growth.

Moreover, while in earlier stages of China's development, it could manage financial and capital markets so that it could intervene in the exchange rate without worrying unduly about inflationary pressures or circumvention of exchange controls (as speculative capital markets attempted to take advantage of expected appreciation), this may be increasingly difficult. Still, China needs to be aware that much of the rhetoric in the West about "market-determined exchange rates" is, at best, somewhat naïve. Even in countries where there is no *direct* intervention in the exchange rate, the exchange rate is affected by a host of government policies, such as interest rates and tax rates. Were, for instance, China to simultaneously tax short-term capital gains, especially those arising from exchange rate changes, impose taxes on property, lower interest rates, impose a high withholding tax on returns, and allow pension funds to invest more abroad, the "market-determined" exchange rate might even be lower than the current level.

Direct intervention to stabilize the exchange rate may be necessary, but the government should consider carefully how the exchange rate is affected by these other interventions.

Alternative measures for moving away from exports

There is a need, for instance, for measures that will correct trade imbalances without simultaneously increasing rural–urban differentials. One such measure is an export tax or reduced export rebates,[41] which have the further advantage of providing additional revenues that could be directed at other social objectives.

Many of China's exports are energy-intensive, with societal costs that go well beyond the costs borne by firms. Raising the price of energy (and imposing a carbon tax and other environmental taxes, to be discussed at greater length) would help adjust the structure of the economy—including helping China move away from exports—and again provide additional revenues that could be directed at other social objectives.

Institutional reforms

Exchange-rate adjustments and export and environmental taxes are only three of a number of instruments for moving China away from its excessive dependence on exports. Earlier in this chapter, we identified several other growth-enhancing strategies that would support such a transformation. Most of these require institutional developments. The three most important categories of macroeconomic changes are: (i) lowering household savings rates; (ii) increasing the share of household income in GDP; and (iii) increasing domestic investment.

The household savings rate would be reduced if the government created: (i) better institutions for social protection, including for health and retirement; (ii) better public educational institutions; and (iii) better financial institutions, including better insurance (reducing the need for precautionary savings) and access to credit for small and medium-sized enterprises. As credit becomes more available, new regulatory institutions will need to be created to prevent the kinds of abuses rampant in advanced industrial countries.

The share of household income in GDP could be increased by creating new legal frameworks for corporations that would result in the distribution of more dividends and stronger worker organizations that could better bargain collectively for higher wages. Better systems of corporate income taxation would appropriate for the government more corporate profits without significant adverse effects on entrepreneurship. Some corporate profits are really resource rents—returns on land or other natural resources that were appropriated by corporations in an imperfect process of privatization. Those resource rents now need to be expropriated by the government. (Because, by definition, the supply of such resources is inelastic, there are no supply effects of appropriately designed taxes on resource rents.)

Domestic investment would be increased (and the need for household savings reduced) by institutional arrangements, such as community-based banks and government lending programs, providing better access to credit for small and medium-sized enterprises.

Much of the domestic investment in coming years will necessarily come from the public sector. If there is to be equality of opportunity, government will have to play a major role in education. If all individuals are to have access to health care, government will have to play a major role in that sector, as well. And government also will have to play a major role in managing the continuing urban transition. If China is to improve the living standards of its people, it will be absolutely essential that it creates livable cities, which will require a host of new institutions, from zoning and local planning boards to metropolitan transportation authorities.

THE TRANSITION TOWARD AN INNOVATION ECONOMY

China has recognized that what separates less developed from more developed countries is not only a gap in resources but also a gap in knowledge, and has laid out ambitious plans for reducing that gap and creating a basis for independent innovation. This will be especially important going forward. In the past, growth has been spurred by high rates of capital accumulation. If the reforms suggested in the previous section occur, then savings will diminish and another basis for growth will have to be found. Growth can only be sustained by increasing the pace of total-factor productivity increases.

There is another change: in the past, efforts were directed at closing the gap in knowledge by obtaining knowledge from others; going forward, the focus increasingly will be on moving the frontier outward. Around the world, emerging countries have shown that they can be at the technological frontier.

Innovation is *endogenous*, the result of the allocation of resources to R & D and conscious policies attempting to learn how to produce "at the frontier" (best practices, as it is sometimes put).[42] But resources devoted to research and learning are, like all resources, scarce. Unfortunately, Western firms have directed too much of their research at reducing the input of labor and too little at reducing environmental impacts.

Thus, China needs to create *an innovation system* that both increases the allocation of resources to innovation and ensures that research is directed in socially productive ways. At the center of a new innovation system is the creation of institutions and legal frameworks. A country's innovation system consists of several parts: (i) a strong educational system, beginning with science and technology training at the elementary and secondary levels, but culminating in strong universities with world-class graduate programs; (ii) strong support for basic research, conducted within research universities and independent research institutes; (iii) policies, programs, and institutions that facilitate knowledge development and transfer within the corporate sector, including a balanced intellectual property regime and financial institutions (such as venture capital firms) that help finance innovation; and (iv) policies designed to reduce the risks of innovation or the consequences of failure.[43] Success entails strength in all of these areas, as well as close ties among them.

Government will have to play a large role and one of the key questions is what that role should entail. It should be obvious, for instance, that government will have to finance basic research and provide support for research universities. Even in the United States, widely viewed as having the best research universities in the world, *none* of these universities is a conventional private, for-profit institution. All are supported either by government or by foundations and endowments. China's attempt to create first-class universities and research institutes is an important component in its efforts to create an innovative economy.

The problem with relying on markets is that the social returns on innovation differ from the private returns, both because of distortions in markets and because the private returns on obtaining a patent differ markedly from the social returns.

In the paragraphs below, I describe both the problems of creating a socially productive innovation system and some of the "solutions."

Excessive incentives for labor-saving innovations

High wages in the West mean that there is a high return on reducing labor input. Even in countries where the unemployment rate is high, there are large investments in labor-saving technologies, exacerbating the unemployment problem. If productivity increases at 5 percent a year, output also has to increase at 5 percent a year for employment to remain constant.

For the owners of the firms in the industrial sector, there is another benefit of increasing unemployment: higher unemployment rates serves to depress wages, lowering the cost of production further. For a "harmonious society," however, jobs have to be created to match new entrants into the labor force. In the case of China, the pace of urban job creation needs to be even greater, as labor migrates from the rural to the urban sector. Higher wages are not a bad thing: the purpose of development is to increase the well-being of workers.

Insufficient incentives for resource-saving innovation

By the same token, because American firms do not pay anything for carbon emissions—regardless of the cost imposed on the global economy—they have no incentive to look for innovations that will curb emissions. Making firms pay the full marginal social costs of their activities—the cost, say, of carbon emissions—would enhance incentives for pollution-reducing innovation.[44]

Fundamental problems in designing an innovation system in a market economy

The problem with the innovation system in market economies runs deeper. It is often suggested that intellectual property is at the center of the market economy's innovation system. But the rewards provided by the patent system do not accord well with social returns. The marginal social return on innovation is making the innovation available sooner than it otherwise would have been. But the patent system gives the (temporary) property right to the first person to discover (or more accurately, to patent) the innovation.

For instance, consider the case of the human genome. There was an international effort to map the sequence of human DNA. This ran on track—until some firms decided to try to "beat" the publicly funded project. If they beat Human Genome Project researchers even by one hour, they received all the benefits of monopoly ownership of a gene—even though their marginal social contribution was nil.[45]

In this case, the benefits from the research motivated by the patent are zero and the cost of the patent system to society is huge. Knowledge is a public good and "nonrivalrous." When one person shares a piece of knowledge with another, it does not detract from what the first person knows. Restricting the use of knowledge is inefficient. But the patent system not only restricts the use of knowledge, it also gives the exclusive right to the use of that knowledge to a single party; it creates an artificial monopoly, which distorts resource allocations. In the case of medicines, what is at stake is not only money, but lives themselves. Monopolists may charge a price so high that the poor cannot afford the medicine; thousands, perhaps hundreds of thousands, of individuals may die unnecessarily as a result, especially in the context of an inadequate public health system. As a result of the patent on the gene that indicates a strong likelihood of breast cancer, the owner of the gene insists on a large payment for every test performed. The resulting $3,000 fee puts the test out of the range of anyone without health insurance.

The possibility of dynamic gains is the only justification for the enormous cost of static inefficiency associated with the patent system. But if the intellectual property regime (IPR) is not well designed, the costs will outweigh the benefits. An IPR is defined by a whole set of detailed provisions, which describe what can be patented (or copyrighted), the standards of novelty, the life of the patent, the breadth of the patent, the process by which patents are granted and challenged, and the enforcement mechanism. Indeed, a poorly designed IPR can even stifle innovation, which many worry is happening in America today. The increasing concerns are leading to an active debate about reform;[46] at the very least, those outside the United States should recognize that the mantra of certain corporate leaders and government officials—the stronger the IPR the better—does not reflect the mainstream of thinking among economists and academic intellectual property lawyers (that is, lawyers not in the employ of the corporations that derive so much of their profits from the current regime).

Designing an innovation system for China

Every country must have an IPR—and more broadly, an innovation system—that is appropriate for its own circumstances.[47] A well-designed innovation system consists of a portfolio of instruments, including government-financed research (at universities, specialized laboratories, and even corporations), prizes, and patents. A prize system provides rewards—large prizes for innovations of high social value, such as a cure for a major disease like malaria, small prizes for a me-too medicine—but then the knowledge is made available to anyone who wants to use it (with, perhaps, a licensing fee).[48] The patent system is a prize—the award of a distortionary monopoly power. But while the patent system is *designed* to restrict the use of knowledge and raise prices, the prize system uses the power of the market economy and competition to ensure the lowest possible prices and the greatest dissemination of the knowledge, so that the benefits of the knowledge are enjoyed by as many people as possible.

China needs to have an innovation system that places greater emphasis on prizes and government-funded research and less emphasis on patents (than does, say, the US system), especially because the innovation needs to be directed toward the broad range of social objectives that were noted earlier.[49]

Chapters 8 and 9 in this book discuss more fully what an innovation system and IPR regime for China should look like. The most important lesson is that, as China marches toward a market economy, it should be careful not to imitate those parts of the market economy that are badly flawed; at the very least, it should investigate the flaws, discuss how they can be addressed, and look for alternatives.

THE TRANSITION TOWARD ENVIRONMENTAL SUSTAINABILITY

China's growing population and its demands on resources will, inevitably, put enormous strains on the environment, both within China and globally. Addressing these issues will be essential, both for ensuring that growth is sustainable and that the growth that occurs translates into meaningful improvements in well-being and living standards. There are several mechanisms by which China can ensure that its growth is environmentally sustainable.

First, environmental taxes (carbon taxes, recycling taxes, taxes on the use of commodities) serve double duty: they raise needed revenue while encouraging better use of the environment. It is better to tax bad things (like pollution) than good things (like work). Moreover, such taxes may encourage innovations on how to economize on taxed resources. This is central to creating an "innovation system with Chinese characteristics."

Taxes alone are not likely to suffice. They will need to be complemented by regulations and government investments. Private spending is affected by public infrastructure: a good public transportation system reduces the need for automobiles, which can contribute greatly to pollution.

Some environmental problems are local, but many ecological issues—most notably global warming—affect the entire planet. Global environmental problems can only be addressed on a global scale, though reducing carbon emissions will provide immediate benefits at home, as well as internationally. Because China is now the second largest economy in the world, it can and should play a large role in creating strong frameworks for addressing global environmental problems. It is a large dynamic emerging market, with close ties to the developing world and so can play a particularly constructive role in bridging the gap between developed and developing countries. China can be more sensitive to their concerns because, in some areas, its interests are closely aligned with theirs.[50]

That China should take an active role is a matter of its own interests. Just as China "harmonized" many of its institutional arrangements with those elsewhere as it joined the WTO, further adjustments will be necessary as the world crafts agreements to address global environmental problems. The extent and nature of those adjustments will, of course, depend on the nature of the agreements. A carbon tax may be institutionally easier for China to implement than a complex carbon market, as well as providing an important source of revenue that could help promote development and reduce the importance of some distortionary revenue-raising schemes (such as land sales). It is important for China to push for a global agreement that at least allows for carbon taxes, rather than a cap-and-trade system.[51] China's avaricious appetite for natural resources, such as timber, indicates potentially significant consequences to its actions, which could have strong negative effects on other countries. One concern is the deforestation of slow-growing hardwood forests, without appropriate replanting programs. China has made impressive efforts at reforestation. But in the rest of the world, China has shown less concern about deforestation. It should demand that all lumber sold in China be "certified" and it should take an active role in international efforts to prevent deforestation by supporting the initiatives begun in Copenhagen and Cancun.

This illustrates a central theme of this book: even as China moves away from central planning to a market economy, it must realize that markets on their own do not necessarily lead to socially desirable outcomes. A system of direct control, which never worked perfectly, must be replaced with a system of indirect control—which won't work perfectly, either. But perfection is not the object. Complex systems of indirect control—involving carrots and sticks, incentives (through the price system, modified by taxes), and regulations are the best way to achieve societal objectives. Nowhere are the undesirable effects of unfettered markets clearer than in the environment, upon which they have had a disastrous effect. The growth that results is not sustainable. The question is not whether there ought to be government intervention, but how the set of interventions should be designed and which institutional arrangements will ensure that the policies are effectively implemented.

LIVABLE CITIES

China is rapidly urbanizing.[52] An increasing fraction of China's population is living in urban areas, and how they are designed will have enormous effects on quality of life, the efficiency of the overall economy, and the environment as China continues to grow. Market forces by themselves will not lead to the creation of livable cities, and there are built-in incentives (both for certain government officials and for private-sector entrepreneurs) for the creation of urban sprawls and the design of urban spaces that are counter to the principles underlying livable cities. It is especially important for governments to take action now, with a clear view of long-term consequences of land usage patterns: the decisions made today (e.g., with respect to the design of road networks) will have consequences for decades to come.

China has moved away from the planning model to a market system, but there may not be sufficient appreciation of the limits of the market. This is especially so in land usage. In most Western countries, city planning is critical—the externalities that naturally arise are too large to be ignored and too complex to be dealt with by a simple price system. (The few cities that have tried to do without planning serve as a reminder of why city planning is so important.) To be sure, zoning can be a source of corruption (both in the design of the plan and in the granting of variations), but there is no alternative to implementing strong policies of and institutions for good governance.

INSTITUTIONAL REFORM

China's Eleventh Five-Year Plan recognized that one of government's main responsibilities is to establish the institutional infrastructure required to make a market economy function well. As we noted in the introductory chapter, every society is governed by a set of implicit and explicit rules (institutions, laws, norms, etc.). Those that work well at one time, in one set of circumstances, may not work well in others. Those appropriate for a closed, planned economy are not suitable for a dynamic, market economy.

Creating good institutions is not easy. It's not even easy to define what a good institution is. Many thought that the Federal Reserve, the US central bank, was a "good" institution; yet, its conduct, governance, and performance have been disappointing. Prior to the reforms of 2010, with the committee responsible for nominating the head of the New York Federal Reserve Bank and the other regional banks, including the heads of the major banks that were rescued, there was a clear conflict of interest. The lack of transparency of the Fed—even to the point of fighting requests from Congress and the press for access to information—has been troubling. After the courts and Congress obtained the information, it became more understandable why the Fed had wanted to keep its secrets: the conflicts of interest that many had worried about were now evident.

In the following discussion, we focus on a few of the areas in which institutions will have to be created or reformed. But before looking at each of the specifics, there are seven general observations. First, China simply can't adopt wholesale the institutions of other countries. To repeat what we have said before: one-size-fits-all policies almost never work and transplanting institutional arrangements (such as America's intellectual property regime) to China would be a mistake. Some adaptation is always required, but in many cases, given the differences in circumstances and objectives, the differences in the appropriate institutional arrangements are so large that it would be a mistake to begin with, say, the American model even as a template. There are not only important differences in circumstances but also in objectives: many of the market economies focus on increasing GDP and have policies and institutional arrangements heavily shaped by special interests; China should pursue broader objectives.

Second, there are a range of approaches taken within different Western countries. Those in the West concerned with broader social objectives in particular are themselves often critical of some of the particular institutional arrangements that have been adopted. To take another example, the US recently reformed its bankruptcy law in ways that may significantly disadvantage those who cannot repay what they owe for reasons beyond their control, such as serious illness. At the very least, it is a contentious change that its opponents believe may increase social distress.

As we have noted, there are many different forms of a market economy; the American model is, in many ways, markedly different from the Scandinavian model, the Continental European model, or the Japanese model. These countries differ in their history, their social context, and their articulated social objectives. The Scandinavian model emphasizes social solidarity and social justice and exhibits more concern for the poor. And again, the Scandinavian countries have succeeded in achieving higher levels of performance in terms of broader indicators of societal well-being (such as the UNDP's Human Development Index), while maintaining a high level of innovation, with the penetration of new technologies again scoring toward the top of the list.[53]

Third, even in terms of narrower objectives, Western market models often fail, both in growth and stability. In many market economies, we have seen deficiencies in the institutional infrastructure result in scandals, touching on almost every major accounting firm, large fractions of the major investment banks, and many of the major corporations. America's economy was strong enough to withstand the enormous misallocation of resources that resulted; China's may not be; the costs relative to the size of its economy could be greater. The scandals left many without adequate provision for their retirement, while the bubble to which they contributed in turn fed the growing inequality within America. It was not a question of a few rotten apples: The problems were clearly systemic. China needs to avoid these systemic failures.

Fourth, many discussions on institutional design issues (such as those on property rights) are based not on an understanding of the actual features and workings of those institutions in particular Western countries, but on an academic idealization—a version of those institutions that some extreme groups might advocate, but which would never have been adopted in practice. For instance, while some free-market economists have advocated a basically private retirement insurance program, the United States has repeatedly rejected the notion of even partially privatizing its public social security system, most recently following the proposals of President Bush in January 2005 to partially privatize social security. Government provision entails far lower administrative costs,[54] provides insurance against risks (such as inflation) that private markets typically do not provide, and can achieve redistributive objectives (reducing poverty and reducing intergenerational inequality) that are otherwise difficult to realize.[55]

Fifth, the details of institutional arrangements are often critical (as the English aphorism has it, "the devil is in the details"). We saw this in our earlier discussion of intellectual property rights. Many of the problems with America's intellectual property regime lie in details—about how intellectual property rights are enforced, the breadth of patents, and how patents are granted. A discussion that simply says, "One should have strong intellectual property rights," doesn't make for much progress.

Sixth, especially because the details are so important, there are often unintended consequences of well-intended policies. In solving one problem, new, unanticipated problems are created.

Seventh, an important aspect of institutional design focuses on *duplication* and *risks of mistakes*. In the United States, antitrust oversight resides in the antitrust divisions of the Justice Department, the Federal Trade Commission, and state antitrust authorities. Those injured by anticompetitive behavior can take civil actions with triple damages. (In the area of telecommunications, further oversight is provided by the Federal Communications Commission.) Similarly, there is multiple oversight in banking and securities regulation. There is a cost, but the benefits are far greater because the risk to the economy of institutional failure is enormous. This is particularly of concern in those areas where political influence (including regulatory capture) is likely to occur—clearly areas of concern for both financial market regulation and antitrust oversight.

In the following paragraphs, I comment briefly on several issues that are at the heart of creating the institutional infrastructure for a market economy. Some of the legal issues (such as property rights) are discussed in the previous chapter and elsewhere in this volume, so a discussion of these pivotal institutional issues is omitted here.

Tax policy

China will need additional public revenues to finance its social, environmental, and developmental agenda. Part of its transformation will be toward the service sector, including health and education, two areas for which there will be great demand and which typically entail large public funding.

China clearly could collect a substantially higher fraction of GDP in taxes without adversely affecting growth. Tax revenue as a percentage of GDP went up from 5 percent in 1994, to 6.8 percent in 2000, to 10.5 percent in 2009, according to World Bank figures. (The Scandinavian countries have shown that even very high tax rates are consistent with rapid growth and high levels of innovation.[56])

In a market economy, tax policies play an important role in resource allocation. Well-designed taxes could help achieve the three objectives that we have discussed in this chapter: (i) protecting the environment and reducing resource utilization; (ii) moving away from export-led growth to growth based on domestic consumption and investment; and (iii) redressing growing inequalities. As noted previously, it is better to tax bad things (e.g., pollution) than good things. There are large costs associated with private cars in congested urban areas, and they should accordingly bear high taxes. The imposition of taxes on carbon emissions could help reduce emissions. Other environmental taxes can encourage recycling and discourage other forms of pollution. Given worries about excessive real-estate investment and speculative bubbles, and given the difficulties of designing administrative measures that deal with these risks effectively, it also makes sense to have high capital gains taxes on real estate and other speculative activities.

The current tax structure may disadvantage services, and shifting from a turnover tax to a value added tax (VAT) would both increase efficiency and encourage the development of this sector.

Another set of distortions that has been widely noted is associated with resources in general and land in particular. Local communities use their control of land as a source of revenue, contributing to excess real-estate development. Enterprises seem driven to reinvest their income, some of which is really implicit rents associated with their control of certain resources, contributing to excess supply. If the central government were to impose high taxes on these rents (or, more directly, to take "ownership" of the resources), and to use some of the revenues thus generated to provide finance to local communities, it would reduce the scope of these distortionary activities. (A 5 percent price-based resources tax on oil and gas produced in Xinjiang was in fact imposed in June 2010.)

Similarly, earlier we noted that China no longer needs to continue to build up its reserves. But increasing its exchange rate would have several adverse effects, including lowering the incomes of farmers. Offsetting the effect of America and Europe's huge agricultural subsidies would divert resources needed for other social and developmental objectives. An export tax (or, at a minimum, eliminating export rebates of VAT) would, by contrast, both reduce the trade gap and generate additional revenues.

Why China shouldn't borrow tax policies from others

Around the world, the IMF has been advocating the adoption of a consumption-based VAT. There are some distinct advantages of such a tax, but it also has some distinct disadvantages. The consumption-based VAT is oblivious to the environment, regressive (in the usual definition, since individuals with lower incomes consume a larger fraction of their income), and discourages consumption. Thus, while the tax might make sense for economies that are concerned with encouraging savings, it makes little sense for China.[57]

How tax policy needs to change with changing circumstances

In earlier stages of development, China felt it needed to attract foreign investment; it worried that there was a shortage of entrepreneurs, capital, and technology at home. But this has all changed, and it makes little sense to give foreigners in general preferential tax treatment over domestic entrepreneurs. Indeed, there are arguments to the contrary: spillovers from the expansion of domestic entrepreneurship may be greater, so that some preferences should be given to domestic firms. Moreover, many foreign firms face tax systems in which tax credits are given for foreign taxes paid, so that raising tax rates on foreign firms may have little effect on incentives and would simply constitute a redistribution from foreign governments to China's government. China may not be able to tax foreign firms at a higher rate than domestic firms, but at this stage of its development, except in certain sectors where it might seek the acquisition of technology, it should not tax them at a lower rate.

Equalizing tax rates may not suffice. What matters are the details—provisions, for instance, concerning depreciation and other expenses. Many Western companies are adept at tax avoidance, paying no taxes even though the legislated rate is, say, 25 percent, 30 percent, or higher. Since foreign firms are clever at the use of transfer pricing, China will have to be careful to ensure that they actually pay the taxes that they should.

Financial markets

Financial markets play a key role in any market economy, because of their importance in allocating resources. Financial markets do more than mediate between savers and investors. They gather and process information, determine who is creditworthy, which investments are most likely to yield high (risk-adjusted) returns, and enforce credit contracts. They can also help manage risk. But market failures are endemic when information is imperfect (which it always is), so there is always an important role for government in financial markets. Few today question the necessity of government regulation of banks and securities markets; the only debate is about the form and extent of the regulation. There are a number of reasons, besides the market failures associated with imperfect information, that government regulation is both desirable and necessary. One is the presence of large externalities, so evident in the Great Recession, and earlier, in the East Asia crisis. Bad lending and borrowing practices are often blamed for these crises—but the crises touched everyone in the affected countries, not just the lenders and borrowers.

Government regulation needs to be directed at four objectives: (i) ensuring the safety, soundness, and stability of the financial system, recognizing that many of the economic fluctuations that have marked capitalism since its beginnings are related to problems in the financial system; (ii) protecting consumers (borrowers, investors) against abusive practices—especially important in a context where there are many uninformed and inexperienced investors; (iii) ensuring competition, recognizing that even when there are many financial institutions, the market may be such that there may be limited competition in, say, the supply of loans to SMEs in a particular locale, and that firms often act collusively, either explicitly or tacitly; and (iv) ensuring access to credit, especially for underserved sectors and groups.

In accomplishing these objectives, the government will need to employ a portfolio of instruments, both market-based interventions and administrative measures. For instance, to ensure that banks do not engage in excessively risky lending, risk-based capital adequacy requirements and deposit insurance premiums may be used as part of market-based measures. But unless capital adequacy standards are countercyclical, becoming tighter in booms, they can contribute to economic volatility.

The subject of financial sector regulatory and institutional design is complex. Here, we will look at only four aspects.[58]

Access to credit

The first is that markets, by themselves, often fail to provide credit (or at least provide an adequate supply of credit at reasonable terms) to certain categories of potential borrowers. That is one of the reasons why even in highly developed financial markets such as the United States, government has intervened in financial markets to promote mortgages, student loans, and credit for SMEs, underserved communities, and rural ventures. The argument for such interventions in China, at its current stage of development, is even more compelling. Increasing the flow of credit in these areas is particularly important if China is to succeed in its objective of reducing the large disparities in income; this is an example of a government action that can enhance both growth and equality—and that may even help the structural adjustment of the economy away from exports.

In the United States (and many other countries), interventions have taken on a number of different forms, and China would probably benefit from using a wide portfolio of instruments: the creation of specialized banks and lending agencies; the imposition of lending requirements to underserved communities and sectors (see the US Community Reinvestment Act requirements); or the provision of partial guarantees or limited subsidies. India has imposed requirements, the effect of which has been to increase branches—and the availability of credit—in rural and more remote areas.[59] (Such requirements, if properly designed, can be made consistent with WTO obligations.) In the absence of such regulations, there is a temptation, especially of foreign banks, to engage in "cream-skimming," providing ample credit for large firms, but little credit for domestic small and medium-sized firms. Indeed, some recent studies suggest that, in many countries, the entry of foreign banks has actually led to an overall decrease in credit to these enterprises.[60]

Perhaps the most important thing that China should do is to encourage the entry of small and medium-sized local banks. The key to providing credit is *information*; local banks are more likely to be relatively well informed about local (small and medium-sized) firms.[61] (Of course, China needs simultaneously to develop the capacity to regulate and supervise small and medium-sized banks.)

Risks and rewards of capital and financial market liberalization

The second is to recognize that capital or financial market liberalization may not lead to faster growth, but may contribute to greater economic instability. Even the IMF, in its 2003 study,[62] has recognized that capital market liberalization brought risk without reward to many developing countries. It found the result surprising—contrary to economic "theory"—but it was contrary only to an economic theory based on perfect information and infinitely long-lived individuals. More realistic models, based on imperfect information,[63] are fully consistent with the empirical findings. The implication is clear: China must take extreme care as it liberalizes its financial and capital markets.

Capital and financial market liberalization played an important role spreading the crisis in America's financial markets around the world. In the aftermath of the crisis, unbridled capital flows have given rise to destabilizing currency appreciations. In the spring of 2007, the IMF recognized the desirability of capital account interventions, at least under certain circumstances.

The complexity and risks associated with liberalization mean that to the extent that markets are liberalized, they should be done so gradually. This is especially true because there is a learning process for investors, regulators, and financial firms.

Trade-offs among objectives

The third is to recognize that there may be important trade-offs among various objectives. For instance, one can ensure the safety and soundness of the banking system by requiring banks to hold only short-term government bills; but if that were done, banks would not be able to fulfill one of their main functions, which is providing access to credit.[64]

Adapting to the evolving Chinese market economy

The fourth is to recognize that the quickly evolving nature of China's economy and financial markets will require adaptable regulatory policies. For instance, as part of its WTO accession agreement, there will be entry of foreign financial firms. Previously, the financial system performed a number of social functions. It may not be possible for some of these to be accomplished through the financial system[65]—and the greater transparency, e.g., of hidden subsidies, may be an ancillary benefit. In other cases, the ways in which these objectives are attained will have to be changed; for instance, in order for there to be adequate access to credit by small and medium-sized firms, regulations, such as the credit requirements discussed earlier, may have to be imposed.

One important aspect of China's evolving market economy is a greater emphasis on domestic consumption. As we noted earlier, one of the reasons that export-led growth played such a critical role in China's earlier development was that it allowed the country's productive capacity to expand more rapidly than its capacity to expand aggregate demand—and one of the reasons for the failure of demand to expand is the failure to develop financial institutions with the capability to judge creditworthiness, i.e., ascertaining which consumers who might gain access to credit would be able or willing to repay. Today, strengthened financial institutions have a greater capacity to provide consumer loans, including mortgages. But China should learn the lesson of other countries: financial institutions sometimes prey on uninformed consumers, charging them exorbitantly high interest rates, and this may be particularly the case in situations where consumers have little experience with debt. Moreover, they often lend beyond an individual's capacity to repay, which can lead to stress on the part of consumers, and, when sufficiently large numbers are unable to repay, stress on the financial system as a whole. China needs strong consumer protection legislation, rigorously enforced, and backed up with a *debtor-friendly bankruptcy law* that gives lenders greater incentives to engage in due diligence to ensure that borrowers have the capacity to repay.

Other market institutions

There are a host of other institutions required to make markets work. The previous paragraph referred to one set of institutions, bankruptcy laws.

There need to be good regulations not only for banks but also for securities. America's Securities and Exchange Commission and Britain's Financial Regulatory Agency were often thought to be regulatory models, but their performance in recent years has been disappointing. Too often they seemed to suffer from "capture" (sometimes cognitive capture, i.e., viewing the world through the eyes of those whom they were supposed to regulate). The result was that New York state, not the federal government, took on responsibility for much of the enforcement. Part of New York's success was because it had a better legal framework. The Martin Act (New York General Business Law) and the Executive Law are examples of forward-looking legislation that can play an important role (when combined with active enforcement) in creating the environment necessary for capital markets to function. It will never be possible *ex ante* to specify all of the ways in which businesses may engage in misdeeds, defrauding shareholders or their customers. But it must be possible to enjoin such practices as soon as they become evident and to punish the corporations and their officials who have been involved in perpetrating these economic crimes.

A market economy only delivers the benefits that are promised if there is strong competition. But profits can often be increased most easily by creating a monopoly or weakening competition through the creation of barriers to entry. That is why it is important to have an active and vigilant antitrust authority. Many anticompetitive practices occur at the local level, and so it may be important to also establish local authorities.[66]

Social insurance

One of the reasons that China has such a high household savings rate is the absence of adequate social insurance;[67] there are inadequacies in the public provision of education, health, and retirement programs. Stronger public support of these programs will help China in its move away from export-led growth and in its attempt to reduce the disparities in well-being among its citizens.[68]

Designing a good social insurance system is not easy, especially in a highly competitive global economy. As I noted earlier, the Scandinavian countries have shown that providing a strong social insurance program (including a strong public education system) can actually provide a country with a competitive advantage. Competing in the global market place requires a healthy, educated labor force, able to adapt to the fast pace of changes. With risk-taking so essential to success, a strong social safety net—combined with high levels of employment and education—enhances the ability and willingness of individuals to undertake risk. There is much discussion about the virtues of international trade—the gains provided by a larger marketplace. But the economic gains that result from creating a strong *national* economy are even larger. And a strong national economy requires labor mobility, which in return requires a national social insurance system.

In the past, firms (both in China and elsewhere) were engaged in two separate activities—production and the provision of social services. Competing in the global marketplace requires separating these functions, and that means that the government must undertake an increased role. (As we noted earlier, there are sound economic and social reasons why the provision of at least a basic level of social insurance cannot be left to the market alone.) Fortunately, China's rapid growth means that there should be the resources with which to begin to create a strong, national social insurance program.

Information systems

Well-functioning economies require good information, but there are systematic market failures. Individuals often have incentives not to reveal relevant information, or worse, to provide distorted information.[69]

Some of my recent research has been concerned with information problems that arise within organizations and the public sector.[70] Governments also need to have good information to make good decisions. There are incentives for government officials not to disclose what is going on, either to citizens or to supervisors. There is, of course, a need to have strong laws to avoid conflicts of interest (just as there is a need for such laws in the private sector). Just as successful private-sector managers have learned that there is a need to have a variety of channels of information, so too does the public sector. A vibrant, responsible media can be one such channel. For it to be effective, it must have access to relevant information, which is why right-to-know laws ("freedom of information acts") are so important.[71]

CONCLUDING COMMENTS

China is a huge country, and pronouncements of policy in Beijing often have to be translated into actions at the local level. The balance of interests and concerns that play out at the national level may play out differently at the local and provincial levels. The environmental issues facing the country may be apparent at the national level, but the need to create jobs may seem more paramount locally. Chapters 15 and 16 and the introduction to Part III highlight the role of decentralization and the relationship between central and local authorities.

As China's economy and society evolve, mechanisms for implementing the national plan and for inducing the achievement of national goals inevitably will change. There may need to be greater reliance on incentives of the kind that are commonly employed in federal systems; e.g., national authorities provide financial incentives, both rewards and punishment, for compliance. The price system itself (e.g., through carbon taxes) can be used to induce better environmental policies. It will be important to develop a national consensus behind the goals and objectives of economic reform, as articulated by each five-year plan, something which the widespread discussion of "the plan" is intended to do.

Ideology and interests

As China goes forward with its transition to a market economy, it will increasingly confront a problem that has faced market economies elsewhere in the world: the conjoined influence of free-market ideology and interests to shape a market economy that is *not* in the broad interests of society.

As enterprises grow in influence and wealth, they will try to use political processes to garner more for themselves. They will argue that what they want for themselves is good for the country; they will threaten to move elsewhere or reduce employment if government does not do what they want. They will use these arguments to weaken environmental standards and worker safety protections. And because there is not widespread understanding of economics, such self-serving arguments often prevail, or at least provide sufficient cover for actions that are counter to the general interest.

The tax code of the United States is riddled with provisions that make no economic sense; they are there because of the influence of special interests. The

United States is contributing enormously to greenhouse gas emissions, which lead to global warming; its energy profligacy has made America dependent on foreign oil. There are countries with just as high a standard of living that are using half as much energy per capita as the United States. A carbon tax (or an energy tax) would actually increase overall efficiency. But America's energy industry has used its political influence to keep energy taxes low. Similarly, America's huge farm subsidies—a billion dollars or more to some 20,000 cotton farmers every year—are bad for the environment, costly to taxpayers, and impose enormous costs on developing countries as they contribute to the impoverishment of some 10 million farmers in Africa alone. These policies do not represent good economics, nor are they consistent with any sense of social values or priorities—they are again the consequence of the workings of special interests.

China, as it moves toward a market economy, needs to be on guard against the role of these special interests. Already, some have suggested that such influences are in evidence in some of its policies. If China succeeds in creating a market economy in which these have at the most very limited sway, China will truly have created a market economy with Chinese characteristics.

No idea has had more influence in economics than Adam Smith's invisible hand, the belief that the best way to achieve economic efficiency is unfettered markets. Understanding the circumstances under which that might be true has been the most important quest in economic science over the past two and a quarter centuries, and the success in analyzing systems of the complexity of the modern economy should be viewed as one of the greatest achievements. Like any such achievement in science, it is the result of the cumulative efforts of scholars and researchers. Arrow (1951) and Debreu (1959) showed, for instance, in the mid-1950s that free and unfettered markets lead to economic efficiency only under highly restrictive conditions, and their proofs of the efficiency of markets provided insights into why markets so often fail.[72] Through the work of a host of scholars (to which this author's work on asymmetric and imperfect information and incomplete markets contributed), as well as an array of historical experiences, we know the problems of unfettered markets, and we know that every successful economy has been based on an appropriate balance between the market and government. As I noted earlier, governments play an especially important role in innovation, in providing safety nets, and in maintaining a "harmonious" society, one in which the ethics of social justice and social solidarity are in evidence.

China will be facing some of its most important decisions as it establishes the rules of the game, the institutions that will not only guide it as it makes its next steps, but that also will serve to "govern" the market economy. The debate over these rules will be contentious. There will be those that come forward with self-serving arguments for why it is best to minimize regulations or to have no regulations. And they will come armed with stories illustrating the dangers of excessive regulation. Still, there are two basic propositions that should guide China's policies going forward:

- *There is no theoretical basis for the contention that unfettered markets lead to economic efficiency.* The rejection of that contention has been one of the great achievements of economic science during the past half century. And the experiences leading up to the Great Recession have, if anything, bolstered these theoretical conclusions.

• *Every successful market economy has been based on achieving an appropriate balance between the market and government.*[73]

Many years ago, China set forth on its course of "crossing the river by feeling the stones." It has moved far into the river, and it has felt many stones. It has achieved enormous successes, and yet it faces enormous challenges. China is still a low-income country. In spite of its remarkable successes, even in purchasing power parity, per capita income is only around a sixth of that of the United States.[74]

Now that China has gone more than halfway across the river, the other side is clearer: there are many different forms of market economy—many different places to land on the bank. China can see that its choices will make a great deal of difference in the directions it takes. The kind of market economy it chooses will affect the society it creates.

Even as China crosses the river by feeling the stones, creating a market that is consistent with China's distinct circumstances and objectives will require a "New Economic Model." China's circumstances have changed, which necessitates a different model than that which girds its past successes—and because China's circumstances are different from that of other countries, the model for China inevitably needs to be different as well.

As China continues the journey, as it takes its next steps in crossing the river, it needs to avoid the pitfalls that have befallen others. To achieve its economic and social goals will require clarity of vision and values about the kind of market economy that it wants. Its past success in balancing vision with pragmatic flexibility and its attention to "social harmony" augurs well for its future.

NOTES

1. This paper is based on two lectures delivered at the China Development Forum, in March 2006 and March 2007, titled "Remarks On China's Eleventh Five-Year Plan: Another Major Step in China's Transition to A Market Economy" and "Toward a New Model of Development." I am deeply indebted to Professor Justin Lin, Mo Ji, Xiabio Lu, Anton Korinek, Akbar Noman, Xie Fuzhan, and Zhou Qiren for discussions on the topics examined here, and to Mo Ji, An Li, Eamon Kircher-Allen, and Farah Siddique for research and editorial assistance. The views are solely those of the author. Professor Lin kindly shared with me his extremely informative slideshow presentation, *The Eleventh Five-Year Plan and China's Future Economic Development* and provided detailed comments on these lectures.
2. See the World Bank's *World Development Indicators* for gross national income per capita, calculated via the Atlas Method (current US$), from 1980 to 2009 (the most recent year available). This growth is from $182 to $2,135 in terms of constant 2000 US dollars and is from $250 to $6,890 in terms of PPP.
3. See Crafts (2004).
4. Of course, there are disagreements about the accuracy of the numbers. But almost surely, in some years (2003 and 2004), China's true growth was higher than the 9 percent reported. China's GDP measured in purchasing power parity—adjusting, in other words, for the cost of living in China—is close to four times the official statistic, which

is based on the exchange rate. If one used GDP as measured by the exchange rate, but assumed that the market exchange rate was overvalued by, say, 20 percent in 1998, as the government intervened to prevent its exchange rate falling in tandem with those of the other East Asian countries, and, by 2005, was undervalued by 20 percent, then "real" growth so measured would have averaged another 5 percentage points higher.

5. See the World Bank's Reducing Poverty Sustaining Growth Initiative, <http://www.worldbank.org/wbi/reducingpoverty/index.html>, accessed June 12, 2011.
6. It is often said that China will be the first country to grow old before it grows rich.
7. That is what motivated the adage "cross the river by feeling the stones."
8. The Commission on the Measurement of Economic Performance and Social Progress noted the many ways in which GDP fails as a good measure of well-being. Several of these areas are important in our later discussions. See the Commission's report, Fitoussi, Sen, and Stiglitz (2010).
9. In 2011, US median household income dropped to $50,054 from $50,831 (adjusted for inflation) in the previous year, a level not seen since 1996. See Census Table H-9, available at <http://www.census.gov/hhes/www/income/data/historical/household/index.html>, accessed December 10, 2011.
10. See, for example, Stiglitz (2008).
11. By poverty line at "a dollar a day," poverty in China fell by almost 250 million from 1990 to 2004, a period in which the total poverty reduction around the world was around 270 million. See *The Economist* (2008).
12. One standard measure of inequality is the Gini coefficient. China's Gini coefficient increased from 0.16 (before reform) to 0.47 (after 2005). By contrast, the US Gini coefficient stands at 0.466, Japan's at 0.249, and the Scandinavian countries at around 0.3. See Seligman (2005).
13. See his lecture "Human Development and Health" delivered at Beijing University at the International Conference on Health and Development in October 2006. He also points out that Kerala's life expectancy is higher than that in every province of China except for the urban conglomerates such as Beijing and Shanghai. Infant mortality rates were comparable in 1979; now Kerala's is one-third that of China's.
14. Indeed, China perhaps should be given credit for having done as well as it has, given its low expenditures on health—estimated to be between 2 and 3 percent of GDP. See <http://earthtrends.wri.org/text/environmental-governance/variable-642.html>. (By contrast, the US spends approximately 15 percent of its GDP on health.)
15. I should note that such concerns helped shape both the Eleventh Five-Year Plan as well as the stimulus package that was adopted in response to the Great Recession of 2008. As the discussion elsewhere in this chapter and book suggests, there remains much to be done.
16. World Bank (2005).
17. In the United States, as noted above (n. 9) *median* household income has been falling—so that most Americans in 2009 were worse off than they were in 1997. But if account is taken of the increased health insecurity, with 48.2 million (18.2 percent of Americans) without health insurance, the deterioration in standards of living is even more marked. See US Centers for Disease Control and Prevention (2012). The affordable health care act was to remedy this, but the Supreme Court has allowed states to opt out of Medicaid expansion, which means significant numbers may remain uncovered.
18. See Yang (2010).
19. Following the issuance of the Stiglitz-Sen-Fitoussi report, several governments around the world are attempting to do so.
20. The broad measure—which includes such indicators as life expectancy, mean years of schooling, expected years of schooling, and gross national income per capita—ranks Norway first in the world, the United States fourth, Sweden ninth, and Denmark

nineteenth. Focusing on particular indicators, however, shows some or all of the Scandinavian countries ahead of the United States; in just one example, the life expectancies in Norway and Sweden are 81.0 and 81.3 years respectively; in the United States it is 79.6. Further, in its "inequality-adjusted" list, UNDP ranks all the Scandinavian countries far ahead of the United States. See United Nations Development Program (2010).

21. See United Nations Development Program (2010).
22. The United States has the highest rate of incarceration in the world, with 743 per 100,000 people, followed by Rwanda with 595/100,000. The United Kingdom (England and Wales) incarcerates 150 per 100,000; Germany 88/100,000; and for Denmark and Norway it is only 71. See International Centre for Prison Studies (2011).
23. I provided an economic analysis of these in my books (2003) *Roaring Nineties*, W. W. Norton and (2010) *Freefall: America, Free Markets, and the Sinking of the World Economy*, W. W. Norton (available in Chinese).
24. An example is China's use of the dual price system in the transition from the prices that prevailed under planning to more market-based prices.
25. Greenwald and Stiglitz (2006).
26. This is particularly true because the financial sector in China is dominated by the four big state banks. Only about 1 percent of the firms in China, mainly the large firms, have borrowed money from banks. Due to the underdevelopment of small and medium-sized banks (which typically provide credit to local, small, and medium-sized firms), SMEs and family farms often do not receive financial services from banks and finance their investment through their own savings, contributing to China's high savings rate.
27. It is even more peculiar to think of China having helped finance America's huge fiscal deficit, arising partly from the Iraq War and partly from the tax cut for the richest people in the richest country in the world.
28. I would argue, accordingly, that Korean Chaebols should not be a model of China's business organization.
29. Although it will still be important for China to guard itself against abusive lending practices, and to adopt bankruptcy laws that do not reward financial institutions for making bad loans. There is concern that changes in bankruptcy law in the United States during the (second) Bush Administration did just that and are contributing to stresses among lower and middle-income individuals, who already face problems of stagnant incomes. These problems have been compounded by the fact that some 48.2 million Americans do not have health insurance; some studies suggest that a significant fraction of individuals who are forced into personal bankruptcy have confronted major medical expenses. For example, one study found that 62.1 percent of bankruptcies in the United States in 2007 were associated with medical spending. There are important lessons from these experiences for China.

    See Himmelstein, Thorne, Warren, and Woolhandler (2009). For health insurance statistics, see US Centers for Disease Control and Prevention (2012).

    China is also expanding uncollateralized consumer debt, e.g. credit cards. The experience of Korea provides a cautionary note, which Chinese regulators say they have taken into account.
30. This is especially important if China is to avoid the real-estate bubbles that have characterized most capitalist economies and that have resulted in such high levels of macroeconomic instability.
31. One must be wary of these numbers. Some analysts argue that it represents a gross overestimate of the "true" trade surplus, because a portion, possibly a substantial portion, of the sharp increase in trade surplus is due to overinvoicing exports and underinvoicing imports by the trading companies for the purpose of gaining from the

anticipated RMB revaluation. Two ways to discourage this practice is for the Chinese government to make it clear that the appreciation will not exceed, say 3–4 percent per year and for capital gains taxes to be imposed, at high rates, especially on short-term capital gains associated with currency appreciation. By contrast, some argue that the large *bilateral* trade surplus with the US understates that surplus, because some of the imports to the US from places like Hong Kong are really of goods made largely in China.

32. According to the Asian Development Bank, GDP in 2009 has grown at 8.4 percent, private consumption at 10.1 percent, and total final domestic demand at 14.6 percent. See the Asian Development Bank Statistical Database System, GDP, private consumption at current prices, government consumption at current prices.
33. In 2009, private consumption was 35 percent of GDP in China, but 71 percent in the US. See the World Bank World Development Indicator, household final consumption expenditure, etc. (percent of GDP).
34. Some have argued that China should rely on a privately financed health care system. No country has succeeded in establishing a fundamentally private health care system that is efficient and provides adequate care for the poor. America has among the most privatized health care systems of the advanced industrial countries; health care expenditure as a percentage of GDP is the highest in the world, and health care outcomes are far poorer than those in other advanced industrial countries of comparable income. Standard theories of asymmetric information (particularly focusing on adverse selection) explain why private provision of health care insurance is inefficient, marked in particular by high transaction costs. Some of the recent "reforms" encouraging private insurance have exacerbated problems of "cream-skimming," and are probably contributing to the increasing problems of lack of coverage.
35. See Wei and Zhang (2009).
36. In 2009, household income was 29 percent of GDP in China, 63 percent in Japan, and 57 percent in India.
37. As always, there is some debate about the numbers. Some argue that GDP and savings are both overstated, because included in real-estate investment is the value of land (there are often large capital gains associated with real-estate developments; value of the capital gain on the land should be treated as a transfer payment, but typically is not). Others argue that there is underreporting of services; an earlier correction led to a marked decrease in the savings ratio; some argue that there is still some underreporting. Finally, some believe that there is overreporting of exports and underreporting of imports, as part of circumvention of short-term capital controls. In this view, a substantial part of the current account surplus is speculative capital flows. Taking this into account would again lower the domestic savings rate.
38. See Feldstein (2007).
39. This shift might even make matters worse for the US and for global stability, since it would make the problem of financing the US trade deficit more difficult.
40. It will, in particular, come under pressure both to appreciate its exchange rate and to make its exchange rate more flexible. There is often a confusion between allowing "more flexibility" and "capital market liberalization." The latter has proved particularly problematic, and China has been well served by avoiding the extremes. There are large costs associated with the high volatility of exchange rates, especially in regimes with liberalized capital accounts. Elsewhere, we have argued for the advantages of an export tax, which has similar effects on the trade surplus, but has the further advantage of generating revenue while avoiding the adverse effects on the rural sector (see next note).
41. For an extended discussion of the advantages of export taxes over exchange rate revaluation, see Lau and Stiglitz (2005).

42. Even within the advanced industrial countries, there are huge disparities between best and average practices, implying there is typically considerable scope for increases in overall efficiency.
43. In that sense, even a country's safety net can be thought of as part of its innovation system: it reduces the downside risk of failure. Some argue that the strong safety nets in the Scandinavian countries are part of the reason for those countries' high level of innovation.
44. Environmental taxes are called corrective taxes, which raise revenue as they enhance economic efficiency. A carbon tax would have, in addition, further important advantages. An international agreement on carbon taxes could, moreover, break the international impasse on what to do about global warming. The scientific evidence about the risks of this impending calamity has been mounting. The Stern Report (UK) made a convincing case that the economic benefits—taking into account all the risks—of doing something to mitigate the risks outweighed the costs. The Kyoto Protocol was based on emission targets determined on the basis of reductions from the 1990 levels of emissions. Unfortunately, no one has come up with a set of principles to guide the determination of emission target levels in a fair and equitable way, one acceptable to both developing countries and the US. Because the distributional consequences of a common policy, in which each country agrees to impose a carbon tax at rates reflecting the agreed-upon global social cost of carbon emissions, are much more limited, there may be some hope of a global agreement. (With each country keeping the revenue from its own carbon tax, the distributional consequences arise from the differences in the deadweight losses associated with the imposition of the carbon tax relative to the imposition of alternative taxes. In many cases, the switch toward a carbon tax would actually be welfare-enhancing. The social cost is measured by the difference in the Harberger triangles, and the differences in the social cost are related to the differences in these differences, which are likely to be small.)
45. Interestingly, some countries refused to grant patents for genes—just as mathematical theorems are not patentable. A US federal court ruled in 2010 against the giving of a patent for the genes linked to breast and ovarian cancers. See Schwartz and Pollack (2010).
46. There are several reasons why a poorly designed patent system may impede the pace of innovation. By making knowledge less accessible, the pace of innovation will be reduced. (This can be partially mitigated by disclosure requirements; interestingly, some advocates of strong intellectual property rights have argued that disclosure violates their rights. But all rights are associated with responsibilities, and a responsibility long associated with good intellectual property regimes is full disclosure.) Another reason is that intellectual property can lead to increased monopolization, and it has long been recognized that monopolies have less incentive to innovate than competitive markets. The ability of a monopolist like Microsoft to squash successful innovators (like Netscape, which innovated in the area of browsers, and RealNetwork, which innovated in the area of media players) almost surely has an enervating effect on innovation—another reason why countries need strong antitrust laws. A third problem arises from "patent thickets," when innovators face uncertainties that their innovation will trespass on the intellectual property of others.
47. The fact that there is no single best IP system is exhibited by the conflicts of views over the use of labeling, with many European countries arguing for tight protection of the use of labeling (e.g., of names like *Parma ham*) and the US, which more often copies these labels from other countries, arguing on the other side. For China, the development of strong trademark protection is important in providing incentives for the development of brand name reputations associated with the production of high-quality goods.

48. The prize system works best when there are well-defined objectives—a cure for a disease, a light long-lived car battery, a more fuel-efficient engine. The Royal Society of Arts in the UK has long advocated—and used—prizes for stimulating innovation.
49. For a fuller discussion of the prize system, and the problems with the patent system, see my 2006 book, *Making Globalization Work*, Chapter 5.
50. China should, for instance, support the initiative of the Rainforest Countries to avoid deforestation. This will provide developing countries, whose forests play such an important role not only in avoiding global warming but also in preserving biodiversity, both incentives and funds with which simultaneously to pursue sound environmental policies and aggressive growth policies.
51. On the other hand, China could benefit from the sale of carbon offsets.
52. For instance, the urbanization level increased from 26 percent in 1990 to 36 percent in 2001, to 47 percent in 2009, and is expected to reach 50 percent in 2020, and 75 percent in 2050. This translates to 10 million new urban dwellers per year in the coming years. (The increased percentage of urbanization was larger than that from 1953–78.) See China Development Research Foundation (2007).
53. There is broad consensus within these countries about the desirability of their model, though, as usual, there are differences in views concerning "fine tuning" of the system. Thus, the recently elected government in Sweden has called for some reduction in social benefits—but even with those reductions, the level of social protection will be far stronger than, say, that of the United States.
54. These "transaction costs," of course, provide much of the motivation: they represent an important source of income to financial markets.
55. See, e.g., Orszag and Stiglitz (2001). In the aftermath of the financial crisis, there is widespread agreement that the effects on the elderly would have been even worse had social security been privatized.
56. For comparisons of tax revenue as a percentage of GDP, see World Bank data at <http://data.worldbank.org/indicator/GC.TAX.TOTL.GD.ZS>, accessed December 13, 2012. Of course, the money has to be spent well. The Scandinavian countries showed that this could be done.
57. There are important administrative issues concerning point of collection, which I will not address here.
58. For a discussion of the implications of imperfect information for monetary and banking regulatory policy, see Stiglitz and Greenwald (2003), Hellmann, Murdock, and Stiglitz (1996, 2000), Stiglitz (2001), and Honohan and Stiglitz (2001). For discussions focusing on these issues in the context of developing countries, see Uy and Stiglitz (1996) and Stiglitz (1994, 2004, 2006). For a more up-to-date discussion of regulation (including financial market regulation) in the context of market failure, see Stiglitz (2009).
59. Han Linghui and Denise Hare have argued that the reduction in branches in rural China has had a significant negative impact on credit availability to rural households, and that this in turn has had adverse effects on rural entrepreneurship and self-employment. See Linghui and Hare (2010). For evidence in the context of other countries, see Kochar (1997), Burgess and Pande (2005), and Dupas and Robinson (2009).
60. See, for example, Rashid (2011).
61. Stiglitz and Greenwald (2003).
62. Prasad, Rogoff, Wei, and Kose (2003). These results were confirmed by its later 2006 study.
63. And individuals with finite lives. See, e.g., Stiglitz (2004). For a discussion of why financial market liberalization may not be desirable, see, e.g., Stiglitz and Greenwald (2003). For broader policy discussions of capital market liberalization, see Stiglitz (2000, 2002a), and for theoretical analyses why excessive integration may exacerbate problems of contagion, see Stiglitz (2010a, 2010b).

64. There is an interesting debate within the economics profession: can one create specialized nondepository institutions that could provide loans to SMEs?
65. For instance, subsidizing loss-making state-owned enterprises.
66. This list is by no means exhaustive. Later chapters in this book deal, for instance, with the problem of corporate governance.
67. It is, however, far from the most important reason, because the real reason that national savings are so high has to do with high corporate and public savings, not high household savings. For example, China's household savings in 2005 were 16 percent of GDP (and even at their peak, in 1996, they were only 20 percent of GDP), whereas India's were 22 percent. In 2009 China's household savings were 76 percent of GDP, and were 69 percent and 65 percent in 2008 and 2007 respectively (National Bureau of Statistics of China). What makes China's saving rate so high is corporate saving, which is more than 20 percent of GDP. Still, China's household savings rate—at 38 percent—is among the highest in the world.
68. Better private insurance would also reduce the need for precautionary savings; but especially in the area of health, there cannot be reliance on private insurance, which will devote excessive efforts to "cream-skimming," resulting in high transactions costs and large distortions.
69. Much of my theoretical work has been devoted to understanding the problems that imperfect information poses for the functioning of a modern economy. I have stressed the importance of good accounting systems, as well as the dangers posed by certain conflicts of interest (as well as the perverse incentives to which stock option systems may give rise). See, for instance, my Nobel Lecture (Stiglitz 2002b). An abbreviated version is available in *American Economic Review*, 92/3: 460–501. My book *Roaring Nineties* (2003) provided a popular account of how these information imperfections had led to the bubble of the 1990s, and its subsequent crashing, at such cost to the American economy.
70. See, for instance, Stiglitz (2003b).
71. The press also, of course, must be responsible; designing appropriate libel laws is important. Unfortunately, such laws have often been abused, and in some countries have vitiated the benefits that would come from an active and vibrant press.
72. Work in subsequent decades attempted to show that there were other conditions in which markets might be efficient. These attempts have, by and large failed: the conditions under which markets are in general efficient are now known to be highly restrictive.
73. To be sure, countries have survived short periods in which that balance has been lost; but as that balance gets lost, and the consequences become evident, corrections are set in motion.
74. China's Gross Domestic Product in 2011 based on purchasing power parity (PPP) per capita GDP was 8382 vs US 48366. Source: International Monetary Fund, World Economic Outlook Database, April 2012.

REFERENCES

Arrow, K. J. (1951), "An Extension of the Basic Theorems of Classical Welfare Economics," in J. Neyman (ed.), *Proceedings of the Second Berkeley Symposium on Mathematical Statistics and Probability* (Berkeley: University of California Press).

Burgess, R. and Pande, R. (2005), "Do Rural Banks Matter? Evidence from the Indian Social Banking Experiment," *American Economic Review*, 95/3: 780–95.

China Development Research Foundation (2007), *China: Accelerating Structural Adjustment and Growth Pattern Change* (Beijing: Development Research Center of the State Council).

Crafts, N. (2004), "Productivity Growth in the Industrial Revolution: A New Growth Accounting Perspective," *Journal of Economic History*, 64/2 (June): 521–35.

Debreu, G. (1959), *Theory of Value: An Axiomatic Analysis of Economic Equilibrium* (New York: Wiley).

Dupas, P. and Robinson, J. (2009), *Savings Constraints and Microenterprise Development: Evidence from a Field Experiment in Kenya*, NBER Working Paper 14693 (Cambridge, MA: National Bureau of Economic Research).

The Economist (2008), "On the Poverty Line: Has 'A Dollar a Day' Had Its Day?" (May 22), available at <http://www.economist.com/node/11409401?source = hptextfeature&story_id = 11409401>, accessed June 12, 2011.

Feldstein, M. (2007), "New Directions for China's Growth: The Role of Taxes and Fiscal Policies." Paper presented to the China Development Forum, Beijing, March 18, 2007.

Fitoussi, J.-P., Sen, A., and Stiglitz, J. E. (2010), *Mismeasuring Our Lives: Why GDP Doesn't Add Up* (New York: The New Press).

Greenwald, B. and Stiglitz, J. E. (2006), "Helping Infant Economies Grow: Foundations of Trade Policies for Developing Countries," *American Economic Review: AEA Papers and Proceedings*, 96/2: 141–6.

Hellmann, T., Murdock, K., and Stiglitz, J. E. (1996), "Deposit Mobilisation Through Financial Restraint," in N. Hermes and R. Lensink (eds), *Financial Development and Economic Growth* (London: Routledge), 219–46.

——(2000), "Liberalization, Moral Hazard in Banking and Prudential Regulation: Are Capital Requirements Enough?" *American Economic Review*, 90/1: 147–65.

Himmelstein, D. U., Thorne, D., Warren, E., and Woolhandler, S. (2009), "Medical Bankruptcy in the United States, 2007: Results of a National Study," *American Journal of Medicine*, 22/8: 741–6.

Honohan, P. and Stiglitz, J. E. (2001), "Robust Financial Restraint," in G. Caprio, P. Honohan, and J. E. Stiglitz (eds), *Financial Liberalization: How Far, How Fast?* (Cambridge: Cambridge University Press), 31–62.

International Centre for Prison Studies (2011), "World Prison Brief," available at <http://www.prisonstudies.org/info/worldbrief/>, accessed August 11, 2011.

Kochar, A. (1997), "An Empirical Investigation of Rationing Constraints in Rural Credit Markets in India," *Journal of Development Economics*, 53/2: 339–71.

Kose, A., Prasad, E., Rogoff, K., and Wei, S.-J. (2006), "Financial Globalization: A Reappraisal," IMF Working Paper WP/06/189 (Washington, DC: International Monetary Fund).

Lau, L and Stiglitz, J. E. (2005), "China's Alternative to Revaluation," *Financial Times*, April 25.

Linghui, H. and Hare, D. (2010), "The Link Between Credit Markets and Self-employment Choice among Households in Rural China." Paper presented at a conference in Honor of Larry Lau, Stanford University, November 2010.

Orszag, P. and Stiglitz, J. E. (2001), "Rethinking Pension Reform: Ten Myths about Social Security Systems," in R. Holman and J. Stiglitz (eds), *New Ideas About Old Age Security* (Washington, DC: World Bank), 17–56.

Prasad, E., Rogoff, K., Wei, S., and Kose, A. M. (2003), "Effects of Financial Globalization on Developing Countries: Some Empirical Evidence," IMF Occasional Paper No. 220, September.

Rashid, H. (2011), "Credit to Private Sector, Interest Spread and Volatility in Credit-Flows: Do Bank Ownership and Deposits Matter?" Working paper, UN Department of

Economic and Social Affairs, available at <http://www.un.org/en/development/desa/papers/2011/outline.shtml>, accessed August 11, 2011.

Schwartz, J. and Pollack, A. (2010), "Judge Invalidates Human Gene Patent," *The New York Times*, March 29, available at <http://www.nytimes.com/2010/03/30/business/30gene.html>, accessed January 18, 2011.

Seligman, D. (2005), "The Inequality Imperative," *Forbes.com*, October 10, available at <http://www.forbes.com/free_forbes/2005/1010/064.html>, accessed January 18, 2011.

Sen, A. (2006), "Human Development and Health," lecture at the International Conference on Health and Development, Beijing University, October 2006.

Stiglitz, J. E. (1994), "The Role of the State in Financial Markets," *Proceedings of the World Bank Conference on Development Economics 1993*. Washington, DC: World Bank.

——(2000), "Capital Market Liberalization, Economic Growth, and Instability," *World Development*, 28/6: 1075–86.

——(2001), "Principles of Financial Regulation: A Dynamic Approach," *The World Bank Observer*, 16/1 (Spring): 1–18.

——(2002a), "Capital Market Liberalization and Exchange Rate Regimes: Risk without Reward," *The Annals of the American Academy of Political and Social Science*, 579: 219–48.

——(2002b), "Information and the Change in the Paradigm in Economics," in Tore Frangsmyr (ed.), *Les Prix Nobel; The Nobel Prizes 2001* (Stockholm: The Nobel Foundation), 472–540.

——(2003a), *Roaring Nineties* (New York: W. W. Norton).

——(2003b), "On Liberty, the Right to Know, and Public Discourse: The Role of Transparency in Public Life," in M. J. Gibney (ed.), *Globalizing Rights: The Oxford Amnesty Lectures 1999* (London: Oxford University Press), 115–56.

——(2004), "Banking Disintermediation and its Implication to Monetary Policy (Keynote Address)," in Charles Joseph (ed.), *Banking Disintermediation and its Implication to Monetary Policy: Theoretical Views and Countries' Experiences*, proceedings of an international seminar sponsored by the Bank Indonesia and Asian Development Bank, Denpasar, Bali, December 2004 (Jakarta: Bank Indonesia and Asian Development Bank), 1–11.

——(2006a), "Development and Finance: Insights from the New Paradigm of Monetary Economics," in Eastern Caribbean Central Bank (ed.), *Economic Theory and Development Options: The Legacy of W. Arthur Lewis* (Kingston: Ian Randle Publishers), 191–209. (The Tenth Sir Arthur Lewis Memorial Lecture, Basseterre, St Kitts and Nevis, November 1, 2005.)

——(2006b), *Making Globalization Work* (New York: W. W. Norton).

——(2008), "Is There a Post Washington Consensus Consensus?" in N. Serra and J. E. Stiglitz (eds), *The Washington Consensus Reconsidered: Toward a New Global Governance* (New York: Oxford University Press), 41–56.

——(2009), "Regulation and Failure," in D. Moss and J. Cisternino (eds), *New Perspectives on Regulation* (Cambridge, MA: Tobin Project), 11–23.

——(2010a), "Contagion, Liberalization, and the Optimal Structure of Globalization," *Journal of Globalization and Development*, 1/2, Article 2, 45 pp.

——(2010b), *Freefall: America, Free Markets, and the Sinking of the World Economy* (New York: W. W. Norton).

——(2010c), "Principles of Financial Regulation: A Dynamic Approach," *The World Bank Observer*, 16/1: 1–18.

——(2010d), "Risk and Global Economic Architecture: Why Full Financial Integration May be Undesirable," *American Economic Review*, 100/2: 388–92.

Stiglitz, J. E. and Greenwald, B. (2003), *Toward a New Paradigm in Monetary* Economics (Cambridge: Cambridge University Press). Also published in Chinese complex by Sci-tech Publishing, in Chinese simplified by CITIC Publishing.

United Nations Development Program (2010), "Human Development Statistical Tables," in *The Real Wealth of Nations: Pathways to Human Development (Human Development Report 2010)*, available at <http://hdr.undp.org/en/media/HDR_2010_EN_Tables_reprint.pdf>, accessed January 18, 2011.

US Census Bureau (2010), "Race of Head of Household by Median and Mean Income," Census Table H-9, available at <http://www.census.gov/hhes/www/income/data/historical/household/index.html>, accessed January 18, 2011.

US Centers for Disease Control and Prevention (2012), "Health Insurance Coverage," available at <http://www.cdc.gov/nchs/fastats/hinsure.htm>, accessed December 12, 2012.

Uy, Marilou and Stiglitz, Joseph E. (1996), "Financial Markets, Public Policy, and the East Asian Miracle," *World Bank Research Observer*, 11/2: 249–76.

Wei, S. and Zhang, X. (2009), "The Competitive Saving Motive: Evidence from Rising Sex Ratios and Savings Rates in China," NBER Working Papers 15093, Cambridge, MA.

World Bank (1980–2009), *World Development Indicators*, Washington, DC, available at <http://data.worldbank.org/indicator>, accessed July 17, 2012.

World Bank (2005), *World Development Report 2006: Equity and Development* (New York: World Bank and Oxford University Press).

Yang, H. (2010), "Hitting Green Targets," *China Daily*, December 1, available at <http://www.chinadaily.com.cn/bizchina/2010-12/01/content_11637936.htm>, accessed January 18, 2010.

3

Analyzing Legal Formality and Informality: Lessons from Land Titling and Microfinance Programs[1]

Antara Haldar and Joseph E. Stiglitz

INTRODUCTION

Despite the fact that China has experienced incredible growth, there is a great deal of pressure on it to adopt a more formal legal framework—particularly with respect to economic matters. Chicago School law and economics—emphasizing the importance of formal law for development, particularly the protection of private property and the enforcement of contracts—has been influential in this discourse.[2] This book has argued, however, that Chicago-style law and economics makes assumptions about the economy, as well as what the law is and how it functions, that are highly problematic. Kennedy and Stiglitz in their introduction to this volume, as well as Chapters 1, 4, and 5, highlight some of these limitations and analyze their implications.

Here, we focus on one particular aspect of this legal tradition: the Chicago School underestimates the difficulty of fully articulating a set of legal rules, as well as the role that social norms play in the legal process. As we will show, property rights are fundamentally affected by norms of use, and contracts are never complete.

The primacy traditionally accorded to formal law is called into question by a twin set of factors in recent development experience. The first is the failure of formal law in large swathes of the developing world to effectively reach the majority of its people. Indeed, according to a recent report by the Commission for the Legal Empowerment of the Poor, four billion people are "excluded from the rule of law."[3] India, a proverbial "bottomless pit" of rights—with an elaborate written constitution, a wide array of legislative protections, and a sophisticated court apparatus, but a failure to provide effective access to rights—is a case in point.[4] The second is the unexpected success of unconventional institutional structures. The paradigmatic example of this is China itself—the greatest development success of recent times, achieving its unprecedented growth rates in the absence of clearly assigned private property rights in the Western sense.[5]

The failure of formal law to reach so many in developing countries does not, of course, mean that if we could better reach them, performance (especially as measured by the well-being of the poor) might not be better. Nor does the fact that China has succeeded so well in the past mean that more formal structures will not be necessary in the future. Every country has some institutional design for allocating resources, adjudicating disputes, etc.—designs that are always evolving. China's will too, and almost surely rapidly as it moves into the next stages of its transition to a market economy. As it does, it will be important for it not to fall prey to certain shibboleths, simplistic notions about what legal structures should or must look like for a modern economy.

This chapter looks at recent attempts to extend credit to poor people around the world. Since most legal systems contain elements of both the formal and the informal, the distinction between formal and informal law is largely a false dichotomy. However, in transitioning to developed markets, countries *do* encounter important choices with regard to their strategy for institutional reform.[6] Indeed, although the Chicago School would argue that rapid legal formalization is imperative, there are two very different institutional experiments underway for making this transition—one emphasizing legal formalization, in keeping with the orthodoxy, and the other taking a different, more norm-based approach. The first approach is exemplified by the Hernando de Soto-inspired land titling program in Peru, and the second is illustrated by the trust-based microfinance program of Muhammad Yunus's Grameen Bank.[7] (We refer to Yunus and the Grameen Bank, but we should emphasize that there are other, roughly contemporaneous, microfinance schemes, most notably Bangladesh Rural Advancement Committee (BRAC), headed by Fazle Hasan Abed, which have met with equal success.) We use the Peruvian and Bangladeshi programs as models of alternative trajectories of institutional evolution. Our purpose is to contrast these two experiments to bring the lessons that we learn from them to bear on the critical institutional choices facing China and to underscore the existence of alternatives to the monochromatic focus of the Chicago School on formal law to the exclusion of all else.

The basis for comparing the Peruvian and Bangladeshi programs may not appear immediately obvious, but a closer examination reveals marked similarities between them. Indeed, Yunus and de Soto concur almost entirely in substantive terms: both emphasize the skills of entrepreneurship often displayed within poor communities, the importance of poor people lifting themselves out of poverty rather than becoming dependent on charity, the culpability of institutional mechanisms in maintaining poverty, and, most critically, the importance of *access to credit* for poor people as a means of alleviating poverty.[8] The crucial difference between them, however, lies in their institutional innovations—their choice of mechanism for credit delivery. De Soto prescribes the assignment of formal legal title of land to the names of those who already informally occupy it,[9] to enable them to use the land as collateral to access credit through the formal banking system. Yunus, on the other hand, provides credit to the poor without collateral, mediated only by trust-based peer-monitoring networks whereby borrowers are organized into groups in which the ability of group members to borrow depends on other members repaying. After members are established, however, loans are increasingly issued on an individual basis, relying largely on the borrower's desire to maintain a good reputation with the lender.[10] Although neither is explicitly a legal reform program, if these two schemes are seen in the light of their common goal—to enable poor people to access credit as a means of alleviating poverty—they allow us to conduct a systematic comparison of the regulatory mechanisms that underlie them: one based on formal legal intervention and the other on informal regulation.

This comparison proves extremely important for a number of reasons. First, the fact that the two schemes pick such dramatically different mechanisms, one substantially *informal* and the other substantially *formal*, for achieving the same goal—access to credit—allows us to compare the performance of the two mechanisms against a common benchmark. We realize, of course, that the distinction between formal and informal is far from absolute. While the relationship between the bank and borrower is informal within the Yunus model, the relationship between the bank and state is mediated by formal law—the Grameen Bank Ordinance of 1983.[11] On the other hand, the claim that the de Soto model wants to formalize (i.e., the rights of squatters through *de facto* occupation) is essentially an informal one. In addition, de Soto calls for incorporating elements of the "extra-legal" into the formal legal code, i.e., he advocates introducing elements of prudential informal business and other practices into the formal legal code through close observation of on-the-ground, informal norms, thereby creating a bridge between the formal law and the informal practice.[12] Nonetheless, the thrust of the two programs is different enough to provide core examples of the opposing directions in which legal reform programs can go: a rapid move from informality to legal formality or a gradual building of a code of informal norms that may subsequently be formalized. The real-world implementation of the models—primarily in the form of the Grameen Bank[13] in Bangladesh and the 1996 titling program in Peru[14]—provides empirical evidence on the performance of the schemes. Both programs have had tremendous international influence. De Soto's Lima-based think tank, the Institute for Liberty and Democracy (ILD), has not only advised the Peruvian government's titling program,[15] it is also advising governments around the world on how to replicate it.[16] In addition, international organizations like the World Bank[17] and the United Nations (especially through the work of the Commission for the Legal Empowerment of the Poor)[18] have taken on board de Soto's recommendations. The Grameen Bank, on the other hand, has directly supported the establishment of replicas in thirty-four countries (to say nothing of the hundreds of microfinance organizations that it has inspired all over the world), and has had at least equal influence on international development agencies.[19] The United Nations, in particular, has focused much attention on microfinance, particularly in the context of achieving the Millennium Development Goals, declaring 2005 as the Year of Microcredit.[20] At the same time, the World Bank is the largest investor in microfinance worldwide.[21]

Not surprisingly, given the prominence that the two schemes have attained—and the claims that their advocates have made about their potential to alleviate poverty—this comparison is of enormous academic and policy significance in facilitating the formulation of successful legal reform strategies. Indeed, it is somewhat surprising that despite the amount of academic and policy attention that these programs have attracted and their obvious commonalities, they have been operating in parallel without any systematic attempt being made to explore the equally obvious tensions between them. If we agree that access to credit is an important policy goal, what is the superior way of achieving this—through formal law or informal norms? More broadly, does this comparison tell us anything about the better way of achieving developmental goals and, more generally, other societal objectives?

Although this chapter is essentially theoretical, we use illustrative evidence from the Grameen Bank and the Peruvian titling program based on multiple sources—insights gathered over twenty years spent observing the programs and extensive interviews in the field, as well as the now vast empirical literature.[22] Additional evidence is presented from program replicas in various parts of the world in order to establish a broader generality to the results.[23] We emphasize, however, that context is of the essence: the choice of the regulatory intervention likely to work in a given context is bound to depend on a country's circumstances, such as the type of social capital more readily available and the development of certain market institutions.[24] It is impossible to conclude that one intervention is superior to the other per se, but rather, that a particular intervention works better given a particular set of circumstances. It may be that a program that is appropriate at one stage of development may cease to be so at another. We return to this point later.

We will focus on four central questions. First, how does the de Soto scheme perform? In particular, as the most recent vintage of high-profile formal law reform projects, does it overcome the chronic problems faced by its predecessors—legal transplants that fail to "take root" in the developing world? Second, how does the more informal, community-based Grameen model perform, especially in relative terms? Third, how do these two models relate to the Chinese experience? Fourth, how can the relationship between law and norms be characterized, and what insights do these two experiments have for our understanding of this relationship? To what extent should we view formal law and informal norms as substitutes or complements?

The central task of the chapter will be to draw insights from the comparison of formal and informal means to achieve a common developmental goal—in this case, access to credit—for systems of regulation in general. The chapter is divided into four parts. The first frames the discussion, while the following section compares the two alternative models of institutional evolution—the Yunus and de Soto programs—in terms of their *efficiency* and *equity* impacts and analyzes them in static and dynamic terms. The third section examines how the two models relate to the Chinese experience and the fourth section concludes.

TWO MODELS OF INSTITUTIONAL EVOLUTION

We view the provision of credit as a contract—implicit or explicit—between the lender and a borrower. The lender provides money today; the borrower promises to repay the money at a fixed date in the future, with interest. When the borrower doesn't comply, there are certain consequences. The adverse consequences provide (part of) the motivation for the borrower to repay the loan. The enforcement provisions are central; if there were no way of enforcing a contract (no incentive for the borrower to repay) credit markets could not exist—the lender, knowing that he would not be repaid, would never part with his money. Contracts (implicit or explicit) are never simple. Extreme punishments (such as the death penalty) provide strong incentives for repayment; if individuals could always comply, that would be the end of the story. But events happen that make it essentially impossible for the borrower to fulfill his commitments. If the borrower knew that there would be extreme penalties, regardless of his ability to repay, that too could destroy the loan market. Thus, a well-designed credit contract has some flexibility. In practice, banks will roll over loans, and in some cases, even engage in debt forgiveness. Extreme measures (like debtor prisons) may provide strong incentives, but more flexible contracts may actually be more successful in getting repayment in adverse situations, and the knowledge of such flexibility may facilitate more borrowing.

In a formal contract, the consequences of nonrepayment are set forth; but the enforcement even of formal contracts is governed by norms, e.g., concerning rollovers.

The elements of the property rights approach to extending credit (which, for brevity, we will call the de Soto model) are simple: Property (land) registration enables individuals to put up collateral to obtain credit, thereby overcoming the fundamental problem of contract enforcement—if a borrower does not repay the loan, he loses his collateral. De Soto postulates that the reason that commercial banks have been reluctant to enter into loan contracts with poor people is the lender's fear of nonrepayment; the ability of poor individuals to provide collateral in the form of land ameliorates this problem. Responsibility for enforcing the contract is vested in a third party—the state legal system; the state turns over the collateral to the lender in the event of default.[25]

"Good" contracts have to be well-designed and effectively enforced. Well-designed contracts share risks, provide incentives for repayment, and have sufficient clarity to facilitate enforcement. Central to the success of a credit market is its ability to "solve" the critical problems of selection (who is creditworthy), monitoring (ensuring that the funds are used in the way intended), and enforcement (ensuring loan recovery). The lower the *information costs* of overcoming each of these problems in the two models, the more efficient it is (Hoff and Stiglitz 1990). Design and enforcement are related: lenders are unlikely to enter into a contract unless they consider the promise of enforcement credible.[26]

The two models (Grameen and de Soto) differ in how and how well they solve these problems. From a legal perspective, what is critical are the differences in their modes of enforcement. Some credit contracts that might be enforced under some circumstances in one "model" may not be in the other and vice versa. Differences in enforcement effectiveness affect not only the overall level of lending activity, but also who has access to credit.

Dasgupta (2003) has identified four systems of contract enforcement. The first, "mutual affection," is based on group members caring about each other. The second is "pro-social disposition," based on norms of reciprocity, such as might arise out of evolutionary development and socialization. The third is "mutual enforcement" based on fear of social sanction in the context of long-term, settled relationships in a community where people encounter each other repeatedly in the same situation. These three enforcement mechanisms are central to "informal" legal systems.

The fourth, "external enforcement," relies on an established third-party authority—that is typically, but need not be, the state—to enforce explicit contracts. This is the model represented by formal, Western-style legal systems. The effectiveness of such an enforcement system may rely on a sufficient number of individuals *opting in* to the system of authority (i.e., a social norm to comply with authority, enforced in turn, perhaps, by a system of sanctions for noncompliance); or it may rely on coercive force, e.g., through state power. However, enforcement achieved largely through coercion, even if feasible, is typically highly uneconomical.[27] Thus, interestingly, the line between formal and informal systems is blurred by the fact that the most effective formal system is one that is sustained by the norm of compliance with it.

Although there are obvious gains to be reaped from cooperation, it can often be contrary to individual interest, especially when that interest is shortsighted. That is, cooperation may not be able to be sustained *as an equilibrium*.[28] Further, Hoff and Stiglitz (2008) show that dysfunctional institutions may persist, and a constituency for the rule of law may fail to be established, despite its being in everyone's interests in the long run.[29] Thus, a successful institutional structure will have to set the incentives right to be able to balance the trade-off between short-term costs and long-term gains to achieve compliance and coordination. Key to this calculus appears to be the *beliefs* of agents within the system—beliefs that are themselves affected by the system itself.

Efficiency

We begin by comparing the relative performance of the two models in terms of efficiency. The alternative models will be evaluated in terms of their success in providing credit to low-income individuals who otherwise would not have access to credit. There is, fortunately, an abundance of data on which to base judgments regarding their success.

Although approximately 3.5 million Peruvian households received title under the de Soto scheme,[30] it appears to have largely failed to lead to the postulated increase in access to credit—particularly from the private sector (Field and Torero 2004).[31] Calderon (2004) provides further evidence of the lack of a link between titling and private-sector lending in Peru: he estimates that by 2002 only about 1 percent of titled families had obtained mortgages or mortgage loans (ibid.: 299). Similarly, Galliani and Schargrodsky (2005) find that effects of titling on access to credit are extremely modest in Argentina.[32] In the case of Colombia, Gilbert (2002: 14) finds that "possession of legal title makes little or no difference to the availability of formal finance."

In stark contrast, not only has Grameen entered into informal lending contracts with more than nine million poor borrowers,[33] but the peer-monitoring mechanism has proven to be an extremely effective means of enforcing contracts, with a repayment rate of 98 percent (Grameen Bank; Hossain 1988). Similarly, a study by Sharma and Zeller (1997) finds comparable repayment rates for several other microfinance organizations in the subcontinent.[34] Counter to the theoretical faith vested in formal legal systems, evidence of the relative success of the informal Grameen mechanism in inducing entry into mutually beneficial contracts and ensuring that the contracts are honored appears overwhelming.[35]

The de Soto model

How do we understand the seeming failure of the de Soto model? First, de Soto's assumption that the problem of access to credit is based on the absence of collateral may be flawed. Indeed, in the developed world, most loans are based on future cash flows rather than collateral. Second, even if collateral were a material consideration, the scheme assumes the existence of a complete set of land markets robust enough to support the use of land as collateral, despite much evidence of their absence in most parts of the developing world (Platteau 2000; Gilbert 2002). A partial explanation may be that owners consider their land as family assets rather than as capital (Finmark Trust 2004; Tomlinson 2005).[36] In some places, there may be another reason for the failure of land markets to develop: in several communities in the developing world, land has an ontological meaning as something almost sacred, rather than a saleable asset. Furthermore, good risk markets are absent in many developing countries. Land ownership provides what limited security the poor can obtain. Third, because of high legal costs (of enforcing the debt contract and obtaining the collateral), the value of the collateral to the bank is low—much lower than the value of the land itself. Hence, the attractiveness of the collateral to the bank is limited (Arrunada 2003). Finally, Gilbert (2002) argues that titled families may themselves be reluctant to take loans—being intimidated by bank requirements or fearing the consequences of default—and, consequently, preferring informal sources of credit instead.

Nor does titling ensure that enforcement is credible.[37] There are two problems: the information requirements for effective enforcement and legal capacity. The external enforcement model—or formal law—requires that breaches be both *observable* and *publicly verifiable*. Thus, the information costs associated with it are high, particularly in the context of the information asymmetries of the developing world—making its prospects of success exceedingly weak (Stiglitz 1990; Hoff and Stiglitz 1990). At one level this appears trivial: breaches can be observed easily enough—it simply means that the borrower has not repaid. But within the formal system, observing the breach does not, by itself, justify punitive action. The system entails the further requirement of public verifiability established through the "due process" of the formal legal system—typically a complex and long procedure even when the breach itself is plainly obvious. Further, the formal system views breaches in a binary manner—displaying little sensitivity (especially compared with informal systems) to qualitative factors like the legitimacy (or lack thereof) of the reasons for the breach.

We noted earlier that the efficacy of a formal legal system is ultimately determined by enough agents opting in to it. This is, in turn, determined by the dual factors of confidence in the enforcement agency (in its effectiveness by lenders and in its fairness by borrowers) and trust in the propensity of other agents to comply.[38] Consequently, in the absence of the use of pure coercive force, the determinants of the success of a formal legal system are essentially *internal* acceptance rather than external imposition.[39] The introduction of an isolated legal intervention, as the de Soto scheme attempts, is of limited value in the absence of a "broader respect that exists for legal authority" (Andre and Platteau 1998: 43). Given that the courts are likely to consider the transfer of poor people's property to the banks highly inequitable, they are often reluctant to use compulsion (i.e., seizing collateral) to enforce the formal law. Of course, if that is the case, the *formal* system becomes, in effect, an informal one, relying on norms.

The ability to enforce contracts will depend on the legitimacy of the contract and the authority that is responsible for enforcement. Andre and Platteau (1998: 43–4) note that new legal bodies are likely to face constant contestation, criticism, and harassment not only from the disputant but also from other stakeholders in the customary system, at least in the context of unpopular decisions. Thus, the legitimacy of the reform ends up being crucial to its prospects of success. It is easy for land titling to lose legitimacy; the problem is inherent. If the owner of the title was clear to everyone, titling wouldn't be a big deal. In the process of titling, large numbers of land disputes may have to be resolved. Inequitable resolutions are likely to be highly salient, when citizens have questions about the government implementing the program. Titling programs seeming to come from elites may be viewed as advancing elite interests.

Finally, formal credit contracts, by their very nature, are likely to be more rigid. Increased formality and rigidity of contracts may contribute to the clarity of the contract, but also to its inflexibility. The result of this inflexibility is a higher chance of default, which in turn can lead to higher concentration of land, greater inequality, and more agency problems. In the long run, overall efficiency may be impaired as a result of an increase in agency costs (Braverman and Stiglitz 1989). Moreover, the de Soto approach glosses over the complexities in property rights that are emphasized in Chapters 1 and 4. In particular, the scheme may actually heighten rather than reduce uncertainty as a result of the legal dualism that may be created. In the event that, due to the reasons elaborated at length earlier, the formal legal system fails to decisively trump the customary or informal system, the central goal of the titling process—increasing certainty in transactions—is defeated. Indeed, the abrupt introduction of another tier to the property matrix can greatly increase confusion in transactions (Mackenzie 1993; Platteau 2000; Andre and Platteau 1998).

The Yunus model

There are several factors that have contributed to the relative success of the Yunus model in extending credit. The absence of collateral requirements removes an important constraint. The fact that the terms of the contract are more malleable encourages more people to borrow where they would normally have been deterred by the more strictly constraining terms of a formal contract. On the supply side as well, the trust-based system turns out to be greatly advantageous. In particular, the *flexibility* of the informal system allows shocks to be internalized in a manner that would break the back of a more rigidly formal system. The terms of formal contracts are largely fixed, and changing them is an expensive process involving high information and procedural costs.[40] The terms of an informal contract, on the other hand, are more easily and economically renegotiated.[41] That informal systems have the latitude to absorb these shocks to quite a significant extent is demonstrated by the recovery of Grameen in the wake of its 1998 flood-induced repayment crisis where the redrawing of repayment schedules allowed losses to be recovered in large part.[42] As an ongoing feature, Grameen retains the flexi-loans that allow individual borrowers to renegotiate their repayment schedules if they find it difficult to meet their original targets. (In this sense, informal contracts can actually manage risk better than formal contracts, even though enhanced "certainty" is allegedly one of the benefits of the formal system.)

In terms of enforcement, the Yunus model has significant advantages with regard to the information costs of monitoring. Since the mutual enforcement model or informal law requires that breaches be *observable* but *not necessarily publicly verifiable*, the information costs associated with it are inherently lower. Further, peer monitoring (part of at least the early Yunus model) has significant informational advantages since the community is far better poised than formal institutions to monitor the actions of borrowers (Stiglitz 1990). Peer monitoring is able to overcome both problems of moral hazard (Arnott and Stiglitz 1991) and adverse selection (Ghatak 1999).[43] These informational advantages are critical for the flexibility of design discussed above. Since speculative (sometimes called strategic) defaults (i.e., an attempt at evading repayment by those who could make them) can more easily be distinguished from genuine ones (i.e., some unforeseeable circumstance, such as a natural disaster or sickness in the family), not only do these contracts have a built-in insurance mechanism against risk, but they also allow the lender to give loans to those considered riskier borrowers, making the system inherently more inclusive (Wydick 1999).[44]

The peer structure also contributes to the credibility of enforcement. The threats of social sanction and loss of reputation—amplifying the threat of not refinancing borrowers who default—are far more credible than that of punishment by the state legal system in the context of a country like Bangladesh (Stiglitz 1990; Besley and Coate 1995; Besley 1995). Further, the Grameen's essentially participatory character allows the problem of borrower apathy to be overcome and enforcement to be achieved through *internal legitimacy* rather than external force.[45]

An increasingly important feature contributing to the desire for borrowers to maintain a positive reputation is the progressive interlinking of markets or the expansion of Grameen into other markets that affect borrowers, thereby increasing the stakes in the relationship between bank and borrower (Hoff and Stiglitz 1990; Braverman and Stiglitz 1982).[46] Grameen has now diversified into areas as varied as electricity generation, information technology, education, telecommunications, and textiles. These enterprises are designed to permeate the lives of borrowers in a variety of different ways. Thus, a person may not only be a Grameen borrower, but Grameen may at the same time act as her employer, bank, source of infrastructural facilities, provider of goods and services, and run her daughter's school.[47] Other factors that add to the incentives of borrowers to maintain a good reputation include the attractiveness of the support services provided by the Grameen "bicycle bankers" (Edgcomb and Barton 1998).

Equity

Not surprisingly, the Grameen model performs better not just in terms of efficiency, but also in terms of equity, as assessed by variables such as income, investment, employment, and property ownership of essentially instrumental normative interest, as well as welfare indices of inherent value such as gender equity, access to education, access to health care, nutritional status, and so on. This section also looks at some of the broader economic impacts, beyond increased availability of credit, that may have consequences for efficiency as well as equity.

The de Soto model

Looking first at the economic variables that the de Soto program targets, the evidence is mixed. On a positive note, the program succeeded in accomplishing its objective of increasing land titling—several million legal titles having been distributed in Peru alone. (That means that if credit did not expand, it was *not* because of the lack of titling.) In addition, there were significant improvements in the cost and time involved in the titling process.[48] However, to the extent that this transfer of title involves granting formal rights over property already effectively controlled by poor Peruvians (i.e., it is a land *titling* rather than land *reform* program and is not fundamentally concerned with redistribution), the value of the program derives from gains from the change in *de facto* to *de jure* rights of ownership, i.e., the benefits of legal ownership. The economic benefits of this change in status have already been cast in doubt because of its failure to have the postulated effect on access to credit. However, there is some indication that there may be other economic benefits. First, there is some evidence that titling leads to increased household investment—or investment in the maintenance and improvement of titled property (Galliani and Schargrodsky 2005).[49] Whether overall investment actually increases, given that credit supply does not increase, has been questioned (Carter and Olinto 2003). It may be that the increase in household investment is the product of a reallocation of funds from one category to another, i.e., the increase in fixed investment (in the property) may come at the cost of movable investment (including consumption). The net welfare effects of such a shift are ambiguous.[50] Second, some studies find that titling leads to increased labor force participation rates. It is hypothesized that this is because titled families need to spend less time defending their property, leaving them more time for productive activities (Field 2007; Galliani and Schargrodsky 2005). However, the validity of the finding by Field (2007) on increased labor supply—cited widely by advocates of the program—has been brought into question, especially by Mitchell (2005).[51] Indeed, many other local commentators observe that the foundations for security of occupation may be diverse, and that titling may only have made an appreciable difference in newer, more insecure communities.[52] This accords with studies in the academic literature that establish that titling is most useful in situations where informal rights are weak or in the case of vulnerable households (e.g., Lanjouw and Levy 2002).[53] Nonetheless, even if the economic impacts of titling are indeterminate, it may have certain positive social effects associated with increased security of ownership and the creation of relatively settled communities.

However, there is a downside to titling, with potentially important social and economic consequences: while the program grants more secure rights of ownership to the poor, it simultaneously makes rights of ownership more easily alienable. The social impacts of the potential loss of land by poor occupiers may be extremely adverse. De Soto's model is effectively a strategy of inducing the poor to risk their main asset or resource—land. As their only means of insurance, the impact of the loss of even a fraction of a household's land would likely be disproportionately severe, and the loss of all of their land would result in the social and economic problem of landlessness.[54] The strategy is rendered even more risky because it is proposed in the absence of any accompanying welfare schemes, such as health care or food subsidies or any training or assistance programs that might increase productivity, thereby increasing the likelihood of distress sales of land. (The risk is even greater in the presence of inadequately regulated lenders, who can engage in predatory lending practices, taking advantage especially of those who are less financially sophisticated.) An alternative—less risky—approach would be to offer a part of the produce of the land as collateral instead of the land itself.

Any land titling program has to confront the problem of inequities (and sometimes illegitimacy) of the initial holdings. For instance, it may be inequitable to distribute land to squatter families currently occupying it. Endemic to de Soto's scheme is that the completely landless—the most destitute in a community—are left out of its ambit altogether. Further, it is those who were most successful in breaking the law before the de Soto reform (squatting on others' land), that are not only rewarded by it but also expected to become "law-abiding citizens" overnight. (Titling large landholders who may have obtained their ownership rights from a colonial power may be even more problematic.)

While the economic benefits of land titling seem limited, so too are the ancillary welfare benefits. There is some evidence of a tangential impact on school attendance of children of titled families (Galliani and Schargrodsky 2005; Field 2007), but no direct evidence of other indices improving as a result of participation in the program (except, perhaps, through any increases in income that may result from increased labor force participation).[55]

However, some studies have found that titling has a positive effect on some indices of gender equity. In cases of joint titling, in particular, a positive impact has been found on the woman's position in the household (Field 2003; Datta 2006). In addition, titling has been found to be associated with decreased household size. Again, this is attributed to a reduction in the need to maintain large families for reasons of security (Galliani and Schargrodsky 2005) and to increased contraception use and decision-making power on the part of women (Field 2003). On the other hand, at least in some contexts, titling may have adverse gender impacts. Titling is frequently associated with the loss of the customary rights of vulnerable communities. Since, due to the complexity and nuance of customary rights, it is impossible for registration to merely recognize and record accurately existing rights, it invariably involves some *de facto* reallocation of rights (Barrows and Roth 1989: 21). Further, since the sections of the population likely to have the most significant interface with the formal system are the most privileged, this reallocation is likely to be at the cost of the most vulnerable, leading to a legitimacy deficit in the reforms. In this way, customary rights are likely to be destroyed by the registration process. The erosion of customary law weakens, in turn, other aspects of the "informal" economy, e.g., with respect to risk-sharing. For instance, in many societies, women have an informal entitlement to a portion of the harvest of their husband's land, but these claims are often destroyed by the titling process—with broad implications for the welfare of not just the woman, but also the family as a whole.

Similarly, it is customary in many societies for a woman separated from her husband to be entitled to a portion of her father's land in order to avoid destitution—but again, titling often displaces these rights. The introduction of individualized formal property rights fundamentally disrupts the system of communitarian norms that bind groups (especially families), enabling them to act as an insurance and welfare net—especially in contexts where the state, and formal systems more generally, conspicuously fail to do so. Platteau (2000) and Andre and Platteau (1998) find compelling evidence of these kinds of effects in the context of Rwanda. Cousins et al. (2005) reiterate this in the context of South Africa. Specifically, several studies find that titling has an adverse impact on women's rights where it formalizes already existing inequities of power (Lastarria-Cornhiel 1997) or undermines systems of customary justice (Kevane and Gray 1999; Hare, Yang, and Englander 2007). Further, although some empirical studies find that the social justice problem can be overcome by explicitly registering land in the name of vulnerable groups of people (such as women), there is evidence that it is particularly difficult for these people to access the formal justice system to vindicate their rights (Lastarria-Cornhiel, Agurto, Brown, and Rosales 2003; Fenrich and Higgins 2001).[56] (Indeed, even targeted programs in general tend to benefit the best-off within the class they target; for instance, the Indian system of reservation for the Scheduled Castes and Scheduled Tribes tends to benefit the socioeconomic class within the caste that least needs reform, frequently called the "creamy layer." Thus, despite titling targeting squatters, it may fail to impact the most needy among them.)

Finally, the titling process may be extremely amenable to appropriation by the powerful. The more unequal a society, the greater the likelihood of such exploitation of those who are vulnerable by officials and others.[57] Widespread evidence of this can be found in Thailand (Thomson et al. 1986; Feeny 1988); India (Wadhwa 1989; Viswanath 1977); Latin America and the Caribbean (Stanfield 1990); Uganda (Doornbos 1975); Nigeria (Zubair 1987); and South Africa (Cousins et al. 2005). The inequities of this process are likely to be exacerbated if registration comes at a fee, as in the Peruvian case, rather than being free.

Neither the absence of broader social impacts nor the reinforcement of existing inequities is surprising. Unlike the microfinance program, the de Soto scheme is not attached to any explicit social agenda. De Soto's starting point is the existing power allocation. He is not concerned with inequity, but rather with leveraging existing power allocations to achieve a more efficient outcome—to achieve a Pareto improvement. His primary focus is on the economic losses he associates with the "dead capital" of untitled land in the developing world. Not have titling programs, with their strategy of achieving social change through efficiency enhancement, diversified organically into different social sectors in the way that the microfinance movement has.

The Yunus model

From the start, the Grameen Bank had a social agenda. Its intention was to bring credit to the very poor.[58] It could more easily have delivered credit to poor communities by enhancing access to the credit among the (still quite poor) local elites. But it chose not to do this, and to go the opposite direction, giving credit to the least powerful—women in very poor families. In doing so,

Yunus wanted not just to increase their livelihood, but to alter power relationships. Given these objectives, it is not surprising that, although Grameen started out as a credit access program, its agenda very quickly evolved to become far more broad—adopting what policymakers in Bangladesh are calling a "microfinance plus" approach. Grameen targets economic variables mainly by attempting to increase income through access to credit, but it also facilitates property ownership (both through funding the acquisition of "business assets" and the provision of housing loans), engages in employment-generating activities, and provides direct avenues and instruments of investment and insurance. It is increasingly proactive in its approach to welfare indices of inherent value. Its focus so far has most explicitly been on education—it provides both education loans and scholarships, as well as funding for schools. In addition, it has begun addressing nutritional concerns by getting involved in the production of high-nutrient, low-cost food and clean, low-cost drinking water.[59] It is currently actively working to extend its reach to the health care sector.[60] Its commitment to female empowerment is explicit, lending almost exclusively to women.[61] (We will discuss later a number of other aspects of its female empowerment agenda.)

The evidence is that not only did Grameen succeed in increasing the flow of credit, but that there were broader economic and social benefits.[62] Several studies show that participation in the Grameen program leads to increased household income. Grameen reports that average household income is 50 percent higher for members in Grameen villages than residents of non-Grameen villages.[63] These claims of increased income are backed by objective third-party assessments, although the magnitude of the benefits reported by these studies is typically more conservative (Khandker 1998; Hossain 1988).[64] Second, participation in the Grameen program appears to be associated with a decrease in poverty at the household level. Grameen reports that a significantly smaller proportion of its members live in poverty (20 percent) compared with nonmembers (56 percent).[65] Further, Yunus reports that 64 percent of Grameen members decisively move out of poverty within five years of joining the program.[66] The reach of the program heightens the significance of this achievement—80 percent of poor families are estimated to have access to microfinance in Bangladesh.[67] But while the objectivity of this data may be subject to question, several independent studies also find evidence of reduced poverty indices in Grameen households (Hossain 1988), as well as an improved socioeconomic status (Wahid 1994).[68] There is, however, some controversy about the macro-level impacts of microfinance on poverty reduction. In a well-regarded study using panel data, Khandker (1998) finds that aggregate poverty in Bangladesh is decreasing by only 1 percent per annum. Moreover, Bateman and Chang (2009) have argued more broadly against using microfinance as a systemic poverty reduction strategy on the basis that it detracts focus from a more fundamental state-driven structural transformation of the economy that would ultimately yield deeper and wider returns. But while the microfinance organizations may have overstated their impact on poverty alleviation and it appears unlikely that it can, by itself, substantially impact poverty—the data suggests that microfinance makes at least a modest contribution to poverty reduction.[69] There is evidence, moreover, that Grameen has had positive effects on some important welfare indicators. For instance, various studies have found positive effects on contraception use by women (Schuler and Hashemi 1994; Amin, Li, and Ahmed 1996; Schuler, Hashemi, and Riley 1997).

There are broader economic benefits, especially to women, that arise from how the Grameen program is structured. Grameen membership requires internalizing a number of different types of prudential practices. Potential members must learn to sign their names and memorize a list of sixteen decisions (such as sending children to school, family planning, basic cleanliness and sanitation, vows of cooperation, etc.) before they are eligible for a loan. In addition, although there is little substantive interference with use of loans (though they are limited to production, as opposed to consumption, and the focus on production itself may have broader benefits), members are provided with ongoing assistance in the form of encouragement and troubleshooting advice in the face of financial troubles. There is evidence of these noncredit, participatory aspects having a positive effect on self-employment profits (McKernan 2002). Indeed, the empowerment dimension of the scheme is one of its key assets.

An important contribution of Grameen has been the creation of an entire second generation of beneficiaries. Reportedly, 100 percent of the children of Grameen families were enrolled in school. Grameen is attempting to actively promote a rapid socioeconomic transition of this second wave of beneficiaries through primary school scholarships, of which there are now 64,000 recipients, and higher education loans, of which 23,000 have been distributed.[70]

It is not surprising that, given its focus on empowering women, the Grameen Bank is considered to have made a significant contribution to gender equity, particularly in the context of Bangladesh. The fact that 97 percent of Grameen borrowers are women is an achievement in its own right, especially in a country where women undertaking activities outside the home is itself stigmatized.[71] In addition, studies have found a positive impact on a number of other empowerment indices. Using surveys, Pitt, Khandker, and Cartwright (2003) find that participation in credit programs leads women to take a bigger role in household decision-making, greater access to financial and economic resources, better social networks, improved bargaining power vis-à-vis their husbands, greater mobility, and better spousal communication.[72] Moreover, Hashemi, Schuler, and Riley (1996) find that even the most "minimalist" credit programs—or those that do not emphasize female empowerment—have an emancipating effect on women.[73] Though the impact of microfinance on female empowerment arises partly from the additional economic resources that it puts at the disposal of women, the structuring of the program strengthens these effects. For instance, to consolidate the woman's position in the household, mortgages given out by the Bank are always made in the name of the woman as a disincentive against her husband divorcing her. Moreover, although there is some evidence of increased domestic violence in the short run (Rahman 1999), other studies find that the Grameen mechanism paves the way to greater assertiveness on the part of women and reduced domestic violence, particularly over time (Schuler, Hashemi, Riley, and Akhtar 1996; Schuler, Hashemi, and Badal 1998). In addition, positive impacts have been found on specific welfare indices such as women's health (Nanda 1999). The emphasis on women may have positive effects for the family as a whole. Pitt and Khandker (1998) find that annual household consumption expenditure increases by 18 taka for every additional taka borrowed by women from these credit programs, compared with 11 taka for men.[74]

Finally, microfinance contributes to releasing the untapped economic potential of the female labor supply in Bangladesh. Emran, Morshed, and Stiglitz (2007) explain that microfinance works essentially because of imperfections in the capital and labor markets. As long as two of these markets function perfectly, mobile factors move to the immobile one, ensuring overall efficiency. In the more realistic context of imperfect capital and labor markets, microfinance harnesses the untapped labor power of unemployed women in the home, thereby evening out capital–labor ratios. In this way, a productive section of the population, women, left out of the labor market due to market imperfections, have their productivity enhanced.

We should emphasize that many of the ancillary benefits of Grameen bank are not the inevitable consequence of microfinance schemes, but depend on the particular way the program has been structured; but some are intrinsic to the trust-based approach that emphasizes group lending and peer monitoring. Still, the fact that other Bangladeshi microfinance schemes, most notably BRAC, have not only replicated Grameen's success, but in some dimensions may have exceeded it, suggests both that the model's success is not just the fortuitous result of having good leadership (Yunus), and that it may be replicable. Indeed, BRAC's programs in female legal and health education and its innovative schooling programs have enhanced social benefits and female empowerment; and its economic programs entailing vertical integration (e.g., not just giving members loans to raise chickens, but also entering into the production of chicken feed and the like) have increased its economic impact. All of this suggests that there is something to the traditional not-for-profit microfinance programs that makes for their successes.

Static analysis

Contrary to the predictions of the Chicago School, the Yunus model outperforms the de Soto model in terms both of its efficiency and equity. In this section, we analyze the reasons for this result—tracing them to the fundamentally different visions of development that motivate the two programs.

One of the essential differences between de Soto's and Yunus's approaches is that the latter takes a more *integrated* view of development. By contrast, de Soto's approach falls into the category of linear models of development (of which the Washington Consensus approach is typical)—assuming that targeting certain critical, albeit isolated, variables will bring about development.[75] Indeed, it is this perspective that informs de Soto's assertion that stimulating capitalism in the developing world is merely a question of implementing the strategic intervention of titling to bring "dead capital alive." The problem with this position is its failure to recognize crucial linkages between economic, legal, and social systems.[76]

Further, his exclusive focus on economic variables of *instrumental* interest, rather than welfare variables of inherent interest, stems from a seeming belief that overall efficiency and the well-being of poor people will follow almost automatically, once life is given to the dead capital. There are further distinctions, discussed below, in conceptions of the dynamics of development.

The notion that land titling (and the rule of law more generally) would be decisive in changing the course of development is predicated on the belief that markets in general work well—or would work well—if only there were a rule of law. But market failures are pervasive even in countries with reasonably good legal systems. Given that markets in the developing world are riddled with imperfections—ranging from externalities to information asymmetries—it is not surprising that simply titling, or replicating the external structure of the rule of law, does not, on its own, bring development.

It was not only the economic assumptions underlying the de Soto scheme that were flawed. As the Introduction to this book and Chapter 4 point out, the assumptions about "law" and "property rights" were overly simplistic and unrealistic. For instance, while the working of the titling mechanism is predicated on a well-functioning legal system, the view of the law he adopts is highly *formalistic*—vesting paramount faith in law as written down in the statute books, as well as the formal structures of the law. On one hand, de Soto advocates incorporating into the formal code elements of successful informal practice, thereby paying homage to the dynamism of the informal economy and the informal norms that make such an economy function. On the other, he makes a definitive formalist leap by assuming the inevitability of the need to formalize these norms and practices—irrespective of how well the informal system may be working. This takes for granted, contrary to much empirical evidence, that the process of writing rules down dramatically improves their efficacy. For example, he asks us to "listen to the barking dogs" or to heed evidence of informal delineation of property rights in the developing world—boundaries, he argues, that are well, if informally, established. But, as we have discussed at length, the formalization process is far from trivial—and frequently introduces distortions in the system in its own right. It assumes, further, that once laws are written down, they can be interpreted and applied completely objectively, eliminating any role for norms. Language inevitably entails ambiguity,[77] disputes arise, and those resolving disputes will rely partially on norms. Moreover, he ignores the transaction costs associated with implementing the formal legal system—and the fact that in almost every society, there are costs in getting full access to its benefits. The poor are at a disadvantage. Though the rule of law may protect against some abuses of power, the formal legal system itself favors those who are better off, and especially so in the context of property disputes. (Public legal assistance redresses the imbalance, but only partially, since the quality of legal assistance is almost always markedly less than that available to the rich.)

Finally, and most critically, de Soto neglects the fact that the best way of arriving at a good legal system is not through *external imposition* but rather through drawing agents into the system through a process of building internal legitimacy through active participation of a broad base of stake holders. Too often, it is foreign experts and the country's own elites that push most strongly for titling programs, and this in itself arouses suspicion and can undermine the legitimacy of the whole process: is the objective of the program really to empower poor citizens or to provide another tool through which the wealthy can accumulate more wealth for themselves?

Yunus, while acknowledging the merits of the market mechanism, also recognizes that markets are far from perfect and riddled with barriers to access. Indeed, his whole approach is premised on a set of market failures (access to credit, access to jobs) and the recognition that political and economic inequalities could be self-perpetuating. Thus, his solution to the access-to-credit problem is far more *substantive*, providing loans directly, not just removing what was viewed as the (only) barrier to access, the absence of collateral.

Further, he is focused directly on welfare variables of *inherent* normative interest as a result of both a lack of faith in the market mechanisms to provide them spontaneously, as well as in deference to their importance for the success of the market process. He realized that among the market failures was lack of effective competition; but the imbalance of market power was matched by an imbalance of political power. It would be elites who design the formal legal system, and it is they who implement it. It is they who adjudicate disputes. Inevitably, a formal legal system works to the disadvantage of the poor. Grameen was designed to improve the well-being of the poorest of the poor, in a context in which they lacked both economic resources and political power.

Rather than relying on formal law and coercion to enforce contracts, Yunus constructed a system in which social and economic incentives sufficed to ensure repayment. The system works because it is able to effectively solicit the participation of agents in the enforcement system by drawing them into it through building up *internal* legitimacy. This final point accounts for Yunus's relative success in soliciting cooperative behavior on the part of program participants—all the more laudable in a context in which the formal legal system has found it notoriously hard to establish a framework for cooperative action.[78]

The Grameen experiment showed that informal, norm-based regulatory interventions—more rooted in social context and inherently more participatory—are much more likely to be seen as legitimate and, hence, to be more efficient than the impersonal structures of conventional law. (They are more efficient in that they enabled more individuals to have access to credit and more efficient in having a lower default rate.)

Indeed, the success of the informal Grameen mechanism is not an isolated phenomenon. Earlier, we referred to other successful microfinance schemes. There are a number of other examples where "informal" law replaces formal legal structures. A host of alternative dispute resolution mechanisms have been successfully implemented in various parts of the developing world, illustrating the flexibility, responsiveness, and accessibility of these systems relative to more formal ones.[79] While they may operate in the broader context of a more formal legal framework, their ability to tap into informal resources, such as shared values, community norms, and networks, and their emphasis on consensus-driven conflict resolution enable them to deliver cheaper and more expedient justice than their formal counterparts. At the same time, an emergent voice within academia is starting to call for more innovative—if less ambitious—regulatory solutions.[80] The "rule of law" regime may be the proverbial institutional "cake"—a luxury in the context of much of the developing world that is unattainable, even if it is desirable. But there is a pressing need to focus instead on what Galanter and Krishnan (2004) call legal "bread for the poor"—functional institutional solutions that are realistic in the context of the developing world.

Dynamics

In the previous section we saw that the Yunus model performs better than the de Soto model, at least in the short run: It has been more successful in extending credit, increasing incomes, and advancing a variety of social goals.

These successes come in spite of arguments in favor of the rule of law over the often more arbitrary "rule of persons."[81] But if the Yunus model is to succeed in reducing poverty at a macro-level, it must "scale up" its operations. This can take the form of widening reach in terms of a proliferation of organizations providing microfinance, as well as increasing the scale and range of the ventures that poor families are able to tap into, thereby allowing them to access wider resources and be lifted out of poverty more effectively.

Both developments are currently under way in Bangladesh. In recent years, there has been an explosion of organizations entering the fray to provide microfinance, and Grameen (along with other major microfinance providers, notably BRAC), has been increasingly diversifying into social businesses—higher-scale business ventures that poor families would be unable to establish in their own right that either provide crucial services to the poor at subsidized rates or that allocate part of their surpluses to poor people.[82] This scaling up of operations has, not surprisingly, been accompanied by an increasing move toward formal regulation. The microfinance sector as a whole (particularly following the entry of new organizations into the sector) is progressively more formally regulated—first by the Palli Karma Sahayak Foundation (PKSF) and now by the Microcredit Regulatory Authority (MRA). At the same time, the social businesses sector into which the microfinance organizations are moving are mostly regulated as any other business enterprise, by formal law.[83] These developments indicate that while a trust-based system seems to work effectively in regulating small lending transactions between the microfinance organization and a network of up to several million individuals, as the size of transactions get bigger and the unit of regulation becomes larger (i.e., organizations rather than individuals), formal law may become more necessary.[84] While the microfinance sector in Bangladesh was dominated by a few key players, entry into the sector did not need formal regulation (they had an incentive to behave well, and so long as they were small, the consequences of misbehavior were limited), but as the number of players increased and incidents of fraud began to occur, there arose a need for regulation.[85]

These empirical insights accord with theory. Dixit (2004) has stressed that the expansion of the market may demand a more generalized form of trust that will allow anonymous actors to transact with each other on a wider scale on the basis of mutual trust in the institutions of the economy rather than a network in which names and faces matter. This is somewhat analogous to the move from the barter to the money economy, facilitating exchange on a wider scale. Thus, for instance, a Grameenphone subscriber purchases a subscription not on the basis of a personal trust in the service provider, but rather as a more impersonal market transaction.[86] Moreover, changes brought about by economic growth and development may themselves undermine the effectiveness of informal regulation, which depends, for instance, on stable communities (repeated interaction). With development, individuals move easily in and out of communities, undermining the effectiveness of the social and economic sanctions that can be applied against a party that has broken "trust" (Stiglitz 2000).[87]

The appropriate choice of institution depends fundamentally on the stage of development and context of the society in question. The trajectory of institutional development in Bangladesh illustrates this: as the process of development progressed, the institutional framework changed to adapt to it. Indeed, what is crucial is not whether the mode of regulation is formal or informal, but rather the influence exerted over the actions of agents.[88] Without a transmission mechanism allowing formal law to acquire traction in a host society by altering actions and norms, legal formalization will have little or no effect—as was the case in Peru. In successful legal systems, formal law and social norms work in tandem. Formal legislation has the capacity to shape norms and influence action;[89] but if they are to do this successfully, they cannot be imposed from above or from the outside.

In the context of the developing world, abruptly introduced and isolated legislative interventions are bound to fail to have the same effect that they might in a developed country that adopted them after lengthy political debate and consensus formation, given that these interventions do not emerge out of an organic process of institutional growth and thereby lack internal legitimacy. This is what we observe in the Peruvian case.

While we have stressed the efficiency and equity benefits of the Grameen mechanism, its key contribution in institutional terms is its capacity to make the shift to a cooperative institutional equilibrium by fostering social capital and trust, i.e., by causing a revolution *within* the agents in the system.[90] In the framework of the Hoff and Stiglitz (2008) model, individual expectations with regard to the prospects for establishing the rule of law determine individual support for it.[91]

The Grameen mechanism can be seen to be producing a public good by creating social capital, changing perceptions about social interactions, and possibly altering expectations about the rule of law.[92] This was especially the case for BRAC, which has had explicit programs enhancing participants' knowledge of, and access to, "the law," especially in domains that are vital to their lives.[93]

Dowla (2006) provides a roster of ways in which the Grameen is engaged in social capital creation—by "forming horizontal and vertical networks, establishing new norms and fostering a new level of social trust to solve the collective action problems of poor people's access to capital." Social capital theory predicts that cooperation will beget further cooperation (Hirschman 1984; Putnam 1993; Seabright 1997), and in the instance of the Grameen, this has been the case—both within and outside of the specific program.[94] A notable example of these spillovers is the election of Grameen members to local government bodies. In the 2003 local government election (the Union Porishad), 7442 Grameen members contested the reserved seats for women and 3059 members were elected—this accounts for 24 percent of the total women's reserved seats.[95]

The social capital building initiatives of the early stages of institutional development of the Grameen paved the way for current developments. The successes of both the newer microfinance organizations that entered the fray after the Grameen Bank and BRAC (like ASA, now the third biggest microfinance provider in Bangladesh) and the social businesses run by the bigger microfinance organizations was enabled by the foundations laid by the first-generation microfinance experiment. The familiarity established vis-à-vis the "technology" of microfinance and the improved norms inculcated by the older microfinance institutions greatly reduced the investment of time and effort required of the newer institutions in establishing themselves. At the same time, the positive reputation of the bigger microfinance institutions has been critical both in attracting the investment and creating the client base that has fuelled the social business sector in Bangladesh.

However, a process of informal consensus and social capital building often works to effectively pave the way to more formal legal systems, which will play a more important role in later stages of development. The issue, then, ends up being not one of choosing between the formal and informal system, as the Chicago School posits it, but rather one of determining which type of intervention is more appropriate to emphasize at a particular stage of development.

We end this section on a note of caution: evolutionary processes do not always work in the ways that we would hope. It is not always easy to distinguish the crucial aspects of an institutional arrangement. Consider microfinance. We have argued that its success was dependent not just (or even so much) on the provision of credit to the poor, but there were those who thought otherwise. They thought that microfinance had proven so successful that it could be converted into a profit-making institution, which would provide incentives to extend its reach, providing more finance to more poor people. But the change from a not-for-profit model to a for-profit model fundamentally changes incentives. Many microfinance schemes outside of Bangladesh have been for profit. In that context, the same incentives for predatory lending that marked the US subprime market arise in developing countries. Private firms have recognized that there is money at the bottom of the pyramid, and rather than freeing it up for the benefit of the poor, have done what they could to move it to themselves. Such concerns are central to the de Soto approach, which relies on private markets. If legal systems are controlled by those who profit from the poor, they will do little to stop predatory lending. The legal system will then become an instrument for increasing inequality.

IMPLICATIONS FOR CHINA

The previous section describes and analyzes two alternative models of institutional evolution. One advocated the rapid Westernization and formalization of law; the other adopted an approach of institutional gradualism—building slowly on informal networks. In this section, we return to our original focus and consider the relevance of the foregoing discussion for China.

It is clear that formal law has *not* been a major contributing factor in China's remarkable economic growth (Qian 2003; Clarke, Murrell, and Whiting 2008; Upham 2009). At the point at which China embarked on the reform process in the 1970s, few of its legal institutions had survived the Cultural Revolution and it possessed little substantive law for the courts to enforce, particularly in the realm of private property rights (Lubman 1999). Even though the government started promulgating lawlike rules and regulations in the 1980s, there was no comprehensive protection of private property until the Property Law of 2007 (Lubman 1999). Chinese courts are well known for "local protectionism"—or their refusal to rule against the interests of entities within their own localities. Moreover, they are known to be even less inclined to go against the interests of politically strong entities—and the party-state has the formal power to intervene when important interests are at stake (Liebman 2007). Thus, Chinese courts are unlikely to protect private property against the Party, the state, or even private entities with whom they have close ties (Upham 2009).

How, then, can the Chinese experience be understood? What mechanisms—in the absence of legally defined property rights enforceable in courts—allow economic agents to form the reliable expectations that are the cornerstone of economic transactions? Different authors stress different aspects of the Chinese legal and institutional structures to explain this process. Some have argued China's success demonstrates the irrelevance of property rights. Some argue that there really is a system of private ownership "dressed-up" as public ownership. What is clear is that China's experience is at odds with the claims of the Chicago school, which contends that well-defined property rights (in the de Soto sense) are necessary (and almost sufficient) for robust and sustained economic growth.[96]

Guanxi is one important, albeit intangible, factor in Chinese economic processes. *Guanxi*—which can be loosely translated into "connections" or "relations," but means, in essence, "particularistic ties"[97]—is acknowledged to be an essential, pervasive, and resilient lubricating factor in Chinese social relations and economic transactions (Gold, Guthrie, and Wank 2002). There persist debates about whether *guanxi* is a uniquely Chinese concept or essentially the same as the more generic social capital but, as with social capital, *guanxi* is understood to have both positive and negative connotations.

Much of the literature has tended to take a negative view of it, considering it to be synonymous with corruption and an impediment to the establishment of the formal rule of law. A more positive view can see it as playing a crucial role in Chinese economic processes—providing consistency in transactions that would otherwise be missing in the absence of formal rules. Some view *guanxi* as a substitute for formal law (Wang 1989; Zheng 1986). Indeed, it is argued by some scholars that despite attempts at legal formalization in China, Chinese business practices still view Western-style contracts as a "cage" that the appropriate *guanxi* can unlock (Lubman 1998).

Most significantly, the changing character of *guanxi* in the era of reforms is debated. There is speculation with regard to whether its importance will persist or even expand, or whether it will wither and be replaced by the formal rule of law. Potter (2001) takes that the view that with the emergence of formal law in China, the complementarities between the formal rules of the legal system and the informal rules and norms of *guanxi* relations are starting to be strengthened. *Guanxi* serves to provide predictability and stability in a legal system that is new, in flux, and incomplete.

That China achieved its remarkable growth in the absence of Chicago-style formal legal structures appears uncontroversial. Although debate persists about the precise institutional mechanisms that enabled this growth, it is safe to say that both institutions rooted in China's particular context (such as TVEs, whose "ownership structure" does not fit neatly into the standard law and economics property paradigm) and informal mechanisms such as *guanxi* played an important role. While the pressures of sustaining growth and further integration into the global economy may impose some pressures to follow the conventional path of legal formalization, some caution should be exercised to ensure that this process does not erode the institutional structures that have served China so well for so long and that the formal structures that are adopted are appropriately adapted to China's distinctive circumstances today, as well as to its history.

CONCLUSION

In the context of the policy choices currently confronting China, this chapter critically examines the Chicago School's assertion that formal law is essential for development. This claim was examined by comparing two high-profile credit-access programs—land titling in Peru and microfinance in Bangladesh—representing two alternative models of institutional evolution that China could follow. A close analysis of the two models revealed that contrary to the claims of the Chicago School, informal norms and codes of conduct can support productive economic exchange, and thereby be conducive to development. In fact, the more informal Yunus model proved to be both more efficient and more equitable than the legal formalization program advocated by de Soto. But a system that might work well at one stage of development may not do so at a later stage. We suggest not only that at later stages of development, formal systems may have distinct advantages, but also that earlier stages of social capital building through informal regulation may pave the way to more formalized regulation more effectively than the approach of rapid, and somewhat abrupt, immediate formalization. In reconciling the static and dynamic analysis, the focus of the legal reform process is no longer that of choosing between legal formality and informality as traditionally posited, but, rather, becomes that of determining the pacing and sequencing of reforms, and what mode of regulation works better in a particular context. We have shown the critical role played by the interactive dynamics between the formal and informal systems.

A hallmark of China's development strategy is recognizing this—and constantly adapting its strategy. We have identified arguments suggesting that, over the long run, there may be certain economic benefits associated with formal regulation. But the critique of the de Soto model is of particular relevance to China, as it proceeds in formalizing property rights. We have shown the risks of growing inequality, especially in the context of a society with an inadequate system of social protection; we have seen too the risk of formal legal systems that are disjointed from social norms; we have shown how the rule of law can protect existing inequities, and differential access to legal redress can be used to increase those inequities. By contrast, we have seen how informal institutions can help create "social capital" that promotes equality (a harmonious society) and actually enhances efficiency, with spillovers into other contexts.

Applying the lessons of this analysis to China, we see that as China negotiates its developmental pathway, it should steer clear of the false dichotomies of the Chicago School mode of thinking, noting the failure of attempts to implement the received institutional wisdom of de Soto-style rapid formalization programs, and draw on the experience of relatively successful alternative institutional experiments of the Yunus type. To encapsulate this wisdom in the words of an ancient Chinese proverb: "He who treads softly goes far."

NOTES

1. An earlier version of this paper was presented at the Initiative for Policy Dialogue's China Task Force Meeting in Manchester (June 25–6, 2008). The authors are indebted to David Kennedy, the participants at the meeting, and to anonymous peer reviewers for their valuable comments and suggestions, as well as to interviewees in both Peru and Bangladesh for their help and participation.
2. See, on China, Prosterman and Hanstead (2006). On the institutional prescription of the Chicago School for the developing world, more generally, see Posner (1998). Some scholars, while recognizing that China has done remarkably well without the kinds of legal system (property rights) that they argue are essential, suggest that without legal reforms, China's growth will not be sustainable.
3. Commission for the Legal Empowerment of the Poor (2008: 4–5). We agree with their estimate that the quantum of "legal poverty" is immense, but not with their solution to the problem.
4. See further Haldar (2007) and Pistor, Haldar, and Amirapu (2009). Various attempts have been made to explain the failure of formal legal reform in the developing world; for instance, one strain of literature analyzes the issue in terms of "legal transplants." See Berkowitz, Pistor, and Richard (2003).
5. While it is not obvious that Chinese property rights operate in the same way as Western property rights, attempts have been made to explain its success in terms of setting up Western-style incentive structures at the margins. See, for instance, Qian (2003).
6. Aoki (2001), for instance, entirely sidesteps the formal–informal dichotomy by classifying as an "institution" only things that actually impact the behavior of agents. While this position overcomes many of the shortcomings of a more formalistic approach conceptually, it leaves the question of the functional choice of approach to reform unanswered.
7. We refer not just to the microfinance and titling programs, but also to their architects, Yunus and de Soto, to highlight the fundamental ideological differences that these two eminent figures in development bring to their programs. Indeed, we are interested as much in the theoretical models as the practical implementation of the reform programs.
8. Yunus (1998) and de Soto (2000). We do not evaluate whether increased access does in fact lead to development or whether differences between the two systems regarding *who* gets access to credit shapes economic evolution differently. There is growing consensus that both Yunus and de Soto exaggerated the importance of credit availability, especially for long-term development, though microfinance has had significant achievements in poverty alleviation at the household level.
9. It is not, in that sense, a land or property redistribution reform. An important part of the program in Peru dealt with squatters (on land otherwise "unowned") who were giving formal rights to the land (housing) that they occupied. (One of the problems discussed below is that there are often ambiguities in "ownership," and resolving these may be no easy matter.)
10. This is the main change characterizing the shift from the "classical" Grameen model, or Grameen I, to the "generalized" Grameen model, or Grameen II. This change was put in place between 2000–2 and started as a response to a 1998 repayment crisis resulting from severe floods in Bangladesh. The opportunity was taken, however, to incorporate structural changes to the system in order to make it more flexible. Some of the changes are as follows: (i) The various categories of loans were dispensed with and reduced to the "basic" loan, housing loan, and higher education loan (with a 50 percent reservation for girls); (ii) The rigidity of loan amounts, repayment schedules, and duration were

removed and borrowers could now get customized loans on the basis of their repayment record and the discretion of the banker; (iii) Group lending was replaced with individual lending and groups were retained for the purpose of positive reinforcement only; (iv) The "flexi-loan" was introduced to enable borrowers to deal with repayment problems whereby borrowers facing difficulties were able to merely reschedule repayment; (v) The "Beggar Program" disbursing loans to beggars with no repayment rule attached was started; (vi) The system of positive incentives was reinforced with the "star scheme" for branches and employees that met targets and "gold membership" for borrowers with an untarnished record; (vii) The introduction of a pension and insurance scheme, in addition to obligatory savings. On Grameen II, see further Yunus (2002) and Dowla and Barua (2006).

11. This law was used to remove Yunus from his position as head of Grameen Bank in 2011. See *The New York Times*, March 8, 2011.
12. For instance, ILD bases institutional reform on "proposals . . . that will build on well-established local legal and 'extralegal' practices that all citizens can identify with and respect, streamlining the rules and procedures that govern real estate and business activities, reducing the time and cost to operate in the legal sector." See further, <http://ild.org.pe/>. The modalities of achieving this may, however, be more complex than it initially appears.
13. For a brief history and overview of the functioning of the Bank, see <http://www.grameen-info.org/>.
14. For an overview of the Peruvian titling program, see Calderon (2004).
15. On de Soto's influence in Peru, see Panaritis (2001) and Bromley (1990).
16. Countries currently being advised by ILD include Mexico, Honduras, Haiti, Egypt, Albania, and the Philippines. In addition, ILD reports that there is "demand" for its services in forty-seven countries. See <http://ild.org.pe/en/home>. In addition, a number of countries, such as South Africa, not directly advised by de Soto, are deeply influenced by his advice; see Cousins et al. (2005).
17. See further, Gilbert (2002: 5); Panaritis (2001: 22).
18. De Soto is, for instance, co-chair of the Commission. See further <http://www.undp.org/legalempowerment/>.
19. See Sharma (2005a, 2005b).
20. See <http://www.yearofmicrocredit.org/>.
21. See, for instance, World Bank, 1999.
22. More than twenty years ago, Stiglitz provided the intellectual foundations of the Grameen peer-monitoring system, explaining why it was an effective system of contract enforcement (Stiglitz 1990). In addition, results reported in this paper are based on extensive field research conducted in Peru and Bangladesh between June 2008 and July 2009. More than 100 in-depth qualitative interviews were conducted with stakeholders in the implementation of the programs.
23. To say that the programs have been "replicated" is, however, to gloss over significant differences. While the microfinance model has spread like wildfire, replicas often change institutional aspects of the model. Further, even when the replication is faithful—in form—to the original model, the informal, context-specific aspects cannot be directly transferred. In particular, the focus on social capital building of the initial model has been somewhat lost. Indeed, Seibel (2000), studying microfinance replicas in the Philippines, finds that the most successful replicas are the ones that are most faithful to the social capital building aspects of the original. Some of the replicas of the microfinance scheme shifted from a nonprofit to a for-profit basis, a change that Yunus and others have suggested put at risk the entire program (Yunus 2011). Similarly, in the case of titling, while the formal process can be replicated, other aspects integral to the program, such as the judicial system, cannot just be transplanted.

24. Thus, while Peru might have a better developed market mechanism than Bangladesh, Bangladesh may have stronger community norms. This difference is crucial in determining which regulatory mechanism is more appropriate. See further Besley and Coate (1995).
25. As the problems in America's mortgage markets make clear, matters are somewhat more complicated than this simplistic rendering would suggest. The debt contract has to specify whether the loan is recourse or nonrecourse. A recourse loan means that the collateral serves as a minimum guarantee (one that might have uncertain value, however). The borrower is still liable for repayment, unless he goes bankrupt. Thus, there are background legal structures behind land titling, specifying the terms of enforcement of contracts and bankruptcy. Norms inevitably play some role in enforcement, though the legal structure itself determines the extent to which that is so.
26. Note that lenders might be lured into entering a contract on the basis of a belief in the effectiveness of the enforcement system, but this belief may be false. The recent subprime mortgages crisis is a paradigmatic example of this. On the other hand, lenders might be deterred from entering into a contract because the prospects of enforcement appear unsatisfactory where they might, in fact, be extremely sound. An extremely trustworthy person might not get a loan of $500, even at an excessive interest rate, if others don't believe that the person is trustworthy. It is clear that subjective beliefs are of fundamental importance in determining whether contracts are undertaken.
27. Although an element of coercion is contained in any state legal system, unless mixed sufficiently with a voluntary acceptance of the system, the normative implications of the use of force to keep contracts are highly questionable. This is especially so if the contract is viewed as "unfair," either because of an imbalance of economic power at the time the contract was entered into or because of deception (real or perceived) on the part of one party to the contract. Note that today, sovereign debt contracts have to rely on one of the first three modes of enforcement, though in the nineteenth century, military force was used to enforce them (Stiglitz 2006, 2010). The theory of repeated games shows how cooperation can be sustained in contexts in which it could not be in a one-shot game. See Abreu (1988) and Abreu et al. (1990).
28. See Olson (1965), Ostrom (1990), and North (1991). However, in the context of repeated games (repeated interactions), it may be much easier to achieve cooperative outcomes. See, e.g., Abreu (1988, 1990).
29. How actors behave rests upon their expectations of whether the rule of law will be established. This affects whether contracts will be enforced; and beliefs about enforcement affect where loans will be made. There can exist multiple equilibria.
30. COFOPRI (2008).
31. This study of the Peruvian titling program finds (when titles are asked for in the first place) a small positive impact on public-sector lending and a beneficial impact on interest rates—but no impact on private-sector lending. More specifically, the bulk of this positive impact is accounted for by increased in-kind lending of housing construction materials by the publicly funded Materials Bank (MB). Various hypotheses are put forward for this discrepancy, although the cause remains unclear. While the paper suggests that the MB generally issues large loans and therefore faces relatively lower transaction costs of dealing with titled property, it appears more likely that the differential impact is inherent in the MB being a government bank and adopting an explicit policy of lending on the basis of the titles distributed. As Mitchell (2005) points out, this is an interesting result since the only increase in access to credit that did occur was not through the market process, but most likely through public subsidy.

32. In terms of access to credit cards, bank accounts, and formal credit (from banks, the government, labor unions, or cooperatives), the study finds no difference between titled and nontitled households, with both groups continuing to rely largely on informal credit sources. The small positive effect found is accounted for by 4 percent of titled households receiving mortgage loans.
33. Grameen Bank Annual Report (2009).
34. This study considers the performance of the two biggest microfinance organizations in Bangladesh other than Grameen: the Bangladesh Rural Advancement Committee (BRAC) and the Association for Social Advancement (ASA), as well as the Ranjpur Dinajpur Rural Service (RDRS).
35. These repayment rates are even more impressive when contrasted with the very poor repayment record of the government credit initiatives that pre-dated Grameen. See Dowla (2006: 5–7).
36. There is an implicit contract across generations; using land as collateral risks losing the land (if a bad outcome occurs), and thus violating the implicit contract.
37. Since, in the case of the de Soto model, the credit contract does not, for the most part, come into existence, the discussion of enforcement problems is essentially hypothetical.
38. Dasgupta (2003). Similarly, in the Hoff and Stiglitz (2008) model, a sufficient number of agents have to believe that the "rule of law" will prevail in order to support it and act accordingly.
39. Alternatively, reliance on external enforcement can be very costly.
40. Indeed, the fact that new contract language is often interpreted in a way that is disadvantageous to the party introducing the deviation from the standard contract deters modifications. See Stiglitz (1992).
41. The point here is not that formal contracts allow no flexibility. Indeed, some degree of flexibility is written into formal lending contracts. For instance you may default on an individual credit card payment at the cost of a fine on the next payment and an adverse effect on your credit rating, but to write the degree of flexibility into a formal lending contract that is relatively easily achieved by an informal one would be extremely expensive.
42. On this, see further, Dowla and Barua (2006).
43. Theoretically, at least, peer monitoring may reduce the costs of screening, but it does not eliminate the desire of individuals not to subsidize others; that is, groups of similar individuals—equal risk of default—will form, to eliminate or at least reduce cross-subsidization.
44. There are other specific features of the Grameen model that may contribute to its success, e.g., regular repayment schedules (Armendariz de Aghion and Morduch 2000). A recent paper by Field and Pande (2008) finds, however, that a less stringent repayment schedule does not adversely affect repayment rates. The high repayment rates mean that the default premium built into the interest rate can be negligible for *all* individuals, thus making these loans more widely accessible than under the conventional market system, where, even with collateral, loans viewed as having a high default rate bear a very high premium.
45. More generally, there is a large literature arguing the greater effectiveness of systems of intrinsic rewards rather than extrinsic rewards. See Stiglitz (2001) and the references cited there.
46. Some of the Grameen enterprises include Grameen Shakti (energy), Grameen Communication, Grameen Trust, Grameen Fund, Grameen Shikkha (education), Grameen Telecom, Grameen Knitwear, Grameen Cybernet, and the world's first "social-business enterprise," Grameen Danone. See Yunus (2007).
47. The omnipresence of Grameen and some other leading Bangladeshi NGOs has led to speculation about their having become para-governmental organizations. See *The Economist* (2001).

48. The cost is estimated to have dropped from around $2,000 to $50 and the time taken from fifteen years to six weeks. See Panaritis (2001: 22).
49. Despite this function of titling having been stressed greatly in the theoretical literature (see for instance, Demsetz 1967), it is not clear from the empirical evidence that it is essential for investment. A number of studies show that perceived security of tenure is more important than exact legal status. See for instance, Payne (1989), Razzaz (1993), and Varley (1987). It is common that lenders rely more on their judgments of the borrowers "creditworthiness," as judged by the security of income flows, than on collateral itself. Before the crisis, many lenders switched to more emphasis on the value of collateral, at great cost to themselves and the economy.
50. That is, the possibility of using credit as collateral may distort investment allocations toward the potential asset, even if the social marginal return on this investment is lower than that to the asset.
51. He attacks the Field result on a number of counts. First, he argues that she does not make the case that lack of title gave rise to a particular need to defend the property, especially in a context where legitimacy can have varied bases. Second, he contends that she fails to account for how the new jobs that titled families were purportedly absorbed into were generated—especially in a period of economic downturn. Finally, and most crucially, he argues that the very basis for making the comparison—the fact that the sequence of titling was random—is false. In particular, he points out that a third of the data for nontitled families is drawn from the Huancayo region—the birthplace of the "Shining Path" and the epicenter of political conflict in Peru and that this data is, consequently, not representative. See p. 309.
52. For further evidence see Haldar (2011).
53. Notice that in some such situations, land titling is simultaneously a land reform program, i.e., giving title to property over which others might have legitimate claims. Thus, squatters may be given secure property rights to public land that they have occupied. This is consistent with the remark made in the introductory chapter and in Chapter 4, that typically property rights assignments are *reassignments*, since claims (however ambiguous and uncertain) still have value.
54. Landlessness is an economic problem, because of the presence of agency costs. But when farmers have limited land, even a loss of part of their land may lead to an increase in agency costs, as they turn to other sources of income or seek additional land to work.
55. Galliani and Schargrodsky (2005), however, do not find evidence of increased labor income as a result of titling.
56. Joireman (2008), for instance, emphasizes the displacement of both customary law and women's rights as major drawbacks of the de Soto program.
57. There is evidence, for instance, of ministers in various developing countries using land titling programs to title substantial tracts of land in the names of members of their families rather than the intended beneficiaries. Given the disproportionate power that the wealthy in the developing world wield over formal law, and the fact that formal law is far more removed from social realities than informal norms, it is easier for the wealthy to manipulate *de jure* rights than it is *de facto* ones.
58. Microfinance was originally thought to target the poorest of the poor, but it emerged over time that conventional microfinance works best for those who are slightly better off than those in extreme and abject poverty. In response, dedicated programs aimed at the poorest of the poor have been introduced. Examples include Grameen's "Beggar Program" and BRAC's "Challenging the Frontiers of Poverty Reduction."
59. This refers to the collaboration between Grameen and the French yogurt company Danone to produce low-cost high-nutrient yogurt aimed specifically at overcoming some of the nutritional deficits of Bangladeshi children. See Yunus (2007). Grameen has also recently entered into a collaboration with the French company Veolia to

establish Grameen Veolia Ltd in order to supply low-cost, safe drinking water in Bangladeshi villages. This is particularly crucial because of the presence of arsenic in Bangladeshi water.

60. Initiatives involving healthcare are mainly Grameen Healthcare Trust and Grameen Kalyan. See Yunus (2007).
61. Aspersions have been cast on the motivations of Grameen for lending to women. Mallick (2002) argues that this choice is prudential rather than ideological, since women borrowers are easier to administer than men. This accusation is reiterated by some Bangladeshi NGOs such as Nijera Kori. Whatever the initial impetus for lending to women, it does not detract from the social impact of the choice.
62. Any discussion about the impact of microfinance programs is mired in the methodological controversies of the Pitt–Morduch debate. Using the same dataset, Morduch (1998) arrived at a very different (and largely, much more negative) set of conclusions about the impact of microfinance from Pitt and Khandker (1998). Morduch explicitly challenged their findings, mainly on grounds that were based on a number of methodological flaws (e.g., Pitt and Khandker's calculation of land ownership by beneficiary households, village fixed effects, and so on). Pitt (1999) responded, in turn, with a defense of the original methodology. The exchange illustrates the difficulties that underlie "impact assessments" of development programs in general, including large-scale quantitative studies based on substantial datasets and rigorous econometric analysis, and the consequent difficulty of arriving at a definitive pronouncement on the success or failure of a program. See also Khandker (1998) and Morduch (1999).
63. Grameen Bank website: <http://www.grameen-info.org/index.php?option=com_content&task=view&id=25&Itemid=128>, accessed June 19, 2011.
64. Pitt and Khandker (1998) attempted to correct for selection bias, but Morduch (1998) has questioned whether they were fully successful in doing so. Despite its contribution to poverty reduction, many commentators are critical of the high interest rates that it charges. See, for instance, Ahmad (2007: ch. 5).
65. Grameen Bank website.
66. Yunus (2007: 24).
67. Yunus (2007: 18).
68. Some studies, for instance Ebdon (1995), argue that the pressures of scaling-up and a preoccupation with performance indicators lead to a reluctance on the part of the Bank to make risky loans, even if this means leaving out the most disenfranchised. Grameen II attempts to address these issues through its "Beggar Program."
69. Even critics of the program concede some modest impact of microfinance on poverty alleviation, for instance Morduch (1998).
70. Yunus (2007: 9).
71. Accusations have, however, been leveled against the Grameen with regard to the appropriation of funds by husbands or other male relatives (Goetz and Sen Gupta 1996). Indeed, Rahman (1999) estimates that men, in effect, control as much as 60 percent of Grameen loans. These results have failed to be validated by other studies. However, on a relative estimate, even if that were true, women still have greater access to resources than under the conventional system of loans being made directly to men. In fact, studies by Van Tassel (2004) and Ligon (2002) find that, given the degree of male dominance in Bangladesh, the involvement of the husband in the loan venture might even be financially prudent.
72. See also Osmani (1998).
73. Using a combination of ethnographic and survey methodology, the paper measured women's empowerment in terms of eight indicators: mobility, economic security, ability to make small purchases, ability to make larger purchases, involvement in major household decisions, relative freedom from domination within the family, political and

legal awareness, and involvement in political campaigns and protests. See also Schuler and Hashemi (1994).

74. Taka is the Bangladeshi currency.
75. The ILD, for instance, identifies three "crucial institutions": fungible property rights, legal organization reform, and identity services. In addition, it purports to provide a "5-step" bridge to the "rule of law" and an "inclusive market economy." See <http://ild.org.pe/en/whatwedo>.
76. The disappointment with the first approach led the World Bank, at the end of the 1990s, to formulate its Comprehensive Development Framework. The conviction that successful development required active engagement of those in the country was key to both the CDF and the IMF's Participatory Poverty Reduction Strategies. See Wolfensohn and Fisher (2000) and Stiglitz (1998, 1999).
77. As we have emphasized, just as markets are incomplete, so are contracts and laws. It is impossible to specify what should be done in every contingency.
78. If anything, the Grameen model is being criticized, particularly within Bangladesh, for not adopting an even more all-encompassing approach. The Bangladeshi NGO Nijera Kori, for instance, argues that even the "microfinance plus" model is overly simplistic in thinking that these interventions will alter the fundamental power dynamics within Bangladeshi villages without engaging more closely with structural issues at the community level (see <http://www.nijerakori.org/>). This objection is further articulated in Barkat (2008) and has also been made by Ahmad (2007).
79. An example of an effective alternative dispute resolution mechanism is the Lok Adalat (people's court) system in India.
80. Dixit (2004) stresses the importance of the role of alternative regulation mechanisms; Sage, Adler, and Woolcock (2007) make a strong case for what they call "interim institutions" based on their in-depth engagement and incremental transformations of their political-economic contexts, citing successful examples of regulatory innovation in Cambodia and Indonesia; Rodrik (2008) argues for what he calls "second-best" institutions—which work within the constraints of deep-rooted government and market failure that cannot be removed in the short run—emphasizing that these may be far removed from "best-practice institutions."
81. Very effective systems of informal regulation based on thick social networks can sometimes be rooted in, or perpetuate, normatively undesirable values. Instances of this include the caste system in India based on arbitrary distinctions between groups of people or systems of customary justice that, for example, see honor killings as an acceptable way of resolving disputes (Dixit 2009; Khadiagala 2001). More specifically, the Grameen approach has been criticized by legal-rights activists in Bangladesh for failing to take a more procedural, rights-based approach to lending and loan collection.
82. This is the "microfinance plus" model referred to above. On "social businesses" see Yunus (2007).
83. See further, <http://www.pksf-bd.org/> and <http://www.mra.gov.bd/>.
84. It is well known, of course, how important nonformal aspects of business even between very large organizations are. See, for instance Macaulay (1963).
85. Fraudulent practices on the part of the Bangladesh microfinance organization Jubo Karmasangsthan Society (Jubok), for instance, underscored the need for regulation. The organization attempted to embezzle the Tk. 10 billion that it collected in deposits from 0.15 million clients. See, on this, *The Daily Star*, May 25, 2006. The oversupply of microcredit in the absence of regulation is leading to the problem of overlapping—borrowers who take loans from one microfinance organization to repay loans to another. Concern about this development was expressed repeatedly in personal interviews, see Haldar (2011). The expansion of services, e.g., toward deposit-taking, may

also necessitate greater regulation. There are more opportunities for fraud in taking money from people than in giving them money.

86. Grameenphone is both one of the earliest and most successful of Grameen's social businesses. It is a joint venture between Grameen Bank and the Norwegian telecommunication company Telenor. It is now the largest telecommunications service provider in Bangladesh. The reputation of the Grameen Bank is, however, a crucial factor behind the success of the venture.
87. It was thought that as markets get stronger and communities less close-knit—or at any rate more mobile—the settled communities on which Grameen relies may be destroyed. The experience of Grameen America, the new Grameen Bank branch in Jackson Heights, New York—belies this hypothesis. Despite operating in the US and in an urban context, repayment rates have been around 99 percent. See <http://www.grameenamerica.com/>.
88. This is increasingly emphasized in the literature by, for instance, Aoki (2001) and Grief (2006).
89. A classic illustration of this is, for example, the Health Act of 2006 in the UK. The passing of this legislation in Westminster altered deep-rooted habits such as smoking, sending smokers to the streets from inside bars, pubs, and restaurants virtually overnight. One of the biggest advantages of effective formal law is that it is able to influence norms, i.e., its self-conscious ability to make a positive impact on behavior patterns.
90. On the relationship between trust and cooperation, see Arrow (1972), Coleman (1990), and Dasgupta (2003).
91. And so too systems of sanctions for violations of norms in informal systems require broad consensus. Almost by definition, norms are social conventions supported by broad consensus, which may not (and often is not) the case for formal legal structures, especially when they come from (or are supported by those from) the outside or elites.
92. As Dasgupta (2003) puts it, the generation of trust is "riddled with positive externalities."
93. BRAC's Human Rights and Legal Aid Services program is, for instance, the largest legal aid program in the world.
94. Putnam (1993: 90) contends that "taking part in a choral society or a bird-watching club can teach self-discipline and an appreciation for the joys of successful collaboration." Hirschman (1984) describes trust as a "moral good," growing with use and decaying with disuse. Seabright (1997) presents empirical evidence of cooperation begetting further cooperation. In addition, Dixit (2004: ch. 3) stresses the continuing importance of civic associations.
95. Yunus (2007: 16).
96. Various scholars have cited other critical features, including the design of appropriate incentive structures that are consistent with China's specific conditions. See Qian (2003) and Oi and Walder (1999) for alternative interpretations.
97. See Jacobs (1979).

REFERENCES

Abreu, D. (1988), "On the Theory of Infinitely Repeated Games with Discounting," *Econometrica*, 56/2: 383–96.

——Pearce, D., and Stachetti, E. (1990), "Toward a Theory of Discounted Repeated Games with Imperfect Monitoring," *Econometrica*, 58: 1041–64.

Ahmad, Q. K. (2007), *Socio-economic and Indebtedness Related Impact of Microcredit in Bangladesh* (Dhaka: The University Press Limited).

Amin, R., Li, Y., and Ahmed, A. U. (1996), "Women's Credit Programs and Family Planning in Rural Bangladesh," *International Family Planning Perspectives*, 22: 158–62.

André, C. and Platteau, J. P. (1998), "Land Relations under Unbearable Stress: Rwanda Caught in the Malthusian Trap," *Journal of Economic Behavior and Organization*, 34/1: 1–47.

Aoki, M. (2001), *Toward a Comparative Institutional Change*. Cambridge, MA: MIT Press.

Armendariz de Aghion, B. and Morduch, J. (2000), "Microfinance Beyond Group Lending," *Economics of Transition*, 8/2: 401–20.

Arnott, R. and Stiglitz, J. E. (1991), "Moral Hazard and Non-market Institutions," *American Economic Review*, 81/1: 179–90.

Arrow, K. J. (1972), "Gifts and Exchanges," *Philosophy and Public Affairs*, 1: 343–62.

Arrunada, B. (2003), "Property Enforcement as Organized Consent," *Journal of Law, Economics and Organization*, 19: 401–44.

Bajaj, V. (2011), "Removal of Microfinancing Bank Founder Upheld," *The New York Times*, March 8.

Barkat, A. (2008), *Development as Conscientization: The Case of Nijera Kori in Bangladesh* (Dhaka: Pathak Shamabesh).

Barrows, R. and Roth, M. (1989), "Land Tenure and Investment in African Agriculture: Theory and Evidence," LTC Paper No. 136, Land Tenure Centre, University of Wisconsin-Madison.

Bateman, M. and Chang, H.-J. (2009), "The Microfinance Illusion" available at <http://www.econ.cam.ac.uk/faculty/chang/pubs/Microfinance.pdf>.

Berkowitz, D., Pistor, K., and Richard, J. F. (2003), "The Transplant Effect," *American Journal of Comparative Law*, 51: 163–203.

Besley, T. (1995), "Nonmarket Institutions for Credit and Risk Sharing in Low-Income Countries," *Journal of Economic Perspectives*, 9/3: 115–27.

——and Coate, S. (1995), "Group-lending, Repayment Incentives and Social Collateral," *Journal of Development Economics*, 46: 1–18.

Braverman, A. and Stiglitz, J. E. (1989), "Credit Rationing, Tenancy, Productivity and the Dynamics of Inequality," in P. Bardhan (ed.), *The Economic Theory of Agrarian Institutions* (Oxford: Clarendon Press).

————(1982), "Sharecropping and the Interlinking of Agrarian Markets," *American Economic Review* (American Economic Association), 72/4: 695–715.

Bromley, R. (1990), "A New Path to Development? The Significance and Impact of Hernando de Soto's Ideas on Underdevelopment, Production and Reproduction," *Economic Geography*, 66: 328–48.

Calderon, J. (2004), "The Formalization of Property in Peru 2001–2: The Case of Lima," *Habitat International*, 28/2: 289–300.

Carter, M. R. and Olinto, P. (2003), "Getting Institutions 'Right' for Whom: Credit Constraints and the Impact of Property Rights on the Quantity and Composition of Investment," *American Journal of Agricultural Economics*, 85: 173–86.

Clarke, D. C., Murrell, P. and Whiting, S. H. (2006), "The Role of Law in China's Economic Development," GWU Law School Public Law Research Paper No. 187 (January 27). Available at SSRN: <http://ssrn.com/abstract=878672> or <http://dx.doi.org/10.2139/ssrn.878672>.

——————(2008), "The Role of Law in China's Economic Development," in T. Rawski and L. Brandt (eds), *China's Great Economic Transformation* (New York: Cambridge University Press), 375–428.

COFOPRI (2008), *Annual Report 2008* (Lima: COFOPRI).

Coleman, J. (1990), *Foundations of Social Theory* (Cambridge, MA: Harvard University Press).

Commission for the Legal Empowerment of the Poor (2008), "Making Law Work for Everyone" available at <http://www.undp.org/legalempowerment/docs/ReportVolumeII/making_the_law_work.pdf>, accessed on August 15, 2009.

Cousins, B., Cousins, T., Hornby, D., Kingwill, R., Royston, L., and Smit, W. (2005), "Will Formalizing Property Rights Reduce Poverty in South Africa's 'Second Economy' Questioning the Mythologies of Hernando de Soto," Policy Brief No. 18, Programme for Land and Agrarian Studies, University of Western Cape, Cape Town.

Dasgupta, P. (2003), "Social Capital and Economic Performance: Analytics," in E. Ostrom and T. K. Ahn (eds), *Critical Writings in Economic Institutions: Foundations of Social Capital* (Cheltenham: Edward Elgar).

Datta, N. (2006), "Joint-titling—A Win-Win Policy? Gender and Property Rights in Urban Informal Settlements in Chandigarh, India," *Feminist Economics*, 12/1–2: 271–98.

Demsetz, H. (1967), "Toward a Theory of Property Rights," *American Economic Review*, 57/2: 347–59.

De Soto, H. (2000), *The Mystery of Capital* (London: Bantam Books).

Dixit, N. (2004), *Lawlessness and Economics*. Princeton: Princeton University Press.

——(2009), "A Taliban of our Very Own," *Tehelka Magazine*, 6/32 (15 August).

Doornbos, M. R. (1975), "Land Tenure and Political Conflict in Ankole, Uganda," *Journal of Development Studies*, 12/1: 54–74.

Dowla, A. (2006), "In Credit We Trust: Building Social Capital by Grameen Bank in Bangladesh," *Journal of Socio-economics*, 35/1: 102–22.

——and Barua, D. (2006), *The Poor Always Pay Back: The Grameen II Story* (Bloomfield, CT: Kumarian Press).

Ebdon, R. (1995), "NGO Expansion and the Fight to Reach the Poor: Gender Implications of NGO Scaling Up in Bangladesh," *IDS Bulletin*, 26/3: 49–55.

The Economist (2001), "NGOs in Bangladesh: Helping or Interfering?" September 13.

Edgcomb, E. and Barton, L. (1998), *Social Intermediation and Microfinance Programs: A Literature Review* (Washington, DC: USAID).

Emran, M. S., Morshed, A. K. M. M., and Stiglitz, J. E. (2007), "Microfinance and Missing Markets," available at <http://www.microfinancegateway.org/gm/document-1.9.30449/36.pdf>.

Feeny, D. (1988), "The Development of Property Rights: A Comparative Study," in R. Bates (ed.), *Toward a Political Economy of Development* (Berkeley: University of California Press), 285–96.

Fenrich, J. and Higgins, T. E. (2001), "Promise Unfulfilled: Law, Culture and Women's Inheritance Rights in Ghana," *Fordham International Law Journal*, 25: 259–336.

Field, E. (2003), "Fertility Responses to Land Titling: The Roles of Ownership Security and the Distribution of Household Assets." Unpublished manuscript.

——(2004), "Property Rights, Community Public Goods, and Household Time Allocation in Urban Squatter Communities: Evidence from Peru," *William and Mary Law Review*, 45/3: 837–82.

——(2007), "Entitled to Work: Urban Property Rights and Labor Supply in Peru," *Quarterly Journal of Economics*, 122/4: 1561–602.

——and Pande, R. (2008), "Repayment Frequency and Default in Microfinance: Evidence from India," *Journal of the European Economics Association*, 6/2–3: 501–9.

——and Torero, M. (2004), "Do Property Titles Increase Credit Access Among Urban Poor? Evidence from a Nationwide Titling Program," available at <http://www.rwj.harvard.edu/papers/field/Field%20Do%20Property%20Titles%20Increase%20Credit . . . .pdf>.

Finmark Trust (2004), "The Township Residential Property Market" (Johannesburg: Finmark Trust).

Galanter, M. and Krishnan, J. K. (2004), "'Bread for the Poor': Access to Justice and the Right of the Needy in India," *Hastings Law Journal*, 55/5: 789–834.

Galliani, S. and Schargrodsky, E. (2005), "Property Rights for the Poor: Effects of Land Titling," Working Paper Series No. 7, Ronald Coase Institute.

Ghatak, M. (1999), "Group Lending, Local Information and Peer Selection," *Journal of Development Economics*, 60: 27–50.

Gilbert, A. (2002), "On the Mystery of Capital and the Myths of Hernando de Soto: What Difference Does Legal Title Make?" *International Development Planning Review*, 24/1: 1–19.

Goetz, A. M. and Sen Gupta, R. (1996), "Who Takes the Credit? Gender, Power, and Control Over Loan Use in Rural Credit Programs in Bangladesh," *World Development*, 24/4: 45–63.

Gold, T., Guthrie, D., and Wank, D. (eds) (2002), *Social Connections in China: Institutions, Culture, and the Changing Nature of Guanxi* (Cambridge: Cambridge University Press).

Grameen Bank (2009), *Annual Report 2009* (Dhaka: Grameen Bank).

Grief, A. (2006), *Institutions and the Path to the Modern Economy: Lessons from Medieval Trade*, Political Economy of Institutions and Decisions (Cambridge: Cambridge University Press).

Haldar, A. (2007), "The Capabilities Approach and Women's Rights in India." Paper presented at the Annual Human Development and Capabilities Conference, New York, available at <http://www.capabilityapproach.com/pubs/Haldar07.pdf>.

——(2011), "Rethinking Law and Development: Evidence from Land Titling and Microfinance Programmes," PhD thesis, University of Cambridge.

Hare, D., Yang, L., and Englander, D. (2007), "Land Management in Rural China and its Gender Implications," *Feminist Economics*, 13/3: 35–61.

Hashemi, S. M., Schuler, S. R., and Riley, A. P. (1996), "Rural Credit Programs and Women's Empowerment in Bangladesh," *World Development*, 24/4: 635–53.

Hirschman, A. (1984), "Against Parsimony: Three Easy Ways of Complicating Some Categories of Economic Discourse," *American Economic Review*, 74 (Papers and Proceedings): 88–96.

Hoff, K. and Stiglitz, J. E. (2008), "Exiting a Lawless State," *The Economic Journal*, 118/531: 1474–97.

————(1990), "Imperfect Information and Rural Credit Markets: Puzzles and Policy Perspectives," *The World Bank Economic Review*, 4/3: 235–50.

Hossain, M. (1988), *Credit for Alleviation of Rural Poverty: The Grameen Bank in Bangladesh*, Report No. 65, International Food Policy Research Institute, Washington, DC.

Jacobs, J. B. (1979), "A Preliminary Model of Particularistic Ties in Chinese Political Alliances: *KanCh'ing* and *Kuanhsi* in a Rural Taiwanese Township," *The China Quarterly*, 78: 237–73.

Jain, A. (1996), "Managing Credit for the Rural Poor: Lessons from the Grameen Bank," *World Development*, 24/1: 79–89.

Joireman, S. F. (2008), "The Mystery of Capital Formation in Sub-saharan Africa: Women, Property Rights and Customary Law," *World Development*, 36/7: 1233–46.

Kevane, M. and Gray, L. C. (1999), "A Woman's Field is Made at Night: Gendered Land Rights and Norms in Burkina Faso," *Feminist Economics*, 5/3: 1–26.

Khadiagala, L. S. (2001), "The Failure of Popular Justice in Uganda: Local Councils and Women's Property Rights," *Development and Change*, 32/1: 55–76.

Khandker, S. (1998), *Fighting Poverty with Microcredit: Experience in Bangladesh* (New York: Oxford University Press).

Lanjouw, J. O. and Levy, P. I. (2002), "Untitled: A Study of Formal and Informal Property Rights in Urban Equador," *The Economic Journal*, 112/482: 986–1019.

Lastarria-Cornhiel, S. (1997), "Impact of Privatisation on Gender and Property Rights in Africa," *World Development*, 25/8: 1317–33.

——Agurto, S., Brown, J., and Rosales, S. E. (2003), "Joint-titling in Nicaragua, Indonesia, and Honduras: A Rapid Appraisal Synthesis." Unpublished manuscript.

Liebman, B. (2007), "China's Courts: Restricted Reform," *China Quarterly*, 191 (September): 620–38.

Ligon, E. (2002), "Dynamic Bargaining in Households (With an Application to Bangladesh)." Working paper, University of California, Berkeley.

Lubman, S. (1998), "The Policy and Legal Environment for Foreign Direct Investment in Carol J. Holgren (ed.), "China: Past Accomplishments, Future Uncertainties," in *Private Investments Abroad* (Newark, NJ: Matthew Bender), ch. 3.

——(1999), *Bird in a Cage: Legal Reform in China After Mao* (Stanford, CA: Stanford University Press).

Macaulay, S. (1963), "Non-contractual Relations in Business: A Preliminary Study," *American Sociological Review*, 28/55: 55–67.

Mackenzie, F. (1993), "A Piece of Land Never Shrinks: Reconceptualising Land Tenure in a Smallholding District in Kenya," in T. J. Basset and D. E. Crummey, *Land in African Agrarian* Systems (Madison: University of Wisconsin Press).

Mallick, R. (2002), "Implementing and Evaluating Microcredit in Bangladesh," *Development in Practice*, 12/2: 153–63.

McKernan, S.-M. (2002), "The Impact of Micro-credit Programs on Self-employment Profits: Do Non-credit Program Aspects Matter?" *Review of Economics and Statistics*, 84/1: 93–115.

Mitchell, T. (2005), "The Work of Economists: How a Discipline Makes its World," *European Journal of Sociology*, 46: 297–320.

Morduch, J. (1998), "Does Microfinance Really Help the Poor? New Evidence from Flagship Programs in Bangladesh." Unpublished manuscript.

——(1999), "The Role of Subsidies in Microfinance: Evidence from the Grameen Bank," *Journal of Development Economics*, 60 (October): 229–48.

Nanda, P. (1999), "Women's Participation in Rural Credit Programmes in Bangladesh and Their Demand for Formal Healthcare: Is There a Positive Impact?" *Health Economics*, 8: 415–28.

North, D. C. (1991), "Institutions," *Journal of Economic Perspectives*, 5/1: 97–112.

——(1995), "The New Institutional Economics and Third World Development," in Harriss J. et al. (eds), *The New Institutional Economics and Third World Development* (London: Routledge).

Oi, J. and Walder, A. (eds) (1999), *Property Rights and Economic Reforms in China* (Stanford, CA: Stanford University Press).

Olson, M. (1965), *The Logic of Collective Action* (Cambridge, MA: Harvard University Press).

Osmani, L. N. K. (1998), "Impact of Credit on the Relative Well-Being of Women: Evidence from the Grameen Bank," *IDS Bulletin*, 29/4: 31–8.

Ostrom, E. (1990), *Governing the Commons: The Evolution of Institutions for Collective Action* (Cambridge: Cambridge University Press).

Panaritis, E. (2001), "Do Property Rights Matter? A Urban Case Study From Peru," *Global Outlook: International Urban Research Monitor*, 1 (April): 20–2.

Payne, G. (1989), "Informal Housing and Land Subdivisions in Third World Cities: A Review of the Literature" (Oxford Polytechnic, Oxford: CENDEP).

Pistor, K., Haldar, A., and Amirapu, A. (2009), "Social Norms, Rule of Law and Gender Reality," in James Heckman, Robert Nelson, and Lee Cabatingan (eds), *Global Perspectives on the Rule of Law* (New York: Routledge).

Pitt, M. (1999), "Reply to Jonathan Morduch's 'Does Microfinance Really Help the Poor? New Evidence From Flagship Programs in Bangladesh'." Unpublished manuscript.

——and Khandker, S. R. (1998), "The Impact of Group-based Credit Programs on Poor Households in Bangladesh: Does the Gender of Participants Matter?" *Journal of Political Economy*, 106 (October): 958–96.

——— and Cartwright, J. (2003), "Does Micro-credit Empower Women? Evidence From Bangladesh," Policy Research Working Papers 2998, The World Bank, Washington, DC.

Platteau, J.-P. (2000), *Institutions, Social Norms, and Economic Development* (Amsterdam: Harwood).

Posner, R. (1998), "Creating a Legal Framework for Economic Development," *The World Bank Research Observer*, 13/1: 1–11.

Potter, P. (2001), *The Chinese Legal System: Globalization and Local Legal Culture* (London: Routledge).

Prosterman, R. and Hanstead, T. (2006), "Land Reform in the Twenty-First Century: New Challenges, New Responses," *Seattle Journal for Social Justice*, 4/2: 769–806.

Putnam, R. (1993), *Making Democracy Work: Civic Traditions in Modern History* (Princeton: Princeton University Press).

—— (1995), "Bowling Alone: America's Declining Social Capital," *Journal of Democracy*, 6: 65–78.

Qian, Y. (2003), "How Reform Worked in China," in D. Rodrik (ed.), *In Search of Prosperity: Analytic Narratives on Economic Growth* (Princeton: Princeton University Press).

Rahman, A. (1999), *Women and Microcredit in Bangladesh* (Boulder: Westview Press).

Razzaz, O. M. (1993), "Examining Property Rights and Investment in Informal Settlements: The Case of Jordan," *Land Economics*, 69: 341–55.

Rodrik, D. (2008), "Second-Best Institutions," Working Paper No. 14050, National Bureau of Economic Research, Cambridge, MA.

Sage, C., Adler, D., and Woolcock, M. (2007), "Interim Institutions and the Development Process: Law and Creation of Spaces for Reform in Cambodia and Indonesia." Paper presented at the Law and Society Association, Berlin.

Schuler, S. R. and Hashemi, S. M. (1994), "Credit Programs, Women's Empowerment and Contraceptive Use in Rural Bangladesh," *Studies in Family Planning*, 25/2: 65–76.

——— and Huda Badal, S. (1998), "Men's Violence Against Women in Rural Bangladesh: Undermined or Exacerbated by Microcredit Programs?" *Development in Practice*, 8/2: 144–50.

——— and Riley, A. (1997), "The Influence of Women's Changing Roles and Status in Bangladesh's Fertility and Contraceptive Use," *World Development*, 31/3: 513–34.

————— and Akhtar, A. (1996), "Credit Program, Patriarchy and Men's Violence Against Women in Rural Bangladesh," *Social Science and Medicine*, 43/12: 1729–42.

Seabright, P. (1997), "Is Cooperation Habit-Forming?" in P. Dasgupta and K.-G. Maler (eds), *The Environment and Emerging Development Issues*, vol. II (Oxford: Clarendon Press).

Seibel, H. (2000), "How Value Creates Value: Social Capital in Microfinance—The Case of the Philippines," Rural Finance Working Paper No. B8, International Fund for Agricultural Development, Rome.

Sharma, K. (ed.) (2005a), *Collected Essays and Stories from Grameen Dialogue (Newsletter Issues # 1–50)*, vol. I: *Emerging Ideas, Concepts and Theories—How the Message of Grameencredit Spread Around the World* (Dhaka: Grameen Trust).

—— (ed.) (2005b), *Collected Essays and Stories from Grameen Dialogue (Newsletter Issues # 1–50)*, vol. II: *The Replication Experience—How the Message of Grameencredit Spread Around the World* (Dhaka: Grameen Trust).

—— and Zeller, M. (1997), "Repayment Performance in Group-based Credit Programs in Bangladesh: An Empirical Analysis," *World Development*, 25/10: 1731–42.

Stanfield, D. (1990), "Rural Land Titling and Registration in Latin America and the Caribbean: Implications for Rural Development Programs," Land Tenure Centre, University of Wisconsin, Madison. Available at <http://www.terrainstitute.org/reports.html>.

Stiglitz, J. E. (1990), "Peer-monitoring and Credit Markets," *World Bank Economic Performance*, 4: 351–66.

——(1992), "Contract Theory and Macroeconomic Fluctuations," in L. Werin and H. Wijkander (ed.), *Contract Economics* (London: Basil Blackwell).

——(1998), "Towards a New Paradigm for Development: Strategies, Policies and Processes," 9th Raul Prebisch Lecture delivered at the Palais des Nations, Geneva. Reprinted (2001) as chapter 2 in *The Rebel Within*, ed. Ha-Joon Chang (London: Wimbledon Publishing Company).

——(1999), "More Instruments and Broader Goals: Moving Toward the Post-Washington Consensus," in G. Kochendorfer-Lucius and B. Pleskovic (eds), *Development Issues in the 21st Century* (Berlin: German Foundation for International Development). Reprinted (2001) as chapter 1 in *The Rebel Within*, ed. Ha-Joon Chang (London: Wimbledon Publishing Company). (Originally presented as the 1998 WIDER Annual Lecture, Helsinki, January 1998; also keynote address at Villa Borsig Winter Workshop, February 1998.)

——(2000), "Formal and Informal Institutions" in P. Dasgupta and I. Serageldin (eds), *Social Capital: A Multifaceted Perspective* (Washington, DC: World Bank).

——(2001), "Democratic Development as the Fruits of Labor," in *The Rebel Within*, ed. H.-J. Chang (London: Wimbledon Publishing Company). (Originally keynote address at the Industrial Relations Research Association, Boston, January 2000. Shortened version available in *Perspectives on Work*, 4/1 (2000): 31–8.)

——(2006), *Making Globalization Work* (New York: W. W. Norton and Co).

——(2010), "Sovereign Debt: Notes on Theoretical Frameworks and Policy Analyses," in H. Herman, J. A. Ocampo, and S. Spiegel (eds), *Overcoming Developing Country Debt Crises* (Oxford: Oxford University Press).

Thomson, J. T., Feeny, D. H., and Oakerson, R. J. (1986), "Institutional Dynamics: The Evolution and Dissolution of Common Property Resource Management," in *National Research Council: Proceedings of the Conference on Common Property Resource Management* (Washington, DC: National Academy Press).

Tomlinson, M. (2005), "Title Deeds Not a Magic Wand," *Business Day*, August 10.

Upham, F. (2009), "From Deng to Demsetz: Speculations on the Implications of Chinese Growth for Law and Development Theory," *NYU Journal of International Law and Politics*, 41: 551.

Van Tassel, E. (2004), "Household Bargaining and Microfinance," *Journal of Development Economics*, 74: 465–6.

Varley, A. (1987), "The Relationship Between Tenure Legislation and Housing Improvement," *Development and Change*, 18: 463–81.

Viswanath, C. K. (1977), "Adivasis: Protesting Land Alienation," *Economic and Political Weekly*, 32/32: 2016–17.

Wadhwa, D. C. (1989), "Guaranteeing Title to Land: A Preliminary Study," *Economic and Political Weekly*, 24/41: 2323–34.

Wahid, A. N. M. (1994), "The Grameen Bank and Poverty Alleviation in Bangladesh: Theory, Evidence and Limitations," *American Journal of Economics and Sociology*, 53/1: 1–15.

Wang, X. (1989), "Guanxiwang' di Jingji Fenxi" ["Economic Analysis of *Guanxiwang*"], *Xinhua Wenzhai* [*Xinhua Digest*] (March 2): 49–52.

Wolfensohn, J. D. and Fischer, S. (2000), "The Comprehensive Development Framework (CDF) And Poverty Reduction Strategy Papers (PRSP)." Joint note by the President of the World Bank and the First Deputy Managing Director of the IMF (April 5), available at <http://www.imf.org/external/np/prsp/pdf/cdfprsp.pdf>.

Wydick, B. (1999), "Can Social Cohesion be Harnessed to Repair Market Failures? Evidence from Group Lending in Guatemala," *Economic Journal*, 457: 463–75.

Yunus, M. (1998), *Banker to the Poor* (London: Aurum Press).

——(2002), "Grameen Bank II: Designed to Open New Possibilities," available at <http://web01.grameen.com/bank/bank2.html>.

——(2007), *Creating a World Without Poverty: Social Business and the Future of Capitalism* (New York: Public Affairs).

——(2008), "Grameen Bank at a Glance," Grameen Bank website, <http://www.grameen-info.org/index.php?option=com_content&task=view&id=26&Itemid=175>.

——(2011), "Sacrificing Microcredit for Megaprofits," *The New York Times*, January 14.

Zheng, Y. (1986), "Connections," in R. F. Dernberger et al. (eds), *The Chinese: Adapting the Past, Building the Future*, Centre for Chinese Studies, University of Michigan, Ann Arbor.

Zubair, M. A. (1987), "The Administration of Land, Water and Grazing Rights under Sotoko Caliphite of Northern Nigera: An Islamic Legal Point of View," in id., *Land and Water Rights Issues in Irrigated Schemes in Sub-Saharan Africa and Madagascar* (Paris: Centre d'études juridiques comparatives), 122–35.

Part II

Toward Law and Development Policies with Chinese Characteristics

Sound economic policy in a market economy begins by recognizing two facts. First, markets are structured by law. Markets do not make themselves—they are complex institutions that must be made.[1] Law structures economic opportunities and incentives, just as it allocates bargaining power, access to resources, and exposure to risk. Market transactions take place on the foundation of legal arrangements, in the shadow of legal requirements, and against the background of legal limitations. Moreover, there is no one best way to design these legal arrangements (in the parlance of economics, there can be many Pareto-efficient systems).[2] Different legal—and social or cultural—arrangements will generate alternative modes of market capitalism that may reflect different distributional preferences. As a result, the background legal regimes of property, contracts, torts (liability), or corporate law structure economic actors and their entitlements—and, alongside legislative regulation or administrative action addressed to particular social or other objectives, are crucial tools of economic policy.

Second, no matter how they are structured, in the real world all markets have limits, which imply that the allocations that they generate are not in general (constrained) Pareto-efficient, let alone consistent with generally accepted principles of social justice.[3] Market incentives will not generate adequate provision of public goods. Because of externalities, markets produce too much of some goods (when there is a negative externality) and too little of other goods (when there is a positive externality). Left to their own devices, firms would collude, conspiring to increase their profits at the expense of the rest of society. Left to their own devices, profit-maximizing firms would try to take advantage of consumer irrationalities and ignorance, exploiting in particular the less educated. Information problems and asymmetries are pervasive, with far reaching consequences, particularly evident in complex markets such as those of finance and health. In short, the "ideal" markets that produce efficient outcomes do not exist in reality, and as a result, there is a presumption that markets are in general *not* efficient.[4] And even when they are efficient, the distributive consequences are often unacceptable, e.g., with some individuals not receiving sufficient income to survive. Economic policy will often be required to compensate for these limitations if a market economy is to achieve equitable and sustainable growth—or even just plain efficiency.

Unfortunately, over recent decades, these realities have all too often been obscured in global debates about sensible development policy. An oversimplified language of market absolutism (sometimes referred to as market fundamentalism) has substituted for careful economic and legal analysis. In this orthodox argot, markets are treated as necessarily efficient and self-correcting. Efficiency and growth are conflated as objectives for policy and understood to flow unimpeded from the "free" operations of markets. The prevalence of market failures and the potential for effective government policy are understated. The many crucial *choices* involved in establishing a legal framework for market transactions are obscured by one-size-fits-all recipes for clear background rules and a default preference for deregulation. Such one-size-fits-all formulas are sold on the grounds that they ensure the efficiency *of any economy.*

Distributional concerns are treated as severable from efficiency, ignoring the dynamic significance of wealth effects and background rules allocating bargaining power, access to resources, and exposure to risk. It is assumed that a "rising tide lifts all boats," as trickle-down economics brings benefits to all; and that even if this doesn't occur automatically, governments can and will engage in costless (lump sum) redistributions. But neither hypothesis is correct. There have been many instances in which the poor—or even the middle class—has not benefited from growth. This has been true for the US in recent years; even before the Great Recession, *all* of the benefits of the growth that occurred, and more, went to the top; by 2011, real median household income (income of those in the middle) was lower than it was in 1996.[5] And the concentration of economic power has, not surprisingly, been translated into a concentration in political power. Rather than offsetting the increasing inequality, tax changes disproportionately benefited those at the top.

Just as economic analysis has been oversimplified, so too has the legal analysis. In a particularly striking misreading of Ronald Coase's famous assault on Pigovian welfare economics, the initial allocation of private rights is treated as inconsequential (so long as it is "clear" and enforceable) on the theory that however initially allocated, market forces will drive resources toward their most productive use so long as there is a clear assignment of property rights.

This orthodoxy is wrong. It is not supported by the best contemporary economic or legal theories—nor the historical experience of leading market economies. It has nevertheless been enormously influential in debates about development policy, even in China. As a result, we frame our analysis of Chinese economic policy by addressing the limitations of this unfortunate set of orthodox oversimplifications in the first two articles of Part II. The first examines the economic arguments supporting the neoliberal orthodoxy about the legal foundations for a market economy. The second focuses on the orthodox assertion that development in a market economy requires property rights that are "clear and strong." The remaining chapters examine some of the legal arrangements that have, in fact, supported recent Chinese development. We begin with property rights, in the rural and urban context, and then consider intellectual property rights, corporate entitlements and governance, social and labor rights. The interesting thing is the extent to which Chinese development policy has routinely departed from this orthodoxy already, often with excellent results.

The chapters in this part illustrate the interplay between concerns about efficiency and equity. If there is a single message that we hope emerges, it is this: government has no choice but to structure "rights and obligations"—including the vast array of rights associated with ownership of property, including intellectual property, rights concerning where individuals can live, rights concerning basic conditions of living. These affect how individuals behave—how much they work, how much and in what they invest, and so forth. They have consequences for the nature of the society that emerges today and in the future, for the well-being of different individuals and their families, for the exercise of influence and control. A certain set of precepts has been pushed by the "neoliberal law and economics" tradition, which is neither really coherent nor consistent with modern economic theory. Its major advantage is that it provides simple prescriptions. Those prescriptions may serve some interests well, but are not likely to serve society more broadly. They should be taken with extreme caution—particularly if China seeks to create a dynamic and harmonious society.

NOTES

1. Of course, individuals exchange with each other even in primitive societies. But even these exchanges are governed by customary law, which may circumscribe what can be bought and sold, what happens when a person sells a defective product, or otherwise engages in fraud, etc. The rules governing markets in more advanced societies are correspondingly more complex, especially when it comes to problems posed by intertemporal trades, e.g., when one party makes a promise to deliver something in the future.
2. There are, of course, Pareto inefficient systems—rules that are so bad that there are reforms that could make all individuals better off. But these may be rarer than one might think, especially in the context of governments that cannot make commitments for the future. Reforms that *seem* to be Pareto improvements sometimes turn out not to be, or at least there is a risk that they might not be, e.g., as government commitments to compensate those who lose from the reform are broken. See Stiglitz (1998).
3. The term "Pareto optimality" refers to the fact that no one can be made better off without making someone else worse off—the prevailing concept of efficiency among economists. The term "constrained" Pareto efficiency is used simply to remind the reader that due account has been taken not only of technology constraints (the limitations imposed, for instance, by technology in transforming inputs into outputs) but also of constraints associated with limitations of information and the costs of acquisition of information and of creating and operating markets.
4. More precisely, they are not "constrained Pareto efficient": there are always government interventions that respect the costs of gathering information and creating and transacting in markets that could make all individuals better off. See, e.g., Greenwald and Stiglitz (1986).
5. US Census figures. See "Table H-9, Race of Head of Household by Median and Mean Income," Historical Tables, Households, available at <http://www.census.gov/hhes/www/income/data/historical/household/index.html>.

REFERENCES

Coase, R. H. (1960), "The Problem of Social Cost," *Journal of Law and Economics*, 3: 1–44.

Greenwald, B. and Stiglitz, J. E. (1986), "Externalities in Economies with Imperfect Information and Incomplete Markets," *Quarterly Journal of Economics*, 101/2: 229–64.

Stiglitz, J. E. (1998), "The Private Uses of Public Interests: Incentives and Institutions," *Journal of Economic Perspectives*, 12/2: 3–22. (Originally presented at a Society of Government Economists conference in Chicago, Distinguished Lecture on Economics in Government, January 4, 1998.)

US Census Bureau (2010), "Race of Head of Household by Median and Mean Income," Table H-9, Historical Tables, Households, available at <http://www.census.gov/hhes/www/income/data/historical/household/index.html>.

4

The Economics Behind Law in a Market Economy: Alternatives to the Neoliberal Orthodoxy[1]

Joseph E. Stiglitz

We noted in the Introduction that China, like developing countries all over the world, has been urged to adopt a set of institutions, typically described as "best practices" and thought to characterize the Anglo-American model of market economy. Underlying a successful market economy, it is argued, there exists a rule of law—and by *rule of law* what is meant is not just any legal framework, but a particular one, what we referred to in the introductory chapter as the "neoliberal orthodoxy," based on "Chicago School" economics.[2] It is important to place this approach, which focuses on notions such as "secure property rights," in perspective. It has long been the subject of intense debate among both economists and legal scholars. Although the Chicago School has had enormous influence in thinking about legal and other institutions, it no longer represents the *best* thinking about the relationship between law and economic policy—far from it. As we explained in the Introduction, as a matter of economics, many of the foundational premises of the Chicago School have been challenged. As a matter of law, the institutions thought necessary for market efficiency have been shown to be far more variable and contingent. And there is more to a successful economy than just efficiency. There is not a single best set of institutional arrangements that work for countries in different circumstances with different objectives. Countries face choices about their institutional arrangements, and the choices about strategy and institutional form are critical, particularly as China puts in place institutional arrangements that will have a long-term dynamic effect on the structure of the Chinese market economy. As China sets out to create a market economy with Chinese characteristics, as it sets out to advance its objectives of creating a harmonious society, as it thinks about institutional designs that provide the flexibility for changing course as it advances in its development (in accord with the principle of "crossing the river by feeling the stones"), it needs to think carefully about the full range of consequences of each of the alternatives—not only for efficiency and equity today, but for how current choices are likely to impact its future evolution.

This chapter explains the limitations both of the underlying economics upon which the neoliberal orthodoxy is based and of some of the associated legal principles.

UNDERLYING ASSUMPTIONS AND ANALYSES AND THE CRITIQUES

Underlying the policy stances of the neoliberal law and economics tradition are certain analytics, and underlying those analytics are certain assumptions. In the past three decades, research has called into question the assumptions, showing that the results are not robust—even small changes in assumptions lead to major changes in conclusions, e.g., concerning the efficiency of markets. And events have called into question both the relevance of its underlying assumptions and the conclusions that follow from them.

Neoliberal analysis is predicated on assumptions of rational and well-informed consumers interacting with profit-maximizing firms in competitive markets in a world with perfect risk and capital markets. Under these assumptions (with a few additional ones—the absence of externalities, such as those associated with the environment, and the absence of public goods), markets are (Pareto)-efficient.[3] Subsequently, it was shown that whenever information is imperfect or risk markets incomplete—that is, always—markets are not (constrained Pareto)-efficient (Greenwald and Stiglitz 1986).

The Chicago School responded with a variety of opposing arguments. In the case of externalities, it was argued that markets could and would efficiently "internalize" the externalities. Most influential was the work of Coase (1960), which suggested that in the absence of transaction costs, clear and unambiguous assignments of property rights lead to efficiency (the Coase Conjecture), even with externalities. If nonsmokers are given the rights to the air, then smokers will pay them to be allowed to smoke if and only if the value of what they gain from smoking exceeds the value of what the nonsmokers lose. If smokers are given the rights to the air, then nonsmokers will pay the smokers not to smoke, so long as the value of what they gain from having a smoke-free room exceeds the loss that smokers incur in not being able to smoke. Either system of assigning property rights could lead to economic efficiency in the absence of transaction costs. Where there are transaction costs, the efficiency gains from lowering these costs are often given primacy in determining desirable legal rules. There are, of course, distributional consequences to these alternative assignments of property rights, but these are typically not the focus of the analysis.[4,5]

In response to the critique that markets are often not competitive, Chicago School economists argued that the scope for anticompetitive behavior is limited. Even if there was only one firm, as is the case with a natural monopoly, potential competition was all that was needed to ensure that firms do not exploit their market power. Competition *for* the market replaced competition in the market. The implication was that there was little need for antitrust action (indeed, the risk is that government intervention would impede real competition in the market place).[6] This was called the contestability doctrine (Panzar and Willig 1977; Baumol, Panzar, and Willig 1982). But then, like the other attempts to defend doctrines of market efficiency, this view too was debunked, as it was shown that markets would not be contestable so long as there were *any* sunk costs, no matter how small (Stiglitz 1988). The example highlighted by advocates of contestability—the airline industry—had outcomes that were *highly* noncompetitive.

The Chicago School never came up with responses to other critiques: the failure of markets to be efficient, for instance, when information is imperfect and asymmetric, or that markets are often imperfectly competitive, or that transactions costs are significant, in which case the assignment of property rights did make a difference.[7]

Chicago School economic analytics had some derivative implications, such as: individuals should be allowed to freely contract with each other; the government's only role is to enforce the contracts that have been made;[8] the stronger the intellectual property rights, the better. In this view, the role of government is limited to ensuring property rights and enforcing contracts and actions that are seen as "market-supporting" while avoiding regulation that seems to "distort" market prices. Individuals and firms will have an incentive to make use of assets efficiently and to make the set of contracts that works best for them; and in pursuing their private interests, they ensure the efficiency of the economy as a whole.

As we have noted, modern economic theory has questioned both the underlying assumptions and the derived economic propositions. Information is often imperfect and markets (including futures and risk markets) are never complete. Individuals and firms have been shown to be not fully rational. This was evident in the run up to the 2008 financial crisis—as it has been evident in the periodic bubbles and panics that have characterized market capitalism's history. The consequences of irrationalities and other market failures can be devastating. When profit-maximizing firms exploit these irrationalities, the outcomes are often especially unpleasant—again seen dramatically in the crisis, as banks exploited poor and less-educated borrowers through predatory lending practices. Other market failures are also hard to ignore: many of the major markets (finance, media, computer operating systems, applications, airlines, microprocessor manufacturing) are far from perfectly competitive.

Free contracting does not generally result in economic efficiency; in particular, problems arise when contracts between two parties affect third parties (e.g., a loan between parties A and B affects the likelihood of default with Party C). Competitive contracting equilibriums are also not efficient whenever there are signaling problems (e.g., bankruptcy provisions may be used as a costly and inefficient signal).

"Strong" property rights can even impede economic efficiency. Consider, in particular, intellectual property rights. Knowledge is a public good, and intellectual property rights (giving the knowledge producer exclusive rights over the use of the knowledge that he has produced) can introduce a static inefficiency in the economy.[9] Whether intellectual property rights is in general the best way of ensuring the efficient production of knowledge is a moot question; but poorly designed property rights, giving temporary monopoly power to a particular corporation or individual, can actually impede innovation and distort the short-run allocation of resources.

Since issues of efficiency and distribution cannot be separated (e.g., in the presence of agency costs),[10] then how property rights are assigned can affect the efficiency of the economic system.

Finally, societal well-being may be affected by distributional considerations—which may not be simply and easily altered by political processes. This has been a key point of legal critiques—the background rules will set the market running toward alternative equilibria.

BEYOND THE CHICAGO SCHOOL LAW AND ECONOMICS TRADITION

This chapter explores the consequences of these realities for the key hypothesis of the Chicago law and economics tradition—that the role of government is simply to ensure clear property rights and that property rights and contracts are rigorously enforced. So far, we have argued that this underlying economic presumption is false, that if the government does this, market outcomes will not be efficient. Moreover, we have argued that even if the outcomes were efficient,[11] society cares about the distribution of income and redistributions are not costless.[12]

The purpose of the law is not just to ensure efficiency, but also to enable socially desirable outcomes (in China's parlance, for instance, there is a concern about achieving *a harmonious society*). Indeed, society may be concerned not just with outcomes, but with the processes by which they are achieved.

The Chicago perspective failed not only in its view about the underlying economy, but also about the objectives of law. The two failures get intertwined in the Chicago School's overly simplistic views of property and property rights, of what "security of property rights" might mean, and of what a good property rights system might look like.

Rights and obligations in an interdependent world

As we have noted, the assertion is wrong that *all* the government should do is simply make sure that property rights are clearly assigned and enforced. Such an approach would unbalance the economic system, deferring equity issues while consolidating the authority of some over society's resources. More importantly, however, this approach to property is simply incoherent. Property is not just about "rights." Every right is matched by an enforceable duty upon other actors to respect that right—rights impose costs, and must be understood in relational terms.

A fundamental problem for policy arises from the fact that what each individual does affects others. If an individual smokes, it affects nonsmokers. A building next door may block my sunlight. A car driving down the road forces me to be more careful as I cross the street. A factory's smoke makes life unpleasant for those living next door.

It is simply impossible to say, other than as a matter of political choice, who "caused" the "harm"—the factory that smokes up the house or the household that wants to live smoke-free next door. There would be no "externality" if there were no house next door. Economists argue that individuals should pay the full costs of their actions. This is sometimes put in a temporal context. Assume a house has been constructed, a family has already taken up residence, and a firm is considering constructing a factory. Then the factory presumably should take into account the costs imposed on the adjacent family before it makes a decision to build. But this seems to assign property rights on a first-come-first-serve basis—and if sunk costs are low, there is no reason to believe that this will result in an efficient outcome. Moreover, it could induce an inefficient "race." Consider two adjacent plots of land. If the homeowner builds first, he will receive compensation for the pollution, but not otherwise.

As a legal matter, one must "assign" responsibility somewhere and there ought to be a political or economic or ethical basis for doing so. What makes such an assignment so difficult is that, as Coase points out, there are often joint costs of a set of adjacent economic activities, and we need a larger perspective to assess the impact of various arrangements on the total value of production.[13] Western governments have settled on a set of principles that guide actions, but leave many questions unanswered. In the context of environmental externalities, there is widespread acceptance of the polluter-pays principle. A regulation restricting pollution is simply a more efficient way of inducing good behavior than forcing those engaging in pollution to compensate those who have been damaged. As a society, we have decided that individuals and firms should not have the right to emit air and water pollution. (Part of the reason may be that it would be hard to run a system in which individuals were paid *not* to pollute. Everyone who does not pollute might claim that he *could* and would pollute were he not to receive compensation.)

Most governments have decided that society as a whole should not pay compensation for the loss in market value as a result of the passage of a regulation (a so-called regulatory taking). In a sense, government has certain "residual rights" of control—one cannot restrict the ability of government to pursue the public interest.

Particularly problematic are definitions of rights, obligations, and constraints associated with social constructions, such as corporations and intellectual property.[14]

The legal framework affects the consequences of different actions and therefore frames the actions that will be taken.[15] It may do this in dozens of different ways: by criminal law, tax law, direct or indirect regulation, tort law, or by specifications of the rights, privileges, and duties comprising property law. Provisions may be mandatory, discretionary (with discretion given to the prosecutor or administrative authority), or may require action by the affected parties themselves. Penalties may be mandatory, discretionary (with the judge or other official), may be predetermined and fixed, or may vary with the impact of the injurious activity, or may be subject to bargaining by the affected parties. The law could prohibit a factory from polluting—sending the factory owner to jail if, say, his factory's pollution exceeds a critical level. It can impose criminal penalties, as a strong inducement for the factory owner not to engage in activities that inflict harm on others. It may use zoning, not allowing houses to be built in the vicinity of the factory, so that no one will suffer the impacts of the factory's pollution. It might allow houses to be built, specifying that anyone moving in cannot sue the factory owner. Or it can allow the homeowner to sue for compensation for undoing the damage of the pollution. It can require the factory to pay a price for its pollution—and it can take some of the money received to compensate those who might be adversely affected.

Note that the bundle of entitlements we call "property" famously includes the legal privilege to injure (in certain particular ways) other economic actors without paying compensation. For example, I can set up a competing business on my property adjacent to yours even if it puts you out of business and forces you to sell your land.

There is no avoiding making regulatory choices in the design of a property rights regime which determines just how strict or lenient the duties on others will be—have they a duty to *never* trespass or only to avoid trespass absent an emergency? Must they respect your intellectual property no matter what, or might they make "fair use" of it? When, moreover, will the privilege to injure be limited—can I set up a noxious factory adjacent to your home or only a competing business? Though intellectual property rights give one a temporary monopoly power in the use of that knowledge, it does not give one the right to *abuse* that monopoly power by engaging in anticompetitive practices.

Accompanying "rights" are obligations. An owner of land may have the right to use his land, but he may also have the responsibility to make sure that no one uses his land to dump toxic waste that spoils the underlying ground water. Accompanying intellectual property rights is an obligation to disclose information so that others can build on the knowledge. The owner of a telephone company may have an obligation to provide interconnectivity.

Not only can these questions of policy not be avoided; there is, in general, no one best way to resolve them. There are, of course, efficiency arguments for the assignment of responsibilities (as well as rights): the landowner may be in the best position to monitor its usage; it is a natural by-product of other economic activities, including those associated with ensuring the value of the asset. In this view, it is "efficient" to assign to the owner the responsibility to ensure that his property does not become a toxic dumping site.

Under certain idealized circumstances (e.g., the absence of transactions costs), economic efficiency could be achieved under a variety of rules for assigning property rights, and there has developed a tradition that argues that property rights should be assigned in ways that minimize transactions costs. It would be very expensive for each individual to ascertain who might harm him or her by driving recklessly, seek the potential "harmers" out, and compensate them for not harming. It is accordingly more efficient to give individuals the right not to be harmed, imposing the responsibility of not having an accident on the driver. But such assignments have distributional consequences, and there are costs associated with undoing those distributional costs—which also need to be viewed as part of the "transaction costs" of the system. Thus, there is no way of *simply* focusing on efficiency, in a narrowly defined way.

In the end, how property rights are assigned does affect the nature of the equilibrium that emerges. There are (in the language of economists) wealth effects. The nature of the equilibrium that emerges today affects the equilibria that emerge in the future, which society may care about. These are societal choices, made through political processes.

In short, there *are* choices. One cannot simply devolve responsibility for these choices to economists, viewing them as "societal engineers," looking for the "best design" (least cost) system.

THE COMPLEX NATURE OF PROPERTY

We have argued that property rights and obligations are a social construction, and the task facing any society is how to construct the legal system (here we focus on property rights) in a way that advances societal objectives. The task of the social scientist is to help clarify the set of feasible choices and their consequences. One of the objections to the Chicago School's approach is that it slid over the wide range of choices facing every society, pretending that there was only one "choice," which effectively Pareto-dominated all others (i.e. makes all individuals as well or better off than any of the alternatives). We will look at several examples of these choices—in particular, how they are bundled and how rights can be changed.

Alternative mechanisms for "regulating" behavior

The choices individuals make are affected, as we have noted, not just by property rights but also by regulations (which can in fact be viewed simply as restrictions on the use of property and thus as a part of the property rights system) and taxes. All of these change the opportunity set facing firms and individuals in ways that alter their behavior in order to induce behavior that is more congruent with social objectives. A fundamental result of modern economics is that tax policy can accomplish much of what regulatory policy can, i.e., by shaping the returns that individuals reap from various actions, tax policies shape the actions that individuals take. Thus, we see more holistically property rights, regulatory policies, and taxes as alternative instruments for structuring the behavior of individuals, households, firms, NGOs, etc., including their relationships with each other.

To take one example: one can induce individuals not to pollute either by imposing formal regulations, by taxing pollution, or by making individuals pay for the damage done by the pollution, through a liability system.

Once we recognize that what matters are the consequences, it becomes apparent that, indeed, there may be many functionally equivalent ways of achieving the same outcomes. One can have a mandate, say, that all individuals have health insurance. A mandate is a requirement, enforceable either by a large monetary or civil penalty. Assume there were a \$500 fine for *not* having health insurance, and assume health insurance costs \$2000. One could get the equivalent result by imposing a \$500 tax on everyone, but simultaneously, providing a tax credit of up to \$500 for anyone who purchased (qualified) health insurance.

Government can try to shape the behavior of individuals and firms, not only through ex ante interventions (affecting prices or imposing constraints *before* actions are undertaken) but also through ex post actions (imposing penalties *after* certain adverse consequences arise).

One can go even further: one can allow punitive damages, i.e., the wronged party collects more (sometimes much more) than the losses incurred. He is, in effect, rewarded for acting as a "private attorney general." This provides strong incentives to private citizens to enforce the law and strong deterrence to potential offenders.[16]

Indeed, there is an even broader range of social decisions. One can have a system of taxes to induce "good" behavior or a system of regulations to require it; but society can choose to *supplement* such a system with a liability system. Individuals suffering injury may, under certain circumstances, be allowed to sue even though there is a regulatory or tax system in place; or they may not. Regulating the use of tobacco (a poisonous substance) may relieve tobacco companies of the liability for the harm done by their product and their failure to adequately represent those risks, or it may not.

Each of these regimes has distributional and efficiency costs (broadly defined, to include transaction costs).

One of the problems with many liability systems is that they intertwine the design of incentive systems with compensation systems. The liability penalties that are imposed on individuals when they have an accident to compensate those who have been injured generally do not equal the penalties that we might impose if our objective was to induce individuals to take the appropriate amount of care while driving. An argument can be made for the separation of these two functions. Some countries have adopted a no-fault approach to accidents: individuals are compensated for injury, and individuals who drive recklessly are punished. But there is no necessary link between the amount paid by one party and that received by the other.

Liability systems are thus part of a property rights system: The individual has a right not to be injured, and those who injure him in a particular way are required to pay compensation. As we noted in the previous section, which "wrongs" are subject to compensation is a matter of policy. Of course, the choice of property rights regimes affects the "value" of different assets, both by restricting what can be done by the owners of those assets, changing the consequences of their actions, and by restricting what others can do that might affect the value of the asset (or changing their incentives in ways that alter actions that might affect the value of the asset).[17]

In general, the neoliberal orthodoxy has a strong preference for ex ante price interventions. This is based on the belief that markets, in general, work well, and one of the reasons that they work well is the price system, which effectively communicates information in a decentralized economy. Accordingly, if the government is to interfere with the market, it should do so in the most limited way. If prices don't fully reflect social costs, then the best thing to do is to correct prices.[18] There is, in this view, a presumption against broader regulatory interventions.

Modern economic theory has shown that these presumptions are not in fact valid, e.g., when information is imperfect and markets are incomplete, as they always are. Weitzman (1974) long ago showed that in the presence of uncertainty, quantity regulations may be superior to price interventions. Atkinson and Stiglitz (1976) showed that nonlinear taxation was superior to linear taxation when the government faced information constraints and distributive objectives. (For a textbook exposition of these ideas, see Atkinson and Stiglitz, 1980.)

Similarly, consider the presumption discussed earlier against ex ante regulation. Liability systems attempt to alter behavior by inducing individuals to more fully take into account the costs of their actions. With a fully articulated set of liability laws, regulations directed at least at negative externalities would be unnecessary. There would be no negative externalities; they would all be internalized. But such a system is likely to entail high administrative costs. Perhaps the worst example is provided by the US law concerning toxic wastes, where litigation costs represent more than a quarter of the amount spent on clean-up. It is often difficult to ascertain who is to blame for a particular problem (even with a well demarcated and well designed system of "rights"). And sometimes, it is difficult to ascertain how much the individual should be compensated—sometimes no amount of money would really adequately compensate an individual. Thus, in many cases, it is more efficient to rely on a system of ex ante regulations and inducements. Thus, just as the *assignment* of rights can affect transactions costs (as our earlier discussion emphasizes), so does the *mode of enforcement*.

We now turn to the broader issue of the assignment and definition of property rights.

Slicing and dicing property rights

Property rights can be sliced and diced in different ways, and there may be efficiency consequences (e.g., arising from coordination problems) in how property rights are sliced and diced and how they are bundled. In many places, mineral rights have been separated from land-use rights; use rights to land are separated from rights to reassign those rights; air rights can be separated from land rights. In real estate, there are often covenants and rights-of-way, which impose limitations on the sale or use of the asset, and which give rights to others (such a right of passage). Sometimes rights of passage are assigned to particular individuals (such as those living in the neighboring house). Such rights might be transferable. But sometimes such rights are extended to everyone within a wider class.

More broadly, an ownership right in a corporation or other property can entail a right to an income and a *control* right, that is, a right to determine what can be done with the asset, including rights concerning the transferring of rights. But these two sets of rights are not always bundled together. There are, for instance, nonvoting shares, which provide an entitlement to income, but no control rights. But the rights of the voting shares are circumscribed: they may not take actions which are considered "unfair" to minority shareholders or nonvoting shares. (In a world with perfect contracting, the minority shareholders would know what actions the majority would take before they bought the shares; restrictions would be imposed to protect the interests of the minority. In reality, there are no such protections; they would be impossible to write, and even more difficult and costly to enforce.[19]) Again, there is no avoiding the necessity for policy *choices* in the design of legal institutions for a market economy.

The meaning of control and ownership

With many different individuals having rights relating to a particular asset, the question arises, who "owns" it? Language can often be misleading: It might be better simply to say that many different individuals have rights, and they, in some sense, jointly own the asset. A well-specified ownership contract would say what happens when there is a conflict, when two different individuals ("owners") have different views about what should be done. Often, though, contracts are ambiguous (a point to which we will return later), and the courts are left to resolve such conflicts on the basis of a set of principles and precedents. It should be clear that the way the legal system resolves such conflicts has efficiency and distributive consequences.

To avoid conflict, a particular party sometimes has "residual rights to control," i.e., rights not specified to others belonging to that party. The person with those rights is sometimes described as *the* owner.[20] Typically, he has the right to transfer that right of control to others (the right to sell), but sometimes that right is circumscribed (the owner of a cooperative apartment can only sell it to someone who has been approved by the board of the cooperative). When he transfers his rights, though, the rights of the others in the asset continue.[21]

The problem with the concept of "residual rights to control" is that it is actually very difficult to specify completely what is meant by fully specified control rights (and therefore, what is meant by fully specified property rights); governments, at all levels, have some control rights in the sense they restrict the kinds of actions that firms can undertake. In the case of "real assets," there are a myriad of constraints on the use of property, imposed by zoning laws, the Endangered Species Act,[22] etc. One can think of regulations more generally as constraints on property rights: they restrict and limit what individuals or firms can do with the assets that are under their control. Of course, every private contract imposes constraints on what individuals and firms can do. When a bank extends a loan, it can insist that a firm take certain action—the firm may have little choice but to accept these demands, especially if it has debt obligations that could force it into bankruptcy. (Advocates of unfettered markets often talk as if regulations are a deprivation of property rights. But regulations—restrictions on how property can be used—are better thought of as an essential part of the definition of the specification of property rights. Criticism of regulation should not be that it has deprived someone of a rightful property right, but rather that a particular restriction interferes with desirable outcomes. In the case of appropriately designed environmental regulations, it is clear that they lead to *better* outcomes.)

Ownership, as we have said, typically refers to the party that has residual rights—given all of these other constraints, there may still be some scope of choice, and the "owner" has the right to make a choice among this set. The issue, of course, is often not what actions are "allowed," but the consequences of particular actions. There may be a law that prohibits polluting, but the firm can do it anyway if it pays a fine. More generally, others affect the opportunity set of firms, and thus affect what the firm chooses to do.

One aspect of "ownership" is the right to sell, but an individual's willingness to exercise that right is affected by the returns he gets from the sale. A capital gains tax thus reduces an individual's incentives to sell, though he retains the "right" to do so. A 100 percent tax on the receipts from a sale would be almost the functional equivalent of a prohibition on sale (not quite, because individuals might face obligations from the ownership of an asset, and selling would free owners of those obligations).

By the same token, the legal/regulatory framework not only affects behaviors of private parties, but also the behavior of government authorities. A law that requires the government to compensate firms for "regulatory takings," for the decrease in the value of an asset as a result of a change in regulation, affects government's incentives for regulating. Those who advocate regulatory takings provisions do so knowing that government is less likely to adopt environmental regulations if it has budgetary consequences. Discussions of regulatory takings highlight the intertwining of property rights and incentives, and the complexity of control.

Corporate governance: shareholder capitalism vs stakeholder capitalism

Neoliberal legal doctrines are often associated with a particular form of corporate governance called shareholder capitalism. Corporations are told to maximize shareholder value. That, it is argued, will lead to economic efficiency and societal well-being. There are a large number of derivative propositions that follow. Rules governing takeovers should be designed to ensure shareholder value.

The legal framework on corporate governance provides a case study for what is wrong with the Chicago view. The belief that firms should maximize shareholder value is a corollary of the simplistic competitive equilibrium model underpinning their analysis. The logic is plain: in the simple neoclassical paradigm, workers and the suppliers of other factors have a horizontal supply curve at the competitive market price, so that the actions of the firm have no effect on them. The actions of the firm only affect the residual returns. Thus, the controller of residual rights, in exercising those rights, only affects his own well-being; and that is why allowing him to do so naturally results in economic efficiency. Even within these narrow confines, the result that shareholder capitalism leads to economic efficiency is not in general true. It requires that there be a full set of risk markets (Arrow-Debreu securities) extending for all dates into the future (Grossman and Stiglitz 1977). Indeed, in general, different shareholders will not even agree on what the firm should do to maximize their own interests (Grossman and Stiglitz 1980).

The simple principle that firms should maximize shareholder value (a seeming assignment of property rights to the firm's shareholders) doesn't fully answer relevant legal questions: Whose *judgment* and in what time horizon? Should management be allowed to decide what is in the long-run interests of shareholders? Should the firm be put up for auction continuously, allowing whoever bids the most to be the "owner"? What restrictions should be placed on management, whose actions might adversely affect what bidders might be willing to pay? Or should deference be given to management and its judgment of what is in the long-term interests of shareholders? Economic theory again provides some (limited) guidance: only under very restrictive conditions will (unrestricted) takeover mechanisms be effective in ensuring efficiency, or even stock market value maximization (Stiglitz 1972; Grossman and Hart 1980, 1981).

We have a whole set of laws affecting the behavior of management within corporations. With imperfect information, restrictions on conflicts of interest may lead to increased efficiency. To be sure, in some of these cases, contract terms (with penalties for breach) might do as well, but there are savings in transactions costs[23] in having standard contracts.[24] Such laws would seem to benefit shareholders and bondholders, at the expense of managers. More generally, different rules for corporate governance can have markedly different effects on different stakeholders. Germany's model of stakeholder capitalism is, in many ways, as effective as America's "shareholder capitalism," but workers seem better protected. There is less divisiveness.

We have argued that one cannot defend the "shareholder capitalism" model of corporate governance on the basis of economic theory. But those who argue for shareholder capitalism, as if it is the only natural form of capitalism, make another mistake. They forget that the limited liability corporation (like intellectual property, or property rights more generally) is a social construction with no inherent rights. Governments, in creating these "artifices," can impose any set of constraints they wish. They can, for instance, impose constraints on the governance structure of the corporations. Society grants limited liability, which means that, necessarily, incentives are distorted (the corporations do not bear the full downside consequences of their actions).

Especially in large corporations, control rights are ambiguous, but even if they were well defined and "assigned" to shareholders, there is a problem: If shareholders are dispersed, then the fact that good management of the company is a public good (i.e., all shareholders benefit) means that each shareholder will underinvest in monitoring. Effective control will reside elsewhere, in management and in banks, whose interests may differ markedly from those of the shareholders and workers. It is inevitable that governments will want to ensure that the decisions taken by the firm advance the interests of stakeholders (and society more broadly), and not just those who control the assets.[25] This means that government will want to impose constraints on corporations, on how they make decisions, including how control of the assets is changed. That is why the issues discussed later in this volume on corporate rights are so important.

We emphasized at the beginning of our discussion of property rights that actions taken by any individual affect others. Corporations are large collectivities of individuals, and not surprisingly, managerial decisions affect not just shareholders, but a host of other "stakeholders"—bondholders, workers, suppliers, customers, those in the communities in which it operates. That this is so can be said to reflect a "market failure," but it is worthwhile to ask more specifically why this is the case. Part of the reason is that there is incomplete contracting and incomplete insurance. A worker who goes to work for a firm does not know fully the jobs that will be assigned to him, how difficult or unpleasant the tasks, the hours that he might have to work. The firm might not know either (i.e., there may or may not be asymmetries of information). There are contingencies that cannot be perfectly anticipated. But different actions by the firm can affect the likelihood of more or less pleasant contingencies occurring—and therefore affecting the well-being of the worker. For example, the firm's actions may increase the likelihood that he will be redundant or the worker may have invested in (firm-specific) human capital. But there is no insurance against the destruction of the capital's value should he be fired. Laws protecting worker rights often recognize the importance of asymmetries in bargaining power that disadvantage workers. A society in which firms are able, without restraint, to take advantage of that asymmetry may not only be inequitable, it may be less efficient. Bondholders are aware that the firm may take actions that adversely affect their claims on the firm, and that is why there are typically bond covenants. But it is well recognized that these covenants only constrain a fraction of the possible actions that the firm might undertake to adversely affect the value of bonds.

Actions of firms—including subsequent contracts with third parties—affect the well-being of those who have previously signed (implicit or explicit) contracts. Different governments take different positions on how these externalities might best be dealt with, e.g., through a voice on the boards of directors, restrictions on the kinds of contractual arrangements that can be undertaken, etc., with different distributive consequences.

As an example, some governments require collective action clauses in bonds, which allow a qualified majority (say 85 percent of bondholders) to restructure. It is recognized that there may be circumstances in which renegotiation (a new bond) is desirable, but that in such circumstances, a small minority can hold up what might otherwise be a Pareto-superior renegotiation, demanding a ransom. On the other hand, the ability of a (qualified) majority to restructure the debt contract means that they can, in principle, redesign the contract in ways that work markedly to the disadvantage of the minority, which may not be simply holding up the majority, but may have legitimate differences in interests and perspectives. Regrettably, it is difficult to write a simple legal framework that protects against one abuse without opening up the window to another.

There is another set of "externalities" that may arise, which relate to signaling. Bankruptcy provisions may be used to signal one's likelihood of going bankrupt. Firms that have a low probability of going bankrupt may signal that that is the case by imposing heavy penalties on themselves should they go bankrupt. The resulting signaling equilibrium is not Pareto-efficient. Signals are costly, and in general, signaling equilibria are inefficient. Governments may enforce a better equilibrium by eliminating the scope for signaling, e.g., by imposing a standardized bankruptcy regime.[26]

Finally, it is impossible (and even if technically possible, prohibitively costly) for contracts to anticipate every contingency. All contracts are incomplete, and there is an important role for government to specify what happens in unanticipated contingencies—a set of "defaults" that greatly simplify the writing of contracts.[27]

In addition to these externalities, there are a host of more widely discussed macroeconomic externalities, where decisions by firms have social costs that they do not appropriately take into account (just as firms do not appropriately take into account environmental externalities). For instance, even without unemployment insurance benefits, firms' decisions concerning layoffs do not, in fact, lead to Pareto efficiency.[28] In unemployment systems that are not experience-rated, it is obvious that when a firm lays off an individual, it imposes a social cost on others; but the result holds even when unemployment insurance premiums are based on experience. When a plant closes, workers lose not only their jobs, but, if the firm is a large local employer, property values decrease. In making the decision to close the plant, these externalities are seldom taken into account—and would be disregarded by a profit-maximizing firm.[29]

Not only is it the case that managers in modern corporations often have effective control, they have the incentives and ability to take actions that enhance their well-being at the expense of shareholders and the rest of society. (This is sometimes called the *agency* problem, and can be viewed in part as an externality—their actions have effects on other stakeholders, which they may not fully take into account.)[30] What has emerged in the United States is more akin to managerial capitalism than "shareholder capitalism," with wide latitude given to management, which has resisted even shareholders having a say in pay. Courts have given management wide deference in interpreting what is in the interests of shareholders. It is clear that American-style managerial capitalism often does not serve shareholders and bondholders well, let alone others in society. Rules and regulations limit shareholders' latitude in a variety of ways, e.g., voting, say in pay, poison pills, golden parachutes, behavior of management, the extent of their control, and their ability to exercise that control to advance their interests over those of shareholders or other stakeholders. Such rules and regulations have both efficiency and distributive consequences.

Different countries have chosen markedly different systems of corporate governance. In thinking about what system is right going forward, China should be aware of the range of alternatives. Though the US system is often described as if it were "shareholder" capitalism, it is in fact a system of managerial capitalism. While the theoretical underpinnings for shareholder capitalism are weak, those for managerial capitalism are even weaker. The system of corporate governance that has evolved in the United States leaves much to be desired.

Security of property rights

We have emphasized that the very nature of what is meant by property—rights, obligations, privileges, and constraints—is defined by the government. And just as there cannot be fully specified contracts (defining what each party will do in every contingency), property (with its rights, obligations, and constraints) cannot be fully specified. New contingencies, not fully anticipated, will arise, and decisions will have to be made about whether the rights, obligations, and constraints need to be altered in response. It would be inefficient to totally bind the hand of government, to say that it cannot change the rules of the game, the regulations that affect what individuals can do. (Such a stance would also imply that governments could not change taxes, since that affects the "rights" of what individuals can extract for themselves from their assets.)

The world (and our knowledge of the world) changes. This will necessitate changes in the rules and regulations that govern how resources can be used.[31] It would be wrong to freeze the rights and responsibilities at any moment of time. "Excesses" of property rights (i.e., making it inordinately difficult to change the rights, obligations, constraints, taxes, etc.) can adversely affect efficiency. Assigning land rights to the commune in a way that could not be reversed would have impaired the reforms that set off China's march to a market economy. We want to be able to impose new restrictions when circumstances or knowledge change.

On the other hand, if rights and responsibilities are always changing, then there will be unnecessarily high levels of uncertainty about the value of any asset. Investments will be impaired and people couldn't reliably contract. It would also be inefficient *not* to bind the hand of government to some extent. The question is where to draw the line—getting the balance right.[32] There might be several places to draw the line that might yield efficiency, but with different winners and losers. Hence the extent to which the hand of government should be bound is a question of policy.

Two examples illustrate. Before society was aware of the dangers of ground water pollution, there was no need to impose restraints on the use of land as a toxic waste dump. Once the danger becomes clear, it is imperative that constraints be imposed.

Earlier, we referred to the takings movement that has demanded that government compensate property owners for changes in regulations. Adopting such an approach would be a change in the property rights regime, for the owner of a polluting factory would know that the cost of individuals suing him are such that he could pollute with impunity. It would, in effect, be a transfer of wealth to the owner from the rest of society. So too, the rules governing class action suits could make it either easier (less expensive) or more difficult to sue. Thus, *any* change in the legal framework has effects on the value of property rights. Government needs to be aware of these effects, and it should be cautious in making such changes. But when there are large enough changes in the world or in our knowledge of the world, it would be wrong not to change.

Any government action or change in government action can affect property values and rights, with complex distributive changes. We have noted that governments have a variety of ways (short of outright expropriation) of imposing restrictions and taxes that, in a sense, deprive the "owner" of his property rights. They decrease the (expected present discounted) value of the asset (to the owner). There are always, of course, questions about the extent to which they are likely to do so. If the increase in a tax or a new regulation was anticipated, then there will be no change in market value; and indeed, failure to enact the tax or regulation as anticipated would lead to an increase in market value. We have argued that no government will (or should) fully circumscribe its ability to adopt legislation that will allow it to respond to new information and changing circumstances. If a firm has been polluting groundwater, poisoning others, in a way that was unnoticed (and perhaps even not known), once it becomes known, it should be stopped—and it is not obvious that it should be compensated for *not* poisoning others. The building of a subway increases some property values and decreases others. We typically neither compensate the losers nor appropriate but a fraction of the gains of the winners. The passage of the Endangered Species Act (which restricts the use of land when it adversely affects an endangered species) may have reduced the value of some property. It may have increased the value of some neighboring properties. But the next set of owners who buy the land knowing that the legislation had been passed and assuming (along with the market) that it would stay in place, would be affected in the opposite way if it were to be repealed. The new owner would get a windfall gain, his neighbor (enjoying the preservation of the land next door), a windfall loss.

Insecurity of property rights also arises from private actions. The value of a house may be dependent on the view of the ocean or the peacefulness of the neighborhood, but someone else can build and obstruct the view, or someone with noisy children may move next door. In short, there is as much private interference with property as there is public—all the other people's rights and privileges that may, or may not, be exercised.

Property rights legislation must balance out the costs and benefits of any changes (including the costs of *not* changing) and of the rules that govern how the changes are made. In the United States, recent trends have emphasized paying more attention to the costs (and possible resulting inequities) of changing regulations—though we suspect that this is motivated little by an analysis of the economic costs; legislation forcing those proposing new regulations to quantify the costs and benefits is intended to make the process of adopting new regulations more difficult, reducing the scope especially for environmental and safety regulations.

Legitimacy of property and security of property rights

There are many countries where questions have been raised about the legitimacy of existing ownership claims. Some have advocated that such issues be put aside; it is more important to have secure property rights. Hoff and Stiglitz (2004a, 2004b, 2007) have argued, however, that it is not possible for any society to provide such security. So long as there is a widespread view in society that such rights were obtained illegitimately, there will always be political pressures for property rights reform. And no government can fully bind successors (though they can make it more difficult or more costly for successor governments). One reason for having "good" property rights laws (widely accepted as "legitimate," and not the result of special interests) accompanied by good judicial procedures (see below) is that it enhances the chances that ownership claims will be viewed as legitimate and that property rights will be viewed as more secure. The issue has played out in many transition economies, which have faced difficulties in the initial (re)assignment of property rights. Should they restore property as of 1944, 1945, or 1946? Often, there were series of land redistributions; in each, land changed hands. The date selected for restitution could have large effects on the well-being of particular individuals. Russia is facing another problem: many of the assets held by oligarchs were obtained via methods that were questionable at best. Should one ignore how the property was acquired? In most societies, a person who buys stolen property may still be forced to return it to the original owner. There is a responsibility imposed on the buyer to ensure that the property rights of the seller are "legitimate." Much of the property of oligarchs can be viewed as stolen from the state. But throughout the world, privatizations were often conducted with a certain degree of "illegitimacy," e.g., involving some degree of corruption.

This raises another difficult issue: if we trace property throughout history, there usually comes a point at which questions can be raised about legitimacy. Most of the land in the US was taken from Native American tribes using a variety of dubious methods. Advocates of "strong" property rights rarely reflect on the legitimacy of their own claims.

China faces a similar problem; questions can be raised about the origins of the wealth of many individuals. If their property rights are not secure, then they will have an incentive to take their wealth out of the country as fast as possible (a problem evident in Russia). If they are given full security, it would in effect be sanctioning socially destructive behavior. China must resolve these issues as it defines its property rights regime.

Enhancing the security of property rights

Some "law and development" scholars have given primacy to assigning clear property rights. Failure to develop is ascribed to a lack of property rights. Putting aside the grandiosity of the claim—some countries have grown rapidly even with seemingly imprecisely defined property rights—a formalization of rights, as part of the process of providing more secure property rights, is an example of a change to a legal system that can have profound distributive consequences. In the status quo (*before* "precisely" defining property rights), there are certain outcomes to economic interactions. They may not be perfectly predictable to every potential participant in the market, but there are still patterns that can be ascertained. There is, in effect, an existing set of "property rights," which may not be easily understood by everyone, but are understood by some. While there may be some ambiguity about such property rights before they have been "assigned," it is likely that some ambiguity (as we have emphasized throughout this chapter) will remain *after*. Indeed, formal rights are not clear to everyone either—they are clearer to some market actors than to others; the clarity to foreigners may differ from that to those for whom kinship and informal arrangements are well understood. It might accordingly be better to say that formalizing rights reallocates transaction costs (and, as always, such reallocations have distributive consequences).

Assigning property rights typically (or, I should say, inevitably) means a *reassignment*. And this is also especially true in circumstances where property rights are ill defined, so that it is hard to determine the effective recipient of the returns to the assets or who has effective residual control. In other words, the "clear" assignment of property rights is almost never just a conversion of *de facto* rights into *de jure* rights. And a conversion from *de facto* to *de jure* is itself a reassignment, in that there is a change in terms of how rights are known, remedies for violation, modes of enforcement—the relationship of the "owner" to many people has changed, and indeed, that is precisely the point of doing it. That is why property rights legislation is often so contentious. If it were just a matter of clarifying existing rights, it would presumably be a Pareto improvement, simply because it would lower transactions costs. De Soto (2000) presumes that it is easy to figure out whom to title from customary patterns. If it were so easy, then almost by definition, the property rights question with which he is concerned would not have arisen.

Legal transplants

The property rights movement is an example of an attempt to transplant a legal system that may work well in one context to another. "Legal transplanting"—taking the legal frameworks developed for one country to another—often encounters problems. Another reason (besides those implicit in the previous paragraph) is that there are typically a host of implied rules and understandings that govern the interpretation of language and practice. Even if the formal language is transplanted, the accompanying interpretations are not. What would the parties to the contract reasonably have understood by the words of the contract? What is meant by "due care"?

FROM COASE TO DE SOTO AND BEYOND

The above analysis implies that the slogan that there *should* be well-defined property rights is empty. It is impossible to have perfectly defined property rights; there may be large costs associated with further refinements (removing further ambiguities); it does not specify how rights (and obligations) might change as circumstances and knowledge change; and saying that there should be well-defined property does not say how questions about the relative strength of various rights, duties, and privileges should be answered, e.g., when various rights come into conflict. And how one answers these questions makes a difference.

Those like de Soto (see, e.g., de Soto 2000), who seem to suggest that the most important problem facing developing countries is the assignment of well-defined property rights, fail to compare their reassignment to the preexisting, often informal, social and institutional arrangements, and to assess the distributive consequences of the change. Moreover, they offer little guidance as to how the various choices about how to fashion a property regime ought to be made—how strong or weak to make the various rights, duties, and privileges. Nor do they tend to recognize the importance in mature property regimes of *general standards*, such as "reasonable" or "fair use," which often are understood by reference to the informal arrangements and expectations of economic actors themselves.

It is, accordingly, wrong to think that simply assigning property rights will solve complex social problems. The devil is in the details—*how* are they to be assigned and enforced, *which* rights and obligations are to be included, *what* excuses and limitations are to be recognized? How to redefine property rights when circumstances (knowledge) change, as they inevitably do?

Property rights and credit markets

The one inefficiency that assigning land property rights is often said to solve is credit market imperfections. Using land as collateral facilitates the development of credit markets, and thus improves overall economic efficiency. But giving title to land will not necessarily give rise to a land market, especially one of a thickness that can support its use as collateral. Moreover, local courts may be loath to turn over land to creditors in the event of a default. And there are other ways of improving credit markets, e.g., through the revolving credit schemes used by Grameen Bank and other microcredit institutions, as Chapter 3 points out—schemes that, at least in some circumstances have performed far better than the "property rights" approach. In addition, one can collateralize the *produce* of the land, even if one can't collateralize land itself. It may well be that preexisting social arrangements offer alternative methods for collateralizing informally recognized entitlements that are more effective than the formal system is likely to be. Moreover, formal titling may well effect a redistribution of land, often within the family (from wives to husbands)—in ways which may or may not enhance efficiency.

Imperfect property rights may suffice

Changing the relationship between farmers and their land played an important role in China's success. Moving to the household responsibility system did not give farmers land "ownership."[33] More accurately, we should say that it gave them some rights that they did not have before, but it did not give them other rights (e.g., the right to sell the land to others). It did give them the fruits of their labor, and this had an enormous consequence for productivity. It achieved much of what could have been achieved by full land titling. Individuals could not borrow, using their land as collateral, to buy seeds and fertilizer. But this lacuna was at least partially filled in by government and other arrangements, which ensured the availability of high-quality seeds and some access to credit. Over the longer run, full land titling might have resulted in many farmers borrowing beyond their ability to repay, losing their land, and creating a new class of landless workers—with obvious implications for inequality, but also for efficiency (with an increase in agency costs resulting from landlessness).[34] In the medium term, there were some efficiency issues: lack of security in land ownership may lead to under-investment in caring for the land. Inability to transfer land may mean that land is not deployed in the best way. But as China's development has progressed, one more issue has arisen: who should reap the benefits of industrialization, with the associated large increases in the value of land near cities? If it is given to the farmer farming that land, it is simply a windfall capital gain, unrelated to his own efforts. He benefits at the expense of others whose land was not so well situated. At the same time, if his land is taken away without adequate compensation, that too seems unfair. But then, what is adequate compensation? Enough to buy a similar plot, of equal quality, elsewhere? But the farmer has ties to his community, and there are high social costs of removing him. There are no easy answers to these essentially distributive questions, though gradually societal consensus may emerge. If the choice is between giving money to the poor farmer or to a corrupt politician or a rich land developer, the farmer's claims seem more justified. Today, land titling is seen not just as a means of assuring efficient land usage, but also as a form of protection for poor farmers, ensuring that they get a larger fraction of the benefits that emerge from growth and urbanization.

Distributive consequences of property rights assignments and alternative approaches

By the same token, assigning property rights to the lords in the seventeenth-century enclosure movements may have been one way of avoiding the tragedy of the commons, the problem of overgrazing. But most communities have found more equitable ways of overcoming the tragedy of commons, e.g., by restricting the usage of the commons, for instance by regulation. There were large distributive consequences of the enclosure. It is a political and ethical judgment whether these large distributive changes (typically adverse, from the perspective of equality) were justified by the efficiency gains. (Economists may have simply played into the hands of the powerful, giving them an excuse, a justification, for their land grab.)

Many contend that something analogous is going on today, the enclosure of common knowledge, its privatization through unbalanced intellectual property regimes.[35]

Why less restrained property rights may lead to lower efficiency

The fallacious nature of the simplistic property rights school is deeper, because it may not even result in enhanced efficiency.[36] Consider the consequences of allowing individuals to sell (without restriction) their land and to borrow against the land. To answer this question, one can construct a dynamic model of land ownership, which takes into account the various conditions under which individuals sell or buy land, e.g., illnesses of parents for which there is a medicine that is available, but for which the public sector will not pay. There are large societal costs of inequalities in land ownership—the agency costs associated with a disparity between labor and land ownership. (There are other costs as well—the landless face a much higher degree of insecurity.) Such a dynamic model could describe the incidence of landlessness, the consequences of which in turn may depend on the pace of job creation in the urban sector, and the levels of education in the rural sector.

One could contrast the outcomes of this system of unrestricted property rights with a system in which individuals are allowed to mortgage a fraction of this year's output, but not the land. There would be a short-run static inefficiency, arising from capital market imperfections (the extent of which might depend on other attributes of the capital market), but this inefficiency might be much less than the long-run inefficiency associated with the greater agency costs arising from more extensive landlessness that would emerge in a system with unfettered rights to sell. Long-run output in the system of unrestricted property rights might be markedly lower than in the alternative system. While unfettered rights to sell might lead to enhanced efficiency in a world without agency costs, it may lead to reduced efficiency in a world with agency costs[37] (Braverman-Stiglitz 1989).

PROPERTY RIGHTS MORE BROADLY DEFINED

The role of legal frameworks in shaping rights and responsibilities—and behavior—should now be clear. The discussion so far has focused on property rights, broadly defined to include intellectual property rights and the "rights" and obligations of other social constructs such as corporations. These broadly defined property rights extend to contracts (what are enforceable contracts, the rules for interpreting disputes when they arise, penalties that can be imposed when contracts are abrogated) and bankruptcy laws (what happens when individuals or firms cannot meet the obligations that they have undertaken in a credit contract).

Labor rights

Modern economics emphasizes that the most important asset in modern societies is not financial or physical capital, but human capital. Society puts all kinds of restrictions on the use of human capital—e.g., on the set of admissible labor contracts and how they can be enforced. Workers must receive a minimum wage and they cannot sell themselves into bondage. Governments also enforce minimal working conditions. In China, there is another important set of restrictions on the mobility of labor, called the Hukou System, which is discussed in Chapter 15. Individual decisions about where to live affect others, and so it is natural that society might try to regulate those decisions.[38] Moving into a crowded city with well-paid jobs and public amenities benefits the individual, but may have adverse effects on both the community from which he comes and the community to which he goes. It may lead to excess population and fiscal burdens (to provide adequate education, health, and transportation) in the latter and insufficient population (to maintain essential services and the tax base to support them) in the former. At the same time, restrictions on labor mobility may create economic inefficiencies *narrowly defined*, i.e., labor may not be used in a way that contributes optimally to economic output, with labor productivity in a city being much higher than in the rural area from which the migrant comes. Moreover, the system contributes to inequality, with migrants who are essential for the country's growth being treated as second-class citizens, with their children not entitled to public education and other public services,[39] and with a risk of social problems arising out of the peculiar structure to family life that often results when the family stays behind, and the wage earners migrate temporarily. Reforming this system remains a priority in China's next stage of transition to a market economy.

By the same token, many laws and regulations arise to protect individuals (especially as workers and consumers) against the abuse of market power or, more generally, to enhance the efficiency of the market, when there is some other form of market failure.

Social rights

The Universal Declaration of Human Rights brought to the fore the importance of another set of *economic* rights, affecting access to certain goods, that follow simply from the fact that an individual is a member of a particular community (a citizen of a particular nation state). The constitutions and legal frameworks in different countries have elaborated, extended, and helped to define the scope of these rights. They include rights pertaining to education, health, and minimum living standards for both workers and retirees. As in other areas that have been discussed, the flip side of a set of rights is a set of responsibilities. Resources do not come freely. A set of rights to access certain goods is inextricably accompanied by obligations on others to pay for those goods and perhaps by the recipients to fulfill certain conditions. The link between these rights and conventional "property rights" is highlighted by discussions about the provision of these goods as being part of a "social contract." Some of the key institutional aspects of these sets of rights are taken up in Chapters 13 and 14.

We have emphasized that any assignment of rights has both efficiency and distribution consequences. Neither can be ignored; neither has primacy over the other. One key aspect of social rights is that such rights have important impacts on different generations: guaranteeing higher incomes for the elderly imposes obligations on those working, and may reduce resources available for the young. (See in particular Chapter 14.) These issues become particularly important when age structures change—as they are in China. The one-child policy combined with advances in health extending longevity is quickly leading to an aging population. China is the one country that appears to be growing old before it grows rich. Environmental/natural resource regulation, while it affects the quality of life in China today, also has important implications for intergenerational equity and efficiency which we were unfortunately not able to pursue in this volume.

HAYEK AND THE "SECOND GENERATION" CHICAGO SCHOOL

The neoliberal law and economics (the Chicago School) focused on the design of institutions to ensure economic efficiency. Nonmarket institutions were explained in part as helping to ensure efficiency.[40] There is another "conservative" tradition, derived not so much from neoclassical economics, which focuses on equilibrium models with antecedents in classical physics, as from Hayek, with antecedents in evolutionary biology. The design of an economic system should facilitate growth and change. It too focuses on "efficiency," but often economic objectives are seen as secondary to a broader objective of individual fulfillment, and this necessitates individuals having "freedom" to pursue their own desires and ambitions.

In many ways, this approach is consistent with some of the perspectives in this book. We have emphasized how institutional arrangements affect not just what happens today but how society will evolve. We have argued that one needs to go beyond a narrow emphasis on economic efficiency toward broader conceptions of the nature of society and people and how individuals are shaped by social (institutional) arrangements.

There are several problems, however, with the Hayekian perspective. Focusing on the narrower economic conception, there is, in fact, no theory that unfettered markets will facilitate "efficient" evolution, whatever that might mean. While evolutionary models have not been the object of the careful kind of scrutiny to which the equilibrium models discussed in previous sections have been subjected, it is already clear that many "market failures" are as relevant to evolutionary behavior as they are to equilibrium behavior. A firm that has, for instance, high long-run growth potential may be wiped out by a macroeconomic downturn; it cannot borrow against its long-run profit potential to tide it over its current difficulties. Firms that are weeded out in crises may be just as efficient as those that survive; the main difference may be their choice of financial structures (debt-equity ratios), which may have little to do with their real dynamic potential.[41]

There are at least two problems with the broader Hayekian perspective. First, one individual's freedom may impinge on the rights of others. One individual's right to smoke may take away another individual's right to not die from second-hand smoke. Externalities constitute one of the main reasons for collective action. A broad affirmation of "freedom" is far too vague to resolve questions about whose ox must be gored as choices are made about the trade-offs inherent in any legal regime.

There is another reason for collective action: through collective action, in many cases, in principle, all individuals *can* be made better off, and in practice, most might be made better off, e.g., through collective expenditures on public goods. To be sure, forcing individuals to pay taxes may impinge on their "freedom," but if they were being completely honest they would agree that the benefits they receive more than compensate.

There is a final problem, then, with the Hayekian perspective, perhaps the most important. One individual's "fulfillment" may come only at the expense of constraints imposed on others, not just because of externalities, but because the realization of an individual's potential requires expenditures (on education, food, health care) that the individual may not be able to afford himself. To finance these, taxes must be imposed on others.

Political economy

The focus on *change* is picked up in another strand of what I loosely call the Chicago School. Political decisions are viewed as endogenous. Decisions today (about institutions, or about the distribution of income, or about policies) affect decisions in the future. A decision today about the voting rule (whether a majority is required, or a supermajority for making a particular decision) affects the decisions that will be made in the future. Each decision has to be evaluated for its future consequences, and the most important decisions are those that affect decision-making processes.

Recent discussions of transition from communism to the market have argued that the assignment of control (property) rights, even before there is a clear rule of law that specifies how those rights might be used or abused, will lead to the adoption of a rule of law, with more clearly specified property rights. Hoff and Stiglitz (2004a, 2004b, 2007) have argued, to the contrary, that the way control rights were assigned (under shock therapy, rapid privatization) as well as specific policies that were adopted (high interest rates, capital market liberalization) undermined the demand for the rule of law and help explain why, in so many of the former Soviet countries, a rule of law has not emerged.

Adaptive frameworks

The evolutionary approach rightly stresses change. Just as no contract can fully anticipate every contingency that the parties to the contract may face, no law can fully anticipate all the disputes that might arise. (If the law could anticipate all of these contingencies, so presumably could the parties.[42]) These concerns are especially important for China, which has an economy with distinctive characteristics that is changing rapidly. It can learn from the problems facing other economies, but inevitably some of the issues are *sui generis*.

Problems arise when society and the economy change in ways that make the legal (and other aspects of the institutional) infrastructure inappropriate and unable to deal effectively with new situations. That is why one of the most important features of a good legal framework is adaptability and flexibility, as we noted earlier. At the same time, there is a cost: excessively frequent changes give rise to legal uncertainty. And the frameworks that allow for flexibility often have their own problems. Ordinary legislation requires broad consensus (in the US, for instance, a minority can often effectively veto major pieces of legislation.) Powers are delegated to regulatory bodies to enact regulations that respond to the changing situations. But the regulatory bodies are often captured by special interests, in particular those they are supposed to be regulating.

Some advocate self-regulation as a more flexible alternative. But it is hard for an industry group to reflect adequately the interests of its customers or other parties that might be injured by its actions.[43] (The problems were brought to the fore by the difficulties at the New York Stock Exchange and the attempts at bank self-regulation, embodied in Basel II, which clearly failed so badly.)

There should be flexibility in the degree of flexibility and adaptability, accompanied by regular review processes that highlight problems in the institutional/legal infrastructure, that allow some changes to the regulatory framework under the aegis of a regulatory agency, but which submit more fundamental changes to political processes.[44]

China, in its development strategy has been sensitive to the necessity of this kind of pragmatism. But as China moves to the next stage of its transition, more formal institutional arrangements will have to be adopted to regulate its growing, and growingly complex, economy. Such arrangements will inevitably circumscribe some of the flexibility that might be achieved by more ad hoc approaches. The institutional designers will, however, have to pay careful attention to preserving adequate flexibility to the rapid changes going on, both inside China and in the world around it.

DISTRIBUTIVE CONCERNS

The Chicago/neoliberal School emphasized the role of property rights and other institutions in promoting efficiency. But institutions (and especially those relating to legal structures) have often served another function: they have overtly distributive consequences.

There has long been an overtone of "social justice" by those outside of the Chicago School, emphasizing the importance of the rule of law, which historically circumscribed the ability of the king to act capriciously against the nobles. But institutions and "the rule of law" have also been used to maintain existing inequalities. We have already discussed how the seventeenth-century enclosure movement was more about redistribution of wealth than an increase in efficiency: there were alternative ways in which the tragedy of the commons could have been avoided without the distributional consequences of the enclosure movement. The current movement for the privatization of knowledge may have its roots more in a movement to increase incomes of certain corporations that are dependent on intellectual property than in enhancing innovation. Privatizing knowledge may actually retard innovation. (And if it were primarily concerned with incentives, it would have provided more incentives for the preservation of biodiversity and greater protection of traditional knowledge.) The rule of law was used to maintain racial segregation and economic suppression in the American South. The rule of law enabled banks to engage in predatory lending, and then to foreclose upon their properties.

Whatever rules are adopted will have distributive consequences. If redistribution were costless, this itself might not be of that much concern: the consequences could always be undone by lump sum redistributions. But, as we have seen, efficiency and equity concerns cannot be easily separated.[45]

Matters are worse: often the reason particular rules and regulations and institutions persist is that they have distributive effects that could not be achieved (or achieved easily) in other ways. (This is related to the earlier point: there is always an implicit set of property rights, including entitlements, and a change in the legal framework accordingly inevitably has distributive consequences. One of the problems with formalizing property rights that exist is that by making such rights more transparent, they may make them political unacceptable.[46] Alternatively, by formalizing them, they make rights that should be unacceptable seem legitimate and therefore protect and preserve them. In either case, formalization itself has consequences.)

While property rights (and institutions, rules, and regulations more broadly) may be used to protect existing inequalities, they can also be used to advance social justice. One might argue that it might be more efficient to do this through lump sum transfers, but such transfers are not feasible, and especially in developing countries, there is a high opportunity cost to the funds. Social legislation may be a more effective way of targeting. For instance, affirmative action programs circumscribe what businesses can do; they may, as a result, be viewed as redistributing wealth from businesses (and, since some of these costs are passed on to consumers, from society more broadly) to the disadvantaged group. But the benefits that they bring may be far greater than the value of the profits lost by firms or the slight increase in prices consumers might have to pay.[47,48]

Much social and economic legislation (restrictions on businesses employment practices or anticompetitive practices) arises out of a belief that the unfettered market may be, in some sense, "unfair." Much of this is based on the premise that the economy is not really fully competitive; there are many "bargaining" problems, and in the bargains, the poor and the less educated do poorly. There are rents to be divided, and they get a disproportionately small share of these rents. Rules and regulations can change the outcome, and while there may be some efficiency costs, the redistributive benefits outweigh these efficiency costs.[49]

Similarly, if individuals are imperfectly informed, exploitive firms can engage in predatory behavior (as America's banks have done). Theorems about the efficiency of competitive markets do not apply in such situations. Arguments that not allowing firms to engage in such predations will interfere with the dynamism and efficiency of the market economy are simply wrong. To the contrary, imposing such restrictions might lead them to devote their create energy in ways that enhance productivity or engage in other activities that might enhance societal well-being.

In this view, then, how property rights are designed and assigned can make a great deal of difference, and not just for the efficiency of the economy. Land reform, redistributing land from large landlords to peasants, can increase economic efficiency by reducing agency costs. Making it more difficult for government to use its right of eminent domain to take land away from poor peasants, to be used for development projects which may be of more benefit to others, will ensure that they get a larger share of the rents associated with the redeployment of land.

CONCLUDING COMMENTS

In recent decades, there has been important scholarly progress on the relationship among law, economics, and development. Coase played an important role in helping us think about the consequences of alternative assignments of property rights. Unfortunately, the neoliberal legal tradition, especially simplifications that have gained currency in some traditions within economics, neither reflects an understanding of the limitations of markets, the importance of equity, and the constraints and costs of redistributions, nor the conceptual complexities associated with property and property rights.

In the beginning of China's move to a market economy, there was a discussion of the central ingredients required to make a market economy work. Obviously, many ingredients contribute to success. At a conference in Wingspread, Wisconsin, with a delegation from China's Academy of Social Sciences, there was extensive discussion of the relative role of property rights and competition. Ken Arrow and I urged that the focus be on competition.[50] Russia and many other Eastern European countries chose to emphasize property rights, with little attention to broader legal structures, including corporate governance; some Western advisers supported this strategy, arguing that good legal structures would follow naturally. They didn't, and inappropriately designed property rights provided flawed incentives, leading to asset stripping, impeding development. The contrasting performance of China and Russia is, in large measure, a result of these fundamental choices made early on in the process of transition (see Stiglitz 2000b, 2001b; Hoff and Stiglitz 2004b).

While this chapter—and much of this part of the book, focuses on property rights, it is important to keep this issue in perspective. This chapter has emphasized that not only did the neoliberal law and development literature overly simplify what was entailed when they instructed countries to provide and enforce clear property rights, but they also almost surely overemphasized their importance and underemphasized other institutional reforms necessary to create a successful economy.

This chapter echoes several themes that are raised throughout the book. There is no single "best" legal system; law is not just about enhancing efficiency, it is also about promoting other societal values such as social justice; different legal systems, like different assignments of property rights, have different distributive consequences, and reflect the norms of society. But they also affect how society evolves. Changes in the legal system, even attempts to formalize property rights, have distributive consequences. Countries have choices—there is not a single Pareto-dominant approach—and those choices do make a difference, both today and in the future.

These are important lessons for China to take on board as it develops the legal frameworks "with Chinese characteristics" that will enable it to continue its transition to a market economy with Chinese characteristics.

NOTES

1. I am indebted to David Kennedy for his insightful comments on law and economics, and to Mo Ji for her insights on the application of these ideas to China. Earlier versions of this chapter were presented to various meetings of the IPD China Task Force, with the financial support of the Brooks World Poverty Center and Columbia's Committee for Global Thought. I am indebted to the participants in those task forces for helpful comments.
2. As we noted in the introductory chapter, we use the term "neoliberal" orthodoxy and the "Chicago School" interchangeably, as a simplification to describe a complex set of ideas within which there are many variants. We should emphasize that there are many economists and legal scholars at Chicago who do not subscribe to what has come to be called the Chicago School. While the distinctions among the adherents of neoliberal doctrines are important, in practice, the distinctions are typically glided over. In its heyday, these ideas were extraordinarily influential in shaping development policy, especially the set of policies that were pushed by the World Bank and the IMF in the 1980s and early 1990s (Stiglitz 2002a). Interestingly, John Williamson, who best articulated the resulting "Washington Consensus" was himself skeptical of unfettered markets, in particular of unbridled short-term capital flows. See Williamson (1990, 2008), Serra and Stiglitz (2008), and Stiglitz (2008a).
3. A result that was "conjectured" by Adam Smith, in his famous "invisible hand theorem," that the pursuit of self-interest led, as if by an invisible hand, to the efficiency of the market (Smith 1776). Smith himself was more aware of the limitations of this conjecture than his latter-day followers (see, e.g., Rothschild 2001; Kennedy 2009; Phillipson 2010). It was to take 175 years before Arrow and Debreu (1954) and Debreu (1959) ascertained the limited conditions under which Smith's conjecture was correct. The conditions in which markets did not lead to efficient outcomes were referred to as "market failures" (Atkinson and Stiglitz 1980).
4. Moreover, in the presence of wealth effects, there are real consequences of these distributional differences: the equilibrium that emerges may be markedly different under alternative assignments of property rights. Still, different assignments can generate efficient outcomes. Coase himself was not so naïve as to think that transaction costs could be ignored, recognizing that they are ubiquitous. Law and economics scholars have been obsessed with transaction costs, from the first interpretations of Coase by Calebresi through to today's leading figures; see Calebresi and Melamen (1972). For a brief summary and bibliography of the American law and economics literature, see Kennedy and Fisher (2006: 403–13).
5. One of the reasons that little attention was paid to distribution was that it was typically assumed in simplistic Chicago-style models that redistributions were costless. Hence, all that was required was to ensure efficiency. But redistributions are often very costly, and indeed, often don't occur. The rules of the game thus determine the well-being of

different members of society. See Coase (1960), Stiglitz (1994), and the references cited there.

6. The US Supreme Court decision (*Brooke Group Ltd. v. Brown & Williamson Tobacco Corp.*, 509 U.S. 209, 1993) limiting the scope of claims on anticompetitive predatory behavior is illustrative of the influence of the Chicago School in this area.
7. Sometimes advocates of the Chicago School economics argue (simply as a matter of assertion) that these imperfections and their consequences are *quantitatively* insignificant. One of the main results of the modern theory of the economics of information is to show, however, that even a little bit of information imperfection can have a very large effect and change the qualitative properties of the economy. See Stiglitz (2002b). Chicago School economists also often argue that even if markets "fail," governments often fail too. But such failures are not inevitable—in all the most successful economies government played an important role—and the objective of this chapter (and other chapters in this book) is to enhance understanding of what kinds of government interventions and actions are most likely to work.
8. Some go so far as to point out the inefficiencies that result from restricting bonded labor, with an overtone that perhaps even these restrictions should be eliminated.
9. In Chicago School economics, the owner of IPR could act as a perfectly discriminating monopolist, and there would be no inefficiency. But an individual would not have the information required to act as a perfectly discriminating monopolist, and the resulting distortions can be considerable (see, e.g., Stiglitz 1977 for the inefficiencies arising from monopolies with imperfect information, and Stiglitz 2006 and Henry and Stiglitz 2010, as well as the chapters below, for a discussion of the distortions arising from the IPR system).
10. As we noted earlier, if farmers tend their own land, there is no problem of incentivizing them; but if farmers have no land, then common forms of tenancy lead to large inefficiencies. Sharecropping—in which farmers give the landlord 50 percent (or more) of their produce, attenuates incentives. One of the implications of the Greenwald-Stiglitz (1986) analysis is that market equilibrium in such situations is almost never Pareto-efficient.
11. In the standard sense of Paretian efficiency.
12. Partially because governments do not have the information required to engage in lump sum redistributions (see Stiglitz 1994).
13. There is a further problem of attribution, which has become particularly relevant in the debate over global warming: should the producer or the consumer of the good be charged for the cost of the greenhouse gases emitted? In perfectly competitive markets, it would make no difference. But markets are typically not perfectly competitive, so how such questions are answered has real consequences; see Stiglitz (forthcoming).
14. All property rights are, we have argued, social constructions; the definitions of rights, obligations, and constraints associated with real property have evolved over centuries and therefore are more likely to be taken for granted.
15. We elaborate on these points at greater length in the discussion below on "control."
16. The logic is that since only a fraction of those who commit the wrong are caught and convicted, optimal deterrence requires that the penalty when they are caught be a multiple of the costs imposed in that particular instance; see Becker (1968). There is good reason for using private enforcement: political influence may impede public enforcement. Such concerns were particularly important in the context of antitrust laws, where large monopolies had the resources to try to induce government not to take actions against them.

17. This discussion also helps explain why, ordinarily, there should be no compensation for regulatory takings. If the regulation is directed at limiting a negative externality, the effect on the value of the property will be limited, so long as the individual had previously faced liability for these negative externalities.
18. If it is assumed that the government can't assess the risks and costs of injury-inducing consequences of certain individual behavior, or at least assess it better than private participants, then making them pay the costs of the injury ex post will more likely lead to "correct" decisions, than would be the case if the government imposed a tax.
19. They would have to anticipate every conceivable situation that might arise. It is obvious that this is impossible—how could one have written a contract contingent on an explosion at a neighboring nuclear power plant, before the concept of nuclear energy had even been conceived? There are always ambiguities in language. Even when contracts are tightly written, there are questions about whether a particular circumstance falls within the ambit of a particular provision. Background law specifies what happens when a contingency not explicitly written into the contract occurs.
20. There has been extensive discussion in the US of the consequences of the separation of ownership and control in corporations (Berle and Means 1932). In that context, control is exercised by management (not be shareholders)—even though *formally* management is not the owner. Though in principle, shareholders have the "right" to choose a new management, there are significant impediments to their doing so. See, e.g. Stiglitz (1982b, 1985a). See the discussion in the next section.
21. Though some rights may be contingent on ownership, i.e., when the "owner" sells, other rights terminate.
22. A US law that ensures that the owner of property (such as a forest) does nothing that adversely affects an endangered species.
23. Not only savings in writing contracts, but in interpreting them. Again, standard contractual forms could arise naturally. But difficulties arise with interpreting the (inevitably) incomplete contracts.
24. Additional problems may arise from signaling inefficiencies.
25. There is a large literature on how corporations can try to align the interests of managers with shareholders, e.g., with stock options. But there is overwhelming evidence that these attempts have failed, and that indeed, stock options have provided incentives for managers to distort the information that they provide to the market and have encouraged excessive risk-taking and short-sighted behavior, with consequences that are adverse to the interests of shareholders, bondholders, and other stakeholders. For a discussion of such behavior in the context of the most recent crises and financial scandals in the US, see Stiglitz (2003, 2010). The problems are inherent, arise out of the inevitable information asymmetries and the public-good problem of "good management"; the separation of ownership and *de facto* control has long been a source of concern about economists and lawyers, but this concern has often been given short shrift in the Chicago view (see Stiglitz 1985a; Berle and Means 1932).
26. In technical terms, this is referred to as imposing a pooling equilibrium. A competitive market equilibrium cannot be characterized by pooling (one of the central results of Rothschild-Stiglitz 1976). The inefficiencies in contractual equilibria are, however, not limited to problems of signaling. In moral hazard models, contracts by one party affect reservation levels and behavior within other contracts. See, e.g., Rey and Stiglitz (1993) and Arnott and Stiglitz (1985).
27. Asymmetric information can also explain why the economy may get stuck at an inefficient contractual equilibrium. See Stiglitz (1992a).

28. This is seen most obviously in efficiency wage models, where wages affect productivity either because of effects on incentives, selection, morale, or labor turnover. For instance, in the Shapiro–Stiglitz "shirking" model, firms must pay a high enough wage to induce individuals not to shirk. The requisite wage depends on the unemployment rate and the length of time that individuals remain in the unemployment pool. Firms that have a policy of letting go of labor more easily lead to higher labor turnover, and, at any unemployment rate, a shorter duration in the unemployment pool. This means that the equilibrium wage and unemployment rate will be higher. More generally, it is optimal to throw "sand in the wheels": some friction, e.g., associated with mandatory severance pay. See Shapiro and Stiglitz (1984); Arnott and Stiglitz (1985); Rey and Stiglitz (1993); Stiglitz, (1974a, 1982a, 1992b).
29. In the absence of insider trading rules, it might even profit from the foreknowledge of the plant closing. This is another example of how the legal framework helps shape incentives and behavior.
30. There is a huge literature on agency issues, which can be viewed as the central issue in incentives. See, e.g., Stiglitz (1974b) or Ross (1973).
31. Fifty years ago, we did not know of the risks of global warming or of the dangers of certain toxic wastes.
32. The choice is parallel to that which we discuss at greater length below concerning broader rules of the game. Good systems need clear rules. But when the world changes, the rules have to change. Putting too many of the rules in a hard-to-change constitution leads to societal rigidities, impeding adaptability to changing circumstances—something Europe is learning at great cost.
33. The word "ownership" is in quotes to remind the reader that property rights always are a bundle of rights and responsibilities, and that such bundles can take a variety of forms.
34. See Braverman and Stiglitz (1989).
35. Boyle (2003).
36. As Chapter 8 points out, "strengthened" intellectual property rights introduce static inefficiencies, and if the system of IPR is not well designed, may not lead to offsetting dynamic benefits.
37. More generally, an implication of the Greenwald–Stiglitz (1986) theorem is that privately profitable contracts may not be socially efficient. The set of contractual arrangements that evolved in the US involving first and second mortgages, "serviced" by service providers without due attention to conflicts of interest and the potential need for renegotiation has resulted in large inefficiencies, including large transactions costs.
38. Note that the United States does similar things with different mechanisms—a combination of zoning (of "nonresidential" land, of minimum acreage for housing or single-unit housing, which affects housing costs), vagrancy laws, location and arrangement of transport networks, etc., affects where individuals live. So too do patterns of expenditures on local publicly provided goods, such as education. Still, there is a difference between these indirect control mechanisms and more direct control mechanisms, though the direct control mechanisms work mostly indirectly, through the rights of access to local public services.
39. Such discrimination of immigrants is common; what is perhaps unusual about China is that these are domestic migrant workers, rather than foreign.
40. They were mainly based on assertions, not deep economic analysis. Indeed, nonmarket institutions that might arise in response to a market failure (e.g., imperfect insurance arising out of imperfect information) may actually decrease efficiency—making everyone in society worse off; see Arnott and Stiglitz 1991). For more general discussion of these issues and references, see Stiglitz (2000a, 2001a).

41. Indeed, the evidence in the case of the Korean crisis of 1997–8 is consistent with this perspective. For broader discussions of the inefficiency of evolutionary processes, see Stiglitz (1975, 1994).
42. The issue is more complex than this sentence suggests. It is not just a matter of anticipating different contingencies. There are large transaction costs associated with resolving what should be done in each contingency. It makes little sense to bargain about what to do in contingencies that are unlikely to occur. Moreover, between now and the time that the particular contingency could occur, other information/events may occur that may alter the set of efficient actions in that contingency, or affect the bargaining position. If each individual believes that the intervening events will redound to their favor, it may be easier to reach compromise by postponing the specification of the action to be taken in that contingency. Legal frameworks may specify the permissible degree of ambiguity for the contract to be valid. And again, the legal framework can have distributive, as well as efficiency, consequences. One party may take advantage of another knowing that ex post, the other party will be in a weaker bargaining position, and that the individual does not know that now.
43. Equally, since corporations are represented by their management, it is hard for self-regulation to protect an industry against actions by management that might be adverse to the interests of shareholders and bondholders—which was evident in the 2008 crisis in the US.
44. To put it in another way: we can think of two stages in the analysis, a specification of how the consequences of risk are borne among the parties and a specification of how the allocation of the consequences is borne can be changed. There are distributional consequences to each specification. The latter inevitably entails not just private parties, but public actors.
45. Moreover, inequities of wealth created by an unbalanced legal system can be self-perpetuating: wealth influences political processes to ensure that redistributions do not occur and to push for legal reforms that perpetuate and enhance inequities.
46. This also helps explain why it is often difficult to make seeming Pareto improvements, e.g., converting distortionary agriculture subsidies into a lump sum annual equivalent. Because governments cannot make binding commitments, farmers would not believe that those payments would continue, once their magnitudes become clear—it would almost surely be unacceptable for a rich corporation to receive millions for doing nothing, though it is acceptable for the same corporation to receive similar amounts for producing corn. But there is in fact a double commitment problem: even if the farmers were to agree to take a lump sum payment up front in return for the elimination of their subsidies, it may be difficult to enforce. After they receive the up-front payment, they may once again lobby for subsidies.
47. To return to the "transactions cost" perspective, the costs associated with achieving these distributive outcomes from this implicit legal assignment of rights may be markedly lower than achieving similar outcomes in other ways.
48. There are even some instances in which such legislation can move an economy from one equilibrium to a Pareto-superior equilibrium. There can exist multiple equilibria, some entailing discrimination, others without discrimination.
49. This is especially the case since the original equilibrium was not itself efficient, because of market failures (e.g., the presence of imperfections of competition).
50. My paper (1980) is available in Chinese as part of *Selected Works on Economics by Joseph E. Stiglitz.*

REFERENCES

Arnott, R. and Stiglitz, J. E. (1985), "Labor Turnover, Wage Structure, and Moral Hazard: The Inefficiency of Competitive Markets," *Journal of Labor Economics*, 3/4: 434–62.

——— (1991), "Moral Hazard and Non-Market Institutions: Dysfunctional Crowding Out or Peer Monitoring," *American Economic Review*, 81/1 (March): 179–90.

Arrow, K. J. (1951), "An Extension of the Basic Theorems of Classical Welfare Economics," J. Neyman (ed.), *Proceedings of the Second Berkeley Symposium on Mathematical Statistics and Probability* (Berkeley: University of California Press), 507–32.

—— and Debreu, G. (1954), "Existence of an Equilibrium in a Competitive Economy," *Econometrica*, 22/3: 265–90.

Atkinson, B. and Stiglitz, J. E. (1976), "The Design of Tax Structure: Direct Versus Indirect Taxation," *Journal of Public Economics*, 6/1–2: 55–75.

——— (1980), *Lectures in Public Economics* (New York: McGraw Hill).

Baumol, W., Panzar, J., and Willig, R. (1982), *Contestable Markets and the Theory of Industry* Structure (New York: Harcourt, Brace, Jovanovich).

Becker, G. (1968), "Crime and Punishment: An Economic Approach," *Journal of Political Economy*, 76: 169–217.

Berle, A. and Means, G. C. (1932), *The Modern Corporation and Private Property* (New York: Macmillan).

Boyle, J. (2003), "The Second Enclosure Movement and the Construction of the Public Domain," *Law and Contemporary Problems*, 66 (Winter/Spring): 33–74.

Braverman, A. and Stiglitz, J. E. (1989), "Credit Rationing, Tenancy, Productivity and the Dynamics of Inequality," in P. Bardhan (ed.), *The Economic Theory of Agrarian Institutions* (Oxford: Clarendon Press), 185–201.

Calebresi, G. and Melamen, D. (1972), "Property Rights, Liability Rules, and Inalienability: One View of the Cathedral," *Harvard Law Review*, 85: 1089.

Coase, R. (1937). "The Nature of the Firm," *Economica*, 4/16: 386–405.

—— (1960), "The Problem of Social Cost," *Journal of Law and Economics*, 3: 1–44.

Debreu, G. (1959), *The Theory of Value* (New Haven: Yale University Press).

De Soto, H. (2000), *The Mystery of Capital* (London: Bantam Books).

Edlin, A. S and Stiglitz, J. E. (1995), "Discouraging Rivals: Managerial Rent-Seeking and Economic Inefficiencies," *American Economic Review*, 85/5: 1301–12.

Greenwald, B. and Stiglitz, J. E. (1986), "Externalities in Economies with Imperfect Information and Incomplete Markets," *Quarterly Journal of Economics*, 101/2 (May): 229–64.

Grossman, S. and Hart, O. (1980), "Takeover Bids, the Free-rider Problem and the Theory of the Corporation," *Bell Journal of Economics*, 11/1: 42–64.

——— (1981), "The Allocational Role of Takeover Bids in Situations of Asymmetric Information," *Journal of Finance*, 36: 253–70.

Grossman, S. and Stiglitz, J. E. (1977), "On Value Maximization and Alternative Objectives of the Firm," *Journal of Finance*, 32/2 (May): 389–402.

——— (1980), "Stockholder Unanimity in the Making of Production and Financial Decisions," *Quarterly Journal of Economics*, 94/3: 543–66.

Henry, C. and Stiglitz, J. E. (2010), "Intellectual Property, Dissemination of Innovation, and Sustainable Development," *Global Policy*, 1/1: 237–51.

Hoff, K. and Stiglitz, J. E. (2004a), "After the Big Bang? Obstacles to the Emergence of the Rule of Law in Post-Communist Societies," *American Economic Review*, 94/3: 753–63.

——— (2004b), "The Transition Process in Post-Communist Societies: Toward a Political Economy of Property Rights," in B. Tungodden, N. Stern, and I. Kolstad (eds), *Toward Pro-Poor Policies: Aid, Institutions and Globalization* (New York: World Bank and Oxford University Press), 231–45. In Chinese: *Nanjing Business Review*, 4 (2005): 22–37; in French: *Revue d'économie du développement*, 17/2–3 (2005).

——— (2007), "Exiting a Lawless State," *Economic Journal*, 118/531: 1474–97.
Jensen, M. C. (1998), "Takeovers: Their Causes and Consequences," *Journal of Economic Perspectives*, 2/1: 21–48.
Kennedy, D. and Fisher, W., III (2006), *The Canon of American Legal Thought* (Princeton: Princeton University Press).
Kennedy, G. (2009), "Adam Smith and the Invisible Hand: From Metaphor to Myth," *Economic Journal Watch*, 6/2 (May): 239–63.
Panzar, J. and Willig, R. (1977), "Free Entry and the Sustainability of Natural Monopoly," *Bell Journal of Economics*, 8: 1–22.
Phillipson, N. (2010), *Adam Smith: An Enlightened Life* (New Haven: Yale University Press).
Rey, P. and Stiglitz, J. E. (1993), "Moral Hazard and Unemployment in Competitive Equilibrium." Unpublished manuscript, October.
Ross, S. (1973), "The Economic Theory of Agency: The Principal's Problem," *American Economic Review*, 63/2: 134–9.
Rothschild, E. (2001), *Economic Sentiments: Adam Smith, Condorcet, and the Enlightenment* (Boston: Harvard University Press).
Rothschild, M. and Stiglitz, J. E. (1976), "Equilibrium in Competitive Insurance Markets: An Essay on the Economics of Imperfect Information," *Quarterly Journal of Economics*, 90/4: 629–49.
Serra, N. and Stiglitz, J. E. (2008), "Introduction," in N. Serra and J. E. Stiglitz (eds), *The Washington Consensus Reconsidered: Toward a New Global Governance* (New York: Oxford University Press).
Shapiro, C. and Stiglitz, J. E. (1984), "Equilibrium Unemployment as a Worker Discipline Device," *American Economic Review*, 74/3 (June): 433–44.
Smith, A. (1776), *An Inquiry into the Nature and Causes of the Wealth of Nations* (Dublin: Whitestone, Chamberlaine).
Stiglitz, J. E. (1972), "Some Aspects of the Pure Theory of Corporate Finance: Bankruptcies and Take-Overs," *Bell Journal of Economics*, 3/2: 458–82.
—— (1974a), "Alternative Theories of Wage Determination and Unemployment in L.D.C.s: The Labor Turnover Model," *Quarterly Journal of Economics*, 88/2: 194–227.
—— (1974b), "Incentives and Risk Sharing in Sharecropping," *Review of Economic Studies*, 41/2: 219–55.
—— (1975), "Information and Economic Analysis," in J. M. Parkin and A. R. Nobay (eds), *Current Economic Problems* (Cambridge: Cambridge University Press).
—— (1977), "Monopoly, Non-Linear Pricing and Imperfect Information: The Insurance Market," *Review of Economic Studies*, 44/3: 407–30.
—— (1980), "Information, Planning and Incentives." Paper presented at the CSCCRP Sino-American Conference on Alternative Development Strategies in Wingspread, Racine, WI. (Chinese edition published 1982.) Available in *Selected Works on Economics by Joseph E. Stiglitz* (Beijing: China Financial Publishing House, 2007).
—— (1982a), "Alternative Theories of Wage Determination and Unemployment: The Efficiency Wage Model," in M. Gersovitz, et al. (eds), *The Theory and Experience of Economic Development: Essays in Honor of Sir Arthur W. Lewis* (London: George Allen & Unwin), 78–106.
—— (1982b), "The Inefficiency of the Stock Market Equilibrium," *Review of Economic Studies*, 49: 241–61.
—— (1985a), "Credit Markets and the Control of Capital," *Journal of Money, Credit, and Banking*, 17: 133–52.
—— (1985b), "Information and Economic Analysis: A Perspective," *Economic Journal Supplement*, 95: 21–42.

—— (1988), "Technological Change, Sunk Costs, and Competition," in M. N. Baily and C. Winston (eds), *Special Issue on Macroeconomics* (Washington, DC: The Brooking Institution), 883–937.

—— (1992a), "Contract Theory and Macroeconomic Fluctuations," in L. Werin and H. Wijkander (eds), *Contract Economics* (Oxford: Basil Blackwell), 292–322.

—— (1992b), "Prices and Queues as Screening Devices in Competitive Markets," in D. Gale and O. Hart (eds), *Economic Analysis of Markets and Games: Essays in Honor of Frank Hahn* (Cambridge, MA: MIT Press), 128–66.

—— (1994), *Whither Socialism?* (Cambridge, MA: MIT Press). Originally presented as the Wicksell Lectures, Stockholm School of Economics, May 1990.

—— (2000a), "Formal and Informal Institutions," in P. Dasgupta and I. Serageldin (eds), *Social Capital: A Multifaceted Perspective* (Washington, DC: World Bank).

—— (2000b), "Whither Reform? Ten Years of Transition," in B. Pleskovic and J. E. Stiglitz (eds), *Annual World Bank Conference on Economic Development* (Washington, DC: World Bank), 27–56. Reprinted in 2001 as chapter 4 in H.-J. Chang (ed.), *The Rebel Within* (London: Wimbledon Publishing Company). Summary in *Transition Economics*, 3/12 (June 1999).

—— (2001a), "Challenges in the Analysis of the Role of Institutions in Economic Development," in G. Kochendorfer-Lucius and B. Pleskovic (eds), *Villa Borsig Workshop Series 2000: The Institutional Foundations of a Market Economy* (Berlin: German Foundation for International Development), 15–28.

—— (2001b), "A Comparison of Economic Transition among China and Other Countries," *Economics Information*, 5: 43–6 (in Chinese).

—— (2002a), *Globalization and Its Discontents* (New York: W. W. Norton). (Published in Chinese complex by Locus; in Chinese simplified by China Machine Press.)

—— (2002b), Information and the Change in the Paradigm in Economics," abbreviated version of Nobel lecture, *American Economic Review*, 92/3 (June): 460–501.

—— (2003), *Roaring Nineties* (New York: W. W. Norton). (Published in Chinese complex by Commonwealth; in Chinese simplified by China Financial.)

—— (2006), *Making Globalization Work* (New York: W. W. Norton).

—— (2008a), "Is there a Post-Washington Consensus Consensus?" in J. E. Stiglitz and N. Serra (eds), *The Washington Consensus Reconsidered: Toward a New Global Governance* (New York: Oxford University Press).

—— (2008b), "The Economic Foundations of Intellectual Property," Sixth Annual Frey Lecture in Intellectual Property, Duke University, February 16, 2007, published in *Duke Law Journal*, 57/6: 1693–724.

—— (2010), *Freefall: America, Free Markets, and the Sinking of the World Economy* (New York: W. W. Norton). (Published in Chinese complex by Commonwealth Publishing; Chinese simplified by China Machine Press.)

—— (forthcoming), "Sharing the Burden of Saving the Planet: Global Social Justice for Sustainable Development," in M. Kaldor and J. E. Stiglitz (eds), *The Challenge of Global Governance* (New York: Columbia University Press).

Supreme Court of the United States (1993), *Brooke Group Ltd. v. Brown & Williamson Tobacco Corp.*, 509 U.S. 209, Washington, DC. Available at <http://bulk.resource.org/courts.gov/c/US/509/509.US.209.92-466.html>.

Weitzman, M. (1974), "Prices vs. Quantities," *Review of Economic Studies*, 41: 477–91.

Williamson, J. (1990), "What Washington Means by Policy Reform," in J. Williamson (ed.), *Latin American Adjustment: How Much Has Happened?* (Washington, DC: Institute for International Economics).

—— (2008), "The Washington Consensus Reconsidered," in N. Serra and J. E. Stiglitz (eds), *The Washington Consensus Reconsidered: Toward a New Global Governance* (New York: Oxford University Press).

5

Some Caution about Property Rights as a Recipe For Economic Development

David Kennedy

In recent years, enhancing the security and clarity or formality of property rights has become something of an *idée fixe* among global development policy experts. The legal orthodoxy which has accompanied neoliberal economic prescriptions routinely affirms that "clear and strong" property rights are a prerequisite to a functioning market economy and that stronger and more formal property rights will promote efficiency and growth. It is not surprising that strengthening property rights has become a standard part of the recipe offered by outside experts for China, often on the basis of an assertion that a strong private property tradition has historically been responsible for robust growth and development in today's most developed industrial societies.

This is more ideological assertion than careful history, however. Western economies have experienced periods of aggressive industrialization and economic growth with a wide range of different property regimes in place. Throughout the West, property rights have always been embedded in a complex legal fabric which modifies their meaning and qualifies their enforcement. As one sorts through the technical details of any Western legal regime, moreover, it is notoriously difficult to say just which entitlements are "clear" or "strong." No property law regime is composed solely of "rights"—there are always also lots of reciprocal obligations, duties, and legal privileges to injure. Since all entitlements involve at least two economic actors—the one with a right, the other under a duty—what is strong and clear to one may well seem weak and vague to another.

Nor is there a compelling analytic supporting the suggestion that "clear and strong" property rights lead inexorably to market efficiency or economic growth. The ideas about property law which undergird assertions that strong and clear rights will lead to economic efficiency and growth become incoherent when we begin to translate them into technical legal regimes. In fact, most proposals for strong and clear property rights rest, at least in part, on lay conceptions about the legal order which are simply not warranted. These include ideas like the following:

- that "property rights" have an ideal form which can be disentangled from the warp and woof of social and economic struggle in a society;

- that "private order," including property rights, and "public regulation" can and ought to be cleanly separated, the one supporting the market, the other potentially distorting it;
- that "strengthening" property rights has no distributive implications, if only because property law concerns the "rights" of individuals over things rather than complex relations of reciprocal rights and duties among people with respect to things;
- that concerns about social uses and obligations are only properly pursued outside the property regime, through social regulation of one or another sort;
- that in a well-functioning market economy, all "private" rights can and will be freely rearranged by market forces, rendering decisions about their initial allocation unimportant;
- that the *formalization* of property rights leads cleanly to both efficiency and growth, eliminating the need for policy judgment about the desirability of alternative uses and distributional arrangements.

Each of these six ideas supports the notion that the development of a proper law of property can be accomplished without facing complex questions of social, political, and economic strategy. But each is incorrect. Property law is a critical domain for engaging, debating, and institutionalizing development policy, but it is not a substitute for strategic analysis and political choice. Property law is everywhere a *mix* of formal rules and quite discretionary standards, of strong entitlements to act and obligations restricting one's ability to act, just as property law is everywhere embedded in a complex combination of public and private legal regimes. The result is a dense fabric of rules and procedures for *adjusting* competing claims on and uses for a society's productive resources.

In short, choices about the meaning and allocation of property rights pose the sorts of policy questions familiar to economists thinking about development policy. If we are seeking economic growth of this or that sort, who should have access to what resources and on what conditions? "Clear and strong property rights" are neither an escape from these questions nor a ready-made answer. Property law is simple one place in which struggles over these questions have been carried out. In this short essay, I review these common, if mistaken, ideas about property rights in the West in light of the Western experience. My objective is to place the strategic choices embedded in any property regime in the foreground and to counsel hesitation before accepting conventional neoliberal wisdom about the importance of "clear" or "strong property rights" for economic development.

PROPERTY AND THE HISTORY OF STRUGGLE OVER MODES OF ECONOMIC LIFE

Property in a market economy has no ideal form separate from the warp and woof of social and economic struggle in that society. Before "property rights" can be strong or weak, they must be allocated and defined—a process which in every Western society has been inseparable from struggles over political and social objectives. Moreover, property law is itself a dynamic social institution embodying an ongoing process of technical definition and redefinition. In every society this technical process has been influenced by a wide range of ideas about what law is and how it works. Different modes of technical definition influence the codification and implementation of the entitlements that emerge from social and political struggle. As a result, property law in every developed society is the sedimented remnant of a complex history, full of political and social struggle over the form of society and the modes of economic production.

A pattern of allocation and entitlement may arise out of the long political and social history of a society or may be imposed in a moment of reallocation—as is being contemplated in China. In this sense, given the political will and opportunity, one can always start over. In the history of the West, one has repeatedly started over, inventing new kinds of property, eliminating or qualifying old property rights, and reallocating obligations and entitlements with respect to resources. New kinds of entitlements—new rights, new duties, new privileges and obligations—have been invented for new kinds of actors in new relationships with respect to new kinds of knowledge or resources. Existing entitlements can and often have been reallocated, either slowly or quite precipitously as part of a conscious project of social and historical renewal or struggle. The difficulty, of course, is that those with entitlements from round one will often be able to exercise disproportionate political, economic, or legal influence in round two, making it more difficult to begin again and placing a premium on getting it as close to right as possible whenever the opportunity for reallocation arises.

As one might expect, the result of a society's history of struggle over property is never a uniform system—and usually one quite specific to that country's social, economic, and political experience. Western societies differ in the definition and allocation of various entitlements and duties and in the relative powers of various players. As fortunes have shifted in ongoing economic and political struggles, different people have had different rights against different others. To take but one example, the moment at which women—or corporations—became able to inherit and transfer property on their own marked a break in the economic possibilities for each society in which it occurred. Once allocated, a regime of entitlements in turn helps structure the next round of social struggle. As ideas change—and as the social, economic, legal, and political balance of forces changes—allocations shift and the technical definitions of entitlements are rearranged. The allocation of entitlements in each round establishes actors with interests and procedures for their pursuit which have an impact on the evolution of the society in successive rounds of political and economic development.

Moreover, Western legal regimes have routinely had a variety of quite different property regimes in place at the same time, which often apply to different kinds of entities and assets. Regimes for land, or specifically for agricultural land, common land, residential land, often differ from those for other commodities, for intellectual property or for various forms of finance capital. Property held by trusts, corporations, individuals, cooperatives, partnerships, or public agencies may each be subject to quite different entitlements. Family members often have a variety of different relationships to assets held, in one or another way, by the family itself. And so on. The result is therefore not a simple or coherent Western system of property, but a dense network of entitlements reflecting specific social histories of allocative struggle.

There are numerous familiar historical examples. Across Europe, struggles to "enclose the commons" accompanied and facilitated a transformation in the agricultural system of production. The North American struggle to settle the western regions of the continent was promoted and resisted by a changing set of property arrangements promoting homesteading, restricting native title, removing native inhabitants, and titling vast tracts to those who would cultivate and settle the land. Is uncultivated land legally open for occupation? Does ownership require cultivation? Is unoccupied or untilled land "owned" by the state? May landlords—or the public weal—allow land to lie fallow or do squatters have the right to render it productive? Answering such legal questions one way or the other in turn transformed the political and institutional context for further economic development. Once homesteaders are *there*, the politics of economic policy is altogether different. Once entitlements have been transformed, different players with different interests were in place, in turn transforming the social and political context for further development.

Struggles over economic and social changes are often carried out quite directly in legal terms. By the end of the nineteenth century, there was little common land left in Germany—a fact which provided the context for Proudhon's famous observation that "property is theft." Nineteenth-century German jurists then worried whether land had been held in common "before" the emergence of villages or whether it had been taken and could now be reallocated. In the United States, economic struggles between the worlds of finance and farming, between the urban East and the rural Midwest and West, were also often framed as struggles over the property regime, and in particular, its interaction with banking and bankruptcy law. If a farmer is unable to pay commercial debts, does he lose the farm to the big city bankers, or is the "family farm" exempt from seizure in bankruptcy?

Similar legal questions have arisen recently in local struggles between those favoring an extractive economy and those favoring an economy rooted in recreation and uses of land more protective of the environment. When should private actors be permitted to use public lands for profit—for logging or mining, for grazing, for travel or tourism? When should public power be brought to bear on private land in the name of one or another of these economic futures? As a matter of property law, are all beaches open to the public? Must access be provided by adjacent land owners? If you own a pond, do you own the fish? Is your right to fish exclusive? How much water can you remove from a stream which crosses your property? In the contemporary American West, struggle over the allocation of property rights in water among a range of public and private uses are suffused with questions of economic policy and choices about the mode of production—suburbs or farms, industry or agriculture or recreation, and so on.

Divisions within industries among players with different strategies and different conceptions of the future for their industry and their national economy are often also fought out in the domain of property law. A particularly obvious case in recent years has been the struggle between dominant and upstart players in technology sectors for which intellectual property is an important resource. Should software be protected by a property right, and if so, of what type—copyright, patent? When protected, on what terms—what constitutes "fair use?"

We are all familiar with the struggles of the 1980s and 1990s between American, European, and Asian producers of electronic equipment, computers, and then software. How quickly should emulation be permitted and new discoveries put in competition? The struggle over the European Union software directive in the late 1980s placed Europe between a Japanese and an American model of innovation and production, presenting difficult choices of economic policy. It was possible to design a regime of "clear and strong property rights" compatible with either mode of production. The same kind of struggle has more recently played itself out between the large Western pharmaceutical companies and generic manufacturers—when are pharmaceuticals subject to compulsory licensing, when do patent owners have a right of action against generics? A similar struggle is under way in the fields of art and entertainment. In each field, the outcome will be influenced both by general ideas about the meaning and legal structure of "intellectual property" and by the political and economic strength of the interests involved. The result at each stage in each field will reflect a quite specific regime of property entitlements accommodating these ideas and interests—and influencing the next round of innovation and political struggle.

Legal arrangements can speed or slow changes in modes of economic order. This was a key lesson of the enclosure moment and of the subsequent transition from an agricultural to an extractive and industrial economy. The allocation of entitlements was not only about who gets the asset. With more duties toward tenants, the dismantling of feudal agriculture, migration towards the towns, and freeing of agricultural land for new uses, such as grazing, would be slower. With fewer duties, faster. Similar choices accompanied the struggle between industry and agriculture from the eighteenth through the twentieth century. Complex feudal land arrangements (fee-tails, copyhold estates, etc.) and restraints on alienation and testamentary power seemed to slow transformation of landed aristocracy. This is difficult to interpret. It may have slowed industrialization, delaying the onset of productivity gains and rapid economic growth. But it may also have made industrialization more sustainable in political and social terms, thereby helping to solidify the Industrial Revolution.

For those designing the property regime, the question was both a narrow one of distribution and interest among those favoring more or less restrictive modes of ownership, and a broader one of dynamic economic policymaking. Should the state be "on the side" of agriculture or industry? Should the state favor the economic transformation from agriculture to industry, and, if so, how? By encouraging alienability and lessening duties to traditional tenants? By slowing the process until displaced workers were absorbed in industry, even if that raised wages and made new industrial ventures less profitable? Should the nuisance to neighbors presented by new extractive or industrial uses of property be encouraged, prevented, permitted with compensation? Such questions of legal design present difficult issues of economic policy and political choice.

Economic struggles have also often resulted in new forms of property. The emergence of commodity markets blended contract entitlements with property—"futures" began as warehouse receipts for agricultural produce which became a tradable commodity themselves. Sometimes this leads to standardization and more formal terms for property and contract—the grading of grain and other agricultural commodities to permit it to be traded without inspection. Private or public inspection and guarantee of weights and measures to facilitate transactions have often been part of the story when a market in a new commodity emerged, from grain to biotechnology. Sometimes it leads to a softening of what had been clear rights—through an expansive interpretation of standards like "fair" or "reasonable" use to accommodate new uses. Property law can take these standards on board—or it can resist them, requiring more localized and specific assessments. Again, an opportunity to speed or retard economic transformation.

Struggles over a nation's economic direction and priorities are not all about law, of course. Nevertheless, none of these struggles took place *on top of* an existing and well-settled regime of "clear" or "strong" property rights. These struggles often led to regulations of various sorts—but they were all *also* fought within the framework of defining and allocating property entitlements themselves. They were all struggles about which property rights should be clear and which should remain murky, which duties ought to accompany property rights, when rights should be defined to give way to public—or to other private—interests. Each struggle was a matter of pull and tug, and none was cleanly resolved. The result is a private-property regime bearing the residue of these struggles and the compromises in which they terminated. Consequently, property rights are less a legal "system" than a historical record of winners, losers, and social accommodation in economic and political struggles over a nation's direction. In this sense, neoliberal legal orthodoxy is wrong to suggest that the establishment of property rights of a particular kind is a *precondition* to a market economy. The ongoing allocation and definition of property entitlements is part of the social and political history of any market economy.

PROPERTY AND SOVEREIGNTY: THE FUSION OF PRIVATE AND PUBLIC ORDER

A sharp distinction between a horizontal private legal order among individuals and a vertical public legal order through which the state regulates the activities of private individuals is neither conceptually nor practically plausible. Nor is it analytically possible to distinguish private legal rules which "support" market transactions from public law rules which "distort" market prices. All prices are bargained in the shadow of the law and reflect the respective legal ability of different parties to mobilize the state for or against their economic interests. In the simplest example, a worker's ability to withhold his or her labor, like the capitalist's ability to withhold capital, is a legal entitlement which can be and has been allocated and defined in various ways. The wage toward which they negotiate reflects the relative allocation of legal powers.

The relationship between "property" and "sovereignty" is an ancient issue, which is often said to have arisen in Roman law as the relationship between *dominium* (rule over things by an individual) and *imperium* (the rule over individuals by the prince). In many conventional accounts, the relationship between the legal regimes of *dominium* and *jus* altered over the course of the

Empire: early on, *dominium* was rather separate, by the late Empire, it had been subsumed within the *jus*. One impression which results from this story is that in "civil law" traditions influenced by the Roman law tradition, more weight is given to public law elements in the legal regime, while "common law" traditions place more weight on the autonomy of private legal arrangements. It turns out, however, that the situation is more complex. In every Western tradition, whether civil and common, there has been a continuing struggle over the relationship between public and private arrangements. And property law is more accurately described as a relationship between people enforced by the state which concerns an asset than as a legal relationship between a person and a thing.

Speaking very generally, since the Industrial Revolution, legal theorists have proposed a range of accounts for the relationship between public and private. Some have sought to strengthen the public at the expense of the private by insisting upon the priority of legislation or regulation or by identifying and expanding the points within private law at which officials charged with implementing private arrangements could exercise discretion and recognize or impose social duties on those in private relationships. For others, the goal has been to strengthen the private against the public by treating private rights as constitutional limits upon sovereign powers or otherwise narrowing the opportunities for officials implementing private arrangements to exercise discretion or impose social obligations. But these two poles are not the only, or even the most important, alternatives. There have also been numerous efforts to see the domains as "equal" if distinct, or to imagine a functional "partnership" between them or "balance" among their respective virtues guided by a larger policy objective such as market efficiency or economic development or social welfare or the provision of public goods.

Conceptually, at different moments legal professions have understood public and private law to be more or less distinct from one another. Looking back at the institutional arrangements in place in practice, it is difficult in any period to disentangle the public and private elements with confidence, precisely because the private order relies upon public authority for effect and may itself be put together in many ways, reflecting different social, economic, and political arrangements. In the feudal period, land tenure (which we might think of as private) and hierarchical relations of personal homage (which we might think of as public) were combined in a range of legal doctrines. The feudal baron sometimes had the right to determine the marriage of his ward or to nominate the local priest. In international law, sovereignty and right remained overlapping categories until the nineteenth century. Chartered corporations and privateers exercised "sovereign rights." The idea of a single unified public "sovereignty," universal in its absolute authority over territory, emerged only late in the century.

Although it has often been said that the late nineteenth-century period of classical laissez-faire economics was characterized by a particularly strong theorization of the formal distinction between public and private arrangements, this conception began to break down almost as soon as it was developed as ever more exceptions and divergent practices became integrated into it.[1] The history of twentieth-century legal thought in both civil and common law jurisdictions may be said to have been preoccupied with rebuilding a theoretical appreciation for the connections between public and private authority and rebutting the idea that public and private could, in fact, be analytically distinguished. Repeatedly, economic, social, and other policy considerations we might associate with public regulation and administrative action have become routine components of private law doctrines.

Moreover, over the last century, legal professionals in the United States have become ever more adept at multiplying the number of possible combinations of public and private authority. Indeed, creative lawyering is often about expanding the toolkit of possible institutional arrangements which combine public and private authorities in novel ways. This proliferation of mixed arrangements was made more possible as jurists lost confidence in the plausibility of a sharp analytic distinction between private arrangements—like property law—which reflected the free "consent" of private individuals and public law which entailed coercion through the plenary power of the state.

It is always difficult to date the emergence of such a general understanding, but two jurists writing in the early twentieth century have often been credited. In the United States, Robert Hale stressed the role of state coercion in private law arrangements by focusing on the ways in which those without property could be forced to refrain from using resources owned by others.[2] Hale emphasized that the property rights of owners placed others under a legal duty to make due without access to assets, an obligation which would be enforced by the state should they trespass or seek to convert another's property for their use. There was, he argued, an unavoidable element of coercion and public power in the routine operation of the private legal order.

At about the same time, Morris Cohen argued that because property is a state-sanctioned right to exclude, it is also the power to compel service for use or the payment of rent. He wrote: "We must not overlook the actual fact that dominion over things is also imperium over our fellow human beings."[3] For Cohen, property is more than the legal protection of possession. It also determines the "future distribution of the goods that will come into being,"[4] which we might well have considered exclusively the province of public law and sovereignty.

> The owners of all revenue-producing property are in fact granted by the law certain powers to tax the future social product. When to this power of taxation there is added the power to command the services of large numbers who are not economically independent, we have the essence of what historically has constituted political sovereignty.[5]

This insight made it easy to see the parallel between the sorts of policy questions faced in making "sovereign" regulatory decisions and those faced in the allocation and definition of "private" property rights. For Cohen, economic policy ought to drive decisions about the allocation and meaning of property: "the essential truth is that labor has to be encouraged and that property must be distributed in such a way as to encourage ever greater efforts at productivity."[6]

Here begins a century-long relationship between legal and economic analysis. For lawyers, the discovery of this relationship brought liberation from a professional experience of necessity—the experience that private rights *had* to be arranged this way rather than that, because of the "nature" of property. There were many ways in which they might be arranged, all had economic effects, and each would harness public authority and private power. Cohen was particularly concerned to disentangle the argument for a strong property system from any preconception about who ought in such a system to have which specific rights.

> It may well be argued . . . that just as restraining traffic rules in the end gives us greater freedom of motion, so, by giving control over things to individual property owners, greater economic freedom is in the end assured to all. This is a strong argument . . . It is, however, an argument for legal order rather than for any particular form of government or private property. It argues for a regime where everyone has a definite sphere of rights and duties, but it does not tell us where these lines should be drawn.[7]

Cohen was attentive to a number of specific issues: how firmly to set intellectual property rights to stimulate innovation without preventing the productive use of the knowledge ("patents for processes which would cheapen the product are often bought up by manufacturers and never used") and how to combine property rights with antimonopoly power to prevent "abuse of a dominant position" through compulsory licensing or in other ways. The details of his particular policy preoccupations are less important, however, than the broad terrain opened up for legal analysis by the general acceptance within the profession of the background idea that property and sovereignty perform parallel functions and ought to be thought available for rearrangement in numerous ways depending upon one's policy preferences.

Nevertheless, it is still common to imagine that property rights in some sense come *before* or lie *beneath* whatever public regulation has been added on top. Of course in a sense this is certainly true—property rights are everywhere restrained and modified by a regulatory framework. The law relating to property in every society rests within a broader legal context which affects the meanings property entitlements will have. Numerous adjacent legal regimes affect the meaning of property rights in every system—laws about taxation, bankruptcy, consumer protection, zoning, family law, corporate governance, environmental regulation, and many more. In this sense, the use of economic resources is nowhere the exclusive concern of "property law."

Even if we could imagine the absence of explicit regulation modifying rights, however, the idea that property rights exist before or outside public policy would still not be sound. Hale and his contemporaries were correct that property rights are, in the end, only as strong as one's ability to bring the state into play as their enforcer. The enforcement and definition of property rights depends upon the larger regime of private law and procedure which may be organized to strengthen or weaken various interests in society. Procedural and institutional arrangements make it easy for some and difficult for others to mobilize the state to protect their interests. Moreover, property rights also vary when combined with different "private law" regimes of contract and tort or obligation. A strong tort regime of duties to avoid negligent injury to others may limit one's legal privilege to use one's property to another's detriment. In the end, we must recognize that the private legal order is shot through with public policy commitments, relies upon the state for interpretation and enforcement, and never controls access to resources in the absence of public law restrictions or permissions.

PROPERTY AS DISTRIBUTION: REGULATING RELATIONS AMONG PEOPLE WITH RESPECT TO THINGS

One reason the "strong and clear property rights" idea continues to seem innocent of any allocative public policy commitment is the lay notion that property rights concern the relationship between an individual and "his property." Strengthening and clarifying that relationship does not seem to implicate anyone else. For a legal professional, however, property is not about the relationship between persons and things. Rather it concerns the relationship between people with respect to a thing. The difference is crucial.

When we say that I own my home, what we mean is that I can enforce a series of rights against other people—to "quiet enjoyment" of the home, to exclude others from the land, to remove a trespasser, to contract for the sale of the home, prevent others from selling or renting it without my permission, and so on. Others have duties—not to trespass, not to convert my property to their use. Should they do so, the state may force them to pay me a penalty. At the same time, we may each have legal privileges—they to trespass in an emergency, me to use my property in ways which may prevent them from enjoying their own property or which decrease its market value. I may also have duties—not to allow a hazardous nuisance on my land, perhaps to cultivate or maintain the land. And so on. "Owning" land says nothing about my relationship to the home itself. It says a great deal about my relationship with other people. In this sense, property law distributes rights and duties among people with respect to things. Every time someone has a "strong" property right, someone else faces a "strong" duty. It is in this sense that property entitlements are always reciprocal—and their assignment allocative.

Once we think of a property right as a relationship between two people, moreover, it is clear that the state also has a role as the enforcer of the rights of one against the other. Thought of this way, the distributional dimension in routine enforcement of property rights is quite visible—for every right, someone is under a duty, and we will want a good explanation when we bring state coercion into play to force him to live up to that duty. In this sense, property law analytics can bring issues of social and economic choice to the surface. These are allocative questions, distributional questions, and no property law regime can be erected or maintained without resolving them. Doing so requires a political or economic or social choice—rooted in a conviction about why doing it this way rather than that will be a good thing.

To take a classic example, we all know that two property owners living side by side may often get in one another's way even without trespassing. Playing music too loudly, opening a competing donut shop, running a brothel—if you do any of these things on your property, my enjoyment of my property will suffer, as may its value. But of course my preventing you from doing any of these things will compromise your enjoyment of your property and may reduce its value. We can imagine a variety of legal regimes to settle this issue. There may be general regulations applicable to both of us which solve it—no brothels in the neighborhood. But in the absence of regulation, it will also need to be settled *within* property law. Are owners under a duty to play their music at a reasonable volume and do neighbors have a right to force them to turn it down? Or do owners have a privilege to play their music as loudly as they wish, giving their neighbors no right to interfere? In the abstract, "ownership" is compatible with both regimes and there is no satisfying way to get an outcome from the "logic" of property. An owner may be able to act until bought out at a negotiated price, may be forced to stop unless he negotiates and buys the right to continue, may be able to be forced to pay a given price to continue, may be forced to stop and left unable to buy the right to continue. The complaining party, reciprocally, may be able to offer to buy the loud neighbor out, may be able to get an injunction to prevent it, which he may then waive for a negotiated price, may be able to get specified damages, or may be able to get an injunction which he cannot waive for any price.[8]

Moreover, we might resolve this issue "clearly" (no music after ten) or leave it more open to later interpretation (no unreasonable noise). As the rule comes to be applied, we might be surprised which turns out to be more predictable—judges (and neighbors) might find the "after ten" rule unreasonably restrictive and blunt its effects by exploiting adjacent rules, broader principles, or discretion as to penalties found elsewhere in the legal materials. As we think about penalties and enforcement mechanisms, we have the opportunity to make the initial rule relatively easy, more difficult, or simply impossible to transfer through private bargaining. I may be able to sell you my right to prevent you from playing music for any price we agree, or you may be able to force me to surrender it by paying a sum of damages calculated by a court. It may be a crime for you to wake me up which may or may not be enforced by the sheriff. Penalties may be stiff or lax—and he may or may not take my views into account in deciding to prosecute. We could also make the transaction costs of later adjustment high or low. Can you negotiate with me (or I with you) alone, or must one of us secure the agreement of everyone in the neighborhood? And so on.

Strengthening or clarifying property rights tells us almost nothing about how to resolve issues of this sort which recur throughout the legal system. You need another reason for developing a music-friendly or music-unfriendly regime. Once you have decided on the level of music you want, you can accomplish that through a variety of different legal arrangements, ranging from criminal law through regulation to an appropriate arrangement of reciprocal rights, duties, and privileges among the property owners or bystanders, each one of which may have important economic consequences.

As a result, it is simply meaningless to say that property rights *in general* are "strong" or "clear" without specifying just who ought to have a strong entitlement against whom or for just whom the application of the state's enforcement power ought to be clear and predictable in what circumstances. One might say, for example, that the property rights of foreign investors ought to be "strengthened" by empowering them to mobilize the state to seize the assets of local companies for payment of debts. Or one might decide the local company's "property right" ought to be strengthened by rendering it immune from this type of attachment. Either could be a development strategy—but one would need to articulate a reason why one approach rather than the other will be conducive to development.

As should be clear, moreover, from a legal point of view, property is not one, but a "bundle of rights"—rights to use, alienate, exclude, assign, rent, enjoy, etc. This bundle of property rights can often be assembled and disassembled in various ways and shared among different parties. A great deal of creative legal analysis goes into arranging and rearranging these rights. We all know when we stay at a Hilton Hotel that many corporate and private entities will share in the proceeds from our stay. The entity "Hilton Hotel" is itself a bundle of legal relationships. It will probably be quite difficult to say with precision just who "owns" the building, or the trademark, or has the right to sell alcohol in the restaurant, or who employs the workers, and so on. Just as many will have rights of one or another sort, set by rules of contract and property, many will also have obligations. The more complex a legal scheme becomes, the more difficult it is to say what it could mean for all the rights to be strong or clear—strengthening and weakening, clarifying and muddying obligations and entitlements will be precisely what is at stake in negotiations to assemble capital and labor into an entity called the "Hilton Hotel."

Moreover, it is not at all clear that "business" or "investors" will always be on the side of clear and strong rights. There will be commercial and financial interests on both sides of the discussion at every point. Indeed, we might say that in commercial negotiations, as in war, when one side has an interest in precision, the other will by definition have an interest in something more woolly. Obviously this is not axiomatically the case—there will be lots of win–win possibilities in both directions—but it is often enough true to make it difficult to make sense of any general statement about what business wants or needs in the way of a legal regime to be productive.

It is tempting to say that while rights and duties may be arranged in lots of ways, everyone shares an interest in a regime which can enforce with clarity and firmness whatever they have agreed. But this is also dubious. There will be a further moment, once the Hotel is erected and a dispute arises about who owes what duties to whom, when parties, including the state, may decide to use the legal regime to carry on that dispute. As they do so, their strategic interests will vary—some will benefit from instant and draconian enforcement, others from delay. Some from clarity, some from vagueness. Indeed, in putting the deal together, vagueness may have won out over clarity for a reason. A dynamic observation of the legal analytics involved in the implementation of legal rules also reveals a proliferation of alternative arrangements, deferrals, settlements, and so forth. Allocating property for purposes of national development requires that we form a view about whose interests in such matters ought to be furthered.

Within the domain of "private law," moreover, it is not only property. Property and contract are mixed together in all sorts of ways which affect the shape of property entitlements and the allocation of power among economic actors. In today's legal order, lawyers are adept at disaggregating ownership rights and transforming them into contracts between various parties for sharing in the use or risk or return on an economic activity. The reverse is also possible—transforming a contract right into something to own or sell. Much of our current financial architecture has been constructed in this way, including the parceling out and resale of mortgage debt in numerous ways. The private law regime which is used to reorganize entitlements back and forth from property to contract may, as a matter of policy, make these rearrangements more or less difficult, faster or slower. Moreover, policies expressed through contract doctrine may transform the meaning of property entitlements—and vice versa. A contract regime that imposes duties of care and implied warranties on sellers will also affect the freedom a property owner has to allow property to decay without affecting its value in a later transaction.

These questions of policy are also not amenable to assessment as "strong" or "weak" entitlement protection. They require choices between social and economic interests. The common lay perception that "strong" property rights are best reinforced by a "strong" contracts regime simply obscures the range of choices that need to be made to design these regimes and chart their relationship with one another. A classic example will suffice. The potential conflict between a factory owner's "strong" property right to exclude trespassers (their duty to refrain from entering) and his workers' "strong" right to freedom of contract with other employers, unions, heath-care providers and commercial entities who might seek to enter the premises for purposes of doing business with the workers (the factory owner's duty to allow access) cannot be resolved without facing a question of social policy. How easy or hard do we want to make it for employers to prevent workers from bargaining with others? The intersection between the labor regime governing relations between owners and workers and the property regime governing the "owner's" interest in the factory itself is one which might be designed in numerous ways—calling for "strong" rights of property and contract is simply to refuse to reflect on the trade-offs and possible effects on the wage rate and the mode and efficiency of production of one or another solution.

After a half-century of analysis in this spirit, the complexity of allocating entitlements and the range of plausible legal arguments for their reorganization has expanded dramatically. Boundaries among doctrinal fields have broken down—property, contract, tort, criminal law, all offer opportunities to arrange and rearrange entitlements to encourage and discourage various kinds of transaction. There simply is no baseline "private legal order" on top of which to build a market.

OWNERSHIP AND USE: PROPERTY DUTIES AND THE SOCIAL PRODUCTIVITY OF ASSETS

The idea that rights and duties ought to be arranged with a view to the economic and social consequences for the society as a whole is not new. Throughout the West, there has always been struggle over the relationship between property entitlement and the obligations to use assets productively or for social benefit. The idea that ownership brings obligations for productive use played a role in many significant historical disputes, over church lands, indigenous title, obligations of colonial occupation, and more. One result has been recognition that property law is about duties as well as rights. Not only the correlative duties of *others* not to trespass and so on, but also the many duties of owners in different periods: to cultivate, to allow tenancy, to prevent dangerous conditions, provide light and safety, support the poor, and so on. Indeed, the details of every property law regime reflect decisions about social uses and obligations as much as they liberate owners to use or waste property as they wish.

The idea of property as a source for communal and civic obligations has a wide range of legal expressions. Property may be subject to forfeiture if not maintained or cultivated. Members of the public may have access rights, including the right to squat, cultivate, even to take title by adverse possession in certain circumstances. Indeed, in England, the ability to dispose of land by testament upon death of the "owner" begins only with Henry VII and remains everywhere restricted. Where property is held in "trust," trustees who may possess or use the property will do so subject to various fiduciary obligations towards the beneficiaries of the trust. Trustee relationships have often been created by implication or judicial construction, as in the case of marital property pending divorce. As a form of private social welfare to prevent slaves, servants, children, or spouses from becoming wards of the state, family law has often been a site for the emergence of property duties to protect widows and children. This communal element in the property system is often expressed as a limit on alienability—perhaps precluding sale of the "family home" in divorce or preventing its seizure in bankruptcy.

More broadly, property ownership is often accompanied by obligations arising from other areas of law. Tax obligations are the most ubiquitous and familiar. In the United States property taxes are routinely used as the primary source of financial support for local government as well as primary and secondary education. These could, of course, be otherwise financed—just as other social purposes might well be financed by property taxes of various kinds. Taxes on transfer of property, including value added taxes and sales taxes, also impose social obligations on property owners and may restrict the speed with which property changes hands. Moreover, the use of property tax for these local purposes has all manner of policy implications, among other things on the distribution of (at least nonstigmatized) commercial property, shopping malls, office complexes, and so forth. We might also think of property taxation as a mechanism to encourage dispossession when property is not used productively, akin to very familiar doctrines of adverse possession.

Finally, every Western property system permits the imposition of obligations to sell or relinquish ownership of property for public purposes. Property may be condemned as uninhabitable or unsafe or expropriated. Temporary use by others may be compelled for safety or other public purposes, with or without compensation. Although taxation is generally distinguished from a public taking requiring compensation, at some point, given an owner's use preferences and rates, any tax burden may become confiscatory. Moreover, regulatory changes often alter property values or eliminate property rights altogether. In a dramatic example, when slavery was abolished in the United States, owners were not compensated. Similarly when the right to nominate priests was eliminated from the entitlements of property ownership, when public consumption and sale of alcohol were banned during Prohibition, or when restrictions are placed on the sale or use of guns, tobacco, or other products.

Of course *some* public takings and new regulations may well be compensated. Some may be voluntary rather than compulsory. The point is that a regime of property rights without property duties, and the ability of the state to rearrange those duties, is unknown in the West. What matters for economic and social policy is how those duties are designed and allocated.

INITIAL ALLOCATION AND THE SUBSEQUENT REARRANGEMENT OF ENTITLEMENTS

Property law—and private law more generally—is a particularly important site for thinking about social, political, and economic strategy in a society like China which is rearranging its legal and economic order in what is likely to be a once-in-a-generation way.

It will be useful to strategize carefully about the relationship between modes of property allocation and economic performance. The economic analysis of law has much to offer in comparing the potential consequences of various rule changes. We need to be careful, however, to understand the limits of economic analytics—or to notice the moment when the analytic is transformed into a looser rule of thumb, default suggestion, or hunch. This is particularly true when the opportunity arises to establish a new property regime.

Neo-classical economics offers a variety of analytics for ensuring the efficient allocation of resources within a society. Economic efficiency means efficiency within constraints. An initial allocation of factors and institutions is treated as exogenous or given. It is easy to see that different initial allocations and limitations may lead to different rates of growth and different distributional outcomes for the society as a whole—differences which may compound over time. With different factor endowments we expect different development outcomes. The possibility of gains from trade even for societies with an absolute disadvantage in the production of all goods does not alter the significance of factor endowments. Different initial allocations may place a society on alternative—even if equally efficient—economic paths with very different growth rates or patterns of distribution.

It is easy to think about factor endowments in physical terms—how much arable land, how skilled a labor pool, how much capital, what technology, and so forth. Once we begin to add social endowments and institutions to the list—how effective a government, how comprehensive an educational system—we increasingly recognize that endowments treated as exogenous limits may often be subject to change through strategy. More public goods might be provided, institutions could be strengthened, technological innovations could be encouraged, and so forth.

The crucial point about private law is this: at base, *all* factor endowments are also legal entitlements. A nation only has agricultural or mineral endowments if the entitlements of economic actors vis-à-vis one another are arranged in such a way as to facilitate exploitation and sale of ore, sunshine, water, seeds, and more. Land is only a resource if and to the extent it can be exploited for gain. Someone has to be able to defend their exclusive productive use and offer the produce for sale. Establishing a regime of private entitlements—rules about property, contract, finance, corporate authority, and obligations—is the process by which the initial factor endowment and institutional limitations are established. In a sense, all we ever buy and sell are entitlements—to use, destroy, profit from, assets of various kinds. In this sense, private law is always present at the creation.

The neo-liberal legal orthodoxy recognizes this—that is why they place property rights front and center. But, as we have seen, calling for "strong and clear property rights" tells us almost nothing about how to allocate initial private law entitlements so as to promote development. Should resources be concentrated or dispersed, should their use be exclusive or shared, ought those with neighboring plots be able to undermine one another's profitability through competition, or ought ownership to imply exclusive access to particular markets, and so on. Do we want to encourage the emergence of large national firms or many small holdings?

In my experience, the idea that "strong" rights might substitute for answering such question even when making initial allocative decisions is strengthened by two related but mistaken ideas. The first idea is that one ought to focus first on achieving efficiency—in the sense that, given factor endowments, resources within an economy are moving steadily towards their most productive use—and leave questions of distribution until later. This separation of efficiency and distribution is familiar, if contested, in economics. It makes little sense once we try to translate it into legal terms. There is simply no way to "get efficiency right" without relying on some initial definition and allocation of entitlements. These may be exogenous to the economic model, but they cannot be exogenous to the design of a legal and economic order. Put another way, there would be no price system absent the legal capacity to own, bargain, and contract. Setting up such a scheme *distributes* access to resources and establishes the capacity and respective powers of economic actors. How one does it influences what happens next. Entrenching some powers and players at the expense of others will influence the direction of an economy's development as well as the outcome of future social and political struggle over policy. Factor endowments are routinely treated as exogenous because there simply is no economic analytic for establishing an "efficient" initial allocation. In the real world, however, it must be done, and doing so requires policy, social and economic strategy.

Moreover, it is important to recognize that most economic analysis of legal rules focuses on efficiency rather than growth. This may sound like deferring distributive concerns—"growing the pie before cutting it"—but it is quite different. Indeed, there is no reason to think that the move to an efficient allocation of resources will lead to more than a one-time increase in income. It is easy to imagine a society moving from an inefficient to an efficient allocation of limited resources and ending up in another stable, but still rather low-level, equilibrium. Indeed, it may well be that growth requires the introduction of inefficiencies. Whether efficiency leads to growth will often depend on who reaps the efficiency gain and what they are permitted to do with it—questions whose answers will often be rooted, in turn, in the allocative structure of private law entitlements.

The second and related idea lending support to the "strong and clear property rights" recipe is the notion that in the general run of things, no matter how entitlements are initially allocated, we can count on market actors to rearrange them so as to maximize the productive use of a society's physical assets. As a result, the initial allocation of rights is relatively unimportant, just as the details of a private law regime are less important than the fact that whatever rights are established be "clear" so that the transaction costs of their rearrangement will be as low as possible.

It would be excellent if this turned out to be true—we could avoid any number of social and political struggles about just how to set up the legal regime. Unfortunately, this idea is also mistaken. It is certainly true that when markets work well, actors do respond to price signals and rearrange entitlements to shift resources to more productive uses. When we analyze the impact of entitlement allocations we must always think in socio-legal terms, aware of the ways in which economic actors will respond to our definition of rights and duties—will they rearrange them, ignore them, respect them, and so forth. Of course, not all entitlements are for sale or subject to private rearrangement. You may not sell your bodily organs, empty the coffers of a trust without regard to the named beneficiaries, or, in some cases, sell what are seen to be family assets in divorce even if they are held in your name. More importantly, markets for entitlements routinely fail and transaction costs are ubiquitous. Consequently, in normal situations, we ought not to expect entitlements to flow seamlessly to their most productive use.[9]

The best we are usually able to do is to allocate entitlements so as to mimic as closely as possible the allocations which we can predict might result from bargaining in the absence of transaction costs and market failures. This is itself not at all easy to do, as a generation of law and economics scholarship in the United States has made abundantly clear. Moreover, an initial allocation of entitlements may establish a pattern of relative wealth and poverty which renders the price system an unreliable mechanism for allocating resources to their socially most productive use. Where differences in initial income are extreme, wealth effects may mean that a market price sends completely different signals to the current owner and the potential purchaser. A variety of other cognitive biases may similarly impede transactions in entitlements.

The idea that we need not worry too much about initial allocations is often expressed in a more cautious version, which begins to slide from analytic to practical rule of thumb. One often hears it said that in the great run of cases one can probably count on market forces to reallocate for efficiency more confidently than one can count on government policy to do so. Of course it is true that governments can be terribly inept. We might expect comparative empirical analysis of government and market failure to be helpful here. Unfortunately, the complexity of such an analysis in the real world is so great that it is far more common for the analytic to give way at this point to the more general hunch that private parties are more likely to be get things right by the light of the price system than are bureaucrats navigating by ideology.

In any event, we will have to rely on government for enforcement of the initial allocation enacted by the private law regime—and it will matter how they do it. There is simply no escaping the problem that we have no analytic for assessing the efficiency of the *initial* allocation. In a sense, entitlements can only ever be *rearranged* by markets through buying and selling. Doing so presupposes a regime of property and contract which defines what it means to own, to buy, and to sell. Before we bargain over the price of a particular entitlement, we need to know whether this or that person has the capacity to own or to sell it. We will only be able to bargain once we know just what the state will routinely enforce—whether, for example, ownership entails the privilege to use one's property so as to undercut the value of a neighbor's property or whether his ownership entails the right to force you to desist. Or whether ownership entitlements survive when assets lie fallow, whether entitlements can be alienated at all, or without preserving a share for kin or country, whether owners may or may not remove the assets from the economy by waste or investment abroad, and more. Before we can begin to bargain about price, moreover, we will also need to know whether gifts and promises to pay are enforceable, whether prices must be "just," whether duress vitiates consent, and thousands of other details of what it means to buy and sell settled by contract law.

It might seem plausible to move through the legal order, testing each rule to see whether it allocates authority in a way which mimics what market actors would do in the absence of transaction costs, while holding all the other rules constant. Ultimately, however, in doing so we would still need to treat some ground rules as axiomatic to a market. This is easy to see if we think about all assets being held in common or all laborers being slaves. Without *someone* having the right to exclusive use and sale, or without economic actors having *some* capacity to participate legally in market activity, it would not be possible to analyze how market forces would operate to reallocate entitlements even in the absence of transaction costs. As soon as we speak of someone having capacity, however, we are in the soup of allocation—who, against whom, with respect to what, under which conditions, and so on.

At some point, in other words, the initial allocative decisions are simply exogenous to economic analysis. They require social, political, and economic judgment. Property law is the place where these judgments are written into the fundamental structure of the market—but "strong and clear rights" gives us insufficient guidance to do this well. We will need economic, political, and social strategy which cannot be derived from what market actors would do once the machine is turned on any more than it can be derived from the "nature" of property. You cannot count on the market to reverse-engineer its own most efficient origin. There is no substitute for a careful dynamic analysis of the developmental consequences of various patterns of entitlement. With that, you can design a property regime.

PROPERTY LAW ANALYTICS: "CLEAR" PROPERTY RIGHTS AND THE CALL FOR FORMALIZATION

Among development policy-makers, it is common to attribute the apparent effectiveness of legal regimes in modern and developed societies to the clarity of rules and procedures. It therefore seems sensible in developing economies to urge that informal arrangements be written down and written rules leave as little room for interpretive flexibility as possible so that their implementation will be predictable and automatic. Unfortunately, calls for the formalization of private entitlements, like general calls for ever "stronger" property rights, only obscure the distributive choices involved in constructing a private law regime—choices which ought rather to be carefully analyzed for their impact on economic growth and development.

There is a long tradition of associating legal formality with industrial capitalism and economic growth. The precise economic justifications for legal formality nevertheless remain vague. Seen as a general quality of the legal order, formality has been thought to improve the rationality and effectiveness of bureaucratic instrumentalism, ensure reliability and predictability among private actors, promote openness and transparency for both public agents (through bureaucratic regularity) and private actors (through price signaling and the reduction of transaction costs). Indeed, formality has often been treated as a kind of cure-all elixir, capable at once of restraining bureaucratic discretion and creating markets. Moreover, formalization carries some of the moral fervor of individualism, responsibility, and democracy. Formality will make the exercise of state power open and predictable, the rights and commitments of all citizens easy to understand, interpret, and enforce without the need for further policy judgments or the expertise of professionals.

This can all sound sensible—until you try to define a technical regime to implement it. In fact, developed societies differ a great deal in the relative formality of their legal arrangements and every developed legal regime is a complex mix of formality and informality. Sometimes excessive formalism ("red tape") can seem an obstacle to economic performance. Indeed, the urge to "formalize" law downplays the role of standards and discretion in the legal orders of developed economies and the importance of the informal sector in economic life. Max Weber long ago pointed out the puzzle that industrial development seemed to have come first to the nation—England—with the most confusing and least formal system of property law and judicial procedure. Polyani famously observed that rapid industrialization may have been rendered sustainable—politically, socially, and ultimately economically—in England precisely because law slowed the process down.

The informal sector—a sector governed by norms *other* than those enforced by the state or which emerge in the gaps among official institutions—is often a vibrant source of entrepreneurial energy. This was certainly the case in the post-transition economies of East and Central Europe. In many developed and developing economies, the dynamic economic life of diasporic and ethnic communities often relies on a certain distance from formal state power. Even the commanding heights of the developed economies are often self-consciously antiformal—from the "old boy's network" to free-trade zones. Businessmen in developed economies routinely disregard or sidestep the requirements of form or the enforceability of contracts. Indeed, the American "Uniform Commercial Code" explicitly sought to reflect the needs of businessmen precisely by reference to the "reasonableness" of contractual arrangements as that broad term is understood in the business community.

Moreover, the association of development with formalization downplays the range of possible legal formalizations, each with its own winners and losers. Formalization allocates understanding and shifts access to resources compared to the situation prior to formalization. A clear title may make it easier for me to sell my land. The impact on the price of land is less clear. Formalization of my title might make my land cheaper or more expensive for my neighbor to buy depending upon the value we each place on clarity and the range of other modes of property available. The reliable enforcement of contracts might make me more likely to trust someone enough to enter into a contract. This also may increase—or decrease—the price they can demand for their promise. In the absence of formalization, perhaps I would need to pay a premium to ensure he performed—or perhaps his promise would be worth less if I needed to procure the public good of clarity and enforcement on the private market.

Formalization may reduce or eliminate the chance for productive economic activity for some economic actors. Although clear title may help me to sell or defend my claims to land, it may impede the productive opportunities for squatters now living there or neighbors whose uses would interfere with my quiet enjoyment—or the access members of my family have traditionally had to the same parcel. Clear rules about investment may make it easy for foreign investors—but by reducing the wealth now in the hands of those with local knowledge about how credit is allocated or how the government will behave. An enforceable contract will be great for the person who wants the promise enforced, but not so for the person who has to pay up. As every first-year contracts student learns, it is one thing to say stable expectations need to be respected, and quite another to say whose expectations need to be respected and what those expectations should legitimately or reasonably be. To say anything about the relationship between legal formalization and *development* we would need a theory about how assets in the hands of the title holder *rather than* the squatter, the foreign *rather than* the local investor will lead to growth, and then to the sort of growth we associate with "development."

Moreover, the relative "clarity" of property rights will often be in the eye of the beholder. For local entrepreneurs, informal and technically imprecise arrangements may be far more comprehensible and predictable than any formalization, while a clear set of nondiscretionary rules about property, credit, or contract might make a foreign legal culture more transparent to me as a potential foreign investor. Formalization was often the substantive development program urged upon nations by foreign direct investors. At the same time, formalization of titles—like the adoption of international standards and accounting procedures—may render an economic sector altogether incomprehensible for many economic actors who had previously been active in it. Conventional forms of credit may simply dry up—and there is no guarantee formalization will give rise to a dense enough market to generate new forms of credit responsive to new forms. Although formalization might encourage foreign and discourage local participation in an economic sector—like real estate—it might also discourage foreign investors who might otherwise jump the knowledge barrier to participate in the local market.

In short, the economic consequences of formalization will depend upon a very localized assessment of who benefits and what they do with their new knowledge about and access to resources. In land reform, ought title to be given to the "head of household," to "the family," to the "matriarch," or to the community in common? Before formalization, each may have had some call on the resources of the land. Formalization may place all the eggs in one basket. Whether farm production or urban sprawl—and ultimately GDP—will rise or fall may depend upon just which basket that is.

Moreover, it will not always be the case that increased formality strengthens an owner's title. Indeed, although they are often conflated in discussion, the case for formalization is distinct from that for "strong" property rights. Sometimes an owner's entitlements will be strengthened by the use of a standard rather than a rule—the right to use my property in any "reasonable" way may well be "stronger" than more precise enumeration of prohibited and permitted uses, depending upon the surrounding cultural meanings of "reasonable." When a tangle of precise local rules can only be manipulated by insiders—foreign investors may prefer to rely on vague standards which are given meaning in routine business practice where they come from. Similarly, non-owners may well prefer the ability to make "fair use" of copyrighted material to an enumeration of permitted excerpting practices.

For development policy, it is not enough to defend "formalization" as a technical matter of "good law." The form of property protection everywhere raises allocative and distributional questions requiring political or economic analysis to resolve. All too often, formalization offers itself as a substitute for all the traditional questions about who will do what with the returns they receive from work or investment, how gains might best be captured and reinvested or capital flight eliminated, how one might best take spillover effects into account and exploit forward or backward linkages. Or questions about the politics of tolerable growth and social change, about the social face of development itself, about the relative fate of men and women, rural and urban, along different policy paths.

Over the last years, enthusiasm for formality in legal arrangements has supported various reforms associated with the opening of local economies to global economic forces. In international discussions of economic policy, formalism has meant strict construction of free-trade commitments, the harmonization of private law so as to eliminate "social" exceptions susceptible to differential judicial application, the insulation of the international private law regime from national judiciaries, the simplification and harmonization of national regulations, the substitution of privately adopted rules for public law standards, the development of a reliable system of bills of lading and insurance to permit contracts "for the delivery of documents" rather than goods—eliminating rejection for nonconformity, and the formalization and standardization of international payments systems and banking regulations. At the national level, formalization has meant the regularization—and reduction—of local administrative discretion, the simplification of procedures for access to credit or administrative permission to engage in economic activity, the adoption of internationally recognized accounting, safety and other regulatory standards, as well as of private and commercial law regimes familiar to foreign investors, and the extension of formal land tenure regimes to markets and assets traditionally managed informally.

Although each of these reforms could be seen, at least in some cases, to involve a relative increase in the formality of entitlements, it is difficult not to conclude that they hang together more comfortably as elements of a general project to disestablish the development state and open markets to private investors. In that project, sometimes it will be useful to render some entitlements more formal—while others will need to be relaxed or simply left alone. Conspicuously absent is a nuanced analytic capable of distinguishing entitlements due for formalization from those better left as is. Rather, there is something mesmerizing about the idea that a formalization of entitlements *in general* could somehow substitute for struggle over these issues and choices. This may be why one rarely hears carefully calibrated demands for clarity here, but not there, of these entitlements, but not those. It is in this sense that what may have begun as an analytic devolves into program or slogan.

CONCLUSION: ANALYTICS AND IDEOLOGY IN THE CASE FOR ENTITLEMENT REFORM

We probably ought not to be surprised that policymakers repeatedly fall back on general ideas about "strong" and "formal" entitlements when making development policy. It is extremely difficult to link a rigorous economic analytic to the detailed choices involved in constructing a legal regime. Moreover, it is not as if lawyers themselves know how to make the necessary allocative decisions. In constructing a legal regime, it will often be necessary to choose between two entitlements and, ultimately, two different social actors. For more than a century, in such situations, legal analysts have turned to other fields for insight about what to do. It would be a relief if one could decide simply by preferring strong to weak rights, formal to informal legal arrangements—and end up with economic efficiency, growth, and development!

Lawyers long ago realized that they cannot figure out how to make technical decisions about the structure of private entitlements without assistance from the best political and economic ideas. As a result, lawyers have internalized a whole series of debates which are familiar to economists, sociologists, psychologists, moral philosophers, and other social scientists. The "economic analysis of law" represents one such strand—lawyers borrowing bits of analysis from economics to help resolve technical choices within the legal field. Lawyers do not always do this well, of course. It would be more accurate to say that a variety of slogans and lay versions of economic or social theories have become part of the standard analytic repertoire of the legal profession. But the practice of referring to economic analysis makes it all the more puzzling when economists return the favor by proposing that difficult questions of economic policy be solved by implementation of "good law," "strong rights," or "clear entitlements."

It turns out that for both disciplines, the pretense that legal regimes are designed by the light of careful analytics is exaggerated. In both fields, we often find ideology posing as analysis instead. Land reform offers a good example. The economic and political significance of law is easy to see in land reform programs, precisely because land reform is law reform—a change in the allocation of entitlements among people with respect to land. As a technical matter, "land reform" presents numerous choices. It may involve public or private land, acquired through purchase or expropriation or some combination, with more or less compensation to past owners. The compensation may be current or deferred, linked to alternative productive investment or open-ended. Land reform may be apply to large or small or all parcels, to parcels used in some ways and not others. The new owners may be selected in different ways, and may have a variety of different entitlements—to use, sell, occupy, till, or rent the land, under conditions or unconditionally, individually or collectively. The land may become public or communal property, may be more consolidated or more dispersed after the reform, and so forth. Land reform may disrupt or solidify existing power dynamics within families, may track or disrupt traditional or customary patterns of land ownership and usage. As a practical matter, land reform may involve more or less land, may involve relocation or not, may be more or less effectively implemented, and may be extended beyond its formal terms by popular support, or resisted tooth and nail on the ground. In the postwar period, land reforms differed quite dramatically in all these ways.

None of these choices can be resolved by reflection on the "nature" of property, or the desirability of "strong" and "clear" property rights. It may be that careful economic analysis could clarify which approach to each issue is most likely to generate development in specific situations. To the extent that this is true we might expect land reform programs to reflect careful fine-tuning in light of development objectives rooted in this kind of analysis. In fact, however, postwar land reform in developing countries reflected far more the pull and push of political and ideological struggle. As a general matter, land reform was routinely associated with import substitution industrialization, more a matter of loose ideological fit than careful economic analysis. For contemporaneous economic theories of industrialization and growth the agricultural sector was not in focus. But the expropriation of rural landowners seemed analogous in a general way to the nationalization of industries or natural resources, which were themselves seen as a way to achieve the objective of mobilizing the nation's resources for a big push to industrialization.

Although policymakers argued for "land reform" as a tool for economic development, the specific choices necessary to design a land reform program came to have connotations associated with ideological and political positions. It was then common for technical choices which seemed ideologically analogous (more or less state, more or less collective management) to be linked together—and decoupled from careful assessment of their many possible economic consequences in particular settings. In literature about the details of land reform—paying compensation, allocating land to individuals, families, or communities, and so forth—discussion then focused on the significance of these details for the ideological meaning of the reforms—public or private ownership, expropriation with or without compensation—or their likely impact on rural poverty, itself not a priority for the economic development theories of the day.

In the implementation, political opportunity counted for a great deal. Far-reaching land reform regimes were implemented in postwar Japan and in regions where the collapse of Japanese colonial rule or occupation allowed land reformers to ignore the interests of the landed, who were no longer politically entrenched. Where relatively strong or authoritarian national regimes were independent of landed interests, as in postwar Taiwan, more far-reaching programs were possible. As the great ideological division of the world emerged in the postwar years, land reform was often a marker for a regime's political identity. In Mexico, it was remembered and continued as part of a nationalist and socialist tradition linked to the revolution. Where it seemed "left" or "communist" in many places, in Taiwan and Korea it seemed a moderate alternative to what was understood to be going on in China.

As a result, it has become conventional to analyze particular land reform initiatives by reference to the vectors of political and institutional pressure brought to bear on their design, rather than by seeking to reverse-engineer the economic commitments or policy objectives of their craftsmen. One could align all of the various choices involved in the construction of a land reform on a series of related axes in ways which made one axis seem "more radical" than the other. Large scope, the taking of private land, without compensation, giving it to the least well-off, to hold communally—taken together, these seem to go "further" than their alternatives. But this is ideology speaking. As a matter of economics, it might well be that these choices do not all cut in the same direction when it comes to increasing or decreasing production or income inequality. Nor is it clear that all the details of the regime line up this way. Take offering the title to individuals or families—it is not clear which "goes further" or is "more radical," or even which accords with and which disrupts traditional patterns of landholding or use. The presentation of land reform as either "effective" or "ineffective" depending on whether it "went far enough" obscures more than it clarifies.

This frame can make it seem that we know what an *effective* land reform looks like—how far it does and does not "go." Once we know what land reform was meant to accomplish, any disappointments are easily chalked up to "resistance." By lumping opposing political interests and economic ideas together with historical inertia, this downplays differences among the objectives, as if reducing rural poverty and stimulating export production would naturally be aligned. Attention to the range of legal possibilities within a land reform regime—and to the dynamic relationship between the legal scheme and those operating in its shadow—may help clarify the distance between land reform as an ideal development policy and land reform as a lived social and political practice. A more nuanced legal analysis, attentive to the interaction of informal and formal legal mechanisms, might have been helpful in ensuring that the more complex strategic objectives proposed by heterogenous economic strategies of "dependent development," for example, might have been achieved. Land reform regimes were not exceptional in this regard.

The history of thinking about the relationship between property and development suggests that analysis of legal entitlements relating to property *could* focus attention on political and economic choices significant for development. "Capital," like labor, is a legal institution. Owning and contracting are key pieces in productive allocation of resources. The allocative priorities of any economic theory of development will need to be realized on the terrain of law, and an understanding of the moving parts and levers, both in the formal legal system and in its institutional and social realization ought to be quite useful to development policy-makers.

At the same time, however, precisely this attention to levers and moving parts ought to make us wary of broad claims for the development magic to be wrought by formalizing and strengthening property rights in general. The claims made for formalization—transparency, improved information, and price signaling, facilitating alienation, reducing transaction costs, assuring security of title and economic return, inspiring confidence and trust needed for investment—are all claims about the desirability of returns to some players rather than others. From a development perspective, it will all depend upon what we can expect those benefiting from the allocations embedded in any particular scheme for improving transparency to do with their new access to resources.

Moreover, the phrase "clear and strong property rights" has been used to refer to a very broad bundle of quite different ideas for the design of a legal order. It has been used to refer to the formalization of customary asset usage, the simplification of bureaucratic schemes relating to entrepreneurial activity or access to credit, the initiation of a scheme for clear and registered land titles, reform of contract law to prioritize simplicity and reliable enforcement (whether through standardized contracts, the legal enforcement of well-known business customs, or the displacement of national regulation by private arrangements), the use of rules rather than standards, more deductive and less policy-oriented legal reasoning, a reduction in the administrative or judicial discretion necessary to administer the legal order, the elimination of any regulatory overlay on baseline property or contract entitlements, or a private law oriented to owners and sellers rather than users and buyers.

In particular circumstances, many of these might be good ideas—although none of these ideas is straightforward enough to be implemented without encountering numerous further choices with allocative implications. In no sense do they together comprise a plausible, let alone universal, recipe for development. Each of these ideas obscures the many choices internal to property law—more transparent to *whom*, the squatter or the trespasser? Presented as a general recipe, the demand for clear and strong property rights understates the role of discretion in developed legal orders and the importance of standards (like "reasonableness") even in advanced commercial orders. The use of law to slow or moderate economic change, in the interest of the long-run sustainability of development, is likewise underplayed. Moreover, as an analytic matter, the call for clear rights ignores a series of classic baseline problems which must be resolved to interpret those rights—distinguishing laws imposing "costs on the transaction" from those "supporting the transaction," for example, or distinguishing prices "distorted" by regulation from prices "bargained in the shadow" of regulation.

The call for clear property rights obscures the range of alternative property regimes which have always been at work within the industrialized West, reflecting different resolutions to the management of social/economic/political conflicts. Worrying about the clarity or strength of property rights focuses attention on the current allocation of rights, reducing attentiveness to past and future possible allocations, and making path dependence harder to avoid. The result discourages the more complex analysis necessary to arrange the various elements in the "bundle of rights" so as to encourage efficient productivity, engaging the dynamic potential in both past and possible future allocative arrangements. This in turn obscures the opportunity to choose among alternative, perhaps equally efficient or productive economic models through property right allocation, while underestimating the relationship between property rights and other institutional forms and legal regimes in the society which may alter the meaning of those rights in practice.

In short, there are many reasons for adopting a healthy skepticism about claims that clear or strong property rights are necessary or even possible as a path to economic development. Perhaps the most significant consequence of the property rights mantra has been the propagation of a serious misestimation of the allocative role of law. A property regime, like any other legal order, is all about choices. Small and large, these choices cannot be made by reasoning outward from the nature of property or general ideas about what constitutes "good law." They require economic, social, and ethical analysis, and must be made and contested in those terms.

NOTES

1. Kennedy (2006a, 2006b).
2. Hale (1923).
3. Cohen (1927–8: 13).
4. Ibid.
5. Ibid.
6. Cohen (1927–8: 17).
7. Cohen (1927–8: 19).
8. This set of choices was elaborated in an early classic in the "law and economics" literature, Calabresi and Melamed (1972). In the years since Calebresi and Melamed introduced a typology identifying these choices, legal scholars have proposed a wide range of rules of thumb to resolve this type of allocation problem so as to maximize economic performance. They have proposed assigning the initial entitlement so as to encourage the party able to resolve information problems most cheaply to do so, using property rules where transaction costs are low (a bowdlerized reading of the Coase hypothesis: doesn't matter to whom they are assigned initially) and liability rules where transaction costs are high (multiple parties, holdouts, freeloaders); allowing distributional concerns to encourage placing entitlement on the weaker or poorer party initially; favoring inalienability rules for such "moralisms" as intentional torts, and more. There is nothing in the nature of property and nothing in "strong" or "clear" property rights which would give any indication about how this problem should be resolved. What is required is an analysis of the distributional consequences between the parties and the dynamic consequences for the social and economic system of choosing one or another mode of property protection. The point is by now a familiar one—the turn to "property rights" as an economic strategy returns us to considerations of economic, social, and political choice, this time for reasons embedded in the internal analytics of the legal field.
9. In both legal and economic literatures, Ronald Coase is often cited for the proposition that regardless of how entitlements are initially allocated, things will work out fine in the end if economic actors are allowed a free, unregulated hand in their rearrangement. It is important to remember that this is not what Coase said. He proposed a model in which economic actors could be expected to rearrange entitlements efficiently, but it was a model which he acknowledged departed from the real world of economic policy in crucial respects—most importantly, the absence of transaction costs and the free tradability of all entitlements. See Coase (1960). It was his focus on transaction costs which opened the door to a productive tradition within the economic analysis of law. See, for example, Calabresi and Melamed (1972). Coase was less concerned about entitlements whose sale or transfer was itself subject to legal limitation. Such limits, however, form at least part of every property right.

REFERENCES

Calabresi, G. and Melamed, D. (1972), "Property Rules, Liability Rules, and Inalienability: One View of the Cathedral," *Harvard Law Review*, 85/6: 1089–128. Reprinted with introduction and bibliography in David Kennedy and William Fisher (eds), *The Canon of American Legal Thought* (Princeton, NJ: Princeton University Press, 2006), 403–42.

Coase, R. (1960), "The Problem of Social Cost," *Journal of Law and Economics*, 3/1: 1–44. Reprinted with introduction in David Kennedy and W. Fisher (eds), *The Canon of American Legal Thought* (Princeton, NJ: Princeton University Press, 2006), 355–400.

Cohen, M. R. (1927–8), "Property and Sovereignty," *Cornell Law Quarterly*, 13: 8–30.

Hale, R. (1923), "Coercion and Distribution in a Supposedly Noncoercive State," *Political Science Quarterly*, 38: 470–94.

Kennedy, D. (2006a), "Three Globalizations of Law and Legal Thought: 1850–2000," in David Trubek and Alvaro Santos (eds), *The New Law and Economic Development: A Critical Appraisal* (Cambridge: Cambridge University Press).

——(2006b), *The Rise and Fall of Classical Legal Thought* (unpublished manuscript 1975); published with a new preface by the author (Washington, DC: Beard Books).

6

Rural Land Rights in China

Roy Prosterman

INTRODUCTION

A substantial majority of China's population remains rural and agrarian—despite the highly publicized development of urban centers—and lags far behind by practically every measure. Agricultural land is the principal asset by which this rural majority earns its livelihood. Its relationship to that land, as embodied in law, policy, and actual practice, has been and will remain central to the course of China's economic, social, and political development over the foreseeable future.

The land tenure issue, and what to do about it, continues to be a subject of controversy. As this chapter was being written, articles appeared in the Western media[1] noting that a small but significant movement was afoot—and was facing strong official opposition—to give Chinese farmers full private ownership of the land they till. In one of the same media accounts, a prominent Chinese academic opposed to private ownership was quoted as saying that if the Chinese government wants "the same problems as India has, then they should go ahead and privatize the land," and arguing that "the current system of state [*sic*] ownership"[2] should be maintained.

Actually, both extremes in what has emerged as an ideologically charged debate are probably ignoring the optimum resolution of China's rural land tenure problem. Neither of these polar positions (private ownership vs status quo) seems adequately advertent with respect to the rural land tenure issue, either to recent Chinese history, to the comparative Asian experience, or—perhaps most relevant of all, in the current setting—to the promising intermediate options that are already available under China's legal system, even with that system's many flaws.

The present chapter is written from the disciplinary perspective of the law, and against the background of more than two decades of fieldwork and policy advisory work by the lawyers of Landesa on land tenure issues in rural China,[3] as well as more than four decades of comparative fieldwork and advisory work on such issues elsewhere in Asia and in the world's other major agricultural regions.[4]

The United Nations Food and Agricultural Organization (FAO) estimates that over 800 million Chinese inhabit the agricultural sector, about 65 percent of the population.[5] Some Chinese estimates are lower, but at the time of writing none puts the proportion depending on agriculture as anything less than a majority of the country's 1.3 billion people. The nature of Chinese farmers' relationship to the land they till was critical to bringing the Communist Party to power in the first place, and it remains central to the outcome of a series of fundamental issues that confront the Chinese government today, almost six decades later. These include the urban–rural gap in incomes and in other indicators, the loss of agricultural land to takings for nonagricultural purposes, rural unrest, and the pace and characteristics of urbanization.

To a considerable extent, these problems can be traced to a single fundamental shortcoming in China's rural reforms. For, while China became the first of the collectivized agricultures to break up its collectives into individual family farms (in 1979–84), this was initially done in such a way as to leave the great majority of the now roughly 190 million farm families with insecure and unstable relationships to the individual land parcels they tilled.

Despite the central government's qualified progress in improving farmers' tenure security in the past decade-and-a-half, the majority of farmers still remain insecure, unable to invest in their land, without measurable land wealth, and often at the mercy of local cadres and officials on issues such as (poorly compensated) takings of agricultural land for nonagricultural purposes.

The present chapter will continue with a review of the rural land tenure situation from the accession of the Communist Party to power in 1949 up through the legislative reforms of 1998 and 2002. The following section will discuss the status of tenure reforms as of mid-2005, when a major field survey—the third of a series—was conducted by Landesa, Renmin University (Beijing), and Michigan State University.

The next section will bring the rural land tenure story up to date as of this writing, with the adoption of the Property Law (in March 2007) and new central government actions to protect farmers' land rights. Next we will make the broader, overall argument that farmers' land rights under existing provisions of law—if those laws are effectively implemented—are not sufficiently inferior to full private ownership to warrant a battle over the difference. The following section will then look at what—from a legal and administrative point of view—still appears needed if there is in fact to be full implementation of the long-term land rights for farmers that are presently on the legislative books. Finally, we attempt to answer the following question: if, contrary to expectations, there were a move to full private ownership for farmers within the fairly near term, what regulatory features might be introduced that could make this as beneficial (and carrying as few downside risks) as possible, thus commanding the broadest political support? The last section offers a brief addendum and update.

FARMERS' LAND TENURE RIGHTS SINCE 1949

The Chinese Revolution led by the Communist Party gained much of its support from the deeply aggrieved rural poor, especially the large population of tenant farmers who typically had neither secure nor equitable access to land and who paid high rents to their landlords.[6]

After coming to power in 1949, the Communist Party's initial land reform gave farmers full, individual private ownership of their small farms through the 1950 Land Reform Law and other accompanying regulations. Under this law, China redistributed over half of its arable land to 50–60 million poor rural households, comprising more than 60 percent of its rural population, on an equitable basis. Land certificates or titles were issued to farmers as well.[7]

The success of this, mainland China's initial "land to the tiller" program, in improving agricultural production and farm incomes was impressive. From 1949 to 1956, mainland China's annual grain production increased altogether by an estimated 70 percent, and total farm income rose by an estimated 85 percent.[8] These results, and the use of full private ownership as the form of tenure provided, closely paralleled the post-World War II land tenure reforms being successfully carried out around the same time in Japan, South Korea, and Taiwan,[9] all at that time with majority agricultural populations.

But, just as the land tenure reforms in Japan, South Korea, and Taiwan were being allowed by those leaderships to persist and spread their benefits throughout the rural and gradually the entire economy, mainland China was shifting to a drastically different approach. Mao Zedong made the disastrous decision to reverse the initial reform, choosing to follow in the footsteps of the then-Soviet Union, and introducing a sequence of legal and policy measures designed to bring about the "collectivization" of all farming beginning in 1956. Agricultural production plummeted, and 15 million to 30 million consequent deaths occurred during the years 1958–62.[10] After 1962, the central government geared down to smaller, village-based collectives rather than continuing with giant communes, also allowing farmers to possess small "private plots" on up to 5 percent of the land, but overall production recovered only slowly.[11]

From the late 1970s, several regions of China started to experiment with tearing down the collective farms and giving individual farmers some limited freedom to farm on those formerly collectively farmed lands. After initial success, this system—called the "Household Responsibility System" or HRS—spread rapidly. Technically, the collectives remained as the landowners and contracted out land parcels to individual households to use for private farming for a period of time, usually allocating the land on an equal per capita basis. The contracting farmers, in return, were obligated to fulfill their "responsibilities" of quotas or taxes to the collectives every year (in the form of grain or cash), based on the quantity of land they had been allocated.

The introduction of the HRS unleashed the energy and resources of tens of millions of rural families and jump-started China's agricultural growth. As a result, between 1979 and 1984, average net income for rural residents increased by 11 percent annually, compared to an average annual increase of 8.7 percent for urban residents.[12] The introduction of the HRS led to the smallest income gap (though at much lower absolute levels of income) of the past several decades, at one point reflected in a ratio of rural-to-urban incomes that had narrowed to 1:1.7. The HRS was an enormously successful reform, lifting the living standards of hundreds of millions of rural people, and was the driving force behind the single greatest poverty-reduction achievement worldwide of the past three decades.[13]

However, emerging as a vital "Catch 22," farmers' land rights under the HRS were generally insecure and short term. "Land readjustments" stood out as the top threat to farmers' land tenure security. Although land use rights were theoretically allocated to farm households for a specific period of years, most villages in China adopted the practice of periodically readjusting or reallocating landholdings in response to changes in individual household makeup, total village population, and loss of land through land-takings or expropriations.[14]

Such land-takings or expropriations by government have further undermined farmers' land rights, not only by frequently triggering readjustments that "spread the pain" and generalized the resulting tenure insecurity, but also in paying little, or sometimes nothing, for the land taken. With China's booming economy, more and more agricultural lands have been converted for urban or industrial use. A large majority of land-losing farmers have fared poorly during the process, which is generally nontransparent and affords them grossly inadequate compensation.[15]

Rights to a piece of land subject to periodic and unexpected readjustments or poorly compensated takings cannot be considered either secure or marketable. As Landesa interviews of farmers during the last two decades have indicated,[16] farmers will not make mid- to long-term investments on a land parcel which they may not possess the next year or year after; potential market transactions in land rights are likewise strongly constrained as to the length of the term (let alone the possibility of an assignment or full transfer), from any putative transferee's perspective, because of the unpredictable duration of the possessory right the transferee would be acquiring. With mid- to long-term land improvements severely limited, the initial benefits brought by the HRS tailed off beginning in the mid-1980s and Chinese farmers' income gains started to lag far behind those of urban residents. By the end of 2007 the rural–urban income ratio had steadily worsened to 1:3.33.[17] Nor was the income gap the only indication of the disadvantaged rural sector. For example, two out of every 10,000 rural people can attend college, while the ratio in the cities is more than 280 times higher. Moreover, the life expectancy of a rural resident is approximately twelve years shorter than someone who lives in a big city such as Beijing or Shanghai.[18]

Concerned about the rural land-tenure problem, and its seeming contribution to lagging agricultural growth and the growing urban–rural gap in incomes, the central government began to seek a solution. In 1993, a policy directive was issued, which set as a broad policy that the land should be contracted to farmers for a period of thirty years.[19] But this fell far short of a general, mandatory enactment. Although often followed by the lower government organs, policy directives do not have the binding power of law behind them.

The thirty-year policy was embodied in formal law for the first time as a result of the adoption by the Standing Committee of the National People's Congress of the revised Land Management Law (LML) in August 1998, which explicitly mandates that the land be contracted to farm households for a term of thirty years, accompanied by a written contract.[20] The LML further restricts land readjustments in various ways, including requiring two-thirds approval by village members.

Under these policy and legal reforms, China began the "second round of contracting" that extended farmers' land use rights to thirty years in the mid- to late 1990s (the first round of contracting being the initial HRS), starting slowly and accelerating with the public discussion and then adoption of the LML in 1998. Provinces adopted various implementation regulations pursuant to the LML. Written contracts or certificates spelling out farmers' thirty-year rights were increasingly issued as a part of the second round of contracting, especially with the advent of the LML with its requirement that written contracts be issued.

Then, in 2002, the NPC Standing Committee adopted the Rural Land Contracting Law (RLCL),[21] representing a major breakthrough in the process of strengthening the legal regime for farmers' thirty-year rights to land and the first piece of modern Chinese legislation to exclusively address farmers' rights to this, their most important asset. Going beyond the LML, the RLCL requires an end to the practice of land readjustments in China in all but extreme cases.

The RLCL further requires that both written contracts (executed by the farmer and a representative of the collective) and certificates (unilaterally executed by a representative of level higher than county) be issued to confirm the contracting relationship. In addition, the RLCL spells out in detail the right to lease, assign, exchange, and carry out other transactions of contracted land (except mortgage and, since individual farmers aren't owners, formal sale[22]), greatly improving the legal framework for marketability of rural land. A series of penalties and remedies are also spelled out in the new law, for violations of farmers' land rights, and farmers are given (at least in theory) the ability to go directly to the People's Court with claims that their land rights have been violated.

FARMERS' LAND-TENURE RIGHTS IN RECENT PRACTICE

The latest findings on the implementation and impact of tenure security in rural China come from a seventeen-province survey of 1,962 households, conducted in mid-2005 by Landesa in cooperation with Renmin University (Beijing) and Michigan State University. This was the third such large-scale survey conducted by Landesa since the adoption of the LML, the other two having been carried out in 1999 and 2001.[23] Broadly, the latest findings indicate that there were important positive impacts, including farmer investments in the land, associated with Chinese farmers' possession of documentation for their land rights. We summarize here the chief tenure-related findings of the 2005 survey.[24]

Positive findings include:

- Where farmers have received documentation of their land rights (contract, certificate, or both), their mid- to long-term investment in their land has substantially increased.[25]
- This holds true even more strongly where the documents received comply with law and are in proper form, and more strongly still where document issuance has been accompanied by reiterated publicity for farmers' land rights.
- Publicity has successfully conveyed to large majorities of Chinese farmers certain basic facts as to their land rights, such as that their arable land should be contracted to them for thirty years without readjustment.

- In villages where farmers possess documents, and especially documents complying with law, farmers—although still only a minority—are much more likely to be satisfied with the compensation package received in cases of land-takings.[26]
- There are some indications that a land market may be emerging, including an increasing number of longer-term transfers, accompanied by meaningful levels of payment for land rights in light of comparative Asian land market data. The capitalized value of the annual rents involved in compensated land rights lease transactions suggested a potential market value (for agricultural uses only) equivalent to around $5,000 per hectare might be emerging for full assignment of thirty-year rights.
- The survey indicates that the central government also appears to have successfully brought about a substantial degree of local implementation of the laws and policies it has promulgated in four other land-related areas, as reflected in the decline in prevalence of the two-field system, scale farming, and recontracting,[27] and the effective reduction of taxes and fees paid by farmers.[28] Thus, it appears that a highly credible argument can be made on a context-setting point of vital concern: where the central government focuses, and makes its will clear, *it can succeed in making pro-farmer laws and policies effective*, even on matters where the collective cadres have largely contrary interests.

Nevertheless, the survey also yields multiple negative findings:

- 17 percent of villages have not yet conducted the second round of contracting or given farmers the thirty-year rights in even the most nominal way.
- 63 percent of rural households have received some documentation (contract, certificate, or both) for their land rights, and only 38 percent of households have received both documents, as required by law.
- Only one out of every ten farmers possesses at least one of these documents in a form substantially compliant with law (and it is for this minority group that the rate of land investment has been greatest).
- 30 percent of the villages that have purportedly given farmers thirty-year land rights have subsequently "readjusted" (almost all of them illegally) farmers' contracted land.
- Only 20 percent of farmers have actually heard of the RLCL, and their knowledge of their specific rights varies greatly from subject to subject.[29]
- During the last ten years, the frequency of takings of farmers' land has grown more than fifteen times over, and in only 22 percent of takings were farmers actually consulted about the amount of compensation.
- Processes for redress available to farmers for their complaints about compensation for takings have been highly inadequate, and rarely produce a result favorable to the farmers.
- In early 2007, another serious property-takings problem emerged in several provinces and threatened to spread. It involves the taking of farmers' foundation plots and houses, heretofore considered sacrosanct in terms of security of tenure,[30] "replacing" the houses and plots with rights to apartments in a high-rise buildings. The buildings are often kilometers away. Apart from the issue of destruction of the community, the replacement program often

raises grave problems for farmers' continuing use of their contracted arable land, which is sometimes surrendered as well. This is often called, locally, the "three concentrations": concentrate farmers' living quarters; concentrate land for nonagricultural construction (by consolidating and using the former separate residential plots); and concentrate farmland (if individual farmers have surrendered it as too difficult to use from their new residence location).

THE PROPERTY LAW AND OTHER NEW INITIATIVES

Some, but not all, of the outstanding issues with respect to farmers' land rights have been addressed in the new Property Law, promulgated by the National People's Congress on March 16, 2007, which became effective on October 1, 2007.[31]

Among the positive features of this new law:

- It reiterates and reaffirms the major provisions of the RLCL on securing farmers' land rights, but now embodies them in what is considered a more fundamental law—including its having been adopted at a full plenary session of the National People's Congress, and not just by the Standing Committee of the NPC (as was the case for the LML and the RLCL).
- It further strengthens the conceptual underpinnings for farmers' land rights by defining them as usufructuary property rights (*in rem* rights), something which had only been implicit in the RLCL.
- It allows the farmer to continue contracting his or her contracted land upon expiration of the present thirty-year term.
- It creates the basis for much greater compensation for the land-losing farmers where land-takings occur. This includes compensation for the land itself (not just for standing crops or possible farmer resettlement), reversing the prior rule, under which compensation for the land was to be paid to the collective cadres, who were to use it, supposedly, "for designated purposes of the collective."[32]
- It contains provisions on partitioning common property which may help protect women's land rights.

But there are still many shortcomings and gaps in the new law. It still falls far short of the comprehensive reform of legal rules as to land-takings that is needed; it lacks specific rules both empowering and protecting farmers with respect to their foundation (housing) plots, now under threat from local "three concentrations" efforts; it fails to lift the existing prohibition against mortgage of farmers' rights to arable land (though this prohibition would have been lifted in some early drafts); it lacks specific and functional rules for formal public registration of rural land rights (which probably should be enacted in a separate law); and it would benefit from further clarifications, even as to some of its positive provisions.

Following the adoption of the Property Law, two important steps have been taken that hold further promise of new momentum for the effective implementation of farmers' land rights pursuant to both that law and the RLCL. The first was the announcement of a major new implementation campaign to be carried out jointly by seven ministries and ministry-level entities of the central government.[33] The second was an even stronger and more authoritative mandate for a comprehensive implementation campaign, including many specifics, in the 2008 "No. 1 Document," which sets the priorities for rural work during the year.[34] For the first time, this document is entirely dedicated to the protection and enforcement of farmers' land rights, including their residential land as well as their cultivated land.

The seven-ministry campaign speaks of "specialized rectification conducted on the basis of examination of rural land contracting and land-takings," and sets five overall goals:[35]

1. Implementation of farmers' rural land-contracting rights in terms of documentation. The language refers to both nonissuance of land certificates and absence of land contracts, and sets a quantitative goal for certificate issuance to "be above 90 percent." (Impractically, it adds "by year end," but this has now been extended.)
2. Protection of farmers' land-contracting rights.
3. Enhancing the ability to resolve land disputes. (Our 2005 survey and our separate "rapid rural appraisal" field interviewing have found this in the past to be almost nonexistent.)
4. Strengthening the management of land contracting.
5. Refraining from illegal land-takings.

Reports on progress in the campaign appearing in the Chinese press as of November 2007[36] spoke of initial success in resolving more than 30,000 cases of rural land grievances, and holding liable more than 1,000 officials and others for violating farmers' land rights.

The 2008 No. 1 Document of the Central Committee and the State Council was issued at the end of January 2008, and lays an even broader and more authoritative basis for an implementation campaign, including these points:[37]

- It demands ensuring the issuance of land rights certificates to all farm households.
- For the first time, it raises the need to "speed up establishment of a land contracting and operation rights registration system."
- It reiterates (never done in previous No. 1 documents) the need to "strictly implement legal rules on no readjustment and no taking-back of farmers' contracted land within the contract period."
- It demands "resolutely preventing and correcting the problems of forcing farmers to transfer land and convert the use of such land through transfers," evidently targeting the so-called three concentrations.
- It reiterates the task of "stopping townships and village entities from violating farmer households' land contracting and operation rights through 're-contracting' and other forms of activities."
- It raises the need also for the first time to "strengthen broker service for rural land transfers."
- It calls for "improving the [land management] system concerning land transfer contracting, transfer registration, and filing."

- It highlights the need to reform China's land-takings system through improving procedural safeguards and increased compensation.
- It states in a very tough tone that "absolutely no approval should be rendered [for takings] if compensation is low, compensation is not timely or fully delivered and social security safety net is not implemented in reality."
- It stresses the prohibition of converting farmland through leasing of such land for construction purposes, again evidently targeting aspects of the so-called three concentrations.

ARE LONG-TERM RIGHTS SUFFICIENT?

In light of the renewed debate over full private ownership (now missing for farmland for over half a century) referred to at the beginning of this chapter, it may be useful to separately address the following question: does full, formal, "private ownership" have serious advantages over farmers' present rights under Chinese law? The conclusion argued for here is that existing provisions of law, *if effectively implemented*, provide farmers with land rights that are not sufficiently inferior to the rights they would have as private owners of the same land as to warrant a distracting (and probably losing) fight over the difference. Consider, in turn, each of the following.

Market value or "wealth" effect

Depending on the percentage factor used to discount a future stream of income, the usual formula would assign a thirty-year land right, in year one, roughly 75 to 95 percent of the value of full private ownership.[38] How important is the qualifier "in year one" (rights that commenced under a contract executed in 1998, for example, would reach their thirtieth year twenty years from now, as this is written)? The qualifier is much less important, certainly, than before the new Property Law, which now allows the right-holding farmer to extend the right at the conclusion of the thirty-year term. It would, however, be helpful to have two legal clarifications: (1) that the intended extension would be specifically for a further thirty years (its length is presently left to implication); and (2) that a farmer making a full assignment of his or her land right can effectively convey to the assignee, by expressly saying so in the assignment document, the right to exercise such a power of extension at the end of the term.

Whether full land "ownership" is necessary for a market economy

There are clear counter-examples. Farmers in Hong Kong's New Territories have (and had under the British) fifty-year rights to their land, while Hong Kong's urban skyscrapers are built on land that is usually held with seventy-five-year rights.[39] Most land in Israel is held under forty-nine- or ninety-eight-year rights (the former with a Biblical origin).[40] Both Hong Kong and Israel would generally be considered market economies. So is Australia, where much privately used land (including extensive grazing land in "stations" held by private parties) is acquired for a single lump sum payment from the government for a "leasehold" period of ninety-nine years.[41] Further examples could be cited.

The psychological impact of land "ownership"

This might indeed be significant, given China's land tenure experience over the period since 1949. But any such psychological difficulties seem to have been fully overcome in the urban sector, where private rights now range from fifty to seventy years and are freely bought and sold (and mortgaged).[42] The key need would seem to be, not giving farmers formal ownership, but persuading them of the reality of the thirty-year extendable and nonreadjustable property rights they already possess under present law. This will require precisely the combination of publicity and implementation measures described in the "Further measures" section. (It would be further facilitated by making farmers' land rights mortgageable, perhaps with some exemption for an essential food crop area; but the mortgageability issue would probably have to be resolved in discussions over the rights to be associated with "private ownership" as well.)

Breadth, duration, and assurance

Legal theorists have usefully suggested assessing the extent of land tenure rights (held with respect to any particular parcel of land) in a manner that, regardless of the particular land tenure system, uses three important measures: breadth, duration, and assurance.[43] Breadth refers to the quantity and quality of the land rights held (sometimes analogized to sticks in a bundle, which can be added or taken away in varying combinations).[44] It may include the rights to possess land, to grow or harvest crops of one's own choice, to pass the land on to heirs, to sell land or to lease it to others, to pledge (mortgage) land rights as security for credit, to prevent trespass, to protect against state expropriation, and many other rights. Duration measures the length of time for which these rights are valid. Typically the same duration applies to all of the rights held, but this is not necessarily so. Assurance, the third criterion, is a measurement of the certainty of the breadth and duration of the rights that are held. If an individual is said to possess land rights of a specific breadth and duration, but cannot exert, enforce, or protect those rights, they have no assurance. A land "right" that cannot be exerted or enforced is not a right at all.

In terms of this analysis, Chinese farmers presently hold, under the law, a rather complete bundle of rights in terms of breadth, with the principal omission being mortgageability. Thirty-year extendable and nonreadjustable land rights, while not perpetual in duration (as in full private ownership), nonetheless represent a reasonably close substitute for perpetuity in terms of their market value, potential for investment, and psychological impact, as argued under the subheadings that precede this one. The key element that is lacking, for many or most farmers, is the *assurance* of these land rights, already existing in law, through full and effective implementation.

Since the potential benefits of farmers' thirty-year extendable and nonreadjustable rights, when implemented, thus seem substantially equivalent to the potential benefits of full private ownership, it would seem a pity to focus on the latter—which is seemingly politically unachievable in the foreseeable future—while ignoring the former, which already exists on the law books and enjoys the solid support of the central government in Beijing.[45] The focus, we therefore argue, should be on implementation of these existing rights.

FURTHER MEASURES NEEDED FOR FULL IMPLEMENTATION OF FARMERS' THIRTY-YEAR EXTENDABLE AND NONREADJUSTABLE RIGHTS

A series of further measures of implementation is now required to complement and carry out on the ground what is now strongly present as law and policy through the confluence of RLCL, Property Law, the seven-ministry rectification campaign, and the 2008 No. 1 Document.[46]

First, there is need for full and reiterated publicity of farmers' rights and the means of redress. Landesa's past surveys have shown that television publicity, timed for and geared to the farm household, can have a powerful effect. For more detailed information—more understandable than the language of the land contracts and certificates themselves—a single laminated plastic card, attractive to the eye and suitable to hang on a wall in the house, can convey the essence of farmers' rights and remedies, including where farmers should go to complain if specific violations occur. These were used, in some provinces Landesa visited, in aid of the successful campaign that largely eliminated farmers' taxes and fees.

Second, there is need for a comprehensive monitoring of local enforcement and local violations. Continuing sample surveys can be of great assistance (including identifying whole provinces that are lagging) in keeping the leadership in Beijing well-informed. So can an active flow of complaints from farmers themselves, if a central-government "hotline" were to be established, making use of telephones, the ubiquitous cell phones (including text messaging), and the increasingly available computer. Local officials should also be warned in advance that "hotspots" where complaints were clustered anywhere in the country could expect visits by inspections teams from Beijing pursuant to the seven-ministry campaign and No. 1 Document.

Third, further flowing from this, and the activities of inspectors, all local officials and collective cadres nationwide should be informed that their political careers are linked closely with their implementation of these pro-farmer initiatives. Serious consequences should flow from violating farmers' land rights, including removal from official posts, fines, and civil and (where the offense is sufficiently grave) criminal penalties. These punishments should also be publicized whenever meted out.

Fourth, the most quickly and widely doable improvements in dispute resolution for farmers should be introduced. These might include establishing a "land disputes panel" for the People's Court in each province, and assigning to it fully law-trained judges (many Chinese judges lack legal training, although this is gradually being remedied). The judges should also receive special training on land law, and be made mobile so they can hear farmers' land complaints down at the village level on a publicized, preannounced schedule. More difficult, and probably requiring some time to accomplish, Beijing will need to end the appointment and funding of judges by local governments, which are often the wrongdoers where land disputes occur. Meanwhile, the land-case judges should be drawn from county level or higher, where they are less likely to have ties to the township and village officials who are the most frequent violators of farmers' land rights.

Fifth, and closely related, over the mid-term a system of legal-aid services for farmers needs to be established. Meantime, court rules and judicial training should allow and encourage judges in land cases to take an active role in questioning accused local officials where farmers involved in the dispute have no, or clearly inadequate, legal representation.

Beijing has successfully ended, or greatly restricted, a series of village-level depredations against farmers' land rights over the past decade.[47] Most recently, it has largely ended the assessment of taxes and fees on the farmers. With an adequate focus, and a well-thought-through program of implementation measures, it is not unreasonable to expect that the same can be accomplished in the implementation of farmers' thirty-year nonreadjustable and extendable rights to land.

IF FARMERS WERE TO BE GIVEN FULL PRIVATE OWNERSHIP, HOW MIGHT IT MOST CONFIDENTLY BE DONE?

If, however, contrary to expectations, the central government were to decide to amend the Constitution and give Chinese farmers full private ownership, how could this be structured to achieve maximum net benefits and the highest possible confidence in its beneficial results?

Of course, China had early success with such private ownership by farmers in the first seven years after the Communist Party came to power, 1949–56, as described in the second section above. And land ownership was provided to the former tenant farmers of Japan, Taiwan, and South Korea, shortly after World War II, which has been highly productive, wealth-conferring, and successfully maintained.

The senior Chinese academic quoted in the *Financial Times*[48] as saying that the conferral of such ownership would turn China into an "India," with an impoverished, landless peasantry, is far off the mark in his comparison. India, except for two or three of its twenty-eight states[49] has had little successful land tenure reform in the sixty-plus years since independence in 1947.[50] At independence, there was a high proportion of tenant farmers and agricultural laborers in India's countryside, and that proportion has not shrunk appreciably over the past six decades—

indeed, as between the two non-landowning groups, there are probably fewer tenant farmers and more agricultural laborers (generally the worse-off of the two groups) today.[51] China, by contrast, would begin with a system under which the great majority of rural families now have possession of a parcel or (usually) several parcels of land on a highly egalitarian basis, even though most of them remain insecure as to *which* parcel or parcels they will possess from one year to the next (or from several years to the next several years). There are very few tenant farmers, very few agricultural laborers, and virtually no landlords in today's China. Thus the starting point for any tenure reform in China is wholly different than it was, and remains, in India. (Indeed, one of the hoped-for results of giving Chinese farmers highly secure, long-term land rights with respect to specified parcels of land is to forestall a gradual accretion of landlord-like powers in the hands of the local cadres.)

But, if full private ownership were to be conferred, are there lessons from the comparative experience that might help further to ensure a "safe" outcome, with a minimization of risk of near-term land concentration or a rebirth of pre-1949 "landlordism"—perhaps, opponents might argue, as a result of improvident or undesirable or coerced transfers by the farmers of their new ownership rights? If full private ownership were to be granted to farm households for the same land on which they presently have thirty-year rights (a land-ownership-to-the-tiller program), the following safeguards might be considered for the governing law:

- Do not allow sale, or even lease, of land rights to anyone who would not be a directly self-cultivating farmer. Such a partial moratorium might be applied for an initial period, such as fifteen years, while farmers gained a better sense of land values and the land market (note that the government has not seen any necessity to apply such a restriction on the transfer of the present thirty-year rights).[52] Or even establish the initial moratorium without any time limit, and simply repeal it when the policymakers believed it was time to do so.
- This could be further reinforced with the requirement that any transferee via outright sale (even though a self-cultivating farmer) could not retransfer via sale or even lease, for some significant period of time, such as five or ten years. Or, again, this restriction could be terminated when the time seemed proper to end it.
- Regardless of the extent of restriction on sale, where sales were permitted there could be a "sliding-scale" tax on profits depending on the length of time the land was owned, with a very high percentage tax on sales that were made after a relatively brief period of ownership.
- Farmers, as owners, should be able to capture the value of their land in transfers for nonagricultural purposes, *if* zoning and land-use restrictions were fully complied with: but, again, *taxation* of the profits from such nonagricultural transfers (even where permitted and lawful) could be at a high percentage rate.
- There could also be restrictions—tailored to specific geographical regions and land types—as to the holding of agricultural land (either as owner or lessee) above specified maximum ceilings. Note that there are no such

"ceilings" now, and their absence has sometimes helped pave the way for abuses such as "outside boss contracting" and "scale farming" (note, too, that large farms are *not* generally more productive or efficient, and certainly not in a setting such as China which remains short on land and capital but long on labor[53]).

- Related to the above restriction, there might be a prohibition of any purchase or lease of agricultural land by foreign individuals or foreign legal entities, and perhaps also by domestic Chinese legal entities. Again, many of these restrictions could be for a fixed initial period of time, or could be unlimited in duration and repealed after policymakers gained assurance that this could safely be done, in the more developed and less agricultural China of ten or twenty years in the future.

In sum, if the "full private ownership" approach of 1949–56 were, unexpectedly, reintroduced, a series of mutually reinforcing limits and safeguards could readily be designed to prevent possible abuses by the well-off or well-connected. In the abstract, we might argue that none of these safeguards is really needed—and that none of them, after all, has been broadly introduced as to the present thirty-year rights. But, in practice, it seems likely that any small chance of Beijing introducing private ownership for farmers is likely to be enlarged if at least some of these protections can be offered as propitiation to the skeptical.

ADDENDUM AND UPDATE

Roughly 800 million of China's 1.3 billion people are still rural, and are dependent on agricultural land for a substantial part of their livelihood. Although this rural majority reaped great initial benefits from the breakup of China's collective farms in 1979–84, they have lagged steadily further behind their urban counterparts in the past two decades: per capita urban incomes are now 3.3 times as great, life expectancy in the big cities is twelve years longer, and a city child is orders of magnitude more likely to attend college. Rural consumption of goods and services lags strikingly, and there are tens of thousands of village demonstrations and incidents of instability annually, most of them land-related.

Many of these problems are linked to the continuing insecure and uncertain relationship that most Chinese farmers still have to the land upon which they depend, a legacy of practices introduced at the time of decollectivization and of the continuing role of local cadres in land use and allocation. During the past decade, the central government, deeply concerned over these problems, has crafted a series of laws intended to give farmers secure, long-term land rights—the 1998 revision of the Land Management Law, the 2002 Rural Land Contracting Law, and the 2007 Property Law—together with a series of accompanying declarations and policy decisions. Strong new implementing decisions have now been announced in October 2008 and January 2009.

A crucial tug-of-war has ensued over the past decade, between the center and the local authorities, over the implementation of the legal rules affecting farmers' land rights, a contest on whose outcomes much depends: whether Chinese farmers can safely invest in their land, with accompanying large benefits for farm incomes, consumption, and the rural standard of living; whether the urban–rural gap can begin to close rather than continue to widen; whether farmers will have meaningful land wealth, inter alia to cushion processes of urban migration; whether rural stability will grow or deteriorate; and, most broadly, whether rural China will move increasingly toward being a society where the rule of law prevails.

Of the above considerations, two may be especially salient in the context of the global economic crisis, which worsened after this chapter was first written:

1. Will China's tenure reform take a sufficiently decisive form to trigger land investment, growth in farm income, and increased rural household consumption on a scale, and within a time frame, that provides an important complement to China's various stimulus measures? Certainly the huge potential of the lagging rural market seems the best hope for development of internal demand and reduction of the Chinese economy's heavy dependence on exports.[54]
2. In terms of stability, the need is not only to provide a wealth-and-income cushion via assured land rights to ease long-term rural out-migration to the cities, but also to provide assurance that any large number of new in-migrants to the villages—urban workers who are laid off—have land to come home to. Under the 2002 RLCL, that is clearly the case in terms of formal law (only a tiny fraction of out-migrants can have their land share returned to the collective under the prevailing law: only where every member of the household moved to a large, multidistrict city, and all members have changed to urban registration).[55]

Where do things stand as this is written, in terms of the possible alternatives for Chinese farm households' land rights, as posed in previous sections of this chapter? RDI and its survey partners (Renmin University and Michigan State University) are presently in the process of analyzing the results from a new seventeen-province survey, carried out in mid-2008.[56] In some respects the initial findings seem discouraging: notably, the seven-ministry effort to reach the great majority of farm households with documentation of their land rights appears to have made little progress since the 2005 survey; and new depredations by cadres against farmers' foundation plot (residential) land are spreading in at least several provinces. In some other respects, findings are more encouraging: illegal readjustments appear to be slowing; and farmer land investments appear to be increasing, although still fewer than a quarter of farm households have made such investments.

One possible way forward is suggested by the language of the October 2008 Central Committee decision, which advocates keeping the "current contract relationship stable and for a long time without change."[57] With small refinement, this could be taken as making farmers' rights to the arable land they presently farm perpetual ("forever rights").[58]

Making farmers' rights perpetual, while maintaining formal collective ownership (now clarified as the joint ownership of all members of the collective under the Property Law) might offer a viable compromise between the "thirty-year rights fully implemented" approach and the "full private ownership" approach. Such a change would need to be embodied in formal law, and probably should be accompanied with parallel language protecting farmers' rights to the foundation (residential) plot.

Thus, still a third option may now be in play in providing long-term security to Chinese farmers.

NOTES

1. See, for example, Bajoria (2008), Anderlini (2008), and *The Economist* (2008).
2. Anderlini (2008). "State ownership" is an erroneous characterization: ownership of rural arable land in China is collective, as discussed below.
3. For an account of RDI's (Landesa was formerly known as the Rural Development Institute or RDI) early fieldwork in China, up to the mid-1990s, see Prosterman, Hanstad, and Li (1996a). For a recent update of such work, see, e.g., Zhu, Prosterman, Ye, et al. (2006).
4. See, e.g., Prosterman and Riedinger (1987) and Prosterman, Mitchell, and Hanstad (2009).
5. Food and Agriculture Organization of the United Nations (2004).
6. A substantial majority of those Chinese agricultural families who owned little or no land were tenant farmers rather than landless laborers. See Moise (1983) and Hinton (1967).
7. Land Reform Law of PRC (1950). As to implementation see China Institute of Reform and Development (1999).
8. China Institute of Reform and Development (1999: 32); Gensheng (2001: 3–4).
9. A number of commentators have concluded that the major land reforms in Japan, South Korea, and Taiwan were key to their rapid economic growth in the postwar period. See, e.g., Alesina and Roderik (1992). See generally Dore (1959), Kawagoe (1999), Voelkner (1970), Yoong-Deok and Kim (2000), Henderson (1968), Morrow and Sherper (1970), Koo (1970), Koo, Ranis, and Fei (1981), and Liu (2001).
10. See Weigelin-Schwiedrzik (2003) and Peng (1987).
11. Carter and Zhong (1988); see also Lardy (1986).
12. National Statistics Bureau of China, Annual Reports, also available at <http://www.stats.gov.cn/tjgb/>.
13. Sachs (2005); Chen and Ravallion (2004). Very recent updates by a working group led by the World Bank have, however, revised downward the previous Purchasing Power Parity (PPP) estimates of the size of the Chinese economy—and hence the *average* per capita GDP—by about 40 percent, suggesting that the number of those living under $1/day may be higher than had been thought. See World Bank (2007), Bradsher (2007), and Davis (2007).
14. Li (2008); Zhu and Prosterman (2006). There are two basic types of readjustments. In "big readjustments," a village takes back all land from farmers and then redistributes it in accordance with population changes at both the village and household levels (e.g., if village population has grown, every individual land share will be smaller). "Small readjustments," involve taking land from households that have lost members (e.g., through death or a daughter's marriage out of the village) and giving it to households that have added members (e.g., through birth or a marriage into the village), and does not affect the entire village landholding pattern.
15. Zhu, Prosterman, Ye, et al. (2006: 778–84).
16. See descriptions of some of that fieldwork cited in note 3 above.

17. National Statistics Bureau of China, 2007 Annual Report, also available at <http://www.stats.gov.cn/tjgb/ndtjgb/qgndtjgb/t20080228_402464933.htm>.
18. See news reports available at <http://www.fsa.gov.cn/web_db/sdzg2006/NEWS/DAILY/gcyl28-05.htm>; <http://www.nssc.stats.gov.cn/news.asp?newsid = 435> (October 30, 2005); and <http://www.sz.sx.cei.gov.cn/discuss/20051130/2005113015.htm> (November 30, 2005).
19. See the Central Committee of the Communist Party of China (1993a). See also the more general Central Committee of the CPC (1993b).
20. Law of Land Management (promulgated by the Standing Committee of the National People's Congress, August 29, 1998, effective January 1, 1999), *translated in* LEXIS (last visited October 6, 2006) (P.R.C.).
21. Law on the Contracting of Rural Land (promulgated by the Standing Committee of the National People's Congress; August 29, 2002, effective March 1, 2003) *translated in* LEXIS (last visited October 6, 2006) (P.R.C.).
22. Assignment involves the transfer of the entire remaining period of the thirty-year right, while lease can be anything from a transfer terminable at will up to a transfer of the entire remaining period minus one day.
23. Prosterman, Schwarzwalder, and Ye (2000) and Schwarzwalder, Prosterman, Ye, Riedinger, and Li (2002); the most recent survey is discussed in Zhu, Prosterman, Ye, et al. (2006).
24. Zhu, Prosterman, Ye, et al. (2006) and Zhu and Prosterman (2006).
25. Projected over roughly 187 million rural households, the estimated total number of mid-to-long-term investments in six specific categories for the four-year peak period (1999–2002) would be 34.4 million, versus 7.9 million for the four-year period (1994–7) before the second round of contracting and the accompanying publicity. The peak years of investments closely follow, with about a two-year time lag, the peak years of contract/certificate issuance. This was followed by a post-2002 drop-off in investments, the reasons for which may include some satisfaction of "pent-up" investment desires, the growing time-lag since publicity or document issuance, and the increased negative publicity on poorly compensated land-takings, as well as the growth of illegal readjustments.
26. Even in villages where farmers had received a contract or certificate in law-compliant form, only about two in five (39 percent) said satisfactory compensation had been paid for the most recent land-taking. But this dropped to about one in five (19 percent) for villages where no document at all had been issued.
27. See Zhu, Prosterman, Ye, et al. (2006: 775–8). The two-field system breaks with the typical pattern of distributing all farmland on a per capita basis. Instead, cultivated land is divided into two categories; consumption land and responsibility land. Consumption land is divided in each village on a per capita basis to meet each household's basic needs. The remaining land is contracted to farm households as responsibility land through a variety of methods which in many cases results in a nonegalitarian land distribution. Unlike consumption land, on which farmers are only responsible for collective contributions, an additional contracting fee is typically charged for responsibility land. Scale farming involves the consolidation of small, labor-intensive farms into larger, mechanized farms. Scale farming can be accomplished through a variety of approaches, but typically involves the contracting of large areas of arable land to a few farmers or the operation of large-scale farms by the collective landowner. Recollectivization of farmland was the ultimate goal of at least some experiments with scale farming in the early 1990s. Recontracting is another form of administrative action by village officials who take back some or all of various households' land—usually a

contiguous area—and then lease or assign it for agricultural use to a non-villager (often an outside agribusiness person or entity). The primary motivation behind recontracting is profit for collective cadres, who cannot legally charge a fee when land is contracted to village households but can collect rent or other payments when land is leased to a non-villager.

28. See Zhu, Prosterman, Ye, et al. (2006: 799–800).
29. For example, 79 percent of farmers knew the general principle that their arable land should be contracted to them for thirty years without readjustments. But only 51 percent knew that, when someone in a farmer's household dies, the deceased person's share of contracted land need not be returned to the collective. And only 35 percent knew that, when someone in a farmer's household moves to the city and changes residential registration, his or her contracted land need not be returned to the collective (return would be required only if all members of the household moved to a large multidistrict city and changed to urban registration, and did so without having made a prior private transfer of those land rights). See Zhu, Prosterman, Ye, et al. (2006: 790–92).
30. See the Central Committee of the CPC's "Revised Regulations on Rural People's Commune" (1962), art. 21. This Regulation is universally regarded as the regulatory framework on rural property before China's decollectivization campaign in late 1970s and early 1980s. Article 21 of the Regulation uses the phrase "long time without change."
31. Property Law [Wu Quan Fa] of the People's Republic of China, passed at the fifth conference of the tenth People's Congress on March 16, 2007.
32. Article 26 of the LML Implementation Regulation (effective on January 1, 1999).
33. See news report at <http://news.hexun.com/2007-08-25/100238594.html> (August 24, 2007).
34. See reports at <http://nc.people.com.cn/GB/6843047.html> (January 31, 2008).
35. See reports at <http://www.chinacourt.org/html/article/200708/24/261681.shtml> (August 24, 2007).
36. See reports at <http://www.agri.gov.cn/xxlb/t20071121_924396.htm> (November 21, 2007).
37. See generally Li (2008): this Op-Ed by the Landesa staff attorney who headed our Beijing Representative office discusses the new No. 1 Document.
38. See Zhu, Prosterman, Ye, et al. (2006: 784, n. 47).
39. See Government of Hong Kong (1996) and Lands Department, Government of the Hong Kong SAR (2005).
40. See Israel Land Administration (2007).
41. See ACT Planning and Land Authority, "Leasehold—Lease availability, length and selling" found at <http://www.actpla.act.gov.au/topics/property_purchases/leases_licenses>.
42. The urban rights are now renewable at the end of their term (Article 149, Property Law of People's Republic of China).
43. Place, Roth, and Hazell (1994).
44. Knetsch (1993). A. M. Honore (1961) proposed a list of eleven "standard incidents" that he claims make up private property, including the crucial rights to exclusive possession, personal use, and alienation. Honore's full list of incidents is: (1) right to exclusive possession; (2) right to personal use and enjoyment; (3) right to the capital value, including alienation, consumption, waste, or destruction; (4) right to transmit by gift, devise, or descent; (5) right to manage use by others; (6) right to the income from use by others; (7) right to tenure security (that is, immunity from expropriation); (8) lack of any term on these rights; (9) residual rights on the reversion of lapsed

ownership rights held by others; (10) duty to refrain from using the object in ways that harm others; and (11) liability to execution for repayment of debts. Honore's list is now commonly accepted by property theorists as a starting point in Western market economies, although arguments may persist over the inclusion of one incident or another.

45. However, giving rise to further concern over the strength of political opposition from local officials and cadres, especially opposition to reforms that would give farmers greater influence over takings for nonagricultural purposes, and in particular would give farmers the great bulk of compensation paid for land rights in such takings, is the recently publicized finding that an average of 60 percent of local revenues derive from takings of farmers' land rights. See news report at <http://news.sina.com.cn/c/2008-03-15/100715154418.shtml> (March 15, 2008).
46. See Li (2008).
47. See notes 27–28 supra, and discussion in accompanying text.
48. See note 2 supra, and accompanying text.
49. In contrast to the central law-making power in China on land tenure issues, each Indian state makes its own laws on these subjects.
50. A new initiative to give ownership of micro-plots of 10-to-15-hundredths of an acre (up to roughly one mu or 1/15 hectare in the Chinese measure) is contained in the new Five-Year Plan. See Government of India (2007). But the amount of arable land to be affected is small (less than 1 percent), and the arable land previously redistributed since independence is barely equal to the 5 percent of China's arable land that had been held in "private plots" on China's former collectives from 1962 until decollectivization.
51. See Appu (1996: 82–124).
52. Under the RLCL, "assignment" of the full thirty-year term does require approval by the collective; but this requirement is largely meaningless, since a "lease" for twenty-nine years and 364 days (including one with a lump sum payment up front for the entire term) does not require any approval.
53. See, e.g., Binswanger, Deininger, and Feder (1995); Johnson and Ruttan (1994); Peterson and Kislev (1991); Prosterman, Hanstad, and Li (1996b).
54. What seems an illuminating practical macroeconomic point is the subject of this recent quotation in *Barron's* financial weekly: "'Policy responses to this crisis are worrisome, especially U.S. actions aimed at supporting excess consumption and Chinese stimulus focused on sustaining excess investment,' argues Stephen Roach, chairman of Morgan Stanley Asia. He thinks the U.S. needs to save instead and plow those savings toward infrastructure investment, alternative energy technology and human capital, while China needs to increase domestic consumption. Fighting this inevitable rebalancing will merely return us 'to the very same strain of unbalanced economic growth that got us into this mess in the first place.'" (Tan 2009).
55. Article 26 of RLCL. Moreover, even in those extreme circumstances, any previous transfer out of land rights is preserved in the hands of the transferee.
56. See Prosterman (2009); also Kwok (2009).
57. See Central Committee of the Communist Party of China (2008).
58. Premier Wen Jiabao had already referred to the desirability of perpetual rights for farm households in one earlier press conference. See "Transcript: Premier Wen Jiabao Responds to Domestic and Foreign Journalists' Questions," Xinhua News Agency, March 14, 2005, available at <http://news.sina.com.cn/c/2005-03-14/10106077756.shtml>.

REFERENCES

Alesina, A. and Roderik, D. (1992), "Distribution, Political Conflict, and Economic Growth: A Simple Theory and Some Empirical Evidence," in A. Cukierman, Z. Hercowitz, and L. Leiderman (eds), *Political Economy, Growth, and Business Cycles* (Cambridge, MA: MIT Press).

Anderlini, J. (2008), "Losing the Countryside: A Restive Peasantry Calls on Beijing for Land Rights," *Financial Times*, 20 February, p. 10.

Appu, P. S. (1996), *Land Reforms in India* (New Delhi: Vikas Publishing).

Bajoria, J. (2008), "China's Land Reform Challenge," Analysis Brief, 10 March (New York: Council on Foreign Relations).

Binswanger, H., Deininger, K., and Feder, G. (1995), "Power, Distortions, Revolt and Reform in Agricultural Land Relations," in T. N. Srinivasan and J. Behrman (eds), *Handbook of Development Economics*, vol. 3 (London: Elsevier).

Bradsher, K. (2007), "A Revisionist Tale: Why a Poor China Seems Richer," *New York Times*, December 21, available at <http://www.nytimes.com/2007/12/21/business/21yuan.html>.

Carter, C. and Zhong, F.-N. (1988), *China's Grain Production and Trade* (Boulder, CO: Westview).

Central Committee of the Communist Party of China (1962), "Revised Regulations on Rural People's Commune," Art. 21 (Beijing: Zhongnanhai).

—— (1993a), "The State Council's Policy Measures on the Current Agricultural and Rural Development," Document No. 11, 5 November (Beijing: Zhongnanhai).

—— (1993b), "Decision of the CCP Central Committee on Some Issues Concerning the Establishment of a Socialist Market Economic Structure," adopted by the 14th Central Committee of the CCP at its Third Plenary Session on 14 November, Art. 31 available at LEXIS News Library, BBCSWB File.

—— (2008), "CPC Central Committee Decision on Major Agricultural and Rural Issues," promulgated by the Third Plenary Session of the 17th CPC Central Committee, 12 October (Beijing: Zhongnanhai).

—— (2009), "Opinion on Ensuring Stable Agricultural Growth and Sustainable Increase of Farmers' Income," promulgated by CPC Central Committee and State Council, 28 January (Beijing: Zhongnanhai).

Chen, C. (1961), *Land Reform in Taiwan* (Taipei: China Publishing Co.).

Chen, S. and Ravallion, M. (2004), "How Have the World's Poorest Fared Since the Early 1980s?" *World Bank Research Observer*, 19/2: 141–69.

China Institute of Reform and Development (1999), *History of Changes and Innovations of China's Rural Land System* (Nanhai: Nanhai Publishing).

Davis, B. (2007), "New World GDP Order—World Bank Project Ranks Economies by Comparing Prices," *Wall Street Journal Europe*, December 18.

Dore, R. P. (1959), *Land Reform in Japan* (Oxford: Oxford University Press).

The Economist (2008), "This Land is My Land," 14 February.

Food and Agriculture Organization of the United Nations (2004), *2003 Production Yearbook* (Rome: United Nations).

Gensheng, Zhang (2001), *Rural Reform in China* (Shenzhen: Hai Tian Publishing).

Government of Hong Kong (1996), "Sino-British Joint Declaration: Exploratory Notes on Annex II-III, 7 November, available at <http://www.hkbu.edu.hk/~pchksar/JK/jd-full8.htm>.

Government of India (2007), *Eleventh Five-Year Plan (2007–2012)*, sections 1.105–1.108 (New Delhi: Government of India Planning Commission).

Henderson, G. (1968), *Korea: The Politics of the Vortex* (Cambridge, MA: Harvard University Press).

Hinton, W. (1967), *Fanshen: A Documentary of Revolution in a Chinese Village* (New York: Random House).

Honore, A. M. (1961), "Ownership," in A. G. Guest (ed.), *Oxford Essays in Jurisprudence* (Toronto: University of Toronto Press).

International Bank for Reconstruction and Development, (2007), *2005 International Comparison Program Preliminary Results* (Washington, DC: World Bank).

Israel Land Administration (2007), "General Information," available at <http://www.mmi.gov.il/Envelope/indexeng.asp?page =/static/eng/f_gen>.

Johnson, N. L. and Ruttan, V. (1994), "Why Are Farms So Small?" *World Development*, 22/5: 691–706.

Kawagoe, T. (1999), "Agricultural Land Reform in Postwar Japan: Experience and Issues," World Bank Policy Research Working Paper 2111 (Washington, DC: World Bank).

Knetsch, J. (1993), "Land Use: Values, Controls and Compensation," in E. Quah and W. Neilson (eds), *Law and Economic Development: Cases and Materials from Southeast Asia* (Singapore: Longman).

Koo, A. Y. C. (1970), "Land Reform in Taiwan," in *Land Reform in Japan, South Korea and Taiwan*, AID Spring Review of Land Reform, vol. 3, Country Papers, Washington, DC.

Koo, S. W. Y., Ranis, G., and Fei, J. C. H. (1981), *The Taiwan Success Story: Rapid Growth with Improved Distribution in the Republic of China, 1952–1979* (Boulder, CO: Westview Press).

Kwok, K. (2009), "Nearly Half of Farmers Can't Prove Land Rights," *South China Morning Post*, 12 January.

Lands Department, Government of the Hong Kong Special Administrative Region of the People's Republic of China (2005), "Land Tenure System and Land Policy in Hong Kong," available at <http://www.landsd.gov.hk/en/service/landpolicy.htm>.

Lardy, N. (1986), "Agricultural Reforms in China," *Journal of International Affairs*, 39/2: 91–104.

"Law on the Contracting of Rural Land" (2002), promulgated by the Standing Committee of the National People's Congress, 29 August, effective March 1, 2003, translated in LEXIS.

Li, P. (2003), "Rural Land Tenure Reforms in China: Issues, Regulations and Prospects for Additional Reform," in P. Groppo (ed.), *Land Reform, Land Settlement and Cooperatives* (Rome: Food and Agriculture Organization), available at <ftp://ftp.fao.org/docrep/fao/006/y5026e/y5026e00.pdf>.

—— (2008), "On Solid Ground," *South China Morning Post*, 23 February.

Liu, C. (2001), "Diversification of the Rural Economy in Taiwan," Working Paper 16, The Japan Program Working Paper Series on Priorities and Strategies in Rural Poverty Reduction: Experiences from Latin America and Asia, presented at the Japan Program/INDES 2001 Conference, Japan.

Moise, E. (1983), *Land Reform in China and North Vietnam* (Chapel Hill: University of North Carolina Press).

Morrow, R. B. and Sherper, K. H. (1970), "Land Reform in South Korea," in *Land Reform in Japan, South Korea and Taiwan*, AID Spring Review of Land Reform, vol. 3, Country Papers, Washington, DC.

National Statistics Bureau of China (2007), *2007 Annual Report*, available at <http://www.stats.gov.cn/tjgb/ndtjgb/qgndtjgb/t20080228_402464933.htm>.

Peng, X. (1987), "Demographic Consequences of the Great Leap Forward in China's Provinces," *Population and Development Review*, 13/4: 639–70.

Peterson, W. and Kislev, Y. (1991), "Economies of Scale in Agriculture: A Re-examination of the Evidence," Staff Paper P91-43, Department of Agricultural and Applied Economics, University of Minnesota, Minneapolis.

Place, F., Roth, M., and Hazell, P. (1994), "Land Tenure Security and Agricultural Performance in Africa: Overview of Research Methodology," in J. W. Bruce and S. E. Mighot-Adholla (eds), *Searching For Land Tenure Security in Africa* (Dubuque, IA: Kendall-Hunt Publishing Company).

Prosterman, R. (2009), "The Land Question in Rural China: Results of a 2008 Seventeen-Province Survey." Workshop presentation, 10 January, Renmin University, Beijing.

—— Hanstad T., and Li, P. (1996a), "Can China Feed Itself?" *Scientific American*, 275/5: 90–6.

—— (1996b), "Large-Scale Farming in China: An Appropriate Policy?" RDI Reports on Foreign Aid and Development, no. 90, July, Landesa, Seattle.

—— Mitchell, R., and Hanstad, T. (2009), *One Billion Rising: Law, Land, and the Alleviation of Global Poverty* (Leiden: Leiden University Press).

—— and Riedinger, J. (1987), *Land Reform and Democratic Development* (Baltimore: Johns Hopkins).

—— Schwarzwalder, B., and Ye, J. (2000), "Implementation of 30-Year Land Use Rights for Farmers Under China's 1998 Land Management Law: An Analysis and Recommendations Based on a 17-Province Survey," *Pacific Rim Law and Policy Journal*, 8/3: 507.

Sachs, J. (2005), *The End of Poverty* (New York: Penguin).

Schwarzwalder, B., Prosterman, R., Ye, J., Riedinger, J., and Li, P. (2002), "An Update on China's Rural Land Tenure Reforms: Analysis and Recommendations Based on a Seventeen-Province Survey," *Columbia Journal of Asian Law*, 16/1: 141–225.

Tan, K. (2009), "A Scorecard of Market Destruction," *Barron's Market Week*, 9 March, pp. M2–M4.

"Transcript: Premier Wen Jiabao Responds to Domestic and Foreign Journalists' Questions," (2005), Xinhua News Agency, available at <http://news.sina.com.cn/c/2005-03-14/10106077756.shtml>.

Voelkner, H. E. (1970), "Land Reform in Japan," *AID Spring Review* (Washington, DC: United States Agency for International Development).

Weigelin-Schwiedrzik, S. (2003), *Trauma and Memory: The Case of the Great Famine in the People's Republic of China (1959–1961)* (Leiden: Brill Academic Publishers).

World Bank (2007), *2005 International Comparison Program Preliminary Results* (December).

Yoong-Deok, J. and Kim, Y. (2000), "Land Reform, Income Redistribution, and Agricultural Production in Korea," *Economic Development and Cultural Change*, 48/2: 253–68.

Zhu, K. and Prosterman, R. (2006), "From Land Rights to Economic Boom: A 17-province survey reveals that more secure land rights can boost the incomes and consumption power of China's 850 million rural residents," *China Business Review* (July–August), 44–9.

———— Ye, J. et al. (2006), "The Rural Land Question in China: Analysis and Recommendations Based on a Seventeen-Province Survey," *New York University Journal of International Law and Politics*, 38/4: 761–839.

7

The Role of Property Rights in Chinese Economic Transition

Kenneth Ayotte and Patrick Bolton

INTRODUCTION

It is widely believed that market-based economic activities are best undertaken in a legal environment with strong property rights protections. In his celebrated article on externalities, property rights, and the internalization of social costs through contracts, Ronald Coase (1960) explains that as long as property rights are clearly delineated and assigned, then externalities can be efficiently internalized through private contracting. Whether the polluter has the right to pollute air or the pollutee has the right to clean air does not matter for efficiency, as in either case the polluter and the pollutee will work out an efficient bargain. There may be distributional consequences in a particular assignment of property rights, but no efficiency consequences. Thus, according to Coase, well-defined property rights and freedom of contracting are the bedrock of a well-functioning market economy.

The economics of contracting literature following Coase (1960) also takes the role of property rights as a starting point for contracting. In addition, it emphasizes the role of property rights in creating incentives to preserve, or exploit, the value of assets that an agent owns. Thus, Alchian and Demsetz (1972) and Jensen and Meckling (1976) argue that property rights create incentives for value maximization by the owner, as the property owner is the residual claimant over the cash flows produced by exploiting the asset. That is, the owner receives the entire increment in value generated by his exploitation of the asset. Most recently, Grossman and Hart (1986) and Hart and Moore (1990) underline another important facet of property rights, the residual rights of control over the asset conferred to the owner. They point out that this residual right of control provides an important protection of the value created by the owner through investments in the asset. This protection is especially important in situations where contracts are incomplete due to inadequate legal enforcement of contracts. The owner's right to determine who can use the asset and in what way gives the owner stronger bargaining power in negotiations with third parties and thus allows the owner to extract a bigger share of the surplus from trade with these third parties. Getting a bigger share of the surplus in turn means that the owner gets a bigger share of the added value created by investing in the asset. In sum, the economics of contracting literature sees property rights as an essential institution to protect valuable investments. What is more, property rights are even more important when there is poor legal enforcement of contracts. That is, the economics literature emphasizes the idea that property rights are a substitute for contractual rights. In a world of unconstrained freedom of contracting there would be no role for property rights.

Taking a closer look at Coase's argument, it is not entirely clear what role property rights play in Coase's logic. While contracting and the enforcement of contracts are clearly necessary for the internalization of the social cost, it is not obvious that well-defined property rights are. If one asks what would go wrong in Coase's basic setting if property rights were not well defined or assigned it is not clear what the answer is. Take, for example, Hardin's (1968) *tragedy of the commons* problem in which a group of herders have access to a common parcel of land over which there are no well-defined or assigned property rights. Hardin shows that in such a situation it is in each herder's interest to let his cows onto the common land even if this may result in higher damages to the land than the benefit to the herders. The reason is that while the individual herder gets a benefit from letting his cows feed on the land, he shares the resulting damage with all the other herders. And if all herders make this individually rational choice, the parcel of land will eventually be spoiled, thus resulting in a social cost for all the herders.

It seems that Hardin provides the perfect illustration of what goes wrong when property rights are not well assigned in Coase's situation and that he also offers the obvious solution: *enclosure* of the land and the assignment of the property right to the parcel of land to one of the herders. With enclosure and ownership, the owner can rent the land to other herders and efficiently trade off the rent revenue with the cost of grazing. While enclosure and the assignment of property rights to the parcel of land does indeed solve the *private provision of public goods* problem and ensures that the land does not get spoiled, it is by no means the only solution to the commons problem. Indeed, another solution that has been suggested is to assign responsibility for preserving the land to an agency who has authority to grant access to the land and is supervised by the community of herders: a form of common ownership of the land.

What is more, property rights and their assignment may not be necessary at all to solve the commons problem. Forward-looking herders will be able to see the threat of overgrazing and can prevent this outcome by writing a long-term contract among themselves regulating access by cows and grazing of the parcel of land. This contract can efficiently bind their actions even if none of the herders has any ownership right. This solution is similar to the arrangements squatters find all over the world when they attempt to regulate the collective use by the squatters of a piece of land or a building they do not formally own. In other words, all that may be needed to solve Coase's problem of social cost is freedom of contracting.

Hardin's basic metaphor, however, oversimplifies the commons problem in one crucial respect that calls for a key role of property rights. If there was no property right to the parcel of land then only the overgrazing of the contracting parties would be controlled through the contract. Any new herder that arrives at a later point in time and that has not signed the contract will not be bound by it. The new herder will then let his cows onto the land in the same way as when no one is bound by a contract. The existing herders can, of course, induce the new herder to sign a contract with them and some of the externalities created by the new herder can be internalized in this way. However, the prospect of future herders, not bound by an initial contract, having access to the land will create an inefficiency that cannot be resolved contractually and that requires property rights as a solution. Indeed, if anyone can bring their cows to graze on the land in the future, then current herders will want to appropriate the benefits of the land early rather than share them with future herders. This response by current herders will then lead to overgrazing.

This dynamic form of the *tragedy of the commons* highlights the crucial difference between property rights and contract rights. Property rights are *in rem* rights (or rights good against the world) while contractual rights are rights against contracting parties. In other words, property rights are unique because they bind not only the parties to a contract, but also bind third parties *who lie outside a contracting coalition*. This may seem like a minor distinction but it is fundamental for two reasons. First, when you have a right against the world an immediate issue is how does the world know about the existence of this right. Contracting parties are presumably aware of the rights and obligations they confer on each other, but that is far from obvious for third parties. In this respect a right against the world is fundamentally different from a contractual right. Second, to the extent that a property right is a right against third parties it can only be conferred by the law. Hence, the importance of the new Chinese Property Rights Law (2007). In contrast, contractual rights only require the enforcement power of the state. They do not necessarily involve any other form of legal intervention.

This key distinction between contractual and property rights applies whether the property right is granted to a private party, a corporate entity, or a government body. In this respect property law must deal with the same issues irrespective of how property rights are allocated between individual agents and government entities. Having said this, the timing of the new law passed in 2007, twenty-eight years after the start of market reforms, and following seven years of deliberations, can be explained by the greater need for such a law in the current economic environment, which relies much more on market-based transactions. There is a greater need for such a law, as trade and credit is more difficult without clear and secure property rights. To the extent that the allocation of goods and investment decisions were based more on central planning decisions and less on market-based transactions there was less of a need to clearly delineate property rights.

Economists' writing on property rights does not address the issue of what distinguishes a property right from a contractual right. Indeed, most of the time what is defined as a property right could as easily be described as a particular contractual right agreed to initially by the contracting parties. Thus, a residual claim to cash flows or residual rights of control could be granted contractually and there is no need for a property law to define these rights. The only public intervention envisaged in economists' writings is the courts' role in enforcing contracts. In contrast, recent legal scholarship (Merrill and Smith 2000, 2001a, 2001b; Hansmann and Kraakman 2002) inspired by a long legal tradition going back to Roman Law defines property rights as *in rem* rights distinct from contractual rights, which are seen as only rights *in personam* (good only against the contracting parties themselves).

In a recent paper—Ayotte and Bolton (2011)—we formalize this distinction between *in rem* and *in personam* rights and develop a theory of *optimal property rights* inspired by the recent legal scholarship, which focuses on the key issue of informing third parties of the existence of property rights and liens on assets. Informing third parties of the existence of a property right can be more or less costly. We argue that the role of the law is to balance these information costs against the benefits of strengthening a contractual right to a property right. When a contractual right is elevated to a property right this means that the property right will trump any conflicting contractual right. In many situations, in particular those involving credit transactions, it is important to be able to secure priority by strengthening one's contractual right to a property right. Any time a loan is issued, secured by a given asset as *collateral*, it allows the secured lender to make sure that he will be repaid before other creditors. It is important to be able to secure such seniority to avoid *dilution* of the debt claim by future loans taken out by the debtor. Thus the benefit of elevating a right to a property right is to ensure an efficient outcome by imposing discipline or limited access. The cost, however, is that third parties must then find out whether there are pre-existing property rights in place that might limit a debtor's ability to repay them. We argue that the design of a property rights law is mainly concerned with balancing these costs and benefits. When should the law prevent the elevation of a contractual right to a property right and when not? How should the law regulate the process by which contractual rights can become *in rem* rights? These are the fundamental questions of property law.

In this paper we briefly describe the key elements of the new Chinese Property Rights Law, especially as it pertains to credit markets, and analyze the main provisions of the law in light of our analytical framework. We begin by providing a brief description of our model in Ayotte and Bolton (2011) (AB) and a summary of the main trade-off for the design of a property rights law. We then proceed to a discussion of the new Chinese Property Rights Law, before concluding.

THE AYOTTE AND BOLTON MODEL

In AB we consider the situation of a (risk-neutral) firm with a single project that requires two rounds of financing from two different (risk-neutral) lenders. The firm must raise i_1 from a first lender ($P1$) at date 1 to start the project. Then to be able to continue the project at date 2, it requires an additional cash input of i_2 from a second lender ($P2$). Credit markets are assumed to be competitive and there is no discounting. After the two rounds of financing the project produces a random cash flow at date 3. The cash flow outcome depends on the realization of a state of nature at date 2. In the good state of nature, s_g, which occurs with probability π, the cash flow outcome depends on the firm manager's effort choice $e \in \{0, 1\}$ at date 2. If the manager chooses $e = 1$ then the project yields a final cash flow X with certainty. If he chooses $e = 0$, the project yields the same cash flow as in the bad state of nature. The manager's private cost of choosing $e = 1$ is $c > 0$ and the cost of $e = 0$ is normalized to zero. In the bad state of nature, which occurs with probability $1 - \pi$, the project yields a cash flow of X at date 3 with only probability $p < 1$ and with probability $(1 - p)$ the project yields no cash flow but a liquidation value γL, where $\gamma < 1$. If the project is liquidated at date 2, however, the liquidation value is $0 < L < i_1$.

The owner-manager of the firm A and the first lender $P1$ write a bilateral long-term loan contract at date 1. Similarly, A and $P2$ write a bilateral loan contract at date 2. Each loan contract specifies the amount the principal agrees to lend i_j and a repayment F_j at date 3. The contract between $P1$ and A can also specify a maximum amount Φ_1 of date 3 cash flows A is allowed to pledge to $P2$, and whether the claim F_1 is senior, on par, or junior to F_2. The role of seniority for the claim F_1 is to prevent the firm from overborrowing at date 2 and attempting to continue with the project in the bad state, when it is efficient to liquidate the project. Importantly in this setup, seniority, while helping to mitigate the risk of overinvestment, does not completely eliminate it. The reason is that the firm's manager may be tempted to overborrow and *gamble for resurrection*. Moreover the second lender would be willing to lend provided the lending terms are right. The main party affected by overborrowing is the first lender, who loses a large fraction of the project's expected liquidation value in the bad state. This is why the initial loan contract must also specify a maximum amount Φ_1 the firm is allowed to borrow at date 2. By enforcing this limit on leverage the first lender is able to prevent overborrowing.

The two debt contracts must be optimally structured to make sure that the manager has: (1) an incentive to put in high effort ($e = 1$) in the good state, and (2) can obtain continuation financing by $P2$ at date 2 only in the good state when continuation is efficient. The key question concerning property rights in this setup is whether the seniority of F_1 and the limit Φ_1 on date 3 cash flows the firm is allowed to pledge to $P2$ should be elevated to a property right. When F_1 is elevated to a property right this means that the first loan is a *secured* loan. In this case the first lender has a property right in the *collateral* posted by the firm. The first lender can then simply seize the collateral in case of default and appropriate its full liquidation value. Secured lending is a widespread practice around the world and a form of lending that is now feasible in China under the new property law.

What does it mean for Φ_1 to be elevated into a property right? In concrete terms the issue here relates to the strength of *negative pledge* clauses in debt contracts. The elevation of Φ_1 to a property right would mean that the second lender would not be able to claim more than Φ_1 of the firm's cash flow in the event of default even if F_2 exceeds Φ_1. That is, Φ_1—a contractual clause in the contract between A and $P1$—would be an *in rem* right to the extent that it would also bind a third party, $P2$. As we have explained, in the AB model such a property right can be valuable in preventing overinvestment in the bad state. Yet, in practice the law often refuses to enforce such clauses as property rights.[1] When Φ_1 is not elevated to a property right then it can only be enforced if $P1$ takes legal action against A for violating the terms of its contract with A. This could mean either filing for an *injunction* to block the second loan or suing for *damages*. Unfortunately, however, the latter action is unlikely to have much bite as the firm will have limited resources. If $P1$ fails to take such actions in a timely way, then Φ_1 will simply not be enforced by court against $P2$ should the firm go bankrupt. Thus, a major difficulty for $P1$ when Φ_1 is not elevated to a property right is that it only has bite if $P1$ is able to continuously monitor A at low cost.

One justification for the difference in treatment between a perfected security interest (an *in rem* right) and a negative pledge clause (an *in personam* right) is that there is no system in place to permit the registration of such covenants (Bjerre

1999). As with an unrecorded security the basic reason given for not elevating negative pledge clauses to property rights is that discovery of a negative covenant requires the cooperation of the borrower, which is less reliable than a recording system.

Thus, the key trade-off in AB on whether to elevate a contractual protection to a property right is that the benefit of the stronger protection also imposes a discovery cost on third parties. The second lender $P2$ must know whether there is a negative pledge clause in the first loan agreement Φ_1 such that $\Phi_1 < F_2$ to be able to determine whether the second loan will be profitable. If the discovery or due *diligence costs* for $P1$ are very low then in the AB model it may be optimal to elevate both the seniority of F_1 and the negative pledge clause Φ_1 to a property right. But if this cost is sufficiently high then Φ_1 should not have the strength of a property right, and for very high costs then even the seniority of F_1 should not be elevated to a property right.

AB models the due diligence costs $P2$ faces at date 2 as follows: $P2$ must expend a due diligence (reading) cost $\rho > 0$ to find out anything about how well protected P_1 is. If $P2$ does not spend this cost he does not know anything about $P1$'s contract, while if he spends the reading cost ρ he understands the contract fully with probability $P(\rho)$, which is increasing in ρ. AB also assumes that the due diligence costs actually expended are private information to $P2$ and thus not verifiable in court.

The presence of due diligence costs raises new subtle strategic issues beyond simply taking account of the transaction cost involved in communicating an *in rem* right to the world. Indeed, $P2$ will rationally attempt to economize on reading costs, by not always diligently reading all existing debt contracts the firm has on its books. Sometimes $P2$ will simply guess what these contracts contain to save on transactions costs. Of course, $P1$ and A understand this and may therefore be tempted to take advantage of $P2$'s negligence by inserting a particularly restrictive and exploitative term Φ_1 in the hope that $P2$ will not see it. Also, the firm may seek to signal its good intentions and thus save on due diligence costs by offering to pay for $P2$'s costs. We refer the interested reader to AB (2011) for the full details of the analysis of dynamic contracting with due diligence costs.

The equilibrium outcome of the contracting game with due diligence costs is such that the firm offers to pay $P2$'s due diligence cost up to a level ρ^*, such that the probability of detection by $P2$ of an expropriative clause in the contract following due diligence, $P(\rho^*)$, is sufficiently high that it becomes unattractive for A and $P2$ to insert such a clause into the first loan contract. Should $P2$ discover such a clause then $P2$ simply refuses to lend, so that the firm may not be able to continue in the good state even when it is efficient to do so. This risk for the firm is sufficiently high when the expropriative clause can be detected with probability $P(\rho^*)$ that the benefit from expropriating $P2$, which cannot exceed $(1 - P(\rho^*))F_2$, does not justify the cost of early termination in the good state. Should the firm offer to pay less than the cost ρ^* then $P2$ simply assumes the worst and chooses not to lend.

In general, two inefficiencies arise in the AB model with costly due diligence, which a well-designed property law can mitigate. First, conditional on receiving funding, total social welfare (which is also A's expected payoff, since the firm receives all the gains in equilibrium) falls by the expected cost of the due diligence, $\pi\rho^*$ Second, some firms who would be funded in a world with no reading costs may be credit-rationed if the parameters of the model are such that

$\pi R_1 + (1 - \pi)L - i_1 < \pi\rho^*$. $P1$ is then no longer willing to finance the project, because he is not able to recoup both i_1 and the expected due diligence cost ρ^* which he must contribute up front. Since social welfare is directly tied to the deadweight costs of due diligence, the model suggests that the law can be beneficial if it can reduce ρ^*.

Now, an obvious but nevertheless important implication from a practical standpoint is that ρ^* can be lowered directly by setting up a public *registry* of property titles and liens on assets where it is easy to register property rights, and that is easy to consult and monitor. As obvious as this insight is, it is generally not adequately addressed in practice. The cost of notifying third parties of the existence of property rights and liens could be substantially reduced in many countries by integrating, digitalizing, and standardizing registries.

However, one potential downside of facilitating access to information by third parties about existing property rights, which the AB model does not account for, is reduced privacy rights for the owners. The property rights law will obviously have to balance the value of privacy against due diligence costs for third parties. Clearly, in practice not everyone needs to know about everyone else's ownership. Thus, access to the information on a registry concerning ownership and liens on assets held by a given firm or individual could be circumscribed and made conditional on a loan or other financial transaction of minimum value to be undertaken with that firm or individual. But, once access has been limited in this way to protect privacy, the property law and public registries should be designed in such a way as to minimize the costs of due diligence and the costs of monitoring the validity of the ownership claim.

A somewhat less obvious implication emerging from the analysis in AB is that an optimal property law can also lower ρ^* by excluding the elevation of a contractual clause to a property right when this clause is particularly costly to identify through due diligence and when it is likely to be very redistributive. The condition guaranteeing that it is not in A and $P1$'s interest to slip in a redistributive clause into their loan contract that would be good against $P2$ is given by:

$$X - i_2 - c \geq P(\rho^*)L + \left(1 - P(\rho^*)\right) V_x \qquad (1)$$

The left-hand side of the inequality represents the maximum surplus for A and $P1$ in the good state, should $P2$ extend a second loan at date 2. This is the surplus A and $P1$ can hope to get if they do not include any redistributive clause into their contract. The right-hand side represents what they can gain if they include a redistributive term: with probability $P(\rho^*)$ then $P2$ discovers the clause and refuses to lend, in which case A and $P1$ only get L in the good state, and with probability $(1 - P(\rho^*))$ the clause is not discovered, $P2$ extends a loan and is expropriated at date 3, so that A and $P1$ stand to gain V_x by expropriating $P2$. Thus, if the clause is particularly difficult to detect or if it has very redistributive consequences for $P1$, a much higher due diligence cost ρ^* is required to discourage its use. For such clauses, it may be optimal not to allow their elevation to a property right.

More generally, three broad principles for the design of optimal property rights emerge from the analysis in AB:

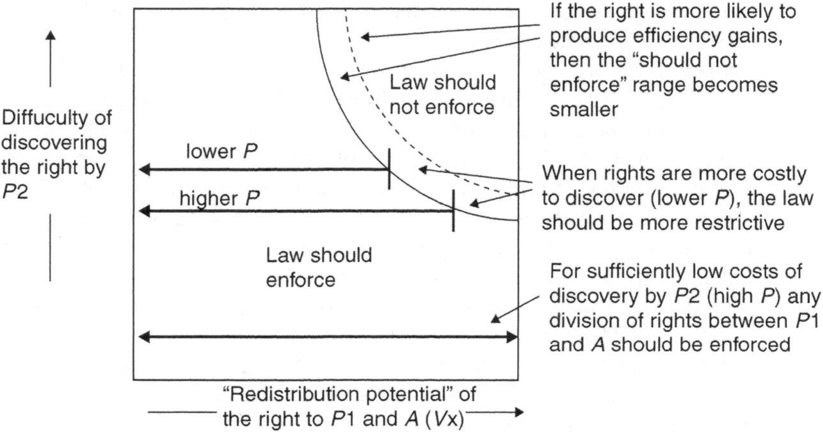

Figure 7.1. Optimal property rights: general principles

Principle 1. The law should be less likely to enforce a right if it is *more costly for third parties to discover* (higher ρ).
Principle 2. The law should be less likely to enforce a right if it is more *redistributive* from third parties (V_x).
Principle 3. The law should be more likely to enforce a right if the *expected efficiency gains* are larger ($(1-\pi)(L - pX - (1-p)\gamma L)$).

These principles are summarized graphically in Figure 7.1.

Note finally that enforcing a negative pledge covenant (or an unperfected security interest) as a property right against *P2* when *P2* has actual knowledge of the covenant may be desirable in the AB model. Thus, if a court can verify that *P2* was aware and understood the negative covenant, then there is no cost to enforcing *P1*'s rights exactly as intended. Importantly, however, an optimal property law should not generally place the burden on *P2* to discover and fully understand negative covenants, as this would unreasonably raise *P2*'s due diligence costs.

AN ANALYSIS OF THE NEW CHINESE PROPERTY RIGHTS LAW

The law passed in 2007 contains five main sections: (1) General Principles, (2) Ownership, (3) Usufruct, (4) Security, (5) Possession. This is a complex but very important piece of legislation for the transition process in China. We shall not attempt a full discussion of all the many elements of the law and shall confine ourselves to a discussion of the fourth section on security which is directly related to our formal analysis in AB (2011). For a broader discussion of the law in English the interested reader may consult Rehm and Hinrich (2008) and Chen (2007).

A major focus of the new property rights law is on the conditions required to obtain an *in rem* property right. These conditions mostly have to do with the requirements concerning *communication* of a right to third parties. As other commentators have pointed out, there are no notaries public in China that can certify and register property rights. Thus, most of the burden of communication of *in rem* rights is put on the country's public registeries. Article 6 of the new law sets the general registration requirements, which are largely inspired by similar requirements in civil law countries.

It also appears that a major focus of the new law is an expansion of the asset classes that can function as security for lending. In particular, the law provides for "mortgages" (nonpossessory security interests) in many classes of both movable and immovable property. Thus, the law explicitly provides for mortgages in currently held and after-acquired equipment and inventory (Article 181). It also seems to provide a mechanism for granting security in intangible assets such as accounts receivable in the form of a "pledge" (a possessory security interest). Our model explains why an expansive approach to security is important, in that it protects a lender from agency problems and overborrowing by a firm. This allows for the expansion of credit that might not be provided otherwise. It also frees up a lender from the need to monitor the firm constantly to prevent this overborrowing, as the law's respect for security provides the firm and new lenders with the incentive to make efficient lending decisions.

Unfortunately, commentators have expressed pessimistic views on the effectiveness of the registry system by which third parties can verify the existence of prior interests in property. Ideally, a system that allows for expansive grants of security would be coupled with a modern, low-cost, electronic, centralized, and standardized registry. Although some proposals for such a system had been floated in the deliberations prior to the passage of the law, the new law only provides for regional registries. Moreover, which public agencies are responsible for administering these registries, what their duties are, whom they are accountable to and what for, and who monitors these critical agencies is largely left undetermined in the law.

As our analysis in AB suggests, there are substantial benefits to be obtained in standardizing the titles and liens that can be registered, so as to reduce due diligence costs for third parties. At the same time, one of the subtle implications of our model is that an optimal property law relaxes the rights of earlier lenders against later lenders when it is very costly for lenders to discover prior interests. Thus, if due diligence cannot be made cheaper, the law might instead decide to weaken protection for earlier lenders. In particular, if some loans are unlikely to be dilutive of earlier lenders, one approach might be to provide a "safe harbor" for these types of loans, allowing a later secured lender to have priority.

An example of such an approach in US law is the purchase money security interest (PMSI) under Article 9 of the Uniform Commercial Code. A lender who provides the borrower with a loan to acquire certain types of new collateral can take priority over an earlier lender who has a security interest in the after-acquired property of the same type. Given that new collateral is being provided to the firm, it is less likely that the new lender will be diluting the value of the prior lender's loan. At the same time, without the guarantee of priority over the new collateral, the later lender might not lend at all, for fear that his rights are (unknowingly) subordinated. Based on our reading of the Property Rights Law, there are no such exceptions to the rule that the first lender to give notice has priority (Article 199).

CONCLUSION

The New Chinese Property Rights Law is an important step in the transition towards a market economy that is fully integrated with the rest of the world. With this law the transactions costs involved in any sale of asset or in any loan can be substantially reduced, especially if the public registries are modernized and operated efficiently. What is more, the risk of expropriation is also reduced to the extent that ownership titles will be easier to establish and verify. As always, of course, the value of a law lies not only in how well the articles of the code have been written, but also in the enforcement of the law. On that front much uncertainty remains and it is not clear at this point how much the passage of the law will, for example, help protect small farmers or small property owners from expropriation by developers with powerful political backing. Another significant uncertainty is how much the courts will get involved in resolving property disputes and in completing the law through precedent.

It is remarkable how much the Chinese economy has been able to develop in the absence of a property rights law and well-defined property rights. To a large extent this has been made possible by an unusually sophisticated reliance on relational contracts and trust, as well as an unusually efficient and business-friendly government. Our analysis in this paper highlights how much can be achieved purely through contractual means, without well-defined property rights.

However, the level of development now reached in China is more and more constrained by its rudimentary financial markets and financial system. As companies need to rely more and more on external financing to stay competitive, the issue of how conflicting debt claims get resolved in financial distress, how to efficiently organize a priority structure of debt, and how to prevent overleveraging by corporations will become increasingly important. It is here that the new law and its enforcement will play a critical role in enhancing development.

NOTE

1. The oldest known case in the US on this subject is Knott v. Shepherdstown Manufacturing, 5 S.E. 266 (W. Va. 1888) in which the court found that the breach of the negative covenant gave rise only to a claim for damages against the borrower.

REFERENCES

Alchian, A. and Demsetz, H. (1972), "Production, Information Costs, and Economic Organization," *American Economic Review*, 62: 777–95.

Ayotte, K. and Bolton, P. (2011), "Optimal Property Rights in Financial Contracting," *Review of Financial Studies*, 24: 3401–33.

Bjerre, C. S. (1999), "Secured Transactions Inside Out: Negative Pledge Covenants, Property and Perfection," *84 Cornell Law Review*, 305: 353–64.

Coase, R. H. (1960), "The Problem of Social Cost," *Journal of Law and Economics*, 3/1: 1–44.

Chen, L. (2007), "The New Chinese Property Code: A Giant Step Forward?" *Electronic Journal of Comparative Law*, 11/2: 1–24.

Grossman, S. and Hart, O. (1986), "The Costs and Benefits of Ownership: A Theory of Vertical and Lateral Integration," *Journal of Political Economy*, 94: 691–719.

Hansmann, H. and Kraakman, R. (2002), "Property, Contract and Verification: The Numerus Clausus Problem and the Divisibility of Rights," *Journal of Legal Studies*, 31: S373–S420.

Hardin, G. (1968), "Tragedy of the Commons," *Science*, 162: 1243–8.

Hart, O. and Moore, J. (1990), "Property Rights and the Nature of the Firm," *Journal of Political Economy*, 98: 1119–58.

Jensen, M. and Meckling, W. (1976), "Theory of the Firm, Managerial Behavior, Agency Costs and Ownership Structure," *Journal of Financial Economics*, 3: 305–60.

Merrill, T. and Smith, H. (2000), "Optimal Standardization in the Law of Property: The Numerus Clausus Principle," *Yale Law Journal*, 110: 1–70.

————(2001a), "What Happened to Property in Law and Economics?" *Yale Law Journal*, 111/2: 357–98.

————(2001b), "The Property/Contract Interface," *Columbia Law Review*, 773: 843–9.

Rehm, G. and Hinrich, J. (2008), "The New Chinese Property Rights Law: An Evaluation from a Continental European Perspective," available at SSRN: <http://ssrn.com/abstract=1132343>.

8

Institutional Design for China's Innovation System: Implications for Intellectual Property Rights

Joseph E. Stiglitz[1]

Thirty years ago, China began its march to a market economy "with Chinese characteristics." At the time, it was not clear what that meant. Even today, what this entails is the subject of debate and discussion. Various chapters in this book have focused on what it might involve for, for instance, the property rights regime.

This chapter focuses on a particular kind of property—intellectual property—and its role as part of society's innovation system. A country's innovation system is the collection of institutions that promote innovation, providing incentives and finance and allocating resources among researchers and research projects. The innovation system is concerned with the production, import, and dissemination of ideas and knowledge throughout the economy and society, including the creation of new products and the improvement of production processes.

There are many components of an innovation system besides intellectual property rights. Much research—and especially basic research, the most foundational—goes on within universities, think tanks, and government laboratories, typically financed by government, sometimes in partnership with the private sector, sometimes supported by foundations. It is important to recognize this, because (as we shall argue at greater length) often too much importance is ascribed to intellectual property.

The design of the innovation system is especially important for China today for several reasons. China has been engaged in transforming its economy, and part of that transformation entails becoming an innovative economy. One of China's main challenges is closing the knowledge gap that separates it from more advanced industrial countries. In spite of huge progress in many areas, that gap remains large. Total factor productivity—output per unit of input—is markedly lower in China, reflected in lower per capita GDP.[2]

Two of the central elements in the Eleventh Five-Year Plan, which took effect in 2006, were creating a more innovative economy and the design of institutions for China's distinctive market economy, including those critical for the innovation economy.

China has always learned from the experiences of other countries, both successes and failures. The Western innovation system has been highly productive, but while the strengths of that system should be obvious, so too should its limits. Research in some areas is, for instance, highly distorted. Consider pharmaceuticals. The system appears highly inefficient, with expenditures on marketing/advertising exceeding that on research; more research is directed at lifestyle improvements (growing hair) than at attacking diseases; research is directed more at addressing diseases of the rich (who can afford expensive medicines) than those of the poor; and much research is directed at "me-too drugs," drugs similar to ones that are already patented, and at "evergreening"—making sure that there is just enough improvement in a drug to extend the life of the patent. The system is costly, with expenditures on patent lawyers rivaling expenditures on research. And, as we shall see, while the patent system leads to short-run inefficiencies (such as monopolies), there is increasing doubt whether, as currently designed, it actually promotes innovation.

As China assesses what kind of intellectual property regime and innovation system is appropriate for it today, it needs to recognize that there are many different intellectual property rights regimes and innovation systems; what works well in one country, may not work well in another. China's circumstances are markedly different from that of the United States and Western Europe. There are at least three distinct aspects of China's current situation:

(i) China is *currently* a net absorber of knowledge, a feature that China shares with most other developing countries.

(ii) Unlike most developing countries, however, China will be moving quickly into the production of new, patentable ideas, from which it can earn rents abroad. Even if the patent system is less central in motivating research within the country, it can be used as an important generator of revenues. There is also a defensive posture: it can facilitate better bargaining outcomes. When a foreign firm has the patent on a standard, it can extract considerable rents. China, with its own technology, can institute its own standard, forcing others to pay it. It may be desirable to do so, even if China's standard may not be as good as the alternative, at least in some dimensions. And the knowledge that China can do this enhances its ability to bargain better terms.

(iii) While most innovation in the West has focused on saving labor, China has an abundance of labor. Little of the innovation in the West has focused on saving natural resources. Doing so, and protecting the environment, will (and should be) a central focus of its research.

The choices that China makes over the next few years may be critical in determining its economic evolution and achieving broader social and economic goals. The wrong intellectual property rights (IPR) regime could make it more difficult to close the knowledge gap, impede China's emergence as an innovation leader, and hamper access to lifesaving drugs. The right IPR system could facilitate China's influence in developing countries, as it provides low-cost generic medicines.

One of the central messages of this chapter is that the dictums emanating from Western governments—that China should imitate their intellectual property regimes and that the stronger the intellectual property regime, the better—should, at best, be viewed with skepticism. To a large extent, they represent the perspectives of certain special interests (such as the pharmaceutical and entertainment industries) that benefit from America's current intellectual property regime. Those with less of a vested interest have not only pointed out the short-run inefficiencies associated with this but also argue that it may slow down the overall progress of innovation.

When I served on President Clinton's Council of Economic Advisers, we provided our assessment of the TRIPS agreement, the intellectual property provisions of the 1994 WTO Uruguay Round agreement, which sought to impose an American-style intellectual property regime on developing countries. Both we and the Office of Science and Technology Policy within the White House basically opposed TRIPS, believing that it was bad for American science, global science, and the economies of the US and developing countries alike. Many of America's own innovative firms are trying to change its IPR regime, which is designed to maximize not innovation but rents from those who have had the good luck receiving a patent (and the two are not the same).

I believed then, and I believe even more so now, that there was a need for reform in the American IPR regime and that it would be wrong to impose such a flawed regime on others. As badly designed as America's IPR regime is for America, it is even worse suited for China; but even if America's IPR regime *were* ideal for the US, that does not mean that it would be ideal for others. What China needs is a development-oriented intellectual property regime, designed specifically for China's stage of development.

COMMON THEMES

This chapter is of interest both because of the central role that the institutional structure of China's innovation system will play in China's future and also because an analysis of the innovation system illustrates several of the general and central themes of this book.

Institutional transplants don't work. Institutional structures that are appropriate for one country may not be the best for another. One-size-fits-all prescriptions don't work in general,[3] but this is one area where they may work particularly badly. Institutional structures have to be sensitive to differences in objectives—a difference to which we have already alluded. Any particular institution (treating IPR, for the moment, as an institution) also must fit in with a broader set of institutional arrangements, which inevitably differ from country to country, shaped by circumstances and history.

Even the World Intellectual Property Organization (WIPO)—an organization that in the past seemed to act as if the stronger the intellectual property, the better—has recognized that the intellectual property regime that is appropriate for the developed countries is not appropriate for developing countries. On October 4, 2004 the General Assembly of WIPO decided to advance an IPR agenda that was, for the first time, explicitly developmentally oriented. The adoption of the Brazilian and Argentinean proposal for a development agenda was a major step forward for several reasons. First, it recognized that intellectual property "is not an end in itself."[4] Second, it reiterated WIPO's mission to "promote creative intellectual activity" and "the transfer of technology to developing countries." The new development agenda calls for ascertaining how different intellectual property regimes affect developing countries. The set of provisions appropriate for the advanced industrial countries are different from those appropriate for the least developed, and both are different from those that would work best for emerging markets, such as China. It is not just a question of "strong" or "weak" intellectual property rights, but rather the design of the whole intellectual property regime, with its myriad of provisions, that matters.

Institutional details matter. Key parts of any country's intellectual property regime entail large elements of interpretation and judgment and are typically defined as much by courts as by legislation. For instance, there is general agreement that patents should only be granted for true innovations, attaining some standard of novelty. But what should be the minimal standard of novelty? Conflicts around such issues between developing and developed countries (and within developed countries) already abound: the US is willing to grant patents for traditional knowledge (such as traditional medicinal uses of certain plants), which developing countries argue should not be patentable. The patents on neem oil, basmati rice, and the medicinal uses of turmeric have been widely criticized by developing countries.[5] India refused to grant a patent for a time release version of a drug whose patent was about to expire. Opponents of the granting of the patent (rightfully, in my view) claimed that this innovation was obvious, significantly so that it did not deserve patent protection; the objective of the "innovation" was simply to extend the patent life of an existing drug.

Rights and restrictions. We have noted (Chapter 1) that all property rights come with restrictions; they are never unfettered. In the case of intellectual property rights, there are restrictions associated both with abuses—they cannot (or should not) be used to unduly restrict competition—and also with public uses—compulsory licenses can and have played an important role in ensuring access to knowledge when it is deemed central for the public interest. Different countries may come to different judgments about which abuses are unacceptable or which public interests are essential.

The central point is that *intellectual property rights*—like other institutions—are social constructions that need to be adapted to the circumstances, history, and objectives of each country. In evaluating alternative innovation systems, there are several criteria. The ultimate objective is the well-being of society. That, in turn, is affected by the pace and direction of innovation and the efficiency with which resources devoted to research are used. But the innovation system does not exist in isolation. It can, for instance, affect the competitiveness and efficiency of the entire economy, the extent of inequality in society, and the health of its citizens. It can even have large budgetary consequences, as in the United States, as government pays pharmaceutical companies large amounts for drugs, the production costs of which are but a fraction of what the government pays—in some cases, even for drugs based largely on government-financed research. The US may be able to afford such largesse (though that is increasingly being questioned); for a developing country like China, the opportunity cost of these funds is enormous—the money could have been better spent promoting education or innovation—and there are even better ways to spend the government's health budget.

This chapter will provide an outline of an innovation system, and its associated intellectual property regime, that may be suited for China's circumstances. The next section explains the basic economics of knowledge, arguing that knowledge is different from ordinary goods, such as steel, where markets can be relied upon. Intellectual property rights introduce static inefficiencies into the economy, but unless IPR regimes are well designed, these inefficiencies can be compounded by slower innovation and distortions in the allocation of scarce research resources, contrary to the claims of its advocates. The following section views IPR as part of a broader innovation system and describes what such a regime might look like—including the advantages and disadvantages of various ways of financing and providing incentives for research.

Following the earlier observation that *details matter,* the next section examines a number of the critical details in an IPR regime. The final two sections focus on the design of intellectual property regimes that promote development, and on the challenge posed by the creation of a global intellectual property regime.

KNOWLEDGE AS A PUBLIC GOOD: INCENTIVES AND INEFFICIENCIES

Knowledge does not come free; resources must be expended on its production and dissemination. It has long been recognized that some form of intellectual property protection can play an important role in providing incentives for innovators, writers, and other creative artists. But intellectual property rights are different from other forms of property rights. While they provide an incentive to innovate, they cause an economic distortion by inefficiently restricting the use of knowledge and creating a (temporary) monopoly power. Ordinarily, property rights are argued for as a means of achieving economic efficiency.[6] Intellectual property rights, by contrast, result in a static inefficiency, justified (in the eyes of its advocates) by dynamic benefits.

The analysis of IPR thus consists of (i) assessing the nature and magnitude of the static inefficiencies to which it gives rise; (ii) evaluating whether it does in fact give rise to dynamic benefits; (iii) determining whether there are ways of designing IPR regimes that reduce the static costs and increase the dynamic benefits; and (iv) assessing whether there are *alternative* ways of financing and creating incentives for innovation, without the drawbacks of IPR.

The central arguments of this chapter is that (i) the static costs are significant; (ii) the dynamic benefits are less than its advocates claim; (iii) there are reforms to the intellectual property regime—institutional structures that are markedly different from those that characterize the US IPR regime—that would enhance the benefits and reduce the costs; and (iv) there are alternatives to the IPR regime that, in many contexts, are superior. The IPR regime should be viewed as part of a portfolio of arrangements for financing and rewarding innovation—a portfolio that in the US and some other countries is currently unbalanced, with too much weight placed on a poorly designed IPR regime.

Basic economics: knowledge as a public good

The analysis of the economics of research begins with the observation that knowledge is a public good—at least in the sense that there is no cost to an additional individual having that knowledge.[7] Economists refer to this as non-rivalrous consumption.[8] If I eat a candy bar, you cannot eat it; only one of us can consume it. But if I know something, you can know it too. To deny you that knowledge, or the right to use that knowledge, gives rise to an inefficiency. Intellectual property is based on such an exclusion. In fact, knowledge is a *global* public good, that is, it is of potential benefit to anyone in the world. There is a global social cost in depriving anyone in the world the right to use available knowledge.[9]

These global social costs are high: They include the value of the lives of the thousands of people who die because they cannot afford AIDS drugs at the high/monopoly prices that the drug companies might charge. Standards of living in the developing world are kept low, because those in developing countries confront barriers to accessing enduring knowledge that would improve productivity and standards of living.

There is another cost: intellectual property rights can give rise to monopoly power. Monopolies interfere with the efficiency of the economy and lead to lower levels of production and higher prices than would prevail with competition. At one time, it was thought that this cost was low, for the monopoly power would only be temporary. In Schumpeterian competition, competition in the market is replaced by competition for the market. And there was even a dynamic benefit: competition for the market led to faster research.[10] Some went even further, arguing that even if there was a single firm in the market, *potential* competition would suffice to ensure efficiency. Each of these assumptions was shown to be wrong, so long as there are any sunk costs (Stiglitz 1988). Potential competition did not suffice to ensure efficiency, and besides, patents preclude potential competition. Incumbent monopolists could, and would, extend their monopoly power, which was often far from temporary. And given the sunk-cost nature of research expenditures, an incumbent could deter competitive entry with only a limited amount of research, so that innovation with monopoly could be substantially lower than with more competition.[11]

Basic economics of innovation: discrepancies between social and private returns and distorted incentives

There is a second key aspect of the economics of innovation: there are marked discrepancies between social and private returns within any patent system, though the magnitude of the discrepancy will be larger with poorly designed IPR regimes. In a well-functioning market economy, there is normally a close congruence between marginal private and social returns. But this is not true in the case of returns generated by intellectual property rights.

The social return to an individual's research is not the invention or innovation that might be produced; rather, it is the fact that the invention or innovation was produced *earlier* than it otherwise would have been. The patent system is a winner-takes-all system: if there are a large number involved in a patent race, the winner gets the entire return; the losers typically get nothing. But if the winner had not done his research, the invention would have been discovered by one of the other researchers, only slightly later. It is not even the case in general that the *average* compensation under the patent system corresponds to what compensation would have been, had we been able to base compensation on marginal contribution.

Particularly if the patent is broad, or if monopoly power in one area can be leveraged into monopoly power in another, the private return may substantially exceed the social return. Many patents (and the research behind them) are focused not so much in producing a product that is better, valued more by consumers, or cheaper, but rather in enhancing market power, e.g., by extending market dominance. Patents can, and often are, used as a barrier to entry. The social return to such innovations can even be negative. At the same time, patents sometimes give rise to research of limited social value, as others try to innovate around a patent. The social return on a me-too invention (designed simply to circumvent an existing patent) is zero.[12] Similarly, there may be relatively low—or even negative—social benefits to allowing patents of traditional knowledge. Such patents obviously don't generate new knowledge, but they may impede the use of knowledge.

In short, the patent system not only does not reward inventors on the basis of their marginal contributions, but sets up a distorted set of incentives for innovations, where inventive activity is directed first at creating market power, and then, by others, at overcoming the artificially created market power. At the same time, the fact that innovations give rise to spillovers and externalities, which are not captured even by strong intellectual property rights, suggests that in many circumstances, the private returns are less than social returns.

The lesson that emerges from this discussion is that, unlike other areas where markets can be relied on to produce efficient outcomes, this is not the case for research. Government has to play a role—indeed, even market advocates argue that government has an important role in creating an intellectual property regime. But a good intellectual property regime tries, on average, to align private and social returns, and to minimize the static costs and maximize the dynamic benefits. Sometimes, as we shall see, it is better to turn to other ways of providing incentives and financing research.

Does IPR actually promote innovation?

While the costs of IPR in terms of static inefficiency are unambiguous, the benefits, in terms of increased innovation, are ambiguous. A poorly designed intellectual property regime can actually lower the pace of innovation. In these cases, there is considerable social cost and little social benefit—dynamic or static—to the patent. The economy loses twice, both from dynamic and static inefficiency.

There are several reasons that strong IPR may impede innovation. The first we have already noted: the monopoly power to which intellectual property rights give rise may actually lead to less innovation, because monopolies may have insufficient incentives to innovate.[13] Moreover, monopolists have incentives—and the ability—to suppress the innovation efforts of others, which critics of Microsoft, for instance, have argued that its policies have done.[14] Second, because research is the most important input into the product of knowledge, by increasing the "price" of knowledge, the pace of knowledge production may be reduced.[15] Even in the United States, there is considerable concern that, for instance, patenting the human genome may impede follow-on research.[16]

The value of many patents arises in part from "enclosing the commons," creating even more severe problems.[17] Often the patent covers knowledge that already exists. While in principle, patents are supposed to be granted only for new knowledge, defining *new knowledge* is not always easy. The criticism of patenting traditional knowledge is that the knowledge covered was previously known. Of course, it may not be known to the patent examiner, and it may not have been published. Indeed, it may not be easy to publish knowledge that is so widely known as to be considered "common knowledge."

Moreover, increasingly innovators face the problem of the "patent thicket," the risk that any innovation "trespasses" on others' intellectual property rights, or at least so they might claim. The most famous recent case involved BlackBerry, whose maker, Research in Motion, was forced to pay hundreds of millions of dollars, under the threat of being forced to shut down, for trespassing on patents, most of which were ultimately declared invalid.

Finally, no matter how well designed the patent law, intellectual property inevitably involves ambiguity—not only over whether there is a legitimate patent (e.g., has the novelty standard been met?), but over the scope of the patent. While it is generally relatively easy to define ownership rights over and boundaries of physical property, this is not so for intellectual property. Did or should George Baldwin Selden's original patent for a four-wheel self-propelled vehicle include all such vehicles, or only the one he sketched out?[18] A potential producer may be uncertain about whom he needs to pay to have the right to produce. He may pay party A, only to find out that party B also has a claim. Patent conflict can impede, and in the past has impeded innovation. Conflicting airplane patents held by the Wright Brothers and Curtis impeded the development of the airplane until World War I, when the government forced the pooling of patents.

The resources devoted to litigation are part of the transaction costs associated with running an intellectual property regime. Financial resources devoted to these costs—which can be considerable—could have been used more productively on research itself. At the very least, the potential of such conflicts adds uncertainty to the innovation process and discourages investment in research.

There are other costs to the patent system. Because rewards are based on who wins the "race," market participants have every incentive not to help others and to hinder competitors. The basic research community rests on principles of openness, transparency, and sharing knowledge; patents lead to secrecy and closed communities—which are antithetical to the progress of science.[19]

Balancing static inefficiencies and dynamic gains

Advocates of intellectual property rights have recognized rights' static costs, but they claim that the costs are more than offset by the social benefits from the resulting induced innovation. A balanced intellectual property regime weighs static and other costs against dynamic benefits. "Balance" must affect every feature of the intellectual property regime, from what can be patented, to the life of the patent, to the breadth of the patent,[20] to the standard of novelty invoked in granting a patent. An unbalanced intellectual property regime—say one with an excessively long patent life—leads to overall inefficiency. The increases in incentives to innovate, from the increased present discounted value of profits from the extension of monopoly power, say from twenty to eighty years, are almost surely of less importance than the present discounted value of inefficiencies to which such an extension of patent life gives rise.

Too often, the advocates of IPR underestimate static losses, overestimate dynamic benefits, and disregard "balance." Even as they note that it may create monopoly power, they emphasize its temporary nature, ignoring the research (noted above) showing that such power can persist and that even attempts to maintain monopoly distorts resource allocations. In the discussions leading to the TRIPS agreement, this careful balancing was totally missing. The argument was essentially: the stronger the intellectual property rights, the better. This is wrong.

IPR AND CHINA'S NATIONAL INNOVATION SYSTEM[21]

So far, our discussion has focused on the potential disadvantages of the IPR system—that it inevitably gives rise to static inefficiencies, and excessively strong, poorly designed property rights may actually impede innovation and growth.

This brings us naturally to the critical question: are there better alternatives to IPR for producing and financing knowledge than the system, with its attendant distortions, of incentives through patents and copyrights?

Advocates of stronger intellectual property rights give the impression that they are essential for innovation. A moment's reflection should make it obvious that there are many alternative ways to finance and reward innovation. There are, for instance, other ways of appropriating returns from innovation (trade secrets, first-mover advantage) besides patents and copyrights, and in many areas these are highly effective. In fact, many of the most important advances in knowledge are not protected by intellectual property rights and were not motivated by monetary gains. The basic mathematic advances that provided the underpinnings of the computer are but one of a large number of examples. Mathematical theorems cannot (and, I would argue, should not) be patented.

There are other ways of financing and providing incentives for research. The US and other governments finance much of the basic research upon which pharmaceutical companies base their innovations. The Internet, which has spawned myriad innovations since the 1990s, was based on research that was supported, and largely conducted, by US and European governments. The fact that so much of the successful innovation in the United States has occurred in research parks adjacent to universities suggests that these firms are benefiting from knowledge produced in the universities; and university research is, by and large, funded by foundations, government, and university endowments—but not motivated by the search for profit.

More recently, the open-source movement in software has been an important source of innovation. While its original successes were in software, it is now demonstrating its effectiveness in other arenas, such as biotechnology.[22]

Alternative ways of financing knowledge production

We can think of IPR as a method of funding research—a highly distortionary method. Price exceeds marginal cost by a considerable amount, for a limited period of time, and the resulting monopoly profit not only provides the incentives, but also the resources for innovation. This gap between price and marginal cost can be thought of as a tax, part of the proceeds of which are used to finance research. In the last seventy-five years, there has been considerable research into the optimal way of raising (tax) revenues. There is no research suggesting that the "implicit" taxation of IPR (even if *all* the proceeds were devoted to R & D) has any optimality properties. Its principal virtue is that it is a benefit tax, that is, only those who benefit from the innovation pay for it. But in most arenas, we do not employ benefit taxes, largely because the additional distortions associated with such taxes are generally not viewed as worth the slight gain in "equity." In the area of lifesaving drugs, such an argument is even more compelling, since typically those who need the drugs are already suffering from having a life-threatening disease. In the case of drugs, the "monopoly tax" is an inefficient way of funding research for yet another reason: a large fraction of the revenue does not reach its target—it is spent on marketing and advertising, rather than on research.

While within the United States the distortions in consumption and inequities associated with monopoly pricing as a basis of research-funding for medicines may be limited, because so much of the funding for health care is from third parties, and there may be accordingly little price elasticity, internationally this is not true. And even in the United States, there are large distortions arising out of rent-seeking—in the quest to garner monopolistic returns. But especially in developing countries, high prices effectively deny access to lifesaving drugs for large numbers of people. More generally, the in-effect benefit tax is regressive. A more equitable system of financing would be progressive and those more able to pay would pay more—and indeed a larger share of their income. Indeed, one can argue that in countries such as China where individuals have to pay a larger share of their drug costs, not charging prices above marginal cost for lifesaving drugs may be a desirable way to provide assistance to poorer people who have the misfortune of suffering from disease. Governments around the world now directly or indirectly pay for a large share of the cost of drugs. A system of direct payment for the underlying research combined with marginal cost pricing would make what is going on more transparent, would be a more equitable system of finance, and would lead to better resource allocations.

Production vs finance

The issues of production and finance can largely be separated. Production can be undertaken privately or publicly; finance can be undertaken privately or publicly. At one extreme are government research laboratories—publicly financed research that is also publicly "produced." The IPR system is often described as the polar opposite, a private-sector solution combining private funding and private finance. But this description is misleading in two respects that we have already noted. First, much of the innovation is based on basic research that is publicly funded and often publicly produced or at least not produced by for-profit entities. And second, in the case of both health and defense, even the seemingly "private" funding under an IPR regime is really public funding, since all defense expenditures are from the public purse and since the government provides most of the funding for health care expenditures in most countries. Even in the most market-oriented country, the United States, much of the funding comes from government: the National Institutes of Health represent publicly financed and publicly produced research; and government spending on health care, both through its program for poor people, Medicaid, and its program for elderly people, Medicare, represents a large share of total health care spending.[23]

Prizes

The prize system represents one alternative to the patent system for providing incentives for research. This entails giving a prize to whomever comes up with an innovation, or at least those innovations that meet announced objectives. For instance, the person who finds a cure or a vaccine for AIDS or malaria would get a big prize. Someone who comes up with a drug with slightly different side effects than existing drugs (but which is otherwise no more effective) might get a small prize. The size of the prize is calibrated by the magnitude of the contribution.

The idea is an old one. The UK's Royal Society for the Encouragement of Arts, Manufactures, and Commerce has been advocating and using prizes to incentivize the development of needed technologies for more than a century. For instance, an alternative was needed for chimney sweeps, those small, underfed boys who used to be sent down chimneys. It was not good for their health, but not cleaning chimneys meant increasing the risk of fire, with serious consequences. So the Royal Society offered a prize to anybody who invented a mechanical way of cleaning chimneys. The prize provided an incentive—and it worked. A patent system might also have motivated the development of a mechanical device (though it did not), but if it had, there would have been a problem: the owner of the patent would have wanted to maximize the return on his innovation by charging a high fee for its use. That would mean that only rich families could have afforded to use the mechanical device, and young boys' lives would have continued to be put at risk. With the prize system, everyone could benefit from this socially important innovation.

The current patent system is, of course, similar to a prize system, but it is an inefficient one, because the "prize" is a grant of monopoly power, and with monopoly power there are incentives to restrict the use of the knowledge. One of the characteristics of a desirable innovation system is that the ideas and innovations, once developed, are widely used and disseminated; the patent system is designed to restrict the use of knowledge. With the prize system, the competitive market ensures efficient dissemination; giving licenses to a large number of people uses the force of competition to drive down the price and to increase the use of the knowledge. With both patents and prizes, market forces are used: one is the incentive of a monopoly to restrict knowledge and raise prices, the other is the force of competitive markets to drive down prices and extend the benefit of knowledge widely.

Moreover, the prize system has the advantage of creating fewer incentives to waste money on advertising and to engage in anticompetitive behaviors designed to enhance monopoly profits. Drug companies spend more on advertising and marketing than they do on research. These marketing expenditures are designed to reduce the elasticity of demand, which allows the owner of the patent to raise prices and increase monopoly profits. From a social point of view, these expenditures are dissipative.

The patent system also distorts the pattern of research: drug companies have insufficient incentives to develop medicines for the diseases that tend to afflict poor people, simply because there is no money in those drugs. One of the widely discussed ideas for addressing this problem is a guaranteed purchase fund, in which the World Bank or the Gates Foundation would guarantee one or two billion dollars to the person or people who develop a vaccine or cure for AIDS, malaria, or some other disease afflicting the developing world for the purchase of the drug. In effect, there would be a certain market. The guarantee of one or two billion dollars for the purchase of the drug would act as a prize, and a sufficiently large guarantee would provide a clear motivation for research. These guaranteed purchase funds, however, would still maintain the inefficiency of the monopoly patent system, unless there was an accompanying commitment that would make the patent accessible to all at reasonable royalties for purchases beyond the guarantee. The discoverer receives his "prize"—the monopoly profits—by charging monopoly prices. The poor, who get the drugs through the guaranteed purchase fund do not, of course, pay the monopoly price. But the funds are limited and when they are used up, without such a commitment, a government that wants to provide to its citizens, say, the malaria medicine that has been bought through the guarantee purchase fund, will have to pay the full monopoly price.

Money spent purchasing this drug at the monopoly price is money that cannot be spent on the country's other health needs. It may be far better to use the money for the guarantee purchase fund in a way which spurs competition in the provision of the drug, to offer a prize, or to buy the patent, and to allow anyone willing to pay a limited licensing fee to produce it.

In areas where there are well-defined needs (such as the need to develop a malaria vaccine) both the prize system and the patent system can provide comparable incentives to undertake research. Both have the advantage over government-funded research that no one has to pick who should undertake the research: there is a process of *self-selection*; those who think that they have the best prospects of succeeding (and are able to finance the research and willing to bear the risk) undertake the project. The prize system uses the force of competitive markets to ensure the widespread dissemination of the benefits of the innovation; the patent system uses monopoly power, restricting the usage, and often distorting the markets in other ways.

A PORTFOLIO APPROACH TO INNOVATION

Intellectual property rights should be part of an innovation system that also includes prizes and government-supported research and grants (which are probably the most important component of the innovation system in supporting basic research). Each of these has its strengths and weaknesses. Table 8.1 provides a chart of some of the attributes of these three alternatives.

As we noted, any innovation system has to solve the problems of finance, selection (who gets research money), and incentives. There are, in addition, problems of coordination of research efforts. How these tasks are solved will affect the efficiency of the system—including the uncertainty and transaction costs facing market participants.

Every country should have a portfolio of instruments, but in our view, too much weight has been assigned to patents in the current portfolio in the US. As China thinks about its own innovation system, it has the opportunity to redress this imbalance, reducing the role of patents and increasing the role of prizes and government-sponsored research.

The first attribute listed is *selection*. One problem facing any innovation system is how to select those to engage in a research project. The advantage of both the patent and the prize system is that they are decentralized and based on self-selection. Those who think that they are the best researchers make the decision to undertake the research. They make the investment, risking their own money, in the belief that they have a good chance of winning the prize (the formal

Table 8.1. Comparing alternative systems

	Innovation System		
Attribute	Patent	Prize	Government-Funded Research
Selection	Decentralized, self-selection; lacks coordination	Decentralized, self-selection; lacks coordination	Bureaucratic; more coordination possible
Finance (tax)	Highly distortionary and inequitable	Can be less distortionary and more equitable	Most efficient
Risk	Litigation risk	Less risk	Least risk
Innovation Incentives	Strong but distorted	Strong, less distorted; requires well-defined objectives	Strong nonmonetary incentives
Dissemination Incentive	Limited—monopoly	Strong—competitive markets	Strong
Transaction Costs	High	Lower	Lower

prize or the prize of the patent). The prize and patent systems have this advantage over government-funded research, in which there is a group of peers (or bureaucrats) deciding on the best researcher. There is obviously also a concern about "capture" of the research-awarding process, e.g., by political or economic interests whose agendas may be separate or counter to the advancement of science and technology.

With respect to *finance,* the patent system is the worst of the three systems. It is highly distortionary and inequitable in the way in which funds to support research are raised—by charging monopoly prices, e.g., on the sick. By the same token, the transaction costs (especially those associated with litigation) and the distortions in the economic system are much higher with a patent system than with the other two.

Regarding the *dissemination* of knowledge and its efficient use, government-funded research is best (because knowledge is generally made freely available); the prize system is second (though there may be little difference compared to government-funded research if, after the prize is awarded, knowledge is made freely available or if, with government-funded research, the government charges a licensing fee); and the patent system is the worst, given that it relies on monopolization, which entails high prices and restricted usage. In short, under the prize and the government-funded research systems, knowledge, once acquired, is more efficiently used. These are among the key advantages of these alternatives.

There is a big difference in the nature of the *risk* faced by researchers operating in the three systems. One of the disadvantages of both the patent and the prize systems is the lack of *coordination*. From a societal point of view, there is a risk of excessive duplication.[24] The lack of coordination increases the cost of doing research. One of the *risks* that each researcher faces is not knowing how many other people are engaged in that research. This increases the risk that someone else will make the discovery first, and thus get the patent or prize. Government-funded research can be more coordinated. The patent system imposes a second risk, that of costly litigation. Thus, with respect to risk, the patent system is the worst and the government-funded system is the best, because it has the advantages of paying for the input rather than the output. That is to say, a researcher gets money for his time and other resources spent doing the research, whereas in the prize and the patent systems researchers are rewarded only if their research is successful—and successful before their rivals.

One of the reasons that risk is important is that in equilibrium consumers have to pay for the risk borne by researchers. People and firms[25] are risk-averse, and if they must bear risk, they have to be compensated for doing so. The patent system makes society bear the cost of that risk in an inefficient way. Under the government-financed research system, not only is risk lower, but it is shared by society in a more efficient way.

Innovation incentives are strong in the patent system, but they are distorted, whereas the prize system can provide equivalent incentives that are less distorted. (They are distorted, as we have noted, because there are incentives to engage in research to innovate around a patent and to spend money in ways that extend the effective life of the patent. These innovation distortions are in addition to the other market distortions, such as those associated with expenditures attempting to make demand curves less elastic.)

On most accounts, the prize system dominates the patent system; but the prize system has one limitation: it does not work when the objective is not well defined. (There are, however, many areas, such as health, energy conservation, and carbon emissions reductions, in which there are well-defined objectives.) That is why the prize system will never replace the patent system. At the same time, in basic research—the foundation on which everything else is built—government-funded research will continue to remain at the core of the innovation system. No one has proposed otherwise: the costs of restricting the usage of knowledge associated with the patent system far outweigh any purported benefits. The debate today revolves only around applied research, which often entails translating the knowledge acquired in basic research into applications.

LEGAL AND POLICY FRAMEWORKS

The first part of this chapter outlined some of the economic principles foundational to a balanced and development-oriented intellectual property regime. Such principles get translated into action through legal and policy frameworks. In designing these frameworks, details matter. Unfortunately, many of the current frameworks do not reflect the kind of balance for which we have advocated, and may actually hinder development and innovation. The problem arises partly from a failure to understand the economics, partly from a failure to understand property rights, and partly because the agenda of those pushing for stronger intellectual property rights is concerned more with rent-seeking than with efficiency and equity.

The following discussion focuses mostly on details concerning the IPR regime. As the conclusion of the preceding section emphasized, IPR should be viewed as part of an innovation system, and there are many government actions besides the IPR legal framework that affect the structure of the entire system. These include government support for research and teaching (including research universities) and the creation of a prize system for needed innovations in areas such as energy efficiency and health. Earlier, we noted the open-source model as an alternative to IPR. Some governments have actively promoted open-source software by, for example, requiring all government computers to have only open-source software. There are occasions in which the open-source legal framework comes into conflict with the closed IPR framework, and where the two conflict, it is important to resolve in favor of open source.

There are also strong arguments for a publicly funded and managed system of pharmaceutical testing, a key component of the current innovation system for drugs (Jayadev and Stiglitz, 2009, 2010). In the current system, drug companies test their own drugs, an arrangement fraught with expensive, distortionary conflicts of interest.

Many details of an IPR regime are critical: what can be patented, the standards used for granting patents, the length and breadth of the patent, restrictions on the patent, how the patent is enforced, and rules governing the granting of the patent. In each dimension, there are complex trade-offs, e.g., between providing incentives for innovation on the one hand and introducing inefficiencies in the dissemination of knowledge and impeding follow-on innovations on the other. One of the reasons that there is a broad consensus against patenting mathematical theorems or other insights from basic research is that the disadvantages of patenting far exceed the advantages. Other patents, such as those for business processes, impose other costs, e.g., in terms of litigation risks.

Recent changes in IPR regimes have not always carefully balanced costs and benefits. The extension of the life of copyrights probably imposed more costs than any benefits from improved incentives. With weak standards of "novelty" and "obviousness" patent owners can "evergreen" their patent, thereby extending its life. There is a legitimate debate about the optimal length of the life of a patent[26]—but such indirect ways of extending it almost surely have greater costs than any associated innovative benefits. The costs can be particularly high in the case of drugs in developing countries.[27] There have been some excessively broad patents (as we noted earlier in the context of the original US automobile patent); the greater the breadth, obviously, the greater the value of the patent, but the greater the impediments for follow-on inventors. China should be particularly wary of broad patents.

Other details of the IPR regime can reduce the costs relatives to the benefits. Historically, to get a patent, knowledge had to be disclosed, which meant, in principle, that others could make use of that knowledge for their research. Patent rights can be viewed as an exchange, where the "public" grants a temporary monopoly right, circumscribed, in return for the revelation of information. More recently, some in the software industry have been arguing for stronger intellectual property rights *without* disclosure. China should insist on strong disclosure requirements. In the end, some may choose not to seek intellectual property protection, preferring to rely on trade secrecy.

The following sections focus on a set of key issues in the design of an IPR system.

What can be patented

Only certain things can be patented. The applicant is supposed to demonstrate, for instance, a certain standard of novelty. Even then, theorems cannot be patented. Some countries have restricted the granting of patents to *processes* for producing chemicals, not to the molecules themselves. An American court recently rejected the right to patent certain genes (that rejection was overturned shortly before this book went to press, a decision which is itself under appeal at the time of writing).[28] This is a position taken by many other countries. America's business process patents have been widely criticized as extending the reach of patents too far.

Breadth of property rights

A common misperception is that, once a patent is granted, the grantee has the right to do anything with it during its lifetime, an uncircumscribed ability to exercise monopoly rights. Property rights do not in general, and should not, give the owners of property uncircumscribed rights, as we have emphasized throughout this book, and this is especially true for intellectual property rights. IPRs are not an end in themselves; they are a social construction, a means to an end—to promote societal well-being—which is accomplished through careful definition and design.

Examples in which public interest concerns circumscribe ordinary property rights abound; the general principle is that I cannot do things with my property that might adversely affect others. This provides, for instance, a justification for zoning. In these cases, there is a balancing of public interest and private rights.

US patent law illustrates these issues by excepting patent protection for government use. Under 28 USC 1498, the government is authorized to use any patent or copyright, which can be extended to any contractor, subcontractor, or employee working for the government. While there is extensive debate about the justification for this, the view taken by the United States Court of Federal Claims in the 1990s is telling: it recognized that the granting of a patent was a limited grant—just as it was limited in time, so too it was limited in use. Government use represents a power reserved to the government when it initially grants the patent: "... the government cannot 'take' what it already possesses, the government [has] the absolute power to take a compulsory, nonexclusive license to a patented invention at will."[29] While other courts have challenged this interpretation, the Court of Federal Claims decisions make clear that reasonable people, even in advanced industrial countries, balancing interests and looking at the costs and benefits of stronger intellectual property rights, have come to the conclusion that these rights should be heavily circumscribed.

The question, accordingly, is not whether intellectual property rights need to be circumscribed to advance broader social objectives, but how much, and in what manner. The answers to this question for China are not necessarily the same as for the US or other advanced industrial countries.

Curtailing abuses of market power through limitations on intellectual property rights

For instance, intellectual property rights, by definition, create a monopoly power over the use of knowledge; but this is not a license for monopoly abuse. But what is meant by an *abuse* of monopoly power? And what should be the appropriate remedy? There is a broad consensus that Microsoft overstepped the boundaries by leveraging its market power over operating systems into other arenas. But while both American and European antitrust authorities have concurred on this, they have proposed different remedies, perhaps partly based on differences in judgments about the "balancing" of static and dynamic effects.

One of the responses to abusive, anticompetitive practices has been to restrict the use of patents, effectively insisting on compulsory licensing, sometimes through forming patent pools. In the consent decree in the case of the antitrust action against AT&T in the 1950s, AT&T had to make its patents available to anybody wanting to use them.[30]

Another proposed reform that has gained favor among some academics is limiting the life of intellectual property protection as a way of limiting abuses, increasing market competitiveness, and spurring innovation. If Microsoft's operating system had only a three-year protection, then it would be spurred to make significant improvements in each subsequent release.[31]

Again, what is clear is that there is no unanimity even among the advanced industrial countries on what appropriate balancing entails. China (and many other emerging markets and developing countries) should be particularly wary of monopolization; in certain sectors, because markets are less perfect, the threat of monopolization is greater. Monopolies, once created, tend to persist.

Compulsory licenses

Beside the restrictions arising from the threat of excessive monopolization, the two most important instances in which patent rights have been circumscribed have been when there is a threat to public health or in response to global warming. The 1992 Rio Agreement created a framework for addressing problems of climate change by providing for compulsory licenses for obtaining access to technology related to mitigation of emissions. The 1994 TRIPS agreement provided for compulsory licenses for lifesaving medicines.

Rule of reason versus per se

A key question in defining an intellectual property regime concerns *presumptions.* In standard antitrust policy, there are some areas in which per se rules apply—price-fixing is per se illegal. In other areas, the courts are asked to engage in a rule of reason, to balance competitive losses against any efficiency gains that might result from a vertical restraint.

While it may eventually be possible to devise simple rules for judging when, for instance, a compulsory license should be granted, intellectual property rights, especially in developing countries, are at an early stage of development. Simplicity—and the limited capacity of developing countries to engage in expensive litigating—argues that there should be strong presumptions in favor of limiting intellectual property rights when there is an apparent health, competition, or developmental objective. That is, the burden of proof should be placed on the original holder of the patent that there is not a legitimate health, competition, or developmental objective. For instance, in granting pharmaceutical patents, China should reserve the right to grant a compulsory license for any lifesaving or life-extending drug. To be exempt from this provision, the patent applicant would have to state that the patent does not cover any such medicinal use; and if subsequently such a use were established, the government would have the right to issue a compulsory license, limited, of course, to sales for such usages.

The process of granting and enforcing patents

We have argued that institutional details matter. Nowhere is that more evident than in the way that patents are granted and enforced. Different countries have approached these issues in different ways, and China should learn from these experiences, as well as from proposals that have been made to remedy the weaknesses in current prevailing practices. In Europe, there is a process of *opposition*: those who believe the patent should not be granted have an opportunity to express their views to the patent office *before* a patent is granted. There is no such provision in the US, exacerbating the bias toward excessive patenting that arises from the very structure of the patent system. Patents, as we have noted, privatize knowledge; but challenging a patent converts what is a private good into a public good. Thus challenging is itself a public good and, as in other arenas, the private sector will underinvest in the provision of this public good.

Once granted, the owner of the patent can exclude others from using his intellectual property *until the patent is overturned.* This has become a source of special concern, given the large number of bad patents—patents which should not have been issued, some of which are eventually overturned. Those who have such patents can impose extortionary demands on those who wish to make use of their patents. These "patent owners" can even insist that those to whom they grant license not sue—eliminating a major source of challenge to patents.

There are alternatives. For instance, under the "liability system," those who use another's intellectual property have to pay compensation, but the owner of the intellectual property cannot exclude someone from using the property. For an emerging market such as China, access to knowledge is essential for its future growth. Intellectual property cannot be used as an impediment to its development. The liability system (in effect, granting a compulsory license at fair compensation for the use of knowledge) is one way of preventing this from happening. Even more modest reforms, such as allowing the use of intellectual property so long as there is a challenge (with appropriate compensation paid if the patent is upheld) would be preferable to the existing system.[32]

De jure *and* de facto *fairness*

Legal systems often look fair on paper: everyone has a right to a day in court. In practice, obtaining justice is expensive, and those who cannot pay often cannot get it. That is why societies increasingly provide legal aid to those who cannot afford it. While there are still enormous imbalances, the system is fairer than it otherwise would be. In the West, because the patent system has become enormously expensive, it serves as an barrier to entry and is unfair to small firms. They already face disadvantages in obtaining finance for research; but under the patent system, they face further costs in attempting to get a patent. Worse still, when they have a successful product, they face the risk of being sued by a well-funded large enterprise for some patent infringement. And if there is no public enforcement of patent infringement, the well-funded enterprise can simply infringe on the patent of a smaller firm, knowing that in the legal battle that ensues, it is likely to prevail simply because of its greater resources.

China, if it wants to create a dynamic, innovative economy within a harmonious society, must ensure that there is *de facto* as well as *de jure* justice. Part of this must entail creating a legal system that does not give undue advantage to rich corporations and providing economic assistance to small and medium-sized enterprises in obtaining and enforcing patents.

This section has discussed an array of institutional details that are central to determining how the patent system works and whether it achieves the right balance between providing incentives and enabling new research versus the inherent costs associated with the restrictions on the use of knowledge.

TOWARDS AN INTELLECTUAL PROPERTY REGIME THAT PROMOTES DEVELOPMENT

For China, every issue that is up for discussion—from what is patentable, to the scope of the patent, to the novelty standard, to the limitations of intellectual property rights, to when governments have the right to grant compulsory licenses and on what terms—needs to be addressed from the perspective of development, in order to create a dynamic, innovative, competitive economy with a healthy population. Focusing on the developmental consequences of intellectual property provides a new lens through which to appraise each of these aspects of the intellectual property regime. The fact that intellectual property requires balancing a variety of concerns implies that one country's appropriate intellectual property regime may be different from that of another.

For instance, a development-oriented intellectual property regime might well recognize the right to grant a compulsory license when doing so promotes development, e.g., when it enables the country to reduce the technology gap that separates it from the more advanced industrial countries. For China, as it strives to create an innovation economy, to improve the health of its citizens, and to address the myriad of environmental challenges that it confronts, these issues are of particular importance.

A development-oriented IPR agenda would pay attention to:

(i) The importance of ensuring effective competition. There is even greater risk of limitations in competition in developing countries, where markets are by definition smaller than in Europe and the United States, so that even greater weight should be given to the risks that patents pose in decreasing competition.

(ii) The importance of ensuring access to lifesaving medicines. With strong budgetary limitations on both the household and government levels, higher prices translate directly into loss of life. Moreover, money spent in purchasing expensive drugs is money that is not available for other purposes, such as promoting developing through investments in education, health, technology, or infrastructure.

(iii) The importance of ensuring the transfer of technology. Unless the gap between developed and less developed countries in technology and knowledge can be closed, there will be no successful development. What is required is not only access to products and technology, but also the ability to learn how to produce with more advanced technologies, which may not be feasible without compulsory licensing.

(iv) The importance of ensuring protection of traditional knowledge, recognizing the special problems in establishing patents in this area and the dangers here of "fencing in the commons."

(v) The importance of protecting genetic resources. Much of the world's biodiversity resides in developing countries and emerging markets. These countries must have incentives to maintain their biodiversity. In doing so, they provide a global public good, which they are currently being asked to provide without receiving any compensation. Their desire to develop puts these resources at risk. Providing property rights in the genetic material that is derived from these sources can be an important part of a global framework for providing incentives for developing countries to protect their biodiversity.

This chapter has explained that intellectual property rights are one part of a country's innovation system and that in the design of IPR, there are complicated trade-offs, e.g., involving static and dynamic considerations. There is no single "best" IPR system. How these trade-offs are balanced does, and should, differ according to the circumstances of each country. We have called for "balance" in intellectual property rights, a balance that will differ among countries. But that means that we need an international system that *allows* each developing country to choose the IPR regime that is appropriate for its own circumstances.

A one-size-fits-all regime is, accordingly, inappropriate. While there may be some advantages from a harmonization of standards, there are also marked disadvantages. In the Commonwealth-IPD report on the Development Round, we called for a "conservative principle"—that common standards only be adopted where there are overwhelming gains, especially to developing countries.[33] Inevitably, in bargaining over standards, developing countries would be put at a disadvantage, and this was especially so when the number of items on the agenda increased. The developed countries have argued that all countries should adopt strong IPRs, claiming they are in the interests of the developing countries themselves. If that is the case, then they should be presented with evidence that this is so, and presumably, if the evidence is as overwhelming as the United States claims, countries will voluntarily undertake these standards. In fact, the agenda that the United States Trade Representative has pushed is *not* designed to benefit developing countries, to maximize their growth or the well-being of the people living there; it is designed to maximize the transfer of rents from others to the United States and to maximize the rents enjoyed by certain sectors within the United States. The United States is right in emphasizing the importance of intellectual property rights, but it is only one part of a country's innovation system, and it has to be carefully designed if it is to promote development and societal well-being.

China should be wary about borrowing economic or legal frameworks from others in any arena, but especially so in intellectual property, where almost surely the standards that are appropriate for advanced industrial countries are different from those appropriate to developing countries, and in which special interests have played such a large role in determining the standards elsewhere. It would not be in the interests of developing countries in general and China in particular to adopt standards that reflect, say, the balancing between static efficiency and dynamic gains (or among various political forces) in the US. China needs to remember that the US IPR regime reflects the influence of particular interest groups, not a well-considered balancing of static and dynamic, efficiency, and equity trade-offs.

IPR AND NATIONAL INNOVATION SYSTEMS: GLOBAL PERSPECTIVES

Most of this paper focuses on the design of China's innovation system, and in particular on its IPR regime, which inevitably will be viewed within the context of IPR regimes being adopted around the world. As China's influence in the global economy increases, it will be important for it to fight for a global IPR regime that supports its own interests. But it should simultaneously fight for a global IPR regime that is consistent with the interests of other developing countries. The previous section argued for a global regime that allows developing countries to design their own IPR regimes. This section elaborates on what an appropriate global IPR entails. Our discussion focuses on the implications of the fact that knowledge is a global public good, as well as on global institutional arrangements.

Financing knowledge as a global public good

We know that knowledge is a global public good. If we were to ask what is a fair and efficient way of financing such a global public good, standard principles of public finance would suggest that the costs be borne by those most able to bear them, and that the market not be distorted by imposing prices in excess of marginal costs. For those in the advanced industrial countries to bear the burden of financing basic research may be a highly effective way of providing foreign assistance to the poorest countries of the world.

Under current arrangements, American taxpayers providing foreign assistance for health in developing countries indirectly are providing funds that go to American drug companies, as the health care budgets of the developing countries pay a "research tax" in the form of a price in excess of marginal costs. And taxpayers in developing countries supporting their countries' health budgets are also helping to finance American drug companies. Thus, the patent system is not only distortionary, but also inequitable, with transfers from the poor countries to the rich, an inequitable system of funding research.

TRIPS and intellectual property rights

There is a broad consensus among academic economists—including some who are strongly in favor of multilateral agreements liberalizing trade between developed and less developed countries—that intellectual property should never have been included in trade negotiations.[34] The World Trade Organization is supposed to promote trade; many of the provisions associated with enforcing IPR entail restrictions on trade. Unlike traditional trade liberalizations, where tariff reductions benefit both the exporter and the importer, intellectual property rights represent a transfer; the holder of the intellectual property right is better off and the user is worse off. To be sure, advocates of intellectual property rights try to claim that in the long run everyone is better off, but such claims are hard to substantiate, especially when the IPR regime is unbalanced and not well designed.

Most importantly, the parties involved in negotiations at the WTO are trade ministers who are not well suited to engage in the careful balancing that is required if we are to have well-designed intellectual property rights. As noted, this was evident during the Uruguay Round, when the concerns of developing countries, the scientific community, and health advocates were given short shrift in favor of the interests of America's pharmaceutical and media industries. Nowhere were the problems with TRIPS more evident that in the treatment of lifesaving drugs. The original text contained ambiguities—the developing countries thought that they had the right to force compulsory licensing for lifesaving drugs that otherwise would not be affordable. The United States thought otherwise. Eventually, a world outcry forced the drug companies to step back, and in Doha, there was an agreement that this was to be one of the issues to be addressed. But just a month before the meeting in Cancun, the United States still was reluctant to go very far. The key question was whether a small country facing an AIDS epidemic, such as Botswana, could purchase from South Africa generic drugs that it was too small to produce itself. Would it have to pay the high American prices? Or could it import lower-priced drugs produced under compulsory licenses from South Africa? While the United States eventually gave in to the global consensus, the dispute made clear the nature of the disagreements about the appropriate framework for intellectual property rights. Clearly, in this case, the position taken by the United States was not "developmentally oriented." But the eventual agreement still fell far short of a minimal developmentally oriented agreement because the United States continued to insist that access be given only in the case of an epidemic. It is, and should be, a concern to developing countries that their citizens are dying needlessly because they cannot get access to lifesaving drugs at affordable prices, whether there is an epidemic or not. It is certainly a legitimate position for developing countries to insist on compulsory licensing for lifesaving medicines when monopoly pricing on the part of the patent holder leaves prices at levels substantially above the costs of production. That developing countries could not get American acquiescence on this fundamental principle even in a round of trade negotiations that was called the "Development Round" suggests that such matters need to be taken out of the WTO and put into other venues.

Even from the outset, it was recognized that the TRIPS agreement was unbalanced, with costs imposed on developing countries almost surely greater than the benefits and with intellectual property protection concerns of developing countries being given short shrift. While developing countries would have to pay more for drugs, the drug companies invested little in the diseases afflicting poor people, especially those in developing countries. There was little protection afforded to the traditional knowledge of developing countries, and drug companies' oppositions to paying for the value of the knowledge associated with the genetic material obtained from developing countries led to the refusal of the United States and other advanced industrial countries to sign the Convention on Biological Diversity.

Access to health

In 2003, the international Commission on the Social Dimensions of Globalization, recognizing the severe potential adverse impact of TRIPS on health conditions in developing countries and how lack of access to knowledge could impair their development, called for a rethinking of TRIPS.[35] The problems were rightly anticipated to worsen as developing countries rewrote their intellectual property laws to conform to TRIPS. Producers of generic drugs still covered by patents in their countries of origin, so critical to the provision of low-cost medicines in developing countries, might be forced out of business. Meanwhile, there were worries that even the "flexibilities" built into the Uruguay Round agreement (supposedly to allow countries to balance other concerns, such as access to health) would be undermined, as the US and Europe might subtly threaten developing countries that exercised their rights to issue compulsory licenses, even when the country is complying with all the rules of TRIPS—and there are a variety of actions that the developed countries can undertake against any developing country going against the wishes of the advanced industrial countries that are very costly to the developing countries.[36] So, it is not just how the rules were designed, but also the ways in which they are being implemented that has made it more difficult to get access to these generic medicines. All of these fears and worries have proven justified.[37]

If the WTO really were interested in making sure people have access to generic medicines, the set of procedures would look very different. There might, for instance, be a list of lifesaving drugs, or drugs that address debilitating disease, which any generic producer could sell in any country whose income was below a critical threshold. Even better would be the reverse presumption: any generic producer could sell any drug in any country whose income was below a critical threshold, unless the owner of the patent substantiated that it was a lifestyle drug, of little value in addressing either life-threatening or debilitating diseases.

Rather than the rebalancing of intellectual property regimes (toward something called TRIPS minus) that the Commission on the Human Dimensions of Globalization called for, these obligations have been extended as part of bilateral agreements; these regimes have been dubbed TRIPS plus. So far, these have embraced a relatively small fraction of global trade. Still, it is very disturbing that so many of them require developing countries to agree to an intellectual property regime that is even more unbalanced than TRIPS, that restricts further, for instance, access to generic drugs.[38] For these countries, the globalization of intellectual property has had severe consequences: increasing havoc in their public health systems, draining royalties toward rich countries, undermining the availability of resources available to address other health or developmental needs, and decreasing access to health.[39]

The examples provided illustrate the gulf in interests between the advanced industrial countries and the developing and emerging markets with respect to IPR. The IPR regime that has emerged globally largely reflects the interests and perspectives of the former—and the special interests within them. There is a need to give greater voice to the concerns of the developing world. This is a matter of both efficiency and equity. Unless this is done, there is the prospect of an ever-increasing gulf between the developed and less developed worlds.

Giving emerging markets and developing countries more voice in the design of their intellectual property regimes will not suffice. They will also need financial assistance. Resources are required to design and implement an intellectual property regime. As in other areas of the law, access to the benefits that might be provided requires resources; given the disparity in access to resources, even a seemingly fair IPR regime may lead to unfair outcomes. Earlier, we discussed how the intellectual property regime could, *de facto*, serve as an entry barrier, discriminating in practice against small firms. The same logic applies internationally. We have already alluded to some of the resulting inequities. It is not just that the legal framework formally does not give adequate recognition to traditional knowledge; it may also be difficult for a developing country to challenge a patent on traditional knowledge. If the international community is really committed to a development-oriented IPR agenda, it will have to recognize:

(i) The importance of the need for impartial technical assistance.
(ii) The need for financial assistance in creating an appropriate IPR regime within each country.
(iii) And legal assistance (financial and technical) to challenge patent applications and to obtain patents in more advanced industrial countries. Without such assistance, there cannot be fairness and there is a risk that whatever the legal framework, the interests of the developing countries will be given short shrift.

This will go only part of the way toward achieving a level playing field. The advanced industrial countries have a number of ways in which they can apply pressure to developing countries. They can threaten to cut off foreign aid or restrict preferential trade access; the international economic institutions too can try to force more stringent intellectual property regimes as a condition for assistance. In some cases, simple pressure may work without the threat of explicit sanctions. For instance, developing countries are told—and sometimes believe—that without strong IPR regimes, foreign investment will not come. The fact that there has been so much foreign investment in China, in spite of allegations of inadequate IPR protection, is evidence to the contrary.

A more balanced intellectual property regime, one which reflects the concerns within developing countries and that gives them more scope for pursuing a developmentally oriented intellectual property regime—as part of a broader developmentally oriented innovation system—is in the interests of the world. It would facilitate the closing of the gap between the haves and the have-nots. A balanced regime is required, moreover, if the kinds of aspirations that were articulated in the Millennium Development Goals are to be achieved.

CONCLUDING REMARKS

Intellectual property is important, but is only one part of a country's innovation system. This paper has discussed several critical features relevant to the creation of an innovation system—including intellectual property rights—designed to enable China to continue its remarkable success, including its ability to achieve its ambition to become an innovation economy and its broader social goals of harmonious growth, including the reduction of inequality and protection of the environment.

The IPR regime that has come to dominate in much of the world is not even well designed for the broader interests of the advanced industrial countries from which it emanates; rather, it is largely designed to maximize the profits of a few sectors that derive their returns largely from intellectual property rights. Not surprisingly, such an intellectual property regime is not in the interests of China. Different countries, facing different circumstances, need to design intellectual property regimes that are appropriate to their circumstances. China's circumstances are distinctive, and so it will have to look for an innovation system and an IPR regime that is correspondingly distinctive—an intellectual property regime "with Chinese characteristics." For instance, given the importance that should be placed on innovation to protect the environment, an arena in which market prices do not reflect social values, there needs to be even less reliance on market-induced innovation (supported by the IPR regime) and greater reliance on public funding.

China is still at a stage in its transition to a market economy where those with vested interests in a flawed IPR system do not play the role that they do in the US. Nor are the flawed ideological presumptions that have played such a central role in shaping America's IPR system as influential. China, at this stage in its transition, has the opportunity to learn from the mistakes of the advanced industrial countries. It should, for instance, take the portfolio approach stressed in this paper, with greater emphasis on a prize system and less on the patent system.

Designing an intellectual property regime (and more broadly, an innovation system) appropriate for China is not an easy task, especially since so much depends on details. We have seen how a poorly designed intellectual property regime may (i) impair static efficiency, both through the creation of impediments to the usage of knowledge and enhancing monopoly power; (ii) lower the pace of innovation and growth; (iii) distort the allocation of resources to research; (iv) lead to inefficiently high expenditures on litigation; (v) lead to a less healthy population; (vi) while simultaneously increasing public expenditures on health.

In the aftermath of the Great Recession, there has been a change in the global economic balance of power. China will play an increasing role in shaping the global economic regime. As part of that role, it needs to help create a global intellectual property regime that is more development-oriented, more flexible, more sensitive to the differing circumstances confronting different countries.

China is an emerging market economy, better off than the least-developed countries, not as well off as the advanced industrial countries. In other arenas, it has become an effective advocate for the interests of the less developed countries. It should do so in this area as well, arguing for an intellectual property regime that is globally fair and efficient. It can do so more effectively if it adopts an intellectual property regime consistent with these principles.

Doing so will be important for the world, and especially for other developing countries. But doing so is also important for China itself.

NOTES

1. This chapter is a revised and adapted version of a keynote address presented at the Ministerial Conference on Intellectual Property for Least Developed Countries, World Intellectual Property Organization (WIPO), Seoul, October 25, 2004, and of a talk titled "Institutional Design For China's Innovation System: Implications For Intellectual Property Rights," Beijing University, March, 2007. This chapter also draws heavily upon chapter 4 of Stiglitz (2006, 2008) and Henry and Stigliz (2010). Many of the ideas discussed here are developed further in Cimoli et al. (forthcoming). I am indebted to Jamie Love for discussions and comments, to Francesco Brindisi for research assistantship, and to the Ford, MacArthur, and Mott Foundations for financial support.
2. In 2010, per capita GDP in China was US$4,382 (PPP $7,519), compared to $47,284 per capita in the US.
3. This was one of the central messages of Stiglitz (2002a).
4. Statement by Brazil on September 30, 2004 before WIPO General Assembly at the introduction of the proposal for a development agenda.
5. The patents on basmati rice and the medicinal uses of turmeric were eventually overthrown, but the costs of litigation were significant (see Stiglitz 2006 and Brand 2005). Indeed, even the US courts have recognized these costs. In *United States v. General Electric Co.*, 115 F. Supp. 835, 844 (1953) the court, in arguing for compulsory licensing with zero royalties, noted that "small firms desiring to stay in or gain a foothold in the industry... may well be unequipped to engage in litigation on the validity of one patent after another at what could be incalculable expense. In order to avoid it they could be required to shoulder royalties which could prove to be the very factor that would push them out of the competitive circle of the market" (cited in Love 2004). See Stiglitz (2006) and Perleman (2002).
6. See, e.g., Coase (1960).
7. Though the concept of a public good is intuitive, it was first formalized by Samuelson (1954) as a good for which the marginal cost of an additional individual using the good is zero (referred to as nonrivalrous consumption) and for which the cost of excluding someone from usage was high (nonexclusivity). The view of knowledge as a public good is discussed in Stiglitz (1987).
8. Jefferson described the public good characteristics of knowledge in the following way: "...no one possesses the less because everyone possesses the whole of it. He who receives an idea from me receives [it] without lessening [me], as he who lights his [candle] at mine receives light without darkening me" (quoted in Meier 1981).
9. A global public good is one whose benefits can extend to everyone in the world (as opposed to a local public good, the benefits of which accrue only to those in a particular locality, or a natonal public good, the benefits of which occur only to those within a country) (see Stiglitz 1995). The idea that knowledge is a global public good is developed in Stiglitz (1999).
10. See Dasgupta and Stiglitz (1980) and Gilbert and Newbery (1982).
11. See e.g., Dasgupta and Stiglitz (1988); Fudenberg et al. (1983); and Farrell, Gilbert, and Katz (2003).

12. In practice, there is usually some value to a me-too innovation—for instance, there may be some patients for whom the side effects are less—but still, the social return to such innovations is very limited and less than the private returns.
13. See Arrow (1962). One of the reasons is that monopoly reduces the scale of production, and at a reduced scale of production, the benefits of, say, cost reductions are smaller.
14. Microsoft was able to leverage its monopoly power in operating systems (protected by intellectual property rights) to squelch innovators in browsers and media players. Potential innovators, knowing this, have less incentive to innovate. See Stiglitz (2006).
15. If the owner of IPR could engage in perfect price discrimination, he would always charge the highest royalty that would still induce innovation. Such perfect price discrimination is not feasible, and with imperfect price discrimination, the licensing fees that would be optimal will be so high as to discourage some of those in developing countries from adapting the technology to their economy or some of those who might otherwise undertake follow-on research from doing so. Moreover, even with perfect discrimination, the high royalties will have an adverse effect on development, simply because of the large transfers.
16. See for instance "Public Comment on the Unites States Patent and Trademark Office N.41," 03/22/2000 by Bruce Alberts, president of the National Academy of Science, available at <http://www.uspto.gov/web/offices/com/sol/comments/utilguide/nas.pdf> (accessed on October 12, 2011).
17. See Boyle (2003).
18. He in fact used his patent to try to organize an automobile cartel. Had the patent not been challenged by Henry Ford, who wanted to create a low-priced car, the development of the automobile would have been greatly impeded. For a discussion of this and other problems with the patent system, see Stiglitz (2006).
19. There is even a reluctance to share data.
20. For example, a very broad automobile patent would extend to any self-propelled vehicle, a narrow patent to the specific kind of car that was constructed.
21. The discussion of this section is adapted from Stiglitz (2008).
22. See Henry and Stiglitz (2010).
23. In 2009, Medicare and Medicaid spending were \$502.3 billion and \$373.9 billion respectively, which consists of 20 percent and 15 percent respectively of the total national health care spending.
24. I say "excessive" because it may in fact be optimal to have several independent, parallel research efforts.
25. The evidence is that capital markets do not fully spread risks faced by firms, because of imperfections of information. See for example Greenwald and Stiglitz (1990), who discuss the effect of information imperfections on firm behavior and argue that informational problems in the capital market cause firms to act in a risk-averse manner. There is also considerable empirical evidence that markets do not efficiently distribute risk, i.e., firms act in a risk-averse manner, even when risks are uncorrelated with the market. See, e.g., Stiglitz (1982).
26. For instance, in the case of "orphan drugs," the life of the patent was extended, because it was thought that the benefits from greater incentives to innovate exceeded the costs. A still better way of creating incentives for such innovation, however, could have been provided through the prize system.
27. India was right, I think, in its recent decision concerning Novartis's attempt to evergreen its patent. In June 2009, India's Intellectual Property Appellate Board ruled

that Novartis's patent on the cancer drug Glivec is not valid in that country; it marks the third time in four years that Novartis has failed in attempts to claim patent on its best-selling cancer drug. Concurring with earlier decisions, the board ruled that Glivec is nothing but a crystal modification of an older drug that was initially patented in 1993 and therefore does not qualify as a new invention. Under patenting rules that India began implementing in 2005, only drugs invented after 1995 are eligible for patent protection.

28. The suit, The Association for Molecular Pathology et al., v. United States Patent and Trademark Office, et al., had at the time of writing been decided favorably for the defendants—of which Myriad is one—holding that companies can obtain patents for genes. In April 2010, the US District Court for the Southern District of New York invalidated patents on a pair of genes linked to breast and ovarian cancer held by Myriad. See Stiglitz (2010). But in July 2011, the Court of Appeals for the Federal Circuit overturned this decision (Pollack 2011). The decision has been challenged twice, and at the time of writing the appeal was to be heard by the US Supreme Court.
29. See Brunswick, 36 Fed. Cl. at 207; cited in Love (2004: 13). Since the government already possesses the right, exercising the right is not a "taking" requiring compensation.
30. *United States v. W. Elec. Co.*, 1956 Trade Cas. (CCH) 68,246, at 71,139 (D.N.J. 1956).
31. Under a US law called the Tunney Act (Antitrust Procedures and Penalties Act, 15 U.S.C. §16), members of the public have an opportunity to comment on a proposed settlement of a civil antitrust suit before it is accepted by a court. At the time of the proposed Microsoft settlement, I filed an affidavit together with Jason Furman (later the Deputy Head of the US National Economic Council) explaining why limiting the length of the patent would be a preferable way for addressing the anticompetitive abuses. See Stiglitz (2002b).
32. See, e.g., Reichman and Lewis (2005) and Shapiro (2007).
33. See Charlton and Stiglitz (2004, 2005).
34. See Bhagwati (2002, 2004).
35. See World Commission on the Social Dimensions of Globalization (2004).
36. They can, for instance, withdraw preferential trade provisions or not support bilateral or multilateral assistance packages.
37. Critics of India's new intellectual property law argue that it went beyond what was required by the TRIPS agreement. Court decisions, e.g., against Novartis's attempt to "evergreen" its patents have maintained some balance.
38. The provisions on data exclusivity that have been included in many of the bilateral trade agreements that the United States has signed have also exacerbated the problem of access to generic medicines. Even if a compulsory license is issued, there is an attempt to restrict the use of data that might be required to establish the safety and efficacy of the generic drug. Although there are changes to the regulatory structures that might allow developing countries to circumvent the restrictive impact, e.g., simply by requiring generic producers to show the bio-equivalence of their product to products that have been shown to be safe and efficacious in the US or Europe, developing countries appear to be under pressure not to make the necessary regulatory changes.
39. See World Bank (2001).

REFERENCES

Alberts, B. (2000), "Public Comment on the United States Patent and Trademark Office N.41," March 22 (Washington, DC: National Academy of Sciences).

Arjun, J. and Stiglitz, J. E. (2009), "Two Ideas to Increase Innovation and Reduce Pharmaceutical Costs and Prices," *Health Affairs*, 28/1: 165–8.

——— (2010), "Medicine for Tomorrow: Some Alternative Proposals to Promote Socially Beneficial Research and Development in Pharmaceuticals," *Journal of Generic Medicine*, 7/3: 217–26.

Arrow, K. J. (1962), "Economic Welfare and the Allocation of Resource for Invention," in R. Nelson (ed.), *The Rate and Direction of Inventive Activity: Economic and Social Factors* (Princeton: Princeton University Press for the NBER), 609–25.

Bhagwati, J. (2002), "Afterword: The Question of Linkage," *The American Journal of International Law*, 96/1: 126–34.

—— (2004), *In Defense of Globalization* (New York: Oxford University Press).

Boyle, J. (2003), "The Second Enclosure Movement and the Construction of the Public Domain," *Law and Contemporary Problems*, 66/33: 33–74.

Brand, R. (2005), "The Basmati Patent," in E. U. von Weizäcker, O. R. Young, and M. Finger (eds), *Limits to Privatization: How to Avoid Too Much of a Good Thing* (London: Earthscan Publications).

Charlton, A. and Stiglitz, J. E. (2004), *The Development Round of Trade Negotiations in the Aftermath of Cancun*, prepared for the Commonwealth Secretariat, the Initiative for Policy Dialogue (New York: Columbia University).

——— (2005), *Fair Trade for All* (New York: Oxford University Press). Published in Simplified Chinese by China Renmin University Press.

Cimoli, M., Dolsi, G., Maskus, K., Okediji, R., and Reichman, J. (forthcoming), *Intellectual Property Rights: Legal and Economic Challenges for Development*, IPD Book Series (New York: Oxford University Press).

Coase, R. H. (1960), "The Problem of Social Cost," *Journal of Law and Economics*, 3 (October): 1–44.

Dasgupta, P. and Stiglitz, J. E. (1980), "Uncertainty, Market Structure and the Speed of R & D," *Bell Journal of Economics*, 11/1: 1–28.

——— (1988), "Potential Competition, Actual Competition and Economic Welfare," *European Economic Review*, 32 (May): 569–77.

Farrell, J., Gilbert, R. J., and Katz, M. L. (2003), "Market Structure, Organizational Structure, and R & D Diversity," in R. Arnott, B. Greenwald, R. Kanbur, and B. Nalebuff (eds), *Economics for an Imperfect World*—Essays in Honor of Joseph E. Stiglitz (Cambridge, MA: MIT Press).

Fudenberg, D., Gilbert, R., Stiglitz, J. E., and Tirole, J. (1983), "Preemption, Leapfrogging and Competition in Patent Races," *European Economic Review*, 22: 3–32.

Gilbert, R. J. and Newbery, D. M. G. (1982), "Preemptive Patenting and the Persistence of Monopoly," *American Economic Review*, 72/3: 514–26.

Greenwald, B. and Stiglitz, J. E. (1990), "Asymmetric Information and the New Theory of the Firm: Financial Constraints and Risk Behavior," *American Economic Review*, 80/2: 160–5. Also NBER Working Paper No. 3359.

Henry, C. and Stiglitz, J. E. (2010), "Intellectual Property, Dissemination of Innovation and Sustainable Development," *Global Policy*, 1: 237–51.

Jayadev, A. and Stiglitz, J. E. (2009), "Two Ideas to Increase Innovation and Reduce Pharmaceutical Costs and Prices," *Health Affairs*, 28/1: 165–168.

——— (2010), "Medicine for Tomorrow: Some Alternative Proposals to Promote Socially Beneficial Research and Development in Pharmaceuticals," *Journal of Generic Medicines*, 7/3: 217–26.

Love, J. (2004), "Compensation Guidelines for Non-Voluntary use of a Patent on Medical Technologies." Mimeo, September 7.

Meier, H. A. (1981), "Thomas Jefferson and a Democratic Technology," in C. W. Pursell (ed.), *Technology in America: A History of Individuals and Ideas*, 2nd edition (Cambridge, MA: MIT Press).

Perleman, M. (2002), *Steal this Idea: Intellectual Property and the Corporate Confiscation of Creativity* (New York: Palgrave).

Pollack, A. (2011), "Ruling Upholds Gene Patent in Cancer Test," *The New York Times*, July 29, available at <http://www.nytimes.com/2011/07/30/business/gene-patent-in-cancer-test-upheld-by-appeals-panel.html?_r = 1&scp = 1&sq = ruling%20upholds%20gene%20patent%20in%20cancer%20test&st = cse> (accessed October 12, 2011).

Reichman, J. H. and Lewis, T. (2005), "Using Liability Rules to Stimulate Local Innovation in Developing Countries: Application to Traditional Knowledge," in Keith E. Maskus and J. H. Reichman (eds), *International Public Goods and Transfer of Technology under a Globalized Intellectual Property Regime* (Cambridge: Cambridge University Press).

Samuelson, P. A. (1954), "The Pure Theory of Public Expenditure," *Review of Economics and Statistics*, 36/4: 387–89.

Shapiro, C. (2007), "Patent Reform: Aligning Reward and Contribution 33–35," Working Paper No. 13141 (Cambridge, MA: National Bureau of Economic Research), available at <http://papers.nber.org/papers/w13141> (accessed October 12, 2011).

Stiglitz, J. E. (1982), "Ownership, Control and Efficient Markets: Some Paradoxes in the Theory of Capital Markets," in K. D. Boyer and W. G. Shepherd (eds), *Economic Regulation: Essays in Honor of James R. Nelson* (East Lansing: Michigan State University Press).

——(1987), "On the Microeconomics of Technical Progress," in J. M. Katz (ed.), *Technology Generation in Latin American Manufacturing Industries* (New York: Macmillan Press). (Presented to IDB-Cepal Meetings, Buenos Aires, November 1978.)

——(1988), "Technological Change, Sunk Costs and Competition," *Brookings Papers on Economic Activity*, 18/3: 883–947.

——(1995), "The Theory of International Public Goods and the Architecture of International Organizations," Background Paper No. 7, Third Meeting, High-Level Group on Development Strategy and Management of the Market Economy, UNU/WIDER, Helsinki, Finland, July 8–10.

——(1999), "Knowledge as a Global Public Good," in I. Kaul, I. Grunberg, and M. A. Stern (eds), *Global Public Goods: International Cooperation in the 21st Century*, United Nations Development Programme (New York: Oxford University Press).

——(2002a), *Globalization and its Discontents* (New York: W. W. Norton).

——(2002b), Declaration of Joseph E. Stiglitz and Jason Furman, *United States v. Microsoft Corp.*, 97 F. Supp. 2d 59 (D.D.C. 2000) (Nos. 98–1232, 98–1233), available at <http://usdoj.gov/atr/cases/ms_tuncom/major/mtc-00030610c.pdf>.

——(2006), *Making Globalization Work* (New York: W. W. Norton).

——(2008), "The Economic Foundations of Intellectual Property," Sixth Annual Frey Lecture in Intellectual Property, Duke University, Durham, NC; *Duke Law Journal*, 57/6 (February 16): 1693–724.

——(2010), "Declaration of Joseph Stiglitz," Amicus filing, Case 1:09-cv-04515-RWS Document 224 Filed 01/20/2010.

World Bank (2001), *Global Economic Prospects and the Developing Countries: Making Trade Work for the World's Poor* (Washington, DC: World Bank).

World Commission on the Social Dimensions of Globalization (2004), *A Fair Globalization: Creating Opportunities for All* (Geneva: World Commission on the Social Dimension of Globalization), available at <http://www.ilo.org/public/english/wcsdg/docs/report.pdf>.

9

The Evolution of China's IPR System and its Impact on the Innovative Performance of MNCs and Local Firms in China

Zheng Liang and Lan Xue

INTRODUCTION

The year 2008 marked the thirtieth anniversary of China's openness and economic reform, which has generated astonishingly high economic growth in China for the past three decades. According to World Bank statistics (2003), the average growth rates of China's Gross Domestic Product (GDP) during the 1980s and the 1990s were 10.1 percent and 11.2 percent, respectively, making China one of the fastest-growing economies in the world. The abandonment of centralized planning and the establishment of market institutions were credited as key reasons for this growth. However, as a key institution for stimulating innovation in a market economy, the intellectual property rights (IPR) system has been the subject of frequent controversies in discussion about China's transition to a market economy (Maskus and Dougherty 1998). While complaints about China's IPR system have been abundant, systematic studies and analysis have been relatively rare. In this paper, based on some unique data, we intend to analyze the evolution of China's patent system, the bedrock of China's IPR system, and its impact on the innovative behavior of multinational companies and domestic companies.

The conventional wisdom about IPR is that strong IPR protection generates incentives for investment in Research and Development (R & D) and hence for technological progress in a society (Arrow 1962; Nordhaus 1962; Scherer 1972). In addition, IPR protection also helps to disseminate technical information and reduce social cost (Machlup 1958), which is always referred to as the "information disclosure effect." At the same time, protecting IPR through assigning monopolistic rights to knowledge also entails economic costs. The monopoly position on a technology deters other firms from trying themselves to invent "in the neighborhood" (Scotchmer and Green 1990; Green and Scotchmer 1995). The fact that granting IPRs is not costless to society implies that one should not grant IPRs where benefits do not exceed the costs (Mazzoleni and Nelson 1998), which maybe particularly true for developing countries (Commission on Intellectual Property Rights 2002).

During recent years, the process of economic globalization has enabled intellectual property to cross international boundaries more easily. For many developed countries, IPR-intensive goods and services constitute a rising share of the income they derive from their presence in foreign markets. It is therefore not surprising to see forces of political economy at work in these countries, leading governments to raise IPR protection as a key negotiating issue in international trade agreements. Rules on how to protect patents, copyrights, trademarks, and other forms of IPRs have become a standard component of international trade agreements. Most significantly, during the Uruguay Round of multilateral trade negotiations (1986–94), members of what is today the World Trade Organization (WTO) concluded the Agreement on Trade-Related Aspects of Intellectual Property Rights (TRIPs), which sets out minimum standards of protection that most of the world's economies must respect. IPR is also a key issue between China and other foreign countries during bilateral talks, such as the second Sino–US Strategic Economic Dialogue (SED) held in May 2008.

Understanding the role of IPR in China is further complicated by the fact that the Chinese economy in the reform era has been far more open than those of many other countries at a comparable stage. From the very start, the IPR system in China has faced the double challenge of meeting the demand of multinational companies, which required strong protection of IPRs, while at the same time satisfying the appeals of domestic companies which favored an IPR regime conducive to technology transfer and diffusion. In the reminder of this paper, using some empirical evidence from China, we will try to describe how China's IPR system has evolved since the economic reform and analyze how domestic and multinational firms have responded to the changing IPR system in China. The remainder of the paper is organized as follows: the following section describes the evolution of China's IPR system with a special focus on China's patent system; the next section analyzes the patenting behavior of China's domestic firms; and subsequently we analyze the patenting behavior of multinational firms. The final section concludes.

THE EVOLUTION OF CHINA'S IPR SYSTEM WITH A SPECIAL FOCUS ON THE PATENT SYSTEM

While China began to adopt legal protection of intellectual property as early as the 1960s, it was not until China embraced openness and reform in the 1980s that it realized the importance of the need to protect intellectual property in a market-based economy. Three major forces have shaped the evolution of China's IPR system over the last two decades. First of all, the transition from a centrally planned economy to a market economy provided strong impetus for the development and improvement of China's IPR system. Second, the openness of China's market for FDI and the increased success of Chinese products in the overseas market generated pressure for China's IPR system to accelerate its development to be in line with international standards. If the first two major forces have been pushing China's IPR system in the same direction, the third force, the slow warm-up on IPR protection on the part of Chinese firms and the passive attitude toward enforcement of IPR regulations at the local level, has played the counterbalancing role.

The development of China's IPR protection system since economic reform

The IPR regime in China was developed in the general context of opening up and economic reform. It was considered part of the institutions that a market economy needs to promote innovation and integration with the global market. Chronologically (see Figure 9.1), China's IPR system began in April 1963 when the Trademark Control Act was promulgated. However, it was not until 1980 when China became a member of the World Intellectual Property Organization that China's IPR system began to develop full-speed. The Trademark Law was published in August 1982 and the Patent Law was publicized in March 1984. China entered the Paris Convention for the Protection of Industrial Property in 1985 and the Madrid Agreement Concerning the International Registration of Marks in 1989. China promulgated its Copyright Law in June 1991 and entered the Universal Copyright Convention in 1992. China became a member of the Berne Convention for the Protection of Literary and Artistic Works in 1992 and entered the Patent Cooperation Treaty in 1994.

Apart from building up the legal system protecting IPR, China has also entered into agreements and memoranda with other countries regarding the implementation of these laws, notably the United States, including the Agreement on Trade Relations in 1979, the Memorandum of Understanding on Enactment and Scope of Chinese Copyright Law in 1989, and the Memorandum of Understanding on the Protection of Intellectual Property Rights in 1992, under which China agreed to update intellectual property protection and join major international conventions (La Croix and Konan 2002). In March 1995, after some serious disputes, China entered into an agreement with the United States regarding protection of intellectual property rights, in which China made commitments to publish all laws, rules, regulations, administrative guidelines, or other official documents concerning any limitation on, regulation of, or permission for engaging in the above-referenced types of activities. Finally in 1999, China and the United States reached an agreement on China's accession to the WTO. China also subscribed to fully implement the TIRPs (Trade-Related Aspects of Intellectual Property Rights) Agreement after its accession to the WTO in 2002. Today, the scope and level of IPR protection in China is substantially in line with international standards and practices (OECD 2005).

The evolution of China's patent system: retrospect and prospect

As mentioned previously, China enacted its first patent law in 1984 which came into force in April 1985. There were hot debates on whether China really needed a patent law at that time. The opponents argued that the time for introducing the patent law in China had not arrived yet, because the technology gap between

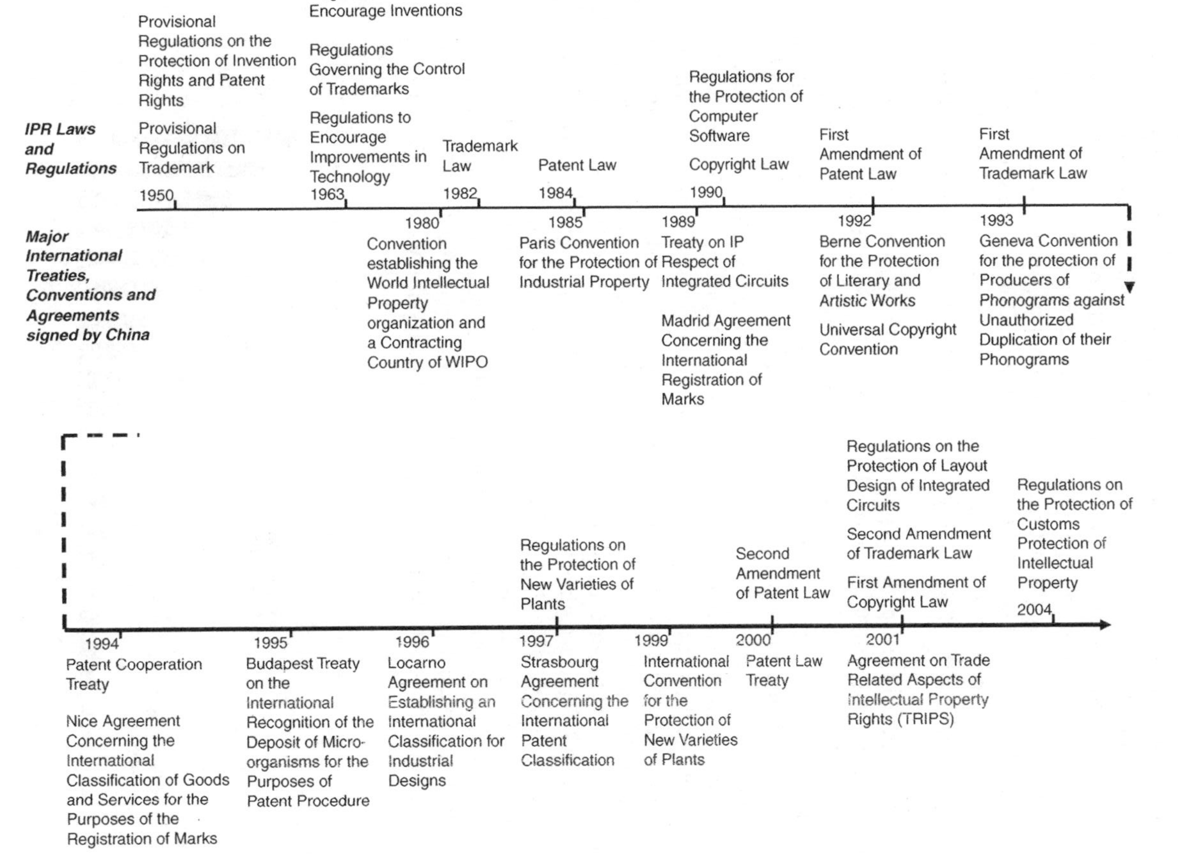

Figure 9.1. Timeline of major national and international IPR laws and regulations

Source: OECD (2008: 410, figure 9.2)

China and western countries was still very large: the protection of IPR would create hurdles for technology borrowing and knowledge diffusion. Others clung to the idea that knowledge is public wealth and should be free. However, the proponents of the Patent Law argued that without better protection of IPR through the Patent Law, it would be very difficult for technology transfer and knowledge dissemination in a market environment. In addition, protection of IPR was seen as very important to attract FDI to China, which was a key strategy for China's economic reform and openness. The debate continued until Deng Xiaoping intervened and decided that China should adopt a patent law. After several years of analysis of patent laws of other countries and China's own situation at the time, the drafting committee presented the draft of the first Patent Law in China, which was revised and approved at the National People's Congress on March 12, 1984.

In general, the Chinese patent system shares more similarities with the Japanese patent system than with that of the United States. For example, the primary purpose for China's patent law is to facilitate diffusion of new technologies, which is demonstrated by the kinds of patents allowed (invention, design, and utility model), their shorter grace period, the adoption of the principle of "first-to-file" instead of "first-to-invent," public disclosure of the invention after eighteen months, and mixed requirement of single and multiple claims. Typically, the adoption of "petit patents" such as utility models and designs is mainly intended to encourage inventing-around behavior and to lower the barriers to utilizing this system, especially for the native applicants. This ambition had been achieved partially according to some empirical studies (Liu et al. 2003; Hu 2006).

As Figure 9.2 depicts, China's patent system evolved through three stages. The first, which is the founding stage of China's IPR system, spanned the years 1985 to 1992. Before 1985, China only had a management system for the fruits of science and technology, which presumably belonged to the entire country. While China's first patent law made it possible for individuals to file patents, it was difficult for them to extract monopoly rents, but it promised material rewards (Alford 1995).

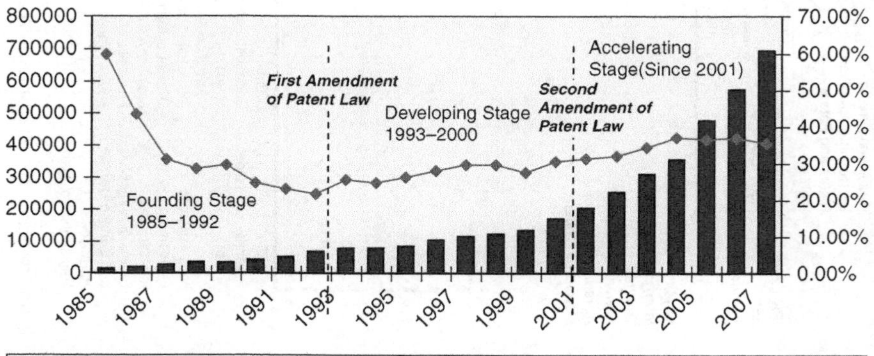

Figure 9.2. The three stages of China's patent system development

Data Source: SIPO Patent Statistical Yearbook, 1986–2007

At the same time, without the permission of administrative department, state-owned enterprises (SOEs) couldn't deal with their patents autonomously, for example, licensing out. These limitations dampened the enthusiasm of SOEs as well as their technical staffs who were key players in industrial R & D. The first Patent Law also excluded chemical, pharmaceutical, and alimentary or process inventions from patent coverage, which were regarded as showing a partiality towards domestic industries and giving additional disadvantages to foreign applicants. These issues reflected the dynamic balances between stimulating indigenous innovations and sharing worldwide knowledge pools by the enforcement of patent protection. They were considered as deficiencies that needed to be corrected in the future revision of the Patent Law.

The second stage lasted from 1992 to 2000, during which time China's patent system made substantial progress. In the first revision of Patent Law in 1992, the duration of patent protection of inventions was extended from fifteen to twenty years and the duration of utility model and design patents was extended from five to ten years; food, beverages, flavoring, pharmaceutical products, and substances obtained by means of chemical processes were also covered by patent protection. Domestic priority for filing applications was also added. As Figure 9.3 shows, all these amendments inspired a rapid rise in applications.

The third stage, from 2001 to 2007, issued in another major revision in China's Patent Law in 2001. In this revision, state-owned and privately owned enterprises were given equal treatment when applying to obtain patent rights and individuals were allowed to own patents for inventions during work time if an agreement was made between individuals and employers. And other amendments were mainly made to fit the requests of the WTO, especially TRIPs. Based on these factors, patent applications surged after 2001 and patent development accelerated.

In 2005, the State Intellectual Property Office (SIPO) began to revise the Patent Law for the third time. The draft of the new version was sent to the National People's Congress for approval in August 2008. The new revision of Patent Law and other legislation is an important step for implementing National IPR Strategy, which has been drafted since 2004 and was formally issued by the State Council in June 2008. In this initiative, the fertilization of capabilities on IPR creation, utilization, protection, and management was given first priority. The core ambition is to induce domestic enterprises to create and grasp the intellectual property rights of key technologies. Thus, although the draft is still in discussion, this revision of Patent Law presents three major changes. First, the precondition for patent granting has been changed from "Relative Novelty" to "Absolute Novelty," which means that the granted patents should not only be novel in China, but also novel in the world. Second, it strengthens the protection of hereditary resources and traditional knowledge. The invention or creation based on illegal acquisition of hereditary resources and traditional knowledge would not be granted patent. Third, articles have been added on the prohibition of misuse of patent rights. All these revisions could be regarded as responses to the changes in internal and external environments which China has faced. In early 2006, China issued a National Medium and Long-Range Science and Technology Development Program and initiated a national strategy for building an innovation-oriented country through cultivating indigenous innovation capabilities. As enterprises have contributed more than half of total R & D expenditure in China, the stricter patent-granting standard will undoubtedly improve the quality of patent applications in China. Furthermore, as we will discuss later, the way patents have been deployed by multinationals in China, including the "Patent Thicket" strategy and the misuse of patent rights, has been a serious problem which may distort normal competition and harm the cultivation of indigenous innovation capabilities. This could be partially the reason for the latter two revisions. As a result, it is possible to imagine a relatively low increase in patent application numbers if these amendments are approved compared with the surges in previous stages. Then China's IPR system might enter a new developing stage, characterized by a change from increased quantity to improvement in quality.

The patenting behaviors of different players under China's patent system: an investigation based on SIPO data

As discussed above, the evolution of the patent system in China has reflected the needs of different entities. Once founded, it has been inevitably molded and affected by the behavior of these entities, even though they may have totally contrary motivations. The different reactions by multinationals and domestic firms under the same patent system are among the main concerns of this paper. Here, we have used the annual data issued by SIPO to reveal the general state of China's patent application and granting processes, especially the different behaviors of domestic and foreign applicants.

Figure 9.2 depicts the general trends of patent applications in China. We can observe that patent applications have grown very fast in China, especially after the second revision of Patent Law in 2000. But if we transfer our attention from the total amount to the structure, from Figure 9.3 we discover that, although the share of inventions in total patent applications has risen gradually since the establishment of the patent system, even today invention application ratios are still under 40 percent although they have risen from the low in 1992 and increased about 14 percent. This is quite different from the experience of developed countries; there, most patent applications, at least 70 percent to 80 percent, are inventions. As we explained above, this is mainly due to the character of China's patent system, especially the adoption of "petit patents," which provide more incentive for incremental innovations and knowledge dissemination.

From Figure 9.3 we can also observe another unique phenomenon. Although the ratio of utility model applications in China decreased linearly after it reached a peak at the beginning of 1990s, the ratio of the other kind of "petit patents," design applications, has increased consistently since 1985 and reached its peak in 2007 (38.54 percent). This is contrary to what was predicted to happen. As estimated, the ratio of invention patents should have increased in line with the improvement of China's native applicants' innovative capabilities, and the ratios of utility models and designs were expected to decline (SIPO). What is the reason for this abnormal result? More detailed analysis in following sections may answer this question partially.

If we compare Figure 9.3 with Figure 9.4, we find that, although the share of invention patents among all patent grants in China has risen since 2000 with the

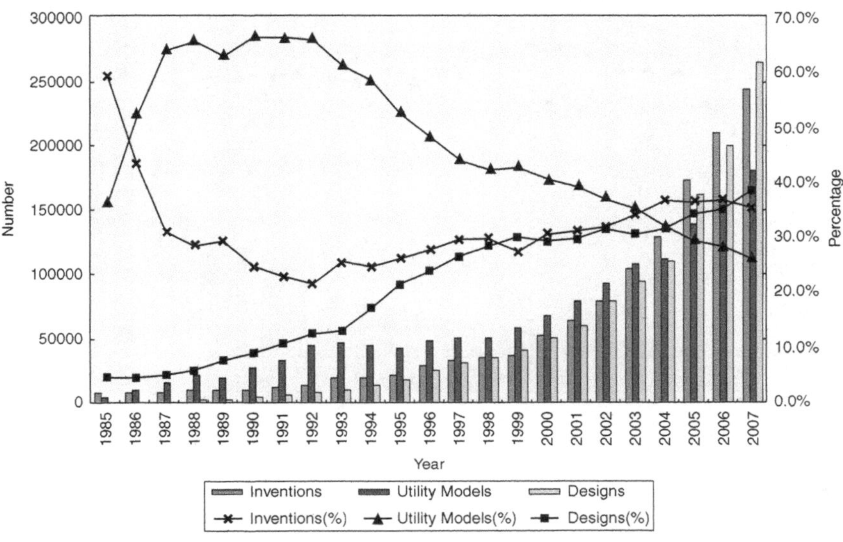

Figure 9.3. Distributions of annual applications for three kinds of patents received by SIPO

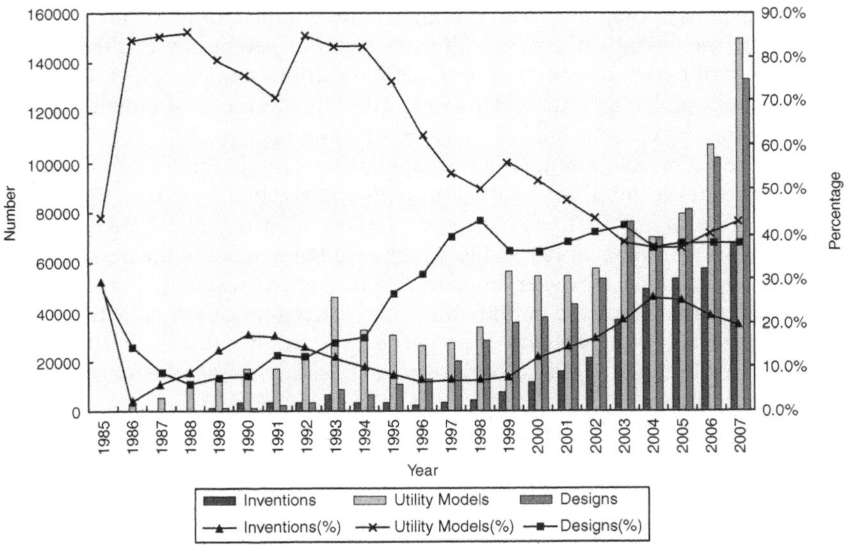

Figure 9.4. Distributions of annual grants for three kinds of patents received by SIPO

second revision of patent law, reaching its peak in 2004 (25.95 percent), the ratio of invention patents in total grants is still much lower than its ratio in total applications. As Figures 9.3 and 9.4 show, this may be partially attributable to the increasing number of invention patents granted not having kept pace with an even faster increase in the number of applications, which reflects the relatively poor quality of applications for invention patents in China. On the other hand, it

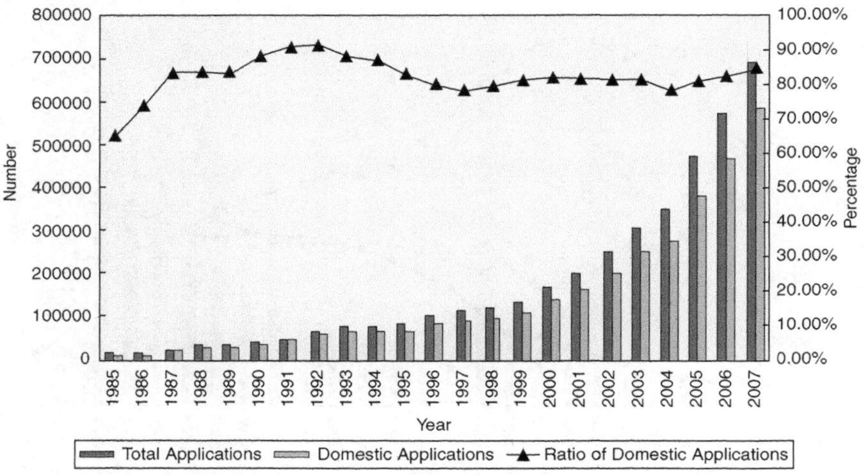

Figure 9.5. Total applications for three kinds of patents received from home and abroad

may also be due to the easier approval of patents in the areas of utility model and design, which have caught up with the surge in their applications. From Figure 9.4 we can also see obvious declines in all three kinds of patent grants after the first amendment of patent law in 1992, especially for utility models, which decreased for four years and rose again after 1997. The improvement of patent-granting standards may be one reason, but more proof should be sought.

As Figure 9.5 reveals, among the total applications for all three kinds of patents in China, domestic applications are dominant and reached a peak in 1992 (92.04 percent). We also find that, after the first revision of patent law, there emerged a faster increase in foreign applications, which resulted in a fall in the percentage of domestic applications. However, it seems that the second revision of patent law in 2000 induced a fast increase in domestic and foreign applications synchronously, which is reflected in the stability of domestic application ratios from 2000 to the present. The different emphases of these two revisions may be the main cause of these developments.

More interesting findings become apparent when we pay attention to different kinds of patents. From Figure 9.6, we can see that domestic applications for inventions were higher than foreign applications until 1994 although the ratio of domestic applications reached its peak in 1992 (69.55 percent) and then began to fall rapidly. As mentioned previously, the main changes in 1992 Patent Law were an extension of the patent protection duration and expansion of the patent protection scope, so as to coincide with standards in most other countries. It seems that this revision roused the enthusiasm of foreign applicants, especially for invention applications. So the fall in the percentage of total applications which related to domestic invention applications was the result of a more rapid rise in applications from abroad. As Figure 9.6 reveals, after bottoming out in 1997 (37.76 percent), the ratio of domestic applications in total invention applications rose and reached a new high in 2007 (62.43 percent). Domestic applications also

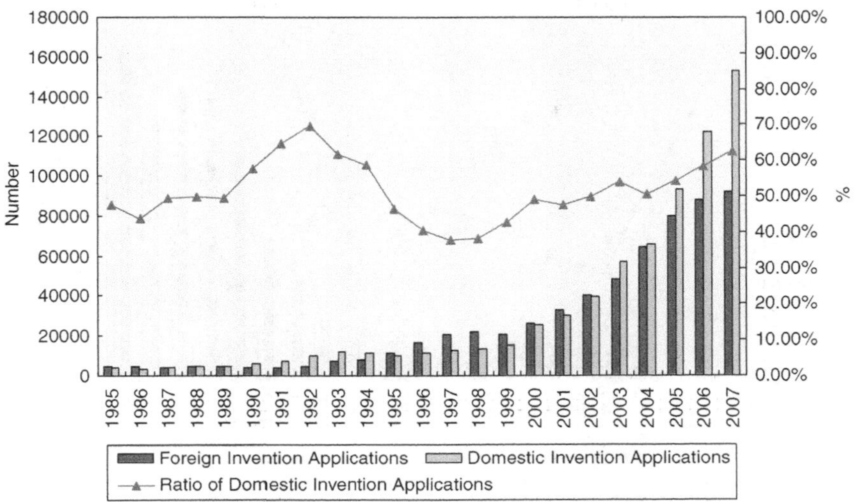

Figure 9.6. Distribution of annual applications for inventions received from home and abroad, 1985–2007

outpaced foreign applications in 2003. As we will also discuss in the following sections, this mainly due to the maturation of domestic firms and a greater social awareness of the importance of IPRs.

As Figure 9.7 depicts, invention patents granted to foreigners are still higher than those granted to native applicants, although the gap has narrowed quickly in the past five years. As suggested above, this may be mainly due to the rapid increase in domestic applications in recent years. Figure 9.7 also reveals distinct fluctuations in invention grants during the past twenty years. In particular, decreases in the number of invention patent grants are apparent for several years immediately after the first revision of Patent Law. Furthermore, compared to the drop in domestic grants, the decrease in foreign grants is faster and resulted in the first rise of domestic ratios in total invention grants during the period 1990 to 1996. Because there is a time lag between patent applications and grants, we conclude that the amendment of Patent Law has had an effect on foreign patent grants in China.

But if we look at the behavior of foreign and domestic applications for utility model and design patents, we find very big differences. As Table 9.1 depicts, since the founding of the patent system in China, more than 99 percent of applications for utility models, and more than 94 percent of applications for designs, have been issued to domestic applicants. The same results can be found on the granting side. It seems that the original design of the three-tier patent system worked: the "petit patents" were utilized mainly by domestic players, which gave them incentives to facilitate incremental innovation and the diffusion of knowledge, just as Figures 9.3 and 9.4 depict.

Figures 9.8 and 9.9 give us a clearer picture of the different behaviors of foreign and domestic patent applicants. As Figure 9.8 depicts, the distribution of three

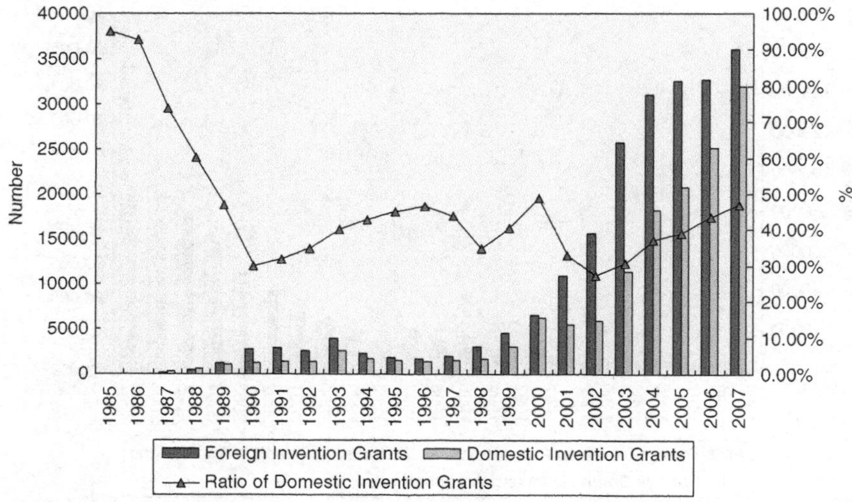

Figure 9.7. Distribution of annual grants for inventions received from home and abroad, 1985–2007

kinds of patent applications issued by foreigners have been very stable during the past twenty-three years, with invention applications dominant. In most years, invention applications accounted for more than 85 percent of the total applications. We can also find another interesting phenomenon; foreign applicants have seldom applied for utility model patents, although they were regarded as part of inventions under China's Patent Law. But foreign firms have applied for quite a few design patents, although their ratio in total applications never exceeded 18 percent after reaching their peak in 1994 (17.42 percent). Even in 2007, foreigners submitted just 1,325 utility applications, no more than fourteen times the number issued in 1985 (97). But during the same period, their invention applications in China expanded twenty times (4,493 to 92,101), and design applications expanded nearly thirty-eight times (371 to 13,993).

As Figure 9.9 shows, the distributions of domestic patent applications are very different from foreign ones. Although utility models have been dominant over the long term, their ratio in total applications began to decrease continuously after reaching a peak in 1988 (77.64 percent), due to the faster increase of invention and design applications, especially designs. Figure 9.9 depicts a surge of invention applications that has occurred since 2000, but it appears that design applications have increased even more quickly. As a result, among all patent applications received from home in 2007, designs are dominant (43.21 percent); utility models rank second (30.69 percent); and inventions account for only 26.1 percent. Furthermore, if we compare Figure 9.9 with Figure 9.3, we can clearly see that the big changes in patent application structures in China were mainly caused by domestic players.

The structural changes of domestic patent grants are very similar to domestic applications. Utility models and designs together account for nearly 90 percent,

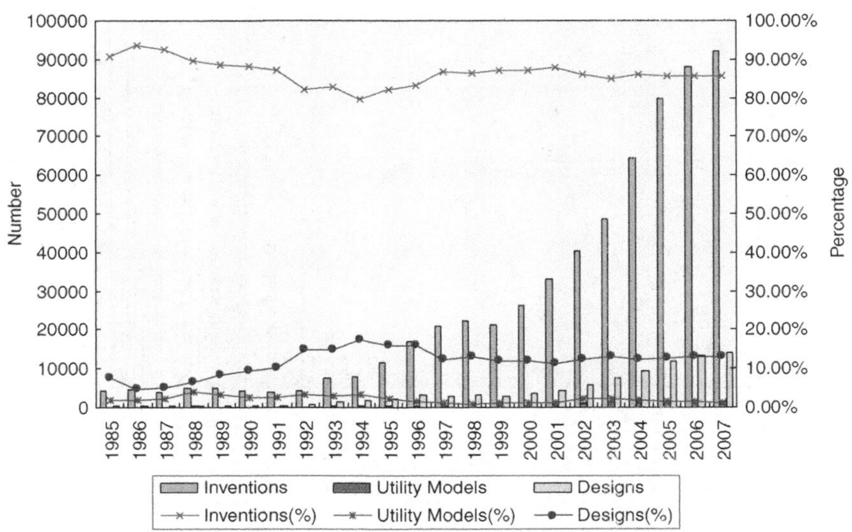

Figure 9.8. Distributions of annual applications for three kinds of patents received from abroad

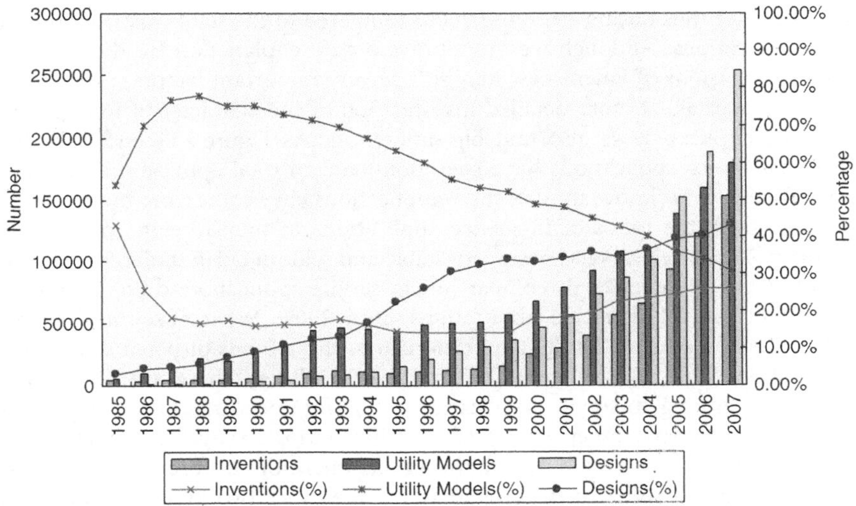

Figure 9.9. Distributions of annual applications for three kinds of patents received from home

even as recently as 2007 (89.41 percent). This also reveals the relatively low granting ratios to domestic invention applications. But from Figure 9.10, we can observe a very different situation regarding changes in the distribution of foreign patent grants in China. The most interesting finding is the granting valley between the two amendments of patent law. As Figure 9.10 depicts, after reaching a peak in

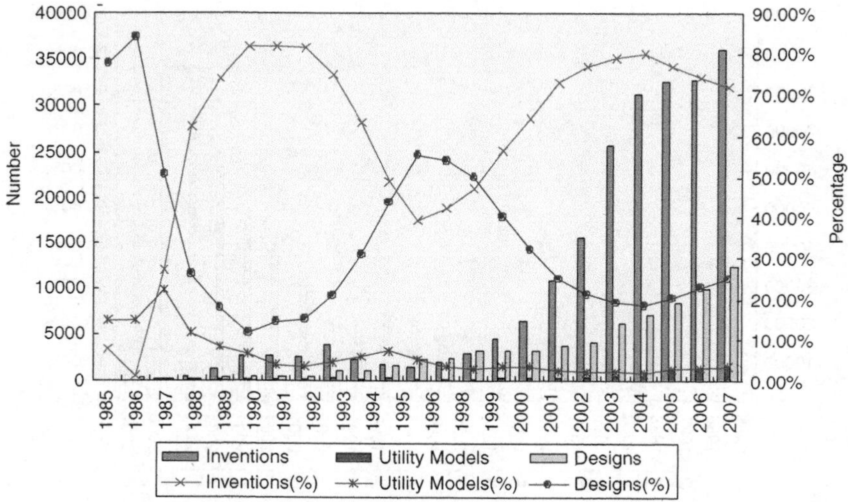

Figure 9.10. Distributions of annual grants for three kinds of patents received from abroad

1993 (3,922), the quantity of invention patent grants to foreigners decreased for three years and rose again from 1997, which resulted in the reversal of invention patent grant ratios during 1992 and 2000, compared to the stable distributions of their applications. Although we cannot give a clear explanation for this reversal here, the revisions of Patent Law may still be very important factors.

If we undertake a more detailed investigation of the character of foreign and domestic applicants, we also find big differences. As Figure 9.11 and Table 9.1 show, in-service applications have been dominant in total applications received from abroad; as we know, most of these applications have come from multinationals. Moreover, the ratios of in-service applications in total foreign applications during past twenty years has been very stable and seldom fallen under 90 percent, just as Figure 9.11 depicts. By comparison, in-service applications didn't exceed 50 percent of annual domestic applications until 2007. What accounts for this difference? If we divide all the applications into three kinds of patents, a clearer explanation could be forthcoming. As Table 9.1 shows, there are no distinct differences among in-service application ratios for the three kinds of patents issued to foreigners, except the relatively low ratios for utility models (78.7 percent). As we have already found, the annual quantities of foreign applications for utility models were much lower than for the other two kinds of patents. It would seem that multinationals didn't care about utility models. On the other hand, we can observe nearly opposite behaviors in domestic applications for different kinds of patents. Among total domestic applications for inventions, more than 60 percent were in-service. But for utility models, this ratio was less than 40 percent, and for designs, the ratio just exceeded 40 percent. So we can conclude, even today, that most of the "petit patents" in China are developed by domestic individuals, not firms or other organizations.

But the character of applicants has not been constant; there have also been great changes during the past twenty years. Take invention as an example: from

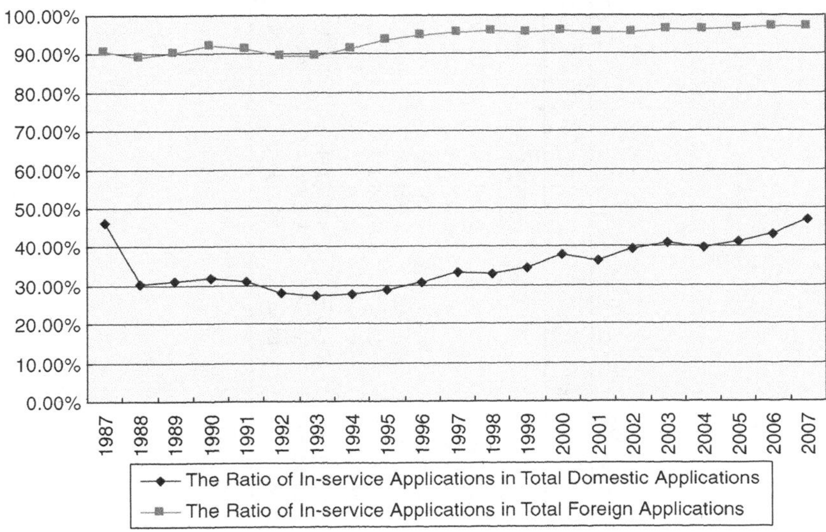

Figure 9.11. Comparisons of the ratios of domestic and foreign in-service patent applications

Figure 9.12 we can see a surge of domestic invention applications, accompanied by an obvious increase of in-service application ratios, right after the second revision of the Patent Law. The ratio of in-service invention applications reached a peak in 2007 (70 percent), from its low in 1995 (less than 30 percent). As we have already mentioned, one of the major revisions in the 2000 Patent Law was to give in-service inventors or designers financial incentives and allow them to own the patents they developed during work time based on agreements with their employers. This factor, plus the improvement of domestic firms' capabilities and their increasing recognition of IPRs, may partially explain the synchronous increases in domestic invention applications and the ratio of in-service applications since 2000.

So far, we have mainly investigated the patent applications and grants under China's patent system from different angles such as the kinds of patents, the sources of applications (home or abroad), and the characters of applicants (in-service or nonservice). And we have found very different behavior models, especially among foreign and domestic players. We will now examine whether there are any differences in implementing and utilizing these patents between foreign and domestic patent holders. We will try to answer this question from three sides.

VALIDITY

As we know, once a patent has been granted, the patentee must pay annual fees to maintain the validity of this patent. Generally said, the patentee will pay this fee only when he estimates the return from this patent will exceed the cost to

Table 9.1. The total applications for three kinds of patents received from home and abroad, May 1985–December 2010

		Invention		Utility Model		Design		Total	
		Number	%	Number	%	Number	%	Number	%
Total	Subtotal	2,325,012	100.0%	2,414,324	100.0%	2,298,238	100.0%	7,037,574	100.0%
	Service	1,825,487	78.5%	969,048	40.1%	1,011,142	44.0%	3,805,677	54.1%
	Nonservice	499,525	21.5%	1,445,276	59.9%	1,287,096	56.0%	3,231,897	45.9%
Domestic	Subtotal	1,429,648	100/61.5	2,397,523	100/99.3	2,173,289	100/94.6	6,000,460	100/85.3
	Service	960,761	67.2%	955,832	39.9%	891,690	41.0%	2,808,283	46.8%
	Nonservice	468,887	32.8%	1,441,691	60.1%	1,281,599	59.0%	3,192,177	53.2%
Foreign	Subtotal	895,364	100/38.5	16,801	100/0.7	124,949	100/5.4	1,037,114	100/14.7
	Service	864,726	96.6%	13,216	78.7%	119,452	95.6%	997,394	96.2%
	Nonservice	30,638	3.4%	3,585	21.3%	5,497	4.4%	39,720	3.8%

Source: <http://english.sipo.gov.cn/statistics/szslzljb/201101/t20110125_570591.html>

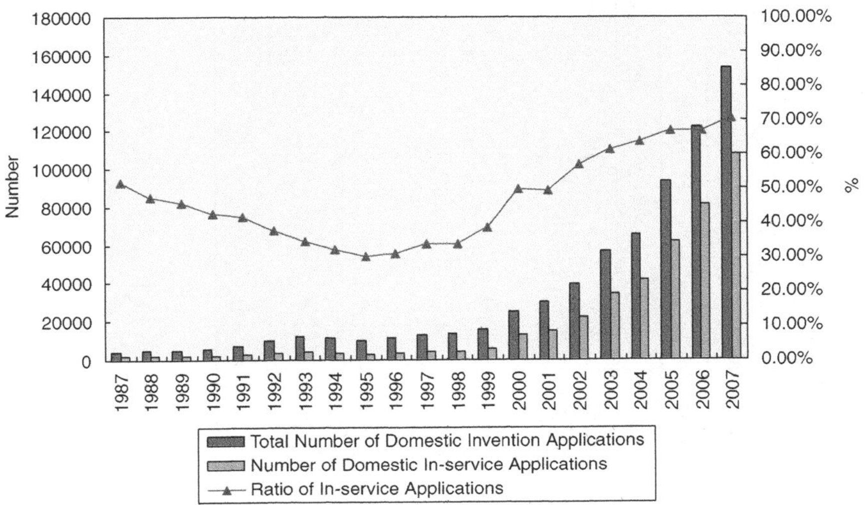

Figure 9.12. Domestic applications for inventions according to service and nonservice, 1987–2007

maintain it. So, we can partially estimate the value of one patent and its utilization from its validity. As Table 9.2 depicts, among all granting patents by SIPO in the twenty-three years through 2007, only 40 percent were still valid (in force). The valid ratios of the three kinds of patents granted to foreigners are all higher than the ones granted to domestic patentees. The gap in inventions is not very big (66 percent to 80 percent) compared to the huge ones in utility models and designs. These gaps reveal that, although domestic applications and grants of "petit patents" grew very fast in China and contributed to the total increase of patents, the quality was still poor compared to the same kinds of patents held by foreigners. Quite a lot of "petit patents" were given up by the patentees themselves after a short term of maintaining them. From Table 9.2 we also find that, whether foreign or domestic, the valid ratios of invention patents are highest. It proves the potential high value of inventions.

PATENT IMPLEMENTATION

There is no acknowledged definition of patent implementation or utilization. In our opinion, patent implementation means making benefits by utilizing patents in different ways, whether the advantages are business profits or competitive advantages. This definition is a little extensive, because it doesn't require putting the patent into production and transferring it into concrete goods. Various patent models and strategies have emerged over the years, for example, "patent thicket," "patent trolls" etc. All these could be regarded as different means of patent implementation. Because there are no official statistics on patent implementations

Table 9.2. Total applications/grants/in force for three kinds of patents received from home and abroad, April 1985–December 2007

		Total		Invention		Utility Model		Design	
		Number	percent	Number	percent	Number	percent	Number	percent
	Application	4,028,284	100	1,334,676	33.1	1,471,191	36.5	1,222,417	30.3
	Grant	2,089,286	100	364,451	17.4	988,264	47.3	736,571	35.3
Total	In Force	850,043	100	271,917	32	299,242	35.2	278,884	32.8
	Grant/Application		51.87		27.31		67.17		60.26
	In Force/Grant		40.69		74.61		30.28		37.86
	Application	3,314,355	82.3	718,207	21.7	1,460,557	44.1	1,135,591	34.3
	Grant	1,790,379	85.7	144,387	8.1	980,029	54.7	665,963	37.2
Domestic	In Force	622,409	73.2	95,678	15.4	294,463	47.3	232,268	37.3
	Grant/Application		54.02		20.1		67.1		58.64
	In Force/Grant		34.76		66.26		30.05		34.88
	Application	713,929	17.7	616,469	86.3	10,634	1.5	86,826	12.2
	Grant	298,907	14.3	220,064	73.6	8,235	2.8	70,608	23.6
Foreign	In Force	227,634	26.8	176,239	77.4	4,779	2.1	46,616	20.5
	Grant/Application		41.87		35.7		77.44		81.32
	In Force/Grant		76.16		80.09		58.03		66.02

Source: SIPO Patent Statistical Yearbook

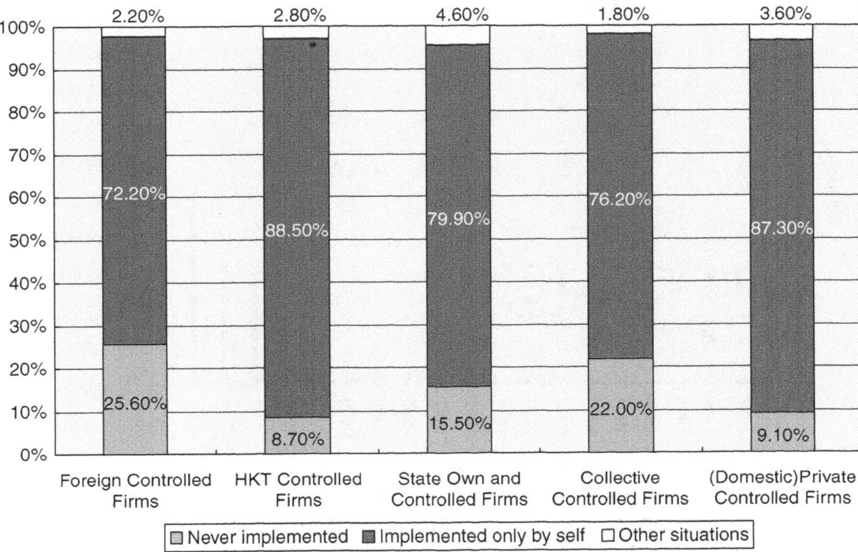

Figure 9.13. The situation of patent implementations of different kinds of firms

in China, the data used here are mainly based on a full-sample survey on the status of patent applications and implementations of China's enterprises, which was performed by SIPO in 2006. This survey included all the firms that have made patent applications in China since 1985, 110,112 firms in total. A database was founded based on this survey, which included 310,554 patent applications issued by 43,383 firms. This may be the largest and most recent sample available regarding the patent implementation situation in China. In the survey, the patent implementations were divided into five modes: never implemented; implemented only by self; only licensed to others; self-implemented and also licensed to others; and transfer of patent privileges. From Figure 9.13 we can clearly see that among different kinds of firms, the patent-implementing ratio of foreign-controlled firms is lowest; nearly 26 percent of total patent applications had never been implemented. Firms controlled by companies in Hong Kong, Macau, and Taiwan (HKT-controlled) and (domestic) private firms have high implementing ratios (more than 85 percent). For these two kinds of firms, less than 10 percent of their total patent applications had never been implemented. And for all kinds of firms, the dominant implementing mode is self-implemented exclusively. For most firms except foreign-controlled ones, nearly 80 percent to 90 percent of the total patent applications had been implemented only by themselves. Among all the invention patent applications by foreign-controlled firms, more than half (51.8 percent) had never been implemented. This ratio is much higher than any among other kinds of firms, especially the HKT-controlled firms (15.7 percent) and private firms (less than 20 percent). Then, because most of the foreign patent applications are inventions and issued by multinationals, we can make another important deduction: compared to domestic firms, multinationals' patent applications in China are more strategic. Patents are not only figured as carriers or tools to protect

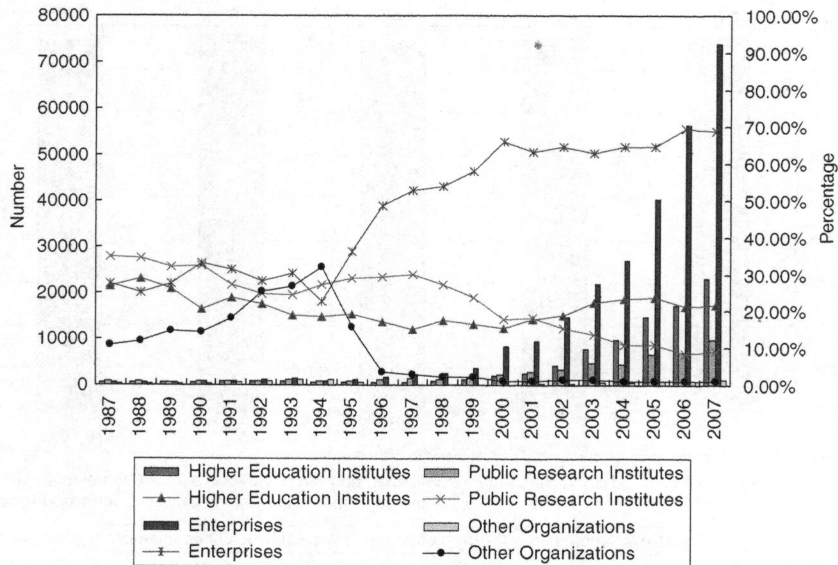

Figure 9.14. Domestic in-service applications for inventions according to character of applicants, 1987–2007

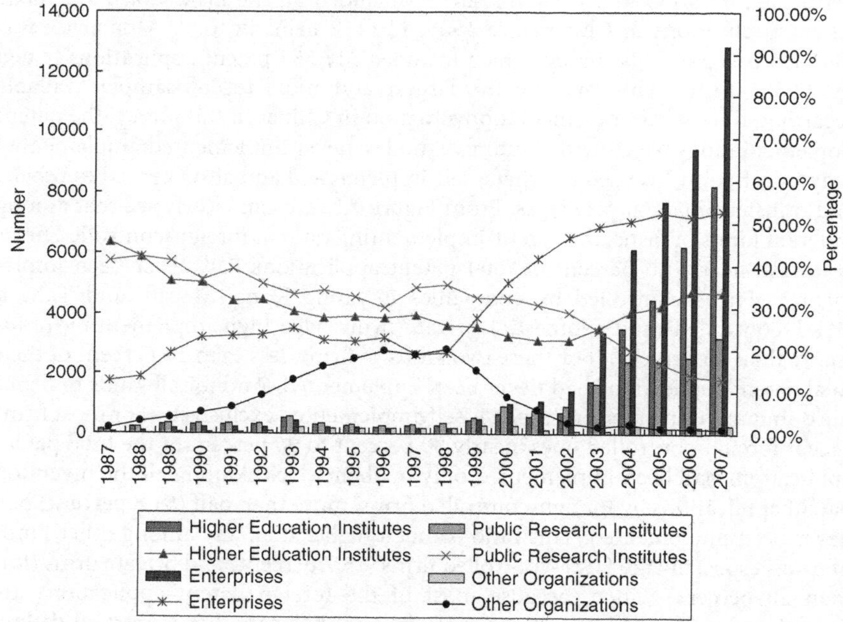

Figure 9.15. Domestic in-service grants for inventions according to character of patentees, 1987–2007

technologies; they are increasingly utilized as the tools to achieve competitive advantages and the embodiments of business strategies by multinationals. Most of the domestic firms in China have not yet entered this stage.

LITIGATIONS

Figure 9.14 depicts another fact in the process of China's patent evolvement. Different from most counties, especially developed countries, the main applicants and gainers of service patents are not only companies, but also universities and research organizations. As we can see from Figure 9.15, industrial enterprises obtained the dominant position after more than ten years. Research institutions, the former dominant players, have seen their share in the granted service inventions decrease very quickly over the past ten years. Besides system reform and policy reasons, this could also reflect the changes of innovative capabilities of different performers.

ADAPTING TO CHINA'S IPR ENVIRONMENT: STRATEGIES OF MULTINATIONALS IN CHINA

A brief overview of China's opening and FDI development

In the December 1978 Third Plenum of the Eleventh CCP Congress, China's leadership adopted economic reform policies known as the Four Modernizations. These tenets aimed at expanding rural income and incentives, encouraging experiments in enterprise autonomy, reducing central planning, and attracting foreign direct investment in China.

In 2002, China received the most FDI in the world, outstripping that of the United States for the first time. In 1983, when China was still in its initial stage of reform and opening, China's real use of FDI only stood at $636 million. In 2002, the figure soared to $52,743 billion, an increase of eighty-two times over 1983.

According to the data available so far, foreign-funded enterprises in China are generally running well. The growth rate of their major economic indices, including industrial added value, export volume, tax contribution, favorable balance in bank Forex settlement and sales, are all above the national average. The ratio of these businesses in the national economic aggregates is growing, especially in the economic increment.

As pointed out above, IPR strategy has been incorporated into enterprises' business strategies. MNCs in China are pioneers of IP strategies. In this section we have a closer look at MNCs' IP strategies, especially patent strategies, and their impacts in China. We aim at analyzing the specific techniques MNCs used to gain technical, economic, and market advantage at the cost of the industry.

Similar to the sample we used above, we use the Fortune Global 500 list (2006) as our population of investigation. From the list provided by SIPO of domestic firms that have made invention[1] applications, we selected 775 related corporations. We then searched SIPO's database and found 108,747 invention applications by these firms from April 1, 1985 to December 31, 2004. For each application, we obtained the following information from it: application date, grant date, prior right, patentee, inventors, residence of inventors, IPC section number, and IPC class number.

An analysis based on patenting activities

During the twenty-year period, the sample foreign firms applied for 108,747 inventions in China, about ten times the applications by the sample of domestic firms. Figure 9.16 shows the annual number of foreign sample firms' invention applications. From the figure, we observe that MNCs' invention applications in China have two upsurges, the first around 1993, and the second around 2001. After 1993, foreign applications increased by over 50 percent annually. From 1997 to 2000, MNCs' invention applications accelerated moderately and even decreased in 1999. After the second upsurge from 2002 to 2004, 56,432 inventions were applied for in total, taking up over 50 percent of the overall applications.

Figure 9.17 compares invention applications of the sample domestic firms and the sample foreign firms in China. It is obvious that before 2000, there was strong contrast between the two parties. Applications by domestic firms were less than 1/15 of those of foreign firms. After 2000, however, applications by domestic firms increased dramatically and reached 1/5 of those of foreign firms. From invention application data, we see that the technology gap between domestic firms and MNCs is large.

With regard to parent country distribution, Japanese MNCs rank first with 50,779 invention applications, taking up 46.7 percent; US MNCs rank second

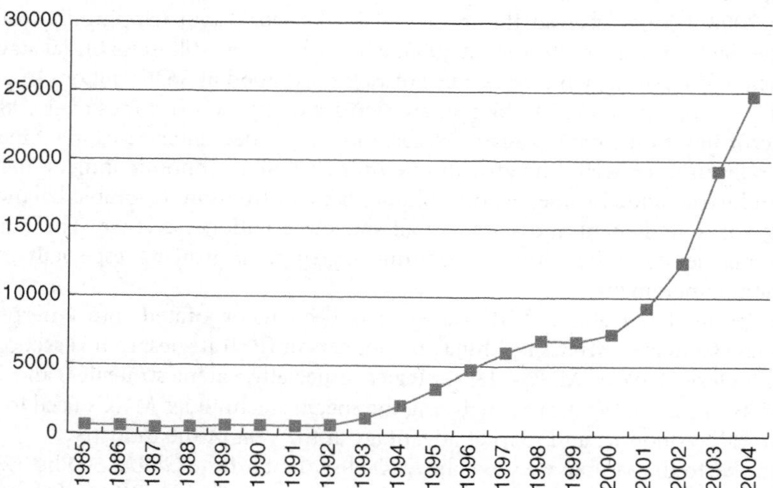

Figure 9.16. Invention applications of foreign firms, 1985–2004

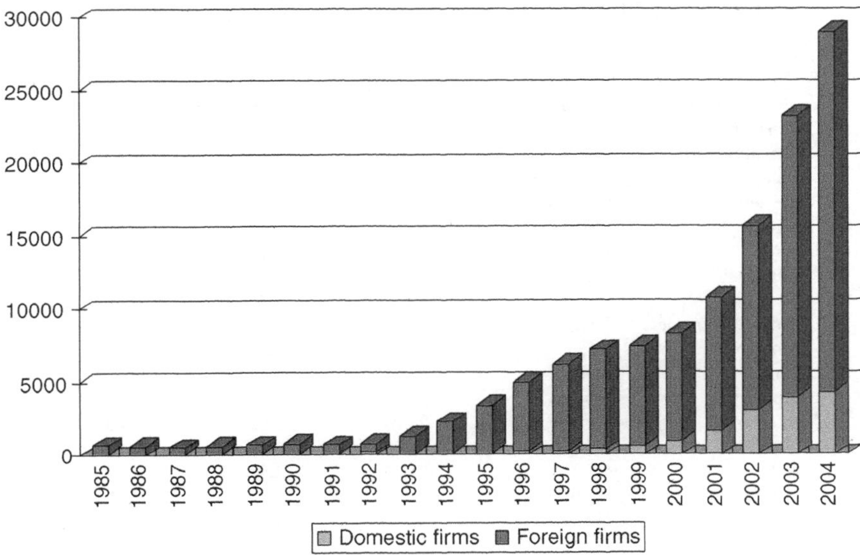

Figure 9.17. Invention applications of domestic firms and foreign firms, 1985–2004

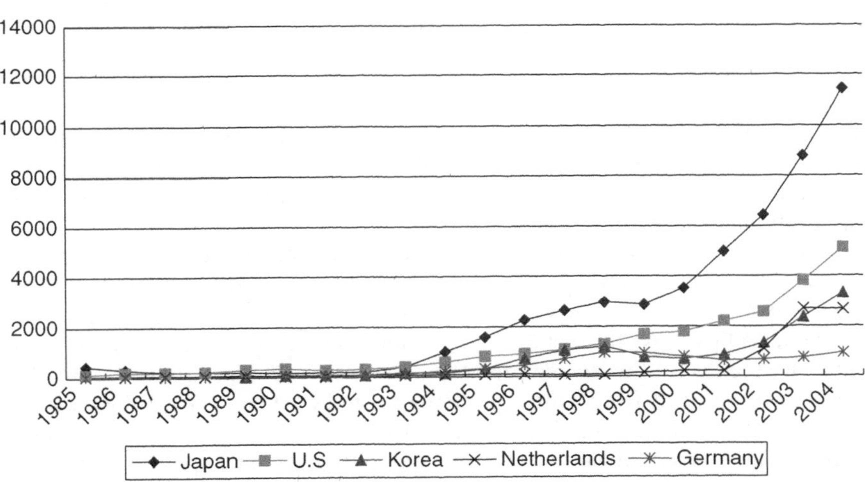

Figure 9.18. Annual invention applications of five countries, 1985–2004

with 24,001 invention applications, or 22.1 percent; Korean MNCs rank third with 13,115, or 12.1 percent. MNCs from the Netherlands and Germany rank respectively fourth and fifth. MNCs from these five countries apply for over 95 percent of the total foreign inventions. Figure 9.18 describes annual invention applications of the above five countries from 1985 to 2004. It can be observed that before 1993, there were barely any invention applications. Korean sample firms applied for their first inventions in 1989, indicating their lateness in entering the

Table 9.3. Foreign firms with over 1,000 invention applications

Patentee	Parent Country	Invention Applications	Percentage	Accumulative Percentage
Panasonic	Japan	12,644	11.63	11.63
Samsung	Korea	9,998	9.19	20.82
Philips	Netherlands	5,586	5.14	25.96
Siemens	Germany	4,713	4.33	30.29
Mitsubishi	Japan	4,454	4.10	34.39
IBM	US	4,119	3.79	38.17
Canon	Japan	4,117	3.79	41.96
Sony Electronics	Japan	3,832	3.52	45.48
Sanyo Electronics	Japan	3,122	2.87	48.36
Motorola	US	2,769	2.55	50.90
Sony	Japan	2,762	2.54	53.44
Honda	Japan	2,559	2.35	55.79
Intel	US	2,199	2.02	57.82
DuPont	US	2,183	2.01	59.82
GE	US	2,135	1.96	61.79
Fujitsu	Japan	2,060	1.89	63.68
P&G	US	1,817	1.67	65.35
3M	US	1,557	1.43	66.78
Shell	Holland	1,458	1.34	68.13
Sharp	Japan	1,424	1.31	69.43
Microsoft	US	1,011	0.93	70.36
Sumitomo Chemical	Japan	1,009	0.93	71.29

Chinese market. After 1993, Japanese firms applied for many more inventions every year. Comparatively speaking, US firms' invention applications accelerated rather moderately. It is also interesting to notice that German firms' invention applications decreased in these years.

Table 9.3 lists foreign firms with over 1,000 invention applications during 1985 to 2004. Panasonic from Japan applied for 12,644 inventions, ranking first of all, taking up 11.63 percent; Samsung ranks second at 9,998 inventions, taking up 9.19 percent; Philips ranks third at 5,586 inventions, taking up 5.14 percent. From the table, we see that out of the ten top MNCs, five are from Japan, two from the US, and one respectively from Korea, Netherlands, and Germany. Generally speaking, the intensity of applications from Japan is strong compared to US firms. Samsung, Philips, and Siemens all compose a large amount of the total application number of their parent countries.

Comparing the patentee distribution of foreign firms with that of domestic firms, we observe much more concentration in domestic firms' applications. For example, Huawei Technology, just one company, takes up one third of domestic firms' overall applications, while the top five foreign firms take up the same percentage of foreign firms' applications.

Invention application origins of foreign firms are very different from their equivalent applications in parent countries. While most of their applications in parent countries are the result of their most recent R & D, which is highly

Table 9.4. Correlation coefficients between patenting and market data of eleven industries

	Total revenue	Total profit	Foreign revenue	Foreign profit
Chemicals	0.640558**	0.189004	0.523921	0.124240
Automobiles	0.914830***	0.795736***	0.876022***	0.872337**
Household durables	0.964147***	0.886973***	0.921190***	0.870688**
Food production	0.625978**	0.317207	0.666105	0.464172
Biotechnology	0.945453***	0.789591***	0.945668***	0.892328**
Pharmaceuticals	0.917804***	0.876112***	0.929821***	0.770316**
Software	0.963375***	-	-	-
Communication equipment	0.847333***	0.511915*	0.837822**	0.612826
Computer peripherals	0.973225***	0.960712***	0.955277***	0.962078***
Semiconductors	0.822729***	0.674993**	0.793686**	0.730509*
Telecommunications	0.904428***	-	-	-
Average	0.865442	0.666916**	0.827724	0.699944

Note: * The level of statistical significance is 10 percent.
** The level of statistical significance is 5 percent.
*** The level of statistical significance is 1 percent.
Source: Zhu and Liang (2006a: table 7).

technology-oriented, their applications in China are mainly inventions with priorities, which are highly market-oriented.

During the twenty-year period, 104,091 out of 108,747 inventions have priorities, or 95.7 percent. This means over 95 percent of foreign firms' invention applications in China have been applied for before in foreign countries, mainly the firms' parent countries. As a result, when MNCs bring forward invention applications to SIPO, they do not need to wait for the technology to be perfect but rather for the market to be ready. Additional research performed by our team also proved this point (Zhu and Liang 2006a).

We took 135 companies that have set up independent R & D subsidiaries in China as the sample[2] and did a correlation analysis between their patenting data and the total revenue, total profit, foreign revenue, and foreign profit respectively of each of their eleven industries. The results are presented in Table 9.4. It is notable that in all eleven industries, MNCs' patenting activities are highly correlated with total revenue, or the overall size of the Chinese market. This strongly supports the standpoint of Sun (2003) that foreign patents in China are largely driven by demand factors. Moreover, in most industries, there is high and significant correlation between foreign patenting and foreign profit data. Ernst (2001) concluded that MNCs' active patenting behavior leads to excellent market performance. We observe that the relationship between patenting and market performance can be seen as a virtuous cycle: the former guarantees the latter, which in turn requires more patenting for further expansion.

MNCs' IPR strategies in China and their impact

In the above section, we talked about the characteristics of MNCs' patent applications in China. We will further analyze their IPR strategies, mainly patent strategies in China, discuss their impacts, and analyze why these strategies can be successful, as well as what the institutional loopholes are that allow MNCs to succeed.

Licensing strategy

When MNCs don't implement technologies themselves, they can transfer or license them to domestic firms to gain great profits. Given that China's overall scientific and technological development level is lower than the world average, years-old MNC technologies are sometimes applicable to the Chinese market and still have great potential.

During the process of IP transferring and licensing, since MNCs take hold of kernel technologies, domestic firms have little capability to argue about prices, but must passively accept the prices MNCs propose. Naturally, overpricing is a common problem. For most of the time, even though IPs are being transferred and licensed, domestic firms take pains to master these technologies. When they meet problems, MNCs usually choose to dispatch experts to domestic firms to solve the problems on site rather than teach domestic firms how to deal with them. It is hard, or even impossible, to enhance their technology capabilities through patent transferring. The original intention of domestic firms to exchange technology for market share is nothing but a dream.

Take the automobile industry for instance; China adopts very strict market admittance requirements. Foreign firms may enter the Chinese market only in the form of joint ventures. In the early 1980s, in order to upgrade domestic automobile R & D capabilities, foreign capital was encouraged to flow into China on a large scale. Domestic automobile firms were anxious to import advanced technologies and cooperate with foreign giants by setting up joint ventures. The pilot attempt was the alliance of Beijing Auto Factory and AMC Motor in 1983. Shanghai-Volkswagen, Changchun FAW-Volkswagen, Dongfeng Peugeot Citroën Automobile, Shanghai General Motor, so on and so forth, were established in succession.

Twenty years of joint venture experiences show us that foreign automobile firms make full use of their technology advantages and spare no effort to gain actual mastery over joint ventures. They monopolize key technologies and make the technology transfer process a black box so as to control technology overflow to a minimum degree. Joint ventures, consequently, are no more than merely technology end-users, knowing little about the details of the technology development process. They fail to enhance their R & D capabilities, which was the original intention of this kind of cooperation.

As Tables 9.5 and 9.6 depict, compared with the scarcity of patents owned by joint ventures, the foreign partners' parent companies usually file large number of patents,especially invention patents, in China. They usually transfer technology to joint ventures at very high prices without disclosing the developing process and related details (Zhou et al. 2006). Foreign parent companies are the absolute dominators of the China–foreign alliances. They remain at the upstream of the technology chain while Chinese partners stay downstream.

Not only are foreign automobile partners reluctant to share their key technologies, they are also reluctant to innovate in China, continuously introducing outdated or even eliminated technologies to the Chinese market. Further, because

Table 9.5. Three kinds of patents owned by China's top ten automobile firms

Firm	Total	Share	Invention	Utility Model	Industrial Design
Shanghai General Motors	54	11 percent	0	0	54
Shanghai Volkswagen Motors	58	12 percent	8	21	29
FAW-Volkswagen	0	0 percent	0	0	0
Beijing-Hyundai Automobile	0	0 percent	0	0	0
Guangzhou Honda Motor	1	0 percent	0	0	1
Tianjin FAW-XiaLi Automobile	5	1 percent	0	0	5
Chery Automobile	272	56 percent	15	70	187
Dongfeng Nissan Automobile	0	0 percent	0	0	0
Geely Automobile	50	10 percent	6	9	35
Dongfeng Peugeot Citroën Automobile	50	10 percent	3	9	38

Note: All data are to July 31, 2006.
Source: Zhu and Liang (2006b: table 3)

Table 9.6. Three kinds of patents owned by parent automobile companies in China

	Total	Invention	Utility model	Industrial design
General Motors	231	230	0	1
Volkswagen	291	254	0	37
Hyundai Motor	489	460	0	29
Honda Motor	3,861	3,000	57	804
Toyota Motor	1,994	1,260	41	693
Nissan Motor	3	3	0	0
PSA/Peugeot-Citroen Mobile	18	14	0	4
Total	6,887	5,221 (76 percent)	98 (1 percent)	1,568 (23 percent)

Note: All data are due to July 31, 2006.
Source: Zhu and Liang (2006b: table 4)

there is strict market admittance of private capital in China's automobile industry, there are very few privately owned automobile firms in China. Consequently, there is barely any competition in this industry. Joint ventures can sell their old-fashioned cars at very high prices and gain big profits.

Sometimes, the MNCs' IPR overpricing results in a deadlock during technology transfer negotiations with domestic firms. Since January 2004, domestic telecom firms together with Ministry of Information Industry (MII) have been negotiating with foreign telecom firms on 3G technology transfer but haven't made remarkable progress so far. The main problem is that Qualcomm has dominant advantages in this field and overcharges during negotiations.

Generally speaking, licensing is a basic strategy of IPR owners. If the owner wishes to license and at the same time reaches an agreement with other firms or institutions that require the technology, it is a win-win business. In China, however, because of the unbalanced technology levels of MNCs and domestic firms, licensing is accompanied by a lot of unfair terms. The original goal of improving a firm's technology level through licensing is hard to reach. Thus, licensing actually inhibits innovation.

Litigation strategy

Just as Merges and Nelson (1990) pointed out, it matters less that every patent is a potential contribution to innovation than that it may infringe or be infringed. IP infringement and litigation has long been in existence and is a means of power in competition with other firms. In China, the deployment of MNCs' IP is very aggressive. Generally speaking, at the start-up of the domestic market, foreign firms apply for a large number of patents. In the case of domestic firms' and individuals' piracy behaviors, foreign firms pretend not to notice. Actually they are secretly waiting for the market to grow large enough. When their patents are granted by SIPO, they bring lawsuits against their Chinese rivals. Most of the time, they receive high compensation fees and even forbid domestic firms from production. In this way, they successfully expand their markets at the cost of domestic enterprises.

Take Microsoft as an example. When it entered the Chinese market, piracy of Windows and other software was everywhere in China, but Microsoft chose to let it be. When market share of Windows was large enough, reaching about 95 percent, Microsoft announced it would crack down on piracy and urged the Chinese government to help. By this IPR strategy combined with other business strategies including litigation, Microsoft became the leading software provider in China. Most other domestic software firms are squeezed out of the market, leaving Microsoft as the monopoly.

Besides litigation in China against domestic firms, MNCs also bring litigation against domestic firms during their expansion in the international market.

In the past and in traditional business operation, litigation was an active strategy to protect firms' technologies and products. Today, litigation has somehow gradually become a passive strategy, which means that firms sometimes secretly wait for other firms to infringe their own patents, and then sue the infringers for a large amount of compensation. MNCs are skilled users of this strategy in China. In China, domestic firms still have little awareness of IPR and piracy is pervasive. Actually, most of the time, domestic firms do not regard IPR as a very serious thing. By the time they do realize it, it is too late. The losses to them are not limited to monetary compensation but loss of the markets that they took pains to cultivate. Thus, litigation is unfavorable to competition and further fosters monopoly. In the absence of antitrust laws, it might be harder for domestic firms to fight for their rights.

Alliance strategy

Foreign firms in China broadly construct their own technology alliances and bind their patents together. Inside alliances, foreign firms cross-license to cut down their technology costs. Outside the alliances, however, high fees need to be paid to have access to those packaged patents. Take the DVD industry, for example: alliances including 6C, 4C, DTS, and MPEGLA have imposed large amounts of patent fees on domestic firms (Table 9.7), making margin profits for each DVD less than ¥30 ($4.40).

Scholars and technicians have investigated the patent package of DVD alliances such as 6C and 4C. They found many patents are actually trivial and do not add

Table 9.7. Patent fees domestic firms need to pay for each DVD

Alliance name	Member companies	Fee ($)
6C	Hitachi, Panasonic, Mitsubishi, Toshiba, AOL Time Warner, JVC	4
4C	Philips, Sony, Pioneer, LG Electronics	0.0375
—	Thomson	1
DTS	DTS Digital	10
—	Dolby	4.95

Source: Collected by the authors

Notes: The practical licensing fee structure is a bit complicated and alterable according to production volume. The calculation here is based on assumption of a very low volume.

value to the overall package. Also included in the package are a number of patents that have already expired. For example, in December 2005, Zhang Ping, an IPR professor at Peking University, attacked a patent of Philips that was part of the 4C DVD pool, because it was alleged to be not essential. This strategy of mixing expired and trivial patents in patent pools is illegal. However, China's current institutional arrangements lack the laws needed to regulate these behaviors.

Standard strategy

Standard specifications are elaborated by diverse stakeholders in order to provide common ground for the future development of new technologies. This common ground consists not only of standards to reduce the variety of possible technological trajectories to a minimum, but also compatibility standards which allow the exploitation of network externalities and quality standards for increasing consumer acceptance. Patent giants are trying their best to persuade standard unions to include their patents when editing standards. In this way, they can have a stronger voice in standards constitution and charge more money.

In China, with help and support from the government, domestic enterprises and research institutions have started to construct national standards to break through the MNC's technology and IPR barriers. These standard organizations include GPRS, TD-SCDMA, AVS, e-home, etc. MNCs have participated in most of the above standard organizations, but as observers instead of formal members. They do not want their high-quality IPRs to be mixed up with domestic firms' low-quality IPRs in the patent pool. At the same time, they don't want to miss the chance to take advantage of favorable government policies. With regard to international standards, however, domestic firms have contributed no more than 0.2 percent.

THE CASE OF HUAWEI

Given the overall picture of patenting behaviors of domestic and multinational firms in China, it is necessary to examine how individual firms in China develop their innovative capabilities. The case of Huawei is an interesting example not only because it adopted an aggressive strategy to innovate, taking advantage of the

IPR system, but also because it has evolved into a multinational company operating abroad in the process.

Huawei Technologies may be the most well-known high-tech company in China, and is also one of the world's leading suppliers of communications equipment. The company has 83,000 employees, of whom 43 percent are dedicated to R & D.[3] It realized global contract sales of $16 billion in 2007, an increase of 45 percent over 2006, and international markets accounted for 72 percent of all sales revenues. Huawei has built up wide product portfolios and advantages in such fields as mobile networks, broadband networks, optical networks, telecom value-added services, and terminals. It has become one of the top three suppliers in the global GSM market; it also earned 44.8 percent of all new contracts in the global CDMA category in 2007.[4] It ranked No. 1 in the MSAN market with a 45.5 percent market share in 2007, ranked No. 2 in shipments of optical network products, and was one of the top three suppliers of routers and Ethernet switches for the operator market.[5] Today, Huawei is a leader in providing next-generation telecommunications networks, and serves thirty-five of the world's top fifty operators, including Vodafone, British Telecom, Telefonica, France Telecom/ Orange, and China Mobile, with over 1 billion users worldwide.[6]

When it was founded in 1988 in Shenzhen, Huawei only had six employees and 24,000 RMB in registered capital. It was one of thousands of small companies, and initially operated as the sales agent for HAX company telephone switches imported from Hong Kong. Unlike his peers, the founder of Huawei, Ren Zhengfei, decided to develop Huawei's own switch products while still selling the imported goods. Huawei's initial knowledge about switches was learned from HAX's engineers when they delivered maintenance services for clients. Mr Ren's foresight was proved in the near future. When HAX took back the dealership at the beginning of 1990, Huawei had developed its first product, a small-capacity user switch—BH03. One year later, it put out a more advanced product, the 512 lines user switch—HJD48, and the crossbar central-office switch—JK1000. Due to the fast growth of the domestic telecommunication market and the cost advantages compared with imported goods, these products brought huge benefits for Huawei. Total revenue exceeded 100 million RMB in 1992 and profit exceeded 10 million.

But Huawei didn't rely on the existing advantages. Mr Ren decided to make a big bet: to invest almost all the revenues in the development of large-capacity digital automatic switches. This decision might have been fatal to Huawei if it had not achieved success. Mu and Lee described the development process of China's first central-office-level digital switches—HJD-04, which was developed in 1991 by a domestic research institute (CIT/ZIIE) in cooperation with SOEs (LTEF, PTIC). They also explored the technological links between HJD-04 and Shanghai Bell's System-12 (Mu and Lee 2005). The general idea is that the success of HJD-04 led to further knowledge diffusion, mainly through the interflowing of engineers and related persons, which finally led to successive development of four other types of digital automatic switches (C&C08, EIM-601, ZXJ-10, and SP-30) by other indigenous firms (Huawei, ZTE, and Datang). For example, Huawei's location in Shenzhen and its higher salary levels attracted skilled manpower from Great Dragon (the original manufacturer of HJD-04). But less attention was given to the hardship during Huawei's development process of the C&C08.

After losing 60–100 million RMB on this project, in 1994, after two years' untiring efforts, Huawei finally developed its 2,000-line digital automatic switch system—C&C08, the first milestone product in its history (Lin 2007).

The great success of C&C08 imbued confidence to Huawei for its innovations based on in-house R & D. In an essential document which played crucial roles during its early development, "The Fundamental Law of Huawei," Huawei set a rule to guarantee that the annual R & D expenditures not fall below 10 percent of total revenue. Huawei followed this rule strictly even in 2002 when the whole telecommunication industry fell into recession. According to data from Gartner, Huawei's R & D intensity was 17 percent that year, even exceeding the ratio at Cisco and Nokia.

So, although technology dissemination from foreign companies and other local peers played important roles in the early development of Huawei, a deep understanding of China's local market, especially the lower-level market, and a focusing of effort on technology learning, absorption, integration, and improvement, were essential to Huawei's success. For example, most MNC or JV products focused on markets in capital cities, not in the country or rural cities, which are several times larger in China. They couldn't resolve the problem of low telephone penetration rates and intensive use for each telephone in rural markets, which was opposite of their experiences in developed countries or big cities. Furthermore, the screen menu of all the foreign systems was in English. Outside the big cities, it was difficult to find operators who could read English. Like other major domestic competitors, Huawei also developed its own digital automatic switches with a simple machine–operator interface and a Chinese-based screen menu. It mainly focused on the lower-level markets in the mid-1990s, where 90 percent of Huawei's products were installed, according to Shenzhen Special Zone Daily (Mu and Lee 2005: 777). So, based on this market which was huge but neglected by the MNCs, Huawei bolstered its capabilities by fully exploiting local cost advantages and fulfilled a fast market expansion. In the domestic central-office switching market, Huawei surpassed Shanghai Bell and became the largest digital automatic switch manufacturer in 1998.[7] Cultivation of China's local market not only brought considerable benefits for Huawei, which supported its continual and intensive investment in R & D, but also endowed it with unique competences abroad.

As indicated above, Huawei's great success was owed to its customer focus strategy. On its website, Huawei promised to meet the projected and actual needs of customers by providing excellent products, solutions, and services in order to consistently maximize customer's benefits and value. To keep the promise, Huawei lured enormous talent for its R & D. At the beginning, it had fewer than 200 workers and 500 R & D researchers. But by the end of March 2007, there were over 35,000 employees engaged in R & D.[8] It founded twelve global R & D centers with locations in Bangalore, Silicon Valley, Dallas, Stockholm, and Moscow, in addition to those in Beijing, Shanghai, Nanjing, Shenzhen, Hangzhou, and Chengdu in China. Huawei worked with leading consultancies such as IBM, the Hay Group, and PricewaterhouseCoopers to carry out management transformation and keep abreast of international industrial benchmarks. Through implementing advanced management tools such as Marketing Management (MM), Integrated Product Development (IPD), Integrated Supply Chain (ISC), Customer

Relationship Management (CRM), and IFS (Integrated Financial Service), Huawei diminished the waste in its R & D process and improved its response speed to customers.

The improvement of management also reflected in the management of Intellectual Property Rights (IPRs). Although Huawei had founded an independent department for IPR management in 1995, the recognition of IPRs' importance did not reach a high level until 2002. By the end of 2002, Huawei had filed 2,154 patent applications; among them, 198 were PCT patent or foreign patent applications.[9] Huawei was a pioneer even among other peers. Its invention patent applications ranked first among Chinese firms that year. The main target of Huawei's IPRs management was to protect its own technologies and R & D results.

A turning point came with Cisco's litigation against Huawei in early 2003. Cisco alleged that Huawei misappropriated its IOS(r) Source Codes, Command Line Interfaces (CLI), technical documents, and five patent technologies relating to Cisco's Router Protocols. Cisco's accusations involved eight sorts, including patent infringement, copyright infringement, business secret infringement, common law misappropriation, trademark law infringement, unfair competition, etc., which covered all manner of IPR laws. The focus of the lawsuit was Huawei's Quidway Routers, which had been the subject of eighteen suits sold in the United States. Most analysts regarded this as a business strategy by Cisco to prevent Huawei's fast infiltration into the Cisco-dominated, high-level market and to slow down Huawei's worldwide expansion. So, although Cisco withdrew the lawsuit and both companies ultimately resolved all patent litigation, it also raised the alarms for Huawei's R & D and IPR strategies. For example, from the first-generation products through today, the core source codes of Huawei's Routers are completely different from Cisco's. But they are actually very similar at the peripheral technologies and designs such as consumer interfaces, CLIs, and appearances, which is partly due to follower-and-imitation strategies of product development in early stages. As mentioned previously, Huawei's early-stage products looked like the MNCs' products but with a Chinese menu.

Through this case, Huawei also realized that IPR could be used not only as the umbrella of protection, but also as the means of attack. The direct outcome was that Huawei accelerated the pace of patent applications dramatically, especially abroad. In just one year, 2003, Huawei filed 226 patent applications under the WIPO Patent Cooperation Treaty (PCT) and more than 200 foreign patent applications, exceeding the accumulative total through the end of 2002.[10] By the end of 2004, Huawei had filed nearly 6,000 patent applications accumulatively, about three times that of its total two years previously.[11]

Cisco's litigation also stimulated the formulation of Huawei's IPR strategy, "protect and utilize autonomous IPRs, respect others' IPRs, improve corporate core competence, and strongly support global product strategy."[12] Huawei actually implemented this strategy through different ways. First, it founded the pre-research department which employs more than 1,000 persons and gives more emphasis to cutting-edge technology research. The Key Performance Indicators (KPI) for the pre-research department include patents and standard proposals. Second, it strengthened patent analysis and concentrated on the breakthrough of technologies with comparative advantages. For example, Huawei started the prototype development of the third-generation wireless communications system (3G) as far back as 1995. But through patent analysis, Huawei found almost all the core technologies in this field had been covered by Qualcomm's patents. Even if Huawei could receive all these patents, it couldn't establish competitive advantage. So, Huawei signed a licensing agreement with Qualcomm. Although the rate of the licensing fee was 6.75 percent for each item of CDMA (Code Division Multiple Access) equipment sold abroad, due to its powerful development abilities in product application, Huawei still earned almost 100 million dollars in this field from abroad by the end of 2005.[13]

Similarly after analysis, Huawei selected Wideband Code Division Multiple Access (WCDMA) as its major direction in 3G R & D and took the Application Specific Integrated Circuit (ASIC) chips as the breakthrough technology. According to estimation, Huawei has invested more than 6 billion RMB in 3G R & D[14] and more than 6,000 employees have participated in its development. Huawei has mobilized its whole global R & D system and its affiliates and joint ventures in more than forty counties to support the R & D of WCDMA. The R & D centers in Silicon Valley and Dallas took charge of the development of chips; Russia's R & D center was responsible for the radio technologies; the Sweden Institute undertook the development of core technologies, and the India Institute led the development of core software. At the same time, the native R & D centers in Shenzhen, Beijing, and Nanjing devoted about 2,500 researchers to the development of WCDMA systems. As a complement, Huawei also collaborated with top universities such as Tsinghua University, Peking University, and China Science and Technology University on the key technology research for mobile communication systems including WCDMA. Huawei applied the IPD model during the development of WCDMA system, and all the software development centers participating in the R & D passed Capability Maturity Model for Software Level-5 (CMM5) certifications. Through the application of these advanced management tools, the efficiencies and quality of R & D improved much more.

As a result, Huawei finally developed ASIC chips for WCDMA with autonomous IPRs and reduced its procurement cost from $200 to tens of dollars per unit.[15] Today, Huawei possesses the full set of technologies for the WCDMA system, from the core technologies to the IC designs, and the whole-set mobile communication solutions including GSM, WCDMA, CDMA2000, and TD-SCDMA. The company has filed thousands of patents regarding 3G; its filed applications for UMTS 3G essential patents rank among the world's top five.[16] Huawei has become the global leading provider in the 3G field, according to the following measures:

- won 45 percent of all new UMTS/HSPA contracts to become the leader in these next-generation mobile networks;
- won 44.8 percent of new CDMA contracts, making it the market leader;
- 12 commercial WiMAX networks deployed around the world.[17]

Third, Huawei improved its collaborative innovation model, founded partnerships with most of the industry peers, and obtained technologies through patent licensing and mergers and acquisitions (M & A). As introduced on its homepage, Huawei works "closely with leading multinationals such as TI, Motorola, IBM, Intel, Agere, ADI, Altera, SUN, Microsoft, Oracle, and HP to improve the time to market of our products, and to incorporate the latest technologies and best management practices into our company."[18]

Right after Cisco launched the infringement litigation, Huawei established a joint venture with 3Com to deliver data communication products in the international market. Also in 2003, Huawei set up a joint venture with Siemens which focused on the research, production, sales, and services of TD-SCDMA. Jointly with Motorola, it set up a UMTS research center in Shanghai, which is engaged in providing global customers with more powerful UMTS products and solutions and HSPA. For the terminal, Huawei cooperated with Infineon Technology to develop the low-cost mobile platform of WCDMA.

Huawei also recognized the importance of mergers and acquisitions in technology obtainment. In early 2002, Huawei accomplished the buyout of OptiMight, enormously enhancing its own technology capabilities in optical transmission. The acquisition of Cognigine also strengthened Huawei's R & D capacity in switches and core processors for routers. All these M & As were based on the assessment of technologies and IPRs and their complementarities with Huawei's technology portfolios.

Fourth, Huawei, giving more emphasis to cutting-edge and future technologies, has actively participated in the process of establishing international standards. Despite having achieved great business success, Huawei has clear recognition of its actual capabilities. In an internal publication, Huawei revealed that for the past eighteen years, it hasn't made any original inventions by itself—all its core technologies were obtained through M & A or patent licensing. In other words, Huawei's products and technologies are mainly based on the modification of existing R & D results by others.[19] Due to this, Huawei takes future technologies such as the All-IP Telecommunication Network (IPTN), Next Generation Network (NGN), Fixed and Mobile Convergence (FMC), etc. as windows of opportunity to leapfrog ahead and deploy patents in advance. Huawei is now a member of 83 standardization organizations (including ITU, 3GPP, and 3GPP2) with over 100 positions accepted. In 2007, a total of 3,072 proposals were submitted, including over 800 proposals in fiber transmission, access network, NGN, IP QoS, and security, and more than 1,500 proposals in mobile core network, service application, and radio access.[20] Huawei accounts for 7 percent of essential patents in 3GPP; as of 2005, it had declared 46 essential patents for ETSI.[21] Now, Huawei's standard patents account for 5 percent of its total patents.[22] More than 300 employees from Huawei participate in the creation of international standards.

The effects of Huawei's IPR strategy is reflected in its patent applications. As mentioned above, Huawei filed nearly 6,000 patent applications accumulatively by the end of 2004. But in just one year, 2005, it filed 5,043 patents, almost 5/6 of the accumulative numbers. As of 2011, Huawei had filed 36,344 patent applications in China, 10,650 under the Patent Cooperation Treaty (PCT), and 10,978 patent applications overseas.[23] The huge increase occurred not only at home, but also abroad. As mentioned before, Huawei's PCT patent applications reached 226 in 2003, placing China in the top tier among developing countries. In 2005, it filed 249 applications under PCT, 2.4 times Cisco's number, ranking China thirty-seventh globally. After one year, its application number doubled and reached 575, exceeding Ericsson and Samsung, just behind Nokia and Qualcomm among all telecommunication firms. Its position on WIPO PCT patent top applicants ranking list moved up from thirty-seventh to thirteenth and accounted for 14.7 percent of China's total PCT applications that year. Finally, as the best symbol of Huawei's successful internationalization and corresponding IPR strategies, according to WIPO, Huawei moved up nine places to become the fourth-largest patent applicant under the WIPO PCT, with 1,365 applications in 2007, following Matsushita, Philips Electronics N.V., and Siemens. It also accounted for one quarter of China's total applications under PCT in that year.[24]

CONCLUSION

Over the last two decades since China's patent law was enacted in 1984, China's IPR system has experienced fundamental changes. Under the same patent system, the responses from domestic and multinational firms operating in China have been very different.

Domestic Chinese firms have followed the route of gradual innovation by taking advantage of design and utility patents in China's patent system. Most Chinese firms have not been able to become true innovators in their corresponding industries, as evidenced by the low number of invention patents granted to Chinese firms, with a few exceptions such as Huawei.

For the most part, multinational companies operating in China have not relied on China's patent system to protect their core technologies. Most multinational companies protect their core technologies through trade secrets and importing key parts from outside China. They use China's patent system to file patents that provide them with strategic competitive advantages rather than to gain monopoly rents from their technological advantages.

However, as Chinese companies' innovative capabilities grow, the responses from the two groups of companies may converge. Huawei's story is a case in point. It followed a competitive strategy, not only relying heavily on IPR protection of its core technologies, but also using its technological advantage to integrate global innovation resources. In the process, it has developed new collaborative relationships with MNCs.

NOTES

1. Here we use invention data instead of patent data because inventions represent the most technology creation compared with the other two forms of patents: industrial designs and utility models.
2. The sample is the same as in our project "Globalization of R & D by MNCs in China" which was commissioned by the Beijing Municipal S & T Committee and carried out in 2004–5.
3. The number at the end of March 2007; see <http://www.huawei.com/corporate_infomation.do>, accessed on September 19, 2012.
4. See Huawei Annual Report (2007: 4).
5. Huawei Annual Report (2007: 27).
6. Tai (2007).

7. See Mu and Lee (2005: 779, table 6).
8. See Huawei Annual Report (2007: 8).
9. Hu and Ran (2003).
10. Guo (2004).
11. *Shenzhen Shangbao* [Shenzhen Business News] (2005).
12. Qiu (2008).
13. Lin (2007: 41).
14. Tai (2007).
15. Hu and Ran (2003).
16. Huawei Annual Report (2007: 8).
17. Huawei Annual Report (2007: 27).
18. Huawei Technologies Co., Ltd (2006), *Annual Report 2005: To Enrich Life through Communication*, p.12, available at <www.huawei.com/mng/ruru/dl?f=626>, accessed on September 19, 2012.
19. Fang (2006).
20. Huawei Annual Report (2007: 8).
21. *Computer Business News* (2005).
22. *Shijie Shangye Baodao* [World Business News] (2007).
23. Source: <http://www.huawei.com/en/about-huawei/corporate-info/research-development/index.htm>, accessed on September 19, 2012.
24. WIPO (2008).

REFERENCES

Alford, W. P. (1995), *To Steal a Book Is an Elegant Offense: Intellectual Property Law in Chinese Civilization* (Stanford: Stanford University Press).

Arrow, K. J. (1962), "Economic Welfare and the Allocation of Resources for Invention," in R. R. Nelson (ed.), *The Rate and Direction of Inventive Activity* (New York: Princeton University Press), 609–26.

Commission on Intellectual Property Rights (2002), *Integrating Intellectual Property Rights and Development Policy* (London: Commission on Intellectual Property Rights), available at <http://www.iprcommission.org/graphic/documents/final_report.htm>.

Computer Business News (2005), "Huawei Leiji Shenqing Zhuanli Tupo Baqian Jian" ["Huawei's Accumulative Filed Patent Applications break through 8,000"], CBINews, September 23.

Ernst, H. (2001), "Patent Applications and Subsequent Changes of Performance: Evidence from Time-Series Cross-Section Analyses on the Firm Level," *Research Policy*, 30: 143–57.

Fang, W. Y. (2006), "Shishiqiushi De Keyan Fangxiang Yu 20 Nian De Jianku Nuli" ["The Practical and Realistic R & D Directions and 20 Years' Hard Efforts"], *Huawei Ren* [*Huawei Person*], 182 (December).

Green, J. and Scotchmer, S. (1995), "On the Division of Profit in Sequential Innovation," *RAND Journal of Economics*, 26: 20–33.

Guo, H. F. (2004), "Huawei vs. Sike, Quanjing Huifang" ["Huawei vs Cisco, Panorama Retrospect"], *Zhongguo Qiyejia* [*China Entrepreneur*], September 28.

Hu, A. (2006), "What and Why do they Patent in China?" Workshop on Greater China's Innovative Capacities: Progress and Challenges, Mimeo (Beijing: Tsinghua University).

Hu, M. and Ran, Y. P. (2003), "Huawei, Hexin Jishu de Tupo Zhilu" ["Huawei, the Breakthrough Road of Core Technologies"], *Remin Rebao* [*People's Daily*], July 28.

Huawei Technologies Co., Ltd (2008), "Annual Report 2007: Enriching Life Through Communication," available at <http://www.huawei.com/ucmf/groups/public/documents/annual_report/092582.pdf>.

La Croix, S. J. and Konan, D. E. (2002), "Intellectual Property Rights in China: The Changing Political Economy of Chinese-American Interests," *The World Economy*, 25/6: 759–88.

Lin, G. X. (2007), "Enterprise Innovation and its Mechanism—Based on the Case Study of Huawei Co. Ltd.," Thesis for Application of Masters Degree of Ji'nan University, Guangzhou, May 8 [in Chinese].

Liu, Y., Xia, M., and Wu, X. (2003), "Measurement Research on Patent of Chinese Top 500 Foreign Investment Corporations and its Influence," *Forecasting*, 22/6: 19–23 [in Chinese].

Macdonald, S. (2004), "When Means Become Ends: Considering the Impact of Patent Strategy on Innovation," *Information Economics and Policy*, 16: 135–58.

Machlup, F. (1958), "An Economic Review of the Patent System," Study of the Subcommittee on Patents, Trademarks, and Copyrights of the Committee on the Judiciary, US Senate, 85th Congress (Washington, DC: Government Printing Office).

Maskus, K. E. and Dougherty, S. M. (1998), "Intellectual Property Rights and Economic Development in China," NBR Regional Studies, Chongqing, 1–30.

Mazzoleni, R. and Nelson, R. R. (1998), "The Benefits and Costs of Strong Patent Protection: A Contribution to the Current Debate," *Research Policy*, 27/3 (July): 273–84.

Merges, R. and Nelson, R. (1990), "On the Complex Economics of Patent Scope," *Columbia Law Review*, 90/4: 839–916.

Mu, Qing and Lee, Keun (2005), "Knowledge Diffusion, Market Segmentation and Technological Catch-up: The Case of the Telecommunication Industry in China," *Research Policy*, 34/6: 759–83.

Nordhaus, W. D. (1962), *Invention, Growth, and Welfare: A Theoretical Treatment of Technological Change* (Cambridge, MA: MIT Press).

OECD (2005), "Intellectual Property Rights in China: Governance Challenges and Prospects," in idem, *Governance in China* (Paris: OECD), 403–32.

—— (2008), "OECD Reviews of Innovation Policy: CHINA" (Paris: OECD).

Qiu, D. K. (2008), "Huawei, Housike Shidai Qiangzhan Zhigaodian" ["Huawei Has Occupied the Commanding Height in Post-Cisco Times"], *Minying Jingji Bao* [*Private Business Newspaper*], July 14.

Scherer, F. M. (1972), "Nordhaus's Theory of Optimal Patent Life: A Geometric Reinterpretation," *American Economic Review*, 62: 422–7.

Scotchmer, S. and Green, J. (1990), "Novelty and Disclosure in Patent Law," *RAND Journal of Economics*, 21: 131–46.

Shenzhen Shangbao [*Shenzhen Business News*] (2005), "Huawei Yanfa Meinian Touru 30 Yi" ["Huawei Invests 3 Billion in R & D Annually"], *Shenzhen Shangbao* [*Shenzhen Business News*], July 21.

Shijie Shangye Baodao [*World Business News*] (2007), "Huawei Meinian Jiqian Xiang Zhuanli Cong Nali Lai Ne?" ["Where did Huawei's Thousands of Patents per Year Come From?"], *Shijie Shangye Baodao* [*World Business News*], January 21.

Sun, Y. (2003), "Determinants of Foreign Patents in China," *World Patent Information*, 25: 27–37.

Tai, T. T. (2007), "Huawei Qiji" ["Miracles of Huawei"], *Zhongguo Pinpai* [*China's Brands*], (July): 36–8.

WIPO (2008), "Unprecedented Number of International Patent Filings in 2007," Geneva, February 21. Available online at: <http://www.wipo.int/pressroom/en/articles/2008/article_0006.html>.

World Bank (2003), *World Development Report 2003: Sustainable Development in a Dynamic World* (New York: World Bank and Oxford University Press).

Zhou, Z., Zhong, H., and Li, J. (2006), "Analysis on Automobile MNCs' Control over China's Joint Ventures," *China's Foreign Trade*, 12: 20–2 [in Chinese].

Zhu, X. and Liang, Z. (2006a), "Patenting Behavior of MNCs in China: An Analysis Based on Panel Data," 15th International Conference on Management of Technology (IAMOT 2006), "East Meets West: Challenges and Opportunities in Era of Globalization," May 22–6, 2006, Beijing.

——— (2006b), "Technology Innovative Capabilities of China's Automobile Industry: A Patent Perspective," in H. Shuhua, Y. Jingdong, and H. Renyong (eds), *International Conference on Auto Industry Innovotion* (Wuhan: Hubei People's Press), 1–6.

10

Property and Intellectual Property Exchanges (PIPEs) in China since the 1990s: An Analysis of the Emergence and Regulatory Resolution of PIPEs and Their Comparative Advantage Over OTC Markets

Heping Cao

INTRODUCTION

This paper seeks to examine a market as a whole—China's Property and Intellectual Property Exchanges (PIPEs)—instead of the behavior of an agent in that market. It looks at the manner in which an individual agent's behavior qua actor in an informal, over-the-counter-style exchange (or "trading spot") is combined with that of his homologues and forged into *integrated action*; this unitary concept takes on different characteristics to a simple market agglomeration of individual choice and ignites reactions from its peripherally connected markets, securities, and credits, etc., and triggers regulation and enforcement. As a result, a market is generated and its border defined, given an institutional matrix.

This being the case, it would challenge the orthodox understanding that the best way for a market to evolve to equilibrium is via the agglomeration of individual choices given a particular regime of private property. In PIPEs, the capital trade market is generated by *group choices*, which, once combined with public-style good elements, demonstrate advantages over a model of individually driven market evolution.

This paper consists of five parts: (1) a literature review of the development of PIPEs with reference to relevant academic schools of thought and a brief overview of its political economy; (2) a short history of PIPEs, taking in the impact of state-owned enterprises (SOEs), restructuring, and 320 over-the-counter (OTC)-style markets; (3) an analysis of the shift from OTC markets to PIPEs, focusing on the interaction between institutional change and public-style goods shortages; (4) a summary of the current status of PIPEs, looking at regulatory gaps and their advantages over OTC markets; and (5) conclusions, including policy proposals and suggestions for further study.

LITERATURE REVIEW AND MINISTERIAL POLITICAL ECONOMY

Studies on PIPEs are few and far between in existing economic literature due to their novelty and the rudimentary nature of the Chinese capital market, which has lagged far behind the fast-growing goods market.

Two closely related schools

Studies from two related schools of thought dealing with China's spectacular growth provide a useful background to understanding the development of PIPEs. The *decentralization* school privileges the increase in local autonomy as a causative factor of Chinese economic growth; the central authority devolves autonomous power to localities, which includes fiscal decentralization and control rights over a substantial amount of resources, regionalizing economic revitalization and expansion (Granick 1990; Naughton 1994, 1995; Qian and Xu 1993; Shirk 1993; Oi 1999). The genesis of decentralization has been traced as far back as the end of 1950s, right after the Great Leap Movement (Xu 2007). The *federalism* school builds on the idea of decentralization. It contends that economic decentralization is coupled to a central appointment and promotion mechanism for officials. This effectively demarcates the economic and political spheres, creating a degree of decentralized market freedom while maintaining executive control through personnel management: a federation-comparable system in economy[1] (Maskin, Qian, and Xu 2000; Lin and Liu 2000; Jin, Qian, and Weingast 2005; Li and Zhou 2005).

These concepts of decentralization and federalization have remained macroeconomic and have not yet been extended to an examination of individual choice under these regimes, especially in the context of capital markets. This paper seeks to do so in relation to PIPEs, which developed owing to decentralization and federalization that began in the early 1990s.

Ministerial political economy and the development of PIPEs

This paper takes a heterogeneous view of political economy: that is, the government is not an atomic unity composed of departments that pursue public interests in a homogenous fashion (Fisk 1985). Rather, branches of the government have heterogeneous interests; when these interests (and branches) compete with each other, their choices (often representing group interests) can drift away from those of the public. This means that ministerial economic policy may be a trade-off between national and group (or ministry) interests, which could leave the locals to fulfill public purposes (if regional gains exceed costs, the local pursuit of development in regards to a specific project or industry is usually compatible with the goal of national growth).

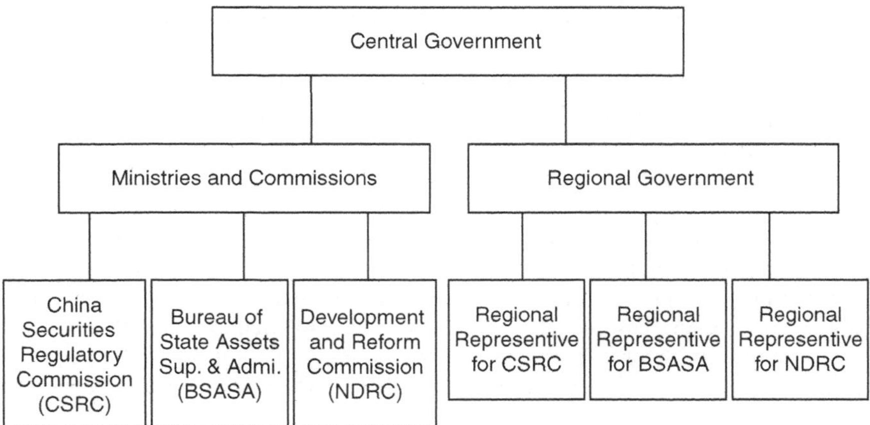

Figure 10.1. PIPEs-related ministries and commissions

Such a scenario represents the development of PIPEs. As shown in Figure 10.1, there is a set of two crucial principal-agent problems. The first lies between the central government and its ministries. In the 1990s, the rapid expansion of OTC-style markets (situated at trading spots), scattered around the country, improved the efficiency of national capital markets and increased local revenue. However, these markets were owned by locals and under the supervision of the Bureau of State Assets Supervision and Administration (BSASA).[2] They thus represented an encroachment on the supervisory power and jurisdiction of the China Securities Regulatory Commission (CSRC), a central body. The CSRC therefore suppressed over 90 percent of these markets.

The second principal–agent problem lies between the ministry and its regional branches. The ministry is the principal and its local branches are the agent. However, the agent's personal appointments and promotions are controlled by local governments. In instances when the principal's interest deviates from that of the public (for example, as it competes for supervisory and regulatory powers at the national level and runs into a political impasse), local agents could stand by their local interest to gain benefits from the local government. Such an institutional dynamic shaped the expansion of PIPEs in the 1990s.

THE GENESIS OF PIPEs: SOE RESTRUCTURING AND 320 OTC-STYLE MARKETS

In the middle of the 1980s, China's agenda of reform for its SOEs began to incorporate and require an understanding of corporate governance. This produced a *de facto* precursor to PIPEs—an early capital market for SOEs.

Prelude: two separations of SOEs and Zhucheng's dare

Vertical and horizontal separations

Under the Chinese planned economy, SOEs were controlled by a *vertical* bureaucratic system, which directed planning, pricing, resource allocation, and even wage rates. Such a system made SOEs the "workshops" of administrative branches, distant from market frontiers. Managerial teams were thus to deal with the task of internal resource allocation. SOEs were also *horizontally integrated* into a bureaucratic welfare regime: they were designed to undertake social roles, such as providing job opportunities, housing, schooling, medical care, etc., for employees. With so many competing imperatives built into their corporate structures, any attempt to divorce SOEs from these horizontal and vertical structures (Zhengqi Fenli) would be a mammoth task of reform for SOEs as economic entities.

Zhucheng's dare

In 1991, a young man, Guang Chen, was nominated as the party secretary of Zhucheng, Shandong Province (a northern near-coastal city). During his first routine inspection of SOEs after assuming his new position, he was surprised to notice that more than 99 percent of them were losing money following the years-long reform of vertical and horizontal systems governing SOEs. Shocked and determined to act, Chen dared to essay a reform, selling all of the SOEs to insiders, including the employees and managers (Xiong 2008).

The sell-off was partially brave and partially awkward. It was brave as it sold SOEs to individuals, breaking a social taboo in a society that was not ready to accept individuals holding state-owned assets; it was awkward as those individuals were insiders (to provide sufficient incentives for employees working in high efforts). This ambiguity can be justified as a compromise to ensure the (reserved) acceptance of the central authority as part of its incentive goal and budget alleviation. Importantly, however, the central authority did not see Zucheng's reform for what it really was: a dare, creating a capital trade market (albeit limited to insiders).

The genesis of 320 OTC-style markets

With no general market to serve as a vehicle for capital allocation amongst these SOEs, it was assumed that local leaders, the most informed "insiders," would take the position of market-makers. The sell-off opened up opportunities for restricted capital goods reallocation while creating rent-seeking opportunities.

Insiders' and outsiders' stock-bonds

Starting in 1985, however, enterprises tried shareholding experiments: companies issued shares (called "Guquanzheng") to insider employees to replenish liquid capital. With the rate of dividend and the payback dates of the principal specified, this was in essence a corporate bond plus an equity option (a "stock-bond," "stock," or "share"). The share-owner could execute the shareholder's option before the debt was repaid. Although no transfer right was attached, the Guquanzheng was tradable in nature due to its divisible, bipartite structure. However, owing to the ambiguity of its classification as debt or equity, the issuance of Guquanzheng did not violate the most fundamental of central prohibitions: that of selling off SOEs to the private sector.

Following this, Sichuan, a southwestern province, was allowed to carry out an experiment in the late 1980s: transforming internal corporate stock-bonds into certified instruments (i.e., standardization). Furthermore, "outsiders" were allowed to participate in the experiment, buying what were called "original stocks." Over a three- to five-year period, similar experiments were carried out across the nation.

A restricted equilibrium

As a precaution, the central government kept a close and watchful eye on the experiment. In 1992, the National Reform Committee issued an order: *A Proposal Regulation for Shareholding Firms (PRSF 1992)*. This specifically prohibited the trade of stocks held by insiders, except those sold to outsiders. In PRSF 1992, the central government clearly deemed stocks to be securities with two separate functions: (1) to be sold to outsiders for fundraising; and (2) to be issued to insiders as an incentive. They were not a form of property with trading rights.

The Shenzhen and Shanghai stock exchanges provided the institutional framework for the trade of outsiders' stocks (most of them associated with institutional investors) in the beginning of 1990s. However, two-thirds of the total shares owned by the state and employees were not traded on markets, meaning that activity at the Shanghai and Shenzhen exchanges was low. The reason for low trading levels was that the majority of shareholders considered their stocks to be dividend generators, or a dividend-based bond; PRSF thus created a restricted equilibrium in the stock market.

Hongmiaozi Market: individual behavior integrated into group action

The upshot of the restricted equilibrium was that a large number of stocks were waiting for the right trading opportunity. Then, in 1992, Shanghai and Shenzhen's stock markets began to boom. Stock prices were pushed up much higher than their book price. The holders of nontradable shares realized that there should be a trading right attached to the piece of paper alongside the dividend right. In April, news leaked out that Sichuan Chemical Salt Industry Group Co. Ltd (SCSI) would be listed in Shenzhen. Speculators began to purchase SCSI stocks from insiders at local trading spots, doing so over book value. This purchasing behavior quickly extended to general outsiders.

On one street of Chengdu, Hongmiaozi, local residents gathered together to trade unlisted stocks. The turnover rate at Hongmiaozi was surprisingly high as investors tried to harvest returns through price differences between trading spots on various dates. At first glance, the trading spot at Hongmiaozi was a typical

OTC market,[3] in which limited information was revealed and market-makers played a dominant role.

At the spot, a stock was registered under its owner's name. If a holder intended to exercise its trading right, he was required to present the stock with the owner's identification documents. At this point, it was uncertain whether the company whose stock was to be traded would list on Shenzhen Exchange. The owner's ID was thus required, as the local OTC-style market could not otherwise grant the holder legal status to exercise dividend and re-trade rights. In other words, trading a stock at a trading spot required the stock-owner's ID, which guaranteed the protection of defined property rights.

This model created two interlinked problems. On one hand, the seller's interests could be harmed by the unlawful use of his ID. On the other hand, if the seller claimed his ID was lost and applied for a new one, the buyer might not be able to exercise his rights deriving from the bought stocks. The potential for moral hazard and subsequent adverse selection stopped the market from expanding beyond trades between colleagues, neighbors, and friends.

These problems led to the integration of an individual trader's choices or preferences into *group action* to solve the two problems: market participants unanimously demanded that local authorities accept as valid copies of identification documents. Roughly in the middle of 1991, a copy of the owner's ID along with a letter of authorization began to be accepted when executing trades. Both the moral hazard and adverse selection problems were thus solved. This innovation, simple as it was, decreased transaction costs dramatically and, hence, increased participation and trade volume.

Genesis: a concession and the emergence of 320 OTC-style trading spots

Later in the year, the authorities in Hongmiaozi conceded, accepting copies of ID for stock registration. In other areas, similar group actions were taking place. In 1988, Wuhan, the capital of Hubei, a central province, established the Enterprise Mergers and Acquisitions Service, a primary OTC market. In 1990, Beijing set up a similar system, the Stock Trade Automated Quotation (STAQ); in 1993, Zibo, a city in the northeast of Shandong province, set up a local version of the STAQ system (ZBSTAQ); in the same year Shenzhen, a special economic zone next to Hong Kong, set up the National Electronic Trade (Net) System. It was estimated that by the end of 1993 there were about 320 OTC-style markets across the country.

FROM OTCs TO PIPEs: INSTITUTIONAL MUTATION WITH PUBLIC-STYLE GOODS SHORTAGES

Group action at trading spots can be conceptualized as a market force, demanding a set of public-style goods[4] otherwise missing from the economy. The interests of the various branches of the public sector were not aligned with the public desire for the provision of such services; group action thus directed trading spots towards another channel of transformation.

The failure of the 320 OTC-style markets

Central and local interests were in conflict with regards to the trading of stocks. The center preferred to make SOEs profitable by solidifying, rather than selling off, its administrative control. Even when stocks were sold, the central administration preferred that this happen in Shanghai or Shenzhen, where trading was limited to the one-third of stocks owned by outsiders. This stopped the center from losing control over SOEs; furthermore, Shanghai and Shenzhen were directly under the control of CSRC. By contrast, the 320 trading spots could potentially remove control of SOEs from the center and threaten Shanghai and Shenzhen's trade volume.

In contrast, local authorities had little incentive to enforce central orders restricting OTC-style markets as they gained two distinct benefits: (1) attracting funds and mobilizing local savings; and (2) relieving budget burdens by restructuring SOEs. Furthermore, the use of copied IDs had become accepted practice; if local authorities suddenly decided to enforce central edicts restricting this, the impact on markets would be severe and previous trades would be invalid, causing uncertainty and possibly unrest. As local authorities acquiesced to the operation of OTC-style markets, regional trading spots survived and even developed to varying degrees.

This expansion led to new problems: (1) many employees, teachers and students, and even officials sought out spots with beneficial trade margins. This affected their primary job or activity and led to the trading of insider information for money and power; (2) the loan and borrowing markets were significantly affected as savings in local banks were withdrawn to purchase stocks; (3) companies issued stocks in local markets without accompanying permissions or regulation over information disclosure. For example, the author learned from a field investigation that a central provincial hospital issued stocks and sold them in a market for 4.00 RMB a share. When the fraudulent nature of the transaction was revealed, thousands of buyers rushed to the hospital seeking compensation, to local offices seeking to complain, and to public sites seeking to protest. This was not an isolated incident, and the resultant chaos was repeated in many locations.

The market for missing public-style goods

This chaos demonstrated a shortage in the provision of particular public-style goods. If a database and an agent were provided through which copies of ID could be verified, the Hongmiaozi trading spot would be more efficient and its reach expanded. Such public-style goods could be supplied either by existing authorities (governmental branches) or by legal structures enforceable by a benevolent court of law that would form part of this enterprise.

Private firms could also provide most of these public-style goods, such as database services and transaction notifications, but the sunk costs would be high and the legislative process allowing for private provision would be lengthy. Given either mechanism of provision, a nonrival and nonexcludable or nonrival but excludable (a Buchanan-style club) set of public-style goods that filtered out noncredit stocks and certified valid ones would assist local spots in growing into an integrated OTC-style market.

In the late 1990s, the public sector was the institution that provided such public goods at low cost. Given the heterogeneity of interests of local branches of government and the fragmented nature of the database, however, even central enforcement of efforts to integrate a database would be insufficient to provide reliable information for firms. The institutional infrastructure and the intermediary market for a set of these public-style goods simply did not exist.

The turmoil caused by improper stock issuance created a situation in which local administrative interests became congruent with those of the center: the combination of mass withdrawals of savings from local banks and gatherings of traders at public sites would damage local reputation and growth. In March 1993, the State Council of the PRC issued an order prohibiting the issuance of equity stocks to insiders without official permission; further, it required locals to take action to stop illegal trading in stocks and restrict trading spots. The link between local trading spots and the two national stock markets was severed. As expectations that local stocks would be listed on the national market in the near future died away, levels of speculative investment withered and the OTC-style markets suffered. In 1998, it was estimated that there were approximately thirty trading spots, less than 10 percent of their peak. The local public interests that backed the trading sports were disbanded as well. In 1998, the East Asian financial crisis provided an opportunity for the center to close down the BSASA (the precursor to today's SASAC), the body that directed and supported the trading spots at the national level in competition with CSRC.

The renaissance of capital markets: OTC's institutional mutation to PIPEs

During this period, the internet revolution was taking place and the network economy was booming. The central government was aware that it had been left behind. Around the turn of the century, the Ministry of Science and Technology set up intellectual property exchanges (IPEs). IPEs were designed to facilitate the trade in intellectual property. Their market practices and profit-driven nature led them to employ many former staff from the network of dismantled OTC trading spots, particularly as their trade framework was based on that of the old OTC markets. It was estimated that there were more than 200 IPEs, which conducted most of the business relating to former OTC stocks. In retrospect, it seems that IPEs' institutional genetic material was taken from the OTC markets.

At this point, locals began participating in unlisted equity trading again (albeit quietly). Over the years, many locals realized that the Shanghai and Shenzhen stock exchanges did not provide enough services to satisfy their needs.[5] The creation of IPEs was an ideal conduit for them and restored the operation of a type of OTC-style market. It lacked one feature of the old system: speculative capital was not as forthcoming as under the old regime, as the link between local spots and national markets was severed.

On March 24, 2003, SASAC was established, incorporating the employees of its now-defunct predecessor, BSASA. On March 31, 2003, the State Council issued the Enterprise's SOE Shares Transfer and Management Code. Former trading spots were reconstituted as Property Exchanges (PEs), in order to avoid a continuation with the names of the old OTC-style system. Later that year, PEs and IPEs were combined by localities into joint exchanges: the Property and Intellectual Property Exchanges (PIPEs). Today, it is estimated that there are over 250 PIPEs.

As IPEs, PEs, and PIPEs developed, they became in essence an enlargement of, a genetic mutation from, the former OTC regime, in which almost everything that carried information asymmetries could be traded: private equity, intellectual property, real estate, instruments, paintings, and even lucky number plates. More recently, this institutional regime has expanded to cover the trading of waste products, pollution emissions, forest rights, precious teas, etc. PIPEs consist of the processing and trading of, and the regional information networks for, a whole spectrum of capital assets.

THE CURRENT STATUS OF PIPEs: REGULATORY GAPS AND ADVANTAGES OVER OTCs MARKET

The growth of PIPEs has benefited locals and created a regulatory space for related ministries. Moreover, public participation in PIPEs has increased the effectiveness of several public-style goods: the mechanisms for disclosure and auction surpass their forebears in the OTC-style system, meaning the monopoly enjoyed by a market-maker is minimized.

Ministerial negligence and power-sharing incentives

The early stages of PIPEs' extraordinary growth took place in the context of indifference and negligence at the ministerial level. This led to regulatory gaps and induced conflict between departments for power and control over the new exchanges. SASAC, the institution that put its weight behind PIPEs from the start, aggressively claimed supervisory and regulatory jurisdiction over the new exchanges despite the fact that its official, legislated-for terms of reference envisage it acting on behalf of the state to hold state-owned assets, rather than to regulate and supervise capital markets (Cao 2009).

The supervisory domain of CSRC (the body that shut down the OTC-style markets) was threatened by SASAC and the new exchanges. In response, CSRC single-handedly invested a substantial amount of capital in an electronic system supporting OTC trades around the country. This was envisaged as a competitor to the locally-focused PIPEs but was never put into use.

The National Development and Reform Commission (NDRC), with a department supervising small- and medium-sized SOEs, also jostled for regulatory position, seeking to take administrative power and reduce the influence of SASAC and CSRC. Given its existing supervisory role, any extension in its jurisdiction to cover PIPEs would make it both player and umpire as regards the exchange, creating a no-win situation for others.

The fight for power over PIPEs extends to a heterogeneous wealth of other ministry-level agencies, such as the National Intellectual Property Agency, the Ministry of Science and Technology, the State Administration of Taxation, the State Administration for Industry and Commerce, and the Government Offices Administration of the State Council. The most interesting political development has seen the Disciplinary Committee of CCCPC, in charge of Party anticorruption issues, supporting the development of PIPEs from the macro perspective of state welfare rather than the Committee's own interests.[6] Owing to these power disputes, no coordinated political will has been applied to stimulate PIPEs' development. It is possible to view this through the lens of collective action, seeing the lack of political coherence as creating a power equilibrium in which PIPEs operate.

The advantages of PIPEs over OTC-style markets

The volatile transformation of capital markets during the first three quarters of the 1990s left the PIPEs isolated from the stock market, becoming a wide-ranging capital trade market and requiring the disclosure of asymmetric information. PIPEs have several advantages over an OTC-style market when fulfilling this role.

Traditional OTC markets offer an alternative mechanism to trade financial instruments. Two of their most important attributes are limited publicity and the monopoly enjoyed by market-makers (Walter 1957). Limited publicity curtails speculative activity while market-makers benefit from monopolies thanks to price discrimination, acting as an intermediary between the parties to a trade and harvesting the rents from asymmetric information. PIPEs get around (or at least reduce the effects of) these problems owing to local public participation and information transparency (through its system of auctions and charge of a flat-rate fee). Transaction costs are thus lower than a typical OTC market.

A final advantage is found in the treatment of capital goods. Some capital goods are created and processed using local public goods. For example, if a product whose value contained a large intellectual property component was to be traded on a PIPE, it may require patent registration and a start-up firm undertaking experimental production may be granted funds and services. The IP product, packaged with its experimental production sites, could easily be traded on a capital market through equity transactions. PIPEs thus acts like a capital goods superstore while OTC-style markets are analogous to old retail stores.

POLICY PROPOSALS AND FURTHER STUDIES

Policy proposals

The survey has shown both the development and deviation of PIPEs from a typical OTC market. It has also shown that this is the consequence of conflicts of interest amongst central administrative branches and of public-style goods shortages. The PIPEs system is currently unavailable to listed companies. However, given local support, it can provide more public goods and play the role of a capital goods supermarket. Further analysis should be focused on how to homogenize the interests and incentives of the ministry-level agencies. The best solution may be to build a new institution by combining all relevant departments, such as SASAC's PIPE department, the CSRC's OTC electronic division, and NDRC's small and medium-sized enterprises division. A unified institution could better execute the mandates of the legislative process, helping to solve policy gaps at the national level.

Further studies

This survey has shown how Chinese PIPEs play a crucial role in refining theories of development economics and political economy. Perhaps the most important lesson is that the pure rival goods of the Arrow–Debreu model need to be revised when in the context of a capital market in which any tradable good is a combination of rival and nonrival elements. Further studies might take the following form: first, a systematic re-examination of the definitions and functions of Chinese central government and regional government. An analysis of conflicts of interest between central ministries and regional governments should provide a reasonable explanation for the late development of Chinese capital markets. Second, a close study of the intersections between and overlaps of the functions and duties of different ministries and commissions will give a new perspective to those seeking to understand the poor efficiency of government institutions. Finally, the extension and application of traditional club theory to capital markets such as PIPEs and OTCs would shed new light on that old concept.

APPENDIX

PIPEs transaction process

The process of a typical PIPEs transaction can be summarized as follows (see also Figure 10.2).

1. Transferors entrust brokers to draw up entrustment contracts.
2. Then, they apply for registration in a PIPE for publicity.
3. If a potential transferee so desires, they will register conditions of sale with the property exchange. The exchange will handle these conditions and list them on its board, usually for a month (22 working days).
4. The property exchange accepts bidders who meet the conditions, confirms check deposits, selects transfer methods, and organizes the selected transaction method (chosen from several different methods, including agreements, bidding, auctions, network competing, etc.).
5. The two parties sign the Contract of Equity Transaction (CET) and settle price and payment after the transaction.
6. The property exchange issues a transaction certification after completion of the auction, with which the two parties could present for equity transfers.

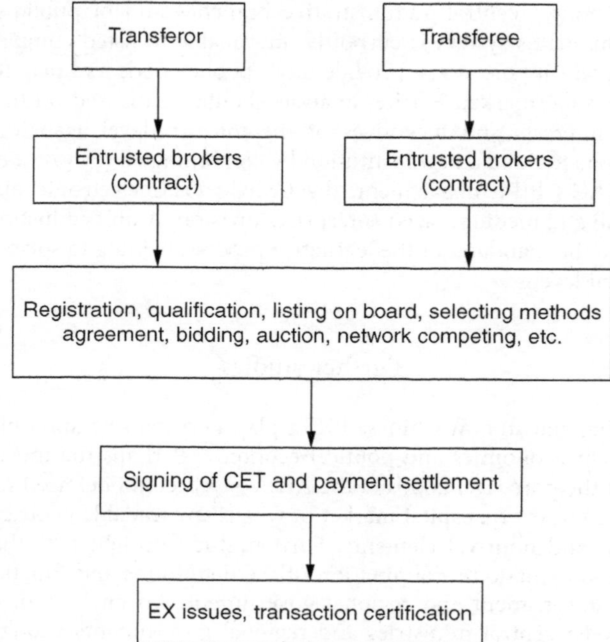

Figure 10.2. Transaction process in a typical property exchange

NOTES

1. Federalism is a system in which the power to govern is shared between national and central (state) governments, creating what is often called a federation. Proponents are often called federalists.
2. The agency changed its name to the State-owned Assets Supervision and Administration Commission (SASAC) in 2003.
3. Over-the-counter trading involves the direct trading of financial instruments between two parties. Information is usually limited and market-makers benefit from monopolies.
4. A useful example of a nonexclusive, nonrival public good is a streetlight. There are, however, examples that are nonrival but enjoy potential exclusivity, such as a coded TV broadcast, a certification network, etc. I denote goods that fall into these two broad categories "public-style goods" rather than public goods, as they can be provided by the private or local public sectors.
5. Over a decade, the listed companies on the two exchanges numbered fewer than a thousand. It is estimated that there were some 700,000–1,000,000 businesses that would have qualified for such a listing but who lacked direct access to channels of finance.

6. The Committee's interests and the interests of the state are compatible with regard to this issue, as the sell-off of SOEs' assets is more transparent through PIPEs.

REFERENCES

Baumol, W. and Sidak, J. G. (1995), "Transmission Pricing and Stranded Costs in The Electric Power Industry" (Washington, DC: American Enterprise Institute (AEI) Press).

Bratland, J. (2004), "Contestable Market Theory as A Regulatory Framework: An Austrian Postmortem," *Quarterly Journal of Austrian Economics*, 7/3: 3–28.

Cao, H. (2009), "PIPEs Development, Theory, Current Status and Policy," in H. Cao (ed.), *Annual Report on the China's Property and Intellectual Property Exchanges* (Beijing: Social Sciences Academic Press).

China M&A Market Almanac 2005 (2005) (Shanghai: Shanghai Science & Technology Literature Publishing House).

China M&A Market Almanac 2006 (2006) (Shanghai: Shanghai Science & Technology Literature Publishing House).

China M&A Market Almanac 2007 (2007) (Shanghai: Shanghai Science & Technology Literature Publishing House).

Fisk, D. M. (1985), "Productivity Trends in the Federal Government," *Labor Review*, 108: 3–9.

Granick, D. (1990), *Chinese State Enterprises: A Regional Property Rights Analysis* (Chicago: Chicago University Press).

Groves, T. and Ledyard, J. (1977), "Optimal Allocation of Public Goods: A Solution to the Free Rider Problem," *Econometrica*, 45: 783–810.

Jin, H., Qian, Y., and Weingast, B. R. (2005), "Regional Decentralization and Fiscal Incentives: Federalism, Chinese Style," *Journal of Public Economics*, 89/9–10: 1719–42.

Li, H. and Zhou, L. (2005), "Political Turnover and Economic Performance: The Incentive Role of Personnel Control in China," *Journal of Public Economics*, 89: 1743–62.

Lin, J. and Liu, Z. (2000), "Fiscal Decentralization and Economic Growth in China," *Economic Development and Cultural Change*, 49/1: 1–21.

Maskin, E., Qian, Y., and Xu, C. (2000), "Incentives, Information, and Organizational Form," *Review of Economic Studies*, 67/2: 359–78.

Naughton, B. (1994), "Chinese Institutional Innovation and Privatization from Below," *American Economic Review*, 84/2: 266–70.

—— (1995), *Growing Out of Plan: Chinese Economic Reform, 1978–1993* (New York: Cambridge University Press).

Oi, J. (1999), *Rural China Takes Off: An Institutional Foundations of Economic Reform* (Berkeley: University of California Press).

Qian, Y. and Xu, C. (1993), "Why China's Economic Reform Differ: The M-Form Hierarchy and Entry/Expansion of the Non-state Sector," *Economics of Transition*, 1/2: 135–70.

Shirk, S. L. (1993), *The Political Logic of Economic Reform in China* (Berkeley: University of California Press).

Varian, H. (1974), "Equity, Envy, and Efficiency," *Journal of Economic Theory*, 9: 63–91.

—— (1992), *Microeconomic Analysis*, 3rd edn (New York: Norton & Company).

Xiong, Y. (2008), *Ziben de Shengyan* [A Carnival of Capital Trade] (Peking: Peking University Press).

Xu, C. (2007), "Chinese Reform and Chinese Regional Decentralization," mimeo, LSE and HKUST Hong Kong University of Science and Technology.

Walter, J. E. (1957), *The Role of Regional Security Exchanges* (Berkeley: University of California Press).

Zhang, S. (1996), *Case Studies in China's Institutional Change* (Shanghai: Shanghai People's Publishing House).

11

The China Aviation Oil Episode: Law and Development in China and Singapore

Curtis J. Milhaupt and Katharina Pistor

INTRODUCTORY COMMENTS

The case study on the "China Aviation Oil (CAO) Episode"[1] has been included in this volume for two reasons. First, it introduces a new methodological approach to the comparative study of legal systems that contrasts with the dominant paradigm of best-practice standards espoused by the law and finance literature and the World Bank's "Doing Business" indicators. Second, it sheds at least indirect light on the governance challenges China faces as it embraces marketization and globalization and in the process increasingly interfaces with the governance regimes of other countries.

NEW METHODOLOGY: INSTITUTIONAL AUTOPSIES

In the 1990s a particular approach to comparative legal and institutional analysis and policy advice gained much currency. The basic premise of these literatures is that all systems face essentially similar tasks in promoting economic development, but that some systems have been better at developing optimal institutional structures to pursue those tasks than others. This literature identified the protection of investor rights as a critical ingredient for financial market development (Shleifer and Vishny 1997); some even drew the direct connection to economic growth (Mahoney 2001).[2] If only countries could design institutions that would adequately protect investor rights, financial markets would flourish and economies would develop.[3] Consistent with this reasoning, a database was created that purportedly measures the quality of investor rights—initially for forty-nine countries around the world (La Porta et al. 1998). This and subsequent studies informed the World Bank's "Doing Business" indicators, which now consists of a substantial database of legal indicators.[4] The quality of law is largely associated with a country's legal origin. Common-law countries are said to have by and large better legal institutions than do civil law systems. Legal origin in this context is defined as a "style of social control of economic life" (La Porta, Lopez-de-Silanes, and Shleifer 2008), which is largely path-dependent (Glaeser and Shleifer 2002). Nonetheless, proponents of the legal origin theory still express confidence that specific legal devices may be transferred from one legal system to another and achieve positive economic outcomes (La Porta, Lopez-de-Silanes, and Shleifer 2008).

In *Law and Capitalism: What Corporate Crises Reveal about Legal Systems and Economic Development Around the World*[5] we take a very different approach to the analysis of comparative legal systems. Building on the literature of comparative capitalism (Hall and Soskice 2001) and the growth experiences of countries in Asia and Europe in the second half of the twentieth century (Wade 2003; Pistor and Wellons 1999), which remains largely unexplained by legal origins theories, we postulate that there are many ways in which legal systems interact with and can support economic growth and development. We also suggest that law is not only about protecting individual property rights and providing institutions for enforcing such rights. Instead, law can perform multiple functions with some legal systems emphasizing certain functions more than others.

We identify three other major functions of the law in addition to protection, namely coordination, signaling, and credibility enhancement. Coordinative law refrains from allocating well-delineated individual rights and instead gives parties a place at the bargaining table. In this sense it is not "unprotective," but places greater emphasis on participatory over individually enforceable rights and interests. Signaling refers to the use of law as a means for conveying a general intention to follow certain principles or policies. Laws that are meant to signal may embrace certain normative goals, but not necessarily offer effective mechanisms for their implementation as implementation is left to nonlegal governance mechanisms. Finally, using legal devices for implementing policies may enhance the credibility of such policies, at least in countries where law is regarded as authoritative.

Not only does law perform different functions in different systems, but legal systems are also organized differently. Some are highly centralized with limited access to influencing lawmaking and law enforcement processes. Others are highly decentralized leaving the initiation of lawmaking and law enforcement processes to dispersed individuals and/or interest groups. Neither the function nor the organization of the legal system is static. Both change over time and in response to broader socioeconomic change that affects the composition of constituencies, which may or may not support a particular configuration of law and legal system.

This framework does not lend itself to simple tests using binary variables that might be added up to aggregate indices. It requires an alternative approach, one that we have labeled "institutional autopsy." An institutional autopsy is a case study that uses an event, such as the breakdown of governance at a firm or of a market, as the starting point for analyzing the systemic vulnerabilities of the underlying governance system. Understanding the event itself is secondary to using the event as a means for investigating the governance regime. Indeed, a critical aspect of the analysis is to demonstrate that the event is not an outlier in the sense that it does reveal critical aspects of the system. The obvious parallel is an academic clinician who performs an autopsy not simply for identifying the cause of death in a patient, but for learning something about a complex system, in this case the human body. In our case, the complex system is the legal system and its interface with the political and economic system.

We employed this analytical approach to a number of corporate crises, which in addition to CAO included cases from the United States, Germany, Japan, South Korea, and Russia. Our conclusions can be summarized as follows. First, many crises have similar symptoms (i.e., fraud, misappropriation of assets), but their root causes differ across systems. Second, a specific legal rule (the equivalent of a legal indicator in the World Bank's "Doing Business" database) hardly ever explains why a system fails or what it takes to put it back on track. Any such analysis requires taking seriously the notion that law is a system of social ordering. It requires identifying the key players involved in the crisis, their interest in using law or alternative governance mechanisms prior to or in response to the crisis, and their relation to those in political or economic positions of power with their own preferences for certain modes of social ordering. Third, important differences in legal systems can be captured by focusing on the organization of legal systems (whether they are centralized or decentralized) and the dominant function law performs in these systems, in particular whether law is more "protective" or more "coordinative." Fourth, while there is some affinity between legal origin and the organization of legal systems, we find that there is as much variation among countries belonging to the same legal family as there is between representative countries of different legal families.

THE CAO CASE: LESSONS FOR CHINA

CAO is a subsidiary of the Chinese holding company (CAOHC) from mainland China. The company was incorporated in Singapore and traded on the Singapore Stock Exchange. The story of CAO's collapse and its eventual recapitalization and relisting on the Singapore Stock Exchange allowed us to analyze the role of legal governance not only in Singapore, but also in China. The story is recounted in full below, but it might be worth emphasizing the major lessons we draw from the crisis especially for China.

First, CAOHC's attempt to rescue CAO may have been fully consistent with governance priorities and practices inside mainland China where parent companies tend to take responsibility for their subsidiaries (i.e., their "children"). The very same strategy, however, turned out to be in conflict with insider trading rules Singapore had adopted and that now prevail in many countries around the world.[6] The fact that CAOHC tried to rescue CAO by placing part of the shares it held in the company with private investors in order to raise fresh capital for CAO—without disclosing to them the dire state of CAO's finances—suggests that it seriously misjudged the possibility that legal rules prevailing in Singapore might have implications not only for CAO, but also for its parent company. Third, while CAOHC ultimately had to pay a fine for insider trading, this was part of a broader package aimed at revitalizing CAO and thereby protecting more important interests that Singapore and China share. The Singaporean authorities were interested in signaling to global investors that they would enforce investor rights impartially. At the same time, they were undoubtedly aware of the fact that

Chinese companies account for a significant proportion of new listings on the Singapore Stock Exchange. This helps explain why Singapore's sovereign wealth fund Temasek recapitalized CAO at the same time that regulatory authorities slapped CAOHC with a fine for insider trading. After all, Temasek also holds a large stake in the Singapore Stock Exchange.

China had equally complex interests, some of which were congruent with those of Singapore while others were not. The CAO case illustrates that governing companies that are located abroad is more challenging than governing them at home. Many of the mechanisms that operate domestically, including information channels and oversight by party officials inside a company, are not as easily available for companies that operate outside that system. This implies that parent companies may face greater agency problems and potential abuse by foreign subsidiaries. They may therefore want to piggyback on foreign governance regimes to control subsidiaries. However, this does not imply that they wish to expose their domestic governance regime to foreign regulatory control. Mitigating these conflicting interests requires coordination with foreign regulatory authorities.

In Singapore coordination was possible, because Singapore's own governance regime is fairly centralized and highly coordinative. While Singapore is formally a common-law country, the enforcement of investor protection primarily takes the form of central regulatory intervention and coordination, not individual rights protection. China's governance regime also displays strong features of centralization and coordination. In China, the major "coordinator" is the Communist Party; in Singapore it is the founding family and an elite core of government bureaucrats. A major question that China faces going forward is whether coordination with foreign authorities can resolve regime conflicts that may be exposed by subsidiaries located in countries around the world. In countries where enforcement is more dispersed this may be more difficult and could expose parent companies to greater legal challenges than they faced in Singapore. A related, and perhaps even more challenging question is whether a highly centralized coordinative regime can be effective in the long term for a country of the size of China. As the economy grows and becomes more complex, so do the challenges of governance. Most of the successful coordinative systems we know (Japan, Germany, South Korea, Singapore, etc.) were tested in much smaller settings. As we point out in our book, even in these countries economic growth, and in particular the process of globalization, have put strains on these systems—mostly by new entrants, whether foreigners or domestic agents, embracing alternative norms and mechanisms of governance. Similar processes are under way in China and will need to be addressed eventually. An important question is how open the existing governance regime is to contestation by new entrants, which we identify as a critical mechanism for change in law and governance over time.

THE CHINA AVIATION OIL EPISODE: LAW AND DEVELOPMENT IN CHINA AND SINGAPORE

China is the latest and biggest of the economic miracles. Since its market opening in 1978, the Chinese economy has grown at an average annual rate of almost

10 percent, lifting perhaps hundreds of millions of people out of poverty. It accomplished this without a legal system that meets conventional notions of functionality and predictability. Surely the experience of China can tell us a great deal about the relation between law and economic development.

This institutional autopsy begins with the collapse of a company called China Aviation Oil (CAO), which was listed on the Singapore Stock Exchange (hereinafter SGX) but controlled by a mainland Chinese holding company with close ties to the state. The events of interest are not the problems that triggered the collapse of CAO but what these problems—and the parent company's response—reveal about the governance structure of Chinese state-controlled firms. The response included the sale of a substantial block of CAO shares owned by the parent company in an off-exchange placement to raise capital for a bailout of CAO—without accurately disclosing the financial status of CAO or the reasons for the share placement. Also heavily involved in the episode were Singaporean financial regulators and Temasek Holdings, a Singaporean state-owned investment company (hereinafter Temasek). Thus, the CAO case also provides an interesting perspective on the role of law in Singapore, one of the "Asian tigers." Singapore's model of law and growth, in turn, raises tantalizing suggestions for China as it continues to reform its legal and economic structures.

THE STORY

On 29 November 2004, CAO announced that it had suffered losses of US$550 million in oil derivatives trading and sought bankruptcy protection from its creditors in Singapore. Singapore's Securities Investor Association called the event a corporate governance disaster comparable to an earthquake registering 7 to 8 on the Richter scale and likened the incident to the collapse of Barings after the revelation of massive rogue trading losses, also incurred in derivatives trading in Singapore.[7]

The tale of massive derivative losses stemming from misguided trading strategies is a familiar one around the world. Less commonplace is the origin and ownership structure of CAO. The firm was formed in Singapore in 1993 as a joint venture between the China Aviation Oil Supply Corporation (CAOSC), the China Foreign Trade Transportation Corporation, and Singapore-based Neptune Orient Lines. In 1995 the company became a wholly owned subsidiary of CAOSC. In June 1997, the Chinese executive Chen Jiulin was appointed managing director and chief executive officer of CAO. He reinvigorated the firm, which had been dormant, and resumed its operations as an oil-trading company. The Singapore government granted CAO a preferential tax rate on income generated through oil trading in 1998, the first year in which it reported profits. In December 2001, CAO launched an initial public offering in which 25 percent of its shares were sold to the public, and the shares were listed on the main board of the SGX. The successful IPO brought the company gross proceeds of S$80.6 million (US$44.8 million). Company information disclosed at the time stated that the main business of CAO consisted of jet fuel procurement, international oil trading, and oil-related investment. In February 2002, CAO was ranked by the Singapore-based *Business Times* as the top company listed on the Singapore exchange in 2001.

Beginning in early 2003, the company began to diversify from oil trading into derivatives trading. This decision was apparently not shared with or approved by the company's board. PricewaterhouseCoopers (PwC), the auditing firm asked to investigate the matter on behalf of the SGX, concluded in its report that there was "no evidence" that CAO received formal approval from its board when it began options trading in March 2003 "without fully appreciating the risks associated with the instrument."[8] The lack of experience and expertise and the absence of effective oversight allowed CAO to fall prey to its initial success in derivatives trading. The first transaction, a bet on declining oil prices, occurred in the fall of 2003. After this trade proved to be profitable, CAO launched an aggressive and ultimately disastrous strategy of betting against the market, predicting that oil prices would continue to fall. But the price of oil reached a series of new highs. By the first quarter of 2004, the company faced losses of US$5.8 million, which breached CAO's internal trading loss limits. Rather than writing off the loss and correcting its strategy, CAO increased its bet on declining oil prices.

While the company was reporting record profits to investors for the second quarter of 2004 (48.6 percent year-on-year growth), it was piling up additional derivatives trading losses and had to respond to a series of margin calls by counterparties to the derivatives transactions. The losses continued throughout the fall but were suppressed in the company's financials. By October 2004, CAO's total position reached 52 million barrels at a time when oil prices reached a historic (nominal) level of US$55 per barrel.[9] Late in the month the counterparties to the derivative transactions began closing out their trades with CAO. Between October 29 and November 24 alone, margin calls amounted to US$247.5 million. On November 13, CAO released its third-quarter financials, which showed an unprecedented 15 percent decline in earnings. The company attributed the drop in part to losses in derivatives trading but did not disclose the amount of the losses. A few days later it publicly announced that it was ceasing speculative trading and would close out all positions by the end of the month. Trading losses subsequently reached US$381 million. On November 29, 2004 CAO filed for court protection from creditors.

Up to this point, the CAO episode is an all-too-familiar story of a company's rise and fall as the result of a poor business decision, greatly aggravated by ill-conceived attempts to recoup and then conceal the ensuing damage. One major aspect of the episode, however, distinguishes this from similar events: CAO's relationship to its parent company, CAOSC, a Chinese state-owned company affiliated with China's Civil Aviation Administration. After the initial public offering of CAO shares, CAOSC transferred the remaining 75 percent stake in CAO to China Aviation Oil Holding Company (CAOHC), established in the restructuring of China's aviation sector. Shares of CAOHC are held by state-owned enterprises in the aviation industry. According to CAO's 2003 annual report, its twenty largest shareholders included CAOHC, with 75 percent, and nineteen others (including Singapore subsidiaries of Citibank and HSBC), each holding an average of 0.82 percent, and none more than 1.78 percent, of the shares.[10] The high dispersion of the publicly traded shares left little doubt that CAOHC controlled CAO. How closely the parent monitored CAO's operations is not clear. What is apparent, however, is that CAOHC learned of CAO's financial difficulties before any of the other shareholders or prospective investors learned of them. In early October 2004, CEO Chen Jiulin turned to the parent company for assistance. According to Chen, he sought support for a possible rescue by British Petroleum or a cash infusion by the parent itself. But CAOHC rejected both proposals.

In order to rescue the company, CAOHC asked other investors to facilitate a bailout. This move is not uncommon in China but is sanctioned as insider trading and securities fraud in Singapore and many other developed market economies. The parent company decided to sell 15 percent of its stake in CAO through a block trade on the market, a strategy that did not require full disclosure of CAO's financial statements at the time of the placement.[11] The sale, which generated S$185 million (US$108 million) in proceeds, was conducted on 20 October at a 14 percent discount off the previously quoted market price. The proceeds went directly from the parent to CAO in the form of a loan to meet its trading partners' margin calls.

The placement was underwritten by Deutsche Bank. Some business reports voiced skepticism about the quality of Deutsche Bank's due diligence process, which may have been compromised by its eagerness to establish itself as a major player in Asian markets. But there is also evidence that the documents it reviewed were forged by Chen in a scheme to defraud Deutsche Bank.[12]

The sale was conducted a little more than a month before CAO filed for bankruptcy protection. The share placement triggered an investigation against CAOHC by the Singaporean authorities after CAO had filed for bankruptcy. On August 19, 2005, CAOHC admitted to civil liability for contravening section 218 (2)(a) of Singapore's Securities and Futures Act (SFA)[13] and paid a civil penalty of S$8 million (US$4.4 million) to the financial regulatory authorities without court action. While accepting responsibility for violating Singaporean laws and regulations prohibiting insider trading, CAOHC submitted that the placement of CAO's shares in October 2004 "was not motivated by a desire to trade on inside information but to rescue CAO from its financial crisis." It also agreed to transfer to minority shareholders of CAO the shares in CAO that it was to receive under a debt–equity swap that was agreed to by CAO's commercial creditors.[14]

This was the first time a Chinese state-owned company had ever been penalized by Singaporean authorities. The official announcement of the civil penalty enforcement stated that CAOHC had placed CAO's shares on the market "while being in possession of material price sensitive information concerning the financial condition of CAO that was not generally available."[15] Apparently, CAOHC's stated motivation of rescuing CAO was recognized as a mitigating circumstance by the Monetary Authority of Singapore (MAS).

KEY PLAYERS AND THEIR STRATEGIES

The massive trading losses that brought down CAO suggest major oversight and compliance problems within the firm. We analyze the source of these corporate governance problems below, but the aspect of the episode that is most revealing is what transpired after CAO's problems became apparent. Thus, we focus our analysis on the rescue attempt by CAOHC, the fallout from this rescue attempt, and the ensuing restructuring of CAO, CAOHC, and the Chinese aviation fuel industry. Three groups of players are at the core of our analysis: the primary protagonists, CAO and CAOHC and their respective leaders, Chen Jiulin and Jia Chiabing; the Singapore regulators and enforcement authorities; and, perhaps most important, the actors behind the scenes—the Chinese political authorities who oversaw CAOHC and Temasek, which emerged as CAO's savior.

CAO, CAOHC, and Their Leaders

Chen Jiulin, managing director and CEO of China Aviation Oil, was until the company's downfall a highly praised Chinese entrepreneur. He joined CAOSC, the company that served as cofounder of CAO, in 1993 as chief negotiator and project manager. In 1997 he was appointed managing director of CAO and was later promoted by the Work Committee of Enterprises of the Communist Party of China to vice president of CAOHC, which became CAO's parent company in 2002. The early success of CAO was largely attributed to Chen. The World Economic Forum voted him one of the "New Asian Leaders" in 2003, and the prestigious Singapore Institute of Management elected him as one of its new members in April 2004. As late as August 2004, newspapers hailed Chen as the man behind CAO's success.[16] According to these accounts, Chen's major assets were his entrepreneurial spirit and the management methods he brought to CAO.

The China Aviation Oil Holding Company was established in 2001 as part of China's effort to commercialize its aviation industry. Its shares were held by a variety of state-owned enterprises, including China Aviation Group, China Eastern Aviation Group, and China Southern Aviation Group. The chairman and president of CAOHC was Jia Changbin, who also served as chairman and non-executive director of the board of CAO. Jia spent the early part of his career in the Civil Aviation Administration of China, having been appointed to its Shanghai branch in 1973 and promoted to deputy director in 1984. In 1990 he became deputy general manager of CAOSC and in 2000 was brought to CAO. In 2002 he was appointed president of CAOHC.

Both companies were products of China's transition to a market economy. Neither firm was a state-owned enterprise as traditionally understood—an enterprise directly controlled by state bureaucrats. Rather, they were "corporatized" firms (that is, distinct legal entities that issued shares and were formally governed by a board of directors) with complex ownership structures and similar in form to corporations in developed market economies, but their shares were ultimately owned by the state. By turning state-owned enterprises into stock corporations, the government created the potential for future privatization and, at least on paper, new governance structures. One of the reasons for listing shares of state-owned enterprises on foreign exchanges was to expose management to new forms of discipline not possible if the ultimate owners of the firm consist exclusively of agents of the state (Clarke 2003).

Throughout the 1990s, companies in China were not permitted to freely list their shares on a domestic stock exchange, much less on a foreign exchange.

Access to the capital market was limited to state-owned enterprises. These companies were vetted by local bureaucrats as well as national securities regulators before they were allowed to issue their shares to the public (Pistor and Xu 2005). In this respect CAO differs from the typical Chinese corporation in that it was established as an offshore joint venture with foreign partners. Its listing on the Singapore Stock Exchange came much later. Moreover, because the company was organized in Singapore, the exchange was domestic rather than foreign. Nonetheless, given the company's control by the Chinese holding company, listing ultimately had to be approved by CAOHC and state bureaucrats.

Given the close connection of their companies with the Chinese state bureaucracy, it is not surprising that the chief executives of the two companies were also products of China's hybrid system of state control and market elements. Jia, the older of the two, launched his career when China still had a centrally planned economy with little room for entrepreneurship and few legal mechanisms of governance. He seems to have ridden successfully on the waves of reform that swept the country, as suggested by his appointments to CAO and CAOHC, both creatures of the transition to a market economy. Still, it is worth noting that all of Jia's appointments—as well as his ultimate dismissal—were initiated by state bureaucrats, not private investors.[17]

Chen, though hailed as a proponent of China's new generation of entrepreneurial capitalists, also spent his career in companies that were directly or indirectly controlled by the state. Nevertheless, he appears to have been much more aggressive in pursuing new strategies and sidestepping the constraints imposed by state controls where possible. His posting in Singapore facilitated this agility, and postgraduate training at the National University of Singapore—which featured him on its website as a star alumnus—may have given him an appetite for freewheeling business strategies. His biography does not suggest that he ever operated in an environment where legal constraints were more important than bureaucratic controls or where shareholder concerns played a significant role in managerial decision-making.

Singaporean Enforcement Authorities

In Singapore, the CAO case triggered enforcement actions by several organizations. First in line was the SGX, which had admitted the company to its main board in 2001 and was responsible for monitoring listed companies' compliance with listing and disclosure requirements. The Singapore Stock Exchange is a demutualized and integrated securities and derivatives exchange inaugurated in December 1999 following a merger between the Stock Exchange of Singapore and the Singapore International Monetary Exchange. Through SEL Holdings, Temasek indirectly holds almost 24 percent of SGX's shares and in 2004 controlled up to 20 percent of the companies listed on the exchange.[18]

The main goal of the SGX is to develop into a leading financial center in Asia. An important component of this strategy has been to attract listings by mainland Chinese firms. In 2000 there was only one listing from mainland China; there were five in 2001. By the end of 2004 there were thirty-three listings representing 7 percent of the combined market capitalization of the exchange.[19] Another thirty-four new listings from China were added in 2005.[20] Chinese firms were particularly attractive to investors in this period because they generated high rates of return, in contrast to many local firms in the aftermath of the Asian financial crisis.

There have been growing concerns about possible conflicts of interest posed by the exchange's aggressive recruitment of firms from mainland China while fulfilling its role of investor protection. The collapse of CAO, the poster child of successful Chinese listed firms, was a wake-up call. The exchange reacted swiftly, appointing PwC to conduct an investigation into CAO. The report produced in March 2004 was a blistering attack on CAO's top management, lack of transparency, and ineffective governance structures.[21]

Enforcement actions against CAO and its representatives were ultimately left to state regulators and criminal enforcement agents. As noted above, CAOHC entered into a settlement agreement with the Monetary Authority of Singapore, which serves as the country's central bank and main financial market supervisor. According to the revised Securities and Futures Act of Singapore, MAS has the authority to bring civil actions against natural as well as legal persons for alleged misconduct in financial markets.

At first, criminal enforcement agents moved only against Chen, who was arrested immediately after returning from China on December 6, 2004. In March 2006 he was sentenced to four years in prison.[22] To the surprise of most observers, however, criminal investigations were also initiated against other members of the CAO board, Jia Changbin, Gu Yanfei, and Li Yongji. They were required by a Singaporean judge to pay fines in the amount of US$247,000 (Jia) and US$92,600 (Gu and Li).[23]

According to press reports, it had been widely assumed that Chen would bear the brunt of Singaporean law enforcement efforts in the CAO scandal. Earlier episodes involving Chinese corporations that were listed on foreign exchanges and embroiled in corporate governance scandals suggested that implicated managers in the overseas offices would be replaced or punished but that high-level managers in mainland China would be shielded from law enforcement actions by foreign authorities. A case in point is the response to the fraud scandal that embroiled Bank of China's New York branch in 2004. The manager of the New York branch office received a twelve-year prison sentence for embezzlement and accepting bribes. Other local representatives of the bank in New York were indicted in a federal court in Manhattan.[24] No company officials at the Chinese parent company were implicated. This time, however, enforcement actions were taken against an important mainland corporate manager and party bureaucrat.[25]

The timing of the enforcement action was also notable. China Aviation Oil had tried to settle its debts with creditors since its collapse in December 2004. An earlier settlement proposed by the company in January 2005, which would have required the creditors to write off 58.5 percent of their debt, was rejected by creditors, some of which moved to sue CAO in various jurisdictions to recover on the debt. In late May a new proposal to write off 44.4 percent of the debt, with CAO to pay back $486 million over five years, gained the support of creditors. To finalize the deal, which was later approved by the High Court of Singapore,[26] CAO's board members traveled on June 8, 2005, to Singapore, where they were arrested at the airport. All of the directors were subsequently released on bail so that the agreement with creditors could be finalized, but the event solidified Singapore's reputation for tough law enforcement, including enforcement against powerful Chinese actors. Press reports suggest, however, that the highly publicized arrest of Jia in particular could not have proceeded without at least tacit approval from mainland China. As one reporter put it, the Chinese government allowed Singapore to "throw the books at them" in a willing sacrifice.[27]

This move seems to have served two interests. First, it allowed China to reinforce a warning to its own companies about risky investment strategies. In fact, the entire CAO debacle has been depicted by Chinese bureaucrats as a problem of excessive speculation, without much attention to the securities fraud and insider trading aspect of the scandal. Second, sacrificing Jia may have been the result of a compromise between the authorities in Singapore and China. As noted above, CAOHC escaped with what many considered to be a rather light fine, and the price may have been allowing the Singaporean police to take action against Jia directly. Moreover, subsequent reports that Temasek would rescue CAO by taking a 15 percent stake in the company suggest that China had a keen interest in ensuring that CAO would emerge from bankruptcy as a viable company.

By contrast, private enforcement actions initiated by investors did not play a role in the scandal in Singapore. The only private action against CAO and its affiliates was filed in the US District Court for the Southern District of New York as a class-action suit, but it was ultimately dismissed for lack of jurisdiction.[28] Class-action suits are not recognized under Singapore law. Instead, MAS is authorized to initiate civil penalty actions and collect the penalties. This does not necessarily imply that investors go away empty-handed. In fact, CAOHC's penalty decree provided that it would compensate minority shareholders of CAO in kind by turning over to them the shares that CAOHC was to acquire from CAO as part of the company's debt-restructuring plan.

An alternative to US-style highly decentralized class-action suits may be found in lobbying efforts and potential legal actions by the Securities Investor Association of Singapore (SIAS). The association is a nonprofit organization established in June 1999 when more than 170,000 retail investors in Singapore had their investments in Malaysian securities frozen by the Malaysian government in the aftermath of the East Asian financial crisis.[29] The emergence of the SIAS mirrors similar developments in other East Asian markets, where the fallout of the financial crisis triggered the formation of nonprofit investor protection organizations. In Korea, Taiwan, and even Japan the organizations have emerged as powerful agents of good corporate governance, launching lawsuits against selected companies and leveraging the combined force of an organization in systems where securities class-action or derivative suits are often unavailable (Milhaupt 2004).

In summarizing the enforcement actions that were taken against CAO, it seems fair to say that Singapore's regulators and criminal enforcement agents moved swiftly against individuals such as CAO's chief executive officer and representatives of its parent company. In the absence of a more viable system for private party enforcement, much depended on the effectiveness and political will of state regulators. The sequence of enforcement actions taken and the level of sanctions applied suggest that these actions were aimed at confirming Singapore's reputation for law enforcement while disturbing as little as possible the country's economic relations with mainland China. Given Singapore's dependence on

Chinese markets, this is not surprising. But the episode highlights the limits of strategies aimed at outsourcing law enforcement, in this case by listing a Chinese company on a foreign stock exchange and thereby subjecting it to a more robust legal regime. This strategy has been the subject of a growing literature in recent years. The basic intuition of arguments pointing to the benefits of outsourcing law enforcement is that firms located in weak corporate governance environments, particularly firms in emerging markets and developing countries, may mitigate these problems by obtaining listing on a foreign stock exchange (Coffee 2002; Gilson 2000). In so doing, the theory goes, the firm bonds itself to the better disclosure regime and governance standards of the foreign country, simultaneously signaling to investors that its management has the capacity to abide by higher governance standards than those practiced in the home country.

Although there appears to be considerable empirical evidence in support of this theory (Reese and Weisbach 2001), the CAO case appears to be an inversion of the theoretical model: weak corporate governance practices of the home country are exported to the foreign listing environment. Rather than receiving additional protections, minority investors are (at least potentially) victimized by a distant parent company operating according to very different rules. In this case the parent company exploited a gap in the listing jurisdiction's law that allowed it to privately place shares without full disclosure in order to raise capital to cover its subsidiary's accumulated losses—all in the name of saving both the subsidiary and its Chinese parent from disgrace.

Perhaps the circumstances of the case are unique and unlikely to be replicated in other markets where Chinese companies are listing their shares. On the other hand, about seventy-eight Chinese companies are listed on foreign exchanges around the world, including twenty on the New York Stock Exchange as of 2007, and some estimate that Chinese IPOs will soon become the second most important source of IPO investment banking fees worldwide after the United States.[30] With so much at stake, the temptation for foreign stock exchanges and underwriters to overlook uncomfortable features of the Chinese corporate governance model may not be limited to the CAO case. Indeed, author discussions with practitioners representing Chinese companies indicate that the US Securities and Exchange Commission and the New York Stock Exchange are concerned about losing Chinese firms to other stock markets and as a result are granting exemptions from various securities law requirements and listing standards.

Chinese Authorities and Temasek

The preceding discussion alludes to crucial behind-the-scenes players in this episode: the Chinese political authorities and Temasek, which is closely linked to Singaporean political authorities. Both sets of players were deeply involved in managing the rescue of CAO, and their efforts are likely to have influenced the law enforcement response. Not surprisingly, however, little information is publicly available about the precise nature of their involvement.

Although it remains a matter of speculation whether Chinese interests had a direct influence on the outcome of Singaporean law enforcement actions, the denouement of the crisis is highly suggestive of a strategy pursued by the Chinese authorities. Such a strategy would have entailed rescuing CAO, downplaying the crisis as a one-off event resulting from excessive speculation, and avoiding the impression of a systemic governance failure that would implicate a breakdown of the Chinese model of company transformation. To pursue this strategy, the Chinese government was willing to play by Singapore's rules, at least to a point. This required sacrificing not only the frontline protagonist Chen—a typical response to corporate governance scandals—but also the more politically connected Jia, while forcing CAOHC to take responsibility for violating Singapore's insider trading rules.

Yet CAOHC's response to the insider charges, which in this context can be equated with the response of the Chinese authorities, is highly suggestive of the difference between the norms operating in the Chinese model and the legal rules of developed financial markets. In the Chinese model, where stability is more important than enforcement of individuals' rights, rescuing a company is the primary goal. Using a share transfer as part of a rescue scheme is not uncommon. Chinese state-owned or affiliated entities are often asked to participate in rescues of individual firms (Chen 2003; Green and Ming 2004). More recently, foreign investors have agreed to bail out Chinese entities (primarily in the financial sector) as a means of gaining access to more lucrative investments in the Chinese market. A telling example is Goldman Sachs's bailout of Hainan Securities in 2004.[31] What the Chinese authorities overlooked in the CAO episode is that the purchasers of the CAO shares sold by CAOHC in October 2004 were not other state-controlled entities but private investors in foreign markets who were unconstrained by expectations of subordination to larger state interests.

There was one important exception, however: Temasek. Although organized as a private limited liability company, Temasek is owned by the state of Singapore and is typically referred to as the government's investment arm.[32] Created in 1974, it took over assets managed by the Ministry of Finance. Over the course of the past thirty years, Temasek has developed into a major holding company with investments in key industry sectors, including financial services (38 percent of total investments), telecommunications and media (23 percent), and transport and logistics (12 percent). Temasek has controlling stakes in a number of firms (including 100 percent of a leading telecommunications company and the largest broadcasting company in Singapore), but it often invests in combination with private investors. As of 2007, 38 percent of all investments of Temasek were located in Singapore, with 40 percent in the rest of Asia outside Japan. Temasek portrays itself as an active investor with concern for the long-term prospects of the companies in which it invests. The company expects to reduce its investments in Singapore to one-third of total holdings over the next eight to ten years, largely by expanding investments in other parts of Asia.

According to the company's reports, it is pursuing an aggressive strategy of expansion into China. In early July 2005 it announced that its wholly owned subsidiary, Asia Financial Holdings, had entered into a strategic partnership with China Construction Bank (CCB), a major state-owned bank that launched an initial public offering at the end of 2005. Asia Financial Holdings committed to investing $1 billion in the bank and purchasing "certain existing shares" from China SAFE Investment Ltd, subject to regulatory approvals.[33]

Temasek's governance structure reflects the philosophy of state–public partnership and close linkages among companies belonging to the Temasek Group. Numerous members of the board are chairmen of companies in which Temasek holds major stakes.[34] Others are senior government officials, including the permanent secretary of the Ministry of Finance and a member of the Council of Presidential Advisors. Temasek is not only wholly owned by the Ministry of Finance; it also enjoys family ties with Singapore's "founding father," Lee Kuan Yew. The current executive director and CEO of Temasek, Ho Ching, is married to the prime minister, Lee Hsien Loong. Loong happens to be the son of Lee Kuan Yew.[35]

When CAOHC sold 15 percent of its shares in CAO in October 2004, Temasek and several of its affiliates purchased a 2 percent stake.[36] Although the investment was relatively small, it was the largest single purchase of shares in the placement, and the fact that Temasek purchased shares was viewed by market participants as a sign that CAO was still a good investment. As a stockbroker linked to a local firm put it, "Small investors often look to government-linked corporations such as Temasek for what stock to buy.... They seem to think that they have better information sources than the market would."[37] Whether it had better information or not, like other shareholders Temasek had to write off its investment when the firm's stock collapsed only a month later.

But this did not end Temasek's involvement in CAO. Only one week after CAOHC settled with the MAS, Temasek announced its willingness to acquire a 15 percent stake in CAO. Press reports about the pending deal suggested that the investment would fit Temasek's China expansion strategy, referring to the company's recent commitment to invest in China Construction Bank.[38] A slightly broader reading of events is that Temasek was serving as a proxy for Singapore's long-term interest in promoting business ties with China. Temasek had participated indirectly in the establishment of CAO in 1993. After having sold the initial stake back to the Chinese parent in 1995, Temasek participated in the share placement in October 2004. There were rumors that Temasek might inject millions of dollars in an attempt to get CAO out of bankruptcy when the first credit-restructuring plan was floated in January 2004.[39] It is also suggestive of the cooperative climate between China and Singapore that none of the bank creditors controlled by Temasek filed suit against CAO or the parent company to recover their loans. They stand in contrast to other international banks, which initiated legal action against CAO (although they ultimately settled their claims).[40] This would be puzzling if Temasek were simply viewed as a burned investor. It is far less surprising considering Singapore's broader interests in promoting closer links with mainland China (see Figure 11.1). Consistent with this strategy, Temasek emerged as a guardian angel for CAO. Seen in this light, Temasek's role is not fundamentally different from the role many parent companies in China (also with state backing) have assumed with regard to their "offspring."

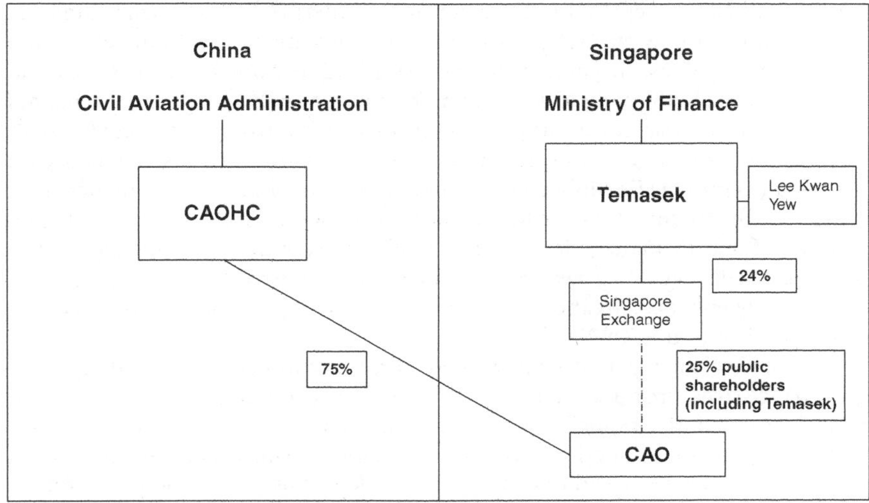

Figure 11.1. CAO's ties with China and Singapore

CHINA'S MODEL OF CORPORATE GOVERNANCE

Until 1978, China had a socialist economy relying primarily on central planning and government control over the means of production. Reforms introduced in the following decade were centered on the agricultural sector as well as the rationalization of the state sector, along with some opening for entrepreneurial activities, particularly in coastal areas and in the vicinity of large urban centers. In the ensuing decades the economy gradually grew out of the plan (Naughton 1995). The relative share of the exclusively state-owned enterprises (SOEs) in the economy declined, while new entrants, including hybrid structures co-owned by state entities and nonstate actors, accounted for the bulk of economic growth (Qian 2000; Walder and Oi 1999). An important step in the reform of the SOEs was the "corporatization" of state-owned enterprises—their legal repackaging and the listing of some firms on domestic or foreign stock exchanges to raise capital (Lichtenstein 1993). According to standard theory, the formation of separate legal entities with shares held by outside owners facilitates several efficiency-enhancing measures. Professional managers pursuing business rather than political objectives could be recruited to run the enterprises. Investors could supervise management through a board of directors. Finally, the public listing of firms would not only bring capital into the firm but also would expose management to the discipline of the capital markets.

In practice, China developed a distinctive model of governance for publicly traded firms in the 1990s. Most of the nearly fourteen hundred companies currently listed on the Shanghai and Shenzhen stock exchanges are still controlled by the state. On average, less than 40 percent of the shares of these "public" companies are publicly traded. Typically, 60 percent or more of the shares are held by the state or by state-controlled enterprises and agents. Until 2006, these shares were not tradable except among state-controlled enterprises.[41] Though technically most shares are now tradable, shares held by the state and its affiliates are not widely traded. Thus, in contrast to the privatization campaigns in Russia and Eastern Europe in the early 1990s, China's motive for establishing stock exchanges and listing firms was not to move assets from state control into private hands.[42] Instead, the goal was to create an alternative to enterprises' exclusive reliance on debt finance provided mainly by China's state-owned banks. Equity finance from a large number of investors would provide such an alternative, as well as perhaps a measure of outside managerial expertise, while allowing the state to retain control over the listed assets. As a sweetener for investors, the listed firms' prospects were often greatly enhanced by the fact that they held monopolies in key sectors of the economy (Pistor and Xu 2005).

The major challenge that Beijing faced with this approach was the design of a governance structure for listed firms. Thus far, that structure can be best described as an "administrative model" performing mainly coordinating functions. Bureaucrats thought to have superior information and monitoring capacities with respect to a given firm played a lead role in selecting which firms to list. There is historical precedent in China for this type of official bureaucratic supervision and sponsorship of enterprise as a substitute for a legal regime (Goetzmann and Koll 2006).[43] The model appears to have worked reasonably well at the listing stage, but it has been much less effective for continuous monitoring of companies thereafter. The explanation is straightforward: local and regional bureaucrats have strong incentives to bring firms to the capital market. If the IPO is successful, the firm raises new capital and thus relieves the local budget of the burden of funding its investments. Additional incentives result from the fact that the local bureaucrats' own career prospects are closely tied to their region's performance (Huang 1996), including the performance of firms from that region on the stock market.[44] Because the central government controls access to the stock market, local bureaucrats have strong incentives to invest enough in the selection process ex ante to avoid failure of the firm, which would reduce future access by other companies from the same region. A potential downside of using regional competition in the selection process, however, is that once a company has been listed, the same incentive structure induces local and regional bureaucrats to cover up negative information that might reveal failure and necessitate a costly rescue. Moreover, the state-owned companies and their representatives who serve as shareholder-monitors often do not have the capacity to closely oversee the actions taken by the listed company. This is evident in the CAO case, in which the younger, more aggressive, and financially minded—if ultimately misguided—management team outran the monitoring capacities of bureaucrats at the parent company.

FORMAL LAW AS A GOVERNANCE DEVICE FOR CHINESE COMPANIES

There is little doubt that China's growth has been supported by nonlegal substitutes, some of which have deep historical roots. Some researchers have gone as far as to suggest that formal law has played virtually no role in the nonstate sector, which has been largely responsible for the rapid growth and development of the past two to three decades. Allen et al. (2005), for example, use the shareholder and creditor rights indicators compiled by La Porta et al. to assess China's formal legal system and suggest that formal law is weak at best. They also document the fact that China's state-owned sector, for which much of the transitional legislation has been adopted (including the company law of 1994, revised in 2006, and the securities law of 1999) contributes only a small share to economic growth and investment. The major source of growth is the nonstate sector, which includes hybrid structures such as Township and Village Enterprises that are often co-owned by public and private agents. This sector has flourished largely beyond the reach of formal laws promulgated by the central government.

Still, it may not be quite accurate to conclude from this analysis that formal law in China has been irrelevant. The indicators devised by La Porta and colleagues may not be the appropriate benchmarks to use. One reason is that a focus on laws and regulations enacted by the central government misses regional and local rules and regulations. The special economic zones, for example, were authorized to develop a set of rules and regulations aimed at promoting investment as well as exports. The scope of autonomous regulation at this level typically included tax incentives, joint venture regulations, land use rights, and the governance of imports and exports (Sonoko 1983). Outside these zones, regions were free to enact their own law, at least in areas where lawmaking was not preempted by central government legislation. Regional company laws, securities regulations, and bankruptcy rules typically preceded centrally enacted laws, which were often criticized for imposing greater controls and higher costs on economic agents (Pistor and Wellons 1999). Another reason why using the indicators of La Porta et al. as benchmarks might mislead is that it assumes that law is used for similar purposes in different settings. There is little doubt that in terms of sheer volume formal law has expanded rapidly in China in the past thirty years. It is therefore important to analyze the various functions to which formal law was put to use by different actors.

We begin with the supply side. Formal law has developed into an important tool for the central government to use in managing the state-owned sector. The 1994 Company Law's primary purpose was to create a framework for the re-organization of state-owned enterprises into corporate entities (Fang 1995). Previously, state-owned enterprises functioned as legal entities that could act in their own name, but their governance and control structures within the state apparatus were ill defined. By transforming these enterprises into corporations, the government could streamline relations within the state-owned sector. Shares of the corporation were allocated to particular government agencies or organizations controlled by the agencies. These public shareholders were vested with the right to hire and fire management and to take critical decisions, such as triggering a bankruptcy proceeding. In 2006 a revised company law entered into force.[45] It is much more focused on the internal governance structure of firms and the protection of minority shareholder rights, and thus it is more like Western models than the 1994 version.

Another example of using formal law in an attempt to improve the state's control over the state-owned sector is the 1987 Bankruptcy Law.[46] As with the

1994 Company Law, it targeted state-owned enterprises, not the nonstate sector, even though subsequent changes in the civil procedure law expanded its application (Li 1999). It would be difficult to directly link the enactment of these and other laws to economic growth in China. But they were not entirely irrelevant, either. Thousands of companies were incorporated after the 1994 law was enacted, and more than thirteen hundred state-controlled entities were listed on China's two official stock exchanges by the end of 2004. Between 1998 and 2001 these companies raised more US$61 billion (Pistor and Xu 2005). Between 1989 and 1997 the number of state-owned enterprises that entered bankruptcy proceedings increased from eighty-nine to more than five thousand per year (Li 1999). Like the Company Law, the Bankruptcy Law was revised recently and for the first time explicitly targets private companies, not only state-owned enterprises.[47]

Although the central government has increasingly used formal law as a governance device for the state-owned sector, it has shied away from giving law primacy over other governance mechanisms. The rules set forth in the 1994 Company Law stipulating the conditions under which a company could issue shares to the public and seek listing on a stock exchange were complemented shortly afterward by a set of regulations promulgated by the State Council and the China Securities Regulatory Commission (CSRC), much to the dismay of legal observers in China who viewed this as weakening the commitment to the rule of law (Fang 1995; Gao 1996). The governance structure that emerged on the basis of these rules and regulations was more administrative than legal. Its foundation was the quota system, which was used to allocate scarce resources including energy, credit, and now access to equity finance among China's regions.

Given the lack of reliable company-specific information and the absence of a well-developed legal system for stock markets, this may have ultimately been a sensible strategy, at least for the early days of China's stock market development. The fact that it reinforced state control over listed companies at a time when they were seeking capital from nonstate investors is unlikely to have been an oversight. From the perspective of investors, this was not necessarily a negative consequence. In light of the pervasive influence that state agents continued to have in these companies, the quasi insurance of the implicit bailout guarantee that regional governments made when bringing their companies to the market gave investors some measure of protection against abuse. In short, the legal system was highly centralized and coordinated. Little thought was given to the development of legal protections for investor interests.

Once enacted, however, law often takes on a life of its own as different agents begin to explore how it might advance their own interests. Shareholders and investors who were defrauded began to take the law into their own hands. The first series of investor lawsuits was filed in the summer of 2001 by law firms in Beijing. This clearly came as a surprise to government officials. The first response was to deny investors access to the courts. The Supreme People's Court issued guidelines stating that in light of the legal and regulatory uncertainties surrounding these cases, China's civil courts were not in a position to hear investor lawsuits at that point in time (Chen 2003).[48] Only a few months later, however, in January 2002, the court reversed this position in part. The new guidelines of the Supreme People's Court allowed lower courts to hear securities actions for false or misleading statements—not other types of securities fraud—but only if the firm had already been administratively sanctioned by the CSRC or the Ministry of Finance or if company officials had been found criminally liable. The motive for this apparent change in position seems clear: the incompetence argument was untenable over the long term. If the government wanted to retain control over the litigation and the companies against which suits could be brought, it had to devise a better strategy. This was achieved by giving these three bodies a *de facto* veto right.[49] In fact, even after the Supreme People's Court issued a set of detailed guidelines for investor suits, litigation was brought against only about 20 percent of the companies eligible to be sued between 2001 and 2006 (Liebman and Milhaupt 2008). In the absence of a clear mandate for class actions, the costs of litigation are substantial, although some bundling of cases by investors against the same company is possible (Chen 2003). Where lawsuits have been filed, the courts have sometimes used the strict causation requirements set forth in the guidelines to deny plaintiffs recovery. Many cases appear to have been settled or complaints have been withdrawn. Without information about the settlement details it is difficult to assess whether settlement in the shadow of the law, which is also common in the United States, is of greater benefit to plaintiffs or defendants.

As this example suggests, China has been willing, within limits, to experiment with legal reforms and to decentralize lawmaking and enforcement. Some of these experiments may have a Trojan horse effect unanticipated by the lawmakers.[50] The pattern (legal change designed to improve state economic governance leads to a loss of control over the legal mechanisms) can be found elsewhere in China. For example, in 1989 China enacted the Administrative Litigation Law, allowing individuals and nongovernmental organizations for the first time to sue government agencies for violation of existing laws and regulations (Potter 1994). The law was not intended to fundamentally alter the relation between state agents and citizens or to be a commitment to a rights-based system subjecting government actions to strict legal scrutiny. Its major function was to reform the state bureaucracy and bring corruption under control. The government hoped to instrumentalize administrative litigation for its own purposes. This move, however, also had unintended consequences. Since the Administrative Litigation Law was promulgated in 1989, People's Courts of first instance have heard more than one million cases brought by aggrieved citizens, with plaintiffs winning about 30 percent of the cases (Conk 2005).

Of course, not all judgments are successfully enforced against government officials. Nonetheless, the possibility of bringing legal action against state officials has advanced the notion that there are individual rights that may be upheld against intrusion by the state (Pils 2005). Another example is media control. By empowering the media in China to uncover and report on abuse of investors rights, the Chinese government has unleashed the powers of the so-called fourth branch of government. Once again, the motive was to create a check against abuse, but the actions taken by some of the media have created serious challenges to government control over news and information (Liebman 2005).

Closer inspection reveals that the very function of law in China today is far from settled. The lawmakers view law primarily as a means to control and coordinate the economy and society. Law's control function is exercised by either vesting government agencies with legal (in addition to bureaucratic and political) rights of control or at times by allocating some rights of control to individuals (litigants in administrative procedures or the media) as a check on the vast bureaucratic machinery that rules the country. But lawyers have used the possibilities provided by the decentralized approach to legal governance (however modest) and have begun to explore the possibility of invoking the protective function of law.

This ambiguity is heightened by the signaling function of law. In China, as elsewhere, legal reform has a tendency to take on a life of its own because the signals received by law's consumers are not necessarily limited to the ones intended by state actors. Through two decades of steady legal reform in the economic sector, China's leadership has signaled that the country is moving (unevenly and imperfectly, to be sure) in the direction of market-oriented institutions and legal governance. Although the leadership has clearly determined that legal governance in the economic sphere is "safer" and more manageable than reforms in the political and social arenas, it is proving difficult for those in power to rein in all of the connotations that any move toward the "rule of law" entails, which, at least according to Western standards, would include using the law to control governmental actions. Plainly, the protective function of law is still a work in progress in China; developments to date have not fundamentally altered the predominant role of law as an instrument of state control and state coordination. But it is not accurate to claim, as many have, that law has played no role in China's economic growth. The law has provided important information about the direction of future reforms, raised societal expectations about the protective capacity of law, and laid a modest platform for individual initiative and experimentation (what we call contestability)—sometimes even directed against state actors.

INTERLUDE: LAW AND GROWTH IN SINGAPORE

The CAO case provides insights not only into China's legal and market development but also that of Singapore. The case is particularly interesting because of the interface between China's unabashedly centralized administrative governance model and the Singaporean system of financial market governance, which seeks to emulate protective features of more highly developed market economies. Singapore is widely depicted in the corporate governance literature and surveys as an example of an emerging common-law country with strong investor protections and effective financial regulation.[51] Yet the actual governance structure employed in Singapore's economy is more complicated than this depiction would suggest. Singapore does have an "English origin" common-law system that has been hailed for having investor rights that are superior to those of civil-law systems (La Porta et al. 1998). But the ability of individual investors to enforce their rights in court is in fact severely constrained. Law enforcement rests firmly in the hands of regulators and criminal law enforcement agents, not civil courts or private plaintiffs. Moreover, the good reputation of the Singapore legal system in perception indices notwithstanding, the CAO episode suggests that Singapore relies heavily on centralized administrative mechanisms other than law. Though formally governed by Singapore's bankruptcy and corporate law regime, the final outcome of the CAO crisis depended on the intervention and support of one

Singaporean governmental entity—Temasek—in consultation with other such entities—MAS and SGX. Indeed, with the exception of the important criminal prosecution of the executives involved, resolution of the financial crisis at CAO rested on a negotiated solution among governmental entities and affiliates from Singapore and China. Put differently, investor protection was achieved not principally by enforcement of corporate and securities laws but through political mechanisms.

To the extent that law was invoked in the CAO case, it was used to punish individuals such as Chen and Jia. The outcome of the case has puzzled some observers who expressed surprise that a parent company based on the mainland was implicated at all. At the same time, most commentators suggested that the punishment of both CAOHC and the individuals involved was rather mild.[52] These contradictory impressions reflect the dilemma that Singaporean regulators and law enforcers faced in this case. Given its aspiration to become a leading financial market, Singapore had little choice but to adhere to the dominant Western model of financial market regulation. For the Singaporean authorities, it was therefore crucial to demonstrate that insider trading rules were taken seriously and would be enforced against any violator. Indeed, in sentencing Jia and other CAO officials for insider trading, the judge explicitly remarked that the case was about "a larger issue, and the broader public interest in good corporate governance."[53] At the same time, Singapore could hardly afford to offend Chinese authorities. The future of the SGX depends on its ability to attract a constant flow of firms from mainland China. Moreover, key players in the Singapore market, foremost among them Temasek, have a keen interest in investing in Chinese markets. It is impossible to imagine that enforcement agents in Singapore were not conscious of Temasek's involvement in CAO or the strong national interest in maintaining good relations with China when taking enforcement actions in this case.

THE ROLE OF LAW IN CHINA'S ECONOMIC SUCCESS: A VIEW FROM SINGAPORE

China's 10 percent annual growth for more than two decades is remarkable. For most observers it is even more remarkable given that China lacks a well-developed legal system. Not surprisingly, some observers predict that China will eventually either converge on the dominant Western model or experience considerable setbacks in economic development (Dam 2006).

Our institutional autopsy of the CAO case, however, suggests that this may be a false choice. In particular, our analysis of Singaporean capitalism demonstrates that there are viable alternatives to the ideal-type market economy, in which law has a primarily protective function for individual rights holders. Singapore has successfully marketed itself as a leading capitalist system in East Asia and received high scores on indices of institutional quality. Yet Singapore's commitment to the protective function of law is highly state-centered and state-administered.[54] Personal relationships and coordination of state- and private-sector interests are key components of the economic governance structure. Indeed, the very efficiency of the legal system appears to derive from the highly state-coordinated nature of enforcement. The CAO case was resolved within ten months, from the date CAO filed for bankruptcy in November 2004 to the Temasek-orchestrated capital injection in August 2005. Within this time frame, CAO settled with other creditors, CAOHC was fined for insider trading, and a criminal action was brought against Chen, Jia, and other board members of CAO (although it took an additional seven months to reach sentencing). This quick resolution demonstrates the advantage of close coordination among economic players and government agents in resolving a case so as to maximize common interests.

Such an approach does not come without costs, however. Viewed from a Western rights-based perspective, the system exposed individual shareholders to the risk that their financial interests might be sacrificed for whatever Temasek and its partners in government and business might deem to be the greater social good. In the end, the minority shareholders were compensated in kind (by CAOHC's transferring to them the shares it had received in the debt-equity swap), but the deal was brokered by state regulators. Minority shareholders cannot easily recover damages in their own right in Singapore.

Singapore's model of market coordination and limited private enforcement in conjunction with its more authoritarian political system is likely to be much more appealing to officials in Beijing than a decentralized rights protection regime based on the US model. Indeed, China's legal and political reform strategy appears to reflect key features of the Singaporean model or that of other countries in East Asia that were traditionally characterized by strong government coordination such as South Korea (Wade 2003; Amsden 1989). Legal reforms are injected where necessary to advance the project of economic growth and development, particularly in order to bolster the confidence of foreign investors and to hold in check the untrammeled authority of state agents. Individual rights protections are used only sparingly as a governance device, and they tend to be paired with veto powers exercised by the state or its agents. Recent history has shown that this model can produce dramatic economic growth and the perception of governance by the rule of law.[55]

A critical question, of course, is whether a country of 1.3 billion people can emulate the governance structure of a city-state. As a tiny country without substantial resources, Singapore must remain economically competitive. It has little alternative but to foster and market its role as a leading financial center. Market forces may therefore place enough pressure on firms and government agents to ensure that coordination strategies enhance rather than reduce the competitiveness of Singaporean entities, whether private or (partly) government-owned. And finally, the small size of the country facilitates the operation of informal governance mechanisms, including reputation effects and mutual monitoring, thus restraining abuse of dominant positions.[56] In this sense, Singapore is not unlike the state of Delaware.[57] Roe (2005) argues that Delaware's governmental actors are keenly attentive to the competitive implications of changes to its corporate law, because the state has no alternative but to retain its leading position in this field. Economic actors can thus be confident that other interests reflected in the political process will not be allowed to undermine the quality of its corporate law over time.

By virtue of its size, China is in a very different position. The country does not have to vie for foreign investors because they have proved willing to pay substantial "admission fees" to gain access to its huge potential market.[58] In other words, in many respects China is a price setter, not a price taker, and by implication is less subject to external market pressures than Singapore. Nonetheless, China's leadership is acutely aware of the fact that its future depends on delivering sustained economic growth. It is therefore in the Communist Party's interest to ensure continuous growth and build a reputation for clean and neutral enforcement rather than intervening in ways that might undermine the country's prospects for growth. At times these considerations have caused officials to tolerate or even encourage governance mechanisms that—like a Trojan horse—may ultimately turn against the current leadership's hold on power. This need not imply that China must turn to an elaborate rights-based governance regime built around an independent judiciary. As the example of other countries examined in this book suggests, few countries have decentralized and "judicified" governance and enforcement to the extent of the United States. Instead, many successful systems place greater confidence in state regulators and prosecutors. Thus, although formal legal governance may play an increasingly important role in China, administrative coordination of state- and private-sector interests is likely to remain the dominant feature of Chinese law, even in a capitalist China.

NOTES

1. The study was originally published in C. J. Milhaupt and K. Pistor (2008), *Law and Capitalism: What Corporate Crises Reveal about Legal Systems and Economic Development Around the World* (Chicago: Chicago University Press). © 2008 by The University of Chicago, reproduced with permission.
2. Note, however, that the studies at the core of this law and finance literature do not explicitly emphasize the relation between "good law" and economic growth. See La Porta et al. (1998).
3. The extent to which the current global financial crisis has challenged these very premises shall be left to separate research.
4. Data are available on the World Bank's web page at <http://www.doingbusiness.org/>
5. Supra note 1.
6. It is worth noting, however, that the enactment of insider trading rules in many well-developed market economies is of relatively recent origin and enforcement continues to remain rather weak. See Beny (2007).
7. "China Aviation Oil's US$550 million Derivatives Disaster," SIAS newsletter, December 1, 2004, <http://www.sias.org.sg>.
8. Quoted in John Burton, "CAO's 'Risky Gambles' Made Losses Worse," *Financial Times*, March 30, 2005, at 27.
9. Energy Intelligence Group (2004). For an overview of historic oil prices, see <http://www.oilnergy.com/1opost.htm#since78>, last accessed September 8, 2012.
10. At this time Temasek apparently did not own any shares in CAO. But the company acquired some of the shares that CAOHC placed on the market in the ill-fated transaction of October 2004. For details, see note 32 below and accompanying text.

11. A *New York Times* article suggested that block trades "exist in a legal twilight in Singapore" (Wayne Arnold and Keith Bradsher, "Bank Says Chinese Assured It Filing Company Was Healthy," *New York Times*, December 6, 2004, at A5). Nevertheless, under existing rules the company was obliged to disclose any "material" information to its investors.
12. See "China Aviation Oil's Suspended Chief Executive Freed on Bail: Reports," *Agence France Presse*, June 11, 2005, <http://www.singapore-window.org/sw05/050611af.htm>.
13. Section 218(2)(a) of the SFA prohibits a person who is in possession of material price-sensitive information concerning a corporation (to which he is connected), which he knows is not generally available, from subscribing for, purchasing, selling, or entering into an agreement to subscribe for, purchase, or sell the securities of that corporation.
14. The role of CAOHC as one of CAO's creditors came about when it lent the proceeds of its October 2004 offering of CAO shares to CAO. At the time CAO filed for bankruptcy, the company's main creditors included MERM (Mitsui & Co.), Fortis Bank, Barclays Capital, J. Aron & Co. (Singapore), Standard Bank London, Sumitomo Mitsui Banking, and Macquarie Bank. See Energy Intelligence Group (2004).
15. See press release by Monetary Authority of Singapore, "MAS Takes Civil Penalty Enforcement Action Against China Aviation Oil Holding Company for Insider Trading," August 19, 2005, <http://www.mas.gov.sg/en/News-and-Publications/Enforcement-Actions/2005/MAS-Takes-Civil-Penalty-Enforcement-Action-Against-China-Aviation-Oil.aspx> (last accessed September 8, 2012).
16. For example, "CAO's Shine All Due to One Man," *Business Times* (Singapore), August 19, 2004.
17. The extent to which Jia's conduct was still informed by China's state-controlled system is suggested by allegations made by Chen concerning Jia's handling of the CAO crisis. According to Chen, Jia was incommunicado during a critical request for assistance because he had turned off his cell phone during a Communist Party training session. When CAO sent an emergency request a few days later, it took a week for managers at CAOHC and Communist Party leaders to look into the case. Mure Dickie, "Ex-CAO Chief Attacks CAOHC," *Financial Times*, February 19, 2005, at 6.
18. Energy Intelligence Group (2004). See also Singapore Exchange Limited Annual Report FY 2004–2005, at 64, <http://sgx.com> (hereinafter SGX 2005 Annual Report).
19. Elliot Wilson, "Scandal Cools Taste for China Plays," *Standard* (Hong Kong), March 7, 2005, <http://www.thestandard.com.hk> See also SGX 2005 Annual Report.
20. SGX 2005 Annual Report, at 59.
21. The report by PricewaterhouseCoopers is not publicly available. Press reports, however, have detailed its findings. See, e.g., "CAO's 'Risky Gambles' Made Losses Worse," *Financial Times*, April 10, 2005.
22. "China Aviation's Chen Gets 4 Years, 3 Months in Jail," *Bloomberg News*, March 21, 2006.
23. "Oil Firm Officials Ordered to Pay Fines," *China Daily*, March 3, 2006 (reporting that jail time would be served only if the convicted were unable to pay the fines).
24. "Three Chinese Indicted in New York for BoC Fraud," *China Daily*, February 15, 2005.
25. Mure Dickie, "CAO Arrests Fade from Official View: Emphasis Is on Good News Not Bad on Industry Website," *Financial Times*, June 10, 2005, at 27.
26. "The High Court Approved the Debt Structuring Plan of Chinese Jet Fuel Importer China Aviation Oil (Singapore)," *Petroleum Intelligence Weekly*, 44/25 (June 20, 2005).
27. Tom Grimer, "China's Taking Notes on Corporate Justice, Singapore-Style," *Globe and Mail* (Toronto), June 15, 2005, at 2.

28. Burke v. China Aviation Oil (Singapore) Corp. Ltd., 421 F. Supp.2d 649 (S.D.N. Y. 2005).
29. The SIAS defines itself as an investor lobby group and a financial market watchdog committed to ensuring transparent and fair treatment of investors in Singapore and throughout Asia. The organization currently has sixty-one thousand members. It was quick to respond vocally to the CAO scandal but did not take any legal action. For details see <http://sias.org.sg/index.php?option=com_content&view=article&id=5&-Itemid=6&lang=en>, last accessed September 8, 2012.
30. Douglas Wong, "China Second-Largest Stock Issuer after U.S.," *Bloomberg News*, June 7, 2005.
31. David Barboza, "Horse Trading for a Venture in China," *New York Times*, March 5, 2005, at C1.
32. The company, though not publicly traded, has adopted governance practices that are on a par with best practices in publicly listed companies and proclaims a firm commitment to enhance shareholder value rather than the interests of the Singapore government. Yet as a nonpublic company the firm has considerable discretion in the content and timing of disclosure. In fact, Temasek only began issuing annual reports in 2004. See "In Issuing First Annual Report, Investment Vehicle Aims to Move Further onto World Stage," *Asian Wall Street Journal*, October 12, 2004, <http://www.singapore-window.org/sw04/041012aw.htm).
33. "China Construction Bank and Temasek Holdings Established Strategic Partnership in Beijing," July 4, 2005, <http://www.temasekholdings.com.sg/newsroom/press speeches /05 07 2005.htm>.
34. The chairman of the board, S. Dhanabalan, is also chairman of DBS Group Holdings, a financial institution in which Temasek holds a 28 percent stake. Also serving on the board is the chairman of Singapore Airlines, which is controlled by Temasek.
35. See <http://www.temasekholdings.com.sg/about temasek/board of directors.htm>.
36. Temasek acquired 0.5 percent directly; the remaining 1.5 percent was acquired by other companies belonging to the group. See Jake Lloyd-Smith, "Temasek Keen to Finish Talks with CAO Parent: Agreement with Scandal-Hit Chinese Jet Fuel Importer May Be in Sight," *Financial Times*, 24 August 2005, at 24.
37. Energy Intelligence Group (2004).
38. "Temasek Keen to Finish Talks with CAO Parent," *Financial Times*, August 23, 2005.
39. John Burton et al., "Creditors to Recover 40% under Bail-Out China Aviation Oil," *Financial Times*, January 24, 2005, at 23.
40. Jake Lloyd-Smith and Andrew Yeh, "CAO Head Was Kept 'in the Dark'," *Financial Times*, February 2, 2005, at 17.
41. In 2006 China implemented a scheme aimed at reducing state holdings in listed companies. Many of the previously nontradable shares were converted into tradable ones, and outside shareholders received a proportion of the newly traded shares. For a detailed account of this scheme, see Kister (2007).
42. To be sure, Russian privatization posed its own acute problems, the consequences of which are still being felt in the political economy. We explore these consequences in our institutional autopsy of the Yukos case in chapter 8 of Milhaupt and Pistor (2008: 149–72).
43. Before 1985, industrial enterprises required not only permission but active sponsorship and supervision from the government and its agents, the bureaucrats. A century earlier, new firms established in the 1870s and 1880s were known as *guandu shangban* (government supervision and merchant management enterprises). In a close parallel to today's listed firms, merchants put up the capital and managed the firms under the

supervision of government officials. The merchants bore the financial risks of the enterprise and were forced to operate under the supervision of officials who followed their own agendas, frequently leading to corruption and poor corporate management (Goetzmann and Koll 2006).

44. Pistor and Xu (2005) present descriptive data and some correlation coefficients suggesting that regions whose companies perform better on the stock market obtain higher IPO quotas from the central government in future years.
45. For an English-language version of the law, see <http://www.novexcn.com>
46. According to the 1987 bankruptcy law, the debtor had the primary right to file for bankruptcy and required approval by the relevant ministry, which typically functioned as its controlling shareholder. See art. 7, Law of the People's Republic of China on Enterprise Bankruptcy, adopted December 2, 1986. According to arts 17 and 20 of the same law, the "superior departments in charge of the enterprise" have the power to initiate and supervise reorganizations. An English-language translation of the 1987 bankruptcy law is available at <http://www.novexcn.com/enterprise_bankruptcy.html>. A new bankruptcy law was adopted in August 2006.
47. See "China: More on Chinese Legislature Adopts Corporate Bankruptcy Law," BBC Monitoring Alert, source: *Xinhua [China View] News Agency* (Beijing), August 27, 2006 (CISNET China CX160378). The law entered into force on June 1, 2007.
48. In English translation, the relevant parts of the court's guidelines read as follows: People's Supreme Court Notice on the Temporary Suspension on the Hearing of Securities Related Civil Compensation Cases . . . : Our country's capital markets are in a period of continuous standardization and development and a number of problems have arisen including insider trading, cheating, market manipulation and other behaviors. These behaviors harm the fairness of the securities market, infringe upon investor's legal rights, and have influenced the safe and healthy development of capital markets and should be progressively normalized. Currently, in the court's administration of justice, this new situation and these new problems that require attention and research have already emerged. However, under current legislative and judicial limits, courts still don't have the conditions to accept and hear this type of case. As the result of research, civilian compensation cases arising from the aforementioned behavior temporarily should not be heard. (Translation provided by Daniel Magida.) See also Magida (2003).
49. This is not to say that civil courts in China are beyond the reach of the party or state bureaucrats. In the long term, however, decentralized litigation brought by nonstate agents may be more difficult to monitor and control than actions brought or enforced by state agents such as prosecutors or regulators.
50. The Trojan horse effect was, however, anticipated or hoped for by many foreigners who advised China about legal reforms. See Stephenson (2000). Note that throughout the book we use the term "lawmaker" generically without referring to a particular institution such as a parliament or legislature.
51. In the original investor protection ranking by La Porta et al. (1998), for example, Singapore scores 4 out of 6. Singapore ranks fifth in the world on Transparency International's Corruption Perception Index and second in the Economic Freedom Index.
52. See Cris Prystay, "Executives on Trial: Three CAO Singapore Officials Are Fined in Derivatives Case," *Wall Street Journal*, March 3, 2006, at C4.
53. Ibid.
54. This is reflected in Singapore's location in the upper left-hand corner of the matrix reproduced in Milhaupt and Pistor (2008: 183, figure 9.1).

55. In this context "rule of law" is understood as law establishing the rules of the game. It does not include the use of law to constrain government actors.
56. A similar point has been made for Sweden, where the Wallenberg family has been a dominant shareholder without displaying strong tendencies to expropriate minority shareholders. See Högfeldt (2003).
57. We are grateful to Donald Langevoort for suggesting this analogy to us.
58. For a discussion of the willingness of foreign banks to pay substantial premiums for minority stakes in state-owned banks, see World Bank, "Financial Sector Policies and Development," *China Quarterly Update*, November 2005, at 13; <http://www.worldbank.org> under "Countries and Regions."

REFERENCES

Allen, F., Qian, J., and Qian, M. (2005), "Law, Finance, and Economic Growth in China," *Journal of Financial Economics*, 77: 57–116.

Amsden, A. H. (1989), *Asia's Next Giant: South Korea and Late Industrialization* (New York: Oxford University Press).

Beny, L. (2007), "The Political Economy of Insider Trading Isolation and Enforcement: An Empirical Contribution to the Theoretical Law and Economics Debate," *Journal of Corporation Law*, 32/2: 237–300.

Chen, Z. (2003), "Capital Markets and Legal Development: The China Case," *China Economic Review*, 14: 451–72.

Clarke, D. (2003), "Corporate Governance in China: An Overview," *China Economic Review*, 14: 494–507.

Coffee, J., Jr. (2002), "Racing Towards the Top? The Impact of Cross-Listings and Stock Market Competition on International Corporate Governance," *Columbia Law Review*, 102/7: 1757–831.

Conk, G. W. (2005), "People's Republic of China Civil Code: Tort Liability Law," *Private Law Review*, 5/2 (The 10th Issue): 77–111, Fordham Law Legal Studies Research Paper No. 892432, Fordham Law School.

Dam, K. (2006), "China as a Test Case: Is the Rule of Law Essential for Economic Growth?" John M. Olin Law and Economics Working Paper No. 275, University of Chicago, Chicago.

Energy Intelligence Group (2004), "Trading Turbulence Downs China Aviation," *International Petroleum Finance*, 27 (1 December): sec. 12.

Fang, L. (1995), "China's Corporatization Experiment," *Duke Journal of Comparative and International Law*, 5: 149–269.

Gao, X.-Q. (1996), "Developments in Securities and Investment Law in China," *Australian Journal of Corporate Law*, 6 (July): 228–45.

Gilson, R. J. (2000), "Globalizing Corporate Governance: Form or Function," Working Paper 174, Center for Law and Economic Studies, Columbia Law School, New York.

Glaeser, E. L. and Shleifer, A. (2002), "Legal Origins," *Quarterly Journal of Economics*, 117/ 4: 1193–229.

Goetzmann, W. and Koll, E. (2006), "The History of Corporate Ownership in China: State Patronage, Company Legislation, and the Issue of Control," in R. K. Morck (ed.), *A History of Corporate Governance around the World: Family Business Groups to Professional Managers* (Chicago: University of Chicago Press), chapter 2.

Green, S. and Ming, H. E. (2004), "China's Stock Market: Out of the Valley in 2004?" *The Royal Institute of International Affairs Briefing Paper* (February): 1–11.

Hall, P. A. and Soskice, D. (eds) (2001), *Varieties of Capitalism* (Oxford: Oxford University Press).

Heritage Foundation (2006), *Economic Freedom of the World* (Washington, DC: Heritage Foundation).

Högfeldt, P. (2003), "The History and Politics of Corporate Ownership in Sweden," ECGI Working Paper available at <http://papers.ssrn.com/sol3/papers.cfm?abstract_id = 449 460>.

Huang, Y. (1996), *Inflation and Investment Controls in China* (Cambridge: Cambridge University Press).

Kister, S. P. (2007), "Note, China's Share-Structure Reform: An Opportunity to Move Beyond Practical Solutions to Practical Problems," *Columbia Journal of Transnational Law*, 45: 312–63.

La Porta, R., Lopez-de-Silanes, F., and Shleifer, A. (2008), "The Economic Consequences of Legal Origin," *Journal of Economic Literature*, 46/2: 285–332.

——————and Vishny, R. W. (1998), "Law and Finance," *Journal of Political Economy*, 106/6: 1113–55.

Li, S. (1999), "Bankruptcy Law in China: Lessons from the Past Twelve Years," *Harvard Asia Quarterly*, 5, 1. Available online at <http://www.leggicinesi.it/dottrina/LiShuguang_Bankruptcy.pdf>, last accessed September 8, 2012.

Lichtenstein, Natalie (1993), "Enterprise Reform in China: The Evolving Legal Framework," Policy Research Working Paper No. 1198 (Washington, DC: World Bank).

Liebman, B. L. (2005), "Watchdog or Demagogue? The Media in the Chinese Legal System," *Columbia Law Review*, 105/1: 1–157.

——and Milhaupt, C. J. (2008), "Reputational Sanctions in China's Securities Markets," *Columbia Law Review*, 108 (May): 929 ff.

Magida, D. (2003), "Establishing an Effective Regulatory Regime: Corporate and Securities Case Studies from Russia and China," Columbia Law School, mimeo on file with the author.

Mahoney, P. (2001), "The Common Law and Economic Growth: Hayek Might be Right," *Journal of Legal Studies*, 30 (June): 503–25.

Milhaupt, C. (2004), "Nonprofit Organizations as Investor Protection: Economic Theory, and Evidence from East Asia," *Yale Journal of International Law*, 29/169: 169–207.

——and Pistor, K. (2008), *Law and Capitalism: What Corporate Crises Reveal about Legal Systems and Economic Development Around the World* (Chicago: Chicago University Press).

Naughton, B. (1995), *Growing Out of the Plan: Chinese Economic Reform, 1978–1993* (New York: Cambridge University Press).

Pils, E. (2005), "Land Disputes and Social Unrest in China: A Case from Sichuan," *Columbia Journal of Asian Law*, 19: 235–92.

Pistor, K. and Wellons, P. (1999), *The Role of Law and Legal Institutions in Asian Economic Development* (Hong Kong: Oxford University Press).

——and Xu, C. (2005), "Governing Stock Markets in Transition Economies: Lessons from China," *American Law and Economics Review*, 7/1: 184–210.

Potter, P. B. (1994), "The Administrative Litigation Law of the PRC: Judicial Review and Bureaucratic Reform," in P. B. Potter (ed.), *Domestic Law Reforms in Post-Mao China* (London: M. E. Sharpe), 270–310.

Qian, Y. (2000), "Government Control in Corporate Governance as a Transitional Institution: Lessons from China," in J. Stiglitz and S. Yusuf (eds), *Rethinking the East Asian Miracle* (Oxford: Oxford University Press), 295–323.

Reese, W. and Weisbach, M. (2001), "Protection of Minority Shareholder Interests, Cross-Listings in the United States, and Subsequent Equity Offerings," NBER Working Papers No. 8164 (Cambridge: National Bureau of Economic Research).

Roe, M. J. (2005), "Delaware's Politics," *Harvard Law Review*, 118 (August): 2491–543.

Shleifer, A. and Vishny, R. W. (1997), "A Survey of Corporate Governance," *Journal of Finance*, 52/2: 737–83.

Sonoko, N. (1983), "China's Special Economic Zones: Experimental Units for Economic Reform," *International and Comparative Law Quarterly*, 32: 175–85.

Stephenson, M. C. (2000), "A Trojan Horse Behind Chinese Walls? Problems and Prospects of U.S.-Sponsored 'Rule of Law' Reform Projects in the People's Republic of China," *UCLA Pacific Basin Law Journal*, 18/1: 64–97.

Wade, R. (2003), *Governing the Market: Economic Theory and the Role of Government in East Asian Industrialization* (Princeton, NJ: Princeton University Press).

Walder, A. and Oi, J. C. (1999), "Property Rights in the Chinese Economy: Contours of the Process of Change," in A. Walder and J. C. Oi (eds), *Property Rights and Economic Reform in China* (Stanford: Stanford University Press), 1–24.

West, M. (2001), "Why Shareholders Sue: The Evidence from Japan," *Journal of Legal Studies*, 30: 351–82.

12

Legal Deterrence: The Foundation of Corporate Governance—Evidence from China

Zhong Zhang[1]

INTRODUCTION

After an initial period of euphoria, the stock market in China was faced with the challenge of surviving until the year 2005. Notwithstanding the fact that GDP increased on average by more than 9 percent every year between 2001 and 2005, both the share indexes of Shanghai and Shenzhen Stock Exchange and the total value of market capitalization lost more than half.[2] Among the 70 million plus registered stock investors, a number which for China had taken no more than ten years to reach, about 70 percent had sold out their investments and withdrawn from the markets by 2005.[3] Before 2001, on average more than 100 companies launched IPOs every year, but the number substantially decreased after 2001. In 2005, IPO activity virtually stopped.[4] The government's policy to reform medium and large state-owned enterprises (SOEs) by way of corporatization and listing, which initiated the growth of the market, had to be brought to a halt.

Why did share prices fall drastically while the macroeconomy was growing rapidly? Why were IPOs not feasible while massive amounts of money were deposited in banks earning negligible interest?[5] Why did so many investors flee from the markets? Clearly the downturn of the stock market had a linkage to a series of corporate scandals that had broken since the end of the 1990s.

This paper analyzes the market mechanisms that were adopted by the Chinese government in order to address problems of corporate governance, and it calls for renewed attention to the need for strong legal deterrents as essential conditions for any corporate governance reform.

Usually companies involved in fraud imploded after a scandal was revealed, and unsophisticated minority investors suffered huge losses. Embezzlement was widespread, and it was common for companies to lose money soon after an IPO. Lack of transparency by covering up bad news was a routine practice and accounting figures were blatantly falsified. Many corrupt company managers fabricated stories about their companies' business prospects in order to collaborate with crooked market traders to manipulate share prices. Clearly investors' confidence in the integrity of the market as well as in the management of listed companies was fading away.

Because of the scandals and frequent company failures, the Chinese government finally learned that corporatization and listing are not the panacea for the illnesses of SOEs. Influenced by Western conceptions of the role of markets, the government recognized the importance of good corporate governance to the success of companies, which in turn is fundamental to the sustainability of the stock market. Since the beginning of the new millennium, corporate governance has become a hot topic in China and attracted a lot of attention. Thus the government has been endeavoring to improve corporate governance in China.

Interestingly, the usefulness of market-based corporate governance mechanisms has been well accepted. The staple governance tools prevalent in the West, such as product and factor markets, independent directorship, institutional shareholder activism, performance-based managerial pay, etc., have been highly regarded by the government and many academics. The dysfunctional stock market as well as the lack of other market-based governance tools have been widely blamed for poor corporate governance in China. Therefore, the Chinese government has focused its efforts to promote good corporate governance largely on making the disciplinary function of the stock market operational and introducing other market-based governance measures.[6] On the other hand, the government seems not to be very interested in tightening legal sanctions, notwithstanding widespread misappropriation and fraud.[7] Legislation remains extraordinarily lenient in terms of criminal punishment and administrative penalties against corporate crooks. Enforcement remains erratic and sporadic. As far as private legal actions are concerned, the government is extremely cautious and the conditions imposed for shareholders to bring derivative actions or securities litigation are inhibitive, excluding private legal actions from playing a role in corporate governance in China.

Is this the right policy to strengthen corporate governance in China? Will the market-orientated efforts alone bear the results expected by the government? Can market mechanisms function properly where deterrence from legal sanctions is intrinsically weak? To answer these questions, it would be helpful to reassess the validity of the theories from the West which advocate the usefulness of market mechanisms for good corporate governance[8] and to ascertain whether they are applicable in China. No doubt the Chinese government in formulating its policy is heavily influenced by such theories and by corporate governance practices from the West. In particular, the unbalanced efforts of the government clearly correspond with the theory favoring markets over legal liability. To assess the validity of the theories, this paper in turn undertakes a re-examination of the working mechanics for market mechanisms to ensure good corporate governance, which is the basis upon which the theories are constructed.

The finding of this paper is that the value of market-based corporate governance mechanisms may have been oversold. They are incapable of disciplining serious misbehaviour such as misappropriation and fraud. Even their ability to discipline less serious misbehavior such as managerial shirking is conditional on the fact that managers are not amenable to misappropriation and fraud. On the contrary, legal deterrence is the only effective way to curb misappropriation and fraud. In addition, by deterring such misbehavior, it also provides for the condition upon which market mechanisms may function properly to discipline managerial shirking. In this sense, legal deterrence is fundamental to good corporate governance. China's current experience of corporate governance confirms this finding.

This paper is organized as follows: the second section provides some background information about the legal framework and practice of corporate governance in China and recent market-oriented reforms. The third section analyzes the working mechanics of competitive markets and other market-based mechanisms in an economic approach and examines the relationship between legal deterrence and market mechanisms. The fourth section discusses the current poor situation of corporate governance and underdeterrence in China. Finally, a conclusion is drawn.

Legal deterrence in this paper indicates the disincentive resulting from legal liabilities. Legal liabilities are in the form of criminal punishments, administrative penalties, and civil liabilities. Legal liabilities imposed when managerial misappropriation is sanctioned deter further misappropriation. Legal liabilities against violation of disclosure requirements mandated by securities law are also critical, though indirectly, in deterring managerial misappropriation.[9] Besides market discipline, this paper examines particularly three market-based corporate governance mechanisms: shareholder activism, performance-based remuneration, and independent directorship. As market discipline, these mechanisms differ from legal deterrence in that they are not compulsory and are not backed by the machinery of the state. They work in a manner similar to market competition or rely on markets to work, so they are termed "market-based corporate governance mechanisms,"

THE LEGAL FRAMEWORK AND PRACTICE OF CORPORATE GOVERNANCE IN CHINA AND RECENT MARKET-ORIENTED REFORM

The issue of corporate governance in China was ushered in by the corporatization reform of SOEs in the early 1990s. Before this, the Chinese government had experimented with several reform policies (Tenev and Zhang 2002) with the aim of boosting poorly performing SOEs, but all ended in failure. The corporatization policy was formally announced by the Communist Party in 1993 with a degree of caution,[10] but it was soon established as the guiding principle for medium- and large-sized SOE reform. It was later decreed that all medium and large SOEs should be corporatized and that, except for a few, the majority should have multiple shareholders.[11] To achieve this, large and medium SOEs were encouraged to issue and list shares on the two stock exchanges in Shanghai and Shenzhen which were opened in 1990 and 1991 respectively.

Originally, almost all listed companies were former SOEs. The common practice of listing is that an SOE sets up a new company and acts as the sole or principal promoter. The founding SOE apportions part of its assets to the new company and becomes its majority shareholder. It may also invite others to join the new company as co-promoters and minority shareholders. The rest of the shares are issued for public subscription. As a result, the state is the ultimate majority shareholder in the bulk of listed companies. It is estimated that the state controls approximately two-thirds of the total shares of listed companies (Qiang 2003).[12] However, this figure must have declined now, because in recent years the state has given up its stakes in many companies that ran into financial distress after listing.

The shares controlled by the state may be owned directly by the governments, but not all by the central government. Different levels of local governments also own a substantial number of shares of listed companies. Shares owned by governments are termed state-owned shares and are actually registered under the name of governmental departments or shareholding companies created specifically for holding and administrating state-owned shares.[13] Further, substantial numbers are also owned by various nonshareholding SOEs and nonprofit institutions like universities, as well as by their subsidiaries. These shares are termed "state-owned legal person shares."[14] Legally, the SOEs and institutions or their subsidiaries are the owners and enjoy the ownership rights, but governments have some control over the exercising of the rights in these shares. For example, the SOE-controlling shareholders of a listed company may have to seek government approval before they sell their shares, and the authority to appoint top managers may be the mandate of the government.

State-controlled shares, as promoters' shares, are not publicly tradable on the exchanges. They can only be bought and sold privately. The fact that the majority of listed companies' shares could not be traded on the exchanges had been strongly criticized and widely regarded as responsible for the failure of the stock market to exert any disciplinary function (Yun 2004).[15] Responding to the criticism, the China Securities Regulatory Commission (CSRC) launched a wave of belated reforms in April 2005 to enable all shares to be publicly tradable. Basically, the guiding rules[16] adopted by the CSRC require that nontradable share owners pay tradable share owners some "consideration" in order for their shares to be publicly tradable, but both how much and in what form this "consideration" takes depend on the result of negotiation between the two types of shareholders, being finally determined by the voting of tradable share owners. It is also stipulated that not all nontradable shares of a shareholder become tradable instantly, but rather over a three-year phased-in period.[17] The reform was said to be very successful and had largely been completed by the end of 2007. But it is doubtful that the alleged goal of invigorating the disciplinary function of the stock market can be achieved where the bulk of shares of listed companies are still in the control of the state. A more significant consequence is that the reform has opened the possibility that the state can reduce its ownership in listed companies through selling on the stock exchanges.

Initially, households were the main group of public investors. They trade via securities companies but hold shares in their own names. That the majority of investors were individuals was blamed for the wild fluctuation in share prices, because individuals are not, it was said, long-term investors. Partly to stabilize the market and partly inspired by shareholder activism associated with institutional investors in Western countries, the Chinese government adopted a policy to encourage the growth of institutional investments. Qualified foreign financial institutions have been allowed to invest in the domestic exchanges since December 1, 2002.[18] National Social Security Funds,[19] insurance companies,[20] and enterprise pension funds[21] have also been permitted to do so. Most extraordinarily, both the number of securities investment funds and assets held by those funds grew rapidly as a result of encouragement by the government.[22] By the end of November 2005, the paid-up capital of securities investment funds had reached about half of the total market value of tradable shares.[23] In a short period of time, institutional investments in China have increased to a percentage comparable to some developed economies.

A basic legal framework for corporate governance has been established in China. The Company Law was passed in 1993 and took effect on July 1, 1994. The Securities Law was passed in 1998 after being delayed for several years. Before that, a regulation adopted by the State Council was the governing law.[24] The Securities Law heavily borrowed from America, and the approach it takes to regulating the stock market is mandatory disclosure; but the law also requires that the CSRC conduct a "merit" review before a public offering is permitted. The CSRC is the designated government agency responsible for the implementation of the Securities Law. But it was set up long before the Securities Law was passed. In October 2005, both the Company Law and the Securities Law were amended extensively to boost corporate governance, but their basic frameworks have not been changed.

The governance structure and power distribution within Chinese listed companies are rather confusing. The old Company Law did not envisage any role for independent directors in corporate governance and thus there were no provisions concerning independent directors. Rather, it stipulated a dual board system. But this dual board system is totally different from that prevalent in continental Europe. The supervisory board has no power to appoint and dismiss members of the managerial board. They are elected and dismissed by shareholders' meetings,[25] just as in the Anglo-American unitary board system. Supervisory directors themselves are partially elected by shareholders and partially elected by employees.[26] The law actually did not seriously expect supervisory directors to play a big role in the governance of companies, as it provided them with virtually no powers. As a matter of fact, the supervisory board was mere window dressing and negligible in corporate governance in China before the Company Law was amended in 2005 (Miles and Zhang 2006).

When the CSRC took on the issue of corporate governance, the Anglo-American system had become dominant and the inclusion of independent directors on the board had become a common practice around the world. In 2001, the CSRC issued a guiding rule mandating that listed companies should have at least two independent directors on their managerial boards by June 30, 2002 and that by June 30, 2003 one third of directors should be independent.[27] This rule was considered by some as important to improve the governance of listed companies, while others were more suspicious (Shen and Jia 2005). The requirement has been endorsed by the new Company Law.[28] But at the same time, the new Company Law furnished supervisory directors with some new rights, albeit still short of the power to appoint and dismiss members of the managerial board. For example, the supervisory board now has the right to propose resolutions to shareholders' meetings to dismiss members of the managerial board and take legal actions against them on behalf of the company after receiving a demand from shareholders who meet specific conditions.[29] Thus under the new Company Law, both independent directors and supervisory directors are entrusted with the responsibility of monitoring managers. The effect of this arrangement combining elements from both the Anglo-American and German systems has yet to be tested, but the overlap is obvious and conflicts are probable (Miles and Zhang 2006).

The Chinese government has also made other moves that can be described as market-oriented in its campaign for good corporate governance. For instance, in 2002, the CSRC adopted a detailed corporate governance code aiming to promote best practice concerning governance structure, shareholder voting, board composition, the conduct of board and shareholders' meetings, etc.[30] Further, in response to calls to introduce performance-based remuneration schemes, in 2005 the CSRC issued a rule allowing listed companies to pay their managers with stocks and stock options.[31]

AN ECONOMIC ANALYSIS OF THE WORKING MECHANICS OF MARKET DISCIPLINE AND MARKET-BASED CORPORATE GOVERNANCE MECHANISMS

The core issue of corporate governance is the agency problem resulting from separation of ownership and control (Shleifer and Vishny 1997). Managers from companies where ownership and control are separated may not work hard for the interests of shareholders as a whole, but for their own benefit (Berle and Means 1933; Jensen and Meckling 1976). The primary concern of corporate governance is how to ensure managers maximize shareholder value and refrain from engaging in behavior that may damage shareholders' interests (Shleifer and Vishny 1997).

There are different types of misbehavior with which managers may sacrifice shareholders' interests for their own benefits. Generally, corporate law classifies directors' duties as the duty of loyalty and the duty of care, and thus managerial misbehavior can be accordingly divided into duty-of-loyalty violations and duty-of-care violations (Davies 2003; Scott 1983). Duty-of-loyalty violations are primarily conflicting-interests acts such as unfair self-dealing, enjoying excessive perks, misappropriation, etc., while duty-of-care violations do not involve conflict of interests.[32] Economists dub duty-of-care violations as managerial "shirking," which means slackness and avoidance of uncomfortable changes (Alchian and Demsetz 1972). As for duty-of-loyalty violations, some academics divide them further into traditional conflicts of interests and positional conflicts (Eisenberg 1989). Traditional conflicts arise from dubious transactions entered into by managers with their companies or from diversions of company assets (tangible or intangible), while positional conflicts mean that managers maintain or promote their positions by way of such misbehavior as empire building, takeover defense, etc., even at the expense of shareholder interests (Eisenberg 1989).

When Berle and Means wrote their seminal book, they did not investigate governance mechanisms other than law which may have the effect of discouraging managerial opportunism. Since then, inspiring economics scholarship has exposed a number of nonlegal governance mechanisms which are nevertheless able to deter managers from engaging in opportunistic behavior. First, various competitive markets (i.e., the capital, Jensen and Meckling 1976; Fama 1980), corporate control (Manne 1965), product (Eisenberg 1989) and labor markets (Fama 1980) and then performance-based remunerations were revealed to be able to function as constraints on managerial discretion (Jensen and Murphy 1990). More recently, shareholder activism associated with institutional investors (Black 1990; Roe 1994; Romano 2001) and independent directorship (Cadbury 1992) stole the spotlight. In the end, competitive markets and market-based governance mechanisms have acquired particular prominence and been widely accepted as critical to addressing the agency problems resulting from separation of ownership and control. Some law and economics scholars who studied corporate law in a "contractarian" perspective went a step further to even suggest that legal rules are negligible, because of the existence of various market-based substitutes (Easterbrook and Fischel 1996; Fischel and Bradley 1986). They argued that mandatory legal rules are superfluous where private persons can bargain for themselves with market forces being in place. Indeed, they suggested that, because of different costs associated with legal liability, markets have comparative advantages over legal liability and thus market mechanisms are preferable to legal liability. Their arguments are best described by the phrase "market primacy." The theories suggesting the efficacy of market mechanisms in general and the market primacy theory in particular are so influential as to have made an impact on the Communist government of China in its formulation of corporate governance policies.

There is already a vast amount of literature debating the pros and cons of markets. The essence of traditional criticisms is that, because of the existence of such problems as informational asymmetry, transaction costs, judgment and collective action, etc., markets are not perfect and may fail to work (Ferran 1999; Cheffins 1997). This paper is not intended to join the traditional debate. Rather, in an aim to evaluate the effectiveness of the Chinese government's policies and efforts to promote good corporate governance in China, it seeks to find out whether market-based corporate mechanisms can be expected to work effectively and play a significant role in corporate governance where legal deterrence is intrinsically weak. To do that, it first takes a closer look at how markets work to ensure good corporate governance.

(1) *The disciplinary function of markets*

It is said that market competition can function to discipline management from engaging in opportunistic behavior. Managerial misbehavior gives rise to additional costs and makes products of a company less competitive. Managers of uncompetitive companies could lose their jobs by being dismissed for poor performance or as a result of company failure, or at least lose the benefits generated through career advancement when business is successful (Eisenberg 1989; Butler 1989; Fischel 1982). Costs also accrue with poor governance in the form of more expensive capital or not being able to raise new capital at all, where the capital market is competitive. Further, if the management of a company performs poorly, the share price of the company would drop to a level where it is profitable for other companies to take it over. After a hostile takeover, inevitably the old management would be replaced (Manne 1965). Even if hostile takeover does not happen, underperformance of a company's share price would lead to discontent among shareholders who would eventually revolt to evict the undesirable management. Finally, a competitive labor market also plays a role in corporate governance in that competition compels managers to deliver their best performance in order to keep their existing employment and to promote their marketability for more lucrative future jobs (Jensen and Murphy 1990; Dooley and Veasey 1989: 511; Coughlan and Schmidt 1985). It is thus clear that the disciplinary function of markets stems from the potential threat that misbehaving managements would lose their current and future employment. In economic terms, managerial misbehavior imposes costs on miscreant managers in the form of losing the benefits associated with career preservation and advancement. For simplicity, hereafter we refer to this cost as the unemployment loss. As rational men, managers would try to avoid this cost and thus an incentive is created which drives them to act honestly and work hard for the interests of shareholders.

However, managerial misbehavior would not necessarily entail only cost. It may also produce benefit. While misappropriation, self-dealing, empire building, or shirking may result in loss of unemployment, they may also afford misbehaving managers financial benefits or the satisfaction of self-fulfillment or leisure time. If a manager is really rational, he would calculate both the loss and benefit an action would bring to him, and only when the benefit is smaller than the present value of loss of benefits from future employment would a manager choose to avoid suboptimal behavior. Otherwise, he would choose to misbehave. Hence, we can see that the disciplinary functions of market competition espoused by market efficacy theories are based on the assumption that the present value of unemployment loss to a manager is more than the benefit he gains from the misbehavior. The assumption can be described as:

L (unemployment) > B (misbehavior)

Is this assumption true? The answer is indeed yes where managerial misbehavior involves only shirking or violations of duty of care. A manager may have more leisure time and avoid stress from demanding work when he engages in shirking, but shirking does not directly afford him financial gains. Thus, in terms of financial benefits,[33] a manager derives no gains directly from the misbehavior where it involves only shirking, but the possibility of losing his job still exists. Thus a misbehaving manager would lose more than he gains. As a rational man making the best deal for himself, he would choose to be diligent and dedicated to his job rather than slack and inattentive. So, where misbehavior involves only shirking, the assumption is correct and markets are effective to discipline. The formula can be elaborated as follows:

L (unemployment) > B (misbehavior)
Because: B (misbehavior) = B (shirking) = 0

Where positional conflicts are in question, the answer is not so certain. A manager may not directly derive financial benefits from acts involving positional conflicts, but he may gain indirectly. For example, where empire building is in issue, he may reap higher remuneration when a company expands. On the other hand, such misbehavior may eventually lead to decline or even collapse of a company, and a misbehaving manager may thus lose his job. The net gain or loss from positional conflicting acts is difficult to assess, and a manager may be confused in calculating the costs and benefits of a positional conflicting act. As a result, it is unclear whether markets are effective to discourage positional conflicting acts.[34]

However, the situation changes when traditional conflicting acts are considered. When traditional conflicts are involved, certainly there exists the possibility that the benefits from misbehavior may outweigh the costs. Let's assume that a manager in a Chinese listed company currently receives annual remuneration of $80,000 and the present value of the future annual income from employment on average is $100,000; further assume that his remaining working life expectancy is thirty years and he would lose his current job and never find a new job following a misappropriation.[35] Thus his total potential loss would be $3 million. If market discipline is the only force governing his behavior, he will choose to commit the misbehavior rather than to work hard honestly to advance his personal interests if he can successfully divert to himself more than $3 million from the company.[36]

Is it possible for him to do so? Obviously, if the total assets of the company are worth less than $3 million, the answer is no. But it would be a rare case that the total value of assets of a company is less than the employment value of a manager. Further, the markets may be very efficient, and the negative information about misbehavior may be transferred quickly onto the markets so that a manager loses his job before he can divert sufficient corporate assets to himself. But, to circumvent this situation, there are various tactics for him to employ. He may misappropriate a sum big enough on one or two occasions. Or he may defraud and cover up his misbehavior and engage in a series of misappropriations. Both types of misbehavior can be regarded as one-off misbehavior, in the sense that the misbehaving manager may derive from such misbehavior financial benefits sufficient enough for him to withdraw from the management job market altogether.[37] Under these circumstances, benefits to a manager from engaging in traditional conflicts may well outweigh the value of loss from unemployment. From this, we can see that, if markets are the only governing force, a manager can gain more by engaging in misbehavior than by honest and hard work. As a result, the disciplinary function of markets would fail to work. In other words, markets alone are not effective to discourage one-off misbehavior, i.e., large-scale embezzlements and nonsubstantial but fraudulent misappropriations. Thus, the formula has been changed as follows:

B (misbehavior) > L (unemployment)
Because: B (one-off misbehavior) > L (unemployment)

Worse still, when traditional conflicts are not controlled, markets are not effective in disciplining managers from shirking or engaging in positional conflicts. If a manager can easily enrich himself by embezzlement or self-dealing, why should he compel himself to work hard to advance his personal interests and refrain from positional conflicts? There is no longer the need for him to work hard to advance his personal well-being if opportunities are ample for him to become rich by way of one-off misappropriation. In other words, when a manager can compensate his loss from unemployment with benefits from one-off misappropriations, he no longer needs to concern himself with how to avoid the cost. He thus loses the incentive to work hard. As such, the only function of markets to discipline managerial shirking is lost. This situation can be described as follows:

If: B (one-off misappropriation) > L (unemployment)
Then: B (misbehavior) > L (unemployment)
Because: B (misbehavior) = B (shirking + positional conflicts + traditional conflicts)
and B (traditional conflicts) = B (one-off misappropriation + other traditional conflicts)

That is, if markets are the only governing force, a manager can gain benefits larger from one-off misappropriation than the unemployment loss. When the benefit from one-off misappropriation is larger than the unemployment loss, the total benefits from various misbehaviors (shirking, positional conflicts, and traditional conflicts) would always be larger than the unemployment loss. Thus the condition for markets to work effectively (i.e., the present value of unemployment loss is more than the benefits from misbehavior) is no longer present. Accordingly, the disciplinary function of markets no longer exists.

In conclusion, market competition alone is not effective to discourage traditional conflicts of interests, particularly large-scale embezzlements and fraudulent misappropriations. When such misbehavior is not constrained, markets would even lose the ability to discipline managerial shirking.

The analysis in this section takes an economic approach[38] and is based on the model of separation of ownership and control. It does not discuss the possible role of social norms or morality in guiding the behavior of management.[39] Further, the economic analysis has been simplified. On the one hand, it is a purely economic analysis which considers only financial gain and loss. Nonfinancial utility as well as disutility (such as leisure time, avoidance of stress, loss of reputation,[40] etc.) have not been taken into account. On the other hand, it assumes that markets are perfectly efficient so that the unemployment cost resulting from misbehavior is accurately priced and timely imposed on liable managers. As purely economic and simplified as the analysis is, it is nevertheless sufficient to conclude that market competition is not omnipotent, and even its limited value to control managerial shirking is based on the prerequisite that the opportunities for managers to enrich themselves by way of misappropriation are rare. If such opportunities are ample and managers have no concern regarding punishment for fraud, the disciplinary function of markets can be ignored. These propositions seem to be common sense, and one does not need to be an economist to appreciate them;[41] but they seem to have become obscured with the rise of market efficacy theories. A sketchy re-examination of the working mechanics of market competition, however, shows that such common wisdom should not be dismissed lightly.

(2) *Institutional investor activism and performance-based remuneration*

The growth of institutional investments and a number of high-profile shareholder revolts led by institutional investors in the 1980s gave rise to the expectation of change in traditional shareholder passivity. Shareholder activism was thus proclaimed to have arrived by some commentators. Many claim that institutional investors play an important role in corporate governance (Black 1990; Roe 1994; Romano 2001), while others are less optimistic (Bainbridge 2005; McCormack 1998). Some empirical studies show that institutional shareholder activism matters little in improving corporate governance (Black 1995; Karpoff 2001). Whatever the controversy, in theory institutional shareholders should be more active in corporate governance, because they hold a much bigger stake in companies compared to individual shareholders.

However, shareholder activism suffers the same problem that markets do: it is incapable of disciplining one-off duty-of-loyalty violations. To a large degree, the mechanics of institutional investor activism to encourage good corporate governance are very much like those of markets. Institutional investor activism means that institutional investors actively participate in company elections; as a result, entrenched underperforming managers are ousted. Because managers have a concern that they may be banished for underperformance, they are pressured to maximize shareholders' interests and not to engage in opportunistic activities. It can be seen that the function of institutional investor activism in encouraging good corporate governance is very similar to the disciplinary function of markets. To be accurate, markets and shareholder activism are one combined mechanism rather than two. On the one hand, market discipline needs the help of shareholder voting to oust incompetent managements. On the other hand, active participation in the corporate elective process by shareholders is informed by information from markets. Because the working mechanics of shareholder activism are similar to or combined with those of markets, the impotence of markets is shared by shareholder activism. Specifically, institutional shareholder activism in the form of active participation in the corporate elective process is not effective to deter managers from engaging in one-off misappropriation. The ability of shareholder activism to discipline managerial shirking is also lost where fraudulent self-enrichment is not brought under control and gains for managers from misbehavior outweigh the present value of future income from employment.

Possibly, performance-based remuneration such as stock options plays a more significant role than institutional investor activism in encouraging good corporate governance (Jensen and Murphy 1990; Dooley and Veasey 1989; Coughlan and Schmidt 1985), though after Enron and WorldCom its downside has attracted more criticism (Coffee 2004). The merit of performance-based remuneration is that, it is said, it restores the connection between the interests of management and shareholder. By linking remuneration with corporate performance, the performance-based remuneration scheme ensures that the interests of shareholders and managements are aligned and incentives are thus created for managements to maximize corporate value.

However, reality is not as simple as that. Actually, it is fair to say that the interests of managers and shareholders are never separated in a competitive market economy: the increase in company value brings benefits not only to shareholders but also to managers, because by enhancing company value managers reap the benefits from job preservation and career advancement. Even without performance-based remuneration, markets align the interests of managements and shareholders. What performance-based remuneration does is to increase the magnitude of benefits from productive behavior and the costs from counter-productive behavior for management. It is thus clear that the mechanics for performance-based remuneration to encourage good corporate governance are not new and not different from those of market competition. Both seek to induce productive behavior by feeding managers benefits and to discourage counter-productive behavior by imposing costs on them. Both are voluntary rather than compulsory. Therefore, performance-based remuneration is similarly not effective as a means to discourage one-off managerial self-enrichment.

This is not difficult to understand. When there are opportunities for a manager to engage in self-interested activities such as misappropriation, the benefit he can obtain may be more than that provided by a performance-based remuneration scheme. As such, performance-based remuneration may not be attractive enough to induce a manager to shun opportunities for misappropriation. When a manager decides to commit misappropriation, it is unimaginable that he can be persuaded by a performance-based remuneration scheme to work hard for the interests of shareholders. Hence, where misappropriation is not deterred by other means, performance-based remuneration adds nothing to managers' incentive to promote the interests of companies. Worse still, performance-based remuneration may be counter-productive where misappropriation is not deterred. When a manager is amenable to misappropriation, it is almost predictable that he may fraudulently inflate accounting figures and thus collect the benefit provided by a performance-based remuneration scheme. As a result, shareholders suffer more loss with than without performance-based remuneration.

In summary, just as market competition, both shareholder activism and performance-based remuneration are not effective in discouraging managers from engaging in one-off, duty-of-loyalty violations. If one-off, duty-of-loyalty violations are not deterred, managerial shirking cannot be disciplined. Further, introducing performance-based remuneration schemes may be counter-productive, if one-off, duty-of-loyalty violations are not controlled and if fraud is not deterred.

(3) *Governing by independent directors*

It is clear from the foregoing discussion that bringing under control one-off, duty-of-loyalty violations is crucial to good corporate governance. Not only is such misbehavior fatal to the success of companies, but it is also a precondition for markets and market-based institutions to work. So, the critical question is how the fraudulent diversion of company assets can be reduced to a minimum. The foregoing discussion has demonstrated that markets, shareholder activism, and performance-based pay cannot be relied on to curb such misbehavior. Therefore, solutions should be sought from other areas.

Independent directorship has now become a paradigm institution of corporate governance and corporate governance codes all over the world require that listed companies should instate some independent directors on their boards.[42] One aspect of the importance of independent directors is that, in theory, they can monitor the executives (Higgs 2003). Specifically, in relation to the prevention of diversion of corporate assets by executives, independent directors are better positioned to decide whether a transaction entered into by executives with their company is a good deal for the company. Because independent directors do not participate in the day-to-day business of a company and usually have no personal interests in the company apart from the directorship, they can exercise an impartial judgment over the fairness of executives' self-dealings. As a result, by requiring that transactions entered into by executives with their company are approved by independent directors, unfair transactions can be avoided. It has been a norm of corporate law that transactions involving conflicts of interests should be decided by disinterested directors, and interested directors should abstain from participating in the decision-making (Enriques 2000). By taking away from executives decision-making power regarding such transactions and giving the power solely to independent directors, managerial misappropriation by way of self-dealing can be prevented.

However, the argument holds only if executives are honest. If they are dishonest and determined to line their pockets with company money, tactics are many for them to escape monitoring by independent directors. They may conceal the fact that they are interested in a transaction. They may disclose false or misleading information concerning the terms of a transaction. Or, they may execute a transaction secretly and not go to the board for approval of a transaction that is required by law or company charter to do so. These are tactics that are currently routinely employed by management or controlling shareholders of listed companies in China.[43] Indeed, if custodians decide to steal properties entrusted to their custody, who can prevent them from doing so? Certainly not independent directors. Independent directors can be monitors, but it is too much to expect them to assume the role of the police. It is unreasonable to expect that they can stop or uncover deliberate fraud perpetrated by executives. They rely on executives for information. If executives do not provide information or supply false information, what can independent directors do? As commentators have rightly pointed out, "If auditors are nervous about their ability to detect fraud when they have full access to the corporate books, how can an independent director be expected to detect dishonesty hidden in the neat and professionally turned-out documents presented to him for board meetings?" (Shen and Jia 2005).

It can be seen that, if managers are determined to misappropriate, independent directors are powerless and cannot be relied upon to control fraudulent diversion of company assets. Independent directors may have a role to play to check dubious managerial self-dealings, but they are useless in combating fraudulent managerial misappropriation. The other monitoring functions of independent directors, like monitoring the authenticity of financial information disclosed to the public, would similarly fail if managers are not afraid to cheat and also auditors have no concern regarding legal liability for failing to live up to the professional standards required by law. The inability of independent directors to protect companies from being looted by crooked managers implies that independent directors have a role to play in corporate governance only if executives are honest or deterred from fraud by other means.

(4) *Legal deterrence as the foundation of corporate governance*

Why are markets and market-related governing institutions not able to discourage one-off managerial misappropriation? It is because they do not possess the ability to take away illegitimate benefits from corrupt managers. This is, in turn, because they are voluntary institutions, not backed by the machinery of the state. So far it is clear that, in order to direct managers to behave in one way but not another, markets provide managers with a benefit larger than the other, rather than deprive any illegitimate benefits they may have gained. For example, markets induce managers to work hard by affording them a financial benefit larger than that from shirking. Obviously, this strategy cannot always be successful. If people are allowed to take property from others, the benefit they receive may well outweigh the benefit that they may gain from restraint. As a result, a person would in all likelihood choose to misappropriate. Because markets are not endowed with the ability to extract illegitimate benefits, they are unable to reverse the calculation of gain and loss and thus fail to induce managers to refrain from misappropriation.[44]

Where misbehavior can generate benefits for managers larger than those that markets can reward them with, the only feasible way to discourage such misbehavior is to take away the benefits it brings. Only legal sanction is endowed with the ability to do this. Because depriving corrupt managers of illegitimate benefits involuntarily would entail the use of physical force and the state has a monopoly on the legitimate use of violent force, participation by the state is needed. This is exactly what legal sanction is. Legal sanction is created and sponsored by the state in order to address illegality and injustice including unjustified benefits and losses. It is the only permissible way to take away involuntarily illegitimate benefits.[45] As a matter of fact, legal sanction may not just take away illegitimate benefits. It may also impose punishment on corrupt managers in the form of fines, disqualification, and/or incarceration, leaving them with negative net gains. As a result, managers are deterred from engaging in misbehavior for fear of suffering losses more than gains. It can be seen that the unique attribute of legal sanction to remove illegitimate benefits (and to impose punishment) distinguishes it from voluntary market mechanisms and enables it to deter one-off misappropriation and fraud. Because bringing one-off misappropriation and fraud under control is fundamental to good corporate governance, and because deterrence by way of legal sanction is the only feasible way to tackle such misbehavior, a conclusion can be drawn that effective legal deterrence is the foundation of corporate governance.[46]

Legal sanctions take the form of civil remedies, administrative penalties, and criminal punishment. They may be imposed separately as well as collectively. There are vast amounts of literature debating the relative merits of different forms of legal sanction. Generally, criminal punishment and administrative penalties are more severe, but various obstacles exist for them to be effectively enforced (Langevoort 1990, 1999; Rider 1988; Naylor 1990). Because of the problem of enforcement, they may not be advantageous in term of deterrence (Becker 1968; Coffee 1980). Civil remedy is less severe, but its deterrent effect is not negligible (Becker and Stigler 1974; La Porta et al. 2006). There exist fewer obstacles for the enforcement of civil law than for imposing criminal and administrative sanctions (Benson 1990; Coffee 1980; Naylor 1990). Nevertheless, the importance of criminal and regulatory punishments should not be rejected, because serious misbehavior has to be dealt with by more severe punishments. As a matter of fact, criminal, administrative, and civil sanctions should be complementary rather than substitutive if an optimal result of deterrence is to be achieved (Braithwaite 1984, cited in Monks and Minow 2003).

Legal sanctions can target managerial diversion of company assets directly and indirectly. First of all, because of the seriousness, criminal punishment against managerial thefts is a staple in criminal legislation around the world, notwithstanding the difficulty of enforcement. In some countries, the government may have the jurisdiction to impose administrative penalties such as fines, disgorgement, or disqualification of managers who misappropriate. As far as deterrence by way of civil sanctions is concerned, it is critical to give shareholders the right to bring a derivative action, because entrenched managements would not sue themselves. Laws stipulating these sanctions target misappropriation directly. Contrastingly, securities law addresses managerial theft indirectly by way of regulating information disclosure. But securities law has become more and more important for corporate governance. In some countries its importance in ensuring good corporate governance may have well exceeded the importance of company law (Thompson and Sale 2003). Indeed some academics argue that improving corporate governance provides the most pervasive justification for ongoing mandatory disclosure (Fox 1999). On the one hand, the functioning of various corporate governance mechanisms relies on the availability of accurately and timely disclosed information. On the other hand, mandatory disclosure deters managerial misappropriation in the first place, because managers who intend to misbehave would worry about the publicity of their misbehavior (Fox 1999). Hence goes the saying, "Sunshine is the best disinfectant" (Brandeis 1928).

(5) *An evaluation of the market primacy thesis*

The problems of the market efficacy theories in general and the market primacy theory in particular have so far been fully revealed. When market mechanisms are incapable of stopping one-off, duty-of-loyalty violations and when their limited value to discourage duty-of-care violations is even conditional on the suppression of managerial misappropriation by legal deterrence, it is not convincing that market mechanisms are superior and more advantageous than legal liability. On the other hand, if legal deterrence is the only feasible way to combat managerial fraud and embezzlement, it is not correct to claim that legal liability can be substituted and is therefore negligible. Because of the vital importance of legal deterrence in combating managerial fraud and embezzlement, it occupies a foundational position in corporate governance upon which the whole system of corporate governance stands.

It was argued that duty-of-care violations are "probably the single largest source of agency costs" (Fischel and Bradley 1986). We should take notice that this argument may be concerning only the experience of the United States. It is true regarding a particular jurisdiction like the United States where duty-of-loyalty violations may have been addressed satisfactorily, but surely it is incorrect if the argument is a general comparison between the two types of violations. Duty-of-loyalty violations in general, fraud and misappropriation in particular, are no doubt far more serious. They are not only destructive to company success, but also destructive to the proper functioning of market-based mechanisms. That is why liability for duty-of-loyalty violations is far harsher than for duty-of-care violations all over the world. It would be wrong for us to draw a general conclusion, based on the US experience, that duty-of-loyalty violations are insignificant and thus belittle the importance of battling duty-of-loyalty violations.

It was also charged that legal liability comes with different costs so that it may not be desirable as a corporate governance mechanism. For example, it was said that legal liability may give rise to a tendency for managers to act in a risk-averse rather than risk-neutral way in managerial decision-making; that the threat of legal liability may cause managers to be less willing to make firm-specific human capital investments; and that there also exist the costs associated with errors made by judges, because judges are not better qualified than managers to decide whether a transaction is in the best interests of shareholders. All of these incidents may harm shareholders' interests (Fischel and Bradley 1986).

First of all, an observation that can be made about this accusation is that it makes no distinction between liability arising from violation of duty of care and duty of loyalty. While the alleged costs may have some relevance with regard to duty-of-care liability (although the costs in this respect have been exaggerated and are not in accordance with reality and the business judgment rule (Schwartz 1986)), they are totally irrelevant as far as duty-of-loyalty liability is concerned. Courts may have difficulty in assessing managerial efforts, but it is hard to claim that they are inferior to managers in assessing the merit of conflicting managerial behavior. The threat from legal sanctions over misappropriation has nothing to do with either risk-taking or firm-specific human capital investments by honest managers. More importantly, it should be pointed out that, because legal sanctions are irreplaceable in deterring managerial misappropriation and fraud, legal deterrence is indispensable even if the alleged costs were true or costs other than those listed above may exist. The correct approach is to see how costs can be reduced rather to reject legal deterrence because of the existence of costs. In other words, costs, genuine or false, are not the reason to downplay the importance of legal deterrence. If legal deterrence is excluded for the reason of alleged costs, corporate governance in a country is destined to be poor.

While academic discourse has not yet clearly indicated that the limited value of market discipline is even based on sufficient legal deterrence, the fact that markets are ineffective to discipline one-off misbehavior has long been recognized (Klein and Leffler 1981; Demsetz 1986). Judge Easterbrook and Professor Fischel, who were the champions of market utility, admitted themselves that market discipline is ineffective so far as one-off managerial misconduct is concerned (Easterbrook and Fischel 1996). But for them, such misconduct seemed only a minor exception to their arguments for the superiority of market mechanisms over legal liability. Why did they ignore that type of managerial misbehavior, despite its seriousness? Why did they not recognize that sufficient legal deterrence is fundamental for market mechanisms to work? We may have an answer, if we can appreciate that their study focused on the United States, where they considered that "the widespread assumption that corporate managers systematically act in ways contrary to investors' best interests is without foundation" and that "the opportunity cost of excess leisure and not working hard is probably the single largest source of agency costs" (Fischel and Bradley 1986). If their assertion is true, sufficient legal deterrence may have already been secured in the United States, and the focal issue of corporate governance is no longer misappropriation and fraud but that of duty-of-care violations.

For duty-of-care violations, market mechanisms may be a better cure than legal sanction (Fischel and Bradley 1986). Indeed, where lack of legal deterrence is no longer a problem, it may be desirable to emphasize the utility of market mechanisms rather than legal sanctions, because of the concerns about overdeterrence. If emphasis is still put on legal sanctions where adequate deterrence has already been secured, the net benefit may be negative in that gains from increased deterrence may be outweighed by associated costs. Furthermore, even if concerns about overdeterrence are unfounded, exploiting market forces to improve corporate governance may be more cost-effective than incurring efforts to increase legal deterrence which has already been substantial. In view of this, it is understandable that legal liability for duty-of-care violations is only nominal (Black and Cheffins 2004) and the business judgment rule is firmly accepted in the United States.[47] So, if we are able to appreciate that the advocates of market utility have focused their study on the United States, where they assumed that managerial misappropriation and fraud may no longer be "systematic," their preference for markets over legal liability becomes comprehensible and criticisms of their market primacy proposition are invalid.[48]

This, however, does not mean that arguments for market efficacy and market primacy in particular are sound as a general theory and universally applicable. Not all countries are in the same position as the United States. At least in China currently, corporate embezzlements are widespread, fraud is rampant, and scandals are recurring realities. For a country like this, it is plainly wrong to claim and detrimental to flippantly accept that market mechanisms are effective and preferable to legal sanction. We should recognize the fundamental difference in corporate governance between China and the United States. Otherwise, those theories will be misinterpreted and the urgent need to enhance legal deterrence to combat managerial fraud and misappropriation will be missed.

UNDERDETERRENCE: EVIDENCE FROM CHINA

So far it has been argued that it is vitally important to deter misappropriation and fraud and that legal sanctions play a unique role in doing so. In this section concrete evidence from China is provided to demonstrate that systematic misappropriation and fraud are not imaginary where legal deterrence is exceedingly weak. This clearly illustrates that market mechanisms alone are ineffective to discourage misappropriation and fraud, and the prevalence and persistence of fraud and misappropriation are better explained by the lack of adequate legal deterrence. The evidence concerns misappropriation of listed companies' funds. Other scandals, such as fabricating accounting figures, manipulating share prices through trading, making up stories about the business prospects of companies, etc., are not discussed here.

(1) *Misappropriations in listed companies*

Generally, corporate governance in listed companies in China is pitiful (Tenev and Zhang 2002; Clarke 2003; Fischer 2005; Schipani and Liu 2002).[49] One acute problem is that funds are routinely channeled out of companies to their controlling shareholders or other related parties not as genuine business transactions. According to a survey conducted by the CSRC at the end of 2002, of the total 1,175 listed companies, 676 had experienced fund tunneling by their majority shareholders, funds misappropriated amounting to 96.7 billion RMB (Ou, Li, and Sun 2005). Up to the end of 2003, the balance of misappropriated funds of 623 listed companies was 57.7 billion RMB (Ou, Li, and Sun 2005). As of June 30, 2005, the majority shareholders of 480 listed companies expropriated corporate funds, and the balance of about 48 billion RMB accounted for more than half of the profits of all listed companies made in the first half of the year. At the same time, more than 1000 listed companies had illegally guaranteed loans of about 42.5 billion RMB borrowed by their majority shareholders (Ou, Li, and Sun 2005).

In a substantial number of cases where funds were tunneled or guarantees offered to majority shareholders, no board decisions were made or resolutions passed by shareholders' meetings even though these may be required by companies' articles of association, administrative regulations,[50] or primary legislation.[51] Such tunneling or guarantees are simply enacted by some executives and concealed both from outside directors (usually independent directors) and the public shareholders. More often than not, such tunneling and guarantees are not authentic business transactions. They are misappropriation, or in plain language, stealing. In 2005, about 180 directors were publicly censured by the two stock exchanges for misbehavior, and more than half were involved in fund misappropriation.[52] At the same time, the requirements of mandatory disclosure stipulated by securities laws are taken extremely lightly and misappropriation is routinely covered up to the last minute. In 2004 and 2005, there were respectively forty-nine and forty-three cases of violations of securities law which were penalized by the CSRC. Among these, about 55 percent involved misrepresentation by listed companies.[53] It should be remembered that violations which have been revealed and punished are only a small percentage of the total. In a study of CSRC penalties and public censure by the two stock exchanges, it is estimated that for every one case of penalty or public censure there are as many as four cases of violations that have not been revealed or pursued (Wu 2005). It is no exaggeration to say that misappropriation is widespread and negative information is routinely concealed by listed companies in China.

Several high-profile cases have been widely reported:

- Kelon (000921): The company's shares are quoted on both the Shenzhen and Hong Kong stock exchanges. The company was originally controlled by a local government in Guangdong Province. In 2001, a private company owned by an entrepreneur bought control of the company, and the same person thereafter acquired control of four more listed companies. After the company was handed over to the private person, there were extensive reports about suspicion that accounting figures were manipulated and funds of the company were misappropriated by the controller. In 2005 the CSRC announced an investigation and, shortly thereafter, six managers including the controller were arrested by the local police. The local government regained control of the company and appointed KPMG to conduct an investigation. After it had examined the occurrences of money transfer above 10 million RMB, KPMG reported that during 2001 to 2005, about 7.5 billion RMB had been transferred in and out of the bank accounts of the company for no business purpose, resulting in a net loss to the company of 592 million RMB. The CSRC's investigation finally uncovered that from 2002 to 2004, 477.18 million RMB in profits were fabricated. The transfers of funds had never been disclosed by the company nor by its auditor, Deloitte and Touche; neither revealed the transfers of funds nor the fabricated profits (Zhang 2006; Luo and Shen 2006).

- Sanjiu Yiyao (000999): Following the company's IPO, from July 1999 to December 2000 more than 2.5 billion RMB were channeled to its controlling shareholder in fund movements that were not true business transactions, representing about 96 percent of the company's total net assets. In the same period, more than 1.1 billion RMB was lent to one of its sister companies at interest rates of between 2.25 percent and 2.925 percent, while it borrowed nearly 1.5 billion RMB from others at interest rates of between 3.504 percent and 9.504 percent. In July 2002, the CSRC handed out a penalty and demanded that the controlling shareholder repay the misappropriated funds. At the end of November 2003, about 1.6 billion RMB had still not been paid back and most of the repayments were in noncash assets.[54] The tunneling had never been disclosed before the CSRC took action. Ironically, after the CSRC's penalty, misappropriated funds increased further. At the end of 2005, the balance was more than 3.7 billion RMB.[55]
- Hou Wang Gufeng (000535): By the end of 1999, while the company's gross assets were only 934 million RMB, about 890 million RMB had been misappropriated by its controlling shareholder. The misappropriation took different forms, including borrowings, receivables, and bank loans borrowed by the controlling shareholder but recorded in the company's account. The company also guaranteed more than 300 million RMB in loans borrowed by its controlling shareholder. In February 2001, its controlling shareholder was declared bankrupt. The company not only got nothing back; it also had to meet its obligations under the guarantee (Shi et al. 2001).
- Pi Jiu Ha (600090): On December 30, 2003 the company made an announcement that its chairman had disappeared. It was also disclosed that the company had guaranteed loans to various companies amounting to 1.787 billion RMB, of which about 1 billion had not been disclosed before. The price of its shares dropped from 16.51 to 3.66 RMB as of July 11, 2004.[56]
- Tuo Pu Software (000583): In 1998, a company owned by an individual acquired a listed company and renamed it Tuo Pu Software. In 2000, the listed company issued new shares and raised about 1 billion RMB with the approval of the CSRC. In the same year, the same individual acquired another listed company and renamed it Yan Huang Online. In 2001, Tuo Pu Software reported huge profits (0.78 RMB per share). But two years later in 2003, it reported huge losses (1.64 RMB per share). An investigation by the CSRC revealed that between October 2003 and April 2004, about 1.4 billion

RMB (100.56 percent of its net assets) were transferred out of Tuo Pu Software to companies controlled by that same individual. In 2003, Tuo Pu Software also guaranteed about 886 million RMB of loans (63.81 percent of its net assets). Yan Huang Online also guaranteed loans to related parties amounting to 286 million RMB (280 percent of its net assets). Both companies were censured by the Shenzhen Stock Exchange in June 2004 for nondisclosure. But by this time the controller had already absconded to the United States. The local regulatory authority "invited" him to come back to China to assist the investigation, but he refused on the grounds of illness. The share price of Tuo Pu Software plummeted from 48 RMB in July 2000 to 4.43 RMB on June 30, 2004.[57]

- De Long Group: A conglomerate owned by four brothers, De Long Group was the largest shareholder of three listed companies and the second-largest of several other listed companies. It also controlled dozens of securities companies, local banks, and trust companies. The Group first acquired one listed company and then misappropriated its funds and caused it to guarantee loans. With the misappropriated and borrowed money, the Group bought a number of other listed companies and financial institutions. Every time a company was acquired, the Group played the same game. Furthermore, securities companies under its control manipulated the share prices of these listed companies to a ridiculously high level with funds from different sources. By offering the inflated shares it owned as collateral, the Group borrowed even more from banks. In this way the Group expanded dramatically in a few years, and in 2003 the brothers ranked 25th on Euromoney's list of China's richest men. But in April 2004 the game was over after national banks were commanded by the central government to cut lending in order to cool down the overheated economy. The Group collapsed spectacularly. The tunneling of astronomical amounts of money was thus officially disclosed. There is little hope that these funds can ever be recovered, because the greater part may have been used to prop up the inflated share prices of the companies and now the value of those shares is negligible (Ling, Cao, and Zhou 2006).

From a general description and these concrete cases, we can gain an insight into the reality of corporate governance in China. It is clear that corporate governance in China is essentially in a state of lawlessness. Misappropriation is widespread; fraud is blatant. A basic level of law and order has not yet been established in corporate China.

(2) *Underdeterrence and misappropriations*

What is the state of legal deterrence in the face of this outrageous criminality? The reality is that legal deterrence is extremely soft. Despite the fact that theft and fraud are pervasive, both criminal prosecutions and administrative penalties are sporadic. It is difficult to estimate how many culprits have escaped punishment, but, as mentioned above, violations which have been penalized by the CSRC or publicly censured by the stock exchanges may be only one quarter of the total number (Wu 2005). Even this figure may overestimate the rate of penalization. There are many suspected violations, many of which are obvious and have been widely reported by the media, but the government has done nothing about them. There are situations where suspected violations had been reported by the media for years, but the government intervened only when the companies involved eventually collapsed. It was reported that from January 2003 to June 2004, ten top managers of listed companies absconded from the country, with it being subsequently revealed that their companies had been looted of funds or caused to guarantee loans amounting to billions (Zhang and He 2004). Surprisingly, there are no criminal actions against these absconders. A few of them have been penalized by the CSRC. The most severe penalty was a 300,000 RMB regulatory fine against a chairman and CEO on the ground that he was responsible for the cover-up of the tunneling of funds and guarantees offered by the company.[58] Compared to the nearly 1 billion RMB of funds of which the company was looted or caused to guarantee, that amount of fine is trivial. Even this trivial amount of fine will not be collected, as the chairman has disappeared and nobody knows his whereabouts. Yet even a fine of this size is unusual. Many violations are settled with private admonishments, letters from the regulator or stock exchanges demanding redress, or public censure by stock exchanges. It is doubtful whether these soft measures have any deterrent effect. For example, among the 477 company directors who were censured by the Shanghai Stock Exchange between April 2001 and November 2004, more than 10 percent were censured repeatedly (tom.com 2004).

As far as private litigation is concerned, deterrence is nonexistent. On the one hand, the old Company Law did not clearly confer on shareholders the standing to sue derivatively, and several attempts to take on derivative actions by minority shareholders have failed as a result of the courts' refusal to accept their cases. On the other hand, shareholders' right to take on private securities actions is substantially restricted by a judicial interpretation adopted by the Supreme People's Court. According to the interpretation, only securities actions against misrepresentation are permissible.[59] Actions can be taken only after a criminal conviction or after administrative penalty decisions have been entered into.[60] Furthermore, both American-style class actions and English-style group litigation are not allowable; actions can only be taken individually or jointly.[61] As a result of these restrictions, there have been only a few private securities lawsuits, all of which have been against flagrant fraud (Hutchens 2003). Damages awarded are insignificant, and it is not clear whether culpable managers have been made personally accountable. In short, legal deterrence against misappropriation and fraud is inconsequential in China. Most violations are not revealed or pursued, and both criminal prosecutions and administrative actions are infrequent. Where actions are taken, penalties are phenomenally light-handed. Finally, deterrence via private lawsuits is nonexistent.

From the above discussion, we may have a better understanding of why fraud and misappropriation are so widespread and flagrant in China. It is true that the reasons are complex and systemic. No single factor is wholly responsible for this unpleasant situation. The stock market is basically devoid of any disciplinary function because of the dominance of state ownership. There have been virtually no hostile takeovers since the stock exchanges were opened. Control is transferred by way of private negotiation, mostly because governments are forced to give up their stakes in listed companies after the companies run into financial difficulties. Share prices have no connection with the performance of companies, and artificial manipulation of share prices is rampant. Similarly, voting by minority shareholders as a disciplinary mechanism is negligible because of the dominance of state ownership. Yet the governments, notwithstanding their majority ownership, have not been able to exercise effective monitoring of the running of these state-controlled companies that in principle private owners should be able to achieve. Further, state ownership very possibly has a psychological impact upon managers. The paradigms of neoclassical economics have now been firmly established in China. As a consequence, state ownership is perceived as illegitimate and regarded as "nobody's" ownership. Managers feel no moral stigma attached to the misappropriation of the assets of listed companies that are under state control. Misappropriation is further exacerbated by the growth of excessive consumerism and individualism. So, state ownership is truly responsible for the prevalence of misappropriation in state-controlled listed companies, not just because state ownership deprives markets of any disciplinary function.

Nevertheless, if legal deterrence remains weak, it would be naïve to expect that corporate governance could be significantly enhanced by divesting the state of its controlling stakes in an effort to restore the legitimacy of ownership and the disciplinary function of market competition. As a matter of fact, plenty of companies suffering from misappropriation and fraud are privately controlled, and the crooks are the private controllers. Of the six cases reported above, three involved listed companies which were controlled by private persons. Recently, the Shanghai and Shenzhen stock exchanges publicized the names of 189 listed companies whose funds have been channeled out of the companies not for business purposes. Among them, sixty-nine are privately controlled companies, a figure which is out of proportion to the share of private companies in the total number of listed companies.[62] It is clear that in too many cases the presence of private controllers has not resulted in good corporate governance. This demonstrates again that private ownership is not a panacea and market mechanisms alone are ineffective. Actually it would be dangerous to commence mass privatization where legal deterrence is weak. The consequence is quite predictable: the country becomes immersed in a state of chaos where dirty wars of asset grabbing and ownership battling ensue, a scenario which occurred during and after mass privatization in some Central and Eastern European countries (Black et al. 2000; Blasi et al. 1997; Boycko et al. 1995). The result would be catastrophic for China, and the effect of illegitimate and corrupt privatization would run for a long time (Stiglitz and Hoff 2005). This indicates that strong legal infrastructure is even critical to the success of privatization. The experience from those Central and Eastern European countries also tells us that dispersed ownership created by privatization is not sustainable where legal deterrence remains weak (Ruehl 2004; Berglof and Pajuste 2003). This confirms that market-based mechanisms have a limited role to play in corporate governance where legal deterrence is not strong.

Actually, some market-based mechanisms are available in China, but they have nevertheless proven to be insignificant. Since 2001, it has been compulsory for listed companies to install independent directors on their boards, and by now at least one third of directors should be independent. However, there are too many cases where the presence of independent directors did not prevent misappropriation and fraud. The first and last cases reported above illustrate perfectly the limited value of independent directors in China. Both involve privately controlled listed companies which were looted of hundreds of millions of yuan by the controlling shareholders. In one case, three independent directors, one of whom is a prominent economist from a top university in China, resigned just before the company was about to collapse. In the other, independent directors resigned after the CSRC announced an investigation. One of the independent directors is a former executive of the Hong Kong Stock Exchange. It is not clear why the independent directors were not able to prevent the misappropriations and reveal the fraud. But in both cases, the resigning directors cited as the reason for resignation "not being able to access the information needed to perform their duty" (people.com.cn 2005). The reason provided seems vague, but it is very possibly that the independent directors themselves were defrauded by the executives and misappropriations were concealed from them. This conforms to the common finding that transactions which are required to be deliberated and decided by board meetings are nevertheless executed secretly by executives. These two cases prove that, where managers are determined to misappropriate and are amenable to fraud, the presence of independent directors matters little.

The same can be said about performance-based remuneration. Again this can be proven by a real case (Tang 2005). Although the CSRC only recently adopted a rule regulating performance-based remuneration such as stocks and stock options for managers of listed companies, the company concerned, which is controlled by a local government, granted its management stock options long before this. It was reported that the annual income of the chairman and CEO, including salary, bonus, and stock options, was worth more than 7 million RMB, an amount that was very generous for a manager in China. But this handsome reward could not dissuade him from misappropriation. In December 2005, he was sentenced to six years in prison for misappropriating tens of millions of yuan worth of funds from the company, which was a rare case of criminal sanction against a top manager of a listed company who perpetrated misappropriation. In an environment where legal deterrence is insubstantial, the effect of performance-based remuneration is predictable.

In summary, "systematic" misappropriation and fraud are not an illusion. They seem inevitable where legal deterrence is feeble in a country. To a large degree, extremely weak legal deterrence has to be blamed for the extent of misappropriation and fraud currently occurring in China. While the stock market is dysfunctional and shareholders do not play a role to ensure good corporate governance in China at present, some market-based governance mechanisms do exist, which nevertheless have proven to be ineffective. It is unrealistic to expect that corporate governance can be significantly improved by only reforming the markets and introducing more market-based initiatives. The urgent need is to curtail misappropriation and fraud. This cannot be done without strengthened legal sanctions.

(3) *The Reasons for Underdeterrence*

Why are legal sanctions infrequent and so lenient in China? Again the reasons are complex and systemic. There are both practical obstacles and problems in legislation which prevent criminals from being called to account (Cai 1999). In practical terms, law enforcement agencies are fragmented in that the CSRC is not responsible for criminal investigation. The responsibility for criminal investigation rests with Public Security Bureaus or Anti-Corruption Bureaus which, on the one hand, are struggling to deal with conventional crimes and, on the other, are controlled by the Communist Party and governments, which are sympathetic to corrupt managers whom they appoint. The courts are also tightly controlled by the party and governments. Corrupt managers enjoy support from party and government officials. Typically top company managers come from the party and government structure, and thus it is possible that government officials and managers are former colleagues and close friends. Moreover, corruption by managers means failure to perform their duties, if not complicity in the corruption, on the part of persons who are entrusted the power to appoint and monitor managers. As a result, party and government officials who have the authority to control law enforcement activities are disincentivized to reveal managerial corruption. For the CSRC, which is entrusted to enforce securities law and has jurisdiction for administrative penalties, the resources allocated for the pursuit of violations is very limited. The CSRC also lacks investigatory powers such as subpoena that the Securities and Exchange Commission in the United States has. Until recently, it had to apply for a court order before it could seize evidence or freeze bank accounts.[63] Last but not least, dismally, corruption also happens within the CSRC.[64]

As far as problems in legislation are concerned, firstly, criminal legislation against misappropriation is full of loopholes, differential treatment and conflicts. The applicable provisions are different with regard to managers from different companies, depending on whether a company is controlled by the state or by private persons. This makes the legislation tremendously complex and uncertain, leaving law enforcers with huge room to act freely. Worse still, there are no explicit provisions against tunneling of funds from which managers do not gain personally.[65] For example, if a company is controlled by the state, managers who tunnel funds out of the company might not violate criminal law if they could not be proven to have received the funds or made profits for themselves.[66] This is one reason why there were so many misappropriations but punishments were sporadic. Secondly, criminal intent is required to be proved for conviction of misappropriation, which is not easy to do. Similarly, criminal legislation against violations of securities law is also porous and mild. It is a crime to provide an IPO prospectus or financial report with fabricated or concealed material information, but punishment is amazingly moderate, with the maximum sentence being imprisonment for five and three years respectively.[67] Even these extraordinarily lenient provisions have been virtually unenforced, with only a few incidences of prosecution to date. For violations of other disclosure requirements stipulated by securities law, they were not criminally punishable. As long as they did not intend to manipulate the market, corrupt managers did not have to be concerned that they might spend time in prison for violating disclosure requirements, even if they deliberately made up information about the performance of their companies, let alone concealed required information.[68] The most severe punishment against individuals for those violations was a 300,000 RMB regulatory fine.[69] In view of both the deplorable legislation and enforcement, it is not surprising to see that the tunneling of funds out of listed companies was widespread and routinely covered up.

As far as private lawsuits are concerned, the restrictions for private shareholders to bring both derivative and securities actions have been discussed above. The new Company Law has clarified confusion about the old law and provided shareholders the *locus standi* to sue on behalf of their companies. However, onerous conditions are imposed. First, only shareholders who individually or jointly hold more than 1 percent of shares are qualified. Second, these shares should have been held for at least 180 days by those shareholders before an action can be taken. Third, shareholders should first serve a demand on the supervisory or managerial board. These conditions are both unreasonable[70] and unnecessarily restrictive. The shareholding requirement would exclude most individual shareholders from being qualified. Considering that supervisory and managerial directors are the main associates and controlled by the majority shareholders, the demand requirement makes no sense. It cannot be ruled out that supervisory and managerial directors may conspire to frustrate a lawsuit. Furthermore, the law says nothing about the issue of funding which is critical for derivative actions to be actually taken. Without a proper rule of funding to address the disincentive inherent with derivative action on the part of minority shareholders, derivative actions would in all likelihood be illusory and not be actually brought (Reisberg 2004).

The obstacles discussed above are only the superficial reasons. To answer the question why legal sanctions are infrequent and lenient, we should look beneath the surface. One important reason that lies deeper is that the government lacks strong will and determination to strengthen legal sanctions against misappropriation and fraud in listed companies. It is widely asserted that the weak legal system in China is attributable to the nature of political institutions and the absence of rule of law. But we should admit that the control of conventional crimes is relatively satisfactory in China. In this respect, the government might be called heavy-handed, and will and determination are not a problem. If the government had the determination to attack misappropriation and fraud just as it tackles conventional crimes, the situation would be different. Why does the government not have the will and determination to tackle corporate crimes? Misreading of the theories from the West which favor markets over law could be a reason. Since the early 1990s when the Communist Party of China announced its intention to establish a "socialist market economy," "market mechanisms" have become fashionable in China. Many government officials, including those from the CSRC, show a strong interest in "market mechanisms." Thus, when they talk about reform policy in public, phrases such as "market competition" and "market mechanisms" are heavily used. Many academics are also obsessed with "market mechanisms." However, as far as corporate governance is concerned, they may have overlooked their limitations as well as the crucial point that, unlike in developed countries, corporate governance in China is still in a primitive stage where misappropriation and fraud are the principal concern. Because of this misguided learning, the urgent need to attack misappropriation and fraud through enhanced legal deterrence has not fully been recognized, hence the lack of strong will and determination to do so.

CONCLUSION

To evaluate the Chinese government's policies and efforts to promote good corporate governance in China, this paper has gone some way to re-examine the working mechanics of market-based governance mechanisms for good corporate governance. The finding is that to rein in misappropriation and fraud is fundamental to good corporate governance, and deterrence by way of legal sanctions is vital to achieving that end. In this sense, effective legal deterrence is the foundation of corporate governance upon which the whole system stands. Currently corporate governance in China is essentially in a state of lawlessness. Misappropriation is widespread and fraud is flagrant. This being so, the top priority is to establish law and order in corporate China by way of legal deterrence. Only once this has been done will the efforts to implement market-oriented reforms bear significant fruit.

The Chinese government should appreciate that the market efficacy and market primacy theses may not be plausible for China. The same may be said for other transition and developing countries where legal deterrence is intrinsically weak. This difference between developed and developing countries should not escape us. Otherwise, there is a danger that those theses are misinterpreted and the urgent need to reinforce legal sanctions to attack misappropriation and fraud is overlooked. From this, a lesson can be learned that a theory should not be accepted frivolously without fully understanding its background.

NOTES

1. This is a revised version of the article originally published in *Corporate Governance: An International Review*, 15/5 (September 2007): 741–67. © 2007 Zhong Zhang; Journal compilation © 2007 Blackwell Publishing Ltd.
2. In Shanghai, the Shanghai Stock Exchange Composite Index was 2245.44 at the peak on June 14, 2001 and was 998.23 on June 6, 2005 (statistics available at <http://www.sse.com.cn>). In Shenzhen, the Shenzhen Stock Exchange Composite Index closed at 635.7310 in 2000 and at 278.7456 in 2005; within the same period, the total market value decreased from 2,116,008.44 to 933,414.96 million RMB, notwithstanding the fact that the issued shares increased from 158,096.84 to 213,364.81 million (statistics available at <http://www.szse.cn>).
3. Statistics available on the website of the China Securities Depository and Clearing Corporation Limited (in Chinese), <http://www.chinaclear.cn/.>
4. Statistics available on the website of the China Securities Regulatory Commission (CSRC), <http://www.csrc.gov.cn.>

5. The one-year interest rate was 2.25 percent and deposits by individuals exceeded 14 trillion RMB at the end of 2005. Statistics available on the website of the Central People's Bank of China, <http://www.pbc.gov.cn/.>
6. See the following section for more information.
7. See the fourth section titled "Underdeterrence: evidence from China" for more information.
8. See the third section titled "An economic analysis of the working mechanics of market discipline . . . " for more information.
9. See subsection (5) in the third section for more information.
10. See the Chinese Communist Party (CCP), *Decisions on Some Issues in Establishing the Socialist Market Economic System* (passed at the 3rd Plenum of the 14th Congress of the CCP, November 1993).
11. See CCP, *Decision of the 15th National Congress of the Communist Party of China* (1997).
12. Empirical research (Liu and Sun 2005) shows that, as at the end of 2001, the state was the largest shareholder in 81.6 percent of listed companies in China, and its average controlling stake in these companies amounted to just fewer than 50 percent. This figure is still only a conservative estimate of the control exerted by the state, as it is likely that the second- and third-largest shareholders are also under the influence or direction of the state.
13. National Administrative Bureau of State-Owned Assets, *Temporary Administrative Measures Concerning State-Owned Shares in Stock Companies* (No. 81, 1994), Article 2.
14. Ibid.
15. See also CSRC, the State-Owned Assets Supervision and Administration Commission, the Fiscal Ministry, the Central People's Bank, and the Ministry of Commerce, *Guiding Opinions Concerning the Reform of Non-Tradable Shares in Listed Companies* (August 23, 2005), Article 1(2).
16. Ibid.
17. Ibid.
18. See CSRC and the People's Central Bank of China, *Temporary Provisions Concerning the Regulation of Domestic Investments of Qualified Foreign Institutional Investors* (November 7, 2002).
19. See the Fiscal Ministry and the Labor Ministry, *Temporary Provisions Concerning the Regulation of Investments of the National Social Security Fund* (December 13, 2001).
20. See CSRC and the China Insurance Regulatory Commission, *Temporary Provisions Concerning the Regulation of Stock Investments by Insurance Companies* (October 25, 2004).
21. See the Labor Ministry, the China Banking Regulatory Commission, and the CSRC, *Trial Provisions Concerning the Regulation of Enterprise Pension Funds* (April 24, 2004).
22. These funds are set up particularly for the purpose of stocks and other securities investments and invite subscriptions from the public. They are licensed by the CSRC. The majority are open-ended.
23. The figure does not even include unlicensed securities investment funds whose value was estimated as being not insignificant (Xia 2001).
24. The State Council, *Regulation on Issuing and Trading Stocks* (April 1993).
25. *Company Law* 1993, Articles 38 and 103.
26. Ibid., Articles 52 and 124.
27. CSRC, *Guiding Opinion on Establishing Independent Director System in Listed Companies* (August 16, 2001), Subsection 3 of Section 1.

28. *Company Law* 1998 (amended 2005), Article 123.
29. Ibid., Articles 54 and 152.
30. CSRC and the State Economic and Trade Commission, *Corporate Governance Code for Listed Companies* (January 9, 2002).
31. CSRC, *Regulative Measures Concerning Listed Companies' Incentive Scheme of Stock and Stock Option* (December 31, 2005).
32. For an argument dismissing the difference between the duty of loyalty and the duty of care, see Fischel and Bradley (1986). It was argued that "there is no difference between working less hard than promised at a given level of compensation (a breach of the duty of care) and being compensated more than promised at a given level of work (a breach of the duty of loyalty)." This argument missed the point that duty-of-loyalty violations directly bring financial benefits to misbehaving managers but duty-of-care violations do not. Thus, in terms of whether financial benefits are directly involved, the distinction between the two duties should not be dismissed. See Schwartz (1986); Scott (1986); Demsetz (1986).
33. In economics the term "utility" is used which is not limited to the calculation of pure financial loss or gain. But nonfinancial "utility" is subjective and different persons have different preferences. For example, shirking may be "utility" for some managers, but others may prefer hard work. Moreover, shirking or hardworking may be both "utility" and "disutility" for the same manager. On the one hand, hardworking may lead to pleasure of self-fulfillment and self-esteem, but on the other hand, it means stress and less leisure time. So it is difficult to say shirking is a gain or loss in general. Because of this, the validity of argument here would not be materially affected without taking account nonfinancial utility, although it can be argued that not all managers work hard primarily for financial benefits. For the debate of the potential role of the so-called "social sanctions" in corporate governance, see Kahan (1996); Skeel (2001); Kahan (2006).
34. In the scenario of "empire building," managers may not act consciously to maximize their personal financial interests but are driven by the desire for self-fulfillment without being aware of the damaging consequences of their behavior. In such a situation, an economic analysis may not be valid. In the scenario of a takeover defense, benefits are obvious for managers, but the potential loss is not clear. Thus market competition may not be effective to discourage managers from taking a takeover defense.
35. Obviously this is less than true in reality. Even if a manager cannot find a new job, he could use the misappropriated assets as capital to open his own business or invest in the businesses of others and thus receive returns from the capital.
36. When the return on the capital is taken into account, the amount that is necessary to lure a manager to misappropriate would be still less.
37. Judge Easterbrook and Professor Fischel (1996) used the term "one-shot" misbehavior but did not elaborate on it. Here it is clear that one-off or one-shot misbehavior is not limited to one-time large-scale embezzlements. A series of nonsubstantial but covered-up misappropriations may also afford a manager financial gains sufficient enough for him to consider withdrawing from the management market altogether. These misappropriations are also one-off misbehavior in nature.
38. In recent years there has been strong interest in the study of behavioral law, which challenges law and economics' fundamental assumptions that human beings are rational and self-regarding, drawing evidence heavily from psychological experiments (Jolls et al. 1998a). In relation to corporate governance, see Stout and Blair (2001); Stout (2003). A detailed discussion of behavioral law is beyond the scope of this paper, but a brief observation is recorded here. First, behavioral law does not suggest, and there is

no evidence to support, that human beings are systematically other-regarding and irrational. It can only be said that there is some irregularity in human beings' rationality. In other words, the rationality of human beings is only bounded. This is admitted even by behavioral law scholars themselves. See Jolls et al. (1998a, 1998b). Second, there are convincing criticisms regarding the applicability of the results of laboratory experiments to real life, the ways such experiments are conducted, and the overstatement and overreading of the experimental results. See Mitchell (2002a, 2002b).

39. There has also been strong interest in the study of social norms in recent years among legal academics. For the debate of the significance of social norm in corporate governance, see *University of Pennsylvania Law Review* 149/6 (2000–1); Eisenberg (1999); Rock (1997).
40. Reputation is not solely a nonfinancial utility. On the contrary, its financial implication is significant and the working of market discipline cannot be separated from reputation. As far as the nonfinancial elements of reputation are concerned, it is doubtful that they can play a big role in dissuading managers from misappropriation and fraud where financial stakes are significant but law is extremely weak. See Kahan (2006).
41. It has been long recognized that market competition is not effective in assuring contractual performance where the short-term gain from nonperformance exceeds the discounted value of future income stream. See Klein and Leffler (1981).
42. E.g. see New York Stock Exchange's Listed Company Manual (2004), s.303a.01; the UK Listing Authority's Combined Code on Corporate Governance (2003), s.1A.3; the German Corporate Governance Code (2005), s.5.4.2; the Italian Corporate governance code (2002), s.2.1 and s.3.1.
43. See the following section for more information.
44. Another explanation is that, according to game theory, market forces are applicable only to repeat market players. Benefits from misappropriation may be big enough to induce a manager to withdraw from markets and become a one-time player. But this explanation does not explain why market forces are only applicable to repeat market players. Information asymmetry is also an explanation, but perfect information is not the reality. The inability of markets to sever illegitimate benefits may be a better and more helpful explanation.
45. As far as civil remedies for duty-of-loyalty violations are concerned, corporate law differs to some degree between common-law countries and continental Europe. In continental Europe, a violation of the duty of loyalty may give rise only to liability for the resulting loss to the company, whereas in common-law countries a duty-of-loyalty violation is also subject to disgorgement of profits. See Enriques (2000).
46. Compared to violent crimes, the proposition that legal deterrence may be ineffective is less valid with regard to managerial misappropriation where managers are highly intelligent and act on careful calculation. Indeed, just as with traditional crimes, white-collar crimes have deeper social roots, and to address the root causes are equally important. But this does not mean that legal deterrence is unimportant. Whatever the social causes are and however well they are addressed, white-collar crimes would not be substantially reduced where legal deterrence is exceedingly weak.
47. A more radical suggestion is to abolish the liability for duty-of-care violations. See Scott (1983).
48. After Enron and WorldCom, there are views that stress the significance of liability for duty-of-care violations. See Fairfax (2005).
49. The International Institute for Management Development in Switzerland surveyed the corporate governance of 60 economies in the world in 2004 and China ranked 25th on board effectiveness, 40th on shareholder value, 57th on insider trading, and 44th on

shareholder rights. Another survey by the World Economic Forum in 2003 ranked China 44th among the 49 economies surveyed. See Liu (2006).

50. See the CSRC, *Guiding Rules on the Article of Association of Listed Companies* (December 16, 1997), Article 94; CSRC, *Notice Regarding Guarantees Offered to Others by Listed Companies* (June 6, 2000), Article 5.
51. See *Company Law* 1993 (amended 2005), Articles 105 and 122.
52. Documents of public censure are publicized by the two stock exchanges (in Chinese) and available on their websites, <http://www.sse.com.cn> and <http://www.szse.cn>.
53. Documents of penalty are publicized by the CSRC (in Chinese), available on its website <http://www.csrc.gov.cn>.
54. See CSRC *Penalty Decision* No. 12 (2002), available at its website <http://www.csrc.gov.cn> (in Chinese).
55. Statistics available on the website of the Shenzhen Stock Exchange, <http://www.szse.cn/> (in Chinese).
56. See CSRC *Penalty Decision* No. 19 (2004), available at its website <http://www.csrc.gov.cn> (in Chinese).
57. See CSRC *Penalty Decision* No. 30 (2005), available at its website <http://www.csrc.gov.cn> (in Chinese).
58. See CSRC *Penalty Decision* No. 19 (2004).
59. See the Supreme People's Court of China, *Notice on Temporary Suspension of Acceptance of Civil Securities Compensation Cases* (September 21, 2001); *Notice on Relevant Issues Concerning the Acceptance of Civil Tort Cases Resulting from Misrepresentation that Occurred in Securities Markets* (February 15, 2002).
60. Ibid.
61. Ibid.
62. It is estimated that among the 1,300-plus listed companies there are about 200 whose controlling ownership has been transferred to private persons after IPOs. See Green (2003).
63. The new Securities Law provides the CSRC such a right without seeking a court order, but with conditions. See *Securities Law* 1998 (amended 2005), Article 180.
64. Recently an officer from the CSRC was sentenced to thirteen years in prison for taking bribes. See Zhou (2005).
65. This loophole has been redressed only from 2006. See *Criminal Law* 1979 (amended 2006), Article 169(1).
66. Ibid.
67. See *Criminal Law* 1979 (amended 2006), Articles 160 and 161.
68. This has been changed only from 2006. See *Criminal Law* 1979 (amended 2006), Article 161.
69. See *Securities Law* 1998 (amended 2005), Article 193.
70. The 1 percent threshold is arbitrary in that shareholders with shareholdings above the threshold are qualified but those under the threshold are not. As for the 180-day requirement, it means that a shareholder may have to wait until the 180-day threshold is met after he has discovered a violation.

REFERENCES

Alchian, A. and Demsetz, H. (1972), "Production, Information Costs and Economic Organisation," *American Economic Review*, 62: 777–95.

Bainbridge, S. M. (2005), "Shareholder Activism and Institutional Investors," Law-Econ Research Paper No. 05–20, University of California Los Angeles, School of Law, Los Angeles.

Bebchuk, L. A. and Roe, M. J. (1999), "A Theory of Path Dependence in Corporate Ownership and Governance," *Stanford Law Review*, 52: 127–70.

Becker, G. (1968), "Crime and Punishment: An Economic Approach," *Journal of Political Economy*, 76: 169–217.

——and Stigler, G. (1974), "Law Enforcement, Malfeasance and Compensation Enforcers," *Journal of Legal Studies*, 3: 1–18.

Benson, B. (1990), *The Enterprise of Law: Justice Without the State* (San Francisco: Pacific Research Institute).

Berglof, E. and Pajuste, A. (2003), "Emerging Owners, Eclipsing Markets? Corporate Governance in Central and Eastern Europe," in P. K. Cornelius and B. Kogut (eds), *Corporate Governance and Capital Flows in a Global Economy* (Oxford: Oxford University Press).

Berle, A. A. and Means, G. C. (1933), *The Modern Corporation and Private Property* (New York: Macmillan).

Black, B. S. (1990), "Shareholder Passivity Re-examined," *Michigan Law Review*, 89: 520–608.

——(1995), "Shareholder Activism and Corporate Governance in the United States," in P. Newman (ed.), *The New Palgrave Dictionary of Economics and the Law* (London: Palgrave Macmillan), 459–65.

——and Cheffins, B. R. (2004), "Outside Director Liability across Countries," Stanford Law and Economics Olin Working Paper No. 266, Stanford.

——Kraakman, R., and Tarassova, A. (2000), "Russian Privatization and Corporate Governance: What Went Wrong?" *Stanford Law Review*, 52: 1731–808.

Blasi, J. R., Kroumova, M., and Kruse, D. (1997), *Kremlin Capitalism: Privatizing the Russian Economy* (Ithaca: Cornell University Press).

Boycko, M., Shleifer, A., and Vishny, R. (1995), *Privatizing Russia* (Cambridge, MA: MIT Press).

Braithwaite, J. (1984), *Corporate Crime in the Pharmaceutical Industry* (London: Routledge & Kegan Paul).

Brandeis, L. (1928), Dissenting Opinion, Olmstead v. U.S., 277 U.S. 438 (1928), Supreme Court of the United States, Washington, DC.

Butler, H. N. (1989), "The Contractual Theory of the Corporation," *George Mason University Law Review*, 11: 99–114.

Cadbury, A. (1992), *Financial Aspects of Corporate Governance* (London: Gee).

Cai, W. (1999), "Private Securities Litigation in China: Of Prominence and Problems," *Columbia Journal of Asian Law*, 13: 135–51.

Cheffins, B. (1997), *Company Law: Theory, Structure, and Operation* (Oxford: Clarendon Press).

——(2001a), "Does Law Matter? The Separation of Ownership and Control in the United Kingdom," *Journal of Legal Studies*, 30: 459–84.

——(2001b), "Law, Economics and the UK's System of Corporate Governance: Lessons from History," *Journal of Corporate Law Studies*, 1/1: 71–89.

——(2001c), "Law as Bedrock: The Foundations of an Economy Dominated by Widely Held Public Companies." Working paper (August).

Clarke, D. C. (2003), "Corporate Governance in China: An Overview," *China Economic Review*, 14/4: 494–507.

Coffee, J. C. (1980), "Corporate Crime and Punishment: A Non-Chicago View of the Economics of Criminal Sanctions," *American Criminal Law Review*, 17: 419–78.

——(1999), "Privatization and Corporate Governance: The Lessons from Securities Market Failure," Centre for Law and Economics Studies Working Paper No. 158, Columbia Law School, New York.

——(2001), "The Rise of Dispersed Ownership: The Role of Law in the Separation of Ownership and Control," *Yale Law Journal*, 111/1: 1–80.

Coffee, J. C. (2004), "What Caused Enron? A Capsule Social and Economic History of the 1990s," *Cornell Law Review*, 89: 269–310.

Coughlan, A. T. and Schmidt, R. M. (1985), "Executive Compensation, Management Turnover and Firm Performance: An Empirical Investigation," *Journal of Accounting and Economics*, 7: 43–6.

Davies, P. (2003), *Gower and Davies' Principles of Modern Company Law* (London: Sweet & Maxwell).

Demsetz, H. (1986), "A Commentary on Liability Rules and the Derivative Suit in Corporate Law," *Cornell Law Review*, 71: 352–6.

Dooley, M. P. and Veasey, E. N. (1989), "The Role of the Board in Derivative Litigation: Delaware Law and the Current ALI Proposals Compared," *The Business Lawyer*, 44/2: 503–42.

Easterbrook, F. (1997), "International Corporate Differences: Markets or Law?" *Journal of Applied Corporate Finance*, 9/4: 23–9.

Easterbrook, F. H. and Daniel R. Fischel, D. R. (1996), *The Economic Structure of Corporate Law* (Cambridge, MA: Harvard University Press).

Eisenberg, M. A. (1989), "The Structure of Corporation Law," *Columbia Law Review*, 89: 1461–525.

——(1999), "Corporate Law and Social Norms," *Columbia Law Review*, 99: 1253–92.

Enriques, L. (2000), "The Law on Company Directors' Self-dealings: A Comparative Analysis," *International and Comparative Corporate Law Journal*, 2/3: 297–333.

Fairfax, L. M. (2005), "Spare the Rod, Spoil the Director? Revitalizing Directors' Fiduciary Duty through Legal Liability," *Houston Law Review*, 42: 393–456.

Fama, E. F. (1980), "Agency Problems and the Theory of Firm," *Journal of Political Economy*, 88/2: 288–307.

Ferran, E. (1999), *Company Law and Corporate Finance* (Oxford: Oxford University Press).

Fischel, D. (1982), "The Corporate Governance Movement," *Vanderbilt Law Review*, 35: 1259–64.

——and Bradley, M. (1986), "Role of Liability Rules and the Derivative Suit in Corporate Law: A Theoretical and Empirical Analysis," *Cornell Law Review*, 71: 261–97.

Fischer, W. A. (2005), "Will China Face Up to its Governance Problem?" *Financial Times*, sponsored reports: Mastering Corporate Governance, June 2.

Fox, M. B. (1999), "Required Disclosure and Corporate Governance," *Law and Contemporary Problems*, 62/3: 113–27.

Gao, H. (2003), News Report (Chinese), Xinhua News Agency, December 24. http://news.xinhuanet.com/stock/2003-12/24/content_1245775_1.htm.

Green, S. (2003), "Two-thirds Privatisation: How China's Listed Companies are—Finally—Privatising?" Briefing Note, December, The Royal Institute of International Affairs, London.

Higgs, D. (2003), *Review of the Role and Effectiveness of Non-Executive Directors* (London: Department of Trade and Industry).

Hutchens, W. (2003), "Private Securities Litigation in the People's Republic of China: Material Disclosure about China's Legal System?" *University of Pennsylvania Journal of International Economic Law*, 24/3: 599–689.

Jensen, M. C. and Meckling, W. H. (1976), "Theory of the Firm: Managerial Behaviour, Agency Costs and Ownership Structure," *Journal of Financial Economics*, 3: 303–60.

——and Murphy, K. J. (1990), "Performance Pay and Top Management Incentives," *Journal of Political Economy*, 98/2: 225–64.

Jolls, C., Sunstein, C. R. and Thaler, R. H. (1998a), "A Behavioral Approach to Law and Economics," *Stanford Law Review*, 50: 1471–550.

——(1998b), "Theories and Tropes: A Reply to Posner and Kelman," *Stanford Law Review*, 50: 1593–608.

Kahan, D. M. (1996), "What Do Alternative Sanctions Mean?" *University of Chicago Law Review*, 63: 591–653.

——(2006), "What's Really Wrong with Shaming Sanctions?" Public Law Working Paper 125, Yale Law School, New Haven, available at <http://www.ssrn.com>.

Karpoff, J. M. (2001), "The Impact of Shareholder Activism on Target Companies: A Survey of Empirical Findings," University of Washington Working Paper, Seattle.

Klein, B. and Leffler, K. B. (1981), "The Role of Market Forces in Assuring Contractual Performance," *Journal of Political Economy*, 89: 615–41.

Langevoort, D. C. (1990), "The SEC as a Bureaucracy: Public Choice, Institutional Rhetoric, and the Process of Policy Formulation," *Washington & Lee Law Review*, 47: 527–40.

——(1999), "Securities Laws and Corporate Governance: The Advent of a Meltdown?" Panel Discussion and Q & A., Reliance National.

La Porta, R., Lopez-de-Silanes, F., and Schleifer, A. (1997), "Legal Determinants of External Finance," *Journal of Finance*, 52/3: 1131–50.

————(1998), "Law and Finance," *Journal of Political Economy*, 106/6: 1113–35.

————(1999), "Corporate Ownership Around the World," *Journal of Finance*, 54/2: 471–517.

———(2006), "What Works in Securities Laws?" *Journal of Finance*, 61/1: 1–32.

Lin, C. (2001), "Private Vices in Public Places: Challenges in Corporate Governance Development in China," Policy Dialogue Meeting on Corporate Governance in Developing Countries and Emerging Economies, OECD Development Centre and the European Bank for Reconstruction and Development (EBRD), London.

Ling, H., Cao, H., and Zhou, F. (2006), "Finale in Sight for Delong Saga," [English] *Caijing Magazine*, 165 (January 9).

Liu, G. S. and Sun, P. (2005), "The Class of Shareholdings and Its Impact on Corporate Performance: Composition in Chinese Public Corporations," *Corporate Governance: An International Review*, 13/1: 46–59.

Liu, Q. (2006), "Corporate Governance in China: Current Practices, Economic Effects, and Institutional Determinants," *CESifo Economic Studies*, 52/2: 415–53.

Luo, J. and Shen, I. (2006), "Kelon executives embezzled US $73 million," *China Daily*, January 24, p. 11.

MacNeil, I. (2002), "Adaptation and Convergence in Corporate Governance: The Case of Chinese Listed Companies," *Journal of Corporate Law Studies*, 2/2: 289–344.

Manne, H. (1965), "Mergers and the Market for Corporate Control," *Journal of Political Economy*, 73/2: 110–20.

McCormack, G. (1998), "Institutional Shareholders and the Promotion of Good Corporate Governance" in B. Rider (ed.), *The Realm of Company Law: A Collection of Papers in Honour of Prof. Leonard Sealy* (London: Kluwer Law International), 131–60.

Miles, L. and Zhang, Z. (2006), "Improving Corporate Governance in State-Owned Corporations in China: Which Way Forward?" *Journal of Corporate Law Studies*, 6/1: 213–48.

Mitchell, G. (2002a), "Taking Behavioralism Too Seriously? The Unwarranted Pessimism of the New Behavioral Analysis of Law," *William & Mary Law Review*, 43: 1907–2021.

——(2002b), "Why Law and Economics' Perfect Rationality Should Not Be Traded for Behavioral Law and Economics' Equal Incompetence?" *Georgetown Law Review*, 91: 67–167.

Monks, R. A. G. and Minow, N. (2003), *Corporate Governance* (New York: Blackwell Publishing).
Naylor, J. M. (1990), "The Use of Criminal Sanctions by UK and US Authorities for Insider Trading: How Can the Two Systems Learn from Each Other (Part ii)," *Company Lawyer*, 5: 83–91.
Oman, C., Fries, S., and Buiter, W. H. (2003), "Corporate Governance in Developing, Transition and Emerging-Market Economies," OECD Development Centre Policy Brief No. 23, OECD, Paris.
Ou, G., Li, H. and Sun, T. (2005), "The Obstinate Disease of Misappropriation of Funds by Majority Shareholders," *Securities Market Weekly* [Chinese], 17: 19–21.
People.com.cn (2005), News report, available at <http://finance.people.com.cn/GB/1045/3537808.html> [Chinese].
Qiang, Q. (2003), "Corporate Governance and State-Owned Shares in China Listed Companies," *Journal of Asian Economics*, 14: 774–5.
Reisberg, A. (2004), "Funding Derivative Actions: A Re-examination of Costs and Fees as Incentives to Commence Litigation," *Journal of Corporate Law Studies*, 4/2: 345–83.
Rider, B. (1988), "Policing the City: Combating Fraud and Other Abuses in Corporate Securities Industry," *Current Legal Problems*, 41: 47–68.
Rock, E. (1997), "Saints and Sinners: How Does Delaware Corporate Law Work?" *University of California Los Angeles Law Review*, 44: 1004 –107.
Roe, M. J. (1994), *Strong Managers, Weak Owners: The Political Roots of American Corporate Finance* (Princeton: Princeton University Press).
——(2002), "Corporate Law's Limits," *Journal of Legal Studies*, 31/2: 233–71.
——(2003), *Political Determinants of Corporate Governance: Political Context, Corporate Impact* (London: Oxford University Press).
Romano, R. (2001), "Less is More: Making Institutional Investor Activism a Valuable Mechanism of Corporate Governance," *Yale Journal on Regulation*, 18: 174–251.
Ruehl, C. (2004), "From Transition to Development: A Country Economic Memorandum for the Russian Federation," World Bank Report, Washington, DC.
Schipani, C. A. and Liu, J. (2002), "Corporate Governance in China: Then and Now," *Columbia Business Law Review 2002*: 1–69.
Schwartz, D. E. (1986), "In Praise of Derivative Suits: A Commentary on the Paper of Professors Fischel and Bradley," *Cornell Law Review*, 71: 322–343.
Scott, K. E. (1983), "Corporation Law and the American Law Institute Corporate Governance Project," *Stanford Law Review*, 35: 927–48.
——(1986), "The Role of Preconceptions in Policy Analysis in Law: A Response to Fischel and Bradley," *Cornell Law Review*, 71: 299–320.
Shang, F. (2005), "Speech addressed to the 4th International Forum on Securities Investment Funds in China on 2nd December 2005 in Shenzhen," *Securities Times* [Chinese], December 2.
Shen, S. and Jia, J. (2005), "Will the Independent Director Institution Work in China?" *Loyola of Los Angeles International and Comparative Law Review*, 27: 223–48.
Shi, Y., Lu, P., et al. (2001), News report, *Xinhua Daily Telegraph* [Chinese], March 24.
Shleifer, A. and Vishny, R. W. (1997), "A Survey of Corporate Governance," *Journal of Finance*, 52/2: 737–83.
Skeel, D. A. (2001), "Shaming in Corporate Law," *University of Pennsylvania Law Review*, 149: 1811–68.
Stiglitz, J. (2002), *Globalization and Its Discontents* (New York: W.W. Norton & Company).
——and Hoff, K. (2005), "The Creation of the Rule of Law and the Legitimacy of Property Rights: The Political and Economic Consequences of a Corrupt Privatization," NBER Working Paper 11772, Cambridge, MA.

Stout, L. A. (2003), "On the Proper Motives of Corporate Directors (Or, Why You Don't Want to Invite Homo Economicus to Join Your Board)," *Delaware Journal of Corporate Law*, 28: 1–25.

——and Blair, M. M. (2001), "Trust, Trustworthiness, and the Behavioral Foundations of Corporate Law," *University of Pennsylvania Law Review*, 149: 1735–1810.

Tang, J. (2005), News report [Chinese], Xinhua News Agency, December 31. http://news.xinhuanet.com/fortune/2006-01/01/content_3997124.htm.

Tenev, S. and Zhang, C. (2002), *Corporate Governance and Enterprise Reform in China: Building the Institutions of Modern Markets* (Washington, DC: World Bank and the International Finance Corporation).

Thompson, R. B. and Sale, H. A. (2003), "Securities Frauds and Corporate Governance: Reflections upon Federalism," *Vanderbilt Law Review*, 56/3: 859–910.

Tom.com. (2004) News report, August 19, <http://finance.news.tom.com/1008/1009/20041130-118787.html> [Chinese].

Wu, X. (2005), "Research on Punishments of Securities Violations," *Caijing Magazine* [Chinese] 136, June 27.

Xia, B. (2001), "Report on the Private Securities Investment Funds in China," *Securities Times* [Chinese], July 6.

Yun, T. (2004), "Wu Xiaoqiu: Eight Inflictions from the Split of Tradable and Non-Tradable Shares," *China Securities Journal* [Chinese], January 12.

Zhang, P. and He, Z. (2004), "Nearly Ten Billions Swept Away in a Year and a Half: Shocking Absconding by Top Managers of Listed Companies" [Chinese], *Beijing Business Today* (June 21), available at <http://www.china.com.cn/chinese/2004/Jun/593302.htm>, last accessed September 8, 2012.

Zhang, X. (2006), News report, *China Securities Journal* [Chinese], A10, July 17.

Zhou, C. (2005), News report, *Shanghai Securities Daily* [Chinese], December 14, <http://www.cnstock.com/cjzg/hgjj/2005-12/14/content_951634.htm>.

13

Generosity and Participation: Variations in Urban China's Minimum Livelihood Guarantee Policy

Qin Gao and Carl Riskin

INTRODUCTION

Property rights, broadly conceived, fit into the context of public policy and social well-being. The institutions that govern the evolution of property rights develop in tandem with those that regulate and limit their reach and create analogous rights to social welfare. Owners of property are often held to counterpart responsibilities, such as payment of taxes whose proceeds finance, inter alia, social welfare programs. These programs can themselves be considered as conferring rights analogous to property rights on their beneficiaries. Such is certainly the case in China, where the evolution of legal protections for private property has gone hand in hand with that of various forms of taxation and of income redistribution, such as unemployment insurance, a pension system, and an urban antipoverty program.

It is the last that concerns this chapter. The Minimum Livelihood Guarantee (MLG) program, commonly known in China as *dibao* (minimum guarantee), has established rights of a sort to income flows on the part of urban poor people for the first time. Previously, control of population movement and a policy of universal full employment in cities effectively prevented abject urban poverty except among those unable to work for reasons of age, illness, or disability, a problem dealt with by a small program (called Assistance to the "Three Without" Households or *sanwu*) administered by city Civil Affairs Bureaus. But the development in the 1990s of a right to fire workers in the new market economy resulted in the emergence of large-scale unemployment and, with it, a new class of urban poor. This in turn required the counter-development of protection against absolute destitution in the form of *dibao*. However, just as "private ownership" must be parsed to reveal its exact content, so too must "minimum livelihood guarantee." What rights and obligations are imposed upon its beneficiaries? Here, in an effort to throw light on how the program works, we examine regional variations in its implementation—specifically, in its generosity and participation rates.

The MLG program was initiated in Shanghai in 1993, in an effort to provide a basic safety net for the city's urban poor, whose numbers were expanding due to increased unemployment, low wages, inadequate pensions, and rampant inflation (Gao 2006; Guan 2005; Leung 2006; Saunders and Shang 2001). Based on the successful experience in Shanghai, the Ministry of Civil Affairs in 1994 encouraged other cities to adopt this program. The number of cities that established MLG rose sharply from twelve in 1995 to 116 in 1996, and then to 334 in 1997 (Information Office of the State Council [IOSC] 2002, 2004; Leung 2006).

In 1999, the central government issued the Regulation on Assuring Urban Residents' Minimum Standard of Living (hereafter "the Regulation") in order to provide a consistent national framework for the MLG program. The Regulation provided an entitlement to basic assistance from the local government for urban residents whose household per capita income fell below the local minimum living-standard line. Local governments were mandated to include MLG expenses in their budgets and those with severe fiscal constraints might get assistance from the central government. Consequentially, by October 1999, all 668 cities and 1,689 counties had implemented MLG (IOSC 2002, 2004; Leung 2003).

The MLG or *dibao* program represents a significant institutional development for China. Part of the newly emerging constellation of social policy institutions, including also a radically altered pension system and unemployment insurance, MLG responds to changed urban conditions in the course of development of a market economy that permit the emergence of substantial urban income inequality and serious urban poverty. It conveys rights for the absolute poor which are counterparts to the emerging property rights that have been complicit in the origin and growth of urban poverty. Moreover, MLG is a particular kind of response, consistent with China's metamorphosis from collectivism to individualism. Unlike China's *rural* antipoverty program, which has always been a program for economic (and sometimes social) development of poor areas, *dibao* is a rigorously means-tested relief program that targets individual families. Reflecting the low social status of its beneficiaries, it exacts a high price for extremely modest help, isolating and stigmatizing its recipients, offering minimal support for their efforts to emerge from poverty, and even actively impeding such efforts. It offers a small amount of money for survival and some other benefits, such as discounted prices for some necessities. But rather than empowering recipients with the means to escape from poverty, it seeks to provide the minimum subsistence that will discourage social unrest and maintain political stability—a primary objective of the program in the first place.

We do not discuss further here these basic characteristics of *dibao* or join the debate over how best to fight urban poverty. We are interested rather in analyzing some implications of the program's structure with a view to suggesting ways of improving it. But it may well be that the outcomes of its structural characteristics are influenced by the program's fundamental conception, a possibility that we return to at the end of this discussion.

Because the MLG policy is decentralized to the city level, its eligibility rules, benefit generosity, and performance outcomes may vary significantly by city, and consequentially by province and region. In this chapter, we examine the trends and intercity variations in MLG generosity and participation using the China Household Income Project (CHIP) 2002 urban survey data as well as aggregate administrative data in 2002 and 2005. In addition, we use multivariate analysis to explore whether and to what extent a city's average living standard and other characteristics affect its MLG generosity and the participation of its residents after other factors are controlled for.

POLICY BACKGROUND AND EXISTING EVIDENCE

Local MLG assistance lines (also referred to hereafter as *dibao* lines), which take the form of monthly amounts of income, are set in accordance with central government guidelines. Based on local per capita income, they are meant to be sufficient to cover such basic needs as food, clothing, and shelter, taking into consideration expenses for utilities, medical care, and tuition (Hong 2005a; Ru et al. 2002). The Ministry of Civil Affairs summarized the basis for the assistance line as including "residents' basic livelihood needs; a city's price level; the degree of development in the region; and that locality's financial ability to contribute to the program" (Solinger 2010: 260). However, in practice a city's fiscal capacity puts an upper bound on its assistance line (Du and Park 2007), which may in poorer cities cause it to fall below the level required to cover recipients' basic needs (Guan 2005).

A variety of methods of determining the *dibao* line has been used by city governments, including surveys of consumption; intergovernmental discussions; imitation of neighboring cities; setting lines with reference to the local minimum wage or unemployment subsistence; or some combination of these methods. The plethora of approaches makes the rationale behind the assistance lines difficult to fathom and causes the *dibao* lines to vary substantially among cities, even within the same province (Hong 2005a).

There have been frequent adjustments in assistance lines in response to changes in consumer prices and local governments' financial conditions. The overall trend in the level of the *dibao* line has been upward, but some cities have had to lower their lines due to constrained fiscal capacity. Compared with average income, however, *dibao* lines are very low, averaging only 14 percent of the average wage and 23 percent of average per capita urban income in 2003 (Leung 2006).

There are two components to the means-testing of a family's eligibility for *dibao* assistance (Hong 2005a). The first is a financial investigation to determine if the family's total financial resources fall short of the local assistance line. "Income" is defined to include not only cash income from any source, but also assets such as savings and stocks. Other indicators may also be considered, such as employment and health status and housing conditions (Ravallion, Chen, and Wang 2008; Du and Park 2007). In some cities (e.g., Beijing), ownership of a pet or of durable goods (such as a motorcycle or cell phone) may render a family ineligible for assistance (Hong 2005a).

The other eligibility test concerns residency status and family formation (Hong 2005a). Official urban residency registration (*hukou*) is required for *dibao* eligibility, thus ruling out MLG assistance to that large fraction of the urban population composed of migrants who retain rural residency status. Cities have also not fixed on a common treatment of adult children still living with their parents: some consider them part of the parental family, while others treat them separately; still others have yet to establish specific rules regarding such cases.

Cash subsidies comprise the bulk of assistance in most cities. The provision of in-kind goods assistance (e.g., food, clothing) has been gradually phased out (Hong 2005a), but some cities provide services such as health care and school enrollment to *dibao* beneficiaries (Ravallion, Chen, and Wang 2008) or discounts in rent and prices of other necessities (Solinger 2010).

Existing literature has identified unemployment, low wages, and inadequate pensions as the major factors associated with MLG participation (Hong 2005a, 2005b; Leung 2006; Tang 2004). Some demographic characteristics, such as low education, bad health (including health problems, disabilities, and chronic diseases), larger household size, and not being a Communist Party member, have also been linked to MLG participation (Ravallion, Chen, and Wang 2008; Du and Park 2007). In addition, higher household dependency rates (measured by the number of children and older persons without pensions relative to the number of working members and older persons receiving pensions) contribute to MLG participation (Gustafsson and Deng 2011).

Recent studies have found that the impact of MLG participation on poverty has been modest due to the limited coverage and delivery of MLG. Further, MLG has had a larger impact on reducing the poverty gap and severity of poverty than on the headcount rate (Ravallion, Chen, and Wang 2008; Du and Park 2007; Gao, Garfinkel, and Zhai 2009; Gustafsson and Deng 2011; Wang 2007). MLG has also helped participating families to pay for education and health care but has been insufficient to cover their rising spending needs (Du and Park 2007; Gao, Zhai, and Garfinkel 2010).

How do city contextual characteristics affect these outcomes of MLG? Using CHIP 2002 data, Gustafsson and Deng (2011) found that the MLG participation rate varied greatly across cities. Specifically, city employment rates and per capita income adversely affected the probability of receiving MLG. The MLG benefit delivery gap (measured by the difference between the entitled MLG benefit and the actual amount received by participating families) also varied across regions. This gap was wider in the least developed western region than in the more developed central and eastern regions (Gao, Garfinkel, and Zhai 2009).

DATA AND METHODS

Building on these earlier findings, this chapter specifically explores the city variations in MLG generosity and participation. We use both micro-level household survey data and macro-level administrative data. Because the micro-data are from the year 2002, we use a compiled aggregate-level administrative dataset for both 2002 and 2005 to compare the results and to study more recent trends. Doing so also allows us to detect if our results using micro-data hold for a different sample and over time.

This study examines two key dependent variables: MLG generosity and participation. MLG generosity is measured by city MLG assistance lines obtained from the Ministry of Civil Affairs. MLG participation is measured by whether families actually received MLG benefits in the micro-data and by city MLG participation rate (i.e., the total number of MLG recipients in the city as a share of total city population) in the macro-data. MLG participation is examined using both data sources, while generosity is examined using the micro-data aggregated to city level, as well as the macro-data.

CHIP 2002 data, variables, and analysis

The micro-level data that we used are from the China Household Income Project (CHIP) 2002 urban survey. CHIP is a national, cross-sectional study collectively designed by a team of Chinese and Western scholars and conducted by the Institute of Economics at the Chinese Academy of Social Sciences. It provides detailed information on demographics, income, and expenditures. Samples of the CHIP study were drawn from larger NBS samples using a multistage stratified probability sampling method. To generate a nationally representative sample, CHIP includes sample provinces from eastern, central, and western regions of China. More specifically, the Beijing municipality and the provinces Liaoning, Jiangsu, and Guangdong represent the eastern region; the provinces Shanxi, Anhui, Henan, and Hubei represent the central region; and the Chongqing municipality and the provinces Sichuan, Yunnan, and Gansu represent the western region. The CHIP 2002 urban sample contains seventy-seven cities, twelve of which are municipalities or provincial capital cities. The dataset has a sample size of 6,835 households and 20,632 individuals. We used regression models to explore the determinants of city MLG assistance lines and families' MLG participation status.

Though rich and reliable, the CHIP data have some limitations. First, the CHIP 2002 data are somewhat dated, especially considering the recent rapid developments in MLG. Second, the CHIP sample size in each city is relatively small: there are typically 50–250 households surveyed in each city, with the exception of Beijing which contained 500 families in the sample. In the regression analyses, this compromised our use of city sample average per capita income to represent actual city per capita income. We used provincial-level characteristics or provincial fixed effects in an attempt to offset some of this limitation and also used the 2002 and 2005 city-level administrative data to analyze the effects of the city living standard. Using the macro-level data also allowed us to analyze trends in more recent years and to detect whether the results based on the CHIP 2002 data still hold.

Administrative data, variables, and analysis

The aggregate administrative datasets for 2002 and 2005 contain MLG assistance lines and participation rates of thirty-five large cities in China, including the four province-level municipalities (Beijing, Chongqing, Shanghai, and Tianjin), twenty-six provincial capital cities (Lhasa is excluded due to data unavailability), and five other large cities (i.e., Dalian, Qingdao, Ningbo, Shenzhen, and Xiamen). The dataset also contains various economic indicators and demographic characteristics of these cities. Economic indicators include city per capita disposable income, GDP growth rate, unemployment rate, and Engel Index (proportion of income spent on food). We also controlled for one major city demographic characteristic, the city population's rate of natural increase (RNI) calculated by subtracting the (crude) death rate from the (crude) birth rate.

We first ran correlation tests between city per capita income and the two outcome variables respectively to understand whether there exists a strong link between city average living standard and these outcomes. We then ran a set of OLS regression models, first controlling for city per capita income and city minimum wage only and then adding in other economic and demographic characteristics. We transformed the MLG assistance line, city per capita income, and city minimum wage into their natural logarithm forms so that the coefficients were estimated as elasticities and were easily interpretable. These three variables were also adjusted by provincial price deflators to account for variations in local cost of living. We adopted these provincial price deflators from Brandt and Holz (2006) and updated the figures for 2005 following their method.

There are in total 668 cities and 1,689 counties in China. However, data are limited on the vast majority of these cities, especially those of smaller sizes. In particular, data on MLG of these cities are very limited. Therefore, our analysis using the macro-level data focuses only on the thirty-five large cities and caution needs to be used in generalizing findings from these analyses.

AGGREGATE TRENDS

Figure 13.1 shows the total MLG expenditures and number of recipients in all Chinese cities during 1996–2007. Total MLG expenditures in urban China

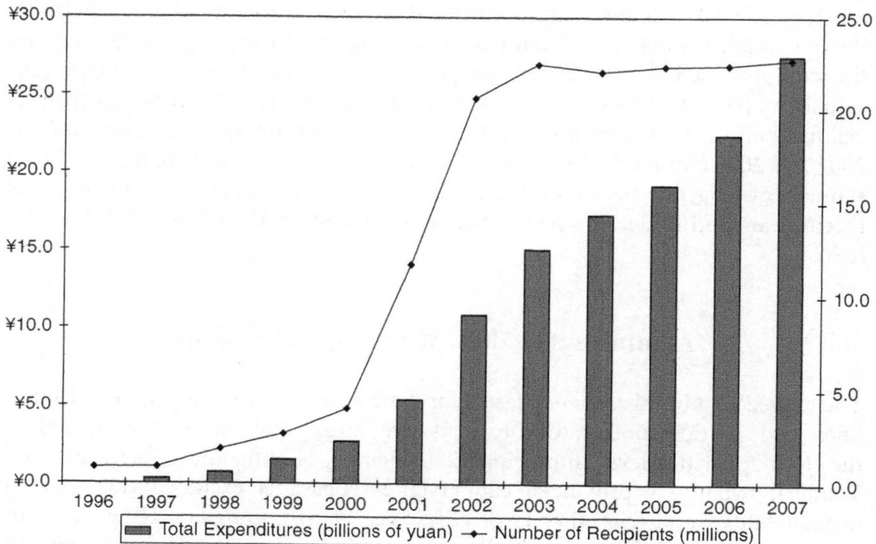

Figure 13.1. Total MLSA expenditures and number of recipients in urban China, 1996–2007
Source: Ministry of Civil Affairs

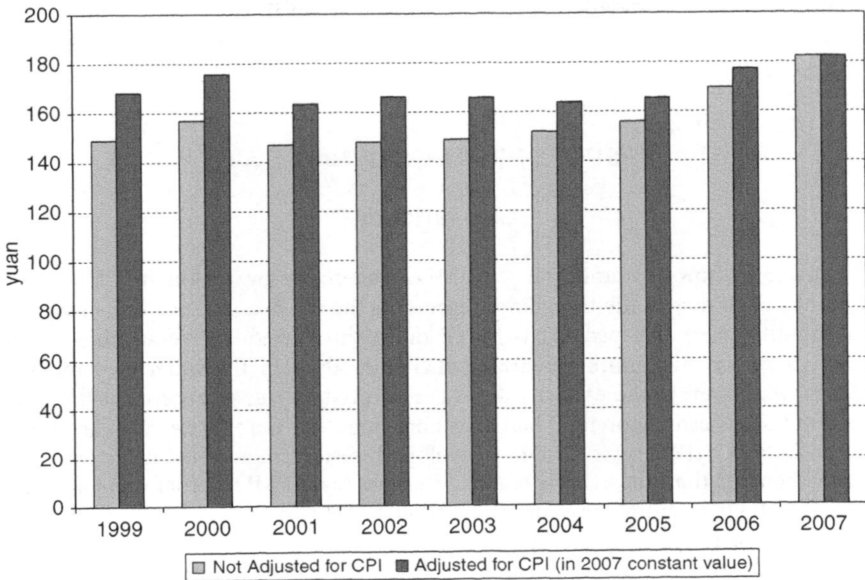

Figure 13.2. Nationwide city average assistance lines (monthly yuan)

Source: Ministry of Civil Affairs

increased steadily during this period, from 0.3 billion yuan in 1997 to 2.7 billion yuan in 2000, 10.9 billion yuan in 2002, 19.2 billion yuan in 2005, and 27.5 billion yuan in 2007. The number of MLG recipients was 0.8 million in 1996 and increased to 4.0 million by 2000. There was a huge jump during 2000–2 to 11.7 million in 2001 and 20.6 million in 2002. The increase leveled off after 2002 and the total number of recipients has remained around 22.5 million since 2003. The period from the program's beginning to 2002 corresponded to its accelerating implementation throughout urban China, but it also corresponded to the burgeoning of the eligible population as the transformation of state enterprises led to massive layoffs and rising urban poverty. The line for "Number of Recipients" in Figure 13.1 thus looks like a classic logistic curve for good reason. By 2002, the rise in urban unemployment and poverty had abated and other social programs (unemployment compensation, shoring up of the new pension system) were also making their contributions. Yet, in the view of some observers (Solinger 2010), the program remains a stingy one, covering only a minority of the "truly indigent urban population."

Despite the increases in the total MLG expenditures and number of recipients, the MLG assistance line remained relatively stable during this period, especially after the Consumer Price Index (CPI) is adjusted for. Figure 13.2 shows the nationwide city average of MLG assistance lines before and after adjusting for CPI during 1999–2007. The average unadjusted assistance line was 149 yuan per month in 1999. It increased to 157 yuan in 2000 but dropped back to 147 yuan in 2001. It increased by about 1–4 yuan per year, hovered around 150 yuan during

2002–5, then rose to 170 yuan in 2006 and 182 yuan in 2007. In constant *yuan*, however, the increases in the assistance line during this period were much smaller.

RESULTS FROM CHIP 2002 DATA

City variations

Figure 13.3 shows variations in city MLG generosity by region in CHIP 2002 sample. Each dot on the three lines represents the MLG assistance line measured in monthly yuan of a specific city in one of the three regions. Overall, cities in the eastern region had more generous MLG lines than in the other two regions. Moreover, seven of the eastern cities (as indicated by the seven dots at the right end of the eastern region line) had assistance lines that were higher than any other cities in the CHIP sample. The less developed western region had more generous MLG benefits than the central region. Western region MLG programs may have received higher central subsidies than other regions, however, which could help explain their relatively greater generosity.[1]

Figure 13.4 presents city variations in MLG participation rate by region in the CHIP 2002 sample. The overall average participation rate across regions was 4 percent. The western region had the highest average participation rate (5 percent),

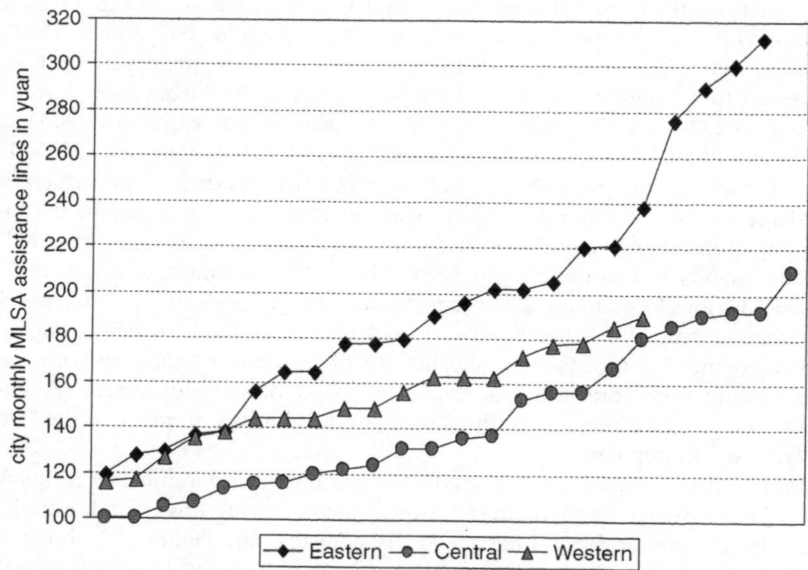

Figure 13.3. Variation in city MLG assistance lines by region in CHIP 2002 sample

Source: Gao, Garfinkel, and Zhai (2009).

Note: Each dot on the three lines represents the MLG assistance line of a specific city in one of the three regions. Some cities have identical MLG lines, but only one symbol for such lines appears on the graph. City MLG lines were obtained from the Ministry of Civil Affairs.

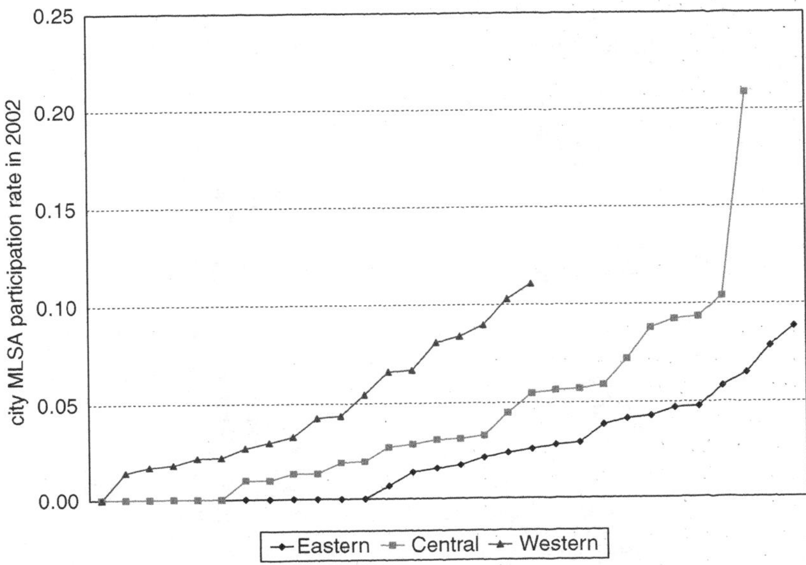

Figure 13.4. Variation in city MLG participation rate by region in CHIP 2002 sample

Note: Each dot on the three lines represents the MLG participation rate of a specific city in one of the three regions.

followed by the central region (4 percent). The most developed eastern region had the lowest participation rate (2 percent). These regional differences conform to expectations. Nevertheless, we note that there might be sampling and measurement errors in the estimates. For example, there are nineteen cities (twelve in the eastern region, six in the central region, and one in the western region) with a zero participation rate. This could be due to an undersampling of poor and eligible families or an underreporting of MLG participation in these cities. We are unable to confirm these speculations about the source of such possible errors. There is another outlier city (Datong city of Shanxi province of the central region) which has an extremely high MLG participation rate of 21 percent. Again, this could be due to oversampling of poor families or overreporting of MLG participation by families in this city.

Associations with city average income level

City MLG generosity (as measured by assistance lines) is expected to be positively correlated to the mean city per capita income. Figure 13.5 presents the correlations between city MLG assistance lines and city mean per capita income by region using the CHIP 2002 data. Overall, despite our reservations about the small city sample sizes, there exists a strong positive relationship between city per capita income and MLG assistance line, with a correlation coefficient of 0.84. This relationship is particularly strong among cities in the eastern region (r = 0.83), followed by the western region (r = 0.70) and the central region (r = 0.56).

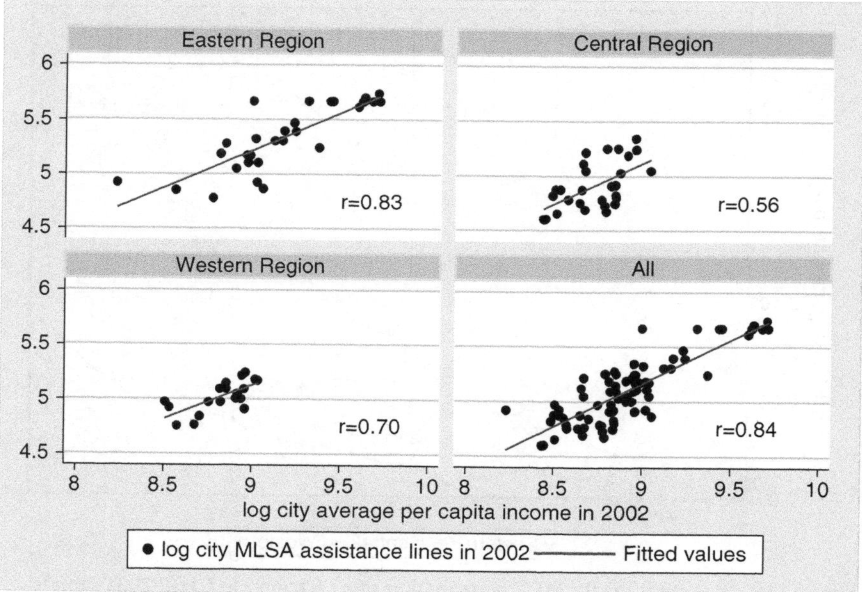

Figure 13.5. Correlation between city MLG assistance line and mean per capita income (annual amount in yuan) by region in CHIP 2002 sample

Figure 13.6 shows the correlation between city MLG participation rate and mean per capita income by region. As expected, the higher the average living standard of a city, the lower its MLG participation rate. Yet it is worth noting that the correlation is much smaller than that between per capita income and MLG assistance line and that there is evidently much besides per capita income that determines participation in the *dibao* program.

Determinants of city variation (A): explaining variations in *dibao* lines

We used regression models to explore the determinants of city MLG assistance lines and families' MLG participation status. In all cases, income and the MLG lines were adjusted by provincial price deflators calculated by Brandt and Holz (2006) to take into account differences in cost of living among provinces. For the "city MLG assistance (*dibao*) line" outcome variable, we ran two OLS regression models, using CHIP 2002 household-level data aggregated to the city level and averaged per city. This enabled us to craft city-level independent variables to explain city-level outcomes. Variables were chosen for which a case could be made for relevance to MLG assistance lines. For instance, number of children would be expected to be related to assistance line, through its association with poverty. However, cities with more children per family might have higher assistance lines

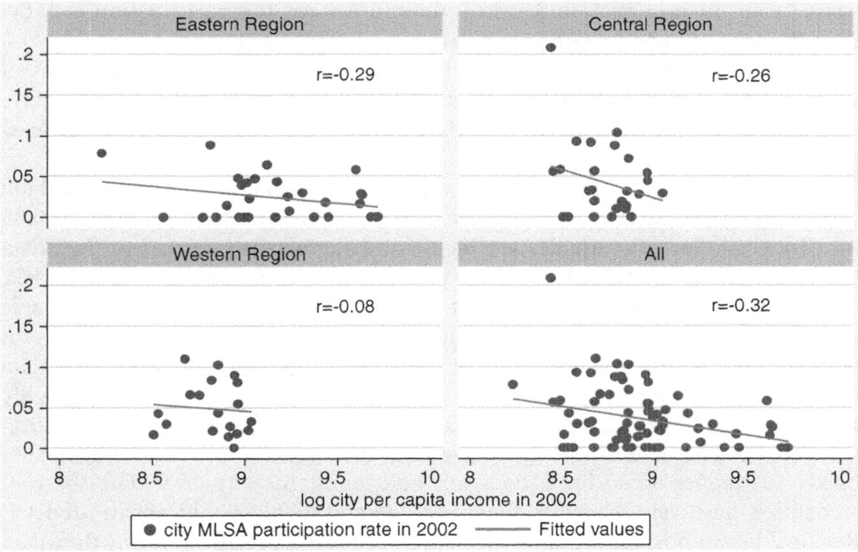

Figure 13.6. Correlation between city MLG participation rate and mean per capita income (annual amount in yuan) by region in CHIP 2002 sample

Note: If excluding the outlier (Datong city of Shanxi province of the central region, with a MLG participation rate of 0.21), the correlation coefficient for the central region becomes −0.02 and the overall correlation coefficient turns to −0.27.

because of greater need, or lower ones because of reduced fiscal capacity (a variable for which we cannot directly control). Both models use the same city average demographic characteristics, including age, years of schooling, household size, number of children in household, number of elder members in household, share of Communist Party members, share of ethnic minorities, enterprise profitability (shares of those at loss or near bankruptcy, those with marginal profit, and those with high profit), employment status (shares of those employed, retired, unemployed, and students), region, and whether the city is a municipal or provincial capital city.

Both models also include three provincial characteristics: GDP growth rate, unemployment rate, and the highest city minimum wage in the province.[2] The GDP growth rate reflects provincial fiscal priorities and the unemployment rate proxies provincial urban poverty, which is related both to the "demand" for MLG assistance and to its supply. The minimum wage is a *substitute* for MLG as a social assistance program. In a labor surplus economy, the equilibrium wage might fall below even a modest poverty line. An enforced minimum wage, by raising earnings, puts wage earners above the *dibao* line. If this relationship holds, then the minimum wage should be inversely related to participation in MLG.

Moreover, the fact that our minimum wage variable consists of the *highest* local minimum wage in each province, means that our minimum wage variable does not account for variation *within* provinces and *overstates* the actual minimum wage of many cities. This suggests that if we possessed and used information on the actual minimum wages of all seventy-seven sample cities, we would obtain a larger "true" inverse relation between minimum wage and participation in MLG than that obtained using our flawed minimum wage variable.

The first model adds province-level per capita income and its coefficient of variation (CV) estimated from the CHIP data. The second model substitutes city-level per capita income and its CV (both from CHIP) for their province-level counterparts.

These regression results are presented in Table 13.1. Both models do a good job of explaining the variation in assistance lines ($R^2 = 0.81$ for Model 1 and $R^2 = 0.85$ for Model 2). Several variables are highly and significantly related to the *dibao* line. Share of enterprises enjoying high profits is a major influence in both models. This is probably the best indication of city fiscal capacity of any of the available variables. Being a provincial capital city is a highly significant positive force in both models. As another indicator of local fiscal capacity, city-level per capita income (Model 2) is also positively related to the assistance line and highly significant, as is provincial per capita income and its coefficient of variation (Model 1). The latter finding, suggesting that greater provincial inequality makes for higher *dibao* lines, does not hold up at the *city* level. The share of students is positively related to the *dibao* line and highly significant in Model 1. Regional location is important, with central location especially *lowering* the *dibao* line (highly significant in Model 2) relative to eastern locations. Provincial GDP growth rate is a highly significant negative influence in both models, possibly because some cities prioritize economic growth rather than welfare provision. It is interesting that the use of city-level rather than province per capita income eliminates the significance of the provincial unemployment rate, while making household size, number of elders, number of members of ethnic minorities, and central location significant. The last is consistent with Figure 13.3 (above), which shows that sample cities in central China had lower assistance lines than either of the other two regions.

In general, these results make intuitive sense. With regard to household size, they suggest that the "demand" factor—the greater need of assistance of large, poor households—is determinative. The number of elders should depress the assistance line, given the expectation that elder care is the responsibility of families. Enterprise profitability, as well as city per capita income, are proxies for city fiscal capacity and prove to be strong predictors of city MLG generosity. Provincial cities are both richer than other cities and the showcases of their provinces and would therefore tend to have higher assistance lines. The lack of significance of unemployment rate in Model 2, once city income is accounted for, may be connected with the questionable official definition of unemployed, which captures only a fraction of those out of work. It is of interest that the coefficient on share of students in the population is positive and significant in both models although number of children is not. One can only speculate about the reason for this relation. Having more students means greater public spending on schools. Cities with larger numbers of students may be more progressive in general. The number of students could also act as a proxy for the state of city finances. Another perhaps not so straightforward result is the strong negative significance of provincial GDP growth rate. Again, we can only conjecture as to why this is. Faster growing provinces may be creating more jobs and experiencing a smaller poverty

Table 13.1. OLS regression results on city MLG (*dibao*) line using CHIP 2002 data

	Model 1	Model 2
City average demographic characteristics		
Age	−1.25	3.73
	(3.22)	(3.03)
Years of schooling	8.85+	3.08
	(4.77)	(4.97)
Household size	27.64	37.83*
	(19.70)	(15.26)
Number of children (<18)	−76.42	−0.95
	(48.77)	(50.63)
Number of elder members (60 +)	−10.52	−64.54*
	(34.18)	(31.81)
Communist Party member	−45.93	1.82
	(33.17)	(34.81)
Ethnic minority	−23.18	−40.37*
	(20.75)	(16.23)
Enterprise profitability (at loss or near bankruptcy omitted)		
Share of those with marginal profit	33.82	50.47*
	(23.69)	(21.43)
Share of those with high profit	98.81**	94.64**
	(32.43)	(26.52)
Employment status (employed omitted)		
Share of retired	160.93*	101.17
	(72.53)	(74.19)
Share of unemployed	−42.46	52.28
	(78.23)	(69.86)
Share of students	265.11**	134.19 +
	(77.67)	(76.13)
Region (eastern omitted)		
Central	−1.37	−18.57**
	(13.46)	(6.47)
Western	3.09	−7.08
	(12.40)	(7.91)
Provincial capital city	20.43**	15.34**
	(6.36)	(5.11)
Province characteristics		
GDP growth rate	−16.52**	−14.68**
	(3.00)	(2.34)
Unemployment rate	8.47*	2.38
	(3.35)	(1.88)
Highest city minimum wage in province[a]	0.08	0.11 +
	(0.08)	(0.05)
Per capita income divided by 1,000	15.78**	
	(5.27)	
CV of per capita income	132.64**	
	(34.64)	
City characteristics		
Per capita income divided by 1,000		10.61**
		(2.13)
CV of per capita income		16.24
		(26.21)
Constant	−112.44	−186.70
	(161.28)	(154.73)
R-squared	0.81	0.85

Note: N = 6,835 households. City *dibao* line, minimum wage, and city/province per capita income are all adjusted by provincial price deflators to account for variations in local cost of living. We adopt these provincial price deflators from Brandt and Holz (2006). Analyses are clustered at the city level with robust standard errors in parentheses. + significant at 10%; * significant at 5%; ** significant at 1%.

[a] Most provinces set several minimum wages, with the highest for the provincial capital city and other large cities and the lowest for the small and less developed cities. E.g., Shanxi in 2005 had four levels of minimum wage (in monthly yuan): 520, 480, 440, and 400. Because we do not know the exact minimum wages of all 77 cities, the minimum wage given here is the highest minimum wage in each city's province.

problem. On the other hand, their public expenditures might be heavily committed to investment with less available for MLG assistance.

One way to think about these results is to group the independent variables into three relevant categories: local fiscal capacity, need, and "other." Poorer macro-regions can afford only much lower MLG lines, *ceteris paribus*, although the poorer Western region does better than the less-poor Central region in this regard because of subsidies from the central government. Provinces (or cities) with higher per capita incomes and more profitable enterprises can afford higher such lines. On the other hand, need may also play a role. Greater household size brings higher lines in the second model. Unemployment cuts both ways, reducing fiscal capacity but increasing need. Indeed the sign on this variable is negative in the first model and positive in the second, but in neither case is it significant. Then there are factors not directly related to either fiscal capacity or need, such as the share of students in the population, which strongly raises the line. Such factors may reflect political and value differences. Local organizational capacity and political exposure may also play a role, for example in explaining why provincial capitals have higher *dibao* lines.

Some of the factors associated with the differences in city MLG lines suggest that these differences are inequitable. This is especially true of the factors pertaining to local fiscal capacity. From a public policy perspective, it would make sense to work toward raising the level of pooling of *dibao* funds as high as possible, at least to the province level, so as to make possible a more equitable assignment of relief levels.

Determinants of city variation (B): explaining variations in household participation

Here we are trying to understand the factors leading poor people to participate in the MLG program, using household-level data supplemented by province and city characteristics or by province dummies, to explain household participation. We extract from the CHIP sample two subsamples based upon alternative definitions of "poor." The first includes persons with household per capita income less than the urban poverty line devised by A. R. Khan (2004) (hereafter referred to as the "Khan poor"). Khan's line is based on the cost of a 2100 kcal diet with an allowance for nonfood basic needs taken from the actual proportion of income not spent on food by the poorest decile of the urban population. The second subsample (called the "*dibao*" poor) consists of persons with income below the local *dibao* line itself.[3] The latter really identifies the *dibao* target population rather than the poor per se. This group is a subsample not only of our entire urban sample, but also of the "Khan poor" group.

In our sample 28.8 percent of people with incomes below the Khan poverty line received *dibao* assistance in 2002, as did 46.6 percent of those below the even lower local *dibao* line (see Table 13.2). Poverty was thus the major driver of participation. These figures are in the range of previous estimates using large-scale household survey data. Specifically, a survey conducted by the Ministry of Civil Affairs in 2000 estimated that about 23 percent of the urban poor (i.e., with

Table 13.2. *Dibao* participation rates by income group, and distribution of *dibao* participants among income groups using CHIP 2002 data

Income group	Percent of income group participating in dibao	Percent of all *dibao* recipients in each income group
Income above Khan line	2.3	59.5
Income below Khan line	28.8	40.5
Income below *dibao* line*	46.6	28.5

*N.B. Those with income below the *dibao* line are a subset of those with income below the Khan line.

income below the *dibao* line) actually received MLG assistance. The percentages varied by cities. For example, the rate for Shenyang was 29.2 percent and that for Bengbu and Xining was around 25 percent (Hussain 2003).

Ravallion, Chen, and Wang (2008) found that 28 percent of the eligible families actually received MLG benefits using a sample of thirty-five of the largest cities from the NBS's Urban Household Survey for 2003/4. The authors argued that, based on international standards, such targeting performance is excellent for a means-tested public assistance program. Using the 2004 Urban Employment and Social Protection Survey containing a sample of fourteen cities of various sizes, Wang (2007) revealed that 39 percent of eligible households were actual MLG beneficiaries. Du and Park (2007) estimated that about 51 percent of eligible households were recipients using data collected from five big cities (Shanghai, Wuhan, Shenyang, Fuzhou, and Xi'an) in 2001 and 2005.

Beyond that, we were looking for the conditions *among the poor* that tend to promote participation. The "family MLG participation" outcome variable in 2002 is the change in probability of participating in *dibao* due to a one-unit change in the independent variable. We also applied the same models to the entire sample containing both poor and non-poor households, in order to identify factors that are significant to participation at this level but that become insignificant when analysis is limited to the poor.

For each sample we ran two logistic regression models. Model 1 controlled for family demographics, city *dibao* line, per capita income and its CV and provincial-level policy contextual variables. The *dibao* line was included to test whether greater generosity evokes greater participation. Family demographics included household head characteristics (i.e., age, education, self-rated health, marital status, ethnicity, Communist Party membership, and employment status) and household-level characteristics (i.e., household per capita income, size, the numbers of children, and older persons in the household, whether the family live in a municipality or a provincial capital city, and region of residence). Provincial-level policy contextual variables include GDP growth rate, unemployment rate, and the highest city minimum wage in the province. Model 2 dropped all province and city characteristics (keeping only the *dibao* line) in favor of province fixed effects to account for all (including unobserved) heterogeneity among provinces.

Table 13.3 presents results of these logistic regressions on household participation in the MLG program using CHIP data. What emerges first from this exercise is the relative difficulty of explaining program participation, compared with explaining city generosity, with the variables at hand. (This was already implied by the lower correlation coefficients of Figure 13.6 compared to Figure 13.5.) Our models, at best, account for 43 percent of the odds of household participation, compared with twice that percentage in the regressions for generosity. Reasonably, that high point of explanatory power occurs for the subsample of *dibao* target population itself. Yet the greater part of the odds even of that population's participation remains unexplained.

This may be partly due to sampling problems. But also relevant is the problem of mistargeting. In our sample, 71.5 percent of *dibao* recipients had incomes that were above the local *dibao* line, and 59.5 percent had incomes above the higher Khan line (Table 13.2). This means that in confining analysis to the poor we are ignoring a majority of *dibao* recipients whose estimated incomes were above either of our poverty thresholds. Part of the reason may be different methods of measuring income, but this can also be an outcome of ineffectiveness in the administration process of the MLG program. Previous research also estimated high rates of mistargeting, ranging between 40 percent (Wang 2007) and 43 percent (Ravallion, Chen, and Wang 2008; Du and Park 2007). Our estimation here is somewhat higher mainly because the detailed income questions in CHIP allow us to estimate income more comprehensively which causes families who are officially at or below the *dibao* line to register higher CHIP incomes and thus appear ineligible.[4]

Under these circumstances, it is difficult to pinpoint the explanatory factors beyond those very obvious ones enumerated above. Related to this issue are the lengthy and demeaning application and means-testing procedures of entry to the program and the severe restrictions imposed on participants, which may provide incentives for many qualified people to avoid participating. In addition, local government officials in charge of the implementation of the MLG program play significant roles in determining which families participate. Some studies suggest that family investigators, who are often local community service center personnel, have conflicts of interest that sometimes corrupt their decisions about access to MLG benefits (Leung 2006; Tang, Sha and Ren 2003).

Second, several characteristics of household heads are highly significant for the entire sample, but not for either of the subsamples. Specifically, bad health is a highly significant predictor of participation in the *dibao* program among all households. Having a household head in bad health increases the odds of a household participating by over 160 percent compared with having one in very good health, a result that is significant at the 1 percent level. Yet among Khan poor or *dibao* target households, while the coefficients on bad health remain large, they are not significant. In the case of unemployed status, the difference is even greater. Among all households, unemployed status for the household head more than doubles the odds of participating in MLG compared with the head's being employed, a strongly significant result. Yet among poor or target households, the coefficient loses significance and its magnitude suggests lower odds of receiving *dibao*, possibly because many unemployed already receive

Table 13.3. Logistic regression results on family MLG participation status using CHIP 2002 data

	Among all families (N = 6835 households)		Among "Khan poor" families (N = 319 households)		Among "*dibao* target" families (N = 138 households)	
	Model 1	Model 2	Model 1	Model 2	Model 1	Model 2
Household head characteristics						
Age (18–29 omitted)						
30–39	0.51	0.54	1.60	3.70	0.82	6.58
	(1.41)	(1.25)	(0.64)	(1.54)	(0.13)	(1.17)
40–49	0.75	0.82	1.93	4.79 +	0.85	10.17
	(0.62)	(0.42)	(0.90)	(1.89)	(0.12)	(1.40)
50–59	0.63	0.71	1.86	4.84 +	0.65	3.76
	(0.96)	(0.67)	(0.73)	(1.67)	(0.29)	(0.87)
60+	0.50	0.53	1.14	1.32	0.41	1.07
	(1.27)	(1.12)	(0.13)	(0.25)	(0.53)	(0.04)
Education (primary school or less omitted)						
Middle school	1.03	1.05	0.97	1.04	1.40	3.37
	(0.11)	(0.20)	(0.07)	(0.08)	(0.41)	(1.14)
High school or secondary technology school	0.95	0.95	1.13	1.37	1.53	6.37
	(0.20)	(0.22)	(0.22)	(0.54)	(0.49)	(1.45)
Two-year college or higher	0.84	0.81	0.40	0.32	2.67	1.62
	(0.51)	(0.63)	(0.86)	(1.13)	(0.61)	(0.28)
Self-reported health status (very healthy omitted)						
Healthy	1.13	1.13	1.49	1.72	2.42	3.14
	(0.57)	(0.55)	(0.75)	(0.96)	(0.80)	(1.01)
Fair	1.17	1.19	1.05	1.10	1.43	1.57
	(0.74)	(0.81)	(0.09)	(0.18)	(0.37)	(0.42)
Bad	2.65**	2.68**	2.07	2.53	4.39	4.93
	(3.74)	(3.80)	(1.23)	(1.51)	(1.36)	(1.42)
Unmarried	1.94*	1.94*	0.88	1.04	0.89	0.76
	(2.32)	(2.26)	(0.18)	(0.04)	(0.10)	(0.22)
Ethnic minority member	1.45	1.32	1.59	0.80	4.01	3.10
	(1.11)	(0.85)	(0.63)	(0.29)	(1.02)	(0.83)
Communist Party member	0.87	0.83	0.70	0.66	0.97	1.37
	(0.77)	(1.00)	(0.71)	(0.68)	(0.03)	(0.22)

(continued)

Table 13.3. Continued

	Among all families (N = 6835 households)		Among "Khan poor" families (N = 319 households)		Among "*dibao* target" families (N = 138 households)	
	Model 1	Model 2	Model 1	Model 2	Model 1	Model 2
Employment status (employed omitted)						
Retired	1.23	1.14	1.25	1.07	1.78	1.93
	(0.87)	(0.57)	(0.41)	(0.13)	(0.72)	(0.80)
Unemployed	2.02**	2.11**	0.66	0.76	0.53	0.56
	(3.23)	(3.49)	(0.99)	(0.59)	(0.93)	(0.81)
Household characteristics						
Household per capita income	0.58**	0.58**	0.12**	0.08**	0.06**	0.02**
(annual yuan divided by 1,000)	(9.67)	(9.77)	(7.23)	(6.79)	(4.14)	(3.49)
Household size	0.94	0.91	0.98	0.72	1.04	0.90
	(0.53)	(0.76)	(0.09)	(1.41)	(0.11)	(0.27)
Number of children aged <18 (0 omitted)						
One	0.82	0.86	0.71	0.94	0.69	0.63
	(1.09)	(0.82)	(0.73)	(0.12)	(0.61)	(0.65)
Two or more	1.29	1.19	0.97	1.17	0.80	0.42
	(0.72)	(0.47)	(0.04)	(0.18)	(0.21)	(0.70)
Number of elders aged >60 (none omitted)						
One	1.22	1.26	1.20	2.46	1.23	2.56
	(0.78)	(0.91)	(0.28)	(1.64)	(0.23)	(0.99)
Two or more	0.74	0.83	0.45	1.32	0.45	1.58
	(0.74)	(0.47)	(0.82)	(0.24)	(0.61)	(0.38)
Region (eastern omitted)						
Central	1.78*	2.94+	1.43	2.44	1.17	1.84
	(2.02)	(1.68)	(0.50)	(0.38)	(0.18)	(0.40)
Western	1.93*	6.06**	0.84	6.28	0.67	1.95
	(2.22)	(2.70)	(0.25)	(0.83)	(0.39)	(0.34)
Provincial capital city	0.68 +		0.52		0.40	
	(1.88)		(1.20)		(1.20)	
Province characteristics						
GDP growth rate	1.14		0.97		1.07	
	(1.37)		(0.15)		(0.19)	
Unemployment rate	1.13+		1.13		1.11	

	(1)	(2)	(3)	(4)	(5)	(6)
	(1.74)		(0.53)		(0.49)	
Highest city minimum wage in province (monthly yuan divided by 10)	0.95*		0.87*		0.91	
	(2.07)		(2.42)		(1.23)	
City characteristics						
Dibao line (monthly yuan divided by 10)	1.15**	1.12**	1.05	1.23**	1.27+	1.54*
	(3.83)	(4.39)	(0.58)	(3.25)	(1.84)	(2.43)
Per capita income divided by 1,000	1.07		1.51*		1.41	
	(0.99)		(2.34)		(1.64)	
CV of per capita income multiplied by 10	0.87+		0.82		0.69	
	(1.86)		(1.30)		(1.42)	
Province dummies						
Shanxi		1.97*		5.89*		24.87
		(2.06)		(2.26)		(1.51)
Liaoning		3.44 +		2.12		2.06
		(1.94)		(0.33)		(0.44)
Jiangsu		1.13		0.59		0.41
		(0.17)		(0.22)		(0.55)
Anhui		—		1.61		—
				(0.63)		
Henan		0.49 +		0.18 +		0.06*
		(1.84)		(1.70)		(2.01)
Hubei		0.81		—		0.18
		(0.61)				(1.51)
Guangdong		2.23		0.99		0.42
		(1.17)		(0.00)		(0.53)
Chongqing		—		0.31		0.35
				(1.30)		(0.60)
Sichuan		0.27**		0.18**		0.15
		(3.48)		(2.62)		(1.31)
Yunnan		0.70		—		4.56
		(1.06)				(1.32)
Gansu		0.77		3.27		—
		(0.73)		(1.54)		
Pseudo R^2	**0.24**	**0.26**	**0.27**	**0.35**	**0.29**	**0.43**

Note: City *dibao* line, minimum wage, and city/province per capita income are all adjusted by provincial price deflators to account for variations in local cost of living. We adopt these provincial price deflators from Brandt and Holz (2006). Analyses are clustered at the household level; odds ratios are presented with robust t statistics in parentheses; + significant at 10%; * significant at 5%; ** significant at 1%.

unemployment insurance or subsistence allowance that disqualifies them for MLG assistance.

Regional location (central or western) likewise is a significant determinant of participation only among the entire sample. The explanation here seems more straightforward: among the population as a whole, being located in the center or west greatly increases the chance of being poor, and therefore of receiving *dibao* assistance. However, among only the poor, living in these regions might actually reduce the chances of receiving *dibao* because poorer regions can afford to provide less assistance than better-off regions.

Among household characteristics, household per capita income is especially potent, and is significant at the 1 percent level for all models and all samples. All of its coefficients (i.e., odds ratios) are well below one, which is analogous to a negative sign on the coefficient, indicating that lower income greatly *increases* the odds of receiving *dibao* assistance.[5] This negative relation is strongest among *dibao* target and "Khan poor" households. Thus, even among the poor, being relatively poorer is the single biggest reason for participating in *dibao*.

On the other hand, at the *city level*, average per capita income is *positively* related to participation (significant only for the Khan poor) because better-off cities are able to enroll more poor in MLG. The local *dibao* line itself is significant for Model 2 for both subsamples (less so for Model 1) and highly significant for the total sample. This suggests that greater city generosity is an incentive to participate in the MLG program and/or it denotes a more serious effort of outreach to the poor. The minimum wage is inversely related to participation (significant for the total sample and the Khan poor). As suggested above, this result is consistent with the minimum wage playing the role of substitute to the MLG program: the higher the minimum wage, the greater family per capita income and the less need (and ability to qualify) for *dibao* assistance. Among the *dibao* targets, however, this relation is not significant, probably because there are very few people in this group who get the minimum wage.[6]

For all three samples, especially for the *dibao* target subsample, the use of province dummies improves explanatory power. Living in Henan and Sichuan provinces greatly reduces the odds of participating, while living in Shanxi increases it. An obvious contrast between these provinces is size: Henan and Sichuan are China's two largest provinces, with populations three times that of Shanxi. Their average per capita incomes are similar. There may be administrative diseconomies of scale in the MLG program that tend to discourage comprehensive outreach and recruitment in the largest provinces.

To sum up, having low household income relative to other poor families is a major reason for participation in the *dibao* program. *Dibao* reaches the poorest although it leaves many of the poor unenrolled. A higher *dibao* line itself encourages more participation. Participation also tends to increase with city per capita income but be depressed by higher minimum wage. Living in Shanxi encourages participation while living in Sichuan or Henan discourages it. Finally, several variables that are generally associated with poverty, such as having a head of household who is unemployed, in poor health, or unmarried, do significantly encourage participation in *dibao* among all households, but not when observations are limited to the poor.

RESULTS FROM THE 2005 MACRO-DATA

City variations

Figure 13.7 shows variations in city MLG assistance lines and in participation rates over thirty-five large cities in 2005. The cities are ranked by assistance line along the horizontal axis from lowest (left) to highest (right). The range is from 161 yuan (Urumqi) to 344 yuan (Shenzhen), a ratio of 1 to 2.1, unadjusted for regional price differences, which are considerable. MLG participation rates are shown for each city, and it is evident that there is negative correlation between level of assistance line and participation rate. The cities on the left with lower assistance lines tend to have higher participation rates than the cities on the right with higher assistance lines. Wealthier cities have fewer participants but can afford to help them more generously.

Associations with city average income level

The association between city income and city MLG generosity in both 2002 and 2005 is indicated in Figure 13.8, which shows the strong correlation between logarithm (ln) of city per capita income and ln MLG assistance line in both years. It is evident that the predicted assistance line for any given per capita income fell from 2002 to 2005. However, the CPI was about 7 percent higher in 2005, so that in terms of real income the two lines would be closer together. China was growing very rapidly during this period, and MLG lines were evidently rising,

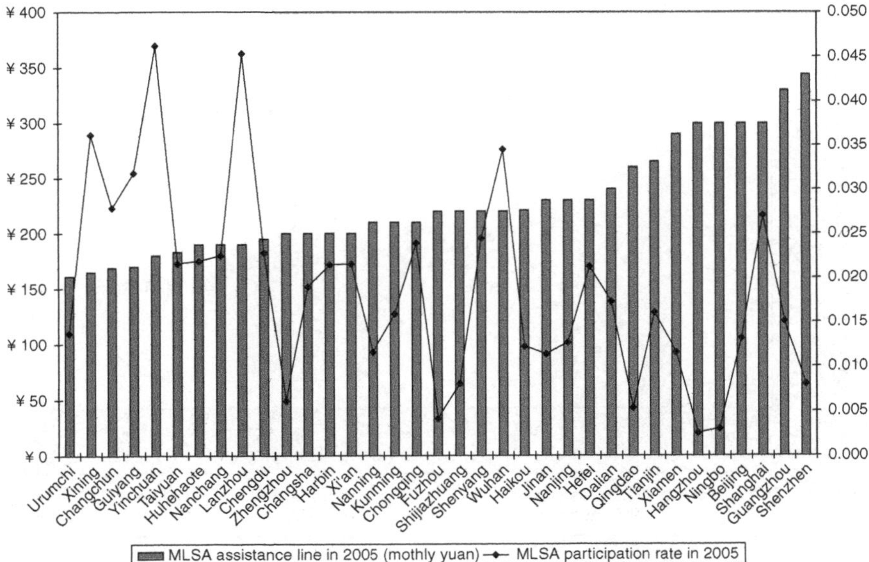

Figure 13.7. Variations in city MLG assistance line and participation rate by region in 35 large cities in 2005

but less quickly than income. Thus, six of the eight highest city lines (see northeast portion of the figure) were those of 2005, while all seven of the lowest (southwest section) were those of 2002. The slope of the fitted line can be interpreted as the average elasticity of assistance line with respect to per capita income. The correlation was almost equally high in both years (r = 0.87 in 2002 and r = 0.88 in 2005).

Figure 13.9 shows the correlation between log city per capita income and MLG participation rate in 2002 and 2005. City income per capita is negatively correlated with city MLG participation rate. The higher a city's income level, the lower the participation rate. This time the fitted line for 2002 lies below that of 2005. For any given per capita income, the participation rate tended to be higher in the later year. In this case, also, the correlation improved substantially between 2002 (r = −0.40) and 2005 (r = −0.54).

Thus, higher city per capita income gives rise to greater generosity with respect to *dibao* line but to lower participation, probably because fewer residents qualify for MLG assistance.

Determinants of city variations: administrative data

Tables 13.4 and 13.5 present OLS regressions for (ln) city MLG assistance line and for MLG participation rate in 2002 and 2005 for thirty-five large cities. The object is to see whether investigation based on administrative data is consistent with our findings using CHIP 2002 data, and/or throws additional light on the variations in

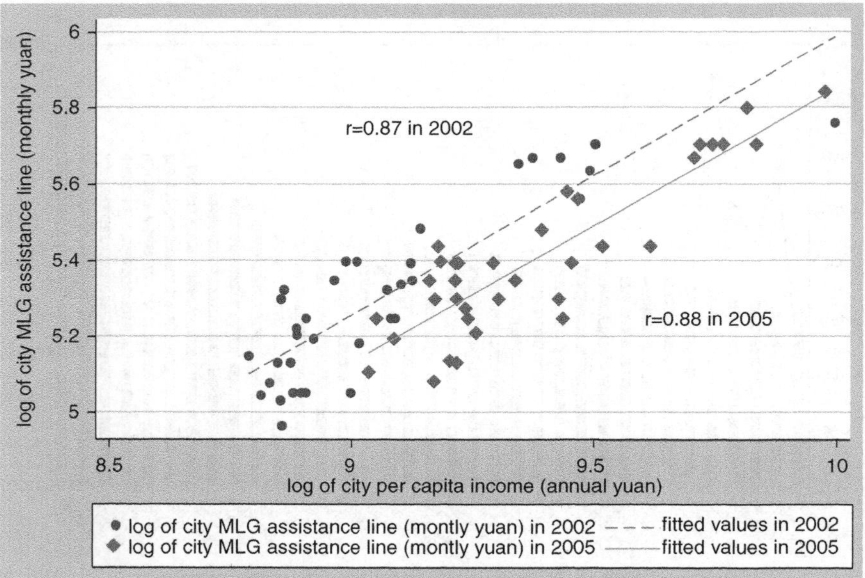

Figure 13.8. Correlation between city per capita income and MLG assistance line in 35 large cities in 2002 and 2005

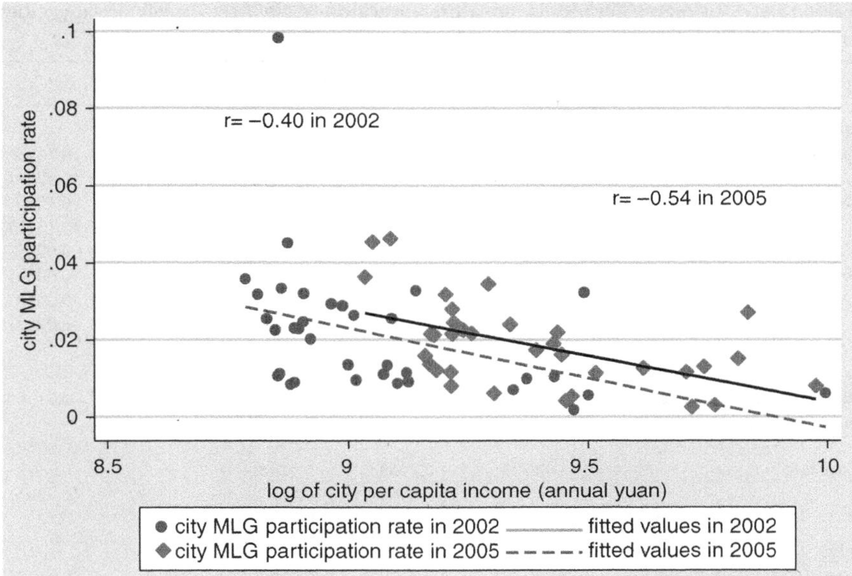

Figure 13.9. Correlation between log city per capita income and MLG participation rate in 35 large cities in 2002 and 2005

Note: Harbin had a participation rate of 10% in 2002.

the dependent variables. With regard to explaining the variation in city MLG assistance line (represented by its natural logarithm) in 2002 and 2005 (Table 13.4), the various models do a good job, with R values ranging up to 0.73. City per capita income is the dominant factor in both years, and is highly significant in all models. In this context, city per capita income proxies for city fiscal capacity. If that is indeed the dominant cause of variation in MLG assistance lines, then the equity principle would dictate raising the pooling level so that redistributive public finance could bring about greater equality in city *dibao* lines.

Minimum wage functions as a proxy for price differences among cities, with which it tends to correlate. It was a significant variable when interregional price differences were not controlled for, but in Table 13.4, which does control for these, its statistical significance disappears. Otherwise, in 2002 only the city Engel Index (Models 3 and 4) and population rate of natural increase (RNI) (Model 5) are significant, the first being positively related to *dibao* line, the second negatively. In 2005, the Engel Index remained significant but the RNI did not.

The Engel Index is a fairly specific indicator of poverty, and its sign indicates that MLG lines tend to be higher where poverty is greater, holding average per capita income (fiscal capacity) constant. In the absence of regional dummies, this could well relate to Figure 13.3, showing that (poorer) western provinces have higher MLG lines than central provinces, the suspected reason being higher central subsidies to the former. As for the RNI, it correlates positively with family size, number of children per family, and, given the income level, with greater

Table 13.4. OLS regression results on natural logarithm of city MLG line in 35 large cities in 2002 and 2005

	Model 1	Model 2	Model 3	Model 4	Model 5
2002					
Ln city per capita income	0.4949**	0.5568**	0.5713**	0.6332**	0.5623**
	(0.1289)	(0.1363)	(0.1265)	(0.1326)	(0.1279)
Ln city minimum wage	0.2476 +	0.1809	0.1964	0.1322	0.1540
	(0.1308)	(0.1395)	(0.1257)	(0.1329)	(0.1315)
GDP growth index		−0.0057		−0.0046	−0.0027
(previous year = 100)		(0.0056)		(0.0053)	(0.0054)
Unemployment rate (%)		0.0265		0.0289	0.0030
		(0.0215)		(0.0202)	(0.0227)
Engel Index (%)			0.0096*	0.0097*	
			(0.0043)	(0.0044)	
Rate of natural increase of population (per 1,000)					−0.0138*
					(0.0062)
Constant	−0.6735	−0.2958	−1.4243 +	−1.1937	−0.3670
	(0.7973)	(0.9865)	(0.8260)	(1.0109)	(0.9265)
R^2	0.66	0.68	0.71	0.73	0.73
2005					
Ln city per capita income	0.6179**	0.6440**	0.6667**	0.6767**	0.6533**
	(0.1203)	(0.1271)	(0.1124)	(0.1189)	(0.1316)
Ln city minimum wage	0.0655	0.0396	0.0795	0.0644	0.0403
	(0.1247)	(0.1312)	(0.1149)	(0.1223)	(0.1332)
GDP growth index		−0.0050		−0.0024	−0.0050
(previous year = 100)		(0.0059)		(0.0055)	(0.0059)
Unemployment rate (%)		0.0014		−0.0027	0.0042
		(0.0247)		(0.0230)	(0.0263)
Engel Index (%)			0.0118*	0.0115*	
			(0.0045)	(0.0048)	
Rate of natural increase					0.0021
of population (per 1,000)					(0.0058)
Constant	−0.8160	−0.3385	−1.7965*	−1.5013	−0.4489
	(0.7762)	(0.9810)	(0.8080)	(1.0323)	(1.0413)
R^2	0.67	0.68	0.73	0.73	0.68

Note: City *dibao* line, minimum wage, and per capita income are all adjusted by provincial price deflators to account for variations in local cost of living. We adopt these provincial price deflators from Brandt and Holz (2006) and have updated the figures for 2005 following their method. Standard errors in parentheses. + significant at 10%; * significant at 5%; ** significant at 1%.

inequality. In China it also correlates with ethnic minority status. Any or all of these are possible routes to the negative impact on assistance lines.

When it comes to explaining variation in MLG participation rates among the thirty-five large cities, a different picture emerges (Table 13.5). We cannot examine *dibao* participation among the poor based upon these administrative data because they lack information about individual household incomes or city income distributions from which poverty rates might be calculated. Therefore, we are able only to examine participation rates for entire city populations. Moreover, the explanatory power of the models is bound to be lower than in the case of city *dibao* lines, since participation is a household-level decision depending upon household circumstances (e.g., household income, health, employment, etc.),

Table 13.5. OLS regression results on city MLSA participation rate in 35 large cities in 2002 and 2005

	Model 1	Model 2	Model 3	Model 4	Model 5
2002					
ln city *dibao* line	0.0526 +	0.0491 +	0.0624*	0.0596 +	0.0629*
	(0.0268)	(0.0278)	(0.0289)	(0.0301)	(0.0299)
ln city per capita income	−0.0671**	−0.0601*	−0.0762**	−0.0701**	−0.0674**
	(0.0207)	(0.0228)	(0.0230)	(0.0253)	(0.0235)
ln city minimum wage	−0.0052	−0.0124	−0.0055	−0.0125	−0.0142
	(0.0244)	(0.0262)	(0.0245)	(0.0262)	(0.0260)
GDP growth index		−0.0007		−0.0008	−0.0009
(previous year = 100)		(0.0008)		(0.0008)	(0.0008)
Unemployment rate (%)		0.0016		0.0012	0.0033
		(0.0032)		(0.0032)	(0.0035)
Engel Index (%)			−0.0006	−0.0007	
			(0.0007)	(0.0007)	
Rate of natural population					0.0012
increase (per 1,000)					(0.0010)
Constant	0.3804**	0.4550**	0.4374**	0.5206**	0.4691**
	(0.1199)	(0.1535)	(0.1350)	(0.1694)	(0.1528)
R^2	0.28	0.30	0.30	0.32	0.34
2005					
ln city *dibao* line	−0.0126	−0.0131	0.0010	0.0014	−0.0119
	(0.0151)	(0.0153)	(0.0161)	(0.0160)	(0.0152)
ln city per capita income	−0.0087	−0.0052	−0.0199	−0.0164	−0.0085
	(0.0131)	(0.0137)	(0.0138)	(0.0139)	(0.0138)
ln city minimum wage	−0.0262*	−0.0275*	−0.0299*	−0.0322*	−0.0279*
	(0.0128)	(0.0130)	(0.0124)	(0.0125)	(0.0129)
GDP growth index		−0.0003		−0.0004	−0.0003
(previous year = 100)		(0.0005)		(0.0005)	(0.0005)
Unemployment rate (%)		0.0026		0.0030	0.0018
		(0.0020)		(0.0019)	(0.0021)
Engel Index (%)			−0.0009 +	−0.0009*	
			(0.0004)	(0.0004)	
Rate of natural population					−0.0006
increase (per 1,000)					(0.0005)
Constant	0.3281**	0.3298**	0.4141**	0.4356**	0.3600**
	(0.0677)	(0.0831)	(0.0786)	(0.0926)	(0.0863)
R^2	0.46	0.49	0.52	0.56	0.52

Note: City *dibao* line, minimum wage, and per capita income are all adjusted by provincial price deflators to account for variations in local cost of living. We adopt these provincial price deflators from Brandt and Holz (2006) and have updated the figures for 2005 following their method. Standard errors in parentheses. + significant at 10%; * significant at 5%; ** significant at 1%.

which are not adequately reflected by the available city-level independent variables. Moreover, the chief determinant of variations in participation is likely to be variations in rates of extreme poverty and, as noted above, we lack information about that for the thirty-five large cities.

Around one third of the variation in city participation rate is explained by our models in 2002 and a little more than one half in 2005. There is a major difference between the two years: in 2002 only the logarithms of city per capita income and of the city *dibao* line are significant. In 2005, however, both of these variables lose significance and the only two significant variables are the logarithms of city minimum wage and the Engel Index. We can only speculate about the reasons for this change. Growing central subsidies to the MLG program may by 2005 have reduced the impact of local fiscal capacity on participation in the program, if not on *dibao* line differences. The same reason could explain the disappearance of significance of the *dibao* line in explaining participation, since this line itself proxies for city fiscal capacity. The city *dibao* line is positive and significant at the 10 percent level in 2002, indicating that higher lines encourage greater participation. In 2002, however, it becomes negative but insignificant. The *dibao* line can have both a positive and negative impact on participation: a higher line encourages participation, but it also indicates a richer city and therefore fewer *dibao*-eligible people.

Model 1, containing only the logarithms of city *dibao* line, minimum wage, and city average per capita income—of which only the last is significant in both years—accounts for 28 percent of variation in participation rates among the thirty-five cities in 2002 and 46 percent in 2005. The coefficient on income is negative, as is to be expected, meaning that higher city per capita income brings lower participation. In 2005, the city minimum wage becomes a significant negative influence on participation. Higher minimum wage brings a lower participation rate. As in our results using CHIP data, the effect of a higher minimum wage is to leave fewer people eligible for *dibao* assistance. Moreover, for reasons explained above, we believe our estimate of the magnitude of this effect to be a lower bound. Finally, in 2005 the Engel Index is significant and inversely related to participation rate. We surmise that the Engel Index stands in for the city poverty rate, so this result appears counterintuitive. As mentioned earlier, we are as yet unable to conduct these analyses among a sample of poor households using the administrative data. Such analyses would enable us to understand these effects better.

OBSERVATIONS AND CONCLUSIONS

The rates of MLG participation in Chinese cities are very low.[7] This is due partly to the fact that China's urban absolute poverty rates are much lower than those of most other developing countries (a subject outside the immediate concerns of this paper). True, China's measured urban poverty omits that among the rural-urban migrants, whose poverty rate is much higher than that of full-status urban residents; however, even if these were included, the overall poverty rate would still be low by international comparative standards. So one reason overall participation rates in the *dibao* program seem low is that the broad target population of urban poor is relatively small. In addition, eligibility for *dibao* assistance does not extend to migrants, which of course suppresses the rate of participation of people who are actually poor. Incomplete coverage of legally eligible recipients by the MLG program completes the explanation of low participation. The first reason is grounds for applause, but the latter two represent weaknesses in this safety net program for the urban poor. Nonetheless, MLG participation rates in the early 2000s were similar to independent estimates of absolute poverty rates among full-status urban residents, both approximating 4 percent of the population, and MLG rates were still growing (Gao and Zhai 2012; Riskin and Gao 2010). Among those whom we identify as Khan poor or *dibao* poor urban residents, we estimate that 28.8 percent and 46.6 percent, respectively, are recipients of *dibao* aid. While mistargeting occurs, its seriousness must be limited by the fact that well-off urban residents are extremely unlikely to be beneficiaries of the program. Perhaps the two biggest weaknesses in the program, therefore, are (1) its conceptual neglect of the migrant population living in China's cities and (2) its limited reach due to the low thresholds used to define both urban poverty and *dibao* eligibility. Subsidiary to this second consideration is the program's design, which tends to discourage participation by anyone not truly desperate (see below).

The determinants of participation in the *dibao* program are difficult to identify. The obvious factors that push people into it, such as low income, unemployment, poor health, living in the west or the center, or being a single head of household together account for part, but only a small part, of the odds of a family participating. Local government fiscal capacity, indicated by per capita income at the city level and province level, also helps explain participation. Odds of participation were lower, *ceteris paribus*, for families living in Henan and Sichuan provinces and higher for those living in Shanxi. These effects are apparent using variables available in the CHIP 2002 data, most of which were not available for the models using city-level macro-data for thirty-five large cities. In these models, city per capita income, *dibao* line, minimum wage, and Engel Index were the only significant variables, depending upon year and model. However, in both sets of models, most of the variation among cities in participation rate, and most of the variation in probability of participation among households, goes unexplained. This raises questions about the targeting of the program, already known to be problematic. MLG is a government program with a complex structure. Many layers of government are involved in it, from the center down to the residents' committees (later amalgamated into "communities"). They all have a chance to exhibit enthusiasm or scorn for the target population. The manner of implementation must have a big influence on participation in ways that are difficult to quantify. Do some localities minimize bureaucratic obstacles, reach out to eligible people, and make it easy for them to get benefits, while others are indifferent or even hostile to the target population? As Solinger (2010: 267) points out, "there are conspicuous variations in the approaches taken by different municipalities in administering the dibao. (For example,) . . . perhaps because of the weak economic base of Lanzhou, that city . . . was more lenient toward sidewalk business than, for instance, Wuhan. In the latter city . . . after 2000 nowhere in the city could shoe repair specialists be found outside, apparently banned by the authorities" (see also Solinger and Hu 2012). It will take good ethnographic work to examine on the ground who is/is not being covered by MLG and why.[8]

City MLG assistance lines are largely predicated on local per capita income, which stands for city fiscal capacity. At the macro level, using administrative data, this was most of the story. The city Engel Index added some explanatory power, which we surmise is because it sharpens the focus upon absolute poverty. Using CHIP 2002 data, which afforded the chance to use demographic characteristics, we found that, in the best-fitting model, the number of elders and central location were negatively related, and the share of enterprises with high profits positively related, to the assistance line. The level of the city *dibao* line presents nothing of the mystery that surrounds participation in the program.

Fourth, because the differences in assistance lines depend so heavily on local fiscal capacity, they are inherently inequitable. Central subsidies already reduce the inequity in local lines but they stop well short of eliminating them. There is therefore a case to be made for raising the level of pooling for *dibao* financing at least to provincial level while increasing central redistributive subsidies.

Finally, we come to the broader social purpose of China's *dibao* program. Unlike China's rural antipoverty program, which has always been conceived of as a development program for poor regions, the MLG program is purely one of relief. It does not seek to enhance the capabilities of the urban poor. Rather than help those poor people who are not seriously incapacitated to find ways of becoming self-reliant, it implicitly or explicitly discourages or forbids efforts to escape from poverty on one's own.[9] Its basic intent, as is made clear by many descriptions of it in its formative days, is to remove a potential source of social unrest by making sure that the urban poor remain pacified. This characteristic of the *dibao* program is perhaps responsible for much of the mystery about participation in it, as it offers strong reasons for those indigent people with any capability of self-reliance to opt out if they possibly can.

NOTES

1. We thank Dorothy Solinger for pointing this out. She states that Lanzhou gets at least 65 percent of its *dibao* expenditures from the central government. See her discussion of central subsidies in Solinger (2010).
2. Most provinces set several minimum wages, with the highest for the provincial capital city and other large cities and the lowest for the small and less developed cities. For example, Shanxi in 2005 had four levels of minimum wage (in monthly yuan): 520, 480, 440, and 400. Because we do not know the exact minimum wages of all 77 cities in the CHIP sample, the highest minimum wage in each city's province is controlled for in these regression models.
3. Local *dibao* lines are obtained from the Ministry of Civil Affairs.
4. Gao, Garfinkel, and Zhai (2009) elaborated on the differences in the income definitions used by these studies.
5. Since in our logistic regression results odds ratios are presented, a coefficient value less than one means that an increase in the independent variable reduces the odds of participation in the *dibao* program.
6. The *dibao* line is usually set below the minimum wage to avoid being a disincentive to work. Therefore, anyone earning the minimum wage would be ineligible for *dibao* assistance. It is possible that a family might contain such an earner while still qualifying for assistance.
7. Some have argued that Chinese participation rates are sufficiently high compared to international standards (Ravallion, Chen, and Wang 2008).
8. Solinger has contributed one such study. Her description of the intrusive process by which applicants are investigated, including physical search of applicant's home, interviews with neighbors and employer, and public posting of the results of the

investigation, provides more than a hint of why some members of the "target population" might choose not to participate. See Solinger (2010: 266).

9. Solinger gives many local examples, such as prohibiting recipients from sending their children to better schools, from owning cell phones or computers, or from trying to run a family business. She argues forcefully that the program's provisions "in many ways confine the payees and their progeny to a long-term life of penury, operatively ensuring that they all be denied any opportunity for upward mobility . . . " (2010: 254).

REFERENCES

Brandt, L. and Holz, C. A. (2006), "Spatial Price Differences in China: Estimates and Implications," *Economic Development and Cultural Change*, 55/1: 43–86.

Du, Y. and Park, A. (2007), "Zhongguo de chengshi pinkun: shehuijiuzhu jiqi xiaoying" ["Social Assistance Programs and their Effects on Poverty Reduction in Urban China"], *Jingji Yanjiu*, 12: 24–33.

Gao, Q. (2006), "The Social Benefit System in Urban China: Reforms and Trends from 1988 to 2002," *Journal of East Asian Studies*, 6/1: 31–67.

——Garfinkel, I., and Zhai, F. (2009), "Anti-poverty Effectiveness of the Minimum Living Standard Assistance Policy in Urban China," *Review of Income and Wealth*, 55: 630–55.

——and Zhai, F. (2012), "Anti-poverty Family Policies in China: A Critical Evaluation," *Asian Social Work and Policy Review*, 6/1: 122–35.

————and Garfinkel, I. (2010), "How Does Public Assistance Affect Family Expenditures? The Case of Urban China," *World Development*, 38/7: 989–1000.

Guan, X. (2005), "Poverty in Urban China: An Introduction," in *Poverty and the Minimum Living Standard Assistance Policy in Urban China*, The Social Policy Research Center, Chinese Academy of Social Sciences, Beijing. Available online at <http://www.chinasocialpolicy.org/Paper_Show.asp?Paper_ID%20=%2040> (in Chinese).

Gustafsson, B. and Deng, Q. (2011), "Di Bao Receipt and its Importance for Combating Poverty in Urban China," Poverty and Public Policy, 3/1: Article 10, doi:10.2202/1944-2858.1127.

Hong, D. (2005a), "The Minimum Living Standard for Urban Residents," in *Poverty and the Minimum Living Standard Assistance Policy in Urban China*, The Social Policy Research Center, Chinese Academy of Social Sciences, Beijing. Available online at <http://www.chinasocialpolicy.org/Paper_Show.asp?Paper_ID%20=%2040> (in Chinese).

——(2005b), "Recent Developments in the Minimum Living Standard Assistance Policy for Urban Residents," in *Poverty and the Minimum Living Standard Assistance Policy in Urban China*, The Social Policy Research Center, Chinese Academy of Social Sciences, Beijing. Available online at <http://www.chinasocialpolicy.org/Paper_Show.asp?Paper_ID%20=%2038> (in Chinese).

Hussain, A. (2003), *Urban Poverty in China: Measurement, Patterns and Policies* (Geneva: International Labour Office).

——(2007), "Social Security in Transition," in V. Shue and C. Wong (eds), *Paying for Progress in China: Public Finance, Human Welfare and Changing Patterns of Inequality* (London: Routledge).

Information Office of the State Council (IOSC) (2002), *White Paper on China's Social Security and its Policy* (Beijing: Information Office of the State Council of the People's Republic of China).

——(2004), *White Paper on China's Social Security and its Policy* (Beijing: Information Office of the State Council of the People's Republic of China).

Khan, A. R. (2004), "Growth, Inequality and Poverty in China: A Comparative Study of the Experience in the Periods Before and After the Asian Crisis," Issues in Employment and Poverty Discussion Paper 15 (Geneva: International Labour Office (ILO)).

Leung, J. C. (2003), "Social Security Reforms in China: Issues and Prospects," *International Journal of Social Welfare*, 12/2: 73–85.

——(2006), "The Emergence of Social Assistance in China," *International Journal of Social Welfare*, 15/3: 188–98.

Ministry of Civil Affairs (MCA) (2006), *Minimum Living Standard Assistance Lines* [*Shehui Jiuji Biaozhunbiao*], available online at <http://dbs.mca.gov.cn/article/csdb/tjsj/>.

Ravallion, M., Chen, S., and Wang, Y. (2008), "Does the Di Bao Program Guarantee a Minimum Income in China's Cities?" in W. Lou and S. Wang (eds), *Public Finance in China* (Washington, DC: World Bank).

Riskin, C. and Gao, Q. (2010), "The Changing Nature of Urban Poverty in China," in S. Anand, P. Segal, and J. E. Stiglitz (eds), *Debates in the Measurement of Global Poverty* (New York: Oxford University Press), 300–26.

Ru, X., Lu, X. et al. (2002), *The Blue Book of Chinese Society 2002* [*Zhongguo Shehui Lanpishu 2002*] (Beijing: Chinese Social Science Press [Zhongguo Sheke Chubanshe]).

Saunders, P. and Shang, X. (2001), "Social Security Reform in China's Transition to a Market Economy," *Social Policy and Administration*, 35/3: 274–89.

Solinger, D. (2010). "The Urban Dibao: Guarantee for Minimum Livelihood or for Minimal Turmoil?" in F. Wu and C. Webster (eds), *Marginalization in Urban China: Comparative Perspectives* (Basingstoke: Palgrave Macmillan).

——and Hu, Y. (2012). "Welfare, Wealth and Poverty in Urban China: The Dibao and its Differential Disbursement," *The China Quarterly*, 211: 741–64.

Tang, J. (2004), "The Situation and Prospects of the MLG," in X. Ru, X. Lu, and P. Li (eds), *China's Social Situation Analysis and Prediction* (Beijing: Social Sciences Documentation Press).

——Sha, L., and Ren, Z. (2003), *Report on Poverty and Anti-Poverty in Urban China* [*Zhongguo Chengshi Pinkun yu Fanpinkun Baogao*] (Beijing: Huaxia Press).

Wang, M. (2007), "Emerging Urban Poverty and Effects of the Dibao Program on Alleviating Poverty in China," *China and World Economy*, 15/2: 74–88.

14

The Intergenerational Content of Social Spending: Health Care and Sustainable Growth in China[1]

Jean-Paul Fitoussi and Francesco Saraceno

INTRODUCTION

The Chinese economy is becoming increasingly unequal.[2] The outstanding long-term growth performance of the country has been obtained partly thanks to the very low priority given to all the other policy objectives, including spatial and sector equality. But the rise of inequalities has been so large that, in the past few years, the phenomenon has triggered a reaction by Chinese authorities fearing that social unrest could undermine the economic performance of the country and its political stability.

This paper argues that growing inequality should be combated also because it may have long-lasting effects on human capital, macroeconomic imbalances, and the overall efficiency of the economy. We suggest that current public spending, in particular social spending (health, education, etc.), has a strong intergenerational content as it affects the distribution of resources among generations, and hence the future level of "well-being" in the broadest possible sense (Stiglitz, Sen, and Fitoussi 2010).

In particular, this paper focuses on health policy. While other categories of social spending in China require attention because of the distortions and inequalities linked to their provision (notably education and social security), none seems to generate the same level of public anxiety as health expenditures. In November 2007, the Chinese National Bureau of Statistics organized the *Seventh Sampling Survey on Public Sense of Security*, interviewing more than 100,000 households.[3] According to the survey, medical care was the top concern (15.3 percent of the respondents), followed by a vaguer "social issues" with 14.3 percent. "Social security" related to the affordability of health and retirement came third with 13.2 percent. The growing public concern about health care access has prompted in the past few years a response from the government, which is rolling back on previous deregulation. The government unveiled a new plan, "Healthy China 2020," in December 2007,[4] with the goal of universal health care and equal access to public services for its 1.3 billion people by 2020. Implementation is so far proceeding more or less as planned (see Meng et al. 2012), and a basic Medicare system is now up and running.

The structure of the paper is as follows. In the next section we discuss the role of China in today's global macro imbalances. We subscribe to the thesis that the source of excess savings—a too-high level of household saving rate—can mostly be traced to the uncertainty about future provision of social goods, which in turn is due to the gradual disruption of the community-based social protection system. The following section discusses the evolution of the health care system in the post-reform period. Next we develop the reasons why current social spending may have strong intergenerational content. The final section gives a snapshot of today's attempts to correct the distortions in the provision of health care, which are based on voluntary adhesion to an insurance scheme. After showing why this attempt would not have the positive effects that the authorities hope for, we conclude by giving some indications about what we believe to be necessary policy and institutional changes for the future, and by trying to assess whether "Healthy China by 2020" is delivering along these lines.

THE SOURCES OF EXCESS SAVINGS

In the debate on global imbalances that rages in the academic literature and in the specialized press, the excess expenditure of US consumers and firms is usually contrasted with the "saving glut" (Bernanke 2005) of other areas of the world, notably East Asian countries. Because of its size, China is usually pointed out as the main example of this world excess saving that helps sustain the current global imbalances. In fact, as Figure 14.1 shows, both the remarkable levels of investment that China experienced since the early 1980s and the recent boom of the current

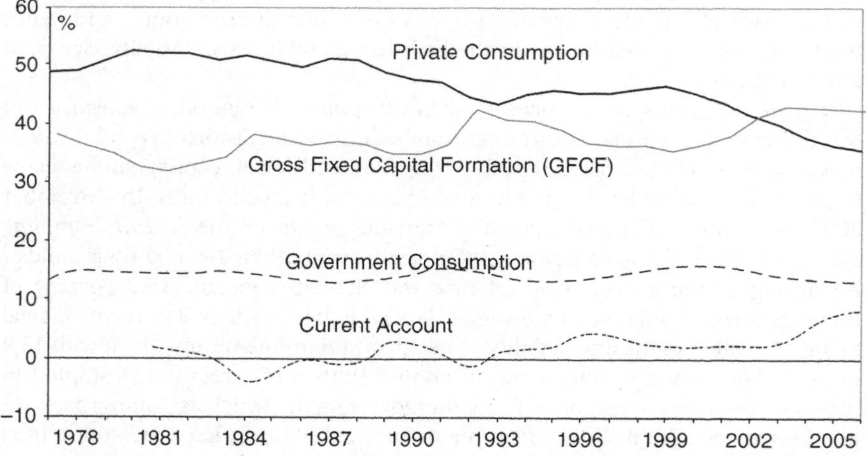

Figure 14.1. Macro aggregates as percentage of China's GDP
Source: Datastream

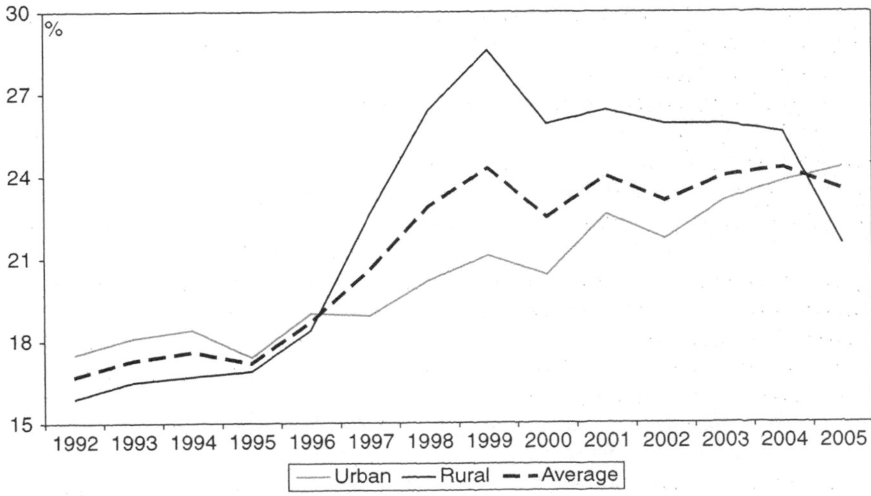

Figure 14.2. Household savings rates in China

Source: Chamon and Prasad (2010)

account surplus happened thanks to an important reduction in consumption, from a level above 50 percent of GDP in the early 1980s to the abnormally low level of 35 percent in 2007. The crisis exacerbated this movement, and the latest available data show a further reduction to 33 percent in 2010. The decrease of current account surplus and the further increase of investment since 2007 can, on the other hand, be explained by the global slowdown, and by the public investment content of the Chinese stimulus plan of 2009.

This aggregate figure hides wide regional and sector diversity, along the well-known differences in growth between coastal and western provinces and between rural and urban areas (for a survey see Lim, Spence, and Hausmann 2006). If we look at the savings rates (Figure 14.2), we can observe two remarkable trends. The first is a generalized increase (that obviously mirrors the decrease in consumption) of savings, which today account for almost 25 percent of household incomes. The second is, within this general trend, a more than proportional increase in savings for rural households. This is somewhat counter-intuitive, as being poorer on average, rural households should on the contrary save less. The saving rate, which used to be lower for poorer rural households, has since the mid-1990s been consistently larger, and has converged only recently (Kraay 2000; Kuijs 2005). Over the same period, their relative income decreased.[5]

While there is some debate as of the causes of this excessive saving (see, e.g., He and Cao 2007, who argue that demand deficiency is to be attributed to a decrease of disposable income and not to the increase in savings rate), the changing behavior of rural and urban households seems to be undoubtedly related to increased income uncertainty and to lower social protection. A high saving rate is then a rational reaction against the increase of both risks. For example, Lim,

Spence, and Hausmann (2006) infer from household surveys that rural household savings are largely precautionary, for retirement and medical expenses, and for life-cycle events such as children's education, weddings, and funerals (see also Kraay 2000 and Kuijs 2005).[6] The precautionary nature of savings would in fact also help to explain the counterintuitive larger savings of rural households, that while poorer, also enjoy lower social protection than urban households. Besides growing uncertainty, Chamon and Prasad (2010) point to the insufficient development of financial markets as one of the main causes of the lack of consumption by Chinese households.

In the same vein, the literature on savings, risk, and insurance (for a survey, see Besley 1995) documents that developing rural economies experience widespread income risk, and that households adapt in order to be protected from this risk, either in the form of self-insurance or of more or less informal risk-sharing contracts with other households. Changing patterns in the social contract, notably in the items that play the role of insuring households against risk, quite naturally affect the expected payoffs of households, and hence the intertemporal consumption-saving choices. Pradhan and Wagstaff (2005) show, for example, that in Vietnam overall consumption was positively affected by the implementation of a public health insurance scheme. This finding is hardly astonishing, since we know at least from Lucas's Critique (Lucas 1976), that changes in policy affect the parameters of a model's behavioral functions. In a more pedestrian way, a transfer from private to public insurance is equivalent to "forced saving," which implies a reduction in (residual) private hoarding.

The intertemporal decisions of households affect among other things the distribution of resources between generations. As we will further develop later, it follows that current spending, notably in social items (education, health, social security), has an important intergenerational content, through its effect on private spending. This content, often neglected, appears to be particularly important in fast-growing economies undergoing deep structural change, like China.

THE EVOLUTION OF SOCIAL SPENDING DURING THE REFORM PERIOD

The health coverage system put in place in the early 1950s by Maoist China was based on the employment units of the workers, mainly state-owned enterprises (SOEs) in cities, and the communes in rural areas. Prevention was given a prominent role, and the system was designed to fit within the dual structure of the economy (Guan 2000). In urban areas, the two main pillars of health care were the Government Insurance Scheme (GIS), which covered current and retired government employees plus selected categories such as students, and the Labor Insurance Scheme (LIS), which applied to SOEs. Both schemes were financed by the government and offered total coverage to employees (and generous, although not total, coverage to their dependents). In rural areas, preventive health action was organized and financed through the Cooperative Medical System (CMS), run by the collective organizations (communes) and subsidized by the government.

The capillary provision of basic health care services, from prevention to cure, was provided through a mass of practitioners with basic training, the barefoot doctors. Finally, hospitals were owned and funded by the government. The three-tiered[7] organization was designed to promote the efficient allocation of health care resources between primary and tertiary care facilities. This system quickly extended basic health care coverage and provided an efficient framework for patient referral and treatment.

To summarize, through subsidies, direct coverage, and low prices, the system provided near to universal health care. As a consequence of the focus on prevention, and on basic health services, the improvement in health conditions of the Chinese population was spectacular. The two most-cited figures are life expectancy, which almost doubled (rising from 35 to 69 years) between 1950 and 1990, and infant mortality, which fell from 200 to 34 per 1000 live births over the same period (Hesketh and Wei 1997; Blumenthal and Hsiao 2005). While limited by the availability of data, the comparison with countries at similar stages of development is striking.[8]

The radical transformation of China's society that began in the late 1970s consisted of a *de facto* privatization of the economy and a far-reaching decentralization process. The main, if not the only, focus of the three decades since 1978 has been economic growth. The issue of a fair distribution of resources has been virtually absent, at least until very recently. As soon as the reform period began, reorganizing the provision of public services quickly became a priority because such services were seen as a source of inefficiency for the economy (Guan 2000). The dismantlement of the pre-reform welfare system was extremely fast, and in some cases, like health care, there was no clear substitute. The main innovation introduced in the early 1980s was a strong reduction of central government involvement in the provision of public services, with the idea of freeing resources to be allocated to more productive uses. Health care expenditure by the government was dramatically reduced, from around a third of total expenditure in 1978 to around a fifth at the beginning of the twenty-first century. In the same time span, private expenditure went from 20 percent to about half, and SOEs and rural communities' spending dropped from almost 50 percent to less than 30 percent.[9] Decentralization also proved disruptive. To compensate for the reduction of transfers from the central government, local communities were allowed to raise funds from some activities like sanitary controls and high-end medical services. As was easily predictable, they focused on the provision of these profitable services, neglecting prevention and unprofitable basic health care. The main effect of this process of decentralization was a dramatic increase in regional inequality both in income and in public goods provision (Kanbur and Zhang 2005; Chou 2007; Qiao, Martinez-Vazquez, and Xu 2008). The metropolitan areas and the coastal regions, being richer, were able to ensure a decent level of public services, while the others experienced serious deficiencies in the provision of even the most basic public goods. Zhang and Kanbur (2005) describe at length the huge differences in education and public health levels that stemmed from this inequality, and Chou (2007) isolates them in a panel econometric model with provincial data. Besides the decentralization of public services' provision and financing, two other specific decisions had an impact on China's health care system. First, the government put in place a partial system of price regulation with the idea of continuing to provide access to basic health care. The price of routine visits and standard diagnostic tests was strictly regulated, while new drugs and technologies were left unregulated. Furthermore, a system of wage incentives was put in place, linking the remuneration of physicians to the amount of revenues generated for the hospitals. This resulted in an exponential increase of expensive drugs sales and high-tech services, and, once again, the neglect of price-regulated basic health care. The second decision impacting the health care system was the dismantlement of the rural communes and the shift from what Guan (2000) calls public ownership to a multiple-ownership economy, which also entailed the disruption of the system of safety nets that had assured basic health services for the mass of inhabitants of rural China. Without the Cooperative Medical System, hundreds of millions of Chinese peasants became uninsured because of their lack of resources. As recently as 2003, surveys highlighted that 36 percent and 39 percent of urban and rural households respectively gave up medical treatment because they were unable to afford it (Markus 2004; Yu 2006; Lim 2006). And a recent assessment of reform effort highlights how costs still remain unbearably high (Meng et al. 2012). Unemployed barefoot doctors were forced into the private sector, where in absence of regulation they found it more profitable to sell drugs or to provide high-end services (for which they were untrained) than to provide basic health care and prevention. As a consequence, the price regulation and the dismantlement of the communes had the unintended effect of skyrocketing prices and out-of-pocket expenditures, together with a substantial deterioration of the quality of the service.

National spending on health care (including public expenditure) almost doubled from 3.04 percent to 5.55 percent of GDP between 1978 and 2004. Nevertheless, in the same year less than one third (27 per cent) of the population had medical insurance, 54 percent of health care expenditures was private, and a vast majority (85.3 percent) of them were out-of-pocket.[10] Furthermore, half of this expenditure was devoted to the purchase of drugs, compared with a worldwide average of 15 percent (Sun et al. 2008). Finally, while the number of health care facilities at the beginning of the millennium was substantially larger than in the 1970s, they were dramatically less efficient and less accessible than they used to be, because of prohibitive costs and lack of coverage. The effect of "reforms" on the cost and the quality of China's health care by the mid years 2000s was quite clear: "To many in the United States, this portrait of pockets of medical affluence in the midst of declining financial access and exploding costs and inefficiency will sound depressingly familiar" (Blumenthal and Hsiao 2005: 1168).

The consequence of this deterioration on public health indicators had to be expected. All the spectacular improvements experienced until the late 1970s were stopped and sometimes even reversed by the reform. Liu, Hsiao, and Eggleston (1999) documented how some indicators (like infant mortality) improved only slightly since 1980, and showed how the general figure hid wide inequalities between rural and urban areas, with mortality rates that actually increased in many poor rural provinces. It does not come as a surprise, then, that at the turn of the century China's overall health system performance ranked only 144th in a pool of 191 countries, well behind the other Asian emerging giant, India, that ranked 112th (WHO 2000; Ma and Sood 2008).

To sum up, the spectacular growth performance triggered by the reform period was not matched by a similar improvement in health care provision. The fading insurance role of the government contributed to the widening of inequality which, in turn, made the absence of social spending and collective insurance more problematic.

This vicious circle did not affect the overall efficiency and growth performance of the Chinese economy. In the next section we argue that this would not have been the case forever, in light of a number of theoretical and empirical results which show how increasing inequality may in the long run harm growth. Therefore, the Chinese government faced no other choice than to rethink its system of health care provision.

THE INTERGENERATIONAL CONTENT OF CURRENT SPENDING

The analysis of business cycles has long been dominated by the belief that nothing substantial would be lost if growth and fluctuations were studied separately. According to this "common wisdom," growth is linked to supply factors (technology, endowments, and other "fundamentals"), while business cycles depend on demand factors. True, no economist would have admitted that the two phenomena were completely independent, and many have expressed the idea that the building of new capacity today (investment) has long-lasting effect on either potential output or growth (cf. e.g. Hahn and Solow 1995). More generally, economists have investigated the mechanisms through which a number of short-term phenomena (like for example unemployment, "false prices" in Hicks's sense, and so on) may have long-lasting effect. But the two frameworks were not really integrated until the emergence of Real Business Cycles (RBC) theory, initiated by Kydland and Prescott (1982). The RBC presents a single model able to account for growth and fluctuations. But this effort of construction of a unifying model was realized at the expense of the demand side that is absent from RBC models, which also attribute short-run fluctuations to supply factors. Hence whether the dichotomy between growth and fluctuations holds or not, economic policy, and in particular social spending, has at best only short-run effects through changes in aggregate demand. This obviously debatable view has been questioned by theoretical and empirical work alike. For example, in a widely known paper, Ramey and Ramey (1995) robustly show using a large sample of countries that higher aggregate income volatility is associated with lower long-term growth (for a general discussion see Fitoussi and Saraceno 2012).

It is worth remarking that in light of the probable discrepancies between the fluctuations of output and those of well-being, some of the consequences (e.g., on health and education) of excessive income volatility may be irreversible. It could then be better to devise policies aimed at minimizing the rate of unemployment and its variation over the business cycle, rather than at maximizing GDP growth. The design of good policies cannot be grounded on the artificial separation between social and macroeconomic policies: if the well-being of the people is the ultimate end, employment, labor market analysis, and income distribution must be central components of the macroeconomic analysis supporting stabilization policies (Fitoussi and Stiglitz 2012).

Fátas and Mihov (2001) further document a strong negative correlation between government size and output volatility across OECD countries and, even more markedly, across US states. This empirical regularity is shown to correspond to a simple new Keynesian model in which consumers are not perfectly rational (Andrés, Doménech, and Fátas 2008). But it may have other interpretations as well. For example, if we assume the level of corruption not to be overwhelming, a higher level of public spending means the provision of more public goods, including social goods, and stronger automatic stabilizers. For both reasons—better collective risk insurance and "built in" stabilization—the volatility of output will be lower.[11]

The most straightforward channel through which public spending reduces income variability is the smoothing of income volatility (for a survey see Creel and Saraceno 2009). It has to be emphasized that income volatility in developing countries, where almost by definition the system of social protection is less developed, may have very disruptive effects on social and productive structures. Sen (2001) argues that in these countries income variability matters more than the growth rate, as a recession may have irreversible consequences on the fate of the more vulnerable fraction of the population.

In particular, social spending strengthens the correlation of current spending and current income, and the reduction of precautionary savings (see, e.g., Creel and Saraceno 2009). On the other hand, one should also consider the opposite effect, namely that excessive income security distorts the incentives and results in a reduction of labor supply. This argument has been used extensively in the European debate on fiscal policy. The argument is more controversial than it may appear (the Scandinavian counterexample shows that incentives are complex); furthermore it can be invoked only for developed countries and has limited relevance for the purpose of this paper. For developing countries, in effect, a vast empirical literature shows that larger social spending increases the level of private consumption and reduces its variability. A number of recent empirical results are an indirect proof of the existence of resource constraints on the poorest households that can be lifted by social spending, thus leading to a more efficient allocation of resources. To quote only a few recent contributions, Dehejia and Gatti (2005) show that schooling duration increases with reductions in parents' income variability. Similarly, Mangyo (2008) shows that in poor households the food intake of children is directly affected by income increases. Increased provision of health care may also bring about a general improvement of the conditions for the creation of wealth. Liu et al. (2008) show a direct impact of household health on income and productivity. In a country like China, where income is growing at unprecedented pace, resource constraints play a relatively limited role for an increasing number of households, but a very important one for those who are not benefiting from growth—a large number indeed. Their effect could become even more important when in the future the average growth rate will inevitably decrease.

Besides its role as insurance against income and consumption fluctuations, especially for poorer households, social spending has a more direct effect.

Increasing the collective supply of public goods would free part of the income that is now saved for precaution, and make it available for investment in both physical and human capital. In other words, social spending could "crowd in" private expenditure and raise the economy's current and future growth rate alike while decreasing its volatility.

Other mechanisms may also play a role. Higher civil servants' wages could make public service more attractive and reduce the extent of corruption.[12] This would increase the quality of public services that are complementary to private spending in sustaining present and, above all, future growth. The same holds for expenditure geared to strengthen the legal system (faster and more equitable trials, larger resources devoted to investigation, legal equipment, etc.), and to set up an effective means to protect property rights.

Furthermore, social mobility ("giving to my children better opportunities than I had") is one of the engines of growth and prosperity. But social mobility is all the more likely if somehow counters are reset, at least partially, at each generation. One of the roles of social spending is a transfer of resources that helps reduce inequalities of initial conditions for the new generations.

When thinking about some of today's challenges—environment and the use of natural resources, population aging, etc.—we frequently reason as if the welfare levels of future and present generations were substitutes. But if we extrapolate for future generations the relationship existing between today's parents and children, we may be led to a quite different perspective concerning the social protection system; in fact, complementarity rather than substitutability seems to us much more appealing in explaining decision mechanisms at the microeconomic level. The hypothesis amounts to saying that if the parents care about their children and the latter about their own children etc., there should be, at least for the kind of expenditures we are discussing here, strong complementarity between the welfare of different generations. Current public spending on all levels of education has obviously an intergenerational content. What is almost universally verified is that the consent to pay by the parents for the education of their children is very high. The health of the parents is almost a precondition for that of their children. Willingly or not, therefore, current spending on health has an intergenerational content. The same can be said of a number of public spending items, including those aimed at fighting unemployment. To belabor the obvious, the conditions of education are certainly disturbed by the unemployment of parents. The improvement of housing conditions through public schemes will also likely benefit the chain of generations.[13]

In fact, the argument should not revolve on whether public spending affects future generations or not. We argue that all current spending may have long-lasting effects, as long as it is not wasteful. Abandoning the artificial distinction between a demand-driven short run and a supply-driven long run would allow a shift in the focus towards the relative efficacy of different types of expenditure in ensuring a sustainable increase in the long-term performance of the economy.

A domain where the welfare levels of present and future generations may be considered to exhibit an important degree of complementarity is social justice. If social justice is not a sufficient condition of complementarity it is at least a necessary condition. There are two reasons why it is so. The first is more of the order of conjecture: in a society where a pervading feeling of injustice prevails, it seems unlikely that there would be space for intergenerational altruism. It would be hard to assume that *intergenerational* equity would preoccupy the members of the society in a context where *intragenerational* equity is not assured. The second reason is a constraint related to the state of inequalities. When these are large and growing, an important fraction of society does not have the means to project itself towards the future, even if it wished to do so (Stiglitz 2012). Day-to-day hardships make it prisoner of the present. It is why a well-functioning social protection system, by giving people a feeling of fairness and allowing them to contemplate the future with less anxiety, would benefit the chain of generations.

This section has outlined a number of mechanisms through which social spending may not only sustain current activity and the standard of living of current generations, but also, and more importantly, affect the potential for future growth and benefit future generations. In the light of this discussion, the next section will describe the recent changes in health policy in China, and conclude on some characteristics that the reformed system should have in light of our analysis.

THE ROLE OF SOCIAL SPENDING FOR SUSTAINABLE GROWTH

The 2008 WHO health report aptly summarizes our argument so far: "Whether by choice or because of external pressure, the withdrawal of the state that occurred in the 1980s and 1990s in China and the former Soviet Union, as well as in a considerable number of low-income countries, has had visible and worrisome consequences for health and for the functioning of health services. Significantly, it has created social tensions that affected the legitimacy of political leadership" (WHO 2008: 17).

The Chinese leadership proved to be aware of these risks. The beginning of the new millennium marked an important change in priorities for the government. The deepening spatial and sector inequality, both in income and in the provision of public goods, was eventually perceived as a potential cause of excessive imbalances, with possible effects on social stability and overall growth. In October 2002, the first China National Rural Health Conference was held in Beijing and a set of reforms in the provision of health care was announced. (Liu and Rao 2006; Wagstaff et al. 2007). The "Healthy China 2020" plan aims at achieving universal coverage by 2020. China is setting up a basic medical and health care system to balance the disparity between medical access and quality of services in urban and rural areas, as well as between different regions, and for people with different income levels.

For rural households, the New Cooperative Medical System (NCMS) is based on voluntary adhesion. The unit of the scheme is the county instead of the village; the increased scale of each unit allows for better risk-pooling and economies of scale in the provision of health care services. To enrol in the program, households have to pay a flat amount per person and per year (changing by occupation and status), which is matched by public subsidies that multiply it up to eight times for the poorest households. (The burden is shared equally by the provincial and the central government.) The level of discretion of each county is very high, from coverage to cost sharing to fees, etc., in accordance with the principle of decentralization of health policy introduced with the reform. The program, although voluntary, has proven extremely successful, yielding an increase in rural insurance coverage from 21 per cent in 2003 to 93 percent in 2008.

The percentage of urban population covered in 2003 was larger (55 percent), but the implementation of the new insurance mechanism Urban Residents' Basic Medical Insurance program (UR-BMI) led to an increase of coverage to 88 percent in 2011 (data for UR-BMI and NCMS are taken from Meng et al. 2012). The mechanism is also voluntary, a large part of it is subsidized by the government, but the premium is higher.

A voluntary insurance scheme is subject to all the typical asymmetric information problems associated with the provision of public goods. These concerns are reinforced by the wide inequalities in income levels and in needs in the recipient population, and by the diversity in economic structures among provinces. From the outset, Wagstaff and Yu (2007) and Wagstaff et al. (2007) remarked that the NCMS budget was too small to significantly affect households' out-of-pocket spending. The per capita contribution, including the subsidies, is around 20 percent of total per capita rural health spending; furthermore, the large deductibles and high coinsurance rates make co-payments large. At the time it was also feared that the excessive financial burden that remained on the insured could induce poor households to avoid enrolling in the scheme, thus excluding from medical coverage the group that is supposed to be the main beneficiary of the program (a phenomenon documented by Jalan and Ravallion 1999, and Wang and Rosenman 2007). By looking at the urban program, Lindelow and Wagstaff (2005) further argued that, because of the distortions in the pricing mechanism and in the widespread practice of fee-per-service reimbursement, higher-end care would remain more profitable and hence overprovided with respect to basic health services (see also Eggleston et al. 2006).

Meng et al. (2012) provide an interim assessment of the reform that only partially confirms the fears that accompanied its implementation. In particular, the programs proved very successful in extending insurance to virtually all the population. This has also led to some decrease of territorial inequality in access to health care and inpatient reimbursement. The main problems, nevertheless, excessive spending and insufficient coverage against catastrophic costs, remain unsolved; in spite of the increase of coverage and of government reengagement (it covered 52 percent of total health expenditure in 2010, up almost 20 points from the 2001 low of 35 percent: WHO website), out-of-pocket expenditure remains a very large share of private expenditure (78 percent in 2010: WHO website). This is mostly because, as predicted by Lindelow and Wagstaff (2005), costs and health care expenditure kept increasing. Finally, and most importantly, Huang (2011) observes that most of the public health indicators have yet to show any sign of improvement, and blames this in part on the governance structure and on insufficient accountability (in particular of local governments).

As the discussion above suggests, these results are hardly surprising. All the standard asymmetric information problems experienced by insurance schemes for the provisions of public goods are likely to be exacerbated in the presence of strong inequalities and high income uncertainty.

This overview of the reform in the health care sector, and of the recent attempts to roll back on some of its more harmful effects, seems to suggest a number of policy conclusions:

1. First, and in general, attention to equality should be paid, in order to obtain income stabilization and provide private households with a less uncertain environment (see also Kuijs and Wang 2006). In particular, for the Chinese case, region/sector inequality seems to be one of the most serious obstacles in the way of continued strong growth. The reform has only started to address this problem.
2. An effective solution to the worsening conditions in health provision seems to be the move toward universal health coverage. Collective insurance seems to be the only way to reduce the huge differences in access to health care. The reform has extended coverage, but the burden that falls on the shoulders of households, especially poorer ones, remains excessive and unsustainable. This does not mean that the provision of health services should necessarily be public. In fact, there is no reason to reduce private involvement in this sector, rather the contrary. (See Eggleston et al. 2006 for pros and cons of the different frameworks.) Nevertheless, in case of private provision, for a socially sensible public good like health care, appropriate regulation is a priority. This may be a problem in China.
3. The spatial inequality that inevitably accompanied the process of decentralization has been a major cause for increased inequality in income and in social conditions (Qiao, Martinez-Vazquez, and Xu 2008). This calls for a central management of the health system, and/or for a system of strong interprovincial transfers (Chou 2007 documents a strong correlation between provincial government deficit and health care provision). The reform so far has not put in place anything like this, and poor countries and provinces struggle to provide even basic coverage. In both cases, problems of free riding and moral hazard should be appropriately taken into account.

To summarize, it is our belief that a reformed health care sector should be centered around universal coverage to be managed centrally or at the provincial level. In this latter case, nevertheless, an interprovincial transfer system would be necessary to guarantee sufficient financing of the insurance scheme regardless of the income level of the provinces. Furthermore, very detailed regulation should be designed prior to further involvement of the private sector in the provision of health care services. A study that appeared in the *Lancet* (2008) reached similar conclusions, noticing on one side that public spending had begun increasing again after reaching the low levels of 2000–1, but on the other that the main challenge was to reduce the disproportionate burden on individuals represented by out-of-pocket expenditure. That has not happened yet.

The plea for universal publicly funded coverage is of course not new. Such experiments in other countries have been met with mixed results. In particular, the risks associated with public intervention (inefficiency, excessive costs, rent-seeking, etc.) may apply. Nevertheless, past experience also shows that, in

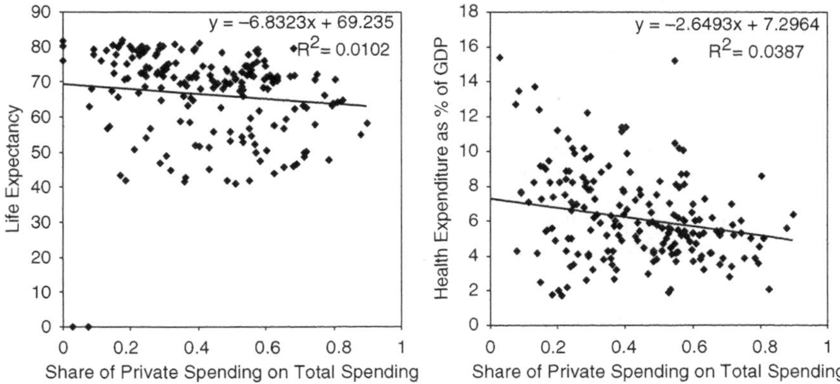

Figure 14.3. Share of private spending and health indicators, 2009

Source: World Development Indicators, World Bank

particular in the field of social protection, the private sector's performance is often at least as poor.

One of our arguments in this paper has been that the main role of social protection is not charity but insurance. The assessment of different systems has hence to go through an evaluation of costs and benefits for private and public insurance schemes. As pointed out by Paul Krugman, with reference to the debate in the United States,[14] a major advantage of universal, government-provided health insurance is lower administrative costs. This is not surprising, as systems based on private insurance have to bear the costs of screening out high-risk clients and of ensuring adequate profits for insurance companies. And in fact, even a casual look at the data confirms this view. Figure 14.3 shows a scatter plot of the share of private expenditure on the total, versus life expectancy at birth (left panel) and health expenditure as a percentage of GDP (right panel). In both cases there is no discernable evidence that increasing the share of private expenditure has effects. Both total spending (that we take as a proxy of cost-effectiveness) and life expectancy (that we take as a proxy of performance) are unrelated to the composition of health expenditure. If anything, life expectancy is *lower* in countries where the share of private expenditure is larger.

To clarify our argument, we can take two particular points in the figure, France and the United States. Table 14.1 summarizes the health indicators for these two countries. Both in per capita terms ($8,361 vs $4,020), and as a percentage of GDP (17.9 percent vs 11.9 percent), the United States spent more than France in health care. In the United States, 45 percent of this expenditure was private, against only 22 percent in France.

Nevertheless, both health performance indicators commonly taken (child and maternal mortality) show that conditions in France are better (the incidence of tuberculosis, on the contrary, sees the United States fare better). In the 2000 WHO ranking, which while controversial in many respects takes into account a whole range of measures, the United States ranks well beyond France. The comparison of any two countries is of course anecdotal, but it serves our illustrative purposes.

Table 14.1. Selected health indicators, 2010

	France	United States
Health expenditure per capita (PPP (constant 2005 international $))	4,020.7	8,361.7
Health expenditure, total (% of GDP)	11.9	17.9
Health expenditure, public (% of total health expenditure)	77.8	53.0
Out-of-pocket health expenditure (% of total expenditure on health)	7.3	11.8
Maternal mortality ratio (modeled estimate, per 100,000 live births)	8	21
Incidence of tuberculosis (per 100,000 people)	9.3	4.1
Mortality rate, under-5 (per 1,000)	4.1	7.5
WHO Ranking (2000)	1	37

Source: World Development Indicators, World Bank

To conclude, a casual look at the data suffices to realize that there is no clear superiority of a privately based social protection system. The standard textbook efficiency argument runs into the problems of huge administrative costs typical of insurance mechanisms. There is no reason, therefore, to believe that a carefully designed public system aimed at universal coverage would be more expensive or less effective than a private one.

By 2020, according to the reform timeline set up by its leadership, China will have completed the establishment of a public medical and health care services network, a universal coverage medical insurance system, a drug supply system, and a medical institution management system. Most of the concerns outlined above would hence be addressed by the plan, which would go in the direction that the present paper envisions.

In particular, two aspects of the plan emerge as new with respect to the current situation.

The first and more important is the commitment to increased involvement of the central and local government in the health sector; this would take the form of an increase in public spending as a percentage of total health expenditure, which in some measure we are already seeing in the data. Such an effort would initially be addressed to increasing affordability of health care for the poorest households and subsequently to improve the quality of service. Increased involvement of the government would also take the form of a more balanced allocation of resources between urban and rural areas, the latter being currently significantly underfunded. According to the plan, the government and households should split the cost of basic medical care, but the burden of specialized medical care would still be borne by patients directly or through private insurance.

The second important innovation of the new plan concerns the management of health care facilities, in an effort to change the incentive structure from profits to public health performance. This is the part of the plan that the government has more difficulties in implementing. We saw above, in fact, that costs keep increasing at an unsustainable pace. The main lines of action are clearer definition of the responsibilities and rewards of public managers, and a disconnection of hospital funding from revenues; the latter should help curb the overprescription of drugs and excessive prices.

Increased dialogue and engagement with the private sector were announced, but so far nothing seems to suggest that this will lead to the much-needed substantial redesign of the regulatory framework.

In the perspective of this paper, the reform undertaken is certainly making important progress in the direction of providing access to basic health care to all citizens, regardless of their means or their region of residence. The remaining burden on households, and the lack of a centralized system of interprovincial transfers have not addressed, so far, the problems of excessive precautionary savings and of regional inequality. If the Chinese leadership can find a solution to these problems, this will contribute to smoothing the current imbalances and ensuring sustainable growth in the years to come.

NOTES

1. Paper prepared for the second Initiative for Policy Dialogue China Task Force Meeting, Manchester, July 4–5, 2007. We thank all the participants and an anonymous referee for comments on an earlier draft. We also acknowledge help from Eswar Prasad, Jun Yao, and Win Lin Chou.
2. A standard measure of income inequality, the Gini Index went from 29.11 in 1981 to 48 in 2009 (source: World Bank WDI). According to the CIA World Factbook, China is today the 27th most unequal country in the world. For comparison, India is 79th.
3. The communiqué summarizing the results of the survey can be found on the NBS website at <http://www.stats.gov.cn/english/newsandcomingevents/t20080109_402457006.htm>.
4. See <http://english.gov.cn/2007-12/26/content_844593.htm>.
5. The ratio between the disposable income of urban and rural households in 1990 was 2.2; by 2005 it had climbed to 3.22 (National Bureau of Statistics of China 2008) and has remained stable since then. For a recent detailed analysis of the increasing income inequality, both across regions and categories, see Wu and Perloff (2005).
6. Modigliani and Cao (2004) argue that following the implementation of the one-child policy, Chinese households substituted investment in human capital with savings; while somehow exotic, this explanation also points to the essentially precautionary characteristics of today's saving rates.
7. In urban areas they were the street (subdistrict), district, and municipal-level hospitals, and in rural areas they consisted of village stations, township health centers, and county hospitals.
8. Life expectancy at birth in 1960 was about 40 years, a level similar to the average of LDCs and slightly lower than the level of low- and middle- (LM) income countries according to the World Bank classification. In 1980, it had risen to 68 years in China and to only 60 and 48 respectively in LM-income countries and LDCs respectively (World Bank, *World Development Indicators*).
9. *China Health Care Statistical Yearbook* 2007. We thank Win Lin Chou for providing the data.
10. *China Health Care Statistical Yearbook* 2007 and the website of the WHO for out-of-pocket expenditure.
11. On this kind of mechanism and other fundamental issues regarding stability, cf. Stiglitz et al. (2006).

12. See for example Chand and Moene (1997). For a different point of view, see Sosa (2004).
13. Many studies have shown that housing conditions play a very important role for the success of children at school, which explains that part of the uneven results of schooling is due to inequalities in present generations. For a survey, see Goux and Maurin (2005).
14. "One Nation, Uninsured," Paul Krugman, *New York Times*, June 13, 2005.

REFERENCES

Andrés, J., Doménech, R., and Fátas, A. (2008), "The Stabilizing Role of Government Size," *Journal of Economic Dynamics and Control*, 32/2: 571–93.

Bernanke, B. S. (2005), "The Global Saving Glut and the U.S. Current Account Deficit." Remarks at the Sandridge Lecture, Virginia Association of Economics, Richmond, VA.

Besley, T. (1995), "Savings, Credit and Insurance," in J. Behrman and T. N. Srinivasan (eds), *Handbook of Development Economics*, vol. 3a (North Holland, Amsterdam: Elsevier Science), 2123–207.

Blumenthal, D. and Hsiao, W. (2005), "Privatization and Its Discontents—the Evolving Chinese Health Care System," *New England Journal of Medicine*, 353/11: 1165–70.

Chamon, M. D., Liu, K., and Prasad, E. (2010), "Income Uncertainty and Household Savings in China," *IMF Working Papers*, 10/289 (December).

—— and Prasad, E. S. (2010), "Why Are Saving Rates of Urban Households in China Rising?" *American Economic Journal: Macroeconomics*, 2/1: 93–130.

Chand, S. K. and Moene, K. O. (1997), "Controlling Fiscal Corruption," IMF Working Paper, No. 97 (Washington, DC: International Monetary Fund).

Chou, W. L. (2007), "Explaining China's Regional Health Expenditures Using Lm-Type Unit Root Tests," *Journal of Health Economics*, 26/4: 682–98.

—— and Wang, Z. (2009), "Regional Inequality in China's Health Care Expenditures," *Health Economics*, 18/2: 137–46.

Creel, J. and Saraceno, F. (2009), "Automatic Stabilisation, Discretionary Policy and the Stability Pact," in J. Creel and M. C. Sawyer (eds), *Current Thinking on Fiscal Policy* (New York: Palgrave Macmillan), 112–44.

Dehejia, R. H. and Gatti, R. (2005), "Child Labor: The Role of Financial Development and Income Variability across Countries," *Economic Development and Cultural Change*, 53/4: 913–32.

Eggleston, K., Ling, L., Qingyue, M., Lindelow, M., and Wagstaff, A. (2006), "Health Service Delivery in China: A Literature Review," Policy Research Working Paper Series (Washington, DC: World Bank).

Fan, S., Kanbur, S. M. R., and Zhang, X. (2009), *Regional Inequality in China: Trends, Explanations and Policy Responses* (London and New York: Routledge).

Fátas, A. and Mihov, I. (2001), "Government Size and Automatic Stabilizers: International and Intranational Evidence," *Journal of International Economics*, 55/1: 3–28.

Fitoussi, J.-P. and Saraceno, F. (2012), "European Economic Governance: The Berlin-Washington Consensus," *Documents de Travail de l'OFCE*, 2012-20, July.

—— and Stiglitz, J. E. (2012), "On the Measurement of Social Progress and Well-being," in F. Allen et al. (eds), *The Global Macroeconomy and Finance: Iea Conference Volume*, n° 150-III (Basingstoke: Palgrave Macmillan).

Goux, D. and Maurin, E. (2005), "The Effect of Overcrowded Housing on Children's Performance at School," *Journal of Public Economics*, 89/5–6: 797–819.

Guan, X. (2000), "China's Social Policy: Reform and Development in the Context of Marketization and Globalization," *Social Policy and Administration*, 34/ 1: 115–30.

Guonan, M. and Wang, Y. (2010), "China's High Saving Rate: Myth and Reality," *Economie Internationale*, 122: 5–40.

Hahn, F. and Solow, R. M. (1995), *A Critical Essay on Modern Macroeconomic Theory* (Cambridge, MA: MIT Press).

He, X. and Cao, Y. (2007), "Understanding High Saving Rate in China," *China and World Economy*, 15/1: 1–13.

Hesketh, T. and Wei, X. Z. (1997), "Health in China: From Mao to Market Reform," *BMJ*, 14: 1543–5.

Huang, Y. (2011), "The Sick Man of Asia," *Foreign Affairs*, 90/6: 119–36.

Jalan, J. and Ravallion, M. (1999), "Are the Poor Less Well Insured? Evidence on Vulnerability to Income Risk in Rural China," *Journal of Development Economics*, 58/1: 61–81.

Kanbur, R. and Zhang, X. (2005), "Fifty Years of Regional Inequality in China: A Journey through Central Planning, Reform, and Openness," *Review of Development Economics*, 9/1: 87–106.

Kraay, A. (2000), "Household Saving in China," *World Bank Economic Review*, 14/3: 545–70.

Kuijs, L. (2005), "Investment and Saving in China," Policy Research Working Paper Series (Washington, DC: World Bank).

—— and Wang, T. (2006), "China's Pattern of Growth: Moving to Sustainability and Reducing Inequality," *China and World Economy*, 14/1: 1–14.

Kydland, F. E. and Prescott, E. C. (1982), "Time to Build and Aggregate Fluctuations," *Econometrica*, 50/6: 1345–70.

Lancet (2008), "A Special Series on Health System Reform in China," launched in Beijing, China, October 20. Available at <http://www.thelancet.com/series/health-system-reform-in-china>.

Lim, E., Spence, M., and Hausmann, R. (2006), "China and the Global Economy: Medium-Term Issues and Options—a Synthesis Report," CID Working Paper No. 126, Center for International Development at Harvard University.

Lim, L. (2006), "The High Price of Illness in China," BBC, Beijing, March 2.

Lindelow, M. and Wagstaff, A. (2005), "Can Insurance Increase Financial Risk? The Curious Case of Health Insurance in China," Policy Research Working Paper Series (Washington, DC: World Bank).

Liu, G. G., Dow, W. H., Fu, A. Z., Akin, J., and Lance, P. (2008), "Income Productivity in China: On the Role of Health," *Journal of Health Economics*, 27/1: 27–44.

Liu, Y., Hsiao, W. C., and Eggleston, K. (1999), "Equity in Health and Health Care: The Chinese Experience," *Social Science and Medicine*, 49/10: 1349–56.

—— and Rao, K. (2006), "Providing Health Insurance in Rural China: From Research to Policy," *Journal of Health Politics, Policy and Law*, 31/1: 71–92.

Lucas, R. E., Jr. (1976), "Econometric Policy Evaluation: A Critique," *Carnegie-Rochester Conference Series on Public Policy*, 1/1: 19–46.

Ma, S. and Sood, N. (2008), "A Comparison of the Health Systems in China and India." Occasional Paper, Rand Center for Asia Pacific Policy, Pittsburgh.

Mangyo, E. (2008), "Who Benefits More from Higher Household Consumption? The Intra-Household Allocation of Nutrients in China," *Journal of Development Economics*, 86/2: 296–312.

Markus, F. (2004), "China's Ailing Health Care," BBC, Shanghai, December.

Meng, Q., et al. (2012), "Trends in Access to Health Services and Financial Protection in China between 2003 and 2011: A Cross-Sectional Study," *The Lancet*, 379/9818: 805–14.

Modigliani, F. and Cao, S. L. (2004), "The Chinese Saving Puzzle and the Life-Cycle Hypothesis," *Journal of Economic Literature*, 42/1: 145–70.

National Bureau of Statistics of China (2008), *China Statistical Yearbook* (Beijing: China Statistics Press).

Pradhan, M. and Wagstaff, A. (2005), "Insurance Health Impacts on Health and Non-Medical Consumption in a Developing Country," Policy Research Working Paper Series (Washington, DC: World Bank).

Qiao, B., Martinez-Vazquez, J., and Xu, Y. (2008), "The Tradeoff between Growth and Equity in Decentralization Policy: China's Experience," *Journal of Development Economics*, 86/1: 112–28.

Ramey, G. and Ramey, V. A. (1995), "Cross-Country Evidence on the Link between Volatility and Growth," *American Economic Review*, 85/5: 1138–51.

Sen, A. K. (2001), *Development as Freedom* (New York: Oxford University Press).

Sosa, L. A. (2004), "Wages and Other Determinants of Corruption," *Review of Development Economics*, 8/4: 597–605.

Stiglitz, J. E. (2012), *The Price of Inequality: How Today's Divided Society Endangers Our Future* (New York: W. W. Norton).

—— Ocampo, J. A., Spiegel, S., French-Davis, R., and Nayyar, D. (2006), *Stability with Growth: Macroeconomics, Liberalization, and Development* (Oxford: Oxford University Press).

—— Sen, A., and Fitoussi, J.-P. (2010), *Mismeasuring Our Lives: Why GDP Doesn't Add Up* (New York: New Press).

Sun, Q., Santoro, M. A., Meng, Q., Liu, C., and Eggleston, K. (2008), "Pharmaceutical Policy in China," *Health Affairs*, 27/4: 1042–50.

Wagstaff, A., Lindelow, M., Jun, G., Ling, X., and Juncheng, Q. (2007), "Extending Health Insurance to the Rural Population: An Impact Evaluation of China's New Cooperative Medical Scheme," Policy Research Working Paper Series (Washington, DC: World Bank).

Wagstaff, A. and Yu, S. (2007), "Do Health Sector Reforms Have Their Intended Impacts? The World Bank's Health VIII Project in Gansu Province, China," *Journal of Health Economics*, 26/3: 505–35.

Wang, H. H. and Rosenman, R. (2007), "Perceived Need and Actual Demand for Health Insurance among Rural Chinese Residents," *China Economic Review*, 18/4: 373–88.

World Health Organization (2000), "The World Health Report 2000—Health Systems: Improving Performance" (Geneva: World Health Organization).

—— (2008), "The World Health Report 2008—Primary Health Care: Now More Than Ever" (Geneva: World Health Organization).

Wu, X. and Perloff, J. M. (2005), "China's Income Distribution, 1985–2001," *Review of Economics and Statistics*, 87/4: 763–75.

Yu, Y. (2006), "Market Economy and Social Justice: The Predicament of the Underprivileged," *Journal of Comparative Asian Development*, 5/1: 131–47.

Zhang, X. and Kanbur, R. (2005), "Spatial Inequality in Education and Health Care in China," *China Economic Review*, 16/2: 189–204.

15

The *Hukou* Reform and Unification of Rural–Urban Social Welfare

Cai Fang

INTRODUCTION

The professed function of the Chinese household registration (or *hukou*) system, formed in the late 1950s, is to register population separately in rural and urban areas. Distinguishing the rural or urban birthplace determines the legitimate residence of any Chinese citizen, which is identified by the *hukou*. The alteration of *hukou* between rural and urban areas is conditional, and the criteria for such an alteration are terribly strict, constraining the rights of free migration for rural residents. *Hukou* was implemented, typically and strictly, before and during the early period of Chinese reform. While it is commonly believed that in the past thirty years, overall economic reform has been accompanied by the reform of the *hukou* system to some extent, the actual development of the *hukou* system has not been recognized fully or properly valued by academia (for example, Chan and Buckingham 2008; Chan 2010). In a more extreme case (Whyte 2010), *hukou*-related rural–urban divide has been mentioned in the same breath as the India-type caste system. Such an underrating of the progress of reform in this area originates from a narrow understanding of the *hukou* system per se. That is, if the *hukou* system is merely viewed as a population registration system distinguishing rural and urban residents, no significant change can be perceived.

However, when scholars advocate *hukou* reform and governments, central and local, actually conduct various reform experiments, their efforts are not confined to only eliminating the regional separation of population. To understand the essential meaning of the *hukou* system, one must explore the primary motive for its initiation, as well as its resultant characteristics (for example, see Cai 2010a). *Hukou* was first introduced to serve as an invisible wall to prevent the rural labor force from moving out of agriculture; thus, it is closely linked to an exclusive employment system in urban sectors. Second, it was adopted to guarantee basic living and minimum social welfare for urban residents, and therefore, it ought to develop an institutional arrangement in order to separate *hukou* residents' entitlements from those of migrants. In taking into account the wider functions of the *hukou* system—instead of viewing it only as population registration—it should be clear that, as the Chinese economy transitions to a market economy, the *hukou* reform should not only progress simultaneously, but also should be carried out on a much wider scope.

As in the other areas of Chinese economic reform, *hukou* reform has been carried out in both bottom-up and top-down ways. On the one hand, seeking higher income and improved standards of living, rural laborers have migrated beyond the resident and employment boundaries set by *hukou* during the reform period. On the other hand, as the reallocation efficiency generated by labor mobility among sectors has become apparent,[1] Chinese governments at various levels first acquiesced to rural laborers' departures from farms and villages and have gradually altered policies over time to actually encourage farmers to leave their rural residences by actively improving the climate for workers who have moved to cities. Since *hukou* reform involves the alteration and abolition of a series of long-standing institutions, the governments' incentives and initiatives are particularly important in the process. Documenting and explaining such reforms requires exploring motives, behaviors, and the interactions of all participants—namely, rural laborers, urban residents, and central and local governments—under an analytical framework of political economy.

The Chinese economy has been undertaking double transitions: a transition from a dual economy to a more integrated economy and a transition from a planning economy to a market economy. The two transitions have imbued *hukou* reform with important characteristics and divided it into three phases. In its first phase, roughly between the early 1980s and mid-1990s, the reform was marginally carried out under the constraints of a planning economy. Spurred by the clearer market orientation of the overall reform laid out by the Chinese leadership, reform accelerated in the period between the mid-1990s and the early twenty-first century, say 2003. As the Chinese dual economy entered a new stage after 2003, a year of significance for the Chinese economy, the reform entered its more pivotal period. While in each of the phases, the reform of the *hukou* system has made some crucial progresses, the latest round of reform has been much more comprehensive, aimed at completely eliminating the *hukou* system and affiliated institutions.

This chapter explains the efforts that have been made for reforming the *hukou* system—as government policies respond to changing conditions—by dividing reforms into three phases. Unlike existing literature that focuses more on the unfinished aspects of reform, this paper positively evaluates progress to date and suggests further tasks by revealing the logic of reform, which is closely related to the changing economic stages. This chapter views *hukou* not only as a population residence regulation, but also as a method for examining changes in the intention and implementation of social welfare programs.

The next part of this chapter depicts *hukou* reform in the context of the transition from a planned economy to a market economy, which happened in the course of a typical dual economy development. The following section discusses the arrival of the Lewisian turning point, a new stage of Chinese economic development, and its implications for migrant workers' demands for new institutional settings and the enhanced motives of governments for *hukou* reform. The final section concludes by identifying some dilemmas and proposing policy suggestions for future reform.

HUKOU REFORM AS INSTITUTIONAL TRANSITION

As is commonly known, Chinese economic reform was initiated in rural areas and was characterized by the introduction of the household responsibility system, which, by solving the long-standing incentives problems, undisputedly enhanced the labor productivity of the agriculture sector, freeing up a new surplus of laborers who had accumulated during the pre-reform period. As a consequence, Chinese farmers, after fulfilling the basic living of their farms, began to seek off-farm work to increase their incomes. Although economic reform at the time did not aim to relinquish the planning system, *hukou* reform actually took place without a clear blueprint of the overall reform: it was represented by labor mobility, from agricultural to nonagricultural sectors in rural areas, as well as from villages to nearby towns.

It is widely believed that the labor transfer had been characterized by local relocation to township and village enterprises (TVEs) before the urbanization policy was later relaxed to allow rural-to-urban migration. It is true that, before the mid-1980s, the central government intended to create a pattern of "leaving the land without leaving the countryside." The development of TVEs, however, was confined to local villages and small towns and was extremely uneven among regions—and therefore incapable of creating adequate nonagricultural employment opportunities for the surplus laborers. In 1985, only 18.8 percent of 370 million rural laborers were engaged in TVEs. According to a scholarly estimation, at the time there were 100–50 million surplus laborers in rural areas, or 30–40 percent of the total rural workforce (Taylor 1993: chapter 8). To tackle such a development challenge, farmers sought to break down institutional obstacles and migrated across regional boundaries, while the governments, both central and local, responded to the desires and actions of rural laborers by relaxing institutional constraints for labor mobility.

As reforms in urban areas were initiated in the mid-1980s, and the development of the TVEs stagnated, rural laborers began to migrate across regions, particularly from rural to urban areas in search of nonagricultural jobs. The gradual abolition of institutional obstacles has been key for increased labor mobility since the 1980s. After observing the rural sectors' narrowing capacity for absorbing surplus labor, in 1983 the government began allowing farmers to engage in long-distance transport and marketing of their products beyond local marketplaces—the first time that Chinese farmers had received legitimate rights for doing business outside their hometowns. In 1984, regulations were further relaxed and farmers were encouraged by the state to work in nearby small towns. A major policy reform took place in 1988, when the central government allowed farmers to work in enterprises or run their own businesses in cities, under the condition that they continued to be self-sufficient in terms of staples, in the light of the still-existing rationing scheme. In the 1990s, the central and local governments relaxed policies restricting migration, which also implied a certain degree of reform in the household registration system as well.

In that period, however, the planning system had not yet been abandoned and the *hukou* system was taken for granted in the institutional setting. That is, any policy adjustment or any action conducted spontaneously by laborers and acquiesced to by the governments was still circumscribed by the strict *hukou* control. In other words, all adjustments and actions outside of the institutional frame were allowed and tolerated only when they fit with certain situations, such as the need for a labor force; when they did not, they were repressed. *Hukou* reform was only marginal and reversible at the time when planning was still in effect.

The official establishment of a market economy as the goal of Chinese reform in the 1990s made the decade a turning point in terms of *hukou* reform. Symbolized by Deng Xiaoping's famous tour of South China, with his speeches during the time, as well as the Fourteenth National Congress of the Communist Party of China in the early 1990s, China's reform and opening-up entered a new era. Because of the accelerated *hukou* reform, labor market development, and population migration, we consider the mid-1990s to be the milestone that distinguishes the first and second phases of *hukou* reform.

In this period, the fast growth of labor-intensive and export-oriented sectors, mostly in the coastal provinces, and the dramatic surge of nonpublic sectors in urban areas, generated a huge incremental demand for labor, spurring a migratory tide of labor that moved from rural to urban sectors and from the central and western to the eastern regions. Conforming to such trends of labor market expansion and integration, a host of reform measures were carried out to eliminate the institutional barriers that deterred labor mobility. For example, the rationing system that was initiated in the mid-1950s to limit supplies of staple foods and other life necessities in cities was abolished in the early-1990s, unlocking one of the most important shackles stopping population migration from rural to urban areas.

Another manifestation of labor market development can be seen in the reform of urban employment policies. Since the mid-1990s, the government granted state-owned enterprises (SOEs) the autonomous powers of hiring and firing employees, which SOE managers took advantage of to break the long-standing "iron rice bowl" (jobs with guaranteed security). During the macroeconomic downturn and East Asian financial crisis, which gave rise to massive layoffs and unemployment in the urban sectors in the late-1990s, the government implemented a layoff subsidy program and built up an unemployment insurance system, a basic pension regime, and a minimum living standard program. While those measures were initiated to protect urban workers, they created an environment for labor market development and liberalized labor market regulations to encourage labor mobility across enterprises, sectors, ownerships, and regions.

In response to the matured economic conditions for labor mobility, in 1998, the Ministry of Public Security gave a green light for the entry of people into cities, such that children could carry out household registration with either parent, couples who had long been separated could get together and obtain a change of household registration, the elderly could obtain city *hukou* along with their children, and so on. Although resistance to these reforms was encountered in some major cities, the future reform of the household registration system was provided with a legitimate basis at the central government level.

China had been typified by its dual economy development before this phase ended: the rural surplus labor force endlessly migrated to urban sectors in coastal areas, seeking nonagricultural wage employment; the wage rates of migrant workers remained unchanged and low compared to their urban counterparts, partially because of the nature of the unlimited supply of labor and partially because of the *hukou* system. Despite the expanded labor mobility and a certain progress in reform, the *hukou* system still played two roles, serving its traditional function.

First, the *hukou* system guaranteed the priority of urban laborers for employment opportunities in urban sectors. Due to the coexistence of rural labor surplus and urban workforce redundancy, there existed to a certain extent job competition between migrant workers and urban unskilled workers, causing the urban governments to protect local workers and treat migrant workers discriminately via *hukou* identification. In an empirical study, Cai, Du, and Wang (2001) found that in the period, urban governments' policies toward inflows of migrants changed cyclically as employment pressures facing local governments changed over time—that is, each time the local unemployment problems became severe, in addition to regular restrictions on migrants' employment,[2] they tended to take measures to supplant migrant workers.

Second, the *hukou* system excluded migrants from obtaining equal access to urban social welfare services. In the course of tackling the employment shock in the late 1990s, the governments built a preliminary social protection system for urban workers, including programs of basic pension insurance, basic health care insurance, unemployment insurance, and a minimum living-standard guarantee scheme. Whereas those programs did not provide full coverage for all urban workers, they *officially* included all workers with urban *hukou* and excluded rural-to-urban migrants. In addition, migrant workers were not entitled to public employment assistance programs and thus exposed to all kinds of employment shocks without formal social protection.

In a dual economy characterized by an unlimited supply of labor, the interests of urban residents typically conflict with those of rural residents, and the urbanites have stronger bargaining power to influence policymaking and thus gain more advantageous status (Olson 1985). That was empirically confirmed in the case of *hukou* reform in that period (Cai 2010d)—that is, when some efforts were made by both central and local governments, they turned out to be futile in the final analysis. Initiated in 2000, *hukou* control of all Chinese small towns was relaxed by significantly lowering the thresholds for residence, while some medium and large-sized cities, including provincial capital cities, such as Shijiazhuang of Hebei province, tried to do the same. Owing to the lack of employment opportunities and capabilities of providing equal social welfare, such as basic pension, health care insurance, access to education, and entrance to higher school for the newcomers, the reform failed to attract many to apply for local *hukou* status. In other cases, where cities abolished the distinction between agricultural and nonagricultural *hukou* identity, due to the remaining unequal social welfare among people living in rural and urban areas, the reform amounted to no more than lip service (Wang and Cai 2010).

LEWISIAN TURNING POINT AND REFORM INCENTIVES

While the mass labor migration from rural to urban sectors has naturally reduced the degree of labor surplus in agriculture (Cai and Wang 2008), and the

Table 15.1. Annual growth rates of selected wages, 2003–8 (%)

	Daily wages		Monthly wages
Grain production	15.1	Manufacturing	10.5
Cotton production	11.7	Construction	9.8
Large pig farm	21.4	Migrant workers	10.2

Source: Wage of hired workers of grains is calculated according to data from Prices Division, National Development and Reform Commission, *Compilation of National Farm Product Cost-Benefit Data* (various years), China Statistics Press. Wage of manufacturing and construction is calculated according to data from Department of Population and Employment Statistics, National Bureau of Statistics and Department of Planning and Finance, Ministry of Human Resources and Social Security, *China Labor Statistical Yearbook* (various years), China Statistics Press. Wage of migrant workers is calculated according to data from Department of Rural Social and Economic Survey, National Bureau of Statistics, *China's Rural Household Survey Yearbook* (various years), China Statistics Press.

demographic transition in China has reached the stage at which the growth rate of the working-age population is declining (Cai 2010b), the fast economic growth has continued to generate huge labor demand, leading to demand for labor exceeding supply. Since 2003, the difficulty hiring migrant workers, or the labor shortage more generally, has become widespread and wages of migrant workers have significantly increased year by year. In addition, the wage rates of hired workers in agricultural sectors have also improved (Table 15.1), indicating the shrinkage of surplus labor in agriculture, the shortage of unskilled workers in urban areas, and ensuing wage increases in all sectors (Wang 2010).

According to the definition set forth by Lewis (1954), those phenomena indicate that the Chinese economy has arrived at its Lewisian turning point—a period of time in which the wages of ordinary workers increase because labor demand exceeds that of labor supply (Cai and Wang 2010). At the same time, the *hukou* reform starts its new phase and is expected to make a more fundamental breakthrough. Because 2003 witnessed so many dramatic changes in Chinese economy and society—e.g., the first labor shortage in China's economic development, the subsequent increase in ordinary workers' wages, the rise of labor cost and fall of labor input in agriculture, and governments' efforts to improve conditions of migrants living and working in cities in response to those changes (Wang 2010)—we take it as a symbolic year indicating the Lewisian turning point and the outset of a new phase of *hukou* reform.

The essential manifestation of a Lewisian turning point is the alteration of the labor market from an unlimited supply of labor to the frequent emergence of labor shortages. That is, the invariable wage rate can no longer maintain the endless supply of labor, on the one hand, and the wage rate increase alone cannot adequately satisfy the workers, who also expect policy reforms in accordance with the changes of development stages. In terms of challenges facing China, this phase of reform can be characterized as follows. First, as the market orientation becomes a clear blueprint of China's overall reform, the *hukou* reform's goal is set to unify the rural and urban labor markets. Second, as the unlimited supply of labor is no longer the property of the Chinese economy, and the structural factors rather than magnitude factors dominate the labor market, the direct conflict in employment between migrant and local workers has been eased. Third, as the social welfare provisions, mainly the social security programs, become pooled based on public finance and individual contribution, there is more compatibility than competition between newcomers and native residents in urban areas. The changes in the reform climate indicate that the governments' intentions and behaviors regarding *hukou* reform are now essentially different from those in the previous phase of reform.

Chinese governments have been conceptualized as a developmental state, in general (Oi 1999; Walder 1995), and local governments as competitive governments, in particular (Herrmann-Pillath and Feng 2004). That is, governments have strong motivation to spur economic growth by various policy measures, including legislation, public policymaking, improving the climate of investment and development, helping local businesses to seek financial resources from domestic and foreign investors and subsidies from higher levels of government, intervention in enterprise management, and sometimes running businesses themselves. As they recognize that the Lewisian turning point is reached and labor becomes a constraint of economic growth, the governments begin to reorient public policy from focusing on employment opportunities to focusing on job decency, and from protecting locals to including migrants, which leads to institutional changes.

More generally, the developmental state with Chinese characteristics has been undergoing a transformation following its own logic of development stages. That is, the Chinese local governments indeed become more and more motivated by Tiebout-type incentives (Tiebout 1956) to try to attract human resources by enriching the contents and adjusting the direction of public services. In those areas, where the booming economy continues to raise demand for labor force, a soundless reform has been undertaken in the building of labor market institutions and social protection mechanisms—incentives compatible with the central government's objective of building a harmonious society (Cai 2010c).

Such a new policy climate has catalyzed the building of labor market institutions in which migrant workers are formally included now. Symbolized by the satisfactory resolution of the legislative problem predicating the Sun Zhigang incident in 2003[3] and President Hu Jintao's intervention in the wages arrears for migrant workers in 2004, labor-related institutions have since evolved in two directions—regulations aiming to protect all workers and deregulations aiming to liberalize labor mobility (Cai 2010a). In tackling the problems of migrant workers' insecure employment, poor conditions of working, low coverage of social insurance, and lack of protection, governments have made various efforts related to *hukou* system reform.

First, the Employment Contract Law came into effect in 2008. This legislation, which attracted worldwide notice, requires enterprises to sign labor contracts with all employees, regardless of their *hukou* status, and to include them in basic social insurance programs. The Labor Disputes Mediation and Arbitration Law issued the same year encourages migrant workers to initiate labor disputes by cutting litigation costs to almost zero.

Second, local governments have increased the frequency and scale of minimum wage adjustments. During the early years of the implementation of this program in the 1990s, the minimum wage standard was low, rarely increased, and hardly applied to migrant workers. As the labor shortage became widespread after 2003, the central government required local governments to adjust the level of minimum wages every other year and to apply the program to migrant workers.

Pressured by labor shortage, municipal authorities have since increased the adjustment frequency and local level of the minimum wages.

Third, one of the efforts made by the central government to enhance migrant workers' coverage in basic social insurance programs is the promulgation of Interim Measures on the Transfer of Continuation of Basic Pension for Urban Enterprises Employees in 2010, which stipulates that all workers participating in basic pension programs while migrating across provincial boundaries will be guaranteed a transfer and continuation of both individual and pooling pension accounts in their new places of work. This new regulation provides institutionally guaranteed portability for migrant workers' pension entitlements.

NEW WAVE OF *HUKOU* REFORM

In a paper about *hukou* reform, Cai (2010c) identifies a dilemma—that is, the more social welfare benefits a *hukou* identity contains, the more difficult it is to push forward the reform; but without *hukou* reform, there is no way to detach social welfare benefits from *hukou* status, which has often brought the reform into stalemate. The reorientation of government functions toward public service provision, spurred by the arrival of the Lewisian turning point, along with labor market institution-building, can help break such a dilemma and boost the new round of *hukou* reform. The fundamental change in the policy climate has made the new round of reform more thorough and plausible. Here, we elaborate the practice and progress of the reforms of the *hukou* system and related institutions since 2003.

The number of migrant workers leaving their home townships for six months and longer increased from 114 million in 2003 to 145 million in 2009, of which 95.6 percent migrated to cities and towns. As Chinese urban residents were statistically defined as those who live in cities for six months and longer when the Fifth National Census was conducted in 2000, the migrant workers and accompanying family members comprised a large part of incremental urban residents during the period. In 2009, the urbanization rate—the share of population living in cities for six months or longer—was 46.6 percent. Those migrants, however, after moving to cities, do not obtain urban *hukou* status and therefore do not have equal access to social welfare as their counterparts with urban *hukou* do. The distinction in social treatment is based on and identified by agricultural *hukou* and nonagricultural *hukou*. In 2007, the share of population with nonagricultural *hukou*, which all native urbanites hold, was 33 percent, twelve percentage points less than the statistical urbanization rate of the year (Figure 15.1).

Taking account of the difference between the statistical urbanization rate and the nonagricultural rate of population, many scholars and policy researchers assert that the *hukou* reform has not made noticeable progress and the urbanization level has been overestimated (for example, see Chan 2010; Chang 2010). Those arguments are partially correct, because whereas long-term migrant workers are counted as urban residents, they are still excluded from equitable entitlement to many public services provided by urban governments. For example, their participation rates in social insurance programs are significantly

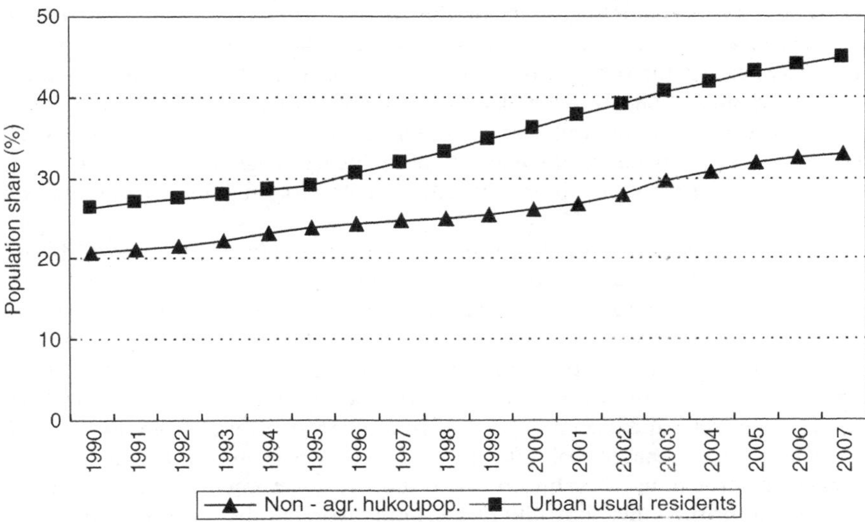

Figure 15.1. Usual urban population vs nonagricultural *hukou* population

Source: National Bureau of Statistics (various years), *China Population and Employment Statistical Yearbook*, China Statistics Press.

Table 15.2. Comparison of social insurance programs between migrant and local workers (2009, %)

	Basic pension	Basic health care	Unemployment insurance	Work injury insurance	Maternity insurance
Urban workers	57.0	52.7	40.9	47.9	34.9
Migrant workers	9.8	13.1	3.7	24.1	2.0

Source: NBS (2009); Sheng (2009)

lower than those of local workers (Table 15.2); their children have difficulty enrolling in compulsory schooling, let alone entering a higher school; and they are not entitled to minimum living-standard guarantee. As we noted previously, however, migrant workers and their accompanying family members now have much better access to public services than they did previously. Moreover, the *hukou* reform of formally accepting migrants as nonagricultural residents in urban areas has been accelerated.

The share of population with nonagricultural *hukou* has increased since 2003, with faster growth than during the previous period. For example, annual growth rates of the nonagricultural population increased from 3.4 percent in 1991–2002 to 4.3 percent in 2002–7. Given that the natural growth rate of population in both rural and urban China has declined to very low levels—that is, the natural growth of population of the country as a whole decreased from 1.3 percent in 1991 to 0.5 percent in 2007—the increase in the share of nonagricultural population is mainly attributed to mechanical growth, or the rural-to-urban migration with *hukou* change. Whereas the expansion of university enrolment may contribute to the increase, because the rural enrolled students can change their agricultural *hukou* to nonagricultural *hukou* by regulation, the share of rural origin in total enrolled students declined dramatically in recent years, meaning that the two factors cancel out each other.[4] Therefore, the majority of the new nonagricultural *hukou* population are those who have been officially accepted for migration to destination cities.

As the Chinese economy has recovered from the 2008–9 financial crisis and then encountered an unprecedented labor shortage, many provinces and cities have initiated a new round of *hukou* reform that is different from the previous ones in at least two ways. First, the motive of the new round of reform is endogenous and strong. In terms of the governments' incentives to reform *hukou*, two facts are worth attention: (i) The shortage of migrant workers, beginning in 2003 and becoming more severe after the recovery from the financial crisis in 2010, has caused real difficulty for enterprises in maximizing production capacities throughout the country. In response, governments in coastal areas, where enterprises suffer difficulty in recruiting workers the most, *hukou* reform has become a policy measure to stabilize labor supply. (ii) Under the strictest control over arable land use, the only means of land exploitation for the local governments who intend to boost urbanization is to reclaim plots of contracted arable land and house sites that migrated households left behind and to use the quota of those plots elsewhere in order to balance the exploitation and reclamation of land. Second, the measures of the new round of reform are more feasible. Since the century began, many areas have announced and piloted *hukou* reform. Despite its effects differing from place to place, the reforms have all been initiated locally to conform to the actual needs of the individual localities. Since the objective of the reform is the institutional format of the dual societal structure, the *hukou* system, the reforms share some common features across the areas in which they have been implemented. That is, reform has been bound to equalize public service provisions and pushed by lowering the threshold-of-entry criteria for in-migrants. Neither high thresholds for migrants obtaining a local *hukou* nor segregated treatments of social welfare between newcomers and natives can make the reform successful. As local governments become more aware of the importance of *hukou* reform as an indispensable engine in pushing urbanization, they tend to substantially ease the criteria for accepting new residents.

While Guangdong, the coastal province of southern China, initiated *hukou* reform in response to a labor shortage in its exports-oriented sectors, the pilot reform in Chongqing, a more agrarian municipality in southwestern China, is a typical example of a city trying to obtain necessary land for urban expansion. A less developed region, Chongqing is bottlenecked more by land than by labor in its efforts to catch up with its more developed counterparts. Since any reform needs to be boosted by incentives and the reform of *hukou* policy that counts on the initiation of government needs to be motivated by governments' will to do it, in particular, linking the *hukou* reform with land development is not only the feature but also the motive for the municipality's reform.

The *hukou* reform initiation in Chongqing is designed to properly relocate the plots of land vacated by urbanized rural families. According to the policies issued by the government, the land relocation includes three steps. First, local governments compensate for the plots of contracted arable land and house sites based on land expropriation regulations and referring to the current price of land voucher.[5] Then the returned house sites are required to reclaim their original localities, their land use quota is traded within the municipality, and the quota may be used as construction land in other localities of the municipality. Next, the claiming right of the land is held for the transferred households for three years in case they return for reasons of employment shock and the like. The unified utilization of the quota of land vacated by official migration from rural to urban areas is the motivation of Chongqing municipal government implementing the *hukou* reform.

The new round of *hukou* reform represented by the experiences in Chongqing and Guangdong in 2010 simultaneously meets the two criteria for reform—low threshold of entry and equal treatment of social welfare. In Chongqing, those migrant workers who have worked and done business for a certain period of time, buy houses, invest, or pay taxes of a certain amount within the destination cities, are eligible to obtain local *hukou* and to get equal access to assistance to employment, social insurance, subsidized housing, education, medical care, etc. In Guangdong, the government converts various criteria into points, such as schooling, working skills, contributions to social insurance, volunteering, and blood donation, which are accumulated to obtain urban *hukou*. In these ways, becoming an urban citizen is no longer a random probability but the outcome of a specific procedure.

CONCLUSIONS, REFLECTIONS, AND POLICY SUGGESTIONS

In the course of China's transition from planned economy to market economy, *hukou* system reform has driven labor mobility from rural to urban sectors and helped the economy reallocate resources and gain efficiency, as well as contributing to the unprecedented growth of the economy. Under the constraints of unlimited supply of labor and scarcity of resources for public services, however, discrepancies in employment opportunities and welfare provisions among urban migrant and local workers have prevented the reform from accomplishing, urbanization from completing, and the floating urbanites from becoming a stable source of labor and consumption. As the Lewisian turning point arrives—that is, economic growth can no longer count on cheap labor and high savings rates brought by a demographic dividend—the central and local governments, seeking a new engine for economic growth, set sights on the potential of deepening urbanization by settling migrant workers. That creates incentives for governments implementing *hukou* reform and the incentives are compatible between central and local governments and between migrant workers and urban native residents. As a result, *hukou* reform pushes forward in both breadth and width.

In the final analysis, different regions' governments have their own motives for carrying out *hukou* reform. They do it to attract and keep human resources in coastal areas, to tap domestic demand in central and western regions, and to break through the land bottleneck in catching-up regions. The different motives have led to dissimilar institutional designs and ways of implementing. The diversity is not only the natural approach to such decentralized reform, it is also what the reform's advantage is based upon. Allowing diversity assures incentives, impetus, and chances of success.

Like the previous rounds of reform, the current ongoing reform has its limitations, which involve the consensus between central and local governments. That is, to initiate *hukou* reform, the local governments not only need incentives, but also legitimacy, in order to have central government's support and approval. As can be seen in the experiences of Chongqing and Guangdong, some shortcomings need to be overcome in this regard. First, the point of intersection between the central government's top concern and the local governments' legitimacy in accelerating urbanization is to retain the designated amount of arable land. Due to the extreme scarcity of arable land in China, neither industrialization nor urbanization can proceed at the expense of shifting land from agricultural to nonagricultural use. The land voucher program coined by the Chongqing government must assure that all plots of land vacated are reclaimed for cultivation in order to be approbated by the central government. The central leaders often doubt the actual reclamation of land declared by local governments, because there have been too many cases of reneging in the process of new village construction. Second, both the central government and the governments of the migrant-receiving cities are concerned about building labor market institutions and social protection mechanisms that prevent urban diseases. As the result of the advent of the Lewisian turning point, migrant workers have become an indispensable source of labor for urban sectors—in other words, nonagricultural sectors' demand for migrant workers has become unvarying, or rigid, on the one hand, and agriculture has rapidly mechanized so that it no longer provides a pool of surplus labor on the other. While migrant workers as a whole cannot revert to agricultural production, individual migrant workers risk becoming urban poor. So *hukou* reform must be a comprehensive package that tackles the risks, from inclusive social protection policy in urban areas to flexible relocation policy of arable land. Third, the coordination among policy measures undertaken by local governments and a holistic vision of the entire country impacts the overall effect of the reform. In the reforms of Chongqing and Guangdong, policies set for migrant workers to officially reside in cities only benefit the residents of the specific province or municipality. In 2009, of the 145 million migrant workers (and their 22 million accompanying family members), 51 percent migrated across provincial boundaries. That the interprovincial migrants can hardly benefit from the *hukou* reform underway in many provinces implies that half of migrants, whose ancestral homes are mostly in the poor central and western areas, are still excluded from the urbanization process.

The *hukou* reform has so far been the initiative of local governments motivated to break through the constraints of local development. As a public policy reform, *hukou* reform requires nationwide harmonization. That is, in addition to encouraging various local reform initiatives, the central government, by generalizing the domestic and international experiences and lessons, should also put forward a general guideline regarding the contents and coverage of social security programs, ways of managing vacated plots of land, and the nexus between the practical policies and overall objectives of the reform.

NOTES

1. Cai and Wang (1999) estimate that, in addition to the conventional contributions made by physical capital, labor, and education, labor mobility from low-productivity agriculture to higher productivity nonagricultural sectors contributed 21 percent to China's GDP growth in the period 1978 to 1998. The World Bank (1997) estimated the contribution of labor mobility to GDP growth was 16 percent.
2. In the 1990s, some large cities issued policies forbidding urban enterprises from hiring migrant workers for certain jobs that would compete with local workers (Cai, Du, and Wang 2001).
3. A 27-year-old university graduate, Sun Zhigang, was detained by the police and beaten to death because of his lack of a local *hukou* or local temporary resident permit. This attracted widespread public criticism of the *hukou* system and led to the abolition of the State Council regulation, "Approaches to the Custody and Repatriation of Urban Vagrants and Beggars," upon which the criminal acts of the law enforcement officers were based (see Cai 2010a).
4. Among the currently enrolled university students, the share of rural origin is 17.7 percent, a big decrease compared to that of more than 30 percent in the 1980s (Li 2009).
5. The land voucher program, an innovative institution in Chongqing, is intended to unify land usage and development on a citywide basis. Namely, the administration issues vouchers for the increase of land area generated by reclaiming the house plots and collective construction land vacated by out-migration from villages and trading them in the government-run land exchange. Those who buy the vouchers get the quota of land use for nonagricultural development within the municipality.

REFERENCES

Cai, F. (2010a), "The Formation and Evolution of China's Migrant Labor Policy," in X. Zhang, S. Fan, and A. de Haan, (eds), *Narratives of Chinese Economic Reforms: How Does China Cross the River*? (New Jersey: World Scientific Publishing Co.), 71–90.

——(2010b), "Demographic Transition, Demographic Dividend, and Lewis Turning Point in China," *Economic Research Journal*, 45/4: 4–13.

——(2010c), "Lewis Turning Point and Reorientation of Public Policy: Some Stylized Facts on Social Protection in China," *Social Sciences in China*, 6: 125–37.

——(2010d), "Labor Market Development and Expansion of Rural and Urban Employment," in F. Cai (ed.), *Transforming the Chinese Economy, 1978–2008* (Boston: Brill).

——Du, Y., and Wang, M. (2001), "Household Registration System and Labor Market Protection," *Economic Research Journal* [*Jingji Yanjiu*], 12: 41–9.

——and Wang, D. (1999), "The Sustainability of Economic Growth and the Labor Contribution," *Economic Research Journal* [*Jingji Yanjiu*], 10: 62–8.

——and Wang, M. (2008), "A Counterfactual Analysis on Unlimited Surplus Labor in Rural China," *China and World Economy*, 16/1: 51–65.

————(2010), "Growth and Structural Changes in Employment in Transition China," *Journal of Comparative Economics*, 38: 71–81.

Chan, K. W. (2010), "The Household Registration System and Migrant Labor in China: Notes on a Debate," *Population and Development Review*, 36/2: 357–64.

——and Buckingham, W. (2008), "Is China Abolishing the Hukou System?" *China Quarterly*, 195: 582–606.

Chang, H. (2010), "Agriculture, Countryside, and Farmers: Challenges Facing the Next Five-Year Plan," *Century Weekly*, 34: 40–1.

Herrmann-Pillath, C. and Feng, X. (2004), "Competitive Governments, Fiscal Arrangements, and the Provision of Local Public Infrastructure in China: A Theory-Driven Study of Gujiao Municipality," *China Information*, 18/3: 373–428.

Jin, H., Qian, Y., and Weingast, B. R. (2005), "Regional Decentralization and Fiscal Incentives: Federalism, Chinese Style", *Journal of Public Economics*, 89: 1719–42.

Lewis, A. (1954), "Economic Development with Unlimited Supplies of Labour," *Manchester School of Economic and Social Studies*, 22: 139–91.

Li, L. (2009), "Why Has the Share of University Students of Rural Origins Been Halved?" *Guangzhou Daily*, January 24.

National Bureau of Statistics (2009), *China Statistical Yearbook, 2009* (Beijing: China Statistical Publishing House).

Oi, J. C. (1999), "Local State Corporatism," in J. Oi (ed.), *Rural China Takes Off: Institutional Foundations of Economic Reform* (Berkeley: University of California Press), 95–137.

Olson, M. (1985), "The Exploitation and Subsidization of Agriculture in the Developing and Developed Countries." Paper presented to the 19th Conference of International Association of Agricultural Economists, Malaga, Spain.

Sheng, L. (2009), New Challenges Migrants Are Faced with on Employment During the Financial Crisis." Paper presented at the conference Urban–Rural Social Welfare Integration, Chengdu, Sichuan Province, April 16.

Taylor, J. R. (1993), "Rural Employment Trends and the Legacy of Surplus Labor, 1978–1989," in Y. Y. Kueh and R. F. Ash (eds), *Economic Trends in Chinese Agriculture: The Impact of Post-Mao Reforms* (New York: Oxford University Press), 273–310.

Tiebout, C. (1956), "A Pure Theory of Local Expenditures," *Journal of Political Economy*, 64/5: 416–24.

Walder, A. (1995), "Local Governments As Industrial Firms," *American Journal of Sociology*, 101/2: 47–70.

Wang, M. (2010), "The Rise of Labor Cost and the Fall of Labor Input: Has China Reached Lewis Turning Point?" *China Economic Journal*, 3/2: 139–55.

——and Cai, F. (2010), "Future Prospects of Household Registration System Reform," in F. Cai (ed.), *The China Population and Labor Yearbook Volume 2: The Sustainability of Economic Growth from the Perspective of Human Resources* (Boston: Brill), 173–86.

Whyte, M. K. (2010), "The Paradoxes of Rural–Urban Inequality in Contemporary China," in M. K. White (ed.), *One Country, Two Societies: Rural–Urban Inequality in Contemporary China* (Cambridge, MA: Harvard University Press), 1–28.

World Bank (1997), *China 2020: Development Challenges in the New Century* (Washington, DC: World Bank).

Part III

Institutional Foundations for the Chinese Market Economy: The State

Over time, the structure of government may be as significant for economic development as any specific regulations, policies, or entitlement allocations. It has been common outside China to treat the structure of the Chinese state as the fundamental factor enabling or limiting Chinese economic performance. For those most influenced by neoliberal orthodoxy about preferred economic policies and legal arrangements, this has meant a small, decentralized state, subject to internal checks and balances and democratic control. For advocates of a small state and limited government, the potential for "government failure" poses the largest threat to strong economic performance. In this view, China's growth spurt resulted from decentralization and a loosening of central control and planning. Looking ahead, China's continued economic development is said to demand the emergence of the kinds of internal checks and balances within the state that are familiar in many Western industrial democracies—in particular, an ever more robust and independent judiciary.

In our view, these accounts underestimate the dangers of private rent-seeking, monopoly power, and market failures, while overstating the significance of both decentralization and separation of powers for economic performance in the Chinese context. An effective state is more important than a small state. Effectiveness requires a balance of centralization and decentralization. It is compatible with many different institutional arrangements and many different roles for judicial authorities. The most dramatic lesson from recent Chinese economic performance has been the range of flexibility, diversity, and learning-by-doing that has characterized Chinese public policy. The state has been, on the whole, effective. That said, this success has dramatically transformed the Chinese social and economic structure in ways that will pose ever greater challenges to effective government. In particular, the emergence of new and often concentrated countervailing economic powers will make it more difficult for the state to maintain an effective balance between centralized and decentralized authority, and between responsiveness to those new economic powers and policy independence.

The third part of this book takes up these two central constitutional issues: how to harness the benefits of relatively more and less centralized public authority, and how to understand the role of judges in the Chinese economy. In Part II, we explained the role of government in setting the rules of the game (such as defining property rights) and why regulations are necessary, both to correct market failures and to promote social justice (to maintain at least a minimal sense of equity). Governments are not always as successful as one would like in achieving goals of either economic efficiency or social justice. The extent to which governments succeed or fail in achieving social objectives depends to a large extent on the system of governance, rules that relate to how decision-makers are chosen, how decisions are made, to whom decision-makers are accountable, the consequences of successes and failures, transparency, etc. The literature on these subjects is vast, and we touch on only two aspects that are of direct relevance to our economic analyses—the first concerning *decentralization* and the second concerning the judicial system for resolving disputes.

DECENTRALIZATION

A hallmark of China's economic reform was a move away from central planning to a market-based system. There is no question that this was accompanied by a movement toward decentralization. It is now widely recognized that no one could possibly have all the information required to make all the allocative (economic) decisions within a society. The crucial point, however, is that decentralization did not necessarily mean an unambiguously less powerful state. On the contrary, the movement toward markets also strengthened *public* decision-making authority at the provincial and local levels. Both *direct* economic decision-making and the public actions that set the frameworks within which enterprises make decisions were decentralized. Indeed, some have argued that "fiscal federalism with Chinese characteristics" was largely responsible for China's success in moving to a market economy with Chinese characteristics. The two papers in this section—one by Justin Lin, Mingxing Liu, and Ran Tao and the other by James Kai-sing Kung, Chenggang Xu, and Feizhou Zhou—provide different interpretations of the role of decentralization. The first argues forcefully against assigning too much credit to "fiscal federalism with Chinese characteristics," pointing out that growth has remained as strong (or even stronger) in the period *after* 1994, when recentralization set in; the second provides a highly nuanced interpretation of central–provincial–local relations, explaining how changes in the institutional structure led to changes in the *form* of development. Both agree that the incentives given to local authorities and the constraints that they faced are key to understanding both the successes China has achieved and the challenges it faces going forward.

We want to put the two papers in context by describing the centralization/decentralization debate more generally, for it plays out, in different forms, in almost every society and at every level. Within firms, too, there are decisions about the extent of decentralization of decision-making. Even if governments decide to allocate decision-making responsibilities downward, there is a question of what level: the state or provincial? Or to the local level? To the level of the neighborhood?

In the end, actions are taken by individuals. But the context in which those actions are taken is structured by those at higher levels—who have only limited information, as well as limited control. If each individual's actions affected only himself, then there would be limited need for having higher-level authorities. If each person's actions only affected his family, then the decision-making authority might reside with the family, but again, there would be no need to confer responsibility to a higher authority. On the other hand, if those at the top level had full information—and their interests perfectly coincided with those below—then those at the top could make all the decisions, and no one below would object.[1] This helps frame the centralization/decentralization debate. Decisions by one party affect others—externalities are pervasive and there is a need for the provision of public goods. This leads to the principle that is often talked about in the context of Europe, of *subsidiarity*, of assigning responsibility to the lowest level possible, within which externalities can be internalized. In the case of public goods, it says that local public goods (goods, the benefits of which only accrue to those living in the area) should be provided by local governments, national public goods should be provided by national governments, and global public goods by the international community.

There are three limitations to this neat assignment. The first we have already alluded to: those at higher levels may have less information about local conditions or local preferences, so there may be a trade-off—better internalization of externalities versus better "quality" of decision-making. But those at the higher level may have better information as well, e.g., concerning the environmental consequences of alternative courses of actions.[2] Second, even if there were no information asymmetries, objectives may differ. The interests (preferences) of decision-makers at each level may differ; those at the higher level may not take actions that are fully reflective of the interests of those below. Indeed, creating suborganizational decision-making units creates *new* interests—those in charge have individual incentives to demonstrate competence and curry favor. One can never succeed in getting interests fully aligned, even with the best-designed incentive structures. Third, decision-making processes themselves matter—when communities are involved in the process, there is more "buy-in," more motivation to ensure that projects succeed.

There are two further considerations that are important in organizational design. Giving more autonomy among organizational units enables the use of competitive forces that can both provide strong incentives and reveal information that would not otherwise be available to those at the center. This is the basis of what is called yardstick competition, particularly important in contexts where the center does not know the difficulty of the tasks to be undertaken.[3] Chapter 17 notes the role that such yardstick competition has played in China's success. The crucial point is that competition can be harnessed or stifled within the public sector as well as the private sector. The market does not have a monopoly on competition.

As economists view these issues, they naturally focus on incentives, and within economics, much of the theory of incentives is based on single-period models; but the real world needs to be viewed as a repeated game.[4] This is important because actions (outcomes) at time t reveal information that can be used in subsequent periods, and agents (whether they are employees or local governments) should know this, which can affect their behavior. If a task is easy and individuals work hard, so that output is high, the employer will infer that the task was easier, and adjust compensation (say the piece rate) correspondingly. But workers know this, and may curtail their effort in order to "hide" the information. If the center could commit on how it would use that information, performance would in general improve. The problem is that higher "authorities" typically cannot commit themselves. Sometimes, however, lower-down units do not fully understand this problem of lack of commitment and ignore the consequences. Eventually they learn, and behavior adjusts—to the adverse interests of the organization.

This dynamic may have played out in the case of China. In the first period of decentralization, before 1994, there was a system of fiscal contracting, in which local levels were able to retain additional revenues that they raised. This provided high-powered incentives for development. Then, the center changed the rules of the game, changed the tax system, capturing much of the "rents" (tax payments) that otherwise would have gone to the local level.

Any organization has a decision-making structure, part of which entails decisions about the decision-making structure. Societies are not simple; there is no fully articulated "map" that assigns responsibilities for decision-making. And, even if there were, the world is always changing, and the decision-making structures need to change to reflect this. Thus, decision-making authority is often contested. Often there is an "official" structure, which specifies who has residual decision-making authority—who makes decisions that have not been otherwise assigned—and who decides when there is a conflict over decision-making authority.[5] Real authority need not correspond perfectly, or even well, with the official structure. In the United States, the Supreme Court arbitrates conflicts of decision-making authority. But as Andrew Jackson, who as president had the executive responsibility to enforce laws, forcefully put it in response to an 1832 Supreme Court decision under Chief Justice John Marshall: "John Marshall has made his decision; let him enforce it now if he can."[6] The justices have no enforcement power—other than their legitimacy—a fact of which they are aware and which may affect their decisions.

In China, the central government retains the power to make decisions about decision-making authority. But all governments represent complex political processes and systems of influence; local and regional authorities have a say in decisions, including decisions about decision-making authority. In China, as Chapter 16 points out, this influence is strengthened by the power of the center to promote those who perform well at the provincial level—which, in part, means performing in accordance with the center's wishes.

The issue of "commitment" is a more general theme in institutional design: one wants the rules of the game not to be always changing, but one also wants rules that change when circumstances change. Circumstances are always changing, and especially in the context of a rapidly changing society—and even more so in a society in which views about what a "good society" might entail and how that might be achieved are rapidly changing, as part of the process of development itself. Europe made a mistake, embedding in its "constitution"—the hard-to-change treaties that created its basic legal frameworks—a set of ideas reflecting the neoliberal orthodoxy of the day. But that has left the EU saddled with a framework that is increasingly out of sync with current ideas and circumstances. Its central bank, for instance, has a single mandate—to keep inflation low. It was thought that low inflation was necessary and almost sufficient for ensuring *real* stability, high growth, and low unemployment. While these ideas were widely criticized at the time, in the aftermath of the crisis, they have become even more discredited. Indeed, in the United States, the dual mandate of price stability and growth/employment has now been supplemented by a third mandate—financial stability.

Constitutions and treaties that make changing the rules of the game difficult need, accordingly, to focus on issues that are likely not to change quickly, with language that is broad enough that there can be adaptability to changing circumstances. This may entail, for instance, broad specifications about powers to correct market failures. Critics of government may worry that this will confer too much power, with too much discretion, on the government. They will argue for circumscribing the powers, e.g., to more narrowly specified activities. The risks of excessive specificity is illustrated by the environment—one of the main concerns of citizens around the world. A hundred years ago, few recognized the fragility of our environment and how it was being despoiled by economic activity. Narrowly specified delegations of authority would not have given the government scope for taking actions which, by most accounts, have been very beneficial.

Institutional design requires carefully balancing—restrictions with discretion, taking into account flexibility in changing the rules and restrictions themselves. The process of this balancing is dynamic. In the aftermath of the crisis, the EU showed flexibility in the interpretation of the Maastricht convergence criteria (specifying levels of allowable budget deficits and debt as a fraction of GDP).

As the Chinese economy grows and becomes more of a national economy, creating national economic, social, and legal frameworks will become increasingly important. With little labor mobility (under the *hukou* system, Chapter 15), there may have been little need for a national social insurance system. There is a high cost to such labor market fragmentation, and part of China's development has been creating a national labor market. As that develops, it will be necessary to have a single social security (public pension) program.

What is remarkable about China's development during the past thirty years is that it has shown this kind of institutional flexibility, evidenced by the discussions in Chapters 16 and 17 on the changing patterns of centralization and decentralization. As the economy grows, though, as we have noted, economic interests will become more influential. There is a question of whether existing interests will impede the natural evolution of the economy from its current stage to the next. Chapters 16 and 17 highlight, for instance, how the change in incentives and constraints before and after 1994 altered development strategies of the provinces and localities. Before turning to that, there is one more general issue to address.

Advocates of strong property rights have always found China's success difficult to reconcile with their theories, particularly in the earlier period when growth centered on state-owned enterprises (SOEs) and township and village enterprises (TVEs). Growth was not based on private property, and property rights were, in this period of high growth, ambiguous and changing. According to the standard theories, growth should not have occurred; if it did, it should not have been sustainable. But it was, for more than thirty years, with one of the fastest rates of growth and reductions in poverty in history. Our discussions in Parts I and II provide the backdrop for understanding these successes.

Property rights are important, but they are not the only thing that matter. Economists emphasize the centrality of incentives in determining the functioning of an economy. Property rights are typically viewed as part of society's incentive system—individuals who work hard get to keep the rewards. But there are other ways of providing incentives. Indeed, not only are financial incentives not the only way of providing incentives, they are very imperfect. In most organizations most individuals work in teams, their contributions to organizational outcomes are hard to measure and often ambiguous, and pay seldom corresponds to the marginal contribution.[7] Even in well-established market economies, there is little correspondence between the pay and performance of executives—made so clear in the recent crisis, in which CEOs who had contributed to the destruction of the market values of their firms and the downturn of the global economy were amply rewarded through bonuses (originally called performance bonuses, but when that language proved unpalatable, the name changed to "retention bonuses," without addressing why firms would retain executives whose performance had been so dismal). Our discussion of corporate governance in Part II highlighted the problems of aligning the interests of management with those of shareholders and other stakeholders.

Thus, property rights are only part of an economy's system of incentives, and a part that, if not well designed, may result in distorted incentives, with outcomes not well in accord with social objectives. At least as important is competition, and China has shown that there can be highly effective competition even in the presence of restrained and sometimes ambiguous property rights. One of the advantages of decentralization is that it engendered competition among local communities and provinces. Decentralization was especially important in the early stages of China's industrialization. The fiscal contracting system provided both incentive structures and resources that enabled the system to work. Local authorities had to create jobs for new entrants into the labor force, who would otherwise have been absorbed into the rural sector with decreasing productivity and income. The system of accountability, resource limitations, and the imperative of job creation restricted the amount that officials could take for their own benefit—funds had to be reinvested to expand enterprises. Those who were successful won respect from others, as well as promotion. The system was almost too successful, for with the possibility of credit creation at the provincial level, inflationary pressures built up. The potential for good projects seemed to exceed resource availability.[8]

These inflationary pressures, combined with increased needs by the center for more revenue, led to a redesign of the system of decentralization. The new system changed local incentives and resources. One more change, introduced a few years later (perhaps not emphasized sufficiently in the chapters), was the privatization of housing. One of the reasons for this was to help promote small entrepreneurship and private businesses (to maintain, repair, and build housing). This effort too was successful—more quickly and more dramatically than most expected at the time, to the point where private home ownership in China now exceeds that in the United States.

While the 1994 reform had taken away fiscal resources from local and provincial authorities, it had left what is perhaps the country's most important natural resource in the hands of local governments—land. Rapid development combined with private home ownership meant that this resource was becoming increasing valuable. Privatizations of state resources have been a source of corruption in most economies, and China, evidently, has almost surely not been an exception. But the privatizations of land also provided a source of quasi-fiscal revenue for local authorities. Sources of revenue affect patterns of development, and not necessarily for the best. The pace and pattern of urbanization may have been more affected by government needs for revenue than driven by a thoughtful analysis of how to create sustainable livable cities.

There is more at stake. China has had a supply-driven model—profits have been used to reinvest, buying land and machines, funding local governments, and creating new jobs. There has been a government–business symbiotic relationship, sometimes at the expense of the environment, but sustained by globalization, which ensured that whatever goods were produced would be purchased.

That model is coming to an end, and yet there are forces that would like it to continue. It is coming to an end partly because of the changing nature of globalization and partly because of China's success: saturation of markets combined with impressive increases in productivity imply that it will be difficult to achieve the necessary employment growth by relying solely on manufactured exports. It may also be coming to an end with increasing internal competition within China, as it succeeds in creating a national economy. Competition among businesses in China will inevitably lead to decreasing rents for localities and provinces, unless somehow that competition is circumscribed. There is the risk of a race to the bottom—the kind of race that occurred in so much of the rest of the world. Only the central government can prevent this from occurring, but there may be other consequences of any such reconcentration of powers.

There are other models that can work, besides the supply- and export-driven model that has predominated for the past three decades. Some entail expanding the service sector and SMEs, which would necessitate strengthening regional banks and committing more lending to this sector by the big banks. *National* policies, like exchange rate adjustments and banking policies, can affect the evolution of the economy in this direction. The central government has announced its commitment to move away from export-led (supply-driven) growth. But during the Eleventh Five-Year Plan, movement was very slow. There are political forces at play—including local and provincial authorities exercising influence over the central authority. Any change in the rules of the game has distributive consequences, and those who stand to lose are never fully compensated and always resist.

Chapters 16 and 17 not only emphasize the importance of the broad issues of centralization and decentralization but also lay out the rich tapestry that has defined the relationship between the center and the provinces and localities, as each level affects the other, and seeks to influence the decisions that are the province of the other and to expand the range of its own control and the extent of its own resources. In China, the processes of change are sped up; what might, in other contexts, be a slow evolutionary process in China occurs in the span of a few years.

DISPUTE RESOLUTION

One important role of government in enforcing justice is adjudicating disputes. Inevitably, there will be conflicts, and how they are resolved is critical in determining the legitimacy of property rights. In Russia, bankruptcy law has been used through corrupt judicial processes to take property "legally." Incomplete contracts are one reason that there are disputes—not all contingencies are specified. *But for the same reason, legal systems are incomplete—they cannot fully specify what should be done in those circumstances in which the contracts themselves do not specify what should be done.* The "law" lays out a set of principles that serve as a guide to judges and that help the litigants predict the outcome. But if the outcome were fully predictable, then the matter would not go to court. Of course, the parties themselves may know the "truth" of the matter, but they also know that the judge has imperfect information, and therefore will not know all the facts and circumstances. In a sense, then, even were the contract complete, disputes can arise, because one party may believe that the facts can be framed for the judge in ways that will lead (with some probability) to a more favorable outcome than would have emerged had the contract been honored.[9] Over time, there may emerge certain patterns and circumstances in which disputes arise with regularity. "Fairness" requires that there be a certain degree of consistency, and most legal frameworks put considerable emphasis on maintaining consistency. The facts and circumstances in each case differ, so that there is always an issue of the extent to which a particular case is sufficiently similar to others that the results of these previous outcomes should guide the current one. Much of legal analysis is directed at precisely this question.

The drive for consistency has one problem: an initially "wrong" decision (from the perspective either of efficiency or equity) can lead to a series of wrong decisions. All humans are fallible, and human fallibility provides one of the justifications of our system of checks and balances (see also Sah and Stiglitz 1985, 1986, 1988). It is one of the reasons that most important decisions are made by large groups (legislatures), often with implicit or explicit supermajority rules. Judicial decisions are, by contrast, made by small panels (sometimes by a single judge). While a judge has, in a particular case, a large degree of power, he is constrained by a set of decisions (and legal frameworks) that have been arrived at by large numbers of individuals.[10] Appellate processes provide some checks and balances (although again, it is typically a limited number of individuals). But the broader implications of the decision are subject to further checks, as similar cases are reviewed by different courts. If they believe that the weight of the arguments and evidence is such as to come to a different conclusion, they will reverse the finding. Finally, the legislature can always override the courts, redefining the "law" in the circumstances at hand.

These processes are slow and cumbersome and, particularly when the world is changing rapidly, there is a risk that laws and interpretations of those laws made for one set of circumstances become ill suited for another. What seemed fair at one time may seem unfair at another; what provided reasonably good incentives at one time may provide distorted incentives at another.

There is another aspect of the fine balance in flexibility and adaptability discussed earlier. A more flexible system (one in which a judge was less constrained by previous decisions) would, at the same time, risk being a more capricious system. The optimal degree of flexibility will differ depending on the pace of change in society. China's rapid pace of change suggests the need for more flexibility than that embodied in many Western systems, which evolved during periods of very slow change. At the same time, to reduce the risk of capriciousness, there must be greater investments in review processes—more review procedures, larger panels of judges, and more frequent reviews of the emerging legal standards by broader legislative/administrative authorities.

Westerners often talk about the importance of having a judiciary that is independent of political influence. This confuses two separate issues. What they mean (or should mean) is that it is important to have a judiciary who makes its rulings based on the "law," rather than on wealth or political connections. What they should *not* mean is that the law itself should be independent of political processes.[11] The judiciary is supposed to interpret the laws passed through political processes. Shouldn't those engaged in these processes have some say in deciding whether the interpretations that courts have provided are consistent with what they intended? Of course, as laws get adopted through political processes, various individuals or groups may have different objectives and understand the law in different ways. Often, ambiguity in interpretation is part of the process of compromise. In a society with a clearer sense of the "consensus," there may be scope for more active reviewing of whether court interpretations are consistent with what was intended, and there may be greater scope for learning. As the consequences of particular rules and regulations become clearer, they should be adapted to ensure that the law is consistent with the intended consequences.

The last two chapters examine the changing role of the judiciary in China. As Liebman notes, the most significant institutional design issues raised by the judiciary in China are quite different from those that preoccupy the literature in the West. Rather than judicial review and the autonomy of modes of legal reasoning from modes of political debate, the most salient issues are the ability of the judiciary, in a variety of forms, to resolve nonsensitive disputes fairly, the level of professionalism in the judiciary, and the ability of the judiciary to play this role without challenging the political structure—improving rather than checking or reducing the state. The judiciary is changing in China, as the result of top-down reform efforts, judicial education, and the interaction of judges themselves. As our authors stress, these changes may—and may not—be related to the establishment of the types of autonomous judicial branches often seen in the West as prerequisites to democracy. Over time, they may present challenges to the authority of other government actors, contributing to the decentralization of the state and shifting the balance of continuity and flexibility in government policy. Liebman and Wu see this potential most clearly in the expanding horizontal networking of judges brought about by technological connectivity. At the same time, they may also contribute to the effectiveness of the judiciary as a component in the existing state and party structure and to the longer-term reliability and effectiveness of government policy.

NOTES

1. This is not quite correct, for individuals may play value on the decision making process itself, and it may affect behavior, as the discussion below illustrates.
2. Moreover, as we argued in earlier parts of this book, there are choices to be made about which externalities should count, and views about this could differ at different levels. It is possible that the center could have a comparative advantage in information (about certain things), and the local level could do a better job at controlling some kinds of externalities.
3. Nalebuff and Stiglitz (1983a, 1983b) show that in situations where there is a common shock affecting various subunits (individuals), and the center (the employer) cannot observe that common shock, then it is optimal to base compensation at least to some extent on relative performance, and in some cases, even to use order statistics (rewarding the best performers, punishing the worst). In some cases, carefully designed incentive structures using such structures can achieve (close to) first-best outcomes.
4. Economists and legal scholars have had to confront similar issues, but they often see the world through a different lens. This book, as well as much of the law and economics tradition, has attempted to bring these two strands of thought closer together.
5. As Chapter 4 pointed out, there are broader ambiguities in the meaning of control.
6. The Court had ruled that the state of Georgia could not impose its state laws upon Cherokee tribal lands.
7. See, e.g., the work of Nobel laureate Herbert Simon (1991) and March and Simon (1958).
8. There are good reasons not to use interest rates as a mechanism for market clearing. See, e.g., Stiglitz and Weiss (1981).
9. I say, "in a sense," because a fully specified contract would presumably take into account what is observable to a third party (the judge), and specify what is to be done in these circumstances, where what is observable to a third party differs from what is observable to the parties themselves. In other words, they would take into account the possibility of dishonesty.
10. In a sense, a judge (or a set of judges) today can be thought of as engaged in a dialogue, over time, with a broader set of judges looking at similar cases, in an attempt to arrive at a "just" (fair and efficient) outcome. Current judges have to make judgments about the extent to which the cases are similar, and whether the circumstances today are similar to those that prevailed at the time of the earlier judgments. Weight is given to the arguments and analysis, not just to the conclusion.
11. There may, in addition, be a desire to insulate the laws from the short term vagaries of political processes.

REFERENCES

March, J. G. and Simon, H. A. (1958), *Organizations* (New York: John Wiley).

Nalebuff, B. and Stiglitz, J. E. (1983a), "Information, Competition, and Markets," *American Economic Review*, 73/2 (May): 278–84.

——— (1983b), "Prizes and Incentives: Towards a General Theory of Compensation and Competition," *Bell Journal*, 14/1: 21–43.

Sah, R. K. and Stiglitz, J. E. (1986), "The Architecture of Economic Systems: Hierarchies and Polyarchies," *American Economic Review*, 76/4 (September): 716–27.

——— (1988), "Committees, Hierarchies and Polyarchies," *Economic Journal*, 98/391 (June): 451–70.

Simon, H. A. (1991), "Organizations and Markets," *Journal of Economic Perspectives*, 5/2: 25–44.

Stiglitz, J. E. with Sah, R. K. (1985), "Human Fallibility and Economic Organization," *American Economic Review*, 75/2 (May): 292–6.

——and Weiss, A. (1981), "Credit Rationing in Markets with Imperfect Information," *American Economic Review*, 71/3 (June): 393–410.

16

Deregulation, Decentralization, and China's Growth in Transition

Justin Yifu Lin, Mingxing Liu, and Ran Tao

INTRODUCTION

China's economic transition of the past three decades has been remarkable. China has transformed itself from a centrally planned economy to an emerging market economy while achieving an average annual growth rate of more than 9 percent. During this period, China's per capita GDP has more than quadrupled and the living standard of ordinary Chinese people has improved markedly. Yet these impressive achievements have been accompanied by widening gaps between rich and poor and across regions, by serious environmental degradation, by poor working conditions, and by a lack of universal social security coverage. These problems have posed great challenges to the sustainability of its economic transition. A better understanding of the progress that has been made and the problems yet to be addressed in China's transition is not only essential for China's future, but also valuable to other developing countries, given the important implications of China's development model to these countries.

An emerging consensus is being reached now in the literature that local governments have played very active roles in China's "growth miracle" by building local infrastructure, encouraging local businesses, attracting investments, and even directly managing enterprises in the early transition period. Much of the literature that tries to explain the rapid growth in the 1980s and the early 1990s has emphasized the importance of fiscal decentralization. By providing revenue incentives for local authorities to benefit from the growth they could foster, according to this view, decentralization encouraged pro-business policies and stimulated economic growth (Lin and Liu 2000; Oi 1992, 1999; Shirk 1993; Wong 1992; Montinola et al. 1995; Qian and Weingast 1997). Some scholars go even further to claim that the Chinese economy has come under the thrall of a "market-preserving federalism with Chinese characteristics," at least up until the mid-1990s (Montinola et al. 1995; Qian and Weingast 1997). This line of argument contends that governments in developing and transition economies have often been the central barriers to development. Therefore, providing local governments with market-preserving incentives is critical to both spark and sustain development.

Other scholars have disputed this view of the positive impacts of fiscal decentralization in China. For example, Wong (1992) argues that decentralization and fiscal contracting have created a variety of microeconomic distortions. Naughton (1999), Young (2000), and Poncet (2003) hold that decentralization in China actually induced local governments to engage in overinvestment, duplication, regional market protectionism, and even more local bureaucratic interventions. In addition, by reducing the central government's ability to redistribute revenues, decentralization and fiscal contraction seems to have increased regional inequality (World Bank 2002).

How can we reconcile these contradictory arguments? If China's growth between the late 1970s and the mid-1990s was mainly driven by fiscal decentralization in the early reform period, why did earlier decentralization policies taken during the pre-reform period not yield similar progress in economic development and living standards? If the "market-preserving federalism with Chinese characteristics" argument holds only for the first half of China's three decades of transition, why has the Chinese economy continued to grow at a high (if not higher) rate since the fiscal recentralization reform adopted in the mid-1990s?

In this paper, we provide a framework for reconsidering China's changing growth patterns both before and after China started its marketization reform and in different phases of economic transition. By examining the evolution of China's institutional arrangements in regulation and intergovernmental relationship, we argue that the regulatory structure under the planned economy was endogenous to the overtaking development strategy adopted by the central government in that period, while the centralization–decentralization cycle in the pre-reform period was an inevitable outcome of information and control problems inherent in the planned economic system. We also argue that without micro-level deregulation during the reform period, decentralization alone would not have brought about sustained economic growth and improvements in living standards.

The rest of the paper proceeds as follows. We start with a discussion of the heavy-industry development strategy pursued in China's planned economy period and the centralization–decentralization cycle that ensued. The following section accounts for China's growth in the early transition phase through an analysis of the deregulation and decentralization moves in this period. Next we evaluate the impacts of changing central–local and state–business relationships on China's growth pattern since its recentralization period from the mid-1990s. The next section offers an alternative interpretation of China's growth in transition, one that contrasts with the view ascribing it to "fiscal federalism with Chinese characteristics." The final section concludes with implications for further reforms that are necessary for China to realize sustainable development in economic transition.

DEVELOPMENT STRATEGY AND (DE)CENTRALIZATION CYCLE IN THE PLANNED ECONOMY PERIOD

After the founding of the People's Republic of China in 1949, the top leadership believed that rapid industrial development, especially in heavy industries, was essential to defend the new socialist system and to help the country catch up economically with the western industrial countries. Learning mainly from the Soviet experience, the Chinese government began in 1953 to formulate and implement the First Five-Year Plan, which gave priority to heavy-industry development. The 156 central and backbone projects of industrial construction in the First Five-Year Plan period were mostly heavy-industrial projects implemented with financial and technical aid from the Soviet Union. Between 1953 and 1957, investment in heavy industries accounted for 85 percent of the total industrial investment and 72.9 percent of the total agricultural and industrial investment (Lin et al. 1999).

The development strategy of prioritizing heavy-industry development was inconsistent with China's capital-scarce and labor-abundant endowment structure, however. If the capital and labor markets had been allowed to operate freely, heavy industrial sectors would not have been viable, because investment would have flowed to labor-intensive light industries (Lin and Tan 1999). To mobilize resources for heavy-industrial development, therefore, the state instituted a planned economic system. According to Lin et al. (1998, 1999), this system had three essential characteristics: (a) a distorted macro-policy environment that depressed interest rates, the exchange rate, and the prices of major industrial inputs; (b) a centralized resource allocation system to guarantee that essential resources flowed to the prioritized sectors (the heavy industries); (3) micro-management institutions depriving enterprises and rural communities of autonomy, so that resource allocation would not deviate from state plans. As a result, a large number of state-owned enterprises (SOEs) and People's Communes were set up in urban and rural areas respectively; these were the micro-institutions whose purpose was to ensure that resources were allocated according to the central plan and to facilitate heavy-industrial development.

After China adopted the heavy-industry development strategy in the 1950s, it set up a highly centralized fiscal system, known as the "unified revenue and unified expenditure." Under this system, the accounting of SOEs was incorporated into the central finance system. The Ministry of Finance was placed in charge of SOE cash flows, while the newly established State Planning Commission (SPC) was granted authority over the allocation of major industrial inputs, as well as the annual formulation of local revenue and expenditure plans. As a result, all government revenue and expenditures had to go through the center, with little budgetary autonomy left to the local governments.

In a country of China's size, however, the task of formulating, administering, coordinating, and monitoring the local and SOE finance at the central level was inevitably overwhelming. It became even more so as the national economy grew and the structure of the planning economy became more complicated. For example, the number of enterprises subordinated to the central government increased from 2,800 in 1953 to 9,300 in 1957, and the number of items in material allocation under central planning increased from 55 in 1952 to 231 in 1957 (Qian and Weingast 1996). Information asymmetries related to control and monitoring naturally emerged. As the economy developed further, with more projects initiated and more enterprises established, the highly centralized plan system became increasingly unmanageable. Because it granted little autonomy to the local and firm levels, this system dampened the incentives both of SOEs and of local governments.

By the end of the First Five-Year Plan period, the central government had recognized this incentive problem and had launched a decentralization process to correct it. In 1957, the center delegated many SOEs to the local level, reducing the share of industrial output produced by SOEs subordinate to the center from 40 percent to 14 percent of the national total. Furthermore, planning was largely shifted from the central level to the local level, with decisions on fixed investment now being made by provinces. Finally, revenue-sharing schemes between the central and the local were now fixed for five years, and the local share of government revenue rose from 25 percent to 50 percent.

This wave of decentralization coincided with the 1958 Great Leap Forward, which called for rapid economic expansion. And local incentives did in fact respond quickly to the decentralization policies, as local small industries supported by the local governments grew quickly. This program did not succeed, however, because the radical decentralization caused serious coordination failures. Under soft budget constraints, local investment expanded excessively and economic overheating soon emerged. The central government had to begin recentralization in 1959, and by 1963, all large and medium-sized industrial enterprises were again controlled by the center, with a concomitant rise in the central government share of revenue.

A second wave of decentralization was initiated in 1970 to meet the high growth target set in the Fourth Five-Year Plan, which reflected the central leadership's perceived high likelihood of Soviet invasion. As in the first wave of decentralization, most large SOEs were again delegated to the provincial and the municipal level. The share of industrial output produced by SOEs under central control dropped from 50 percent in 1965 to 8 percent in the early 1970s (Lin et al. 1999). Local governments again obtained more authority over fixed capital investment and fiscal revenue. Once again, decentralization was followed by overinvestment and overheating, which finally led to a recentralization in the middle 1970s.

In summary, the implementation of a heavy-industry development strategy in a capital-scarce economy made it necessary to establish a distorted macro-policy environment, a centralized resource allocation system, and non-autonomous micro-institutions (the SOEs and the People's Communes). In the initial period, a centralized fiscal system was also necessary to mobilize resources to the prioritized sectors. But this system was highly inefficient, for two main reasons: because the capital-intensive development strategy was incompatible with China's endowment structure, because central planners lacked the information, and because local governments and SOEs lacked the incentives necessary to achieve greater efficiency. The government then had to resort to both fiscal and administrative decentralization by delegating more powers to local governments.

But without a change in the overall development strategy and the planning resource allocation mechanism, decentralization always led to coordination failure. Industrial linkages constructed under the centralized system broke down, and interregional segmentation naturally followed. Under these circumstances, local governments had strong incentives to become self-sufficient by establishing relatively independent industrial systems. Under the typical soft-budget constraint of the planned system, local governments naturally competed for scarce resources from the central planner, while at the same time striving to increase the supply of these resources by establishing small local enterprises such as steel plants, coal mines, and machinery-building plants. As a result of overinvestment and economic overheating, the central government had to recentralize.

Therefore, there are causal links all along the chain, from the heavy-industrial development strategy to the centralized planning system, to low efficiency stemming from a lack of information and incentives, further to decentralization policies that led to overinvestment and economic overheating, and finally to recentralization in the planned system. As long as China stuck to its heavy-industry development strategy, the planned system had to be left largely intact, and decentralization would not be sufficient to tackle the inefficiencies of the system. In fact, administrative/fiscal decentralization without marketization further distorted the socialist economic structure, because it aggravated economic shortages without addressing the problem of soft-budget constraint on local governments and enterprises. This pattern of decentralization–centralization even continued into the reform period, although under different environments and with different implications.

DEREGULATION AND DECENTRALIZATION IN THE EARLY REFORM PERIOD

Deregulation through reform and opening up

The Chinese central leadership recognized the inefficiency in the traditional centralized planning system as early as the 1960s, when the first round of decentralization policies was implemented. But it was not until 1978, two years after the ending of traumatic Cultural Revolution, that fundamental reforms took place. Though at that time the central leadership did not realize that the fundamental cause of China's unsatisfactory development record under state planning was the heavy-industry development strategy, policymakers did recognize the low production efficiency and lack of work incentives in the SOEs and the People's Communes. This explains why China's reforms started from micro-management institutions and focused on improving work incentives.

In rural areas, the Household Responsibility System (HRS) initiated in 1978 granted farmers land use rights and the autonomy to allocate their own labor. As a result, farmers became the residual claimants of their production. Within just a few years, the HRS became the dominant form of microeconomic institutions in rural areas, resulting in the collapse of People's Communes.

In cities, contemporaneous reforms in SOE management focused on power delegation and profit-sharing. To stimulate enterprises to increase production, various pilot reforms allocating more decision-making power to SOEs were carried out from 1979; these reforms included raising the retained share of profits and giving SOE managers more freedom to reward good work performance.

The reform policies taken in SOEs and agricultural sectors in this period can be viewed as gradual deregulatory moves out of the traditional planned system, although central leadership had yet to give up on the heavy-industry development strategy. By granting the micro-units (the SOEs and rural households) more decision-making power in production and allowing them to share in profits or surpluses, these reforms induced rural households and SOEs to invest in labor-intensive industries that had been repressed before and were now extremely profitable due to the shortage of their products in the markets. As China's rapid growth in the late 1970s and 1980s indicates, these policies not only improved the incentive mechanism in micro-institutions, but also helped, in an incremental way, to capitalize on China's comparative advantage in labor-intensive sectors.

Micro-institution reform in SOEs and rural areas was far from the whole story of China's early transition period, however. Two other aspects that made China's transitional experiences in the 1980s and the early 1990s a typical deregulatory process were the policy of opening up in the cities and the rise of township and village enterprises (TVEs) in the countryside. In July 1979, the center decided that Guangdong and Fujian, two southern provinces adjacent to Hong Kong and Taiwan, could pursue reform "one step ahead" of other regions by adopting "special policies" and implementing "flexible measures." This marked the beginning of regional experimentation in China. In 1980, China set up four Special Economic Zones (SEZs)—Shenzhen, Zhuhai, and Shantou in Guangdong Province, and Xiamen in Fujian Province. The SEZs enjoyed not only lower tax rates, but also greater authority to make decisions for local development. While the rest of China was still largely dominated by the planning structure and public ownership, the SEZs were allowed to carry out market operations and to develop private ownership. In 1984, the central government declared another fourteen coastal cities as "Coastal Open Cities," and gave them authority paralleling the SEZs. To attract foreign capital and technology, each of these open cities was authorized to set up local "Development Zones" within its jurisdiction that could implement more liberal policies.

Another fundamental change in this period was the rise of TVEs in the countryside. The earlier agricultural reform through the Household Responsibility System contributed a great deal to rural TVE development, since it not only helped to liberate China's huge rural labor surplus from pure agricultural production to nonagricultural employment in TVEs, but also accumulated the starting capital for rural enterprises. Moreover, the second wave of decentralization in the early 1970s had generated a lot of local government-owned small industries, which laid a foundation for the rapid growth of TVEs in the 1980s. As a matter of fact, the 1980s also witnessed a large number of new local SOEs entering the labor-intensive light-industrial sectors. Along with the booming TVEs, these local SOEs began to produce highly demanded consumption goods whose production had been depressed in the planning period. Therefore, one fundamental reason for the rapid growth of TVEs (and new SOEs) in the 1980s was that local governments were no longer restricted from establishing enterprises in most manufacturing sectors, as they had been during the planning period. Therefore, the key to rapid growth in this period was the deregulation of entry into labor-intensive sectors. This not only helped China to utilize its comparative advantage, but also filled the demand gap left by the traditional heavy-industry development strategy. Between 1983 and 1988, the total TVE output increased by more than fivefold (NBS 2000).

Therefore, in contrast to the policy changes in the late 1950s and the early 1970s, the reforms and liberalization policies taken in the late 1970s and the 1980s were essentially deregulatory policies that turned out to be market-oriented. By 1985, a "dual-track price system"—under which the SOEs could make transactions at market-determined prices beyond the margin, as long as they had fulfilled the state planned production quotas—had been largely legitimized. At the same time, with the rapid entry and growth of new TVEs and SOEs, a more market-oriented track emerged. Booming labor-intensive sectors took advantage of China's abundance of cheap labor.

All in all, the reforms in micro-institutions can be viewed as the first step in China's reform sequencing. By relaxing control over micro-operational mechanisms, the government improved incentives, which produced new streams of resources. Part of the new resources under the control of profit-oriented TVEs and SOEs were then invested in the labor-intensive sectors that had been depressed in the planning period. This helped, in an incremental way, to adjust the distorted industrial structure inherited from the planned period. It also brought more market forces into play by inducing a partial marketization of key production inputs and outputs through the emergence of the "dual-track price system." In other words, marketization was not an intended outcome of China's reform strategy: at least early in the reform period, the Chinese government had no plan to adjust its heavy-industry development strategy, but instead was trying only to improve micro-efficiency through better incentives.

DECENTRALIZATION IN THE FIRST PHASE OF CHINA'S TRANSITION

China's reform and liberalization policies in the late 1970s and the early 1980s were facilitated by corresponding institutional changes in the central–local arrangements—that is, administrative and fiscal decentralization. In fact, the deregulatory policies, including micro-reforms in SOEs and Communes, regional experiments in SEZs and "Coastal Open Cities," and promoting the development of rural TVEs, all necessitated administrative and fiscal decentralization to be supported by the local governments.

China's decentralization in the early period of transition can be characterized as an evolutionary process of decentralizing both administratively and fiscally. The administrative decentralization granted local government officials greater authority over local economic management, including the autonomy to set prices, to invest with self-raised funds, and more importantly, to restructure their firms and issue licenses to new firms. This change was evidenced by the diminishing role of the central State Planning Commission, from approving fixed-assets investment projects to managing only "key projects" (Qian and Weingast 1997).

A second, perhaps no less important, component of administrative decentralization was the delegation of SOEs to local governments at the provincial, municipality, and county levels. This process began in the early 1980s, and by 1985, the state-owned industrial enterprises controlled by the center accounted for only 20 percent of the total industrial output at or above the township level, while provincial and municipal governments controlled 45 percent and county governments the remaining 35 percent (Qian and Xu 1993). Fixed investment for local government-owned enterprises fell naturally on the shoulders of local governments. Since SOEs then also provided a wide range of social services to their employees, a higher share of local SOE ownership also meant that local governments now took primary and final responsibilities for these expenditures.

Administrative decentralization in the 1980s was also accompanied by a fiscal decentralization move known as the "Fiscal Contracting System" between adjacent levels of governments. Between the center and the provinces, for example, this system worked as follows. First, revenues in any given province were divided between: "central fixed revenue," all of which was to be remitted to the center; "local fixed revenue;" and "shared revenue" that was collected by local governments but was to be shared by the center. Although fiscal contracting schemes varied across regions and over time, the main idea was that provincial governments contracted with the central government on the amount of fiscal revenue to be remitted for the next year(s). Once local governments had fulfilled their fiscal obligations to the center, they were permitted to keep any additional revenue. This system remained in place until the end of 1993 (Montinola et al. 1995).

Compared to the "unified revenue and unified expenditure" system commonly found in the planned period, the new "Fiscal Contracting System" indeed granted local government much higher fiscal autonomy. A growing literature on China's growth in transition argues that local governments in the reform period now had incentives to develop local enterprises and to step up their efforts to collect revenues under the fiscal contracting system. At the same time, because they now had the autonomy to invest with self-raised funds and to issue licenses, local governments were stimulated to establish state-owned enterprises, including TVEs.

However, an important complication arises with regard to the operation of the fiscal contracting system. Though this system granted local governments higher marginal retention rates in budget revenue, it was a highly unstable system: the central government could and did arbitrarily change the "rules of the game" and adjust fiscal contracting arrangements in favor of itself. Though China's fiscal system in the 1980s and the early 1990s is generally referred to as "fiscal contracting," this system experienced quite a few significant changes initiated by the center between the late 1970s and the early 1990s. The 1980 fiscal system of "dividing revenue and expenditure with each level of government responsible for balancing its own budget" was introduced because the center found itself in deficit after the fiscal system of "linking expenditure to revenue and dividing extra revenue with fixed share," adopted in 1978.

The 1980 central–provincial fiscal contracts were supposed to last five years. However, the central government started "borrowing" huge amounts of funds from the provinces to alleviate its fiscal problems in 1981 and 1982. These loans were never paid back. Instead, they were transformed into permanent transfers to the center (Tsui and Wang 2004). In 1982 all the contracts were revised, except for those of Guangdong and Fujian, and the budgetary revenue was to be shared between the center and the provinces based on the ratio of provincial expenditure to provincial revenue. A further adjustment was again introduced in 1985 by "changing profit remittances into taxes and dividing taxes into central, local and shared taxes" (Lin et al. 1999). Because central–provincial revenue-sharing arrangements were based on the budget balances of previous years, provinces with surpluses were expected to remit more revenues to the center while deficit provinces could retain more. This system was also intended to increase the central share and strengthen central fiscal controls (Tsui and Wang 2004; Wong 1992). Through this reform, the central government was able to maintain a tight grip over those regions that were the most important sources of central revenue, including Shanghai, Beijing, Tianjin, Liaoning, Jiangsu, and Zhejiang. The revenues from these regions generally grew more slowly than the national average, since the high share of remittances dampened local enthusiasm for expanding the tax base. To mitigate this effect, the State Council adopted a new system in 1988 that introduced six types of central–provincial revenue-sharing methods, each applied to a number of provinces (Qian 2000; Yang 2006).

To sum it up, though under the fiscal contracting system local governments generally enjoyed a relatively high share of marginal revenue, the center did make a number of attempts and in fact eventually succeeded in increasing the scope of central fixed revenues. These moves shrank the revenue pool available for central–local sharing during the 1980s, from about 85 percent to about 60 percent of total budget revenue. Therefore, although under the fiscal contracting system the average marginal retention share of local governments in budget revenue grew from 68 percent in 1980 to close to 90 percent in 1990, local retained revenue as a share of total GDP fell from about 15 percent to 8 percent (Cai and Treisman 2007).[1]

Under the fiscal contracting system, the center resorted to various ad hoc mechanisms to influence revenue remittances from the local governments—for example, by revising fiscal contracts, arbitrarily shifting expenditure responsibilities to local governments, forcing local governments to purchase bonds at lower-than-market rates, and recentralizing locally owned enterprises. These mechanisms led in many cases to perverse reactions from the local governments, which were motivated to conceal their revenue capacities and to raise "extra-budgetary" or "extra-system" funds, which are not considered a formal part of China's consolidated state budget.[2] In the 1980s and early 1990s, revenue concealment could be successful for two reasons. First, as owners of local SOEs and TVEs, the local governments were able to control their cash flows, and to conceal tax and profit from the center. The existence of local extra-budgetary and extra-system funds associated with local government-owned enterprises further facilitated the revenue transfer from the formal to the informal budget. Second, under the fiscal contracting system the local governments were responsible for tax collection and had control over the *de facto* tax rates and tax bases, despite the fact that they did not have the authority to alter the statutory rates and bases (Ma 1995). In fact, local government frequently coordinated with local SOEs and TVEs to understate their profits and to avoid central predation. Having to meet their own ends in expenditure under fiscal contracting but with little bargaining power in rule-setting against the center, the local governments as shareholders of local enterprises preferred to leave the profits with the enterprises or channel them to local extra-budgetary and off-budget accounts that were not subject to central control.[3]

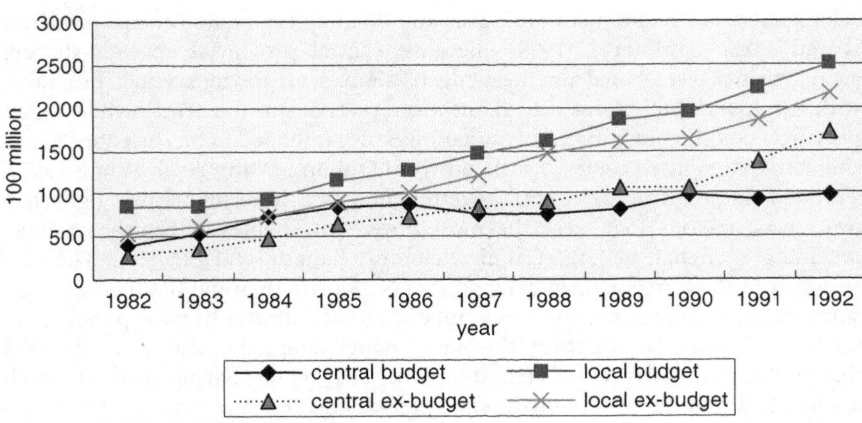

Figure 16.1. Central and local revenue, 1982–1992

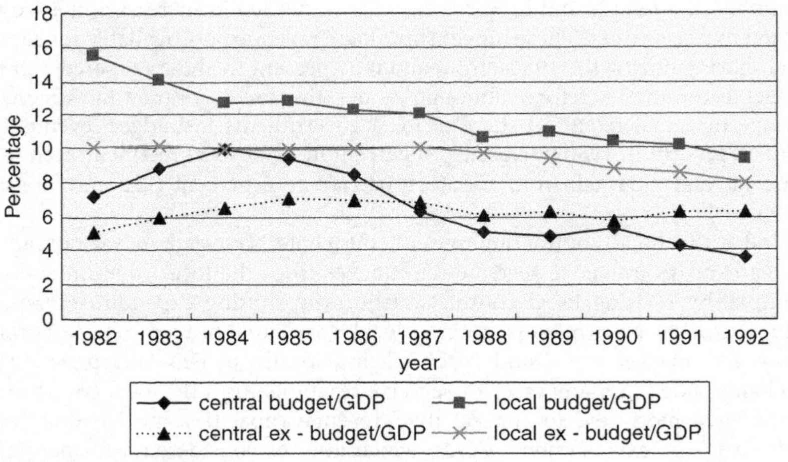

Figure 16.2. Revenue as a share of GDP, 1982–1992

Figure 16.1 shows the central and local revenue and their shares in GDP between 1982 and 1993. As shown in the figure, though both the central and local revenues grew fast in absolute terms, China's budgetary revenue as a share of GDP declined sharply in this period, falling from over 22 percent of GDP in the early 1980s to 11.2 percent in 1994 (this decrease is apparent in Figure 16.2). Declining local tax efforts could explain at least part of this drop.[4] Even when extra-budgetary revenues are included, total government revenue as a share of GDP dropped from 37.8 percent in 1982 to 27 percent in 1992. The share of central budget revenue in total budget revenue fell from a high of 43 percent in 1984 to 22 percent in 1993.

During this period, budgetary revenue grew much faster at the local level than at the center. In the case of extra-budgetary revenue, both central and local, this grew rapidly, surging at an average annual rate of 29.9 percent between 1982 and 1992. By the end of that period, the total amount of extra-budgetary revenue was already 110.7 percent of the budgetary revenue. Local extra-budgetary revenue grew from RMB 53.2 billion to RMB 214.7 billion, registering a much higher growth than that of budget revenue. The dramatic increase in expenditure requirements of local governments—their share rose from around 45 percent in 1981 to over 70 percent by 1992—imposed tremendous fiscal pressure at the local level and encouraged the proliferation of extra-budgetary funds and self-raised funds that were not shared with the center, at the expense of budgetary revenues (Ma and Norregaard 1998).

PROTECTIONIST LOCAL DEVELOPMENTALISM

Besides concealing revenues from the center via extra-budgetary revenues and extra-system funds, local governments in the early reform period also had many other instruments to promote local SOE and TVE development. China in the 1980s and the early 1990s had a highly decentralized financial system in which the local governments could exert substantial influence over banks to provide subsidized credit to local state-owned firms. In the case of the TVEs, local governments went even further to explicitly or implicitly guarantee loans in lieu of collateral. As a result, these enterprises—which were owned by the same local government or community organization—became jointly liable for loans to individual enterprises (Park and Shen 2003). The local governments also pressed state banks to lend to unprofitable SOEs in their jurisdictions. In other words, in the 1980s and early 1990s it was the decentralized financial system, rather than the fiscal system, that led to the soft-budget constraint for both SOEs and TVEs.

The unique roles played by county, township, and village governments in TVE development serve as the best illustration of local developmentalism. During the mid-1980s, when the TVEs saw their golden period of growth, local governments assumed an entrepreneurial role and initiated rural industrial development. Empirical research carried out by Oi (1995) showed that township governments and rural community organizations at the village level made strategic decisions about investment and finance, managerial selection, and the use of after-tax profits for public expenditure. Local officials in this period often spared no effort to circumvent government regulations and grant the maximum tax advantages and exemptions to TVEs, thereby keeping more revenues within the locality and strengthening the competitive advantages of the TVEs. In return, the TVEs provided local governments with funds for locally needed public goods and services.

To promote and protect revenue bases, local governments then also had strong incentives to protect locally owned SOEs and TVEs under their administration against competition from nonlocal enterprises. Taxes, remittances, extra-budgetary and extra-system funds from these local enterprises often constituted a large share of local fiscal revenues (Tsui and Wang 2004). There is a lot of evidence that local governments in this period intentionally closed local markets by implementing restrictive policies for nonlocal commodities, for example by choosing not to create transportation links with other regions (Naughton 1999; Young 2000; Poncet 2003). These policies led in the 1980s and early 1990s to a serious duplication of industrial structure across regions and to growing price dispersion, both signaling substantial interregional trade barriers. Therefore, to the extent this period saw any "regional competition," it came mostly in the form of regional protectionist policies aiming to protect local tax bases by shielding local firms and industries from any real interregional competition.

With the local economy being dominated by local state-owned enterprises, regional competition for mobile manufacturing capital, including foreign direct investment (FDI), was not important in the 1980s and the early 1990s. For the entire 1980s, FDI in China was not only tiny, but also highly concentrated in a small number of large cities and pilot-reform provinces. Between 1983 and 1992, the two provinces of Guangdong and Fujian and the three large cities directly under central control—Beijing, Shanghai, and Tianjin—took in over 70 percent percent of China's FDI (NBS various years). Other regions did little to compete for such investment.

In summary, in this period local governments had access to multiple instruments for supporting SOEs and TVEs, which the local governments owned. Besides tax concealment by hiding profits and/or channeling them extra-budgetarily or extra-system, local governments could also help to provide subsidized credit and free or subsidized inputs (such as land, electricity, and other production inputs) and could even implement protectionist policies to support local TVEs and SOEs. Because they owned the enterprises that were their revenue bases, local governments in this period had strong incentives to protect these enterprises from both central predation and competition from nonlocal enterprises. As a matter of fact, local governments in this period had little incentive to develop private enterprises: ownership rights gave the government control over the financial accounts of firms, and it was easier to extract revenues from those firms than to tax private firms. For the same reason, when local governments controlled firms, it was also harder for the central government to extract revenue from them, and thus revenue was more likely to stay at the local level.

MARKETIZATION, RECENTRALIZATION, AND CONTINUED GROWTH SINCE THE 1990s

Further marketization and privatization

Starting from the 1990s, local government-owned enterprises, including the SOEs and TVEs, began to lose ground as both product markets and financial markets were liberalized. The accelerating market-oriented reforms after 1992 led to a fast-growing private sector, rapidly rising FDI flows, declining inter-regional trade barriers, and a much more integrated domestic market, intensifying product-market competition (Li et al. 1998; Bai et al. 2004; Naughton 1995).

A financial centralization initiated by the central government in 1993 also gradually made it harder for local governments to support the SOEs and TVEs by pressuring local banks to lend. Before 1993, 70 percent of the central bank's loans to state banks were made by the central bank's local branches. But in 1993, the People's Bank of China centralized its operation, and since then, local branches of the central bank have been supervised solely by the bank's local headquarters. And in 1995, China passed the "Central Bank Law" to give the central bank the sole authority over monetary policy. These reforms gradually and substantially reduced the influence of local governments on monetary policy and credit allocation. Financial centralization was one of the major factors that led to the hardening of local budget constraints in the second phase of China's transition (Lin et al. 1999).

As a result of these changes, by the mid-1990s both the SOEs and TVEs had begun to decline. Their problems were exacerbated by overcapacity in manufacturing caused by the duplication of industrial structure and excessive investment under the decentralized fiscal and financial system of the earlier period. As China's product and financial markets became more liberalized, local governments were now losing money from the SOEs and TVEs, so that enterprises that used to be assets for local finance now became liabilities. Large-scale restructuring of SOEs and TVEs had to be initiated in the mid-1990s. For example, by the end of 1996, 70 percent of small SOEs had been privatized in pioneering provinces and half were restructured in other provinces (Cao, Qian, and Weingast 1999; Li et al. 2000). In 1978, nearly four-fifths of the total industrial output in China came from SOEs; by 1997, the share had shrunk to slightly more than a quarter. With the acceleration in SOE and TVE reform, about 25 million employees of SOEs and TVEs were laid off in 1998–2002 (Qian 2003).

Fiscal recentralization

Accompanying the decline of local SOEs and TVEs was a fiscal recentralization initiated by the center in the mid-1990s. Under the earlier fiscal contracting system, the center had seen its share of budget revenue continue to decline. Though the center had worked very hard to increase its share by constantly revising fiscal contracting schemes, local governments responded by lowering their tax collection efforts and concealing revenue from central predation. Overall tax revenue was also declining as a share of GDP (Bahl 1998; Wong 1997; Wong and Bird 2005). In 1994, the central government responded to these problems by introducing a new tax system, commonly known as the "Tax Sharing System" (TSS hereafter). The center's two major goals in adopting the TSS were to raise its own revenue share in total revenue and also to increase total government revenues as a share of GDP.

The TSS changed the way in which fiscal revenues were shared between the central and the provincial governments. It not only introduced several new taxes, but also made a clear distinction between central taxes (such as the consumption tax), local taxes (including the business tax and income tax), and shared taxes (the value-added tax or VAT). Revenues from the VAT, which became the most important tax under the TSS, were to be shared at a fixed rate of 75 percent for the center and 25 percent for subnational governments. With these changes, the TSS successfully replaced the ad hoc contracting arrangements that had characterized China's intergovernmental fiscal relations in the early reform period (Bahl 1998; World Bank 2002).

The TSS also significantly strengthened tax administration. It established separate central and local tax systems, with each responsible for its tax collections of non-shared taxes, and assigned to the Central Tax Bureau the responsibility for collecting the shared VAT (levied on the value-added of manufacturing goods). Thus local governments are now only responsible for collecting local taxes such as the business tax (Wong and Bird 2005; World Bank 2002). These reforms make it very difficult for the local governments to collude with local manufacturing firms to avoid the central taxes and the shared taxes. As Bahl (1998) has pointed out, the changes also undermine at least some of the ability of the local governments to use "backdoor" approaches in revenue mobilization, by making it more difficult for them to transfer budgetary revenues into extra-budgetary or off-budget revenues. The tax instruments available to the local governments for supporting (or competing for) manufacturing firms are now limited to the local share of the enterprise income tax, which constitutes only a very small part of the overall tax revenue. Our recent fieldwork in Zhejiang, Jiangsu, and Guangdong shows that local governments can at most exempt manufacturing firms from the local enterprise income tax entirely for three years and from half the tax for another two years. Further tax exemptions become extremely difficult.

Land developmentalism and continued strong growth after recentralization

Interestingly, after the fiscal recentralization reform in 1994, the Chinese economy continued to grow as rapidly as during the early phase of transition. Fluctuations in China's economic cycle complicate comparisons, but there is no evidence of a slowdown. For example, even as dwindling opportunities for reallocating labor were reducing China's growth potential, the average annual growth rate in the seven years after the fiscal reform (1994–2000) was 8.1 percent, exactly the same as that for the previous seven years (1987–93) (Cai and Treisman 2007). The average growth rate rose in the past five years, to over 10 percent. Contrary to what the model of "fiscal federalism with Chinese characteristics" would predict, it seems that the incentives of local governments to promote development did not fade as the country's fiscal system became more centralized. On the contrary, centralization had the effect of intensifying regional competition for manufacturing investment in the past decade or so, as a "race to the bottom" emerged in which local governments in China competed to offer low-cost land and subsidized infrastructure to manufacturing investors. In the 1990s, and perhaps even more since the early 2000s, local governments across China have established a large number of "industrial parks" and "development zones" by leasing land to industrial users at low prices or even for free.

Considering that after the 1994 fiscal reform, the center began to reap most of the tax revenue from the manufacturing sector, it is difficult to understand this behavior within the framework of decentralization-promoted growth. Why should local governments still have had a strong incentive to promote growth by setting up development zones and industrial parks over the past decade?

The explanation can be found in the fiscal pressures imposed by the fiscal centralization that was not accompanied by corresponding expenditure changes or adequate central transfers to local governments. With the introduction of the TSS, the central government was able to raise its share of revenue from less than 30 percent to over 56 percent after 1994. Yet the TSS has *de facto* maintained the decentralized structure of expenditure duties, to the disadvantage of the subnational governments. In fact, local expenditure responsibilities became much heavier with the restructuring of state-owned sectors since the mid-1990s, as public service and social security responsibilities that had been taken care of by the SOEs themselves were passed to local governments without corresponding resources being set aside to meet them. In the late 1990s and the early 2000s the subnational governments already accounted for more than 70 percent of total public expenditure, while receiving less than 50 percent of total government revenue. Spending on social services was decentralized all the way down to the county level, with the subprovincial tier financing 70 percent of public investment in social services, and provincial and central governments contributing only another 20 and 10 percent respectively (World Bank 2002).

Facing mounting fiscal pressures, provincial governments in turn appear to have taken advantage of the vacuum left by the 1994 fiscal reforms, in the domain of intergovernmental fiscal relations at the subprovincial level. They seem to have defined their fiscal relations with lower-level governments on the most favorable terms for them, that is, claiming a larger share of local fiscal revenues and transferring expenditure duties downwards, while playing a minor role in fiscal equalization at the subprovincial level through fiscal transfers. This has seriously compromised the ability of subprovincial levels of governments to carry out infrastructure investment and to provide for social security and public services (Wong and Bird 2005).

Thus local governments after the 1994 fiscal reform were increasingly pressured to generate revenues on their own. These included both extra-budgetary revenues fully controlled by the local governments, and the formal tax revenues collected from manufacturing and service sectors. Since most of the SOEs and TVEs were already bankrupt or privatized by the late 1990s and early 2000s, the local governments had to generate extra-budgetary revenue from other sources. Collecting land lease revenue, levying administrative charges on firms and individuals, collecting penalty and confiscatory income charges, and in agriculture-based regions directly charging farmers can all be viewed as "entrepreneurial" ways for local governments to extract resources through informal taxation. In fact, these extra-budgetary revenue sources have become essential for supplementing regular budgetary funds and financing infrastructure in urban expansion. In many regions, fees and other revenue from commercial and residential land leasing have become the single most important source of local extra-budgetary revenue. Studies consistently show that land transfer fees account for some 30 to 50 percent of total subprovincial government revenues and in some developed regions they reach 50 to 60 percent of total city revenue (World Bank 2005).

To maximize their own budgetary revenue, local governments promoted the development of local manufacturing and service sectors. After the 1994 fiscal reform, the business tax (levied on service sectors) and the income tax (on enterprise income and personal income) were assigned as purely local taxes, giving local governments a strong incentive to collect them in full. In fact, the incentive was so strong that for several years, revenues from these two sources grew much faster than overall tax revenue, which raised the local share of budget revenue from 44.3 percent in 1994 to 51.1 percent in 1997 (World Bank 2002).

Local governments are also motivated to expand their tax bases by attracting manufacturing firms both from other regions and from abroad. Although local governments receive only one quarter of the VAT revenue levied on manufacturing sector, that share is better than nothing. Our fieldwork in Chinese provinces such as Zhejiang, Jiangsu, and Shandong indicates that local governments believe local service sectors cannot grow without a rapidly expanding local manufacturing sector. Local officials explicitly expressed their expectations of a demand spillover from manufacturing investment to service-sector development. These hopes have intensified regional competition for mobile and mostly private manufacturing capital. Because strengthened tax administration and financial commercialization have reduced their ability to use tax exemptions and favorable bank lending as incentives,[5] however, local governments now rely on subsidized land and infrastructure as the key instrument for attracting investment.

As a result, the period since the late 1990s has seen very rapid growth in "development zones." Local governments at the city, county, or even township level acquire land at low cost from farmers and race to set up different types of "development zones" or "industrial parks," which offer basic infrastructure (water, electricity, and road) and other supporting facilities. By the end of 2003, the total number of local "development zones" and "industrial parks" in China had already reached 3,837. Among these, only 6 percent (232) had been approved by the national government and 26.6 percent (1,019) by provincial governments. A majority of these development zones (2,586) were set up by the city, county, and township levels of governments at their own initiatives. By 2006, the figure further jumped to an astonishing 6,015. Because there are only 2,862 county-level administrative units in China, this number implies that on average each county-level administration has at least two development zones (Zhai and Xiang 2007).

By providing land and infrastructure at negotiated and usually subsidized prices, local governments in China strive to attract industrial investors through "site-clearing"-style packaged development. The land is prepared with infrastructure and leased out for fifty years, usually at only a nominal price or even at a so-called "zero price." Since local governments need to finance the land requisition costs (compensation to dispossessed farmers) and infrastructure preparation costs (costs in building roads and providing access to electricity, water, and heating) ex ante, leasing out industrial land this way inevitably means significant net costs to them.

The impacts of fiscal recentralization and local race-to-the-bottom competition on government revenue are shown in Figures 16.3 and 16.4. The figures present the central and local revenue and their shares of GDP between 1993 and 2005. Although local budgetary revenue registered a decline immediately after the 1994 reform, it has grown rapidly since then, while central budgetary revenue has also been increasing since 1994. Extra-budgetary revenues have seen a divergence, however: whereas central extra-budgetary revenue has more or less stabilized

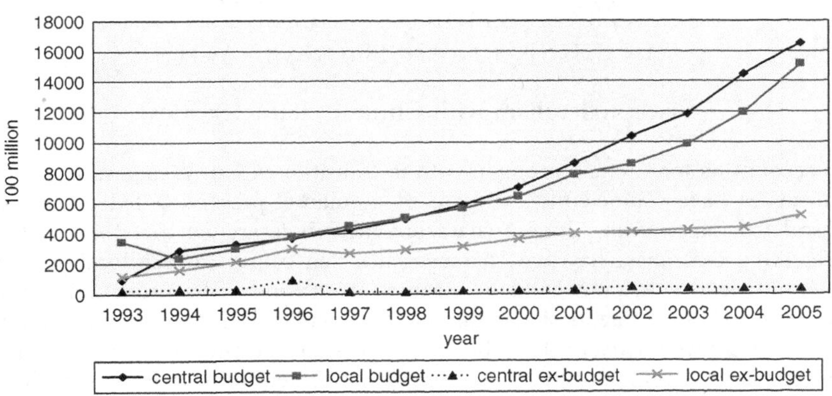

Figure 16.3. Central and local revenue, 1993–2005

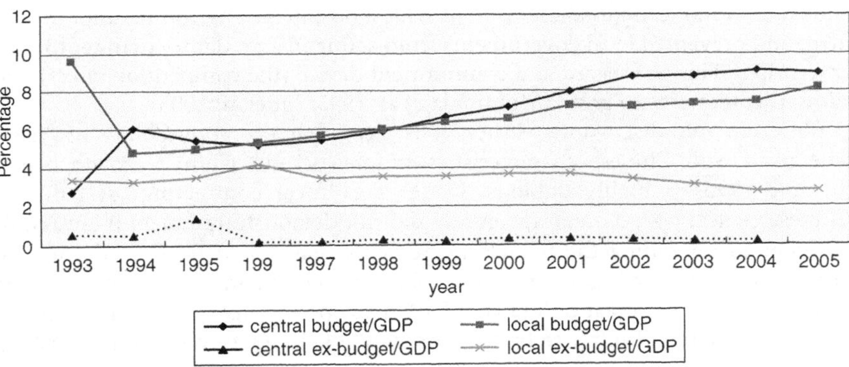

Figure 16.4. Revenue as a share of GDP, 1993–2005

since 1994, local extra-budgetary revenue has grown significantly, despite a reclassification during this period that moved some extra-budgetary revenues onto the budget.

In summary, once they were no longer able to extract resources from local SOEs and TVEs, local governments became keen on cultivating new tax bases by attracting private investment. As most local government-owned firms were privatized, the role of local governments in economic development gradually shifted from serving as shareholder in local state-owned enterprises to collecting taxes on nonlocal government-owned and mostly private firms. Because these firms are apparently much more mobile than the previous locally owned SOEs and TVEs, genuine regional competition for private investment and new local tax bases began to emerge.

DECENTRALIZATION AND DEREGULATION IN CHINA'S TRANSITIONAL PATH

Fiscal federalism with Chinese characteristics?

In accounting for China's strong growth in transition, Qian, Weingast, and their colleagues have claimed the existence of a "market-preserving federalism" or "fiscal federalism with Chinese characteristics." It is argued that this market-preserving federalism has two characteristics that cause Chinese local governments to lend a helping hand to business. First, under the fiscal contracting system, local governments signed durable contracts with the central government and thus enjoyed a relatively stable and high share of budget revenue. Consequently, a "commitment effect" prevented the center from appropriating local revenue and gave local governments strong fiscal incentives to promote growth. Second, in a decentralized system like China, fiscal competition across regions increased the opportunity costs of bailing out insolvent firms. In addition, as competition among jurisdictions extended to factors of production such as capital and labor, it induced jurisdictions to provide a hospitable environment for investment and prevented local governments from acting in a predatory manner toward enterprises. This too served as a commitment device (the competition effect) and allowed enterprises to grow (Montinola et al. 1995; Jin et al. 2005).

But from our discussions earlier, it is clear that the applicability of "fiscal federalism with Chinese characteristics" framework for China's growth before the mid-1990s is highly dubious. Under the "fiscal contracting" system, the Chinese central government apparently did not demonstrate much, if any, commitment to upholding the fiscal arrangements that it had negotiated with (or imposed on) provincial governments. In fact, the center constantly took desperate and ad hoc measures and "nonstandard fiscal policy instruments in order to influence revenue remittance by the localities" (Tsai 2004; Ma 1995). As Wong et al. (1995) and many others have shown, these instruments include "revenue-grabbing outside the (revenue-sharing) system by changing the scope of central fixed revenues, 'borrowing' etc. and unilaterally resetting contract terms in mid-course." In addition, in this period the center also took over profitable enterprises from localities and coerced the latter into purchasing central government bonds. As expected, the ad hoc strategies reinforced the rationale for revenue concealment and further eroded trust between central and local governments (Tsai 2004). Local governments in this period still had incentives to develop, however—not because they enjoyed a relatively high and stable share of marginal revenue, but because they could evade central predation by channeling resources to extra-budgetary and even off-budgetary accounts linked with local government-owned enterprises (the SOEs and TVEs).

Furthermore, precisely because China's financial system was largely decentralized in this period, there could not have much "competition effect." Nothing prevented local governments from bailing out the local state enterprises (the SOEs and TVEs), which dominated local economies in most regions. In this period, capital mobility was inevitably low, since these enterprises were essentially local revenue bases and could not be as mobile as private firms, which are assumed to seek best locations to develop. Therefore, regional competition for mobile capital could not possibly be the right story in this period. On the contrary, local governments had no incentives to predate these enterprises since they were the shareholders.

Contrary to the "fiscal federalism with Chinese characteristics" argument, which would predict that localities would have weaker incentives for promoting growth after the 1994 revenue centralization reform, our analysis helps to account for the apparent continued (or even greater) strength of those incentives after the mid-1990s. Under the new fiscal system, which assigned them a lower tax share and higher expenditure responsibilities, local governments had no choice but to seek new tax bases by taking the new fiscal system as given. Since manufacturing capital is highly mobile and very sensitive to the change of local preferential policies, local governments have had to engage in a race-to-the-bottom competition for manufacturing investment. This has helped to produce new tax revenue, because even though localities can take only a much lower share of tax revenue thus generated, that share is preferable to receiving nothing. Moreover, success in competing manufacturing capital not only brings a relatively stable stream of VAT revenues for the foreseeable future, it may also boost local service-sector development and generate more revenue for local governments. Success in attracting manufacturing investment would further be translated into higher business tax revenue from service sectors, and perhaps higher extra-budgetary revenue from leasing land for commercial and residential purposes. Under such a circumstance, the race-to-the-bottom competition we have witnessed in China since the mid-1990s can be explained from a fiscal perspective.

Deregulation for growth and helping hand for revenue

According to our view, the fundamental cause of China's fast growth in transition can be found in the deregulatory moves that have allowed enterprises to make use of China's comparative advantage in labor-intensive sectors. In the first phase of China's transition, deregulation mainly involved removing barriers to entry in the industrial sector. This was to permit newly emerged SOEs and TVEs to utilize China's cheap labor force and to enter labor-intensive sectors (and consumption goods production) that had been depressed in the planning period. A market track that included the SOEs, TVEs, and foreign-funded enterprises developed outside the plan track. The growth of market elements was made possible by reforms in the farming system (adopting the Household Responsibility System), the SOE enterprise management system (delegating more autonomy to SOEs), the pricing system (adopting the dual-track pricing mechanism), and regional development (experimenting with the SEZs and the Coastal Open Cities). Gradually the coverage of the planned track was narrowed and market mechanisms began to dominate in resource allocation.

It is widely believed that the traditional planning system is inefficient since there is a lack of incentives at the micro-level. However, China's growth in the early reform period came not only from efficiency gains from micro-institution reforms, but also from efficiency gains from overall resource allocation improvement (Lin et al. 1996, 1999). We argue that a more fundamental reason for China's good performance in the early transition period is that government began to allow free entry of enterprises, regardless of their ownership, into labor-intensive sectors. As a matter of fact, not only were most of the TVEs local state-owned firms in the 1980s, but also the output of the SOE sectors continued to grow at an average annual rate of 7.8 percent between 1980 and 1992. The contribution of the SOEs to China's total industrial output was well over 50 percent during that period.[6] This is in sharp contrast with the transition experiences of the former Soviet Union and the Eastern European economies, where transition led to an immediate drop in output and serious unemployment (Lin et al. 1999).

As China's market-oriented reforms deepened over the past decade, high growth has been sustained despite the fact that there was a large-scale SOE and TVE restructuring in the late 1990s and early 2000s. Even though "fiscal federalism with Chinese characteristics" could not be the fundamental cause of China's growth in its early transition, this does not mean local fiscal incentives have been unimportant in China's trajectory of growth. As shown above, the local governments in the early transition period had strong fiscal incentives to promote local SOE and TVE development with their controls over the cash flows of SOEs and TVEs. Since the mid-1990s, changes in the central–local relationship and the state–business relationship have worked together and redefined the choices faced by revenue-maximizing local governments. Fiscal recentralization without corresponding changes in expenditure assignment and sufficient compensating transfers has forced local governments to seek new revenue sources, either from formal taxation on industrial and commercial firms or from extra-budgetary sources such as land-leasing fees (in more industrial regions) and direct taxes on farmers (in agriculture-based regions). The decline of the SOEs/TVEs and the strengthened tax administration during this period not only made it much more difficult for local government to conceal taxes from the center, but also turned these local public enterprises from assets to liabilities. Under these circumstances, local governments naturally resorted to a race to the bottom by grabbing land from farmers and providing subsidized land and infrastructure to attract private manufacturing investment.[7]

As Frye and Shleifer (1997) have argued, local governments can be a "grabbing hand" or they can be a "helping hand" in economic development, depending on their incentives under the given institutional arrangements and endowment conditions. As shown in our previous discussion, on balance local governments have been a helping hand to business throughout different phases of China's transition. The pro-business tendency of Chinese local governments has become particularly obvious since the late 1990s, as local governments anxiously seek new revenue sources by engaging in fierce competition for investment. However, the government's "helping hand" is too often offered to investors at the expense of farmers who tend to see their land requisitioned without adequate compensation, at the expense of workers who tend to face poor labor protection and social insurance coverage, and at the expense of the environment that has degraded seriously in the past decade.

CONCLUSIONS

In this paper, we argue that China's continued growth in the past three decades can be largely attributed to deregulatory policies in different phases of transition. These policies have facilitated a better utilization of China's comparative advantage in labor-intensive sectors. Though at the beginning of China's transition the central leadership did not have a long-term blueprint for reform, deregulatory moves starting with micro-institutional reform have naturally reshaped resource allocation mechanisms. This in turn has helped to adjust the distorted macro-policy environment inherited from the planning system. In an incremental way, the process of marketization led the way and a *de facto* change of development strategy followed.

We also argue that decentralization, in particular the "Fiscal Contracting System" adopted before the mid-1990s, could not be the fundamental source of China's growth in transition. The "fiscal federalism with Chinese characteristics" cannot explain the failure of decentralization moves in the planned economy period, nor can it account for China's strong, if not stronger, growth after the 1994 fiscal recentralization.

Our interpretation of China's growth story does not downplay the roles of local governments in transition, however. Indeed, revenue-maximizing local governments did play an essential role in bringing about China's growth, both in the early transition period and in the second phase of transition. Particular attention needs to be paid to a new form of local developmentalism via offering subsidized land and infrastructure in regional competition after the mid-1990s. In fact, it might not be an overstatement to say that China's growth record in the past decade is somewhat astonishing, partly because the country lacks both necessary regulations on labor and environmental protection and sufficient protection of farmers' land property rights. Therefore, even if bringing in decent labor and environment regulations and strengthening property rights protection for farmers dispossessed by urban expansion may imply slower growth than China is now experiencing, these policies might be essential if China aims to achieve sustainable growth and development in its unfinished business of transition.

NOTES

1. According to Lin et al. (1999), many developing countries, including those socialist countries such as Russia, Eastern European countries, and China, and even many Latin American countries and India that adopted import-substitution strategies, were actually adopting an overtaking and leaping-forward development strategy after World War II.
2. However, the decentralization in the 1970s did have some impact on the reforms starting from the late 1970s. One result of this wave of decentralization was the rise of local small industries (the so-called "five small industries"). For example, more than 300 counties or municipalities set up small steel mills and about 90 percent of counties set up agricultural machinery repair factories. During that period, "mechanization in agriculture" was a catalyst for rural industry, which was the predecessor of township and village enterprises (TVEs) one decade later.

3. The 1988 new fiscal contracting system further raised the marginal revenue share retained by the local governments, particularly those that were major contributors to the central government's revenue. However, the contracts were not strictly adhered to and were revised repeatedly for some regions. In 1991, when the 1988–90 system was supposed to expire, the central government was unable to negotiate a satisfactory replacement; as a result, the 1988–90 system was extended until the end of 1993, when the center replaced the fiscal contracting with a new tax share in its favor.
4. As a matter of fact, the center's move to raise the marginal retention rates can be largely viewed as the outcome of a bargaining game to compensate local governments for the center's revenue grabbing through raising central fixed revenue.
5. Extra-budgetary funds (EBFs) date back to the early 1950s when local governments were permitted to levy nominal fees to finance activities outside of the formal state budget. However, they were minimal before the reform period and only started their dramatic growth during the 1980s. At the provincial and city/county levels, EBFs consisted of the retained earnings and depreciation of local state-owned enterprises (SOEs), as well as various user fees and public utility charges levied by agencies involved in the administration of SOEs. These latter fees generally remained with the levying agencies or departments rather than going to the local government's treasury. Until 1993, the retained earnings of SOEs had a greater impact on local finance, since SOEs were known to collaborate with local officials in taxing the retained earnings or allocating the funds for local capital expenditures. The extra budgetary revenues or "little money lockers" (*xiaojinku*) include fees for specific public goods, profits from township and village enterprises (TVEs), and assorted surcharges and fines collected by townships and villages (Tsai 2004; World Bank 2002).
6. Even the local extra-budgetary revenue was not very secure. In the 1980s, the central government, under fiscal pressure, did make efforts to tap into local extra-budgetary accounts. The collection of the major energy and transportation projects fund and the state budget adjustment fund are examples. Therefore, when the central government found itself under deficit pressure, it changed the rules governing extra-budgetary revenues and tried to draw some fiscal revenues from local governments by rearranging its relationships with the local governments and the SOEs. In response, some local governments used their control of the cash flow of SOEs and TVEs to shift revenues out of both budgets and extra-budgetary accounts. Such efforts prompted local governments to move money into off-budget funds completely outside formal control.
7. In the early 1980s, as an effort to increase enterprise autonomy, the government permitted state-owned enterprises (SOEs) to retain some revenues. After the mid-1980s, SOEs' profitability declined in the face of increased competition.

REFERENCES

Bahl, R. (1998), "Central-Provincial-Local Fiscal Relations: The Revenue Side," in D. J. S. Brean (ed.), *Taxation in Modern China* (New York: Routledge).

Bai, C. E., Du, Y. J., Tao, Z. G., and Tong, S. T. (2004), "Local Protectionism and Regional Specialization: Evidence from China's Industries," *Journal of International Economics*, 63/2: 397–417.

Cai, H. and Treisman, D. (2007), "Did Government Decentralization Cause China's Economic Miracle?" *World Politics*, 58/4: 505–35.

Cao, Y., Qian, Y., and Weingast, B. (1999), "From Federalism, Chinese-Style, to Privatization, Chinese-Style," *Economics of Transition*, 7/1: 103–31.

Frye, T. and Shleifer, A. (1997), "The Invisible Hand and the Grabbing Hand," *American Economic Review*, 87/2: 354–8.

Jin, H., Qian, Y., and Weingast, B. R. (2005), "Regional Decentralization and Fiscal Incentives: Federalism, Chinese-Style," *Journal of Public Economics*, 89/9–10: 1719–42.

Li, Shaomin, Li, Shuhe, and Zhang, W. (1998), "Cross-Regional Competition and Privatization in China," *MOCT-MOST: Economic Policy in Transitional Economies (Economics of Planning)*, 9/1: 75–88.

—— —— —— (2000), "The Road to Capitalism: Competition and Institutional Change in China," *Journal of Comparative Economics*, 28/2: 269–92.

Lin, J. Y. (2001), "Development Strategy and Economic Convergence," The Inaugural D. Gale Johnson Lecture in Chicago, Mimeo, China Center for Economic Research, Beijing University.

—— Cai, F. and Li, Z. (1996), *The China Miracle: Development Strategy and Economic Reform* (Hong Kong: The Chinese University Press of Hong Kong).

—— —— —— (1998), "Competition, Policy Burdens, and State-Owned Enterprise Reform," *American Economic Review*, 88/2: 422–7.

—— —— —— (1999), *The China Miracle*, 2nd edn (Shanghai: Shanghai Sanlian Press).

—— and Liu, Z. (2000), "Fiscal Decentralization and Economic Growth in China," *Economic Development and Cultural Change*, 49/1: 1–21.

—— and Tan, G. (1999), "Policy Burdens, Accountability and Soft Budget Constraint," *American Economic Review*, 89/2: 426–31.

Ma, J. (1995), "Modeling Central-Local Fiscal Relations in China," *China Economic Review*, 6: 105–36.

—— and Norregaard, J. (1998), "China's Fiscal Decentralization." Unpublished manuscript, IMF.

Montinola, G., Qian, Y., and Weingast, B. (1995), "Federalism, Chinese-Style: The Political Basis for Economic Success in China," *World Politics*, 48/1: 50–81.

Naughton, B. (1995), *Growing Out of the Plan* (Cambridge: Cambridge University Press).

—— (1999), "How Much Can Regional Integration Do to Unify China's Markets?" Paper presented at the Conference for Research on Economic Development and Policy Research, Stanford University.

NBS (2000), *China Statistical Yearbooks* (Beijing: China Statistical Publishing House).

—— (various years), *China Foreign Economic Statistical Yearbook*, various issues (Beijing: China Statistical Publishing House).

Oi, J. C. (1992), "Fiscal Reform and the Economic Foundations of Local State Corporatism in China," *World Politics*, 45/1: 99–126.

—— (1995), "The Role of the Local State in China's Transitional Economy," *China Quarterly*, 144: 1132–49.

—— (1999), *Rural China Takes Off: Institutional Foundations of Economic Reform* (Berkeley: University of California Press).

Park, A. and Shen, M. (2003), "Joint Liability Lending and the Rise and Fall of China's Township and Village Enterprises," *Journal of Development Economics*, 71/2: 497–531.

Poncet, S. (2003), "Measuring Chinese Domestic and International Integration," *China Economic Review*, 14/1: 1–21.

Qian, Y. (2000), "The Process of China's Market Transition (1978–98): The Evolutionary, Historical, and Comparative Perspectives," *Journal of Institutional and Theoretical Economics*, 56/1: 151–71.

—— (2003), "How Reform Worked in China," in D. Rodrik (ed.), *In Search of Prosperity: Analytic Narratives on Economic Growth* (Princeton, NJ: Princeton University Press).

—— and Weingast, B. (1996), "China's Transition to Markets: Market-Preserving Federalism, Chinese-Style," *Journal of Policy Reform*, 1/2: 149–85.

—— (1997), "Federalism As a Commitment to Preserving Market Incentives," *Journal of Economic Perspectives*, 11/4: 83–92.

—— and Xu, C. (1993), "M-Form Hierarchy and China's Economic Reform," *European Economic Review, Papers and Proceedings*, 37/2–3: 541–8.

Shirk, S. (1993), *The Political Logic of Economic Reform in China* (Berkeley: University of California Press).

Tsai, K. S. (2004), "Off Balance: The Unintended Consequences of Fiscal Federalism in China," *Journal of Chinese Political Science*, 9/2: 7–20.

Tsui, K.-Y. and Wang, Y. (2004), "Between Separate Stoves and a Single Menu: Fiscal Decentralization in China," *China Quarterly*, 177: 71–90.

Wang, S. (1994), "Central-Local Fiscal Politics in China," in H. Jia and L. Zhimin (eds), *Changing Central-Local Relations in China: Reform and State Capacity* (Boulder: Westview Press).

Wong, C. P. W. (1992), "Fiscal Reform and Local Industrialization: The Problematic Sequencing of Reform in Post-Mao China," *Modern China*, 18/2: 197–227.

—— (1997), *Financing Local Government in the People's Republic of China*. An Asian Development Bank Publication (New York and Hong Kong: Oxford University Press).

—— and Bird, Richard M. (2005), "China's Fiscal System: A Work in Progress," International Tax Program Papers 0515, International Tax Program, Institute for International Business, Joseph L. Rotman School of Management, University of Toronto.

—— with Heady, C. and Woo, W. T. (1995), *Fiscal Management and Economic Reform in the People's Republic of China* (Hong Kong: Oxford University Press).

World Bank (2002), "China National Development and Sub-national Finance: A Review of Provincial Expenditures" (Washington, DC: World Bank).

—— (2005), "China: Land Policy Reform for Sustainable Economic and Social Development" (Washington, DC: World Bank).

Yang, Dali (2006), "Economic Transformation and its Political Discontents in China: Authoritarianism, Unequal Growth, and the Dilemmas of Political Development," *Annual Review of Political Science*, 9: 143–64.

Young, Alwyn (2000), "The Razor's Edge: Distortions and Incremental Reform in the People's Republic of China," *Quarterly Journal of Economics*, 115/4: 1091–135.

Zhai, N. and Xiang, G. (2007), "An Analysis of China's Current Land Acquisition System and Policy Implications," *China Administration*, 3 [in Chinese].

17

From Industrialization to Urbanization: The Social Consequences of Changing Fiscal Incentives on Local Governments' Behavior[1]

James Kai-sing Kung, Chenggang Xu, and Feizhou Zhou

INTRODUCTION

China has experienced sustained economic growth of more than 9 percent per annum during 1978–2005—a record that surpassed even the miraculous growth rate of the group of four East Asian economies in the 1970s and 1980s. What is even more striking is that this sustained growth was, at least until the late 1990s, achieved in large part under predominantly *public* ownership, with township and village enterprises (TVEs) being the most notable organizational form under the purview of subnational governments.[2] Regional decentralization, which drives regional competition or specifically "yardstick jurisdictional competition" and regional experiments, has been a principal force underpinning China's unorthodox growth experience (Xu 2011). Specifically, "yardstick jurisdictional competition" refers to a process that relies on regions facing a similar external economic environment competing with one another on a (more or less) equal footing in a decentralized and nonspecialized environment (Maskin, Qian, and Xu 2000). At an earlier stage, and as part and parcel of China's reform strategy based upon regional decentralization, the central state adopted the specific strategy of fiscal decentralization in the early 1980s. By assigning residual tax-claiming rights to various levels of local governments, this fiscal measure empowered them with positive inducements to promote local economic growth (Oi 1999). Thus, despite the notable absence of private property rights, these regional decentralization-based reforms led to sustained local economic growth.

In this chapter we investigate how the powerful incentive of fiscal stimulus has induced local governments to switch their development focus from industrializing their jurisdictions to urbanizing them, as articulated in the eventual demise of TVEs after their phenomenal rise, followed by the boom and bust of the real-estate sector in recent years. Determined to enhance "state capacity," the central state attenuated the claims of local governments over tax revenues generated by their nonstate, nonprivate enterprises; the 1994 fiscal recentralization reduced the share of local governments' entitlement to an important tax source, namely value-added or transaction tax, by a substantial 75 percent. The overall regional decentralization strategy which underpinned economic growth has not been weakened by this particular fiscal recentralization measure, however. In fact, the incentives of local governments in promoting rural industrialization had remained unchanged up to this stage of the reform. It was only when the central state further reduced the local governments' share in the enterprise profit tax—also by a substantial 60 percent in 2003—that the latter found it no longer profitable to continue to run industrial enterprises that were barely profitable. It was then that many local governments began to pursue the alternative strategy of "urbanization."

Why are local governments interested in urbanizing their localities? More importantly, how do they benefit from such a process, and with what consequences? In the context of highly decentralized rights (both *de jure* and *de facto*) over local resources including land, fiscal revenue incentives provide an important clue to addressing these questions. Specifically, while the central government has since 1994 reclaimed a substantial share of the tax revenues generated by TVEs and subsequently all industrial enterprises regardless of ownership, local governments have been assigned the exclusive right over an increasingly important tax category, the business tax. This tax has been a driving force in China's urbanization process, as nearly half of these revenues are generated from the construction and real-estate sectors. In addition, since urbanization helps spur local GDP growth, it also enhances the career prospects of local officials (Xu 2011).

Indeed, evidence does show that business tax has replaced both value-added and enterprise profit taxes as a new source of local governments' budgetary revenues. However, the *monopoly* right that the central state assigned to local governments over the conversion of farmland to non-arable usages has powerfully whetted the local governments' fiscal appetite. Blessed with escalating land prices (especially for commercial and real-estate developments in premium locations) on the one hand, and artificially low compensations (based on the value of agricultural land use) on the other, many local governments—especially those in the rapidly developing coastal areas—have pocketed windfall profits from this state-induced urbanization process. As with the wide array of fees that users of converted farmland are made to pay to local governments and kept under the "extra-budgetary" or unsupervised category, land conversion income or the market price of land that developers pay for its use is similarly unsupervised. Evidence further suggests that land conversion income constitutes the biggest source of unregulated and unshared revenue for many local governments.

As with the effect of fiscal decentralization on the explosive growth of TVEs in the 1980s, the strong fiscal incentives provided by the aforementioned monopoly right over land revenue have led to two social problems. The first is that this land revenue incentive has predisposed local governments to engage in farmland conversion at rates that not only endanger China's stock of arable land, but also subject large majorities of farmers to losing their primary sources of livelihood with minimal compensation. And that is because, despite them being the nominal owners, the prevailing compensation as designed by the central government confines farmers' land rights to basically agrarian usage; once land use is changed and ownership converted (from the collective to the state), agrarian rights cease to exist. In other words, farmers would only be compensated according to the value of crop production, which is meager in comparison to what the local governments would obtain in selling these converted rights, in particular if the latter are based on commercial and real-estate usage. Clearly, the Chinese government needs to address the twin problems of protecting farmers' property rights as well as halting the unabated loss of arable land.

The remainder of this chapter is organized as follows. In the next section we provide a descriptive analysis of "regional decentralization authoritarianism" as a general context for understanding China's reform strategy, followed by a brief discussion of the fiscal contracting system and the powerful incentive effects it has had on local officials in developing the nonstate local economy (in particular the TVEs). In the following section we show the connection between fiscal recentralization and the demise of TVEs, and subsequently also the waning interest of local governments in promoting enterprise growth. We next examine the new set of incentives that powerfully set the local states to keenly engage in hastening urbanization or specifically land conversion. The problems of this urbanization strategy both from a resource erosion (of farmland) standpoint and from the perspective concerning the violation of farmers' property rights are then looked into. The final section provides a brief conclusion.

REGIONAL DECENTRALIZATION AUTHORITARIANISM

In sharp contrast to all other formerly centralized economies where specialization and monopoly is an outstanding feature, China had never organized its economy in a highly centralized manner—even in its heyday as a command economy (Naughton 2007). This may explain why, when reforms commenced in China, the number of products produced directly under the central plan was a mere 791—compared with over twelve million in the former Soviet Union, and the number of ministries directly under the central government's control less than thirty—compared with sixty-two in the Soviet Union in the late 1970s (Xu 2011). By further devolving the responsibilities of developing the local economies to regional governments, Chinese-style economic reforms only deepened this long-embedded decentralizing proclivity (Shirk 1993). Consisting of a region-based multilevel hierarchy, in 2005 the central government directly controlled less than 4 percent of all industrial employees nationwide—already the largest economic sector in which it has had direct involvement.

An overriding goal of economic reforms is to improve economic efficiency, and the key to achieving that is to invigorate competition. The Chinese state achieved that important goal via regional decentralization, which essentially consists of two core elements. The first is, given its initial conditions (of being already highly decentralized) the state devolved property rights to various levels of regional governments to directly set up and manage enterprises of varying ownership types appropriate to their levels, and have them compete with each other on a regional basis. Secondly, the state has effectively put into place a "nested" system of personnel control by which to reward officials who have proven track records of moving their economies forward with promotion (and "rotation" in some instances). More specifically, this developmental incentive was further invigorated by the adoption of a fiscal contracting system whereby local governments were entitled to retain that portion of the revenue in excess of the remitted amount that it negotiated with the central government:[3] a system with incentive properties analogous to that of a "fixed rental" system and which therefore had the effect of encouraging the "tenant"—the local government—to seek more revenues (more below).

But decentralization does not always create strong incentives to regional officials for regional economic growth. Hence the intriguing question is what makes China *special* in providing strong incentives to regional officials for economic development, and is there empirical evidence to bear upon the effectiveness of a basically decentralized regional economic operation nested within a hierarchy of centralized personnel control? Below we provide some clues to these related questions.

For regional decentralization and competition to work, the center must be able to observe the true effort of regional officials—a dauntingly formidable task given that typically information is "impacted" within regions (Williamson 1985). While the principal is unable to observe effort, fortunately outcome can be observed. Specifically, competition between regional officials can be evaluated among regions of comparable levels of development through a ranking system that resembles a tournament competition; which, as economic theory shows, is an effective mechanism for differentiating effort and accordingly performance. But two conditions must be met in order for a regional tournament competition to be feasible. First, the central government must be able to eradicate collusion between local or regional governments, because collusion among regional officials could destroy competition. Fortunately, this condition is made possible by the fact that Chinese regions—especially those at the county levels—are relatively self-sufficient and nonspecialized. To the extent that each region contains multiple economic sectors, it weakens interdependence between regions, as it enables local governments to carry out and coordinate most economic activities within their own jurisdictions.

Secondly, for regional tournament competition to work, it is also important that each region and the industrial sectors contained therein face broadly similar exogenous conditions. That permits the center to compare the *relative* performance of regions—a more accurate and relevant yardstick for evaluating actual performance.[4] Based on data that contains industry classification codes and location codes for each firm, Maskin, Qian, and Xu (2000) find that the Chinese regions are indeed alike; their empirical results suggest that regional tournaments do work better than the alternative ministerial tournaments—resembling the highly specialized and monopolistic features of the formerly centrally planned economy—in providing incentives to local officials. Similarly, using data covering 344 top provincial officials for the 1979–2002 period, Chen, Li, and Zhou (2005) find that each official's performance relative to her immediate predecessor does have a significant impact on her promotion. Using a panel dataset that covers 254 provincial leaders who had served in twenty-eight Chinese provinces from 1979 to

1995, Li and Zhou (2005) similarly show that regional officials were indeed strongly motivated to promote regional economic growth. Specifically, a higher GDP growth rate in a province significantly improved the likelihood of promotion of provincial leaders—a result that underscores the underlying assumption that the central government makes promotion or turnover decisions based on a performance score of these leaders.

That there exists an intimate relationship between the performance of regional officials and their career prospects is indeed well documented in a number of studies. Tsui and Wang (2004), for instance, show that 60 percent of the targets required of leading provincial officials are related to "economic construction." Moreover, the lower the level of regional governments, the more concrete the stipulated targets become (Edin 2003). At the lowest administrative levels—the township and village levels—party secretaries and township heads are required to fulfill three categories of performance targets, with the fulfillment of the "hard" targets (consisting specifically of economic development plans most notably per capita GDP growth and tax revenue quotas) tied intimately to the award of bonuses and promotions (or political rewards) (Whiting 2000). At the county level, for instance, Edin (2003) has observed that top-ranking township officials have been promoted to positions at the county level, whereas well-performing municipal officials have even transferred to other provinces as governors (Xu et al. 2007). In this context, an important question is whether the incentive embedded in this kind of yardstick competition serves the intended purpose of spurring regional economic growth. Before answering this question it is important that we include in our discussion the unique importance of fiscal decentralization—a core element of regional decentralization—in China's reform process.

FISCAL REVENUE INCENTIVE AND THE RISE OF TVEs

The career incentive embedded in the kind of regional decentralization authoritarianism outlined above explains the powerful incentives bestowed upon regional governments in developing the economies under their jurisdictions. Growth of per capita GDP, employment, and tax revenues, among other performance indicators, are the important metrics upon which their careers within the Party and the government crucially depend. Another important part and parcel of the regional decentralization strategy was *fiscal decentralization.* The fiscal reforms implemented in the 1980s dramatically changed the incentives for local governments. By ceasing to guarantee upper-level budget allocations to meet local expenditures, local governments had to rely primarily on revenues created within their own jurisdictions. They were granted control rights over both revenues and profits generated by these endeavors. An important part of the revenue came from the development of non-farm enterprises (Qian and Xu 1993; Oi 1999). This shared arrangement of fiscal revenues between two immediate levels of government has had the essential incentive property of a "fixed rental" contract, whereby the "tenant" gets to keep more the more revenues it manages to generate.[5]

As part of regional decentralization, fiscal decentralization played an important role in the massive and rapid development of a nonstate sector in the Chinese economy from around the mid-1980s, of which township and village enterprises (TVEs) were a key component (Qian and Xu 1993; Jin, Qian, and Weingast 2005). Indeed, with no more than a modicum of nonagricultural enterprises before the early 1980s, TVEs already counted for roughly 80 percent of output of the nonstate sector in less than a decade. Between 1981 and 1990, total industrial output of TVEs grew at an average rate of 28 percent, and as such had been the main engine of growth of the Chinese economy. It is also well known that the productivity of TVEs was distinctly higher than that of the SOEs (Weitzman and Xu 1994).

County governments benefited enormously from the development of TVEs, primarily because they were able to share tax revenues that these enterprises generated under the fiscal contracting arrangement, and because the lion's share of the increases in tax revenues (the industrial-commercial taxes) had come primarily from township and village enterprises. Starting at a modest base of a little over 2 billion yuan in 1978, taxes grew to 205.8 billion yuan by 1995—an increase of more than tenfold (Oi 1999: 36).[6] As long as the variety of taxes that county-level governments were able to capture was based on production (product tax), income (value-added or transaction tax), and turnover (business tax) rather than profits per se, it had powerful incentives to expand TVEs without paying much regard to their profitability.

A similar incentive existed for the township governments. Not only were they entitled to the bulk of tax revenues (e.g., 70 percent), they were also the keepers of enterprise income or simply profit tax, which formed an additional source of "horizontal" income essential for, among other purposes, financing the provision of local public goods.[7] Depending on the level of tax revenues, local governments did not need to exert the same amount of effort in collecting taxes. By taxing at the minimum rather than maximum levels, which was viable in a context where the economy was still growing, some local governments could decide to provide greater incentives for enterprises under their jurisdiction to become more efficient.[8]

In addition to reaping the direct benefits of increased fiscal revenues, the development of TVEs also had the anticipated effect of accelerating GDP growth, which in turn served to enhance local officials' career prospects (Xu 2011). Thus, local officials were keen to develop the TVEs, such as by procuring loans from financial institutions under their jurisdiction to finance their expansion. In 1995, for example, bank loans accounted for as much as 64 percent of all credit incurred by TVEs; more startlingly, overall debt–equity ratio of TVEs even outweighed that of the SOEs (Kung and Lin 2007: 573). In fact, even up until 1999, when some provinces had already undertaken large-scale privatizations of TVEs, TVEs continued to achieve steady growth in tax revenue; only the "efficiency" of tax revenues—that is, tax revenues measured in terms of per unit of sales and profits—declined (more below on this).

1994 FISCAL REFORM AND THE DECLINE OF TVEs

By the 1990s concerns had mounted that the reform strategy of allowing localities to benefit disproportionately from local economic growth by assigning the regional governments residual income rights over tax revenues and enterprise profits was being achieved at considerable costs; to the extent that the "central state capacity" had been severely weakened. For instance, the central government's share of overall budgetary revenue dwindled precipitously from 40.5 percent in 1984 to 22 percent in 1993. Some scholars even contend that the state had, as a result of fiscal decentralization, lost its capacity to macromanage the economy, which may in turn have led to political instability (e.g., Wang and Hu 1993, 2001). Responding to this concern, the state tightened fiscal control over revenues in 1994 by redefining tax rights between the national and regional governments and taking more in taxes from the localities. In particular, the central government wrestled from local governments the exclusive rights over a newly established consumption tax over such inelastic consumption products as beer, hard liquor, and cigarettes, as well as reassigned a hefty 75 percent of the transaction or value-added tax to itself. As Figure 17.1 clearly shows, this measure drastically altered the proportion of revenues shared between the national and subnational governments. For the latter, the ratio plummeted from an apex of 80 percent before 1994 to roughly 45 percent afterwards and became stabilized at that level thereafter.

While the central government has since the 1994 fiscal reform reclaimed a substantial share of the tax revenues generated from TVEs and other industrial enterprises, local governments were compensated by gaining other rights in the process. Specifically, they were assigned the exclusive right over what is to become an increasingly important tax category, i.e., the business tax. Moreover, at the 15th National Congress of the Communist Party of China, 1997, local governments were given official recognition for being the *de jure* owner of not merely the enterprises established under their jurisdiction but more importantly also of land

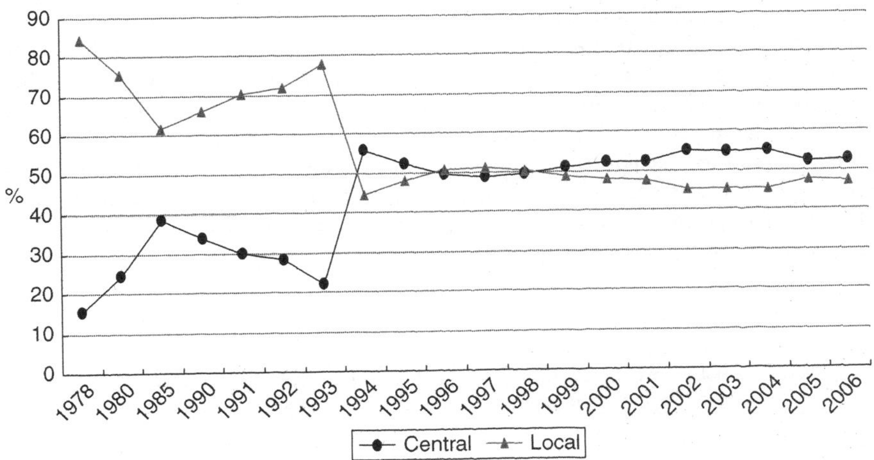

Figure 17.1. Central and local governments' budgetary revenues, 1978–2006

Source: National Bureau of Statistics, *A Compendium of Statistics for the 55 Years of New China, 1949–2004* [*Xinzhongguo Wushiwu Nian Tongji Ziliao Huibian*] (Beijing: Zhongguo Tongji Chubanshe, 2005)

(Research Center on Chinese Communist Party History 2009; Xu 2011); which for some is going to be an enormously important revenue source. As we shall soon demonstrate, the rights which the central state assigned to the local governments both in the disposal of local firms but more so in the conversion of farmland to non-arable usages have crucially shaped the incentives for and accordingly the behavior of the local governments in the post-TVE era.

The implications of the fiscal reform package on local finances and on the development strategy of local governments are profoundly far-reaching. Here we confine our analysis to the eventual demise of TVEs—once an engine of growth of China's economy during the first twenty years or so of the reform. As rehearsed earlier, local officials at both the county and township levels had especially strong incentives to expand TVEs because of the (transaction) tax revenues that these enterprises remitted and their career concerns. These advantages were, however, short-lived; once the central state began to expropriate the lion's share of the tax revenues associated with TVEs, local governments were no longer as enthusiastic in their expansion and from then onwards the entire TVE sector began to decline (Kung and Lin 2007).

The decline of the TVE sector is attributable in particular to both a reduction of investments in, and privatization of, the sector. The reasons behind the reduction of investments and privatization were variegated; here we focus primarily on the impact of the 1994 fiscal reforms.[9] Indeed, despite a secular rise in TVE tax revenues, tax "efficiency" of the TVE sector—measured in terms of tax revenue per unit of sales and profit rate—had in fact declined over time. This is due to a weakening in the local officials' monitoring capacity and their growing inability to obtain credit to help finance TVE expansion. Nationwide evidence indicates that as a result, the relative importance of TVEs declined (Kung and Lin 2007).

The 1994 fiscal reform was one of the major factors that further pushed the nationwide privatization of TVEs. In light of the drastic shift in fiscal rights between the national and subnational governments over particularly the transaction tax (from fully 100 percent before 1994 to only 25 percent thereafter), it is most likely that the benefits of TVE expansion at the margin would decline precipitously, whereas the costs of expansion—in terms of obtaining loans and maintaining profits—would increase markedly. Given other factors, this may further convince local governments to privatize TVEs. The statistical significance of a negative coefficient of time trend in Kung and Lin's (2007) estimations may be interpreted as capturing this secular trend of privatization triggered by the change exogenously imposed by the 1994 fiscal reforms.

FROM INDUSTRIALIZATION TO URBANIZATION: A NEW SOURCE OF FISCAL REVENUE INCENTIVE

In market economies, industrialization and urbanization usually go hand-in-hand. The case in China, however, is somewhat different. Owing to restrictions that the Chinese government has placed upon rural–urban migration (since around the mid-1950s), the two processes have been made artificially separate.

This is especially the case before the 1978 economic reforms, when industrial growth was spatially concentrated in urban areas, on the one hand, and rural–urban migration held tightly in check—via the household registration system or *hukou*—on the other. The physical movement of people has been greatly relaxed in the last quarter century, and urbanization has since proceeded at a much faster clip, as hundreds of millions of villagers have migrated to urban areas to take advantage of non-farm employment opportunities. Yet the *hukou* system—essentially an "apartheid" system that separates the urban populace from its rural counterpart via the rights to a wide range of "entitlements" (such as the right of children to education)—remains restrictive in many respects. Moreover, a case can also be made that urbanization has been slowed by the fact that a good part of China's post-reform industrial growth has been spatially concentrated in townships and villages. While the reassignment of rights over transaction or value-added taxes undoubtedly led the local governments to shed a large collection of nonprivate enterprises, many of which were likely unprofitable, the 1994 fiscal reforms did not stifle rural industrialization. Local authorities were still left with exclusive claims over enterprise income or profit tax, which caused them to focus parsimoniously on enterprise efficiency. It is thus no coincidence that the privatization of TVEs, which began in earnest around 1995, merely led to a change in ownership rather than elimination of many of these industrial enterprises.

What made local governments shift their development strategy from fostering enterprise growth to that of urban growth was the reassignment of rights over enterprise profit tax in 2002. The 1994 fiscal reforms left both local enterprise income tax and individual income tax (alongside a number of other tax categories) to the local governments as sole residual claimants (Oi 1999: 55). Similar in spirit to the 1994 reforms, the central government has proposed to appropriate, from 2002 onwards, 50 percent of the enterprise profit tax (increased to 60 percent in 2003)—a change which has the effect of robbing local governments of the incentive to improve enterprise efficiency regardless of ownership. To make up for the lost revenues resulting from these fiscal reforms, local governments must look elsewhere. Fortunately for the local governments the central state has not proposed to share with them what is to become an important source of tax revenue, namely the business tax, which consists primarily of taxes levied upon the construction and real-estate industry and to a lesser extent the service sector. The Chinese economy continues to grow, and so the country is concomitantly going through a secular process of urbanization. Construction and real-estate development has become the cornerstone of this development process to the extent that it profitably provides a new source of tax revenue to local authorities, who, needless to say, are all too happy to ride on this emerging wave.[10]

The changing relative importance of these two taxes in overall budgetary revenues of local (county-level) governments is reflected in the growing share of business tax from 20 percent in 1994 to 25 percent in 2003 and the decline of transaction tax from 22 percent to 18 percent during the same period (Zhou 2006: 112). As shown in Figure 17.2, the construction and real-estate (CRE) sectors have been a major contributing source of business tax revenue. Moreover, its relative importance had increased over time—from 33 percent in 2001 to almost one half, 45.5 percent, in 2004. It is not surprising, therefore, that one of us found, in an in-depth study of local finance in a rapidly developing county in Zhejiang—a

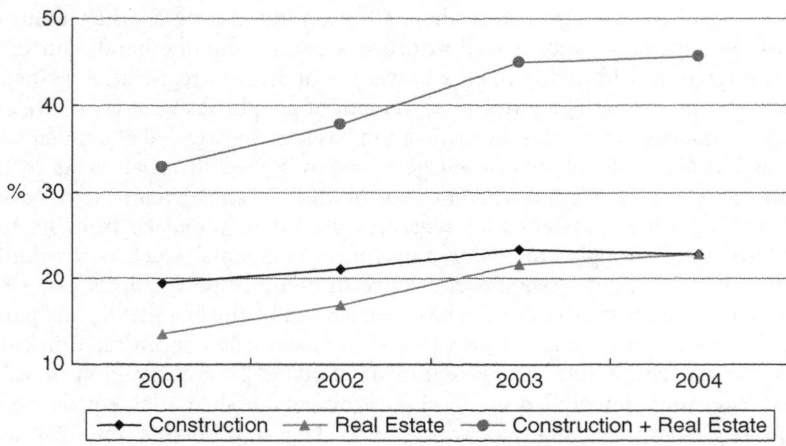

Figure 17.2. Share of construction and real-estate sectors in business tax, 2001–2004
Source: State Administration of Taxation, *The Taxation Yearbook of China, 2005* [*Zhongguo Shuiwu Nianjian*] (Beijing: Renmin Chubanshe, 2005)

province located on the eastern coastal seaboard—that business taxes collected from the CRE sector accounted for 17 percent of land-and-construction-related budgetary revenues, which in turn accounted for nearly 40 percent of total budgetary revenues (38.4 percent of roughly 12 million yuan, Figure 17.3, Zhou 2007). Against this background, it becomes apparent that as much as 17.6 percent of the farmland loss (due to conversion) between 2000 and 2005 was occupied by construction for a variety of purposes, with the magnitude rising over time (more than half, 58.7 percent, of the farmland converted in 2005 was earmarked for construction; Ministry of Land and Resources 2006). The recentralization of fiscal rights since 1994 notwithstanding, the reforms in question have unwittingly left a "tail" for local governments to engage in a gamut of construction and infrastructure projects in China's accelerating urbanization process. But it is land development or specifically the conversion of farmland to non-arable usage that provides local governments with even more powerful incentives to "urbanize" China.

The benefit of pursuing an "urbanization" strategy is by no means confined to being the sole residual claimant of the business tax. By converting farmland for a variety of development projects, local governments are able to both collect fees (*fei*) associated with land conversion and, even more lucratively, be entitled to land conversion income (*tudi churang jin*)—an income stream over which it has been assigned exclusive rights by the central government (more below). As fees are classified as "extra-budgetary" revenues, local governments are allowed to lay exclusive claims over this income source, which as we can see from Figure 17.3 amounted to over half (51.5 percent) of the surveyed county's overall "extra-budgetary" revenues in 2003. For rapidly developing counties that command a price premium on their locations, these "extra-budgetary" land revenues can indeed be substantial, and must have been a useful substitute for the lost revenues which have been channeled to the central government as a result of the 1994 and (perhaps to a lesser extent) the 2002 fiscal reforms.

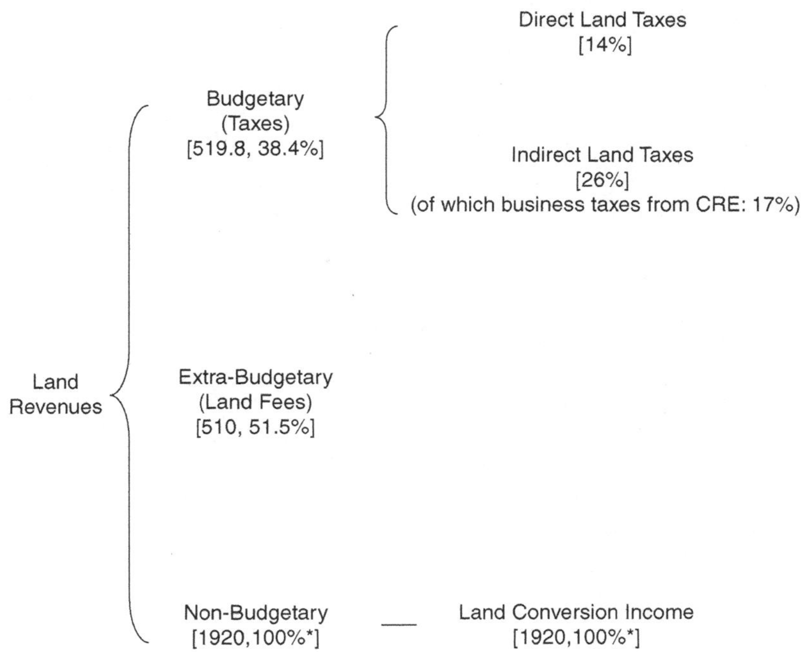

Figure 17.3. Profits from land revenue in S County, Zhejiang Province, 2003 (million yuan)

Note: CRE = Construction and real estate % of budgetary revenue; % of "extra-budgetary" revenue; %* of "non-budgetary" revenue

Source: Zhou (2007)

But the biggest gain of all from converting collective farmland into non-arable usages comes distinctly from land conversion income, also commencing in 1994.[11] Although conversion of cultivated land for urban and rural construction can be dated to the late 1980s, thanks initially to the rural housing construction boom and subsequently to industrial, transport, and urban developments, the magnitude of revenues was miniscule back then. For instance, the amount of fees collected from land-leasing totaled only 242 billion yuan nationwide between 1987 and 1994 (State Land Management Bureau 1998, cited in Lin and Ho 2005), which pales greatly in comparison with the 901 billion yuan or 90 percent of the entire revenue received during the three years between 2001 and 2003.

That the acceleration of land conversion is a recent phenomenon can be clearly illustrated in Figure 17.4, where we plot both the incidence and magnitude of land conversion for the period 1993–2005 from figures provided by the Ministry of Land and Resources. There we can see that it is only after 1999 that both the incidence and magnitude exhibit a steeply upward trend, until 2003 when the state became worried that China would soon deplete its arable land below its lowest threshold required for food self-sufficiency and began to clamp down on the "excessiveness" of land conversion, at a time when land prices—especially those in premier locations—already commanded hefty valuations (more on this below).[12]

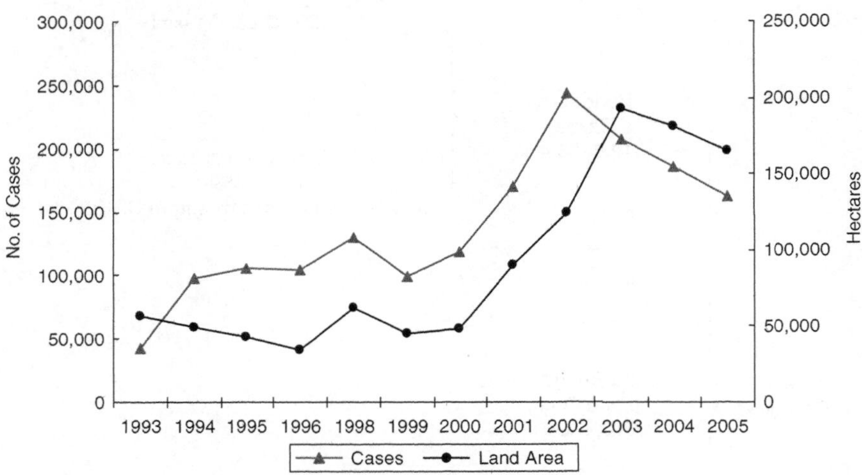

Figure 17.4. Incidence and magnitude of land conversion, 1993–2005

Sources: State Land Administration Bureau, *The Land Yearbook of China, 1995–1997* [*Zhongguo Tudi Nianjian, 1995–1997*] (Beijing: Renmin Chubanshe, 1995–7); Ministry of Land and Resources, *The Land Resource Yearbook of China, 1999–2006* [*Zhongguo Guotu Ziyuan Nianjian, 1999–2006*] (Beijing: Renmin Chubanshe, 1999–2006)

In an attempt to slow down the conversion of farmland by regional governments, the Ministry of Land and Resources set a quota on the maximum quantity of land authorized for conversion in a policy document in 2001, beyond which limit it would be considered illegal. But if Zhou's (2007) micro-study approximates the reality, the colossal magnitude of land conversion fees received by governments in the rapidly developing counties (as large as budgetary and "extra-budgetary" revenues combined) implies that it would not be an easy task for the central government to effectively put a brake on land conversion. The fact that regional governments have been assigned monopoly rights to receive this lucrative, unregulated income source in its entirety must have powerfully whetted the fiscal appetite of regional officials in hastening the pace of land conversion.

This may help explain why, even though authorized (or "legal") land conversion activities declined after 2003, unauthorized (or "illegal") ones rose sharply during the same year; this is especially so with regard to land area (Figure 17.5). Escalating land prices—especially those in premier locations—and the low costs of land compensation were the likely culprits. The prices of land in premier locations appreciated by leaps and bounds; for instance, eight premier sites in the municipality of Hangzhou were expected to fetch 6 billion yuan from cash-flushed domestic developers in 2007 (*South China Morning Post* 2007: 3). Such lucrative revenues have to be set against the exceedingly low costs of land conversion incurred by regional governments—the subject of our next section. For instance, Zhou (2007) finds that compensation for a county government in Zhejiang Province accounted for an extremely tiny fraction, 1.59 percent, of the selling price. Even after paying various fees to the relevant government departments, total costs of land conversion only made up 4.75 percent of overall land

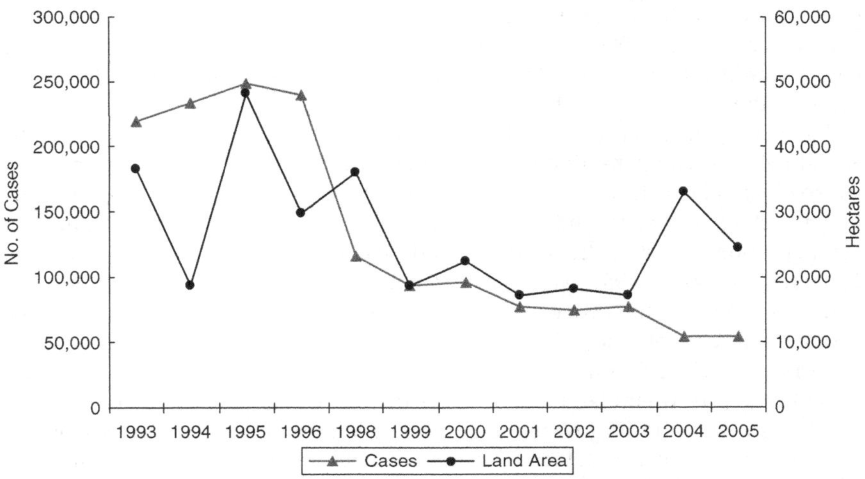

Figure 17.5. Unauthorized land conversion: incidence and magnitude, 1993–2005

Sources: State Land Administration Bureau, *The Land Yearbook of China, 1995–1997* [*Zhongguo Tudi Nianjian, 1995–1997*] (Beijing: Renmin Chubanshe, 1995–7); Ministry of Land and Resources, *The Land Resource Yearbook of China, 1999–2006* [*Zhongguo Guotu Ziyuan Nianjian, 1999–2006*] (Beijing: Renmin Chubanshe, 1999–2006)

conversion revenues. And in the less lucrative instance of residential and mixed (commercial and residential) usages, the pertinent percentages accounted for only 13.84 and 9.16, leaving colossal profits to be reaped by the municipal government. Similarly, Zhou Qiren (2004) has also shown that in selling one *mu* of arable land, the township government of Maichen in Xuwen County in Guangdong Province had to pay only 40,000 yuan, which, when set against the average selling price of 0.88 million yuan per *mu*, the township government there could easily cover the cost from selling only four *mu* of land; the Maichen township government sold 90 *mu* of land in this instance and made a windfall profit.

Small wonder regional governments increasingly turned to auctioning land usufruct rights to commercial and real-estate usages instead of either industrial (in the form of "development zones" or *kaifaqu*) or public welfare projects (*gongyi shiye xiangmu*), such as road and highway construction, schools, and hospitals—the latter a trend until the mid-1990s (Lin and Ho 2005: 424). Regional governments' waning interest in allocating land to public welfare projects can be easily explained by the fact that land is typically provided for free in such instances. Moreover, regional governments have to provide subsidies typically required in developing land for these projects. And while industrial usage is in principle also a revenue generator, fierce competition among localities could easily drive prices down (Zhou 2004), to a point where villagers became so upset with the township government for having charged an unconvincingly low price that they suspected the local officials of corruption. Some villagers were so angry that they even robbed the cadres' houses (*Ming Pao Daily News* 2007a, 2007b). Once again, Zhou's (2007) study of the three municipalities/counties in Zhejiang Province demonstrates this point most clearly. Whereas the average price of industrial land varied only narrowly between 12,000 and 15,000 yuan per *mu* between 1999 and 2003, the lowest commercial price was 34,000 yuan in 2001 and a whopping 182,000 yuan the year after.

The hefty prices that premier locations fetch is, however, not balanced by the appallingly low compensation that farmers receive in relinquishing their land. As we shall explain in further detail in the next section, apart from exceeding the quotas set by the state and the delays in compensating farmers overall, low compensation is part of the institutional design and is thus not illegal. The Land Management Law of 1986, which spells out in detail the exact compensation to be paid to farmers in the event of land conversion, is essentially premised on the agricultural value of land, whereas the sale price of the converted land is determined by nonagricultural value, between which lies a colossal gap in monetary value (especially where land is converted for real-estate development). In other words, as long as local governments convert land within the limits set by the central government and compensate the farmers according to legal stipulations, which is set at 6–10 times the average crop yield of the previous three years, plus a resettlement allowance set at 4–6 times the average yield of the previous three years, and lastly a locally determined crop compensation fee, land conversion conducted in accordance with these stipulations is legal. Indeed, local governments are assigned the rights to retain the profits from land conversion and are expected to deploy them rationally to developing the local economy.

LAND CONVERSION: LOW COMPENSATION A VIOLATION OF FARMERS' PROPERTY RIGHTS?

The extraordinarily strong incentives of local governments to boost fiscal revenues have far-reaching consequences both for China's arable resources and state–peasant relationships with regard to competition over these scarce resources. Although the state has officially set quotas on land conversion, local governments have strong incentives to circumvent the law. For instance, of the 837 appeal letters received by the central government in 2003 concerning land issues, fully 55 percent were related to illegal land expropriation and occupation of collective land (Yu 2005: 23).[13] This finding is consistent with the evidence that unauthorized conversion increased in 2003 amidst the decline in authorized conversion (Figure 17.5). Although it receded in 2004, by 2006 the Ministry of Land and Resources was still forced to issue an urgent circular to local officials who approved new land acquisitions without authorization from the central government. The circular warned them of possible consequences of party disciplinary sanctions, and also called upon the supervisory ministry to ensure better enforcement in the crackdown. In light of the trend that an average 200,000 hectares of farmland had been converted annually into non-arable usage (Chen Xiwen, cited in Wang Hongru 2006: 3), in 2007 China's premier Wen Jiabo warned gravely that China must rigorously protect its arable resources as it could ill afford to fall below the minimum threshold of 1.2 million square kilometers of arable land required for food self-sufficiency.

Even more seriously, as unauthorized land conversions often involved forced evictions of farmers from their land and homes, inadequate compensation, deferred payments, or downright embezzlement, they threatened social stability. Indeed, the "land issue" (*tudi wenti*) topped the list of the three key major agrarian issues (*sannong wenti*)—accounting for 68.7 percent of all responses in a CCTV telephone survey conducted in 2004. It is also not surprising that violent conflicts between villagers and local police over land disputes have repeatedly occurred since the early 2000s, with county and municipal governments being notable villains (Yu 2005).

To better understand the nature of property rights in the Chinese context it is necessary to invoke a little bit of history. In a nutshell, *de jure* private ownership of land with respect to bundle of use, income, and transfer rights ceased to exist in China after the Communist Party came to power in 1949 and collectivized agriculture in successive stages in the mid-to-late 1950s. Since decollectivizing its agriculture in the early 1980s, China's use and income rights have been reassigned to the farm households through land-leasing contracts which farmers signed with village authorities (*cun jiti*). Neither the right to alter the land's usage nor to transfer it to another party was conferred to the farmers, however. This crucial right to transfer the foregoing bundles of rights has remained firmly in the hands of the state and in part the village authorities. But as an increasing number of farmers leave for long-distance off-farm employment opportunities, it becomes apparent that it is necessary for the state to relax the grip placed upon farmers that keeps them from transferring their use and income rights in land—at least temporarily.

It is in this evolving context of development that the state further extended farmers' rights by allowing them to temporarily transfer their use rights or simply rent. According to the new Rural Land Contracting Law (*Nongcun tudi chengbaofa*) enacted in 2002, farm households are allowed to sublease their land to other farm households. To ensure that farmers are able to enjoy this limited transfer right, the state has even gone so far as to prohibit village authorities, the nominal owners, from periodically reallocating land among farm households in response to demographic changes—a customary practice embedded in the collective ownership nature of China's arable land. Unfortunately, this protection of farmers' transfer right is confined to only arable land use; once land is converted to non-arable usage the statutory power of the Rural Land Contracting Law ceases to apply.

In fact, nationalization has been the only legal mechanism by which farmland, which is *de jure* collectively owned, can be converted into non-arable uses. According to Article 63 of the Land Management Law of 1999, the legal statutes governing land conversion, farmers do not possess the right to convert arable land into non-arable usage; only the (nominal) owner, meaning the local authorities, is empowered to do so. Moreover, any non-arable usage of collective farmland requires a corresponding change in ownership—specifically from collective to state ownership (Article 43). Apart from the minimal compensation stipulated by the state, which therefore is liable to legal protection, China's farmers are thus subject totally to the whims of local authorities in the process of land conversion.

As mentioned earlier, even in the best-case scenario where local governments observe the quota limits of land conversion and abide by the procedures of compensation, the massive disparity between the "windfall profits" resulting from selling the farmland for commercial and real-estate development on the one hand, and the measly compensation made to farmers on the other, has created an enormous sense of injustice from the latter's point of view.

In the process of land conversion, local authorities have triggered serious conflicts with the farmers, who feel that they have been robbed of the bundle of rights assigned to them at the outset of the reform. From this vantage point it is thus ironic that, while the state has legislated to protect farmers' use rights by prohibiting local authorities from periodically reallocating land, it accords the same authorities the monopoly right to grab land away from the village community with only minimal compensation. Although they are nominally "members" of the village collective, farmers are basically unable to defend their collectively held land rights against the local authorities. With this power bestowed upon them and, more specifically, with a clearly defined compensation formula stipulated by the central state, many local authorities simply find it unnecessary to negotiate with the peasants for a fair compensation; the major binding constraint in determining compensation appears to be the threshold value of avoiding social unrest. Thus, although local authorities are supposed to act in the interests of the farmers, in particular in guarding their collective land rights, more often than not they have turned out to be robbers of valuable communal resources.

CONCLUSION

China's sustained economic growth since 1978 has occurred in a highly decentralized context of "yardstick competition" among regions facing similar external conditions. While the initial decentralization-based reform led to the phenomenal success of industrial growth (in the form of TVEs) in many regions, the reassignment of fiscal rights over various tax categories and revenues has subsequently induced some local governments to focus disproportionately on "urbanization." The key impetus behind this drive for "urbanization" lies in the conversion of farmland into commercial usage, and the construction and real-estate sectors associated therewith. The exclusive income and monopoly rights of local authorities over land conversion have powerfully predisposed them to maximize their fiscal coffers at the expense of farmers' rights in agricultural land. However, the legal rights with which local officials have been assigned and the biased incentives embedded in these rights have led to ever-worsening social conflicts. To arrest these adverse tendencies, the central government has endeavored both to crack down on land conversion and development and to temper the growing rural social unrest. However, a thorough solution would require more than mere piecemeal attempts to contain these problems; just as in the case of previous reforms, further reforms down the road of transition and growth will require a reconfiguration of existing institutions and their attendant property rights structure.

NOTES

1. Comments from the IPD China Task Force Manchester Workshop, particularly Joseph Stiglitz, Christine Wong, and an anonymous referee, are gratefully acknowledged. We thank Xiulin Sun for helpful research assistance.
2. While the term usually refers to the provincial level and below, in this paper we are mostly concerned with the economic behavior of lower-level government authorities spanning the municipal and township authorities.
3. Jean Oi (1999) describes this revenue-sharing fiscal contracting system most succinctly: "Revenue sharing is a process in which local governments down to the level of township have the responsibility for collecting all nationally set taxes and then turning over a portion of this revenue to the next higher level. Those who have increased their tax revenues are allowed to keep the major portion of the increase. The provisions of revenue sharing are formalized in fiscal contracts between the central state and each of its provinces, between each province and its prefectures, between each prefecture and its counties, and between each county and its township" (p. 29).
4. For example, even if the tasks of agents are similar but outside random factors that agents face do not follow the same distribution, the principal would be unable to compare the performance of one agent with that of the other even if the absolute performance of both can be observed.
5. Oi (1999) notes that the terms of the contracts vary from one place to another; while some areas employ an overall ratio such as 70:30 (with the level of government from which the taxes are collected keeping 70 percent whereas the immediate supervising level keeps 30 percent), others merely pay a fixed lump-sum quota to the next higher level (p. 29). "Regardless of the system of revenue sharing in effect, increased tax collection guarantees a locality an increase in tax revenue" (Oi 1999: 30).
6. Although county-level industrial firms continued to be the bedrock of county-level income and taxes, their tax contribution decreased as a proportion of total revenues over time as TVEs grew (Wong 1991; Naughton 1992).
7. In 1985 enterprise income tax was extended to township and village enterprises in replacing the industrial-commercial income tax (see Oi 1999: 35).
8. Oi (1999), for instance, has found that rich counties tended to grant more tax breaks than did poor counties (p. 38).
9. The existing literature predicts that when the protection of private property rights has improved, when asset markets are better developed, and/or when large-scale migration has occurred, the ownership advantage of TVEs tends to become suboptimal and privatization is more likely to occur. Evidence is consistent with these predictions (Xu 2011).
10. The percentage of the Chinese population classified as "urban"—those residing in townships and above—increased from less than 18 percent in 1978 to 43 percent in 2006 (State Statistical Bureau of China 2007).
11. It was first introduced in 1989 as a shared arrangement between the central and regional governments under the provisional regulation "Temporary regulation on the transfer of use rights of state-owned land in towns and cities." When it was amended in 1994, the state allowed regional governments to appropriate in full the proceeds from transferring the use rights of state-owned land.
12. Statistics show that farmland decreased by as much as 120 million *mu* (1 *mu* = 0.0667 hectare) between 1996 and 2005 or 6.6 percent of the total arable land (Ministry of Land and Resources 2006).

13. The next major reason, which accounted for 23 percent, pertains to compensation being "too low or misappropriated."

REFERENCES

Chen, Y., Li, H., and Zhou, L. (2005), "Relative Performance Evaluation and the Turnover of Provincial Leaders in China," *Economics Letters*, 88/3: 421–5.

Edin, M. (2003), "State Capacity and Local Agent Control in China: CCP Cadre Management from a Township Perspective," *China Quarterly*, 173 (March): 35–52.

Editorial Committee (1995–7), *Statistical Yearbook of China's Land [Zhongguo tudi nianjian]* (Beijing: Renmin Chubanshe).

Jin, H., Qian, Y., and Weingast, B. (2005), "Regional Decentralization and Fiscal Incentives: Federalism, Chinese-Style," *Journal of Public Economics*, 89/9–10: 1719–42.

Kung, J. K. and Lin, Y. (2007), "The Rise and Decline of Local Public Enterprises in China's Economic Transition," *World Development*, 35/4: 569–84.

Li, H. and Zhou, L. (2005), "Political Turnover and Economic Performance: The Incentive Role of Personnel Control in China," *Journal of Public Economics*, 89/9–10: 1743–62.

Lin, G. and Ho, S. (2005), "The State, Land System, and Land Development in Contemporary China," *Annals of the Association of American Geographers*, 95/2: 411–36.

Lin, J. Y. and Liu, Z. (2000), "Fiscal Decentralization and Economic Growth in China," *Economic Development and Cultural Change*, 49/1: 1–21.

Maskin, E., Qian, Y., and Xu, C. (2000), "Incentives, Information, and Organizational Form," *Review of Economic Studies*, 67/2: 359–78.

Ming Pao Daily News (2007a), "Land Expropriation in Shantou Induced Villagers' Attacks of Cadres [*Zhengdi Lianbao Chongtu, Shantou Cunmin Xiguan*]," May 8, A9.

—— (2007b), "Villagers in Shantou Set Deadline for Factory Relocation [*Shantou Cunmin Wei Gongchang Xianqi Banzou*]," May 11, A29.

Ministry of Land and Resources (1999–2003), *Almanac of China's Land and Resources [Zhongguo guotu ziyuan nianjian]* (Beijing: Zhongguo Tudi Chubanshe).

—— (1999–2006), *The Land Resource Yearbook of China [Zhongguo Guotu Ziyuan Nianjian]* (Beijing: Renmin Chubanshe).

National Bureau of Statistics (2005), *A Compendium of Statistics for the 55 Years of New China, 1949–2004 [Xinzhongguo Wushiwu Nian Tongji Ziliao Huibian, 1994–2004]* (Beijing: Zhongguo Tongji Chubanshe).

Naughton, B. (1992), "Implications of the State Monopoly over Industry and Its Relaxation," *Modern China*, 18/1: 14–41.

—— (2007), *The Chinese Economy: Transitions and Growth* (Cambridge, MA: MIT Press).

Oi, J. C. (1999), *Rural China Takes Off: Institutional Foundations of Economic Reform* (Berkeley: University of California Press).

Qian, Y. and Xu, C. (1993), "Why China's Economic Reform Differ: The M-form Hierarchy and Entry/Expansion of the Non-state Sector," *Economics of Transition*, 1/2: 135–70.

Research Center on Chinese Communist Party History (2009), *Major Events in the People's Republic of China, 1949–2009 [Zhonghua Renmin Gongheguo Dashiji, 1949–2009]*. (Beijing: The People's Press [Renmin Chubanshe]).

Shirk, Susan L. (1993), *The Political Logic of Economic Reform in China* (Berkeley: University of California Press).

South China Morning Post (2007), "Officials Warned on Illegal Land Deals," August 15, pp. 3.

State Land Administration Bureau (1995–7), *The Land Yearbook of China [Zhongguo Tudi Nianjian]* (Beijing: Renmin Chubanshe).

State Statistical Bureau of China (2007), *China Statistical Yearbook 2007* (Beijing: Zhongguo Tongji Chubanshe).

State Administration of Taxation (2005), *The Taxation Yearbook of China* [*Zhongguo Shuiwu Nianjian*] (Beijing: Zhongguo Shuiwu Chubanshe).

Tsui, K. Y. and Wang, Y. (2004), "Between Separate Stoves and a Single Menu: Fiscal Decentralization in China," *China Quarterly*, 177 (May): 71–90.

Wang, H. (2006), "Land Disputes Hasten the Reform of Land-Requisition Institutions [*Tudi Jiufen Jicui Zhengdi Zhidu Gaige*]," *China Economic Weekly*, 9.

Wang, S. and Hu, A. (1993), *Report on China's State Capability* [*Zhongguo Guo Jia Neng Li Bao Gao*] (Shenyang: Liaoning Renmin Chubanshe).

—— —— (2001), *The Chinese Economy in Crisis: State Capacity and Tax Reform* (Armonk, NY: M. E. Sharpe).

Weitzman, M. L. and Xu, C. (1994), "Chinese Township Village Enterprises as Vaguely Defined Cooperatives," *Journal of Comparative Economics*, 18/2: 121–45.

Whiting, S. H. (2000), *Power and Wealth in Rural China: The Political Economy of Institutional Change* (Cambridge: Cambridge University Press).

Williamson, O. E. (1985), *The Economic Institutions of Capitalism: Firms, Markets, and Relational Contracting* (New York: Free Press).

Wong, C. P. (1991), "Central-Local Relations in an Era of Fiscal Decline: The Paradox of Fiscal Decentralization in Post-Mao China," *China Quarterly*, 128: 691–715.

Xu, C. (2011), "The Fundamental Institutions of China's Reforms and Development," *Journal of Economic Literature*, forthcoming.

Xu, X., Xianbin, W., and Yuan, S. (2007), "Local Officials and Economic Growth [*Difang Guanyuan Yu Jingji Zengzhang*]," *Economic Research Journal* [*Jingji Yanjiu*], 9 (September): 18–32.

Yu, J. (2005), "Land Issues Have Become the Focus in Peasants' Safeguarding of their Legal Rights—A Special Study of Contemporary Rural Society in China [*Tudi Wenti Yi Chengwei Nongmin Weiquan Kangzheng De Jiaodian*]," *The World of Survey and Research* [*Diaoyan Shijie*], 3: 22–3.

Zhou, F. (2006), "Ten Years of Fiscal Tax Revenue-Sharing: the Institution and Its Impact [*Fenshuizhi Shinian: Zhidu Jiqi Yingxiang*]," *Social Science in China* [*Zhongguo Shehui Kexue*], 6: 100–5.

—— (2007), "The Road to Riches: Governments and Peasants in Land Development [*Shengcai Youdao: Tudi Kaifa Zhong De Zhengfu He Nongmin*]," *The Sociological Study* [*Shehuixue Yanjiu*], 1: 49–82.

Zhou, Q. (2004), "Rural Property Rights and the Institution of Land-Requisition—Critical Choice in China's Rapid Urbanization [*Nongdi Chanquan Yu Zhengdi zhidu: Jisu De Zhongguo Chengshihua Mianlin De Zhongda Xuanze*]," *China Economic Quarterly* [*Jingjixue Jikan*], 4/1: 193–210.

18

China's Network Justice*

*Benjamin L. Liebman and Tim Wu***†‡

INTRODUCTION

China's Internet revolution has set off a furious debate in the West. Optimists from Thomas Friedman to Bill Clinton have predicted the crumbling of the Chinese party-state, while pessimists suggest even greater state control. But a far less discussed and researched subject is the effect of China's Internet revolution on its domestic institutions. This article, the product of extensive interviews across China, asks a new and different question. What has China's Internet revolution meant for its legal system? What does cheaper, if not free, speech mean for Chinese judges?

The broader goal of this article is to better understand the relationship between how a legal system functions and how judges communicate, both with each other and with other parties, including the media, the public, and political actors. Information transmission is an important but poorly understood part of any legal system. A precedent system, *amici* briefs, and the rules on ex parte contacts all serve to regulate how parties in a system communicate and what kind of information "counts." Media and political pressure cannot help but affect a legal system. In the words of Ethan Katsh, "Law is an organism whose lifeblood is information and media of communication are the veins and arteries."[1]

The People's Republic of China stands as a useful case to study the effects of changing means of communications on a legal system. Over the last fifteen years the Chinese legal system has undergone important transformations in the costs and means of disseminating information—the consequence both of new technologies and of the simultaneous commercialization of the Chinese media. This has led to changes in both the information available to judges and the attention paid to the judiciary's decisions. Such changes have come precisely as the Chinese courts are undergoing dramatic reforms, the stated aim of which is to make courts more competent, fair, and authoritative actors in the Chinese political system.

While necessarily an exercise in extrapolation, we can take several predictions from Western communications theory as to the likely impact of changing communications technology for Chinese courts. First, the optimistic side of American communications theory suggests that greater exposure to information and ease of communications will usually be good for a political system, including its legal system. While primarily writing about the United States, writers like Yochai

Benkler, Eugene Volokh, and Glenn Reynolds have argued that cheaper mass communications technology will improve government and lead to healthier political systems.[2] As Benkler writes, "we are [now] witnessing a fundamental change in how individuals can interact with their democracy and experience their role as citizens."[3]

Our study of the Chinese judiciary[4] reveals some evidence to support the optimistic theory—exciting examples of Internet pressure that have uncovered injustice and forced courts and Chinese Communist Party ("Party") officials to take action. But overall, we find a mixed picture that includes both optimistic, headline-grabbing stories and decidedly ambiguous developments.

Second, a different line of American scholars, writing in the 1990s, argued generally that the effects of electronic publishing and communications would be as profound for legal systems as the invention of printing itself. "Broad change is occurring to the law," wrote Ethan Katsh in 1989, "to what it is and how it works, and these changes are linked to the appearance of new methods of storing, processing and communicating information."[5] While this thesis seems weakly supported in the US context,[6] it may find greater strength in China. In other words, it is in the Chinese legal system where judges are treating electronic sources of information in ways different than they have treated print sources. It may be in China where some of the communications-driven changes predicted by Katsh and others have found a home.

We present three groups of findings. The first, under the heading *Net Justice*, are developments in communications between the judiciary and the media, the public, and the Party officials who oversee both the courts and the media. The media and the public's newfound ease in ascertaining what judges are doing has already had important benefits. In cases such as that of Sun Zhigang—a university graduate brutally murdered in a detention center for migrant workers[7]—it is clear that Internet and media pressure led to both judicial action and salutary institutional reform. But on the flip side, the Internet has also been used to generate extreme public pressure and consequent political intervention in reaction to certain types of inflammatory cases. That is, of course, not an entirely new development. The Chinese legal system has long been characterized by party-state intervention in important or sensitive cases. The difference is the rise of cases where public reaction and outrage online leads officials to intervene and predetermine or change judicial action. In one of the examples discussed below, Internet pressure resulted in a convicted gangster, Liu Yong, having the reduction of his sentence from death to life in prison reversed and being swiftly put to death. The same efficiencies of communication that make exposing unfair or unjust decisions easier also facilitate, and make more likely, public pressure and political intervention.

The second set of findings is under *Judicial Networks*, which discusses developments in the communications patterns among judges. There are signs of important changes in how Chinese judges communicate with each other. Chinese judges have traditionally made decisions based on consultation that is mostly *vertical*—with "adjudication committees" within the courts that resolve difficult or sensitive cases or between judges, court presidents, Communist Party Political-Legal Committees, and higher courts. Judges have had limited abilities to consult with other members of the judiciary outside their court, other than those in directly superior courts, and sometimes have had limited access to relevant laws and other legal materials. Today, much is changing, particularly through use of the Internet and other communications technologies. Chinese judges increasingly communicate and consult along *horizontal* lines, including with other judges, and also with academics and the public. Many judges use the Internet from home or web cafes to do extra research, finding either Chinese or foreign cases. Judges report an emerging and informal system of quasi-precedent made possible by horizontal networking. Judges' decisions are also much better publicized through a variety of means, including the Internet, and as a result are subject to more external criticism.

Third, under the section *Innovative Uses*, our study shows that some Chinese judges have begun to use the Internet as a judicial tool in ways that are unusual and perhaps unprecedented in other parts of the world. For example, some judges use chat rooms and email in the course of deciding hard cases, communicating with other judges, academics, and even the public. Other judges and courts maintain blogs that comment on cases, and make their case decisions available to the public and other judges. These types of behavior are relatively unique and may lead to distinctly Chinese judicial communications practices.

The study of China's judiciary yields important and general insights into the poorly understood relationship between judicial power and judicial speech. As generations of American scholars have suggested, the power of the judiciary to act independently from other branches depends on the availability and acceptability of higher principles to which judges may appeal. Whether it be to Herbert Wechsler's "neutral principles," to tradition, or to accepted moral doctrine contemplated by others,[8] the degree to which society and other government actors accept the principles to which judges appeal does much to determine the judiciary's power.

The changes in communications affect both the accountability and the authority of the Chinese judiciary. The claims to legitimacy are strengthened through access to the laws themselves, and through the ease of forming judicial networks. As horizontal, judge-to-judge communications become easier and cheaper, judges can make new claims to the authority to decide cases according to cases already decided. Networked judges, like common-law judges, also gain the ability to learn from other judges.[9] The development of horizontal judicial networking may be a crucial means for strengthening the autonomy and professional identity of courts.

But there is a flip side: cheap communications also affect how accountable judges are, in every meaning of that term. Cheaper speech makes it easier to attack the judiciary and diminish its legitimacy. This is particularly true where, as in China, speech is cheap but not free. In the Chinese example, we see an extreme version—the "Internet manhunt" leading to political intervention—with important lessons for the rest of the world. The dominant writing on Internet criticism in the United States stresses improvements in government and media accountability. Yet not all criticism is socially useful, and when criticism is used as a political weapon against an already weak judiciary it does not improve governance but endangers progress toward a rule of law system. At its worst, and when supported by the state, cheap mass criticism can cause judges to become unwilling to make decisions that run the risk of inflaming the public, thereby causing a surrender of judicial authority to the vicissitudes of public opinion.

This Article is divided into three parts. Part I introduces theoretical background on the relationship between communications technologies and government and judicial behavior. Part II is a study of the Chinese judiciary. Part III discusses the relationship between speech and judicial legitimacy.

I. SPEECH AND INFORMATION IN A LEGAL SYSTEM

A. Free Speech, Information, and Government

Since the early twentieth century, the relationship among communications technologies, government, and free speech has been a field of intense interest. The rise of the telegraph, telephone, and the mass media of the twentieth century led writers from Charles Cooley through Wilbur Schramm and Marshall McCullen to forecast great changes in human governance.[10] This is the field of "communications studies," which in its earliest days tended to optimism. Charles Cooley wrote with moving confidence that technologies such as the telegraph might "make it possible for society to be organized more and more on the higher faculties of man, on intelligence and sympathy, rather than authority, caste, and routine."[11] These ideas reflected both a faith in technological progress and the more general belief in the power of free speech to improve society embodied in the American First Amendment.

One hundred years later, the optimism of the early 1900s was reborn during the Internet revolution of the 1990s. Consistent with the American free speech tradition, commentary has been mostly buoyant. It suggests, with a few exceptions, that cheaper speech will yield a more participatory democratic culture, more attention to public opinion, and generally better and more responsive governments.

A small group of writers in the late 1980s and 1990s confronted the specific impact of changing communications technologies on the operation of legal systems.[12] Included in such arguments is the recognition that a prior change in technology—the birth of printing—played an important role in shaping Anglo-American legal systems, and in forming a common-law system of precedent.[13] Ethan Katsh's writing is the exemplar. He characterized the American legal system of the 1990s as deeply integrated with, and reflective of, print media. "It is not 'fine print,'" wrote Katsh, "that characterizes the law, but print itself. Print affected the organization, growth and distribution of legal information."[14] "Law," writes Katsh, "has been conditioned in many ways by various characteristics and constraints of traditional modes of communication, particularly print." Katsh predicted dramatic changes in the law's operation produced by the different property of the texts themselves. "The electronic media are not to be considered merely as more powerful versions of print. They have different mechanisms for transmitting and processing information, some of which will pressure the law to change course and become a different and not simply a more efficient institution."[15]

In the 2000s, a different and independent body of scholarship promoted the possibilities of Internet communications for improving the nature of national deliberation, in particular by supplementing or replacing traditional media as the primary source of scrutiny of government. One of the first to present what we can now call "blogger theory" was Professor Eugene Volokh, in *Cheap Speech and What It Will Do.*[16] Yochai Benkler presented a full treatment of this thesis in his book, *The Wealth of Networks,*[17] as did writer Dan Gilmour in *We The Media*[18] and law professor and blogger Glenn Reynolds in *An Army of Davids.*[19]

These latter authors present an attractive thesis: in a country where every citizen has the means to act as a critic, the result will be a more responsive government. Roughly, the premise is that the marketplace of ideas has been hindered by barriers to entry. The high costs of communications have stood in the way of regular citizens participating in political discourse, leaving participation to specialized entities such as professional interest groups and the professional media. But since the 1990s, the decreased costs of communication made possible by technological changes have facilitated greater access to the political process, making it possible for amateurs and regular citizens to be involved. As Benkler writes, the rise of the Internet has "fundamentally altered the capacity of individuals, acting alone or with others, to be active participants in the public sphere as opposed to its passive readers, listeners, or viewers. . . . It is in this sense that the Internet democratizes."[20]

The dissent from this view has come in clearest form from Professor Cass Sunstein in his books *Republic.com* and *Echo Chambers.*[21] Sunstein argues that technologies such as the Internet are not aiding national political discourse but splintering it. "If Republicans are talking only with Republicans, if Democrats are talking primarily with Democrats, if members of the religious right speak mostly to each other, and if radical feminists talk largely to radical feminists, there is a potential for the development of different forms of extremism, and for profound mutual misunderstandings with individuals outside the group."[22] A glut of information and the ease of listening to only what you agree with, argues Sunstein, will lead to national factions that generally ignore one another—the fractionalization of the Republic.[23]

China's own Internet revolution has touched off a similar debate. Many argued that, in Thomas Friedman's words, "the Internet and globalization, are acting like nutcrackers to open societies." Bill Clinton argued that the Internet will "democratize opportunity in the world in a way that has never been the case in all of human history,"[24] while George W. Bush argued that, in China, the Internet takes "freedom's genie . . . out of the bottle." However, so far the political change forecast in the 1990s has been far less than predicted. In previous work, we have explored many of the ways the party-state has managed to maintain a grip on political power despite the dramatic changes in communications. We have suggested that, in some ways, the party-state has honed its use and control of information flows for political purposes.[25] Nonetheless, writers from Friedman through Nicolas Kristof continue to argue that the party-state's grip will not survive the Internet revolution. As Kristof wrote in a 2005 column, *Death by a Thousand Blogs,* "the Chinese leadership . . . is digging the Communist Party's grave, by giving the Chinese people broadband."[26]

In this article we come at these debates from a new angle by providing detailed evidence of what is actually happening in China. What much of the present debate misses is what happens when speech becomes far *cheaper*, yet still not *free*—where some forms of criticism are allowed, but not others.[27] In our example of China, direct criticism of Party rule is off limits, yet critiques of the courts are more acceptable. The consequence, as we will see, is a directed form of criticism whose social function is not well appreciated by our existing and dominant means of understanding speech.

This study is also an opportunity to examine the impact of focused criticism not on government in general, but on the courts specifically. Previous writing in this area, with some exceptions,[28] has not devoted much attention to the intricate relationship between mass, inexpert participation made possible by the Internet, and the functioning of a legal system. The American free speech case law does concede the need for restrictions on speech *within* the courts, and in exceptional cases for restrictions on media coverage of court proceedings, but the effects of cheaper speech on the judiciary itself are not as well understood. There is a simple explanation for this. In the United States, the most obvious consequences of the Internet revolution have been for the media and business. Conversely, the operation of the judiciary has been far less affected. This may reflect the American judiciary's particular tradition of independence and relative isolation from the direct influence of public opinion. Aside from better legal blogging, an occasional URL citation in Supreme Court opinions, and greater competition for Westlaw and Lexis, it may be that few of the decision-making methods of courts have changed, so far.

But it is unsurprising that different countries are affected differently by a major change in the costs of communications. The effects of the Internet on the Chinese legal system are arguably far more profound than in Europe or the United States. Yet since these developments are largely not discussed in the West, we find ourselves writing on new ground, with regard to both China and the broader question of how new technologies may be affecting judicial decision-making.

Judges are decision-makers, and to pursue the question of how information affects judging, the tools of information economics will prove useful. For that reason, we turn now to a review of some of the relevant literature on information transmission and decision-making.

B. The Economics of Information and Decision-Making

Fredrich Hayek's 1945 work *The Use of Knowledge in Society* is a starting point for much of what has followed on the relevance of information to decision-making.[29] Hayek argued that the advantages of the free market over a planned economy were largely related to how a free market makes use of information. The free market, he pointed out, is not obviously more efficient than a centralized, planned production, since competition tends to be disorganized, duplicative, and wasteful. Instead, said Hayek, the problem with models of centralized planning is informational: no single actor can possess sufficient information to make all the decisions necessary in a complex economy. Conversely, the market's decentralized decisions about production, while certainly prone to error and waste, are at least made on the basis of much more of the relevant information—leading to, in the aggregate, better decision-making. Market prices, in Hayek's view, were valuable pieces of public information about resource scarcity that a centralized planner had difficulty replicating.

The study of decision-making given imperfect information has developed into an entire field since Hayek's time, often called "information economics."[30] The tools of information economics are valuable for understanding the importance of communications within a legal system.

First, in the information economics literature, a major distinction is made between decision structures that are more horizontal or "polyarchical" in nature, and those that are more vertical, or "hierarchical."[31] That difference in decision structures is, for example, an essential difference between a planned and market economy. Economists Raaj Kumar Sah and Joseph Stiglitz originally focused on the differences between hierarchies and polyarchies for purposes of error correction. But other writers, including economist Jeremy Stein, write about the differences in information transmission in vertically—and horizontally—organized institutions.[32]

One type of decentralized decision-making system of great interest is common-law courts. First, Hayek himself in 1960 argued that the English legal system was a superior institution to the French, based on its decentralized decision-making.[33] Later, Richard Posner described the common-law litigation process as a source of rules—and viewed judges as decentralized decision-makers acting on the basis of local information, whose collective decision-making might, over time, reach efficient results.[34] The challenges to Posner's thesis are well known.[35] Nonetheless, the theory of common-law "learning" and the potential of moving toward better rules has been influential.[36]

A second and particularly useful tool from information economics is the theory of the "rational herd" or "information cascade." The herding literature is interested in the puzzles of mass behavior, like fashion trends, and mass mistakes, such as stock market bubbles or the tendency of mutual fund managers to underperform the market. These theories explain what happens when decision-makers weigh not only their own judgment, but the collective volume of the decisions of others.[37] The phenomenon of rational herding identifies situations where decisions are decreasingly driven by one's own information and increasingly driven by the actions of others.

The notion of rational herding has obvious implications for a legal system. The prospect is that judges may similarly, and rationally, herd around a bad or suboptimal rule, yet due to the weight of cases behind the rule, be increasingly hesitant to run against the crowd. Economists Andrew Daughety and Jennifer F. Reinganum, in their paper on horizontal judicial herding, gave the example of *Eastern Enterprises v Apfel*, where six circuit courts had agreed a law was constitutional but were later reversed by the Supreme Court.[38] The example showed that, perhaps due to herding effects, errors might remain long uncorrected in a common-law system.

The prospect of judicial herding may seem like a serious challenge to the utility of a common-law system. But as we discuss in Part III, doing what other judges have done in similar cases may also be desirable—for it is a means for judges to build their own political power. Herding may also be another way to say "following a rule."[39] As Eric Talley has written, healthy legal systems aim for a balance between blind obedience and learning.[40] They employ devices, like life tenure, or the technique of distinguishing cases, that allow judges to break from suboptimal rules when they deem it necessary. An ideal system ought simultaneously to provide predictability and the capacity to adapt, despite the apparent contradiction.

These tools from information economics literature help us understand what is at stake when we study communications within a judicial system. We now turn to our empirical study of recent developments in the communications practices in the Chinese judiciary.

II. CHINESE JUDGES AND THE INTERNET

Before beginning our analysis of the impact of the Internet on the Chinese courts, we offer a brief primer in the functioning of China's courts and the Chinese media.[41] China has a lot of judges—most estimates say about 200,000, or roughly twice the number of lawyers. Until recently, relatively few Chinese judges had significant legal training: reports in mid-2005 stated that, for the first time, more than 50 percent of judges were university graduates. A decade earlier the figure was just 12 percent. In the past, many judges were retired military officials or government cadres. As of 2002, however, new judges are required to be university graduates and to pass the difficult national bar exam (which has a pass rate of about 10 percent). The Supreme People's Court ("SPC") has also devoted enormous resources to training existing judges. Many of those who lack formal training in law have been required to attend night school or special training programs. Older judges who lack legal training are being pushed into early retirement or are sometimes no longer permitted to hear cases.

For much of the reform period (1978–present), China's courts have remained relatively minor actors in the Chinese political system. Courts lack significant power over other state institutions and have no formal powers of judicial review. Under the Chinese Constitution, only the National People's Congress and its Standing Committee have the power to interpret laws or the Constitution, though in practice the SPC plays an important role in interpreting the law.

China's legal system is national and unitary, with four levels of courts. Most first-instance cases are brought in basic-level courts in counties or in districts within cities. Appeals from such cases go to intermediate courts in municipalities, or *shi*. Intermediate courts also hear certain categories of first-instance cases—generally those involving large sums of money or serious crimes, but also sometimes cases that are politically sensitive. Provincial high courts (and the high courts of municipalities with provincial rank, such as Beijing and Shanghai) oversee the courts in their provinces, hear appeals from intermediate courts, and have the power to rehear cases brought in all lower courts in their jurisdiction. The SPC, with hundreds of judges, manages the court bureaucracy, hears appeals and rehearings, and issues a large volume of interpretive documents intended to guide lower courts in the application of the law. These range from formal interpretations of laws, which often read like statutes themselves, to responses to courts regarding the handling of individual cases pending in lower courts.

Court caseloads have grown significantly since the beginning of legal reforms in the late 1970s—with some stating that China is now experiencing a "litigation explosion." Over the last five years the total number of cases heard in China has held steady at about eight million a year. Courts continue to be one of many state institutions with responsibility for resolving disputes and hearing grievances.

Problems in the Chinese courts have received widespread attention in both the Chinese and international media. Corruption is said to be common, courts often lack the power to enforce their decisions, and external intervention in pending cases is widespread. Intervention comes from a range of sources. Local Party officials frequently pressure the courts in cases involving key local interests. Courts find it hard to resist such pressure, in particular because judges depend on the local Party for their jobs and salaries. Court appointments (and removals from office) are generally made by the local Party branch and government, and court budgets are dependent on local governments. Communist Party Political-Legal Committees, which include senior police, court, procuratorate, justice bureau, and Party officials, exist at each level of the party-state, and discuss (and sometimes issue written suggestions in) major cases. People's Congresses—China's legislatures—have the formal power to "supervise" the courts, and may from time to time issue requests or views to courts regarding cases. Individual officials also may intervene in cases of particular concern, issuing written instructions to the courts regarding pending cases, or sometimes simply discussing cases with court presidents.

In contrast to the courts, the Chinese media have long occupied a privileged position in the Chinese political system. The media serve as both the mouthpiece and the "eyes and ears" of the Party—not only writing public reports that appear in print or in broadcasts, but also "internal reports." Internal reports contain information for officials of a particular rank, and are deemed not suitable for public dissemination. This means that when media views conflict with those in the courts, Party officials tend to side with the media.

Commercialization of the Chinese media in the 1990s resulted in major changes. Thousands of new publications appeared, mostly offshoots of traditional Party mouthpiece newspapers. These commercialized papers compete fiercely with one another, often by providing sensational or hard-hitting reports. They also generate profits for their parent publications, which continue in their "official" or "mouthpiece" propaganda roles. The growth of the Internet brought further competition, with papers and web portals now competing to attract readers online as well as in print, often by providing content that skirts the edges of what is permissible.

China's media regulatory system, although challenged by the growth of commercialized media and the Internet, remains fundamentally unchanged. Regulations restrict who can enter the market—ensuring that the overwhelming majority of publications and broadcasters in China are state-controlled (albeit often in corporatized form). The Party's Central Propaganda Department ("CPD") oversees all media content, relying on both circulars that prohibit certain content, and also on a system of post-publication sanctions that target those who go beyond permissible boundaries. Local propaganda departments at the provincial, municipal, and local level likewise oversee content in local media, often supplementing CPD restrictions with their own local restrictions on content.

The job of the CPD and local and provincial propaganda departments has become much more difficult in recent years. The commercialization of the media means that there is vastly more content available than at any prior point in Chinese history. And the growth of the Internet, as we will show, means that news spreads much more quickly than before—often before propaganda departments can react to impose bans. Chinese authorities have not been passive in response to such challenges. As has been widely reported in the Western media, China devotes substantial resources to monitoring and controlling the Internet. This includes ordering websites to prohibit discussion of certain topics or to remove controversial articles. Sites that go too far are shut down. One result is that self-censorship by commercial Internet news providers is perhaps the most effective means by which authorities maintain control over reporting and discussion of controversial topics online.

The following sections set forth our empirical findings. They are based on extensive review of Chinese writings and on interviews with more than one hundred scholars, reporters, lawyers, and judges about the impact of the Internet on China's courts. Interviews with judges were conducted in three provinces in China and in two cities with provincial rank. Judges surveyed ranged from those sitting on provincial high courts, to well-educated judges in major cities, to judges in small county towns who lacked formal training in law.[42] We freely admit the limitations of our methodology: those likely to interact with us are most likely younger, more liberal, and more likely to use the Internet, than many others in China. Nevertheless, their descriptions of the impact of the Internet provide a crucial base for understanding the important changes we believe are taking place in China's courts.

A. External Pressures

China's own Internet revolution has made it much easier for the public, the media, and the party-state to become aware of and criticize the Chinese legal system and its courts. Although that may sound good, the results, from a rule-of-law perspective, have both attractive and less attractive aspects.

Sometimes cheaper information has meant better accountability and pressure for important reform. As we discuss below, courts or legal institutions that are neglecting or deliberately abusing their duties can be exposed and subjected to public or media pressure. Bad decisions, corrupt judges, and unjust procedures are sometimes brought to light by Internet communications, leading to important reforms.

Yet the same mechanism can create excessive pressure on the courts. As we discuss, unpopular decisions can attract a strong public reaction—the "Internet manhunt"—and subsequent political intervention to quell public outrage. The Internet plays a crucial role in making both Party leadership and the courts aware of public opinion, which is important in a system in which other outlets for public opinion are restricted. But the effect may be more mixed in a system where only one segment of public opinion is being heard, where the media play an active role in generating popular outrage online, and when such opinion is significantly restricted due to Party control and oversight of the media.

1. Greater Accountability

In 2003, Sun Zhigang, a university graduate working as a graphic designer in the southern city of Guangzhou, was detained by police for failing to have the temporary residence permits required of migrant workers. Three days after his arrest Sun was beaten to death while in a local detention center for migrants.[43]

More than a month after Sun's killing, on April 25, 2003, the leading commercial newspaper in Guangdong Province, *Southern Metropolitan Daily*, carried a report on the case, entitled "Only Missing a Temporary Residence Permit, College Graduate Is Beaten to Death." Local Communist Party Propaganda Department officials immediately banned any further discussion of the case in the local media. But the ban was ineffective. The *Southern Metropolitan Daily* article had already been posted to the paper's website on the day of publication, and had been subsequently reposted to numerous other websites. It even showed up on the website of the *People's Daily*, the mouthpiece of the Party.

Within hours, Internet discussion forums filled with discussion of the case.[44] Noting the article in the *People's Daily*, numerous other newspapers subsequently reported on the case, carrying follow-up stories that were also posted and reposted online. On May 13, three weeks after the original report and following weeks of online discussion of the case, authorities announced that they had detained thirteen suspects. A month later, twelve defendants were convicted for their roles in the case, and the two "primary culprits" were sentenced to death and life in prison, respectively.[45]

The impact of the case—and of the Internet—did not end with the trial. Following the arrests in May, a group of academics and journalists launched an assault on the detention system, known as Custody and Repatriation, under which Sun had been apprehended. In an effort coordinated with print and online media, two groups of lawyers and scholars issued petitions calling on the system to be abolished because it was unconstitutional. The petitions themselves were not printed in full in the official media, but were widely available online.[46] Media coverage highlighted their demands, leading to online discussion and reposting of the petition.[47] Reports also noted some of the widespread abuses in the system, including numerous reports of other inmates also being murdered while in detention. Websites provided significantly wider-ranging discussions of the case than those appearing in the traditional media.[48]

Shortly after the June trial of the defendants in the Sun Zhigang case, China's State Council announced that the Custody and Repatriation System was being scrapped and replaced with a system designed to shift the emphasis from punishing migrants to assisting them by establishing "a caring assistance system" of "aid stations" that provide migrants with shelter and food.[49] Although official comments stated that the changes simply reflected changed conditions in China while others involved in the drafting of the new regulations noted that the changes had been contemplated since before the incident, the link between the Sun Zhigang case and ensuing public outcry was clear.

The Sun Zhigang case is an example of how the growth of investigative journalism in China, in particular among the market-driven newspapers that developed throughout the 1990s, combined with the Internet, is resulting in much greater attention to law and the legal system than at any prior point in Chinese history.[50] Prior to commercialization of the media, press reports on the courts tended to be declaratory statements of the outcomes of cases, often written by court officials. Increased competition among the print media brought greater scrutiny to the courts and to legal issues more generally, along with greater critical coverage of decisions perceived as unjust. Yet prior to the growth of the Internet, discussions of cases in one region, even in the commercialized media, often went unnoticed elsewhere, and it was relatively easy for Propaganda Department officials to terminate discussion of cases by banning further media reports. A daring newspaper, such as *Southern Weekend*, might expose gross injustice, but officials could move swiftly to terminate follow-up reports. Otherwise, courts often operated in relative obscurity. Decisions might be reported in a local newspaper, or not at all.

That is changing. As the Sun Zhigang case shows, thanks mainly to the Internet and the birth of competing Internet news sites, cases that might once have been invisible, or have disappeared, can receive national attention, sometimes virtually instantly. In other cases, websites and web discussion forums spread news of cases where local Propaganda Department officials have instructed the official media not to report on such cases. In addition to the famous Sun Zhigang case, numerous other cases of alleged injustice have attracted widespread coverage and discussion on the Internet.

In 1994 a woman named Zhang Zaiyu disappeared. Zhang's family accused her husband, She Xianglin, of killing her. When police found the body of an unidentified woman, which relatives identified as Zhang, in a nearby water tower, they charged She with murder. After She confessed to the murder, allegedly under torture, he was sentenced to death. On appeal, the Hubei Province High People's Court sent the case back for retrial due to insufficient evidence, and She was sentenced to fifteen years in prison for intentional homicide.[51]

Eleven years later, on March 28, 2005, Zhang Zaiyu reappeared alive and married to a different man.[52] An initial report on Zhang's reappearance ran in a local paper in Wuhan, the capital of Hubei Province. Following the report, local authorities banned further reporting on the case pending an official investigation, and instructed the media to use only an officially approved report on the case.[53] But news quickly spread online and to other newspapers. A few weeks later, on April 15, She was released from custody. Media coverage may not have been solely responsible for She being freed—authorities reopened the case immediately after Zhang returned home. But such coverage did appear to assist She in obtaining 460,000 yuan (approximately $57,000) in compensation for his wrongful incarceration. The settlement was reported to be the largest from the state in Chinese history.[54]

As in the Sun Zhigang case, the media linked the case to broader problems in the Chinese criminal justice system. One report on the She case argued such wrongful conviction cases reflected the pressure placed on local authorities to solve cases and assuage popular anger.[55] Official explanations, in contrast, blamed the case on historical circumstances and the weakness of the legal system at the time of She's conviction and praised the efforts of local authorities to resolve the matter.[56]

Another illustrative example is the wrongful conviction case of Nie Shubin. In 1994, a court in Hebei Province found Nie Shubin guilty of rape and murder. Nie was executed the following year. Eleven years later, in 2005, a second man named Wang Shujin confessed to the original rape and murder.

The confession story was originally reported in March by a reporter from the *Henan Commercial News*, reprinted in the *Beijing News* and followed up by a report in *Southern Weekend*.[57] All of the reports subsequently were posted and circulated online. Local authorities refused to reopen Nie's case, and the media began to complain of a cover-up. A report in *Southern Weekend*, for example, asked why the local authorities failed to release details of their investigation into the case, and inquired whether the case would "disappear."[58] The report also noted that all details about the case had been removed from the police website.[59] Likewise, a report in the *Beijing News*, issued on March 15, questioned why the police, procuratorate, and court involved in the case had refused to take any action or to comment on the case.[60] Following the report, Propaganda Department officials apparently ordered the media not to carry further reports on the case.[61] However, reports continued to circulate, both in print and online, suggesting that the ban was either very limited or was widely ignored.[62]

On the same day the *Beijing News* report appeared, the Hebei Province High People's Court launched an investigation into the case. The Court did so after written instruction from leaders of the Political-Legal Committee of the Provincial Communist Party.[63] Although rumors later circulated online that an internal investigation had determined that the case had not been incorrectly decided,[64] as of early 2007 no official decision had been announced.[65]

Nie Shubin's family may still be waiting for justice. But, as with the Sun Zhigang case, the most important effect of the Nie and She cases was not the outcome of the individual cases, but their effect on national policy. At the end of 2005, China's SPC announced that it was revising China's procedures for handling capital cases. Under the new rules, final review of all capital cases will be conducted by the SPC. In the past, such review power was delegated to provincial high courts—which were also responsible for hearing appeals of capital cases. The new procedures create a third tier of review. In addition, the SPC rules require appeals in capital cases to be heard in open court.[66] Although pressure for such changes, both domestic and international, had been building for some time, the wave of public attention to the Nie, She, and other wrongful conviction cases during 2005 appeared to be a crucial factor leading the SPC to make the changes.[67]

Most such cases follow a pattern similar to those of the Sun Zhigang, She, and Nie cases. Traditional print media initially report on the case, the report is posted to the media's official web page, and then is reposted to numerous other websites. The articles create widespread discussion online, in particular in web discussion forums.[68] Such discussion and coverage encourages follow-up reports in the print media, reports that are subsequently reposted to the Internet.

The interaction between print and online media is important. Chinese regulations on the Internet restrict the ability of Internet providers to create their own news content. With just a few exceptions, only traditional media are permitted to generate news stories.[69] The number of websites legally qualified to print original news is unclear; a 2004 report stated that 163 websites were legally qualified to publish news, while another 1400 were permitted to offer "news service"—which generally means they are permitted to reprint articles that have already appeared in the official media.[70] Websites with the ability to generate original news content are generally those linked to national, provincial, and local Party mouthpiece newspapers.[71] Another important difference between the traditional media and online media is that the online media are more likely to carry commentaries on cases while they are pending. The traditional media usually wait to discuss cases until decisions have been made.[72]

An additional crucial feature of the Sun Zhigang, She, and Nie cases is that the Internet facilitates coverage by the media in jurisdictions other than those in which a case occurred. In the Nie case, what might have been a local issue was reported by media from Beijing, Henan, and Guangdong. The significance lies in the fact that in many cases local propaganda authorities will block local media from reporting on local cases.[73]

Another recent example of such transprovincial news coverage is the defamation action brought against the authors of the best-selling—but subsequently banned—book, *An Investigation into China's Peasants*. The book detailed problems facing China's peasants, including abuse and overtaxation by local authorities. A Party official in Anhui Province sued the publisher and author in local court, arguing that the book had defamed him.[74] After an initial flurry of coverage in the print media, the Central Propaganda Department banned further reporting on the case.[75] Despite the ban, widespread discussion of the case continued online—putting the court under pressure not to act too obviously to protect the local official. Continued Internet postings also highlighted the court's ongoing failure to resolve the case.[76]

The *Investigation into China's Peasants* case has yet to be resolved, and the long delay suggests that the court either continues to struggle to determine how to handle the case or has decided to ignore it.[77] According to a widely circulated email written by the defendants' lawyer in April 2006, the court handling the case has decided to leave the case unresolved and not issue any decision. But it does appear that the continued attention to the case, in part via online media, resulted in pressure on the court to follow procedural norms and not to act immediately to protect local interests.

The Sun Zhigang, She, and Nie cases show how the combined efforts of traditional and online media can force authorities to reopen cases and redress long-standing injustices. Meanwhile, the *Investigation into China's Peasants* case shows how online media may help keep discussion alive when traditional media are barred from such discussions, and how email can be used to spread news of cases where reporting has been banned.

2. *Internet Populism*

In the Sun Zhigang case, public pressure led to more attention to the treatment of migrants within China. Media pressure, fanned by Internet discussion, forced authorities to investigate the case, make arrests, and abolish the detention system that led to his death. The case may have resulted in belated justice for Sun. But it was less clear that those accused of being his killers received fair trials. Public pressure resulted in rushed and closed trials of the defendants, with court judgments that appeared preordained by Party leaders. The trial was held in June 2003, just six weeks after the case first came to light. The Guangdong Province High People's Court affirmed the lower court's decision on the case on June 27, and Qiao Yanqin, the principal defendant, was executed the same day.[78]

Only three official media outlets were permitted to send reporters to the trial. Propaganda officials instructed other media to use only reports from the official *Xinhua News Agency*, and Internet portals were told to terminate discussion of the case. Some journalists and other observers questioned the fairness of the trial, arguing that the death sentence imposed on Qiao Yanqin was excessive, and asked why charges had focused on a low-ranking nurse and other inmates in the detention center, rather than on higher-ranking officials. But such discussions were generally not permitted online or in print. Instead, official accounts focused on praising authorities' speedy handling of the case, and on the court's responsiveness to public opinion.[79] And in a final development, the editors of the paper that originally broke the story of Sun Zhigang's murder were later imprisoned, albeit for "unrelated" corruption charges.[80]

In 2003, Liu Yong likewise found that angry online discussion of a case can lead to execution. Liu, an organized crime boss, was convicted in the early 2000s of a range of crimes, including organizing a criminal syndicate, bribery, and illegal possession of firearms.[81] An intermediate court in Liaoning Province tried his case and sentenced him to death. On appeal in 2003, however, the Liaoning High People's Court reduced his sentence to life in prison. One reason for the reduction was the fact that Liu's confession had been obtained through torture.[82]

A Shanghai paper, *Bund Pictorial*, quickly questioned the reduction in sentence.[83] News of the court's decision spread rapidly online—one major Internet portal ran a headline on its news home page, stating in large font "Liu Yong Will Not Die." The media suggested that Liu's ties to officials in Liaoning Province resulted in favorable treatment.[84] Reporters criticized academics who had written expert opinions—in return for sizable fees—in support of Liu.[85] Web discussion forums filled with angry commentary, denouncing Liu's "lenient" treatment.

Following the public outcry, the SPC decided to rehear the case. The SPC invoked a rarely used procedure that permits the court to try de novo questionably decided cases.[86] In a carefully scripted trial, Liu's case was heard on a Friday. The court announced its decision—reinstating the death penalty—on the following Monday morning. Liu was executed the same morning.

Media outlets and some academics described the decision as an appropriate response to popular opinion.[87] Various websites carried morbidly detailed accounts of each step of the case—including, on the date of Liu's judgment and execution, hourly reports that described the court judgment, transportation of Liu to the execution ground, transportation of his body to the crematorium, and then return of his ashes to his family.[88] The *sina.com* page on the case included links to more than one hundred articles and commentaries.[89] Some declared the case a victory for "public opinion."[90]

The official media hailed the Liu Yong and Sun Zhigang cases as examples of successful official responses to public demands demonstrating China's progress toward a more just and democratic society. Yet subsequent cases also demonstrate that Party propaganda officials have become increasingly conscious of the need to manage online discussion of cases, and not let public outrage go too far. In two high-profile cases the authorities went out of their way to demonstrate that public outrage expressed online would not necessarily affect or change court decisions.

What became known as the BMW case began in 2003, when, in the northeast city of Harbin, a peasant accidentally drove his onion-cart into a parked BMW. The driver, a woman named Su Xiuwen, got out, and argued with the driver of the onion cart, Dai Yiquan. After bystanders intervened, she retreated to the car. She then unexpectedly put the car into gear, striking and killing Liu Zhongxai, Dai's wife, and injuring several others.

At trial in Harbin, the issue was whether Su had intentionally or accidentally put the car into forward gear. After a trial notable for its lack of eyewitness testimony, the court ruled the killing an accident and imposed a suspended sentence.

As news of the story spread, the reaction on the Internet was overwhelming. *Sina.com*, a leading web portal, reported receiving more than two hundred thousand web postings on the case—even more than the total number of postings regarding the SARS crisis earlier in 2003.[91] The class difference between the owners of the BMW and the onion-cart drove public outrage, as did the questionable nature of the trial. Many speculated that political connections of Su, the wife of a prominent businessman in Harbin, influenced the outcome.

In January 2004 authorities announced that the case would be reexamined. But authorities at the same time banned further reporting on the case and ordered websites to terminate and remove discussions of the case. There seemed to be a clear effort to establish that Internet rage would not overturn the verdict.

Three months later, official media announced that an investigation led by the Heilongjiang Province Communist Party's Political-Legal Committee had determined that the case had been correctly decided. Although official statements declared that the court's decision in the BMW case had been upheld, observers reported that in fact a number of persons involved in the case were sanctioned internally.[92] The sanctions were never announced publicly.[93] The message can be read several ways. One possibility was that authorities did want to protect Su, the driver of the BMW. But the clear message was that malfeasance will be handled internally, and that Internet anger cannot always be allowed to dictate Party or court decisions.

A similar story came in 2005, when websites carried extensive discussion of the case of Wang Binyu.[94] Wang, a migrant worker, was sentenced to death for murdering four people, including his construction site foreman and three family members. Wang's case became famous nationwide following reports in the *Beijing News*.[95] He was a symbol of the hardship and exploitation faced by China's millions of migrant workers. Wang killed his boss after he repeatedly failed to pay him. Said Wang, "I want to die. When I am dead, nobody can exploit me anymore. Right?"[96]

Many online postings and articles took Wang's side, and argued that he should be spared.[97] As with the BMW case, however, online discussion largely stopped following a Central Propaganda Department instruction.[98] Wang was then quietly executed. Although news of his execution was posted to the official *China Court News* website the day after his execution,[99] domestic media did not report on it. Only after the case received attention in the *New York Times* did the domestic media report on Wang's death.[100]

* * *

From these leading cases, and from interviews with journalists, judges, and academics, we can describe a general pattern. First, the growth of the Internet has made it more difficult for courts to conceal information about cases, and more likely that misdeeds will be noticed and reported. Judges state that courts find it hard to conceal information about cases, which increases pressure on courts to handle cases according to law. Courts and party-state officials that oversee the courts cannot be assured of their ability to silence discussion of cases simply by issuing an instruction banning further reporting. As we've seen, the three most famous cases of Internet influence—the Sun Zhigang, Liu Yong, and BMW cases—all demonstrate how online coverage or discussion can encourage Party officials to intervene. In all of the cases, reports in the print media, reposted to major Internet portals, were enough to set off a chain reaction.

This, in turn, has led to a new type of party-state intervention into the operations of the legal system. The interventions come in response to outrage on the Internet and are marked by a determination to resolve the matter quickly: in the Sun Zhigang case, with the rapid arrest and trial of suspects and then a choreographed closed trial; in the Liu Yong case with the SPC apparently being ordered to rehear the case; and in the BMW case with the investigation of the case by Party authorities.[101] At the same time, Party propaganda authorities curtail any further discussion of the cases other than by officially approved sources—generally by requiring that the media only use dispatches from the *Xinhua News Agency*.[102] Propaganda authorities also order web portals to remove or ban discussion of the cases: one list of terms automatically filtered by one Chinese blog service included both "Nie Shubin" and "Wang Binyu."[103] In the final step, official media declare the interventions and resulting decisions to be successful examples of authorities responding to public opinion.

Given the possibility of public scrutiny leading to unstoppable pressure, political intervention, and even possible punishment for judges, courts are taking some preemptive action to better control information. In recent years, courts have taken steps to restrict media coverage of cases, requiring reporters to obtain court approval prior to attending trials. Courts frequently either draft articles about cases in their court for the local media or require that all such articles are screened by court officials prior to publication. Courts have also retaliated against negative coverage, with both courts and individual judges filing defamation lawsuits in response to critical media coverage. In addition, court propaganda or research departments monitor online discussions of cases involving individual courts,[104] sometimes via daily searches to locate discussions of the cases in the media or in discussion forums.[105] Finally, while it is hard to say for sure, courts may be more inclined to decide cases in ways that are less likely to inflame the public, which in the criminal context often means applying harsh sanctions.

The result is a strange, tense, and slightly rivalrous relationship among the courts and the media, major Internet providers, and the party-state. As we have seen, the courts fear media reports that might result in popular outrage and political intervention. The media, meanwhile, must balance the risk of punishment if they go too far in reporting on sensitive cases with their desire to maximize profit through aggressive or sensational reporting. Party-state officials are concerned with maintaining stability—even at the cost of undermining their claims to be emphasizing rule of law. Unfortunately, this complex web of relationships cannot help but sometimes distract from resolving disputes fairly. The fears of media attention, public reaction, and party-state intervention do make the legal system more accountable, just not necessarily to the parties before the court.

B. Communications Practices within the Chinese Judiciary

Until this point, this article has focused on communications practices between the courts and other actors, including the media, public, and party-state officials. We now turn to the results of interviews with Chinese judges, to see how their communications practices have been affected by the Internet revolution.

1. *Traditional Communications Practices*

To understand how matters are changing, we must first describe the traditional communication practices within the Chinese judiciary. To generalize, Chinese judges have operated in a context in which they had limited access to *horizontal* information—information about how other similarly situated courts were doing their jobs. Instead, their primary source of guidance for handling novel or difficult cases has been *vertical*—consultation with superiors, either within the court hierarchy or in other party-state institutions. Chinese judges have also operated in an environment in which their access to information is restricted in some respects and uninhibited in others. On the one hand, courts have often had limited access to legal materials and the decisions of other judges. Chinese judges not only knew very little about how judges elsewhere were handling cases; in impoverished rural areas they also may have lacked easy access to laws, regulations, SPC interpretations, and other normative documents. On the other hand, judges have been relatively uninhibited in seeking advice on how to handle cases from colleagues, superiors, party-state officials, or academics and experts outside the courts.

Since the start of the reform era in 1978, China's judges have worked in a historically unusual legal environment. During the Mao era, and particularly during the Cultural Revolution, many legal institutions were neglected, left to play minor roles or used primarily as political tools of the state. During the Cultural Revolution, the legal system ceased to function in any recognizable form. Since 1978, great efforts have been made to improve and reform the Chinese legal system. Much of the statutory law was either rewritten or drafted anew. Judges, consequently, have been called on to apply a huge number of new laws, which have often been vague or unclear. Yet despite reform, in many regions judges have continued to lack even the basic legal materials required to resolve cases. What might strike a foreign observer as the most important sources of guidance—legal education, the laws themselves, and decisions of other courts—have often been unavailable or at the least lacking in detail.

Limited access to information has not meant that judges confronting hard cases have had no other sources for guidance. First, within individual courts, adjudication committees provide guidance (or decide outright) difficult or sensitive cases.[106] These adjudication committees, which include high-ranking judges from the court and sometimes procurators (who participate in discussions in some criminal cases, but apparently do not have voting power on the committee),[107] serve as a venue for discussing challenging or sensitive cases. This practice (which has both critics and supporters in China) results in cases that are decided in the first instance by judges who have not heard the case. The practice can be said to reflect the fact that the concept of judicial independence in China refers to courts, not individual judges. In any case, in addition to the formal adjudication committee, judges frequently consult informally with their peers and superiors within courts. Court presidents, who are the most powerful figures within individual courts (and who often lack formal legal training), play a particularly important role in guiding decisions in cases that are perceived to be sensitive or difficult.

Second, lower court judges have also traditionally sought guidance on difficult cases by seeking advice of the superior court through the process known as *qingshi*, or "requesting instruction." Judges encountering a difficult or novel question can contact the higher-level court—often by telephone or in person—to discuss how the case should be handled in the court of first instance. The *qingshi* practice, which bears some resemblance to an informal interlocutory appeal, has been criticized for eliminating the point of an appeals process.[108] However, it continues to be an important mechanism for judges seeking guidance in difficult or potentially sensitive cases.[109] Chinese judges are evaluated based in part on whether their decisions are affirmed or reversed on appeal; a judge who gets a decision "wrong" can be fined or, in serious cases, removed from office. It is thus easy to understand why judges might seek guidance from a higher-level court prior to issuing a decision.

Third, China is officially a civil law system and does not formally recognize court precedent as such. As with other civil law systems,[110] however, written cases and formal guidance from higher courts do play an important role. Official advice as to how cases should be handled is disseminated through public normative documents issued by the SPC—ranging from official interpretations of laws to replies to questions or explanations concerning decisions in specific cases—or by nonpublic instructions issued by the SPC or by provincial high courts. Judges also learn of new legal information and of representative cases through official publications. These include the *People's Court News*, the official newspaper of the court system, which frequently highlights interesting or noteworthy cases handled by lower courts, and the *Gazette of the Supreme People's Court*, which publishes official decisions and cases from the SPC. Numerous collections of cases have also been published, some under the guidance of the SPC that are designed to highlight "representative cases" that courts should follow, and others by academics or individual courts. Some local courts have published case collections, designed to serve as guidance for handling cases—although such volumes have limited reach outside their local areas. A few for-profit websites now also provide collections of cases.[111] There is no formal system for publication of cases in China, nor is there a mechanism for searching the cases that are made publicly available. Thus with the exception of information in the *People's Court News* (which prior to the Internet was not searchable), other similar publications, or the occasional published collection of cases, judges had little information about how to handle cases other than that passed down to them from superior courts.

Finally, senior judges in courts may also discuss cases with the local Party Political-Legal Committee, or with representatives from local people's congresses or government. This is particularly true in serious criminal cases, in cases that have aroused widespread public attention, or in cases that touch on important local interests.

This model, which depends heavily on vertical consultation with superior courts or political officials, continues to predominate. However, today the Internet is changing how many Chinese judges do their job. In the next section we canvass how at least some judges use the Internet in deciding cases, including some of the uses that may seem unusual from the perspective of practice in other nations.

2. *New Communications Practices*

The use of the Internet by individual judges is beginning to transform communications practices within the judiciary, and, consequently, how law is both used and applied in China. Judges who once worked in isolation, without either easy access to national laws or information about how similar cases were handled elsewhere, now are able to access not only the law on the books, but also how such laws are being applied and debated elsewhere.

The Chinese judges interviewed for this article overwhelmingly commented that they use the Internet to conduct research to assist them in handling cases—especially in hard or novel cases. Perhaps the most interesting outcome of such usage is the slow development of what resembles a nonbinding system of precedent in the Chinese legal system. Judges state that they are developing "unwritten precedent" regarding how to handle cases.[112] They note that doing so helps to reduce their workload when they encounter new legal issues.[113] Judges explain that they do not look to other courts' decisions as "precedent," but rather only for the purposes of reference or *cankao*.[114] But even this nonbinding "precedent" may strongly influence decision-making.

The reported use of informal precedent dovetails with a rise in interest in using precedent in the Chinese legal system. Since early 2002, the Zhengzhou Zhongyuan District Court has experimented with a "precedent decision" system whereby the court selects important cases as "models."[115] Similarly, the SPC has within recent years begun referring to its model decisions as "legal precedent." However, the Internet-driven use of informal precedent exceeds the scope of these experiments.

Some of the greatest consequences of these developments may be for the more remote parts of China. For example, judges from places like Qinghai Province, in western China, explained that they frequently consult court websites in more developed areas of China to see how they have handled particular legal issues.[116]

This is a break from traditional practice. Judges encountering new legal questions have traditionally sought assistance from their superiors, either in their own court, or in higher-ranking courts. The growth of the Internet suggests that courts may increasingly be able to look horizontally, to courts elsewhere in China, whereas in the past they would have sought assistance from those above them.

Over the long term, the development of an informal system of precedent may significantly change the Chinese legal system. It may lead to a greater confidence born of national consistency and the authority of acting in concert. That may in turn lead to greater institutional security and autonomy, as judges rely on the strength of the judgment of others, as opposed to mere personal judgment.

Yet the Internet is not only permitting the development of horizontal interactions among judges, but it is also a mechanism for strengthening existing vertical relationships in the courts, and perhaps even control over individual judges by superiors within the courts. Numerous courts in China have established internal court networks, designed to facilitate court work, improve efficiency, and also strengthen oversight over individual judges. In sum, internal networks show how the Internet may also serve the party-state's interests in control.

We first explore ways in which judges are using the external web, and then turn to the impact of internal court networks.

a) Finding cases. The best place for Chinese judges to find useful cases is, ironically, sometimes outside of the courthouse. Few judges in China have access to the external Internet (the Internet as it exists in China) from work, as many courts do not permit judges other than those in court propaganda departments to access the external web from work.[117] In other courts, only the court president has access to the external web.[118] Such restrictions may derive both from concerns that judges will waste time online, and from concerns that judges will use the Internet to reveal confidential or secret information.[119] But in some courts, access to the Internet also appears to be a sign of status—akin to having a car and driver—with only the highest ranking judges permitted to go online from work.

Despite these restrictions, a great many judges say that they use the external network to aid their decision-making, particularly to research legal questions and to see how other courts have handled cases similar to those before them.[120] In the central Chinese city of Xi'an, judges use the Internet to consult cases decided by the SPC, and by the Shaanxi Provincial High People's Court, as well as decisions from other courts.[121] In Shenyang, judges note that they consult both the websites of other courts and media reports for information on cases.[122] Even in areas in which courts lack computers, judges state that they frequently conduct online research when they encounter difficult cases.[123] Some judges have access to the Internet at home; others go to web cafes.[124]

As one judge put it, "the effect is huge."[125] A judge working in a rural county court in central China (which lacks both an internal network and access to the external web) gave the example of determining how to apportion blame in traffic accidents when both sides share liability. Going online, judges "found that in Guangdong there is a standard for the whole province for this."[126] Although not in Guangdong and thus not obligated to use the standard, the court decided to use the Guangdong rule. "In the past we only looked at cases in our court" for guidance, commented the judge. Now the court looks elsewhere.[127]

On the external Internet, judges rely on the same tools that other participants in the legal system use to build legal arguments. Summaries of cases on China Court Web and the websites of individual courts, media reports, and other sources give judges an idea as to how cases have been decided. Judges also frequent prominent academic websites, including the Civil and Commercial Law Website of Renmin University.[128] Judges say that it is often easier to locate legal materials on the web than on internal court networks, which they say are often incomplete or are infrequently updated.[129] Simply making it easier for judges to locate binding law is an important development: in the past, judges often had no easy way to locate relevant laws and other materials. As one judge explained, courts often have one book for hundreds of people, making it difficult for individual judges to actually locate materials.[130]

The most significant examples of Internet research are in cases where the law is uncertain, or in which judges face difficult legal questions.[131] Judges state that they routinely search websites of other courts for examples of cases similar to those before them.[132] For example, a judge specializing in intellectual property cases in Beijing stated that judges hearing such cases will often look online to see how similar cases have been handled elsewhere, including overseas.[133]

Judges are not the only ones using the Internet in this way. Lawyers also say they use the Internet to conduct research, and that they often will provide judges with printouts of materials they locate online, including information about similar cases elsewhere.[134] One lawyer recounted how, in a case in which his client had been sentenced to death in the first instance, he located a newspaper report regarding a case from the same city in which a defendant in a similar case had been sentenced to fifteen years in prison, not death. The appellate court then reduced the sentence.[135] Public-interest lawyers say that they have used websites to link plaintiffs and lawyers who are bringing similar cases nationwide.[136] Lawyers say that law firm websites can also be useful for gathering information about prior cases—and that they sometimes will print out materials from such sites to provide to judges.[137] Likewise procurators say that they frequently use the Internet to conduct research where the law is unclear, in particular in determining the appropriate crime with which to charge a defendant.

Some courts appear to be particularly important sources of precedent. Thus, for example, intellectual property divisions at the intermediate courts in Beijing or in Beijing's Haidian District (home to many technology companies), are seen as being influential.[138] Likewise, judges in the interior say that they often look for guidance to courts in Beijing and Shanghai—where judges are widely regarded as being better qualified than in many other areas of China.[139]

The practice of using the Internet to look for useful precedent or other guidance is among the most potentially significant developments in judicial communications. However, for the most part, what it does is mimic what we see in other legal systems, both civil and common law. In the next part of this section we discuss more novel ways in which Chinese courts are using the Internet.

b) Innovations. Some of the ways courts use the Internet in China may strike a Western observer as surprising or unusual. Here we discuss several examples where judges have used the network in ways that appear distinct from the rest of the world. The first examples involve using court websites for public relations purposes.

In 2004, the Shiquan County Court in Shaanxi Province came under fire from local media when it dismissed the case of migrant worker Xu Dengkai for being eight minutes late for a hearing. Xu contracted silicosis from work at a local factory and sued to challenge a labor arbitration award. The labor arbitration committee had ordered that the defendant factory pay him 6,200 yuan (about \$775), while Xu argued that he was entitled to 217,206 yuan (about \$27,000).[140] On the date of the hearing, however, Xu arrived slightly late.[141] By the time he arrived, the court had already dismissed his case for failure to appear, forcing Xu to forfeit 14,000 yuan (\$1750) in court filing fees that he had already paid.[142]

The *Huashang News*, a leading commercial newspaper in the provincial capital, Xi'an, wrote an editorial entitled "The Legal System Should Not Be Emotionless." The newspaper argued that dropping the case was an unduly harsh punishment for a litigant who was five minutes late.[143] It pointed out that the plaintiff had to travel by train from outside the mountainous county to arrive at the court by eight thirty. It also wrote that the worker was in poor health as a result of the injuries he had suffered at work.[144]

The court, slighted, turned to the Internet to defend itself online. Its first act was to release a report that argued that it had handled the case fully in compliance with the law.[145] Next, court judges responded to and debated with critics on the court's public Internet message board.[146] One comment posted to the court's electronic bulletin board urged the court to admit that its handling of the case had been incorrect. In response, a court official wrote that because the case was still on appeal it could not be said to have been incorrectly decided. In another exchange, a posting complained that the case was "not readable." The court thanked the poster of the message for the criticism, and stated that the court needed to continue to strengthen its ability "to serve social stability and development."[147] Some of the court's postings were identified as coming from the court president, while others appeared to come from other court officials.

Later on, the court backed down and permitted the plaintiff to refile the case without having to pay the court fees a second time. Without mentioning the controversy or criticism, the court posted a report on the case on its website as an example of how the court was working to further the "advanced education" policy of the Party. The court posted a picture of Xu to the court's homepage, with a caption stating, "Our Court Carries Out Judicial Assistance in the Case of Xu Dengkui."[148] The court noted that it had taken account of the plaintiff's status as a worker from outside the county, and had therefore decided to waive the court fee and schedule an afternoon hearing so that Xu would be able to attend. The report also stated that the court had been praised by the parties to the case and the media.[149]

The Xu case is just one example of how courts use their websites for public relations purposes. Hundreds of Chinese courts—ranging from the SPC to rural county courts—have created public websites.[150] Court public websites frequently include information such as an overview of court work and personnel, news from the court, and discussion forums.[151] Although urban courts were first to establish websites, even courts in some rural areas have sites that provide information about the court, judges, and cases.[152]

Court websites focus on providing information about the court, largely to educate the public about such work, and to achieve other propaganda goals. The SPC's website, for example, includes news on the court, primarily focused on the activities of court leaders; an introduction to each branch of the court and to each judge on the court; explanations, interpretations, replies, and other normative documents issued by the court; selected decisions of the court (but none from the past two years); model decisions from lower courts; and the court's annual work reports to the National People's Congress.[153] The website makes it easier to access the same type of information that the court already makes publicly available through the *People's Court News*, the Court's Gazette, and regularly published books of selected decisions from lower courts.

Another important and widely read site is the China Court Web, which is discussed above.[154] The China Court Web carries news articles regarding the courts, laws and regulations, academic legal materials, and online discussion forums and chatrooms regarding legal matters. The China Court Web is a particularly important place for judges to read about what other courts are doing—and to help find the informal precedent discussed above. The site is run by the *People's Court News*, the official newspaper of the SPC, and thus is directly under the supervision of the SPC.[155] The site includes both content in the paper, and also a wide range of material that does not make it into the print version.

Lower court websites are similar. They focus on highlighting court work and educating the public about such work, either through selected opinions from cases or summaries of cases, as well as articles written by judges.[156] Cases included on websites are generally selected by court propaganda officials with a view to highlighting noteworthy or new cases.[157]

Few courts post all or even many of their decisions online. Indeed, only one court is known to have done so: in 2000, the Guangzhou Maritime Court announced that all of its decisions would be made available online.[158] The court website now includes 777 cases decided between 2001 and 2005.[159] Other courts have similarly pledged to make all cases available online, or all intellectual property cases,[160] but such promises appear to have gone unfulfilled.[161] Most courts continue to post only a small number of selected decisions or case descriptions.

Finally, as is common in the West, court sites also provide information to potential litigants—ranging from court rules and regulations, to explanations of litigation procedures, to instructions on how to file cases and the risks and costs involved in bringing lawsuits.[162] Other courts include hearing times,[163] selected laws and regulations,[164] instructions regarding the formulation of legal documents and examples of such documents,[165] and court legal notices.[166] The Shenzhen Intermediate Court includes a link to live broadcasts of selected court hearings, although the system does not yet appear to be functional.[167] Some court websites also provide online mechanisms for citizens to file complaints about the court[168]—although judges say few such complaints are filed.[169]

The growth of court websites reflects greater emphasis on public relations and media management by China's courts.[170] Courts have increasingly found themselves coming under criticism, in particular from China's newly commercialized media. Courts are also coming into conflict with other party-state institutions, including People's Congresses, procuratorates, and administrative actors. Websites provide a mechanism for improving the reputations and images of courts, and perhaps thus for raising courts' status in their interactions with other official actors. Both the courts generally and individual judges—in particular court presidents—have an interest in raising their profiles with higher-ranking leaders and with the public. The development of public websites also reflects rhetorical commitment by the courts to the importance of boosting transparency as a means for raising popular confidence in the legal system, and of boosting legal knowledge among ordinary people so as to make the courts more accessible. Internet sites, and in particular court news sites such as the official China Court Web, do make an enormous amount of information available, both to other judges and to the public. Yet like the embrace of the Internet by the party-state more generally, the content on courts' public websites also suggests a greater emphasis on managing information than on making such information publicly available.

c) Judges online. In 2006, in the Shiquan County People's Court in Shaanxi, an anonymous user posted a message advising the court to ignore a case brought by an elderly woman against her granddaughter for financial support. The message was posted to the court's BBS chatroom, where court officials and sometimes the court president respond to postings from the public (and where the same court had previously defended itself in the Xu Denkai case). The poster argued that that the plaintiff's daughter, an alternative source of support, was alive and in another town.[171] The poster suggested that the grandmother was treating the court president like her grandson—expecting him to provide assistance simply because she was elderly.

In a posted reply, a court official stated that the court would do their best to handle the case. Later, the court president himself responded. He stated that he had resolved the case by contacting the local civil affairs bureau, and asking the bureau to provide financial support. The court president acknowledged that it was not the court's role to take such actions, but stated that he had done so because the plaintiff was old, and because the plaintiff recognized the importance of the courts.[172]

As this example shows, Chinese judges sometimes venture onto public websites to handle cases or discuss legal issues with members of the public.[173] Judges even frequent public chatrooms, such as those on China Court Web.[174] Most judges state that they will not discuss actual cases before them in online forums before such cases are decided. But there are also examples of judges using such discussion boards to help determine how best to decide a case.[175] In one example, a judge reported how a colleague had used online discussions with legal scholars and ordinary people to "obtain consensus" as to how a case should be handled.[176] He praised the use of online forums for facilitating interactions between judges and the masses. And even judges who are cautious about participating in online discussions regarding cases themselves said that they nevertheless will sometimes consult such discussions when deciding cases.[177]

Judges also use email to help decide cases. Judges in relatively remote areas say that they sometimes email leading academics to ask their views of particular legal issues.[178] This was already the practice in major cities like Beijing, where judges frequently consult with academics when they encounter new or difficult legal issues. The growth of the Internet makes it easier for judges in less developed areas to do the same.[179] As an extension of the informal precedent system described earlier, judges say that they also sometimes use the Internet to locate courts that have encountered similar legal issues in the past, and then telephone the judges who handled the cases to discuss how they reached their decisions.[180]

Finally, in recent years, some judges have begun blogging. Web sites such as the China Court Web include blogging sections, where judges discuss a variety of issues, including general views of their work and also sometimes particular legal issues.[181] Some judges appear to be using blogs to advance their own careers—writing in ways that highlight their own work (and how they advance the party-state's goals for the legal system). Many of the blogs appear to serve a mixture of education and propaganda goals. Thus, for example, Judge Wu Jinpeng, a judge on the Henan Province High People's Court, used his blog to describe the court proceedings in a capital case—describing how the court held a public hearing on appeal, and how such proceedings received praise from all parties, including the defendant, who thanked the court for its fair handling of his case.[182] Another judge, identified as Lan Cai, discussed cases ranging from a dispute over an insurance contract, to a claim brought by local residents challenging an administrative regulation.[183] A judge writing under the name Judge Song Zhumei used a blog to discuss criminal cases, asking, in one case, whether particular facts should be treated as an accident or as giving rise to a charge of criminal negligence.[184] And a judge writing under the name Jia Mu used a blog to discuss a range of civil cases, including a claim of harassment via a cell phone message and a medical malpractice case.[185]

All of these cases appeared to be examples of already decided cases—judges do not appear to blog about pending cases. Moreover, none of the judges interviewed for this article mentioned blogs as an important source of information in deciding cases. This is not surprising; the use of blogs in China has exploded during the period in which we conducted our research. But it does appear that blogs are emerging as another important mechanism through which judges both share information about cases before them, and perhaps also interact with the public and the legal community regarding interesting or novel cases.

In sum, Chinese judges are experimenting with a variety of new ways of using the Internet to either handle their legal duties or conduct public relations. The long-term implications of these activities are not clear. Nevertheless, China may serve as an interesting case study for the rest of the world.

3. *Internal Networks*

Use of the external Internet and the development of court public websites represent just one aspect of how Internet technology is changing China's courts. One reason most judges are not able to go on the external Internet from work is that many Chinese courts have constructed internal court networks (another is that many basic level courts lack computers).

The developments we describe above regarding how judges use the Internet have gone largely unnoticed in academic and media writings in China.[186] The Chinese media have, however, covered in detail the development of internal court networks—networks that can be accessed only by court personnel. These networks, known in Chinese as *juyu wang*, generally link judges within a particular court; in some more developed areas they link lower courts with higher courts. In some respects internal networks provide similar types of information and opportunities for interaction that are provided on the external Internet: judges have easier access to laws and regulations and some selected cases than in the past and, in some courts, can share their views about cases with other judges in chatrooms. Internal networks, like the external web, make it easier for judges to do their jobs.

Yet the information on such sites is limited to that selected by court officials, and thus is often far less comprehensive than what is available on the external Internet. Judges using internal networks are limited to seeing those materials that their superiors want them to see. In addition, internal networks are also an important mechanism for monitoring work by individual judges. In this respect courts' use of the Internet may be seen as a parable for China's embrace of the

Internet more generally: more information is available, and judges are able to do their jobs more efficiently (and, one hopes, more fairly), but the Internet is also serving the state's interests in imposing oversight and control.

In a 2002 notice, the SPC instructed all courts in China to set up networks or individual computers with software allowing judges to search laws and other legal materials.[187] Courts have gradually complied with the notice. Reports in 2003 and 2004 on the development of the Internet in China's courts stated that 500 to 600 of China's approximately 4,000 courts had established internal networks.[188] Many more courts appear to have set up internal networks since then, or are in the process of doing so.

Discussions of the role of internal networks focus on their role in making courts more efficient. Thus, for example, reports have noted that developing internal networks raises court efficiency by strengthening information management and "leadership methods" in the courts.[189] Reports have also noted the importance of court networks in facilitating supervision of lower courts by higher courts.[190]

Not surprisingly, courts in economically developed areas have taken the lead in developing such networks.[191] In Jiangsu Province—one of China's richest—a 2006 report noted that computer networks had been established in 116 of the province's 123 courts.[192] Yet courts in less developed areas—ranging from Heilongjiang in the northeast to Tibet—have also developed court networks and have publicized their use in increasing both efficiency in and supervision over local courts.[193]

Many basic-level courts, in particular in rural areas or county towns, lack networks or computers.[194] Judges at a rural county court in Jilin Province reported that the only people in the court with web access are the court president and the vice-presidents; judges have no access to either an internal network or to the external web.[195] Only court leaders have computers.[196] Judges at both a county and an intermediate court in the central province of Hubei commented that they lack any web access, and that many courts lack computers.

In general, internal networks have four primary functions. First, they provide searchable databases of laws, regulations, some cases, and other binding normative documents. Many courts include a database of national and local laws developed in conjunction with the SPC, the *People's Court Press*, and the Chinalawinfo Center at Peking University.[197] The database includes SPC interpretations, replies, and other documents, as well as some cases.[198] Internal networks thus provide judges with electronic forms of the types of materials they have traditionally consulted in deciding cases, making it easier for judges to access such materials.[199] Judges also receive information about new laws, regulations, and interpretations via notices on their internal court networks.[200] Over time, how, why, and by whom the information included on internal webs is collected may have a major impact on how courts function and apply the law. Controlling information on internal networks—which the SPC is doing by requiring all courts to use standardized software—is also a mechanism for controlling how judges decide cases.

Second, some court internal networks include discussion forums in which judges discuss topics ranging from new cases to the quality of food in the court cafeteria.[201] These forums are similar to those that exist on the external web, but are accessible only to judges from a particular court or courts. In some courts judges comment that such discussion forums are rarely used to discuss substantive matters.[202] In others, however, such as in Jiangsu Province, judges say that such internal discussion forums—which are accessible to most judges in the province—have become important forums for discussing new legal issues and, occasionally, pending cases.[203] The system includes numerous discussion forums, moderated by individual judges, where judges can discuss cases (and other issues) anonymously.[204] One judge noted that the forums allow judges to learn about new developments, both in China and overseas.[205] Likewise, all judges in Shanghai can participate anonymously in discussions on the Shanghai court web, which links all courts in the city.[206] In addition, the Shanghai Second Intermediate People's Court's internal network includes a section in which judges can discuss "difficult legal questions" that they encounter in cases. The discussion is also accessible to judges in lower courts under the intermediate court's jurisdiction. A report on the court's website stated that court officers can discuss abstract legal issues encountered in individual cases. The court also organized a team of experienced judges to provide information in response to such abstract questions.[207]

As we have noted, Chinese judges frequently discuss cases that are under consideration with their peers and superiors, including superiors in higher courts. Discussing pending cases on discussion forums is thus an electronic version of the forums of vertical consultation that already exist. Yet such discussion forums may also facilitate debate in which judges might be less willing to engage face to face with other judges or with their superiors. For example, one report on the Liu Yong case[208] recounted how judges on the Liaoning Province High People's Court had discussed the case on their Internet network while it was under consideration—but did so anonymously out of concern for retribution.[209] Nevertheless, such discussion takes place in a controlled environment, one in which only court personnel participate, and one that is monitored by court superiors. It may be that judges are more willing to participate in such discussion when they know it is unavailable to the public. On the other hand, judges may also be wary of speaking too freely in a system run by the courts with an explicit goal of boosting oversight of judges.

Third, internal networks serve to disseminate information to judges, in particular about recent court developments. Internal websites sometimes include representative cases from provincial or municipal high courts, as well as notices and interpretations from such courts.[210] Local court leaders also sometimes include specific materials or cases from their own court on their internal websites.[211] These materials are designed to inform and educate judges; such cases are often selected because they either are particularly good examples and are thus worthy of study, or they carry a particular message.[212] Thus, for example, in Beijing, courts can view interpretations from the Beijing High People's Court, as well as those from the SPC. The Beijing High Court posts descriptions of important decisions (but not court decisions themselves) on its internal website for judges in the city to review.[213]

Fourth, and arguably most important, internal networks facilitate oversight of individual judges and even courts. In many cases it appears that the networks have become a significant mechanism for higher-ranking judges to monitor the work of those below them. In so doing, internal networks reinforce the hierarchical and bureaucratic structure of China's courts. Many internal court networks provide information regarding the status of cases, such as party names, dates on which cases were filed or dates of scheduled hearings, and whether a case has been resolved. In most cases, such information is available only to judges handling such cases and their superiors,[214] although in some courts all judges can view such information.[215] In others, however, such information is available only to court superiors; judges complain of being required to enter extensive administrative information regarding cases into the computer system which they themselves cannot even access. The monitoring function is backed up by other technology. In some courts in Beijing and Shanghai, court presidents, vice presidents, and heads of individual divisions can watch live video streams of the proceedings in any courtroom under their jurisdiction.[216] At the SPC, all judges are required to log in to the court network as soon as they get to the court, so that superiors can monitor who has arrived at work.[217]

Court judgments are likewise usually available only to a limited number of judges and court officials. In a few courts it appears that all judges with access to the internal network can view all or most decisions from their own courts,[218] but most networks only allow court leaders to view decisions (other than those selected by court propaganda officials as worthy of posting on the network).[219] As one court president explained, decisions are not generally available on the internal website because they are "secret."[220] Thus court presidents and vice presidents often can view all cases in their courts, and heads of divisions within courts can view decisions in their division, but ordinary judges have access to only those cases they have decided.[221] As one judge in an intermediate court put it, each judge in the court is allowed to view different information depending on his or her status.[222] In addition, in some jurisdictions in which networks connect lower and higher courts, some higher court judges are able to view decisions in lower courts in their jurisdiction.[223]

In Beijing, for example, only high-ranking judges can view decisions. The situation in Beijing is noteworthy in part because it marks a departure from the more open system that was in place when the Beijing courts first created an internal court network. At the time, judges could view all cases decided by any court in Beijing.[224] Judges could also view cases in their own courts in which they were not involved.[225] The Beijing High People's Court altered the system, creating instead a system that permits only higher-ranking judges to access such information.[226] The progression in Beijing appears to represent a more general trend. As court networks have developed, courts have become more sophisticated about both the type of information provided and the degree to which higher-ranking judges are able to use the system as a tool for oversight.

It would be wrong to view efforts to use technology to improve oversight of judges as entirely pernicious. As we have noted, there are many problems in China's courts—including corruption, incompetence, and other forms of malfeasance. If internal networks are able to ensure that cases are heard and decided on time—within the time limits stipulated in law—it would be a major step forward for the fairness of the Chinese system. The same is true with having live images of court proceedings available to court superiors: the fact that proceedings are on camera may reduce incentives to engage in obvious misconduct. In this regard, however, the development of court internal networks reflects the development of the Internet in China more generally. Restricted access to the Internet serves the state's interests in oversight and control. But restricted access may be better than no access, and in the legal system it may mean courts that function more fairly, more efficiently, and more consistently.

III. JUDICIAL COMMUNICATIONS AND JUDICIAL POWER

What is the relationship among how a judiciary communicates and its position in society? What can we learn from the Chinese example about the relationship between judicial communications, judicial power, and the rule of law?

We suggest a central and important tradeoff for the Chinese or any legal system in a cheap speech environment. First, in a country with a weak judiciary, the ease of criticism made possible by cheap communications technology can pose a serious threat to the legitimacy and power of the courts and threaten progress toward a consistent rule of law. In more developed legal systems, where the judiciary is stronger, such effects may be weaker, and the salutary aspects of criticism more obvious. However, in countries with less developed legal institutions, the power of mass, directed, and cheap criticism to weaken judicial institutions is much clearer.

The criticism born of greater informational freedom can correct injustice, prevent corruption, and otherwise ensure a more fair legal system. But at the same time it can also destroy what little power and autonomy weak courts may have. Where the courts lack authority, the media and courts may become rival institutions, set on a course of repeated conflict. That is what we have seen in China, where courts and the media each contend that their view of the law and the facts is the correct one, and where each claims that the other is beset by corruption and incompetence.

But the same cheap communications can also be used to build judicial power. The easier it is for judges to communicate, the easier it is to develop a consistent set of rules across the country. Cheaper communications make it easier for courts to apply the law consistently—a major and often overlooked problem (at least in Western writing on Chinese law).[227] That, in turn, gives judges the power to appeal to the potent principle that similar cases should be decided similarly. Stated differently, we suggest here that judicial "herding," while considered dangerous by some of the American literature,[228] may be a key component of constructing judicial power.

Horizontal networking among judges also makes it easier for judges to cumulatively improve the law—by passing on best practices to others. It also facilitates the development of professional identity, which may be key to developing the ability to resist external pressure. Those improvements will further strengthen judicial claims to legitimate resolution of cases.

A. Judicial Power

The source of judicial legitimacy and power presents one of the oldest questions in law and political science. What gives courts their political power? The question is not easy to answer. The judiciary, whether in China or other countries, typically lacks either the legitimacy of an elected body,[229] or the command of coercive physical force (like that of an army) to enforce its will. The judiciary's power to make others obey must derive from an appeal to some other source of authority and legitimacy. Invariably judges lay claim to be enforcing some higher principle that transcends the case before the judge.[230] The exact principle may vary across cases, legal systems, and eras. A judge may claim to be effectuating the commands of the legislature, deciding the case the same as a similar case, enforcing basic principles of morality, or perhaps implementing a divine will. The strength of those claims will vary across time and among places. But what these claims have in common is an appeal to an authority beyond the personal discretion of the judge, and a hope that, thanks to the claim, the judge's decision will be obeyed.

From this perspective, a judiciary's power can be said to stem from at least two social factors. The first is how broadly any principle upon which the judiciary might rely is accepted, both by other parts of government, who may have to enforce the ruling, and by the public at large, who choose whether to comply. A second is, even granting the existence of accepted principles, the capacity of the judiciary to assert the claims in the first place, a question that may depend on access to resources. For example, a judge who lacks the relevant statute books will have trouble claiming, as a matter of principle, that she is faithfully implementing the will of the legislature.

Let us turn to the Chinese example, where the courts are weak, both constitutionally and in actual practice, and discuss what makes their claims to higher principle difficult. First, among the simplest claims of principle a court can make is that it is obeying the written law. Yet even that most basic claim is complicated by the vagueness and confusion in many Chinese laws, and by overlapping claims to authority by various party-state institutions. Meanwhile, courts in poorer areas sometimes lack basic legal texts, let alone Internet access. Similarly, judges, especially in rural areas, may lack the legal training necessary to articulate their claims to legitimacy.[231]

Second, as we have already discussed, courts in China have been isolated and largely unaware of what other, similar courts are doing. This deprives the courts of another of the most obvious principles from which they can claim legitimacy: doing what other courts have done. The decisions made by Chinese courts, consequently, have lacked the consistency that might form the basis for a claim to legitimacy and fairness.

Without recourse to these more obvious claims to legitimacy, a popular default, as other Chinese scholars have noted, is for Chinese courts to make the claim to be effectuating the will of the party-state.[232] However, the relatively unclear legitimacy of the party-state itself, along with its control over the courts, means that the authority that may be derived from such claims may be weak. In practice, it appears that injustice in individual cases, and inconsistent application of the law, are widely viewed as undermining popular confidence in the courts.

What our study adds to this discussion of judicial power is a new appreciation of how judicial communications may affect the claims to authority that judges may make.[233] Cheaper communications can both weaken and strengthen judicial power.

B. Net Justice

The blogger theory discussed in Part I makes the classic point that cheaper speech ought to improve government performance. Much of the argument is a high-tech version of the classic view of free speech presented by John Stuart Mill in *On Liberty*, suggesting the now seemingly obvious merits of having orthodoxy challenged by heretical opinion.[234] In its high-tech manifestation, the idea is that the government will commit a given number of wrongful acts. Due to resource limits and agenda, traditional media will only expose a percentage of these errors. In theory, the sheer increase in the number of critics empowered by Internet technology will lead to more government misdeeds being uncovered—in the sense that a nation equipped with more fly-swatters will kill more flies.

Writers like Thomas Friedman and Nicolas Kristof rely on blogger theory and predict that in authoritarian regimes such as China, cheap speech ought similarly to improve government performance—or even lead to the downfall of such regimes. Whether that is actually happening or not is the subject of an ongoing debate. Both of us, in other work, have discussed this subject, emphasizing a loss of specific control yet a maintenance of overall control over political debate within China.[235] More wrongs are being exposed in China, but this does not necessarily mean the Party is any less in control than in the past.

What we have learned in this study sheds further light on this debate. Blogger theory prizes criticism as a remedy for bad governance, which means that the cheaper it is to criticize, the better. This study shows the limits of these views—and urges a better understanding of the role of cheap Internet criticism. We uncover the problems of directed criticism, in particular, of attacks on a weak judiciary in an environment where criticism of other government actors is more effectively barred.

An important assumption of the free speech theory discussed above is that the government actors in question are powerful enough that criticism will, in the end, improve performance. Yet matters may be different when some but not other forms of criticism are allowed and when the criticized actors are weak and face ongoing legitimacy problems. In that context, the public criticisms made possible by cheaper speech can erode the ability of judges to act, in effect, as judges. It can weaken their capacity to act independent of public and political opinion, and weaken the courts' power relative to that of other political actors.

We have seen in this paper that criticism of the judiciary helps maintain the power of the Party. Net-fueled rage provides new reasons and justifications for individual party-state officials to intervene in the operation of the legal system.[236] Although sometimes the party-state will prop up, as opposed to reverse, a judge's decisions, either way, it is the party-state, not the courts, that has the final say. Whatever legal authority might have existed is replaced with a political decision made by the party-state. This creates incentives for the public and the media to appeal to party-state actors to intervene in cases with which they disagree. It also encourages courts to align their decisions with what they believe will be party-state leaders' views.

For judges, political intervention can be embarrassing, and carries the risk of more serious sanctions if decisions are viewed as incorrect by court or Party superiors. In China, in politicized or sensitive cases, the threat of political intervention has always been a check on the power of the courts. Preordained outcomes and Party intervention have long been a feature of the Chinese legal system. The new concern, however, is a type of political pressure that is born not of the narrow political or financial concerns of the Party or of individual Party officials, but of the broader set of issues that inflame public opinion. What is new is the possibility of intervention not only for politically sensitive cases, but for simply unpopular decisions.

At its worst, cheap mass criticism may lead to a legal system where Internet reaction serves as a kind of alternative appellate review. The case of Liu Yong's execution comes closest to that extreme, one that Chinese commentators have compared to the court-free mass justice of the Cultural Revolution. But more ominous still are the cases like Liu Yong's that never come to light, because the ourts do not dare practice leniency for fear of the public reaction.

Courts have several means of trying to avoid such interventions, but most lead in unfortunate directions. First, courts facing cheap mass criticism have every reason to try to prevent the media and Internet sites from stirring up controversy. The result is the spread of false or controlled transparency in China's courts. The courts, as we are seeing, have used new technology and the commercialization of the media to spread positive reports about their own work.[237] They are also making it harder for journalists to cover court proceedings. The emphasis China's courts have put on managing media relations and the flow of information to the media in recent years reflects both the power of the Chinese media and the Internet, and judges' beliefs that media intervention in cases is often illegitimate and unhelpful. The courts thus are now trying to exert more influence on the media, much as the media have tried to influence the courts.

Second, given that courts cannot always control media coverage, courts have an incentive to try to decide cases in a manner least likely to inflame public opinion or attract media attention. As we have said, the real question is how often courts fail to decide cases like the Liu Yong case for fear of public outcry. It goes without saying that such self-conscious efforts to avoid unpopular decisions are a far cry from deciding cases fairly.[238] Instead, the courts may engage (like the media itself) in a judicial version of a self-censorship—or make a deliberate effort to guess what outcomes the media or ultimately the Party might prefer.

What we are saying can be misinterpreted as suggesting that a judiciary is better off absent any external criticism. None of this is meant to suggest that there is no positive side to the new criticisms of China's courts. The optimistic face of web justice is (half) of the Sun Zhigang case, where public attention demanded government reform, or the Nie and She cases, where Internet coverage helped to pressure the SPC to revise procedures for capital cases. We do not advocate further restrictions on speech in China. The problem is not with the courts or the media, but rather lies in hypersensitivity to public opinion and concerns regarding "social stability" among Party officials, and a resulting unwillingness to refrain from intervening when law and public opinion conflict.

* * *

The points discussed here have obvious implications for other developing countries, as well as for legal systems with more robust courts. The blogger theories developed in the West have their limits, particularly when the development of the judiciary is at issue. In many developing countries with weak judiciaries, it must be understood that cheap mass criticism of the courts alone may hinder, rather than aid, the development of an independent judiciary. The case of China shows how important it is for media to respect a judiciary's role in society, and for courts and other state institutions to be able to resist the temptation to yield to public rage. The spectacle of the Internet manhunt as a kind of appellate court of public opinion may have reached an extreme form in China. Yet no legal system can afford to ignore similar dangers.

This discussion also highlights a crucial difference between *cheap* speech and *free* speech. Many observers of China mistake the present volume of speech (cheap speech) as reflecting an inevitable trend toward free speech, when actually the two are distinct. Speech may be cheaper in the new China but at the same time only modestly freer, for while the volume of criticism may be growing, much is in permitted directions. The media has some freedom to incite virulent public attacks on the judiciary (cheap speech), but not to question the legitimacy of Party rule (free speech). Indeed, the very fact that there remain significant restrictions on speech may be what makes permitted forms of criticism so extreme. That is why when we warn of the dangers of cheap speech to the power of the Chinese judiciary, we are not discounting the value of free speech in the political system. We claim only that cheapening speech along one dimension—mass criticism of an already weak judiciary—may not be a healthy development.

C. Judicial Networks

Cheap speech may make it easier to ignite populist campaigns against the judiciary. But, as compared to print media, the flip side of Internet communications is that they can make it easier for judges to learn about and rely on each other's decisions—giving a new basis for claims to independence and legitimacy. The changing costs of information, stated otherwise, affect both the independence and the accountability of Chinese judges in new ways.

Judges who are aware of the decisions of others may make claim to a central principle: that like cases be decided alike. There is obviously far more to a legal system than the "like cases" principle. Nonetheless, the idea that if a case is not different in relevant particulars from a case already decided it should be decided in the same manner is an important starting point.[239]

The recent American literature on judicial precedent cascades, discussed in Part I, has largely warned of the dangers of blind obedience to the decisions of other judges. Our study leads us to a conclusion that is nearly the opposite: imitative behavior may be a crucial route for the Chinese courts to develop their power and autonomy. We argue here that the rise of horizontal communications within the judiciary may slowly give individual judges and courts more confidence in their decisions, as they create more uniformity and consistency within their courts and across the country.

What happens when it gets easier and cheaper for judges to know what similarly situated judges are doing or have done?[240] A judge now has a new source of (external) information, namely, the decisions made by other judges who faced the same problem.[241] This setting—a set of sequential and similar decision-makers facing a similar problem with imperfect information—contains the basic components of the main economic models of herding behavior.[242] And given basic assumptions, the prediction is that judges, like any other actors, will rationally value the information on what other decision-makers did in similar circumstances, or at least count it in addition to local information.[243] Even without a binding rule of *stare decisis*,[244] we might expect the knowledge of what other judges have done to have an effect on judicial decision-making. Certainly this is the case in other civil law systems that at least formally lack a principle of *stare decisis*.[245] This is a complex way of saying that judges will value the acts of other judges as a source of information as to the right decision.[246] As Professor Eric Talley writes, as judges "learn information from previous holdings, they may rationally begin to treat such holdings as binding on them, *even if* not formally required to do so, and *even if* the case they actually hear suggests a contrary outcome."[247]

Most of the American literature on herding and the judiciary presents the possibility of precedential cascades as a threat to the legal system. The argument is that judges may begin to blindly obey what others have done with little regard as to the correctness of the rule adopted. Yet whether this is really a problem depends on the legal system under study. Where consistency and a basic rule of law are taken for granted, herd behavior may be a problem. But where the judiciary is weak and its decisions inconsistent, herding may be an important political strategy. Our theory suggests that information about similar cases—even if not acknowledged as precedent—may make it easier for courts elsewhere to reach similar decisions. The greater availability of information and debate may also make it more likely that courts in different areas of China will apply the law consistently. Courts are increasingly looking for guidance horizontally, to peer courts in other jurisdictions, rather than only looking to their vertical superiors. The fact that judges are increasingly looking horizontally to each other also suggests the possibility of ground-up development of law and courts, greater expansion of court autonomy, and perhaps increased professional identity among judges. All of these may over time encourage courts to further develop their own ability to resist external pressure.

We can present this discussion a different way. As we discussed above, the legitimacy and power of courts stems in part from their adherence to higher or neutral principles.[248] In a mature legal system, it can be easier to find such principles, whether they be the "rule of clear mistake" allowing the judiciary to correct obvious errors made by the legislature and executive, the principle that like cases be treated alike, or some other principle. Yet in a developing legal system the search for such rules may be more difficult. That is why the simplest principle of all—acting as other courts or judges have done—is so important.[249] Lacking any other particular claim to legitimacy, the judge may at least say that the court is acting in a manner consistent with what other courts have done. Courts and legal systems that treat like cases alike would appear both more deserving of and more likely to receive public trust.

A further component of the advantages of judicial networking for judges is the possibility of innovation toward better rules. In a world where judicial communication is difficult, an innovative decision—either a novel resolution of an unclear legal issue or a decision that appears to challenge existing laws or norms—often went unnoticed. Today, some such cases become lively topics of debate online—allowing both lawyers and judges elsewhere to become aware of such decisions.[250] Courts may be more willing to innovate when they know that courts elsewhere in China have done the same. And to the extent judicial networks improve the law in ways that prove popular, judges may lay claim to greater authority and prestige.

The implications of this China-focused discussion for the rest of the world should be clear. Empirically, scholars like Anne-Marie Slaughter have documented the rise of cross-border contacts and networking among judges.[251] Slaughter's work on judicial networks describes the increasing practice of judges in different countries paying attention to each other, and each other's decisions, in a way that is influential despite being nonbinding. What courts in both international and Chinese judicial networks are seeking is the same. They seek the additional power and legitimacy that is the product of judicial conformity. That judges in China and around the world should both seek the comfort of reliance on what other courts have done should be no surprise.

We close this discussion with three caveats. First, our findings are predictive rather than conclusive; we are suggesting that horizontal networking by Chinese judges presents one possible route to strengthening the position of China's courts within the existing political system. Second, the position of courts in Chinese society is the product of many factors, most importantly party-state policy. Third, the interviews conducted for this article do not permit overly broad conclusions regarding how many judges use the Internet, or the degree to which such use of the Internet is fostering informal precedent. Certainly not all judges go online; those who do so tend to be younger, educated, and accustomed to using computers. Many judges in China's courts are older and have had no formal higher education prior to joining the courts. One judge noted that only those judges who are "responsible" will bother to conduct online research.[252] Another judge stated that those judges who do have Internet access are more likely to use the Internet to play online games than they are to conduct legal research.[253] Despite these caveats, we are confident that changes in how judges communicate will, over the long term, affect the operation of the Chinese legal system.

IV. CONCLUSION

The dramatic drop in the costs of communications represented by the Internet revolution has had effects on the world both predictable and unpredictable. In North America, Japan, and Europe, it is the media and entertainment industries that have faced the most radical challenges. But it stands to reason that not every country will change in the same ways. In China, this study shows that the legal system is one area where changing informational practices seem to be having long-term transformative effects, with important lessons for the rest of the world.

The perennial question is whether China's Internet revolution is facilitating the "rule of law." We see mixed results. At its best, judicial networking may strengthen the confidence and autonomy of individual judges, as they network with their peers. Net justice may also be used as a corrective against judicial malfeasance and corruption. But as for the delicate issue of external, political scrutiny of judges, matters may be getting worse before they start getting better. As one of us has noted elsewhere, at the end of the day raising the status and authority of courts is not something courts can do on their own.[254] The central party-state does not appear interested in fundamental changes to the power of the courts. What is emerging, however, is a new and confusing dynamic between a commercial media, better trained judges who are beginning to aspire to the roles played by judges elsewhere, party-state officials, and a reactive public. We do not claim to understand the full implications of that dynamic for the rule of law in China.

The case study of China yields important lessons for the legal systems in developing and developed countries. Every country has a *de facto* speech environment surrounding its judiciary—a mixture of informal and formal rules that control how judges speak, and how people speak about judges. What we learn from the study of China is how vital these speech practices can be for a healthy and fair legal system. The speech norms by which a judiciary lives by may be vital to its power, and their erosion cannot be taken lightly.

NOTES

* Previously published in *The Chicago Journal of International Law*, 8/1 (July 2007).

** We are grateful for comments from participants in a seminar hosted by the Institute of Law of the Chinese Academy of Social Sciences, and at workshops at Columbia, Cornell, and Duke Law Schools. We are indebted to Jennifer Bell, Hu Jianjie, Peng Lingyan, Yang Fuhao, Zhang Lan, and Zhang Wenguang for outstanding research assistance.

We also gratefully acknowledge financial support for this project from the Stanley and Judith Lubman Fund at Columbia Law School.

† Copies of all Chinese language sources cited in this article are on file with the authors.

‡ Many of the websites hosted in China that are cited in this article are frequently unavailable online. Hard copies of these sources were provided by the authors and confirmed by the *Chicago Journal of International Law* staff. Where websites have been unavailable, we have modified our citation format to indicate that copies are on file with the authors, rather than providing the last date on which the availability of the website was confirmed by *CJIL*.

1. Katsh (1989: 3–16).
2. See generally Benkler (2006); Reynolds (2006); also Volokh (1995).
3. Benkler (2006: 272).
4. In China, references to "the judiciary" and "judicial" encompass both the courts and the procuratorates. In this article, we use "judiciary" and "judicial" to refer to the courts alone.
5. Katsh (1989: 3). See generally Katsh (1995); Ross (2002); Collins and Skover (1992).
6. See generally Goldsmith and Wu (2006: vii–ix) (questioning the impact on some of law's operation from changing communications).
7. See Part II.
8. See generally Wechsler (1959); Bickel (1962: 49–65).
9. See, for example, Slaughter (2004: 66–103), describing a global trend toward judicial networking.
10. The field of early communications studies is far too vast to describe here. For an introduction, see Schramm (1997).

11. Cooley (1998: 103).
12. See note 2.
13. Katsh (1984: 631): "The spread of printing led to fundamental changes in legal doctrines, legal institutions, legal values and attitudes about law." Ross (2002: 640–42) summarizes arguments that the development of printing facilitated the evolution of common-law precedent.
14. Katsh (1989: introduction at 14).
15. Katsh (1989: 13).
16. See generally Volokh (1995).
17. Benkler (2006: 272).
18. Gillmor (2004).
19. Reynolds (2006).
20. Benkler (2006: 212, 272). Writers like Benkler focus on Internet-based, mass-political movements that make use of network technology. For example, Benkler tells the story of how a variety of Internet activists managed to make the security of Diebold voting machines a matter of public concern in the 2000s, an issue in which the mass media was originally uninterested (2006: 225–33). Other well-discussed examples are the Internet-driven fundraising behind the Howard Dean campaign in the 2004 election, the exposure of fraud behind various anti-Bush war records, and the purge of Trent Lott from the Senate leadership (2006: 258, 262–5). The general tenor is to suggest that, but for a more democratic "citizen media," history would have taken a much different course.
21. Sunstein (2001a, 2001b); see also Sunstein (1995: 1785–7).
22. Sunstein (2001b: 5).
23. See James Madison, "Federalist 10," in *The Federalist Papers*, ed. Clinton Rossiter (New York: Mentor 1961), 77.
24. William J. Clinton, *Remarks by the President to Business Leaders, and Officials and Employees of Gateway Computers* (September 4, 1998), available online at <http://www.clintonfoundation.org/legacy/090498-speech-by-president-to-officials-of-gateway-computers.htm> (visited April 21, 2007).
25. See Goldsmith and Wu (2006: 87–104); Liebman (2005: 59–64, 82–92).
26. Nicholas D. Kristof (2005), "Death by a Thousand Blogs," *New York Times* (May 24), A21.
27. For more general commentary on the impact of the Internet, see Chander (2002); Ulen (2001); Nadel (2001: 857).
28. See Katsh (1995: 172–94).
29. Hayek (1945).
30. Since Hayek's time the relationship between information transmission and decision-making has received much attention—only the briefest of summaries will be attempted here. Michael Spence, Joseph Stiglitz, and others have developed the field of information economics, which emphasizes economic decision-making under conditions of imperfect information. See generally, Stiglitz (2002). That has led to work on information asymmetries as a form of market failure (and signaling as a remedy), the relative performance of decentralized and centralized decision-makers, the phenomenon of "herding behavior," and other interactions between information and the market. See, for example, Bolton and Dewatripont (1994); Milgrom and Roberts (1992: 113–16); Sah and Stiglitz (1984, 1991); Scharfstein and Stein (1990). Versions of these ideas have reached the public in widely read works such as James Surowiecki's *The Wisdom of Crowds: Why the Many Are Smarter Than the Few and How Collective Wisdom Shapes Business, Economies, Societies, and Nations* (2004).

31. See generally Sah and Stiglitz (1984, 1991).
32. See Stein (2002: 1891–3), arguing that information that might be easier to transmit, or "hard" information, like numbers, can be handled well by a hierarchy, while "soft" information, such as a subjective assessment of managerial ability, might be better processed by decentralized actors.
33. Hayek (1960: 194–6).
34. See Posner (1973: 320–8). See also Rubin (1977); Priest (1977).
35. One obvious point is that judges who choose the wrong rules do not, like firms, go out of business, and few today seem to believe that all common-law rules are efficient. See, for example, Priest (1977: 75–81); Kornhauser (1996: 169–78); Hadfield (1992).
36. Paul Mahoney, for example, has sought to demonstrate empirically that common-law, precedent-based systems create faster economic growth than civil systems. His data show, on average, slightly more than 0.5 percent faster growth in the world's common-law countries during the period 1962–90. See Mahoney (2001: 516). Mahoney controlled for starting per capita GDP, secondary school enrollment, population growth, investment, and other factors (2001: 521).
37. For example, imagine that Restaurants A and B serve similar-quality food, and that ten people, who know nothing about the restaurants, arrive one by one. The first sequential decision-maker D1 might decide randomly to go to restaurant B. The next, D2, if he weights D1's decision heavily, might make the same choice. Over time, restaurant B may be full, a powerful signal of quality having nothing to do with the actual quality of the food. For a more in-depth overview, see Bikhchandani, Hirshleifer, and Welch (1998).
38. Daughety and Reinganum (1999: 159), citing *Eastern Enterprises v Apfel*, 524 US 498 (1998).
39. See Gillette (1998: 822).
40. See generally Talley (1999).
41. This discussion is based on Liebman (2007, 2006, 2005).
42. All interviews were conducted by Liebman. All interviewees were promised complete anonymity, and thus we identify neither their name nor the location in which the interviews took place. [Editorial note: In order to accommodate this anonymity, the *Chicago Journal of International Law* has made an exception to its policy of independently reviewing all cited sources, instead relying on the authors to ensure the proper use of these interviews. Copies of all interviews are on file with the authors.]
43. For details of the case, see Liebman (2005: 82–91).
44. *Southern Weekend*: "Articles on People's Daily Online Strengthen the Determination to Crack the Sun Zhigang Case" ["Nan Fang Zhou Mo: Renmin Wang Wenzhang Zengjia Le Zhenpo Sun Zhigang An De Juexin"], *Southern Weekend* [*Nan Fang Zhoumo*] (June 6, 2003), available online at <http://past.people.com.cn/GB/news/8410/20030606/1010138.htm> (Chinese) (on file with author), discussing the Internet's role in the case; Human Rights Watch: "The Voice of China: The Sun Zhigang Affair" ["Zhongguo Zhi Sheng: Sun Zhigang Shijian"], Human Rights Watch (April 29, 2003), available online at <http://www.hrw.org/campaigns/china/beijing08/voices_ch.htm> (Chinese) (on file with author), stating that tens of thousands of postings protesting the case appeared, on all popular websites in China, and including examples of such postings. See also Teng Biao, "The Sun Zhigang Affair: Intelligence, Media and Power" ["Sun Zhigang Shijian: Zhishi, Meijie Yu Quanli"], *Law Thinker Web* [*Falü Sixiang Wang*] (October 25, 2004), available online at <http://law-thinker.com/show.asp?id=2703> (Chinese) (on file with author), describing online discussions of the case and the important role of the Internet.

45. In addition, twenty-three officials were given administrative sanctions for their mishandling of the case.
46. For discussion of the petitions, see Guo Liang, "Internet Growth in China: Drivers, Actors and Impact on Public Opinion" ["Zhongguo Hulianwang De Fazhan: Dongli Yiji Dui Minyi De Yingxiang"], *China Internet Research Project* [*Zhongguo Hulianwang Yanjiu Xiangmu*] (April 26, 2004), available online at <http://www.wipchina.org/?p1=content&p2=05013000345> (Chinese) (on file with author); Teng Biao, "The Sun Zhigang Affair" ["Sun Zhigang Shijian"] (cited in note 44); Cui Li, "Five Experts' Petitions to the NPC to Initiate Special Investigation Proceedings Regarding Sun Zhigang Case" ["Wu Zhuanjia Jiu Sun Zhigang An Tiqing Renda Qidong Tebie Diaocha Chengxu"], *China Youth Daily* [*Zhongguo Qingnian Bao*] (May 28, 2003), available online at <http://www.npcnews.com.cn/gb/paper7/30/class000700001/hwz236693.htm> (Chinese) (on file with author); "Three Citizens Petition to the NPC Calling for Constitutional Review of the Custody and Repatriation Provisions" ["San Gongmin Shangshu Renda Jianyi Dui Shourong Banfa Jinxing Weixian Shencha"], *China Youth Daily* [*Zhongguo Qingnian Bao*] (May 16, 2003), available online at <http://www.people.com.cn/GB/shizheng/20030516/993964.htm> (Chinese) (on file with author).
47. For discussion of the Internet's role in the case, see Ouyang Bin, "Internet's Impact on the Environment of Chinese Society" ["Hulianwang Chongji Zhongguo Shehui Shengtai"], *Phoenix TV Net* [*Fenghuang Wang*], available online at <http://www.phoenixtv.com.cn/home/phoenixweekly/141/30page.htm> (Chinese) (on file with author); Guo Liang, "Internet Growth in China" (cited in note 46).
48. For example, a well-known Peking University professor engaged in a pointed two-hour online discussion on the case; the transcript is available at He Weifang, "Development of Rule of Law in China as Reflected by the Sun Zhigang Affair" ["Cong Sun Zhigang Shijian Kan Zhongguo Fazhi Fazhan"], *People's Daily Online* [*Renmin Wang*] (June 10, 2003), available online at <http://www.people.com.cn/GB/shehui/46/20030610/1013342.htm> (on file with author).
49. "670,000 Urban Vagrants Get Assistance in China," *People's Daily Online* (December 23, 2004), available online at <http://english.people.com.cn/200412/23/eng20041223_168443.html> (on file with author); "Vagrants Get Aid as New System Begins in China," *People's Daily Online* (August 1, 2003), available online at <http://english.people.com.cn/200308/01/eng20030801_121435.shtml> (on file with author).
50. For discussion of the development of the commercialized media in China and the rise of investigative journalism, see Liebman (2005: 23–41).
51. "From Nie Shubin to She Xianglin: Correcting Wrongful Convictions Cannot Rely Only On Chance" ["Cong Nie Shubin Dao She Xianglin: Cuoan Zhaoxue Buneng Jiwang Yu Ouran"] (April 3, 2005), available online at <http://news.xinhuanet.com/legal/2005-04/03/content_2779236.htm> (Chinese) (on file with author).
52. Id.
53. See Lü Zongshu, "Journalist's Investigation: The Wrongful Conviction of She Xianglin for 'Killing his Wife'" ["Jizhe Diaocha: She Xianglin 'Sha Qi' Cuo An"], *People's Daily Online* [*Renmin Wang*] (July 27, 2005), available online at <http://media.people.com.cn/GB/22114/47850/47855/3572767.htm> (Chinese) (on file with author).
54. Hu Bing and Yan Hua, "She Xianglin Obtains 460,000 Yuan in Compensation" ["She Xianglin Nadao 46 Wan Peichang He Buchang Kuan"], *China Court Web* [*Zhongguo Fayuan Wang*] (September 3, 2005), available online at <http://www.chinacourt.org/public/detail.php?id=176316> (Chinese) (on file with author).
55. "From Nie Shubin to She Xianglin" (cited in note 51).

56. "Jingmen for the First Time Summarizes Publicly the Lessons from the She Xianglin Case: The Crucial Reason Is the Presumption of Guilt" ["Jingmen Shouci Gongkai Zongjie She Xianglin An Jiaoxun: Youzui Tuiding Shi Shouyin"], *Xinhua Net* [*Xinhua Wang*] (July 19, 2005), available online at <http://news.xinhuanet.com/legal/2005-07/19/content_3239399.htm> (Chinese) (on file with author).
57. "'The Case of Nie Shubin's Wrongful Execution' Is Pending, and the Public Calls Out for an External Investigation in Order to Avoid 'Compromising'" ["'Nie Shubin Yuansha An' Xuan Er Wei Jue, Fang 'Goudui' Gongzhong Yu Yidi Diaocha"], *Southern Weekend* [*Nanfang Zhoumo*] (March 24, 2005), available online at <http://www.southcn.com/weekend/commend/200503240006.htm> (Chinese) (on file with author).
58. Zhao Ling, "Nie Shubin Case Will Absolutely Not End Up with No Outcome" ["Nie Shubin An Juedui Buhui Bu Liao Liao Zhi"], *Southern Weekend* [*Nanfang Zhoumo*] (April 28, 2005), available online at <http://www.nanfangdaily.com.cn/ZM/20050428/xw/fz/200504280005.asp> (Chinese) (on file with author).
59. Previously, the Guangpin County public security website had included details of the case in a prominent place. Id.
60. "Real Rapist and Murderer Caught, An Innocent Youth Was Executed Wrongfully 10 Years Ago" ["Qiangjian Sharen An Zhenciao Lou Wang, Wugu Qingnian 10 Nian Qian Bei Zhixing Sixing"], *Beijing News* (*Xin Jing Bao*) (March 15, 2005), available online at <http://news.hexun.com/detail.aspx?lm=1697&id=1068197> (Chinese) (on file with author). See also Zhao Ling, "Nie Shubin Case" (cited in note 58); "'Nie Shubin Case' Needs More of the Public's Continuing and Intense Attention" ["'Nie Shubin An' Geng Xuyao Gongzhong Haobu Songxie De Jinmi Guanzhu"], *Southern Metropolitan Daily* [*Nanfang Dushi Bao*] (April 22, 2005), available online at <http://www.southcn.com/opinion/politics/200504220359.htm> (Chinese) (on file with author) (discussing the case).
61. "The Central Propaganda Department Urgently Circulates Notice Banning Reports of the Case of Nie Shubin's Wrongful Execution" ["Zhongxuanbu Jinji Tongzhi Jinzhi Baodao Nie Shubin Bei Cuosha An"], *Boxun Newsnet* [*Boxun Xinwen Wang*] (March 21, 2005), available online at <http://www.peacehall.com/news/gb/china/2005/03/200503211409.shtm> (Chinese) (on file with author); Fu Yingji, "Twelve Big Pieces of News Deleted from the Chinese Internet in 2005" ["2005 Nian Zhongguo Wangluo Shier Da Bei Shan Xinwen"] (December 31, 2005), available online at <http://forum.chinesenewsnet.com/archive/index.php/t-19858.htm> (Chinese) (on file with author) and <http://www.wangbingzhang.us/forum/wbz/messages/4381.htm> (on file with author). The two sources that reported on the ban are overseas media and may have overstated the reach of the ban. Although both reports stated that the CPD had imposed a ban, it appears more likely that any ban was imposed by local, not national, propaganda department officials. For a collection of commentary on the case, see Xiao Han, "Pay Attention to Nie Shubin's Wrongly Adjudicated Death Penalty Case" ["Guanzhu Nie Shubin Mengyuan Sixing An"], *China Review Web* [*Zhong Pin Wang*] (March 22, 2004), available online at <http://www.china-review.com/tbzt/050322bianzhean.htm> (Chinese) (on file with author).
62. "The Case of Nie Shubin's Wrongful Execution" (cited in note 57); Zhao Ling, "Nie Shubin Case" (cited in note 58); Qian Haoping, "Hebei Reinvestigates the Nie Shubin Case, Stating They Will Reveal the Truth in the Shortest Time Possible" ["Hebei Chongxin Diaocha Nie Shubin An, Cheng Zuiduan Shijian Nei Huan Shishi Zhenxiang"], *Beijing News* [*Xin Jing Bao*] (March 18, 2005), available online at <http://news.hexun.com/detail.aspx?lm=1716&id=1073687> (Chinese) (on file with author).
63. Id.

64. "Hebei Makes Determination that the Nie Shubin Case 'Was Not Wrongfully Decided'" ["Hebei Zuochu Nie Shubin An 'Bushi Cuoan' De Rending"], *Strait Met Newspaper* [*Haixia Dushi Bao*] (April 22, 2005), available online at <http://www.peacehall.com/news/gb/china/2005/04/200504220259.shtml> (Chinese) (on file with author).
65. Zhong Kai, "Southern Metropolitan Daily: Are All the Original Investigation Records of Nie Case Required" ["Nanfang Dushi Bao: Feiyao Zhaoqi Nie An De Yuanshi Xingzhen Jilu Ma"], *Southern Metropolitan Daily* [*Nanfang Dushi Bao*] (January 7, 2006), available online at <http://news.163.com/06/0107/01/26R26J510001124T.html> (Chinese) (on file with author). One report stated that the family of Nie Shubin had heard that officials had determined that there was no error, but had not received any formal notification to this effect. "'The Nie Shubin Rape and Murder Case' Was Not Wrongfully Decided" ["'Nie Shubin Qiangjian Sharen An' Bushi Cuoan"], *Guangzhou Daily* [*Guangzhou Ribao*] (April 20, 2005), available online at <http://gzdaily.dayoo.com/gb/content/2005-04/20/content_2023768.htm> (Chinese) (on file with author).
66. "Yearender: Media's Frequent Exposure of Unjust Cases Promotes China's Judicial Reform," *People's Daily Online* (December 19, 2005), available online at <http://english.people.com.cn/200512/19/eng20051219_229034.html> (on file with author).
67. "Legal Daily: Clicking on Four Key Legal Words in the Year 2005" ["Fazhi Ribao: Dianji 2005 Nian Si Da Falü Guanjian Ci"] (January 10, 2006), available online at <http://news.sina.com.cn/c/2006-01-10/08317940186s.shtml> (Chinese) (on file with author) (discussing the effect of the Nie and She cases).
68. In some cases in which initial reports in the official media are blocked, information on the cases is first posted to websites. Once sufficient public discussion has been generated, and official attitudes toward the case have become clear, the official media will then report on the case. Ouyang Bin, "Internet's Impact" (cited in note 47).
69. The Information Office of the State Council and the Ministry of Information Industry [Hulianwang Xinwen Xinxi Fuwu Guanli Guiding], *Provisions for the Administration of Internet News Information Services, Order No. 37* [*Guowuyuan Xinwen Bangongshi, Xinxi Chanye Bu Di 37 Hao Ling*] (September 25, 2005), available online at <http://law.chinalawinfo.com/newlaw2002/SLC/SLC.asp?Db=chl&Gid=60145> (Chinese) (on file with author) (stating that only websites linked to traditional media are permitted to generate their own news stories); The Information Office of the State Council and the Ministry of Information Industry [Guowuyuan Xinwen Bangongshi, Xinxi Chanye Bu], *Temporary Provisions for the Administration of Internet Websites' Service of Posting News Information* [*Hulian Wangzban Congshi Dengzai Xinwen Yewu Guanli Zanxing Guiding*] (November 7, 2000), available online at <http://info.people.com.cn/EComClnt/index2.jsp> (Chinese) (on file with author).
70. Shi Jiangmin, "'Internet Broadcast' Officially Published in Beijing" ["'Wangluo Chuanbo' Zai Jing Zhengshi Chuangkan"], *People's Daily Online* [*Renmin Wang*] (April 20, 2004), available online at <http://www.people.com.cn/GB/14677/14737/22035/2458358.html> (Chinese) (on file with author).
71. Id. (listing examples); Liebman (2005: 60–1).
72. Interview 2006–26.
73. In mid-2005, China's Central Propaganda Department issued new rules restricting "non-local news." The rules, which ban local media from writing original news content on other jurisdictions in China, is apparently a direct response to the widespread practice of nonlocal media engaging in investigative reporting. Nailene Chou Wiest, "Closing of Loopholes to Further Gag Media," *South China Morning Post (Online)*

(June 11, 2005), available online at <http://www.asiamedia.ucla.edu/article.asp?parentid=25640> (visited April 21, 2007).

74. Ruo Qiao, "Authors of 'Investigation into China's Peasants' Are Sued for Defamation and Refuse to Settle Out of Court" ["'Zhongguo Nongmin Diaocha' Beigao Mingyu Qinquan Yuanshu Zuozhe Jujue Tingwai Hejie"], *Chengdu Commercial News* [*Chengdu Shang Bao*] (February 25, 2004), available online at <http://www.booktide.com/news/20040225/200402250013.html> (Chinese) (on file with author).
75. "Beijing Tightly Controls the Media before the Two Meetings, Bans 'Investigation into China's Peasants'" ["Lianghui Qian Beijing Yankong Yulun Fengsha 'Zhongguo Nongmin Diaocha'"], *Boxun Newsnet* [*Boxun Xinwen Wang*] (February 29, 2004), available online at <http://www.peacehall.com/news/gb/china/2004/02/200402291359.shtml> (Chinese) (on file with author).
76. "Exclusive: Letter to the Chief Judge from Pu Zhiqiang, Lawyer for the Defendants in the 'Investigation into China's Peasants' Case" ["Bentai Dujia Huode 'Zhongguo Nongmin Diaocha' An Bianbu Lüshi Pu Zhiqiang Zhi Shenpanzhang Yi Xin"], *Radio Free Asia* (July 11, 2005), available online at <http://www.rfa.org/mandarin/shenrubaodao/2005/07/11/puzhiqiang/> (Chinese) (on file with author).
77. Chinese courts encountering difficult or sensitive cases frequently either refuse to allow such cases to be filed or simply never decide such cases. For a discussion of the phenomenon, see Liebman (2007).
78. "Final Decision of Sun Zhigang Case Affirms the First Trial Decision: Principal Criminal Qiao Yanqin is Executed" ["Sun Zhigang An Zhongshen Weichi Yuanpan, Zhufan Qiao Yanqin Bei Zhixing Sixing"], *People's Daily Online* [*Renmin Wang*] (June 27, 2003), available online at <http://www.people.com.cn/GB/shehui/1061/1939883.html> (Chinese) (on file with author).
79. See, for example, "The Ministry of Public Security: The Resolution of Sun Zhigang Case is Speedy, Determined and Serious" ["Gong An Bu: Sun Zhigang Anjian De Chuli Shi Xunsu, Jianjue He Yansu De"], *Xinhua Net* [*Xinhua Wang*] (August 7, 2003), available online at <http://news.xinhuanet.com/weekend/2003-08/07/content_1016300.htm> (Chinese) (on file with author).
80. Liebman (2005: 16, 19). The same newspaper, *Southern Metropolitan News*, had also been the first to report on the SARS epidemic in 2003. Observers suggested that the editors were punished for their coverage of both the Sun case and the SARS crisis.
81. "SPC Decision in the Retrial of the Liu Yong Criminal Case (2003) Criminal Retrial No. 5" ["Zuigao Renmin Fayuan Zaishen Liu Yong An Xingshi Panjue Shu (2003) Xing Ti Zi Di 5 Hao"], *China Court Web* [*Zhongguo Fayuan Wang*] (December 20, 2003), available online at <http://www.chinacourt.org/public/detail.php?id=96393> (Chinese) (on file with author).
82. The court stated that it had reduced the sentence in light of the facts and circumstances of the case and noted that torture could not be ruled out. The Provincial High Court Opinion is not publicly available, but the decision is summarized in the SPC's opinion.
83. Li Shuming, "Bund Pictorial: Questions on the Gang Leader Liu Yong's Reduced Sentence of Death with Reprieve" ["Waitan Huabao: Dui Shenyang Heibang Toumu Liu Yong Gaipan Sihuan De Zhiyi"], *Bund Pictorial* [*Waitan Huabao*] (August 21, 2003), available online at <http://news.sina.com.cn/c/2003-08-21/01351583471.shtml> (Chinese) (on file with author).
84. Gao Yu, "Why Is the Shenyang Gang Leader Liu Yong So Aggressive? He has Godparents as Strong Backup" ["Shenyang Heibang Laoda Liu Yong Heyi Ruci Xiaozhang, Gandie Ganma Houtai Ying"], *Sanlian Life Weekly* [*Sanlian Shenghuo*

Zhoukan] (March 8, 2001), available online at <http://news.sina.com.cn/c/202847.html> (Chinese) (on file with author).

85. Zhang Hui'e, "Legal Experts' Analyze Interference in Judicial Justice, Monster Baby is Born By the Malformed System" ["Falü Zhuanjia Lunzheng Ganrao Sifa Gongzheng, Jixing Zhidu Chansheng Guaitai"], *Southern Metropolitan Daily* [*Nanfang Dushi Bao*] (October 9, 2003), available online at <http://news.sina.com.cn/c/2003-10-09/11591884089.shtml> (Chinese) (on file with author). In an online discussion forum on the case, one posting claimed that each expert earned 300,000 yuan for writing in support of Liu Yong. The experts denied this. One of them told journalists that they received only 2000 yuan each. Id.
86. Pursuant to the *tishen*, or "elevation and trial" procedures, the SPC can rehear cases decided by lower courts even absent a request from the parties that they do so. One report stated that the case was the "first ordinary criminal case" in which the SPC had used the procedures; one prior known *tishen* case was the trial of the Gang of Four. Cai Wenquing and Fu Yang, "Two Reasons for the SPC to Retry the Liu Yong Case, Experts Claim It Reflects Major Progress in the Legal System" ["Gaofa Tishen Liu Yong You Liang Da Yuanyin, Zhuanjia Cheng Ci Tixian Fazhi Jinbu"], *Beijing Evening News* [*Beijing Wanbao*] (December 17, 2003), available online at <http://news.sohu.com/2003/12/17/81/news217048181.shtml> (Chinese) (on file with author); "SPC Retries the 'Liu Yong Case' Today, Two Big Questions are Waiting to be Resolved" ["Zuigao Yuan Jinri Tishen 'Liu Yong An,' Liang Da Xuannian Youdai Jiekai"], *Beijing Morning Post* [*Beijing Chenbao*] (December 18, 2003), available online at <http://news.xinhuanet.com/legal/2003-12/18/content_1236925.htm> (Chinese) (on file with author).
87. See, for example, Ouyang Bin, "Internet's Impact" (cited in note 47) (arguing that the death sentence was reinstated due to the combined efforts of Internet and print media); Guo Liang, "Internet Growth in China" (cited in note 46).
88. See, for example, "Shenyang 'Godfather of Black Society' Liu Yong Is Sentenced to Death" ["Shenyang 'Heidao Bazhu' Liu Yong Bei Panchu Sixing"], *Sina* [*Xinlang*], available online at <http://news.sina.com.cn/z/liuyongsy/index.shtml> (Chinese) (on file with author); "Shenyang Liu Yong Case" ["Shenyang Liu Yong An"], *Sina* [*Xinlang*], available online at <http://news.sina.com.cn/z/liuyongsy/1.shtml> (Chinese) (on file with author).
89. "Shenyang 'Godfather of Black Society' Liu Yong Is Sentenced to Death" (cited in note 88).
90. Xiao Yuhen, "Sentencing Liu Yong To Death Is Also the Victory of Public Opinion Supervision" ["Panchu Liu Yong Sixing Ye Shi Yulun Jiandu De Shengli"], *Sina* [*Xinlang*] (December 22, 2003), available online at <http://tech.sina.com.cn/me/2003-12-22/1447271669.shtml> (Chinese) (on file with author).
91. "The Case of 'BMW' Hitting People Gets the Most Internet Reading, Exceeding SARS" ["'Baoma' Zhuangren An Wangshang Dianji Lü Weiju Di Yi, Chaoguo Feidian"], *Xinhua Net* [*Xinhua Wang*] (January 8, 2004), available online at <http://news.xinhuanet.com/legal/2004-01/08/content_1266893.htm> (Chinese) (on file with author). *Sina* first reported on the case on December 31, 2003; ten days later it reported 220,000 online comments. Guo Liang, "Internet Growth in China" (cited in note 46); see also Zhang Shuang, "Analysis of Hot Web Forums Phonomenon Regarding 'BMW Hitting People' Event" ["'Baoma Zhuanaren' Shijian Zhong Wangluo Luntan De Huobao Xianxiang Tanxi"], *News World* [*Xinwen Jie*] (First Colume, 2004), available online at <http://www.thebeijingnews.com/news/2005/0905/11@011747.html> (Chinese) (on file with author) (describing the online discussion forums of the case as "a miracle").
92. Interview 2005–45.

93. The driver in the case, Su Xiuwen, was subject to punishment but was not jailed. But the investigation into the case apparently led to other misdeeds being uncovered. Thus press reports stated that as a result of the investigation into the BMW case, another woman, Han Guizhi, was removed from office and tried for corruption. "The Former President of the Heilongjiang Political Consultative Conference Han Guizhi is Removed from Office" ["Yuan Heilongjiang Zhengxie Zhuyi Han Guizhi Bei Mianzhi Qianhou"], *Beijing News* [*Xin Jing Bao*] (June 24, 2004), available online at <http://news.sina.com.cn/c/2004-06-24/03373503585.shtml> (Chinese) (on file with author); "Han Guizhi Will be Tried in Beijing First Intermediate Court, Several Family Members Have Been 'Double Specified'" ["Han Guizhi Jiang Zai Beijing Di Yi Zhongyuan Shoushen Jiazhong Shu Ren Bei Shuanggui"], *Legal Evening News* [*Fazhi Wanbao*] (March 24, 2005), available online at <http://news.sina.com.cn/c/2005-03-24/14156183789.shtml> (Chinese) (on file with author).
94. For examples, see "Last Wish of a Criminal Waiting for Execution: Paying Attention to Migrant Workers" ["Siqiu Zuihou Yuanwang: Guanzhu Nongmin Gong"], *Beijing News* [*Xin Jing Bao*] (September 5, 2005), available online at <http://www.thebeijingnews.com/news/2005/0905/11@011747.html> (Chinese) (on file with author); Yuan Xiaobing, "In Depth: Peasant Worker Wang Binyu's Anger and Sorrow" ["Shendu: Mingong Wang Binyu De Nu Yu Bet"], *Southern Metropolitan Daily* [*Nanfang Dushi Bao*] (September 11, 2005), available online at <http://www.nanfangdaily.com.cn/southnews/tszk/nfdsb/sd/200509110183.asp> (Chinese) (on file with author).
95. "Last Wish of a Criminal Waiting for Execution" (cited in note 94).
96. Yuan Xiaobing, "In Depth" (cited in note 94).
97. Fu Yingji, "Twelve Big Pieces of News Deleted from the Chinese Internet in 2005" (cited in note 61).
98. Id.
99. Yang Chao, "The Appeal in Wang Binyu's Intentional Homicide Case is Decided" ["Wang Binyu Guyi Sharen An Er Shen Xuanpan"], *China Court Web* [*Zhongguo Fayuan Wang*] (October 20, 2005), available online at <http://www.chinacourt.org/public/detail.php?id=181959> (Chinese) (on file with author).
100. Yuan Xiaobing, "Wang Binyu Killed People" ["Wang Binyu Sha Ren"], *Southern Metropolitan Daily* [*Nanfang Dushi Bao*] (December 31, 2005), available online at <http://www.nanfangdaily.com.cn/southnews/zt/rdzt/zgxwcd/200512310024.asp> (Chinese) (on file with author) (reporting on Wang's execution).
101. "'The Case of Nie Shubin's Wrongful Execution'" (cited in note 57).
102. Consider Fu Yingji, "Twelve Big Pieces of News Deleted from the Chinese Internet in 2005" (cited in note 61) (discussing restrictions on reporting in the Nie Shubin and Wang Binyu cases).
103. "Keywords Used to Filter Web Content," *Washington Post* (February 18, 2006), available online at <http/www.washingtonpost.com/wp-dyn/content/article/2006/02/18/AR2006021800554.html> (visited April 21, 2007).
104. Interview 2005-10.
105. In other areas, however, judges say that they are not concerned about Internet discussion of pending cases, Interview 2005-10—perhaps because there is little such discussion in the less developed areas of China's interior. See, for example, Interview 2005-12 (stating that there is little online discussion of cases in Xi'an).
106. The range of cases considered by adjudication committees varies substantially. In most courts adjudication committees consider any cases in which the three-judge panel responsible for the case can not agree on an outcome. In some courts adjudication committees consider all cases where a defendant has been sentenced to life in

prison or death, as well as all cases in which the panel decided not to impose a prison sentence on a defendant.

107. In China, procurators serve both as the prosecution and as supervisors over the legal system. Technically, the procuracy is a judicial branch of equal rank to the courts. They are not only the prosecution, but also have the power to force courts to retry cases where the procuracy thinks the courts got it wrong. *Organization Law of the People's Courts* (*Renmin Fayuan Zuzhi Fa*), arts 12, 14–15 (effective January 1, 1980, as amended September 2, 1983 and October 31, 2006).
108. See, for example, Wang Lin, "The Judges Have No Boss Other Than Law" ["Faguan Chule Falii Jiu Meiyou Bie De Shangsi"], *Beijing News* [*Xin Jing Bao*] (December 3, 2003), available online at <http://news.xinhuanet.com/comments/2003-12/03/content_1210980.htm> (Chinese) (on file with author).
109. Some courts in China recently have taken steps to restrict the use of *qingshi* procedures, requiring that all such requests for guidance come in writing, or come from lower court adjudication committees (rather than individual judges).
110. See Bell (2006: 69–70), noting that "in practice, even in civil law, there is an acceptance of the concept of 'a leading case', such that particular lines of legal principle are commonly described by reference to the name of the leading case which established them"; Glendon, Gordon, and Osakwe (1994: 207): "Because of the necessity to interpret and apply the so-called written law, the civil law systems are in a real sense case-law systems." See generally Schlesinger (1988: 643–51).
111. Some of these sites claim to have tens of thousands of cases. In our interviews, however, not a single judge mentioned ever having consulted such commercial websites to research cases.
112. Interview 2005–85.
113. Interview 2005–12.
114. Id.
115. See "Constructing a Case-Law System with Chinese Characteristic? A Precedent-Decision System Emerges from Zhengzhou," *China Newsweek* (September 6, 2002), available online at <http://www.chinanewsweek.com.cn/2002-09-06/1/357.html> (Chinese) (on file with author) (Center for Chinese Legal Studies translation).
116. See, for example, Interview 2005–09.
117. Interview 2005–10; Interview 2005–13; Interview 2005–18. See also Interview 2005–51 (stating that at a district court in Beijing judges are not allowed to go online from their offices, but that there is a computer at the court that judges can use to go online if they need to do so); Interview 2005–58 (stating that judges at the Beijing High People's Court do not have access to the external web from their offices, but that they can go to the court library if they want to go online). In economically well-off areas of Jiangsu Province, some offices have two computers—one for the internal network and one for the external network. Interview 2005–63.
118. Interview 2005–64. In other locales vice-presidents also have access.
119. Interview 2005–10; Interview 2005–77.
120. Interview 2005–09; Interview 2005–13; Interview 2005–85; Interview 2006–36; Interview 2006–76. See also Interview 2005–12 (stating that when judges encounter new types of cases they will sometimes go online at home to see how other courts have handled the issue); Interview 2005–51 (judge stating that he will sometimes search online for information regarding how other courts have handled similar cases).
121. Interview 2005–10; Interview 2005–12.
122. Interview 2005–64; Interview 2005–65; Interview 2005–70; Interview 2005–85.
123. Interview 2005–95; Interview 2005–96.

124. Interview 2005–95; Interview 2006–49.
125. Interview 2006–34.
126. Interview 2006–35.
127. Id.
128. Interview 2005–65; Interview 2005–70.
129. Interview 2005–55.
130. Interview 2005–54.
131. Interview 2005–65 (stating that judges in Liaoning routinely look online when confronted with new cases); Interview 2005–78 (stating that judges frequently use the Internet when they encounter issues that existing law does not clearly govern); Interview 2005–84 (same); Interview 2005–82 (stating that judges will look online for cases, news reports, and academic articles when they encounter new legal issues).
132. Interview 2005–17.
133. Interview 2005–49; Interview 2005–104. See also Interview 2005–58 (stating that Beijing High People's Court judges frequently use the Internet to look for cases from overseas); Interview 2005–70 (stating that judges in Changchun will use the Internet to research developments overseas).
134. Interview 2006–31; Interview 2006–45.
135. Interview 2006–17.
136. Interview 2006–25.
137. Interview 2006–37.
138. Interview 2006–04.
139. Interview 2006–67.
140. *Notice of Big and Important Cases 2005 (no. 1)* [*Da Yao Anjian Tongbao 2005(Di Yi Qi)*] (February 24, 2005), available online at <http://www.aaawww.net/select/selectl.php3?id=372207& userid=24245> (Chinese) (on file with author).
141. "Peasant Worker Who Got Silicosis Through Working Withdraws Suit for Compensation, Are Government Officials Suspected of Owning Stocks?" ["Mingong Dagong Huan Xifei Suopei Chesu, Zhengfu Guanyuan Shexian Cangu?"], *Huashang News* [*Huashang Bao*] (September 18, 2005), available online at <http://news.huash.com/gb/news/2005-09/18/content_2222951.htm> (Chinese) (on file with author); Zhang Lu, "'The Legal System' Should Not be Emotionless" ["'Fazhi' Buying Leng Bing Bing"], *Huashang News* [*Huashang Bao*] (January 12, 2005), available online at <http://news.huash.com/gb/news/2005-01/12/content_1564512.htm> (Chinese) (on file with author).
142. Xue Feng and Mu Shi, "Because of Five Minutes Late for Court, Hanyin Peasant Worker is Ruled to Have Withdrawn His Claim for Compensation" ["Zhi Yin Kaiting 5 Fenzhong Nei Wei Dao, Hanyin Mingong Suopei Zao Chesu"], *Huashang Web* [*Huashang Wang*] (January 12, 2005), available online at <http://news.huash.com/gb/news/2005-01/12/content_1564511.htm> (Chinese) (on file with author); *Notice of Big and Important Cases* (cited in note 140). In most civil cases in China plaintiffs are required to pay a filing fee that is a specified percentage of the amount in controversy.
143. "'The Legal System' Should Not be Emotionless" (cited in note 141); "Peasant Worker Who Got Silicosis Through Working" (cited in note 141).
144. *Notice of Big and Important Cases* (cited in note 140); "'The Legal System' Should Not be Emotionless" (cited in note 141).
145. "See How Ankang Shiquan County Court Plunders Peasant Worker" ["Kan Ankang Shiquan Fayuan Zenyang Lueduo Nongmingong"], Shangxi Network BBS Chatroom (January 24, 2005), available online at <http://bbs.sxtvs.com/printpage.asp?BoardID=34&ID=48266> (Chinese) (on file with author) (BBS chatroom). The court argued

that the plaintiff had failed to provide an excuse for being late, and thus the court's action was justified under China's Civil Procedure Law. Id.

146. Interview 2005–16; Shanxi Shiquan County Court Message Board, available online at <http://www.aaawww.net/bbs/index2.php?userid=24245&c> (Chinese) (on file with author).
147. See id.
148. <http://www.sqfy.com/index.php3?file=4> (on file with author).
149. "Shiquan County People's Court Maintains the Advanced Teaching of the Communist Party" ["Shiquan Xian Renmin Fayuan Zai Baochi Gongchan Dangyuan Xianjin Xing Jiaoyu"], available online at <http://www.aaawww.net/select/select1.php3?id=378962&userid=24245> (Chinese) (on file with author).
150. As of August 2006, the official China Court Web site included links to 110 other court websites in 22 provinces. *Courts Online* [*Fayuan Zaixian*], *China Court Web* [*Zhongguo Fayuan Wang*], <http://www.chinacourt.org/fyzx/> (Chinese) (on file with author). The list, however, is not comprehensive. "Brief Introduction of China Court Web and Notice of Web Construction" ["Zhongguo Fayuan Wang Jianjie Ji Jianwang Xuzhi"], *China Court Web* [*Zhongguo Fayuan Wang*], available online at <http://www.chinacourt.org/other/detail.php> (Chinese) (on file with author). For example, although an Internet search found that five courts in Shanghai had public websites, only one was listed on the SPC website.
151. See, for example, *Ankang Intermediate Court* [*Ankang Shi Zhongji Renmin Fayuan*], available online at <http://www.akfy.org.cn> (Chinese) (on file with author) (website of Ankang Municipal Intermediate Court).
152. *Shaanxi Province Shiquan County People's Court* [*Shaanxi Sheng Shiquan Xian Renmin Fayuan*], available online at <http://www.sqfy.com/index.php3?file=4.php> (Chinese) (on file with author); Interview 2005–14. See also *Xingguo County People's Court* [*Xingguo Xian Renmin Fayuan*], available online at <http://xgxfy.chinacourt.org/> (Chinese) (Jiangxi Province Xingguo County Court) (on file with author); *Hebei Province Gu'an County People's Court* [*Hebei Sheng Gu'an Xian Renmin Fayuan*], available online at <http://gaxfy.chinacourt.org/> (Chinese) (on file with author); *Shangdong Province Kenli County People's Court* [*Shangdong Sheng Kenli Xian Renmin Fayuan*], available online at <http://klfy.chinacourt.org/> (Chinese) (on file with author).
153. The website also includes links to pages covering court history and an online video, but both links are empty. The site appears to be under construction, which may also explain the small number of cases included on the site.
154. <http://www.chinacourt.org/> (Chinese) (on file with author).
155. See "About Us" ["Guanyu Women"], available online at <http://www.chinacourt.org/other/aboutus.php> (Chinese) (on file with author).
156. See, for example, <http://www.jsfy.gov.cn/aljx/index.asp> (Chinese) (on file with author).
157. Interview 2005–63.
158. "Guangzhou Maritime Court Posts Decisions Online" ["Guangzhou Haishi Fayuan Panjueshu Shangwang"], China News Agency Website [*Zhongxinshe Wangzhan*] (October 12, 2000), available online at <http://dailynews.sina.com.cn/society/2000-10-12/134098.html> (Chinese) (on file with author).
159. *Guangzhou Maritime Court Judgment Documents* [*Guangzhou Haishi Fayuan Caipan Wenshu*], available online at <http://www.gzhsfy.net/writ/index.php> (Chinese) (on file with author). In a 2005 article, the court stated that it posts "announcements of cases, decisions and introductions to judges" online. Guangzhou Maritime Court

[Guangzhou Haishi Fayuan], *Using Modern Information Technology, Enhancing the Construction of Maritime Judicial Ability* [*Yunyong Xiandai Xinxi Jishu, Jiaqiang Haishi Sifa Nengli Jianshe*], China Foreign-related Com Trial Web [*Zhongguo Shewai Shangshi Shenpan Wang*] (November 23, 2005), available online at <http://www.ccmt.org.cn/ss/news/show.php?cId=6356> (Chinese) (on file with author).

160. For example, the Beijing High People's Court reported in 2003 that all intellectual property cases from all courts in Beijing would be published online. Beijing People's High Court [Beijing Gaoji Renmin Fayuan], "Endeavor to Make the Beijing Court Net A Unique and Excellent Website" ["Niili Jiang Beijing Fayuan Wang Bancheng Tese Jingpin Wangzhan"], *China Court Web* [*Zhongguo Fayuan Wang*] (November 28, 2003), available online at <http://www.chinacourt.org/public/detail.php?id=92553> (Chinese) (on file with author). As of February 2006, the website included 863 decisions—although it is not clear whether that number reflects all intellectual property cases in the municipality. *Judicial Documents—Intellectual Property Cases—Patents* [*Zhishi Chanquan Anjian*], *Beijing Court Web* [*Beijing Fayuan Wang*], available online at <http://bjgy.chinacourt.org/cpws/?sub=2> (Chinese) (on file with author).

161. A 2003 report stated that Beijing courts would begin publishing all decisions from all three levels of Beijing courts online, and would thus become the "first courts in the world" to do so. Gua Zhixia, "All Beijing Court Decisions To Be Posted Online from November, the First In the World to Do So" ["11 Yue Beijing Fayuan Caipanshu Quanbu Shangwang, Cheng Shijie Shang Shouli"], *Star Daily* [*Beijing Yule Xinbao*] (November 3, 2003), available online at <http://www.edisc.com.cn/bike/viewnews.btml?id=16230> (Chinese) (on file with author). Yet as of February 2006 the court's website listed only fifteen cases other than intellectual property cases. "Judicial Document—Other Cases" ["Qita Anjian"], *Beijing Court Web* [*Beijing Fayuan Wang*], available online at <http://bjgy.chinacourt.org/cpws/?sub=8> (Chinese) (on file with author). See also "Guangdong Foshan Court Puts Decisions Online" ["Guangdong Foshan Fayuan Panjueshu Shangwang"], *Southern Metropolitan Daily* [*Nanfang Dushi Bao*] (July 1, 2003), available online at <http://tech.sina.com.cn/i/c/2003-07-01/1059204196.shtml> (Chinese) (on file with author) (statement by Guangdong Foshan Intermediate court stating the types of cases that will and will not be posted online). In an online essay, Peking University professor He Weifang commented that he had found no court in China that made all decisions available without modification online. See He Weifang, "What's the Difficulty of Putting Decisions Online?" ["Panjueshu Shangwang Nan Zai He Chu?"], *Law Thinker Web* [*Falv Sixiang Wang*] (December 15, 2005), available online at <http://law-thinker.com/show.asp?id=3025> (Chinese) (on file with author).

162. Interview 2005–70. See also *Beijing Court Web* [*Beijing Fayuan Wang*], available online at <http://bjgy.chinacourt.org/bjfy/> (Chinese) (on file with author) (introducing the basic functioning of courts in Beijing); <http://www.jsfy.gov.cn/sszn/sscx.htm> (Chinese) (on file with author) (explaining litigation procedures on the Jiangsu Court Network).

163. See, for example, <http://www.shezfy.com/OpenJudge.asp?show=week> (Chinese) (on file with author).

164. See, for example, <http://www.jsfy.gov.cn/sszn/cyfl.htm> (Chinese) (on file with author).

165. See, for example, <http://www.jsfy.gov.cn/sszn/szgs.htm> (Chinese) (on file with author).

166. See, for example, <http://www.shezfy.com/BulletDetail.asp?id=586> (Chinese) (on file with author).
167. Shenzhen Intermediate People's Court [*Shenzhen Shi Zhongji Renmin Fayuan*], *Live Broadcasts of Court Hearings Online* [*Wang Shang Kai Ting*], available online at <http://www.szcourt.gov.cn/tszj.php> (Chinese) (on file with author).
168. See, for example, "Hainan High Court Constructs New Working Platform Hand in Hand with Cisco" ["Hainan Gaoyuan Xieshou Sike Gongzhu Ban'an Xin Pingtai"], *eNet* (October 15, 2004), available online at <http://www.enet.com.cn/article/2004/1015/A20041015352752.shtml> (Chinese) (on file with author) (reporting that courts in Hainan Province have established an online web page through which citizens may report on misconduct by court officials).
169. See, for example, Interview 2005–70 (stating that a court in Changchun receives few complaints via its website).
170. Liebman (2005: 1).
171. Shanxin Shiquan County Court Message Board, available online at <http://www.aaawww.net/bbs/index2.php?userid=24245& c=&infotype=&page=4> (Chinese) (on file with author); <http://www.aaawww.net/bbs/index.php3?userid=24245& c=&infotype=&page=4> (Chinese) (on file with author); <http://www.aaawww.net/bbs/index2.php?userid=24245&c> (Chinese) (on file with author).
172. Shanxin Shiquan County Court Message Board, available online at <http://www.aaawww.net/bbs/index2.php?userid=24245&c=&infotype=&page=4> (Chinese) (on file with author).
173. See, for example, Ge Zhihao, "Shanghai: Yangpu Court Internal Network Enhances Efficiency" ["Shanghai: Yangpu Fayuan De Juyuwang BBS Tigao Gongzuo Xiaolü"], *Shanghai Morning Post* [*Xinwen Chenbao*] (November 17, 2004), available online at <http://news.chinabyte.com/396/1876896.shtml> (Chinese) (on file with author) (noting online meeting between judges and "Internet friends").
174. Interview 2005–65. Judges sometimes self-identify as judges in their postings on bulletin boards and in discussion forums. See, for example, Yang Fan, "Doubts on an Official Embezzlement Criminal Case" ["Dui Yiqi Zhiwu Qinzhan Zui De Zhiyi"], *China Court Web BBS* [*Fazhi Luntan*] (February 8, 2006), available online at <http://bbs.chinacourt.org/ index.php?showtopic=139693> (Chinese) (on file with author).
175. See, for example, Zuoan Tiankong, "An Administrative Case that I'm Adjudicating" ["Wo Chengban Yijian Xingzheng Anjian"], *China Court Web BBS* [*Fazhi Luntan*] (February 21, 2006), available online at <http://bbs.chinacourt.org/index.php?showtopic=141739> (Chinese) (on file with author) (discussion by judge of case after decision, requesting comments from other participants in a web discussion forum).
176. Interview 2005–82.
177. Interview 2006–34.
178. Interview 2005–65.
179. In Shenyang, the largest city in northeast China, an official document from the intermediate court stated that consultations with experts should be done by telephone, letter, fax, email, orally, through seminars and lectures, or through other appropriate means. *Working Methods of Shenyang Intermediate People's Court's Expert Consultation Group* [*Shenyang Shi Zhongji Renmin Fayuan Zhuanjia Zixuntuan Gongzuo Banfa*] (November 17, 2004), available online at <http://cdfy.chinacourt.org/public/detail.php?id=1386> (Chinese) (on file with author). The document, however, only refers to cases in which an official decision has been taken by the court to request the views of an expert; in reality judges in China also consult informally with outside experts.

180. Interview 2005–49; Interview 2005–51; Interview 2005–77.
181. See <http://blog.chinacourt.org/> (Chinese) (on file with author) (homepage for blogs on the official *China Court Web*).
182. <http://blog.chinacourt.org/wp-profile1.php?p=34042&author=130> (Chinese) (on file with author).
183. <http://blog.chinacourt.org/wp-profile1.php?cat=3&author=1494> (Chinese) (on file with author).
184. <http://blog.chinacourt.org/wp-profile1.php?cat=3&author=5008> (Chinese) (on file with author).
185. <http://blog.chinacourt.org/wp-profile1.php?cat=3&author=529> (Chinese) (on file with author).
186. One exception is an interview with us about our research in *Procuratorate Daily*, one of China's leading legal newspapers. Liu Hui, "American Scholars' Discussion about 'Chinese Legal Research'—The Impact of the Internet on Judges and the Rule of Law" ["Meiguo 'Zhongguo Fa Yanjiu' Xuezhe Tan—Hulian Wang Dui Faguan Ji Fazhi De Yingxiang"], *Procuratorate Daily* [*Jiancha Ribao*] (July 24, 2006), available online at <http://www.jcrb.com/n1/jcrb1004/ca530254.htm> (Chinese) (on file with author).
187. "The SPC Notice on Printing and Circulating the 'Regulation on the Administration of the Establishment of the People's Court Computer Information Network System' and the 'Plan for Establishing the People's Court Computer Information Network System'" ["Zuigao Renmin Fayuan Guanyu Yinfa 'Renmin Fayuan Jisuanji Xinxi Wangluo Xitong Jianshe Guanli Guiding' He 'Renmin Fayuan Jisuanji Xinxi Wangluo Xitong Jianshe Guihua' De Tongzhi"] (January 29, 2002), available online at <http://www.yfzs.gov.cn/gb/info/LawData/flfg2002/gfsfjs/2003-02/19/1518560846.html> (Chinese) (on file with author) (stating that all courts should establish internal court networks in order to improve management of cases and case statistics; in theory the networks should connect provincial courts to the SPC). In 2002, the SPC instructed all provincial high courts and intermediate courts to establish court networks by 2003 and to link such networks to the SPC's network, and instructed all local courts generally to establish court networks by 2005. Id. The SPC does not appear to have made public more recent data on progress toward meeting such goals.
188. *Brief Introduction to Technology Criteria for the Establishment of the People's Court Information Network System* [*Renmin Fayuan Xinxi Wangluo Xitong Jianshe Jishu Guifan Tushu Neirong Jianjie*], available online at <http://www.law-lib.com/shopping/shopview_p.asp?id=11349> (Chinese) (on file with author); Beijing Huaxia Telecommuncation Technology Ltd, *Plan and Construction of the National Courts' First Level Special Network Video Conference System* [*Quanguo Fayuan Xitong Yiji Zhuanwang Shipin Huiyi Xitong De Guihua Yu Jianshe*], China Multimedia Video Comm [*Zhongguo Duomeiti Shixun*] (March 5, 2004), available online at <http://www.cmvc.com.cn/list.asp?id=338> (on file with author).
189. *Brief Introduction to Technology Criteria* (cited in note 188); *Plan and Construction of the National Courts' First-Level Special Network Video Conference System* (cited in note 188). See also "Hanbin Court Establishes Internal Computer Network" ["Hanbin Fayuan Jiancheng Jisuanji Juyu Wang"], *People's Court News* [*Renmin Fayuan Bao*] (May 10, 2003), available online at <http://rmfyb.chinacourt.org/public/detail.php?id=49783> (Chinese) (on file with author) (stating that the presence of a court network improves efficiency and quality of the court); Zhang Yigao, "Laishan Internal Network Expedites Trials" ["Laishan Juyu Wang Wei Shenpan Tisu"], *People's Court News* [*Renmin Fayuan Bao*] (March 27, 2002), available online at <http://rmfyb.

chinacourt.org/public/detail.php?id=35107> (Chinese) (on file with author) (noting how a court network has improved efficiency).

190. See, for example, Pei Cong, "Lhasa Chengguan District People's Court Internal Network Construction Passes Inspection" ["Lasa Shi Chengguan Qu Renmin Fayuan Juyuwang Jianshe Tongguo Yanshou"], *China Tibet Court Web* [*Zhongguo Xizang Fayuan Wang*] (August 15, 2005), available online at <http://tibet.chinacourt.org/public/detail.php?id=506> (Chinese) (on file with author) (noting the important role internal networks play in facilitating lower courts' reporting to higher courts).

191. The 2003 SPC notice instructing courts to provide networks or computers on which judges could search for laws and other relevant materials stated that the costs of such infrastructure should be borne by individual courts. See *SPC Office Notice on Promoting and Furnishing the "China Adjudication Law Application Support System"* [*Zuigao Renmin Fayuan Bangong Ting Guayu Tuiguang Peibei "Zhongguo Shenpan Falii Yingyong Zhichi Xitong" De Tongzhi*] (November 4, 2003), available online at <http://www.courtpress.com/subject/s1.php> (Chinese) (on file with author).

192. "Pushing for the New Development of All Courts in the Province" ["Fenli Tuidong Quansheng Fayuan Gongzuo Xin Fazhan"], *Jiangsu Legal News* [*Jiangsu Fazhi Bao*] (February 15, 2006), available online at <http://www.jsfy.gov.cn/fydt/fyyw/fyyw_esw1.htm> (Chinese) (on file with author); *Brief Introduction to the Courts in the Province* [*Sheng Fayuan Jianjie*], *Jiangsu Court Web* [*Jiangsu Fayuan Wang*], available online at <http://www.jscourt.gov.cn/fyjj/index.htm> (Chinese) (on file with author).

193. *Informationized Institutions* [*Xinxihua Jigou*], Heilongjiang Province Information Center [Heilongjiang Sheng Xinxi Zhongxin], available online at <http://www.hljic.gov.cn/xxhsd/xxhjg27.asp> (Chinese) (on file with author) (discussing the establishment of internal court networks in sixty courts in Heilongjiang Province, and noting the role of the provincial high court in inspecting and overseeing internal networks in lower courts); Pei Cong, "Lhasa Chengguan District People's Court" (cited in note 190) (discussing the establishment of an internal network at a district court in Lhasa, the first in the Tibet Autonomous Region, and emphasizing the importance of the network in managing the acceptance, adjudication, and enforcement of court opinions); see also "Hainan High Court Constructs New Working Platform" (cited in note 168) (stating that all courts in Hainan Province have been equipped with internal networks). In some areas court networks connect higher courts with lower courts under their jurisdiction, although this appears to be primarily the case in more developed areas. In Changchun, for example, the intermediate court is linked via an internal network to both the provincial high court and to lower courts. Interview 2005–70; Interview 2005–84. In Xi'an, however, as of mid-2005 the intermediate court's network was separate from and not connected to the internal networks at lower courts. Interview 2005–10.

194. Interview 2005–09.

195. Interview 2005–95.

196. Id. See also Interview 2005–83 (stating that in many rural courts in Jilin there is only one computer for each court, and there is often no internal network); see also Interview 2005–18 (stating that some local courts in Xi'an lack the resources to provide computers for all judges).

197. *"China Judicial Law Application Support System" Order Invitation Form* [*"Zhongguo Shenpan Falii Yingyong Zhichi Xitong" Zhengding Dan*], The People's Court Press [*Renmin Fayuan Chubanshe*], available online at <http://www.courtpress.com/subject/index_5.php> (Chinese) (on file with author); Interview 2005–18. See also Interview 2005–55 (stating that the legal materials available on internal sites are purchased

from the SPC). In 2003 the SPC issued a notice instructing all courts to purchase a database of laws produced by the People's Court Press. *SPC Office Notice on Promoting and Furnishing the "China Judicial Law Application Support System" [Zuigao Renmin Fayuan Bangong Ting Guayu Tuiguang Peibei "Zhongguo Shenpan Falii Yingyong Zhichi Xitong" De Tongzhi]* (November 4, 2003), available online at <http://www.courtpress.com/subject/s1.php> (Chinese) (on file with author). It is not clear, however, what percentage of courts have actually done so. According to one report, the database is in use in all courts in Beijing, Shanghai, Fujian, and Guangxi; in another fourteen provinces it is used by some courts. "Warm Congratulations for the 'China Adjudication Law Application Support System' Winning the 'Third National Electronic Publications Awards'" ["Relie Zhuhe 'Zhongguo Shenpan Falii Yingyong Zhichi Xitong' Ronghuo 'Di San Jie Guojia Dianzi Chubanwu Jiang'"], Peking University Law Information Web, available online at <http://chinalawinfo.com/ad/courtpress/index.htm> (Chinese) (on file with author).

198. Interview 2005–10; Interview 2005–12; Interview 2005–13; Interview 2005–18.
199. Interview 2005–63.
200. Interview 2005–70.
201. See, for example, Chen Shaoquing, *Yuhuan People's Congress Issue General No. 194* [*Yuhuan Renda Zong Di 194 Qi*], Yuhuan People's Congress Web (August 9, 2005), available online at <http://www.yuhuanrd.gov.cn/news_show.php?show_id=986> (Chinese) (on file with author) (emphasizing the use of an internal court network for judges to exchange views with each other and with the court vice-presidents responsible for their division of the court).
202. See, for example, Interview 2005–79 (stating that court chatroom is rarely used); Interview 2005–65 (stating that judges in Shenyang rarely use the internal BBS); Interview 2005–2102 (stating that Beijing judges rarely use their discussion forums to discuss cases).
203. Interview 2005–63.
204. Interview 2005–58. See also Interview 2005–70 (stating that judges in Changchun will sometimes discuss difficult cases on discussion forums on their internal network, but generally only after the case has been decided).
205. Interview 2005–58; Interview 2005–77.
206. Interview 2006–57; Interview 2006–76.
207. Zhu Yong and Pan Sishen, "When Judges Encounter Difficult Questions in Adjudicating Cases: Court Website Offers Discussion Space" ["Faguan Shenpan Anjian Yudao Nanti, Fayuan Wangzhan Tigong Yantao Kongjian"], *Shanghai Youth Daily* [*Shanghai Qingnian Bao*] (April 7, 2005), available online at <http://legal.people.com.cn/GB/42734/43194/3302092.html> (Chinese) (on file with author). All responses must be approved by the intermediate court's research office; the intermediate court will not respond to questions that reveal facts relating to individual cases. Interview 2006–45. Judges in other areas likewise state that they will sometimes use the internal web to discuss pending cases, in particular in courts where every judge has his or her own computer. Interview 2005–83.
208. See text accompanying notes 80–9.
209. Zhang Yue, "Court Opinion Reform Advances Judicial Transparency, Independence of Judges Needs to be Enhanced" ["Panjueshu Gaige Licu Touming Shenpan, Faguan Dulixing Youdai Tigao"], *Oriental Outlook* [*Liaowang Dongfang Zhoukan*] (July 6, 2005), available online at <http://www.china-judge.com/ReadNews.asp?NewsID=3267&BigClassID=17& SmallClassID=25 &SpecialID=0> (Chinese) (on file with author).

210. Interview 2005–70 (stating that in Changchun, the internal network at the intermediate court includes internal notices and announcements to judges, as well as a database of laws). See also Interview 2005–104 (stating that court networks are used to distribute notices and other information to all judges in Beijing); "Luzhou Intermediate Court Opens Forum on Internal Network" ["Luzhou Zhongyuan Juyuwang Shang Kai Luntan"], *People's Court News* [*Renmin Fayuan Bao*] (June 21, 2004), available online at <http://rmfyb.chinacourt.org/ public/detail.php?id=70984> (Chinese) (on file with author) (noting the usefulness of a court internal network for disseminating notices and other information to judges).
211. Interview 2005–10.
212. Interview 2005–77 (stating that internal websites also sometimes include descriptions of cases or opinions in selected cases that court education and propaganda officials have decided to post).
213. Interview 2005–58.
214. Interview 2005–12; Interview 2005–63.
215. Interview 2005–49. See *Administrative System for Court Proceedings* [*Fayuan Ban'an Liucheng Guanli Xitong*], available online at <http://www.spsp.com.cn/chinese/products/chanpcx_dzzw_fy01.htm> (Chinese) (on file with author) (noting the use of court networks to improve management of case information).
216. Interview 2005–48; Interview 2005–58; Interview 2006–36; Interview 2006–76. See also "Luzhou Intermediate Court Opens Forum" (cited in note 210).
217. Interview 2005–2103. See also *Yuhuan People's Congress Issue General No. 194* (cited in note 201).
218. Interview 2005–09 (stating that at one intermediate court in Qinghai judges at the court can use the court's internal network to view all cases decided at the court); Interview 2005–65 (stating that judges in one court in Shenyang may view judgments in already decided cases on the court's internal website).
219. Interview 2005–49 (stating that although individual judges may be able to access certain information regarding cases not before them in their court or division within the court—such as the date of such cases and the names of parties—they do not have the ability to access opinions); Interview 2006–76 (stating that only senior judges can view decisions).
220. Interview 2005–12. See also Interview 2005–18 (stating that the internal website of an intermediate court in Shaanxi includes no cases).
221. Interview 2005–70; Interview 2005–47; Interview 2005–48. In practice, this may not be a significant bar to judges obtaining information: judges seeking information about previously decided cases can also obtain information by asking their colleagues. Id.; Interview 2005–102 (stating that judges can ask their division heads if they want to see additional materials).
222. Interview 2006–76.
223. Interview 2005–47 (stating that in some courts in Beijing the court network allows both higher-ranking judges and judges at the Beijing High People's Court to view decisions from lower courts).
224. Interview 2005–49.
225. Interview 2005–47.
226. Id.; Interview 2005–58 (stating that the heads of court divisions can view case details of cases in lower courts).
227. For discussions of inconsistent application of law, see, for example, Zhang Weiping, "The Function and Structure of Legal Hearings in Civil Litigation" ["Minshi Susong Falü Shen De Gongneng Ji Gouzao"], *Leg Stud Res* [*Faxue Yanjiu*], 5 (2005), available

online at <http://www.civillaw.com.cn/weizhang/default.asp?id=22910> (Chinese) (on file with author); Yu Dongai, "Precedent Legal System? Precedent System? A Specious Judicial Question" ["Panli Fa Zhidu? Panli Zhidu? Yige Si Shi Er Fei de Sifa Wenti"], *Public Law Forum* [*Gongfa Pinglun*], available online at <http://www.gongfa.com/yudapanlifa.htm> (Chinese) (on file with author).

228. See text accompanying notes 36–9.
229. In the United States the majority of judges are elected. However, the most powerful judges, including all federal judges, are generally appointed.
230. This argument is made in many forms in many places. See, for example, Thayer (1893); Wechsler (1959: 1); Bickel (1962: 49–56).
231. See He Lili and Zhang Shouzeng, "Resolve the Problem of Full Payment of Judge's Salary in the Way that Late Payment of Education Funding is Resolved" ["Yao Xiang Jiejue Tuoqian Jiaoyu Jingfei Nayang Jiejue Hao Faguan Gongzi Zu'e Fafang Wenti"], *China Court Web* [*Zhongguo Fayuan Wang*] (July 1, 2004), available online at <http://www.chinacourt.org/public/detail.php?id=121608> (Chinese) (on file with author) (reporting official comments on the poor conditions and low salaries in local courts); Liebman (2007) (discussing inequalities among courts in China).
232. See Liebman (2007) (discussing court commitments to "socialist rule of law" theory and to maintaining social stability).
233. As noted above, there are historical parallels to recent developments in China, in particular in the important role that printing played in facilitating the development of common-law courts. See text accompanying note 4.
234. See Mill (1975 [1859]: 50–2).
235. See Liebman (2005: 1); Goldsmith and Wu (2006: 87–104).
236. We recognize that the party-state is far from monolithic in its views, and that speaking of the party-state as a single institution obscures many important differences within the Party. In some cases intervention furthers the interests of local party-state officials; in others, top leadership of the central party-state intervene at the expense of local officials. Our point is not to suggest that such differences are irrelevant; it is to show that the Internet is in some cases facilitating oversight of and interference in the courts by a wide range of actors at various levels of the party-state.
237. See, for example, "Ni Shouming Sends Words to Our Web: Enhance Management and Positively Develop" ["Ni Shouming Jiyu Benwang Jiaqiang Guanli Jiji Fa Zhan"], Hebei Province Gu'an County People's Court [Hebei Sheng Gu'an Xian Remin Fayuan] (March 31, 2005), available online at <http://gaxfy.chinacourt.org/public/detail.php?id=94> (Chinese) (on file with author) (court official discussing importance of the Internet).
238. Interview 2005-10.
239. See, for example, Dworkin (1986: 176–224); Eisenberg (1988: 10–12, 170 n. 29); West (2003: 107).
240. By assumption, the "other judges" are not superior courts or in any kind of vertical relationship, but equals or higher-ranking courts in other jurisdictions whose decisions are not formally binding in any way.
241. The idea of such a change in technology is not far-fetched—as various historians have pointed out, the common-law system may have only begun to function well after the invention of the printing press, which offered, among other things, a cheaper means of finding out what other judges had done in similar circumstances.
242. See, for example, Bikhchandani, Hirshleifer, and Welch (1998: 152–3); Banerjee (1992).
243. See Daughety and Reinganum (1999: 165–8); Talley (1999: 87).

244. Compare Kornhauser (1989).
245. See discussion in note 110 (discussing case law in civil law systems).
246. A number of writers in information economics discuss why decision-makers (usually in financial markets) will rationally place weight on the decisions made by others in similar situations. One reason is the possibility that the earlier actors knew something—among Choice A and B, they possessed private insight or information suggesting that Choice A was preferable. A second is simply a preference for conformity—that most people prefer to do what others have done, either because it reduces mental strain, protects their reputation, or avoids the risk of being criticized. For these and other reasons, see Bikhchandani, Hirshleifer, and Welch (1998: 152–3). An important point is that we might expect imitation both in the absence or presence of a formal precedent system. For one thing, production of rules is part of the business of the judiciary—so that a judge who does what others have done might be a good judge. Another reason is that judicial power may also be maximized by consistency among judges—a united front that deters political meddling. Third, and maybe the most important for most judges, following may just be easier. It is much easier for judges to do what others have done—in jargon, it minimizes decision costs.
247. Talley (1999: 94). Talley goes on to specify some of the ways that a legal system can mitigate some of the negative side effects of precedential cascades.
248. It stems from these, along with, as Alexander Bickel argued, the power to avoid making decisions. See Bickel (1962: 49–65, 111–99).
249. See, for example, Katsh (1984: 649), noting, with regard to printing in England, that "as court decisions began to be printed and distributed, pressure arose for national uniformity and equal treatment regardless of place."
250. For a discussion of innovation in the Chinese system, see Liebman (2006: 36–9); Liebman (2007).
251. Slaughter (2004: 66–103).
252. Interview 2005–19.
253. Interview 2005–10.
254. Liebman (2007).

REFERENCES

Banerjee, Abhijit V. (1992), "A Simple Model of Herd Behavior," *Quarterly Journal of Economics*, 107: 797–817.

Bell, John (2006), *Judiciaries within Europe: A Comparative Review* (Cambridge: Cambridge University Press).

Benkler, Yochai (2006), *The Wealth of Networks: How Social Production Transforms Markets and Freedom* (New Haven: Yale University Press), available online at <http://www.benkler.org/Benkler_Wealth_Of_Networks.pdf> (visited April 21, 2007).

Bickel, Alexander (1962), *The Least Dangerous Branch: The Supreme Court at the Bar of Politics* (Indianapolis: Bobbs-Merrill).

Bikhchandani, Sushil, Hirshleifer, David, and Welch, Ivo (1998), "Learning from the Behavior of Others: Conformity, Fads, and Information Cascades," *Journal of Economic Perspectives*, 12/3: 151–70.

Bolton, Patrick and Dewatripont, Mathias (1994), "The Firm as a Communication Network," *Quarterly Journal of Economics*, 109/4: 809–39.

Chander, Anupam (2002), "Whose Republic?" *University of Chicago Law Review*, 69: 1479–500.

Cooley, Charles Horton (1998), *On Self and Social Organization* (Chicago: University of Chicago Press).

Collins, Ronald K. L. and Skover, David M. (1992), "Paratexts," *Stanford Law Review*, 44: 509–52.

Daughety, Andrew F. and Reinganum, Jennifer F. (1999), "Stampede to Judgment: Persuasive Influence and Herding Behavior by Courts," *American Law and Economics Review*, 1/1: 158–89.

Dworkin, Ronald (1986), *Law's Empire* (Cambridge, MA: Belknap).

Eisenberg, Melvin Aron (1988), *The Nature Of The Common Law* (Cambridge, MA: Harvard University Press).

Gillette, Clayton P. (1998), "Lock-In Effects in Law and Norms," *Boston University Law Review*, 78: 813–42.

Gillmor, Dan (2004), *We the Media: Grassroots Journalism by the People, for the People* (Sebastopol, CA: O'Reilly).

Glendon, Mary Ann, Gordon, Michael W., and Osakwe, Christopher (1994), *Comparative Legal Traditions: Text, Materials, and Cases on the Civil and Common Law Traditions, with Special Reference to French, German, English, and European Law*, 2nd edn (Eagan, MN: West Group).

Goldsmith, Jack and Wu, Tim (2006), *Who Controls the Internet? Illusions of a Borderless World* (Oxford: Oxford University Press).

Hadfield, Gillian K. (1992), "Bias in the Evolution of Legal Rules," *Georgetown Law Journal*, 80: 583–617.

Hayek, F. A. (1945), "The Use of Knowledge in Society," *American Economic Review*, 35/4: 519–30.

—— (1960), *The Constitution of Liberty* (Chicago: University of Chicago Press).

Katsh, M. Ethan (1984), "Communications Revolutions and Legal Revolutions: The New Media and the Future of Law," *Nova Law Journal*, 8: 631–69.

—— (1989), *The Electronic Media and the Transformation of Law* (Oxford: Oxford University Press).

—— (1995), *Law in a Digital World* (Oxford: Oxford University Press).

Kornhauser, Lewis A. (1989), "An Economic Perspective on Stare Decisis," *Chicago-Kent Law Review*, 65: 63–92.

—— (1996), "Notes on the Logic of Legal Change," in David Braybrooke (ed.), *Social Rules: Origin, Character, Logic, Change* (Boulder, CO: Westview Press), 169–81.

Kristof, Nicholas D. (2005), "Death by a Thousand Blogs," *New York Times* (May 24), A21.

Liebman, Benjamin L. (2005), "Watchdog or Demagogue? The Media in the Chinese Legal System," *Columbia Law Review*, 105/1: 1–157.

—— (2006), "Innovation through Intimidation: An Empirical Account of Defamation Litigation in China," *Harvard International Law Journal*, 47/1: 33–177.

—— (2007), "China's Courts: Restricted Reform," *China Quarterly*, 191: 620–38.

Mahoney, Paul G. (2001), "The Common Law and Economic Growth: Hayek Might Be Right," *Journal of Legal Studies*, 30/2: 503–25.

Milgrom, Paul R. and Roberts, John (1992), *Economics, Organization and Management* (Engelwood Cliffs, NJ: Prentice Hall).

Mill, John Stuart (1975 [1859]), *On Liberty* (New York: W. W. Norton).

Nadel, Mark S. (2001), "Customized News Services and Extremist Enclaves in *Republic.com*," *Stanford Law Review*, 54/4: 831–86.

Posner, Richard A. (1973), *Economic Analysis of Law* (Boston: Little, Brown).

Priest, George L. (1977), "The Common Law Process and the Selection of Efficient Rules," *Journal of Legal Studies*, 6/1: 65–82.

Reynolds, Glen (2006), *An Army of Davids: How Markets and Technology Empower Ordinary People to Beat Big Media, Big Government, and Other Goliaths* (Nashville, TN: Nelson Current).

Ross, Richard J. (2002), "Communications Revolutions and Legal Culture: An Elusive Relationship," *Law and Social Inquiry*, 27: 637–84.

Rossiter, Clinton (ed.) (1961), *The Federalist Papers* (New York: Mentor).

Rubin, Paul H. (1977), "Why Is the Common Law Efficient?" *Journal of Legal Studies*, 6/1: 51–63.

Sah, Raaj Kumar and Stiglitz, Joseph E. (1984), "The Architecture of Economic Systems: Hierarchies and Polyarchies," *American Economic Review*, 76/4: 716–27.

—— —— (1991), "The Quality of Managers in Centralized versus Decentralized Organizations," *Quarterly Journal of Economics*, 106/1: 289–95.

Scharfstein, David S. and Stein, Jeremy C. (1990), "Herd Behavior and Investment," *American Economic Review*, 80/3: 465–79.

Schlesinger, Rudolf B. (ed.) (1988), *Comparative Law: Cases, Text, Materials* 643–51, 5th edn (Westbury, NY: Foundation Press)

Schramm, Wilbur Lang (1997), *The Beginnings of Communication Study in America: A Personal Memoir* (Thousand Oaks, CA: Sage Publications).

Slaughter, Anne-Marie (2004), *A New World Order* (Princeton: Princeton University Press).

Stein, Jeremy C. (2002), "Information Production and Capital Allocation: Decentralized Versus Hierarchical Firms," *Journal of Finance*, 57/5: 1891–921.

Stiglitz, Joseph E. (2002), "Information and the Change in the Paradigm in Economics," *American Economic Review*, 92/3: 460–501.

Sunstein, Cass R. (1995), "The First Amendment in Cyberspace," *Yale Law Journal*, 104: 1757–804.

—— (2001a), *Republic.com* (Princeton: Princeton University Press).

—— (2001b), *Echo Chambers:* Bush v. Gore, *Impeachment, and Beyond* (Princeton: Princeton University Press), available online at <http://press.princeton.edu/sunstein/echo.pdf> (visited April 21, 2007).

Surowiecki, James (2004), *The Wisdom of Crowds: Why the Many Are Smarter Than the Few and How Collective Wisdom Shapes Business, Economies, Societies, and Nations* (New York: Doubleday).

Talley, Eric (1999), "Precedential Cascades: An Appraisal," *Southern California Law Review*, 73: 87–137.

Thayer, James B. (1893), "The Origin and Scope of the American Doctrine of Constitutional Law," *Harvard Law Review*, 7/3: 129–56.

Ulen, Thomas S. (2001), "Democracy on the Line: A Review of *Republic.com* by Cass Sunstein," *University of Illinois Journal of Law, Technology, and Policy*, 2: 317–46.

Volokh, Eugene (1995), "Cheap Speech and What It Will Do," *Yale Law Journal*, 104/7: 1805–50.

Wechsler, Herbert (1959), "Toward Neutral Principles of Constitutional Law," *Harvard Law Review*, 73/1: 1–35.

West, Robin (2003), *Re-imagining Justice: Progressive Interpretations of Formal Equality, Rights, and the Rule of Law* (Aldershot/Burlington, VT: Ashgate).

19

China's Courts: Restricted Reform[1]

Benjamin L. Liebman

Recent developments in China's courts reflect a paradox largely avoided in literature on the subject. Changes to courts' formal authority have been limited, courts still struggle to address basic impediments to serving as fair adjudicators, and they continue to be subject to Communist Party oversight. They have also confronted new challenges, in particular pressure from media reports and popular protests. At the same time, however, the party-state has permitted, and at times encouraged, both significant bottom-up development of the courts and their expanded use as fora for the airing of rights-based grievances, including administrative litigation, class actions, and a small number of discrimination claims filed directly under the Constitution. Some courts have engaged in significant innovation. Judges are better qualified than in the past, and are increasingly looking to other courts and judges, rather than Party superiors, in deciding novel or difficult cases. As a result, courts are increasingly coming into conflict with other state institutions, growing numbers of well-educated judges are developing professional identities, and popular attention to both the problems and the potential roles of the courts appears higher than ever before.

The current and potential future role of China's courts has received wide attention. Discussions in both China and the West, however, have largely avoided two central questions. First, why has the party-state permitted the courts to develop even limited new roles? Secondly, can courts play an effective role in a nondemocratic governmental system? This article surveys recent developments in China's courts with a view to beginning to answer these questions. The focus is on civil and administrative litigation, where reforms have been more significant than in the criminal justice system.

REFORMED COURTS?

Caseloads

Are Chinese courts playing fundamentally different roles in society from those played in the recent past? There is no clear benchmark for evaluating changes in their position within the party-state. As Donald Clarke has noted, "perhaps

Chinese courts are not designed to do, and should not do, the things Western courts do."[2] Courts are one of a number of state bureaucracies with the power to resolve disputes, and lack significant oversight powers over other state actors. Despite these differences, Chinese judges and academic commentators have in recent years looked to Western models of courts and judging in evaluating developments in China's courts.[3]

Reports have noted that Chinese courts are handling more cases than at any time in the past, with some claiming that China is facing a "litigation explosion."[4] The courts reported hearing 8.1 million cases in 2006,[5] more than triple the number heard in 1986. Yet such comparisons overstate the growth of litigation in China: as Table 19.1 shows, caseloads have grown only modestly, if at all, since 1999. The total number of cases heard in 2006 was only 2 per cent higher than in 2005, and the total number of first-instance cases actually decreased by 2 per cent between 1996 and 2006. Similarly, the total number of first-instance civil cases decreased in four years between 1999 and 2006; the total number of administrative cases likewise decreased in four of those years.[6] Lower court judges have confirmed in interviews that caseloads have either declined or grown only modestly over the past five years.[7] The modest increases are striking when set against the backdrop of China's rapid economic growth and widespread reports of a surge of civil disturbances in China. Judges attribute the declines to lack of confidence in the courts, in particular to the difficulties successful litigants face in enforcing decisions, and to private parties' preference for informal methods of dispute resolution.[8]

Nevertheless, the long-term trend appears to reflect a modest increase in the use of the courts, and that a greater range of cases and cases of greater complexity are being brought. Litigants are also increasingly challenging first-instance decisions: appeals have grown at a much faster rate than first-instance cases, with appeals nearly doubling between 1995 and 2006 (see Figure 19.2). The increase in appeals suggests that litigants may be both more familiar with legal procedures, and perhaps more confident that higher courts will issue decisions that differ from those of lower courts.

The modest growth in litigation in recent years suggests that courts are not necessarily playing a greater role relative to other institutions. As Table 19.1 and Figure 19.1 show, the increase in court caseloads coincided with a decline in the total number of disputes resolved through People's Mediation Committees until 2004.[9] Compared to other institutions engaged in dispute resolution, however, the modest rise in the total number of court cases appears less significant. Disputes and complaints of all types have increased in China in recent years, and thus any increase in court caseloads may simply be part of the more general increase in both disputes and grievances. For example, far more grievances are raised through the letters and visits system than through the courts.[10] Commercial arbitration cases, including both domestic and international disputes, increased by more than 20 per cent annually from 2004 to 2006.[11] Labor arbitration cases more than quintupled between 1996 and 2004.[12] The fact that the number of disputes and complaints raised in other institutions has continued to rise suggests that the decrease in the growth of litigation has not resulted from increased clarity of legal norms.

Table 19.1. Number of cases (first-instance and appeals) closed nationwide, 1994–2006

Year	1994	1995	1996	1997	1998	1999	2000	2001	2002	2003	2004	2005	2006
1st criminal	480,914	496,082	616,676	440,557	480,374	539,335	560,111	623,792	628,549	634,953	644,248	683,997	701,379
1st civil[a]	3,427,641	3,986,099	4,588,958	4,720,341	4,816,075	5,060,611	4,733,886	4,616,472	4,393,306	4,416,168	4,303,744	4,360,184	4,382,407
1st admin.	34,567	51,370	79,537	88,542	98,390	98,759	86,614	95,984	84,943	88,050	92,192	95,707	95,052
All 1st inst.	3,943,095	4,533,551	5,285,171	5,249,460	5,395,039	5,698,705	5,380,611	5,336,248	5,106,798	5,139,171	5,040,184	5,139,888	5,178,838
2nd criminal	52,579	53,942	67,087	64,548	70,767	78,803	86,619	98,157,	89,440	96,797	96,204	96,776	94,092
2nd civil	179,687	208,263	243,510	263,664	294,219	339,929	363,522	377,672	357,821	370,770	377,052	392,191	406,381
2nd admin.	7,672	9,536	11,365	12,684	14,220	18,072	19,404	22,149	27,649	25,045	27,273	29,176	29,054
All 2nd	239,938	271,741	321,962	340,896	379,206	436,804	469,545	497,978	474,910	492,612	500,529	518,143	529,527
Letters and visits to courts[b]	5,847,948	6,361,495	6,960,162	7,131,469	9,351,928	10,691,048	9,394,358	9,148,816	3,656,102	3,973,357	4,220,222	3,995,244	Not yet available
Mediation by People's Mediation Committees	6,123,729	6,028,481	5,802,230	5,543,166	5,267,194	5,188,646	5,030,619	4,860,695	4,636,139	4,492,157	4,414,233	4,486,825	Not yet available

Notes:

[a] Prior to 2002 Chinese courts had separate divisions for handling civil and economic cases; they were merged in 2002. The figures for 1994 to 2001 thus include both civil and economic cases.

[b] "Letters and visits" refers to complaints about cases received in writing or in person by courts; for a discussion of the letters and visits system, see below. Complaints about the courts to letters and visits offices at other Party or state institutions are not included in this figure.

Sources: 1994–2005: *Zhongguo falü nianjian* [*China Law Yearbook*] *1995–2006*. 2006: 2007 SPC Work Report (for first-instance data); Supreme People's Court, *2006 Nian quanguo fayuan shenli zhixing anjian qingkuang* (*Details of Cases Tried and Enforced Nationwide in 2006*), available at <http://www.dffy.com/sifashijian/ziliao/200703/20070314163527.htm> (for data on second-instance cases)

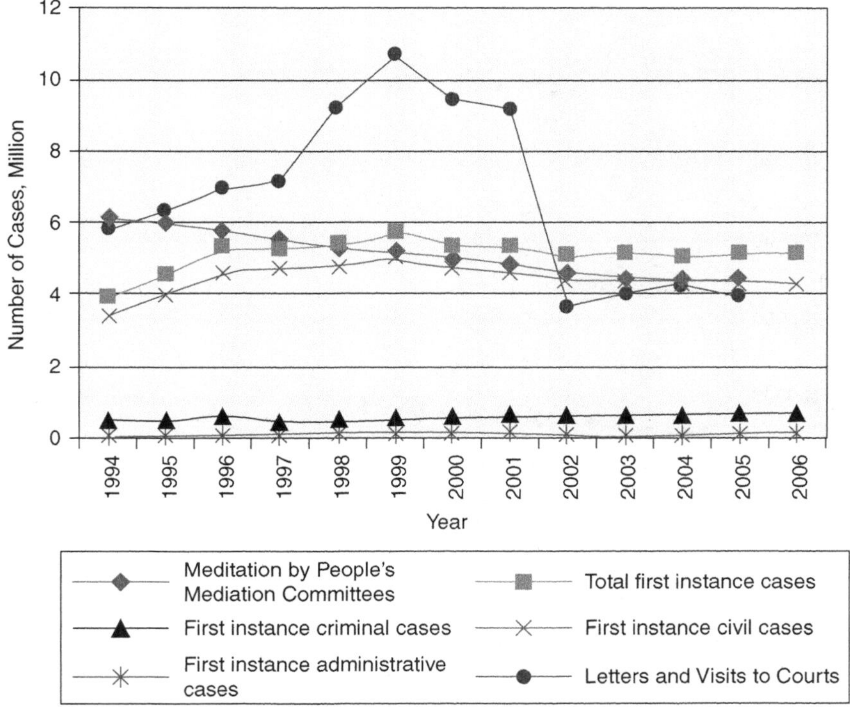

Figure 19.1. First-instance cases, mediation by People's Mediation Committees, and court letters and visits, 1994–2006

Top-down reform

The modest growth in caseloads does appear to reflect a conscious decision by party-state leaders to strengthen the courts' ability to resolve an increasing number and range of disputes.[13] But the party-state has also emphasized reforming other dispute resolution institutions—including the letters and visits system, mediation, arbitration and administrative review. These moves suggest that the party-state is focused on the need to resolve disputes and grievances, and thus preserve social stability. But they do not necessarily reflect an increased role for the courts in comparison with other institutions.

Court reform has, however, received enormous attention over the past decade. China commenced its project of court reform when it began reconstruction of its legal system in 1978. The role of the courts received increased attention in the late 1990s, as China's leadership renewed efforts to strengthen the legal system. Following the embrace of "rule of law" by the 15th Congress of the Chinese Communist Party in 1997, the Supreme People's Court (SPC) in 1999 issued its first five-year plan for reforming China's courts. This brought increased attention to the need to strengthen the courts. The plan set out fifty goals.[14] In late 2005 the

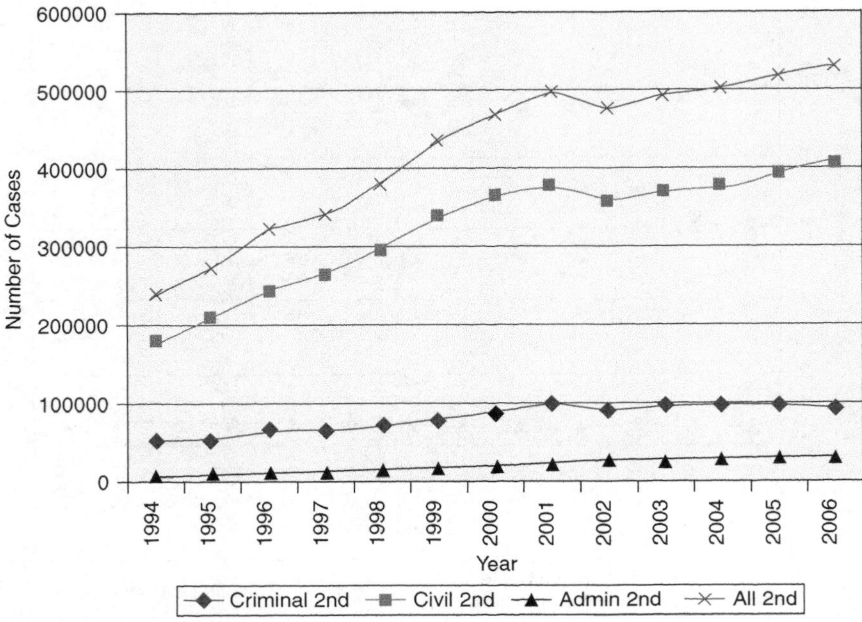

Figure 19.2. Second-instance cases (appeals), 1994–2006

SPC issued a second five-year plan, covering the period from 2004 to 2008, again listing fifty goals.[15]

Both plans address problems in the courts, ranging from judicial training to regularity in court procedures. Such reforms are largely either general and overly abstract, or primarily technical changes designed to address competence and fairness. The goals of the 2005 plan, although similar in number, also appear modest when compared to the 1999 one.[16] The earlier plan embraced some quite significant reforms, including the creation of rules of evidence and the separation within courts of the acceptance of cases from adjudication, and adjudication of cases from enforcement. With one exception—the reform of procedures for capital cases—the 2005 reforms include no major breakthroughs. The 2005 plan does mention the need to address centralizing court appointments, a step towards breaking the link between local authorities, which generally control court appointments, and judges. But it proposes doing so only within "given areas," not nationally. And it raises the topic of centralized financing of courts, but proposes no specific steps towards this goal.

Despite the limited goals of the official plans, courts have undertaken significant reforms designed to strengthen the competence of judges and the professionalism of the court system. Most significantly, the education levels of judges have improved dramatically. Media reports in mid-2005 stated that, for the first time, more than 50 per cent of Chinese judges had university degrees.[17] This marks a sharp increase from 6.9 per cent in 1995. Since 2002, all new judges in China have been required to possess bachelor's degrees. Likewise, in 2002 the Supreme

People's Court stated that sitting judges who were below the age of 40 would be required to obtain a degree within five years or lose their jobs. Older judges who lacked a university education would be permitted to stay only if they completed a training course.[18] Many new judges, in particular at higher-level courts in major cities, now possess graduate degrees in law. New judges in China are also now required to pass the national bar exam, which had a pass rate of just 14 per cent in 2005. Those who became judges before 2002, however, are not required to pass the exam. Court presidents—who generally are the most powerful figures within courts and who take part in deciding major or sensitive cases—likewise are not required to be judges or to pass the bar exam.[19] The SPC has also taken steps to improve the quality of court decisions. In 2005 it issued a notice stating that opinions should include both accurate descriptions of the facts and evidence, and logical arguments and legal reasoning.[20]

Attention to training judges and to well-reasoned opinions appears to be yielding results. Judges comment that greater competence in the judiciary increases the ability of courts to resist external pressure by relying on legal arguments.[21] In addition, judges say that whereas in the past such intervention might have come either formally, in the form of written instructions, or informally through telephone calls, courts increasingly are swayed only by written instructions. Many such instructions tell courts to "emphasize" a case, or handle a particular case "according to law," rather than dictating outcomes, although even instructions in such form may make clear the desired outcome. It is difficult to assess whether interference in China's courts is increasing or decreasing. Some in China argue that external interference is actually growing, reflecting both falling confidence in the courts and the rise of the importance of popular opinion and social protest as means of influence. But it does appear that courts confronted by such pressures are increasingly likely to try to use legal arguments to resist.

Intervention continues, however, and continues to be a legitimate action by Party officials. Greater political sophistication in the courts may also make direct intervention by officials outside them less necessary, because courts are well aware of the cases most likely to be of concern to Party leaders. Improvements have been greater in routine cases than in politically sensitive ones. But the scope of sensitive cases remains wide and includes not only major criminal or political cases, but also those involving the financial interests of the party-state, powerful individuals, or high-profile companies, as well as cases involving a large number of plaintiffs and those receiving media coverage.

Other reforms have been less successful. Lack of enforcement of court decisions continues to be a major problem. Difficulties enforcing decisions reflect problems that courts cannot address on their own: local protectionism, continued intervention in cases by party-state officials and administrative departments, an undeveloped credit system, and weak punishment for noncompliance with court orders. In an acknowledgement of the continuing difficulties in enforcement, the Party's Central Political-Legal Committee issued a notice in December 2005 calling for the cooperation of the police and the procuracy in the enforcement of court judgments and for the establishment of a comprehensive enforcement information system that involves government departments overseeing banks, real estate, vehicles, and other sectors.[22] Similarly, repeated official statements regarding the importance of combating corruption in the judiciary suggest that corruption continues to be a major problem, one that reflects the difficulty of strengthening the authority of courts so long as they remain subject to extensive external influence.

Depoliticization?

Courts continue to be subject to Party leadership. Nevertheless, scholars in China have argued that the courts have gradually shifted from primarily serving as political tools in criminal campaigns in the early 1980s to focusing on providing justice in individual cases today.[23] Court rhetoric has changed over the past decade, reflecting a modest attempt by the courts to shift from being a tool for enforcing Party policy to being a neutral forum for dispute resolution. Many judges have replaced their military-style uniforms with robes—a change viewed as a step forward by some commentators who see it as a signal that judges and courts are not simply another branch of the party-state.[24] Likewise, the new education requirements for judges represent a shift away from primary reliance on political backgrounds in selecting members of the judiciary.

Depoliticization—to the degree it has occurred—may be possible precisely because the courts are not a challenge to Party authority. Local Party organizations continue to oversee court appointments, court presidents are often primarily chosen for political reasons, and the overwhelming majority of judges continue to be Party members. Within the Party hierarchy, the President of the Supreme People's Court continues to rank well below the Minister of Public Security, a pattern generally replicated at local level.

Courts' loyalty to the Party was reemphasized in 2006 with the launching of a new campaign on "socialist rule of law theory" in the courts, procuratorates, justice bureaus, and public security bureaus. The campaign began with a speech by Luo Gan, head of the Party's Central Political-Legal Committee, in which he stated that the goals were to guarantee the legal and political system's "political color" and loyalty to the Party, the nation, the people, and the law. The five elements of the campaign were "ruling the country by law," "implementing law for the people," "maintaining fairness and justice," "serving the overall situation," and "following the leadership of the Party" (p. 9).[25] In the speech Luo appeared to be drawing a distinction between "rule of law" and "socialist rule of law," with the latter emphasizing the legal system's obligation to follow Party leadership, and in particular Hu Jintao's theory of a "harmonious society." The SPC instructed all courts nationwide to educate judges in these principles. In a follow-up speech, Cao Jianming, vice-president of the Supreme People's Court, linked the campaign to the need to avoid the "negative influence of Western rule of law theory"[26]—an apparent reference to those within and outside China advocating Western-style judicial independence for China.

NEW PRESSURES

The recent focus on reinforcing political orthodoxy in the courts reflects the modest reach of top-down court reform. The evolution of Chinese society and governance has also resulted in new challenges for the courts. This section discusses pressures on them that threaten to undermine their already fragile authority.

Media pressure

Over the past decade China's courts have confronted increasingly aggressive and influential media. The media have long been far more powerful actors in the Chinese political system than the courts, serving as both the mouthpiece and the "eyes and ears" of the Party. The growth of commercial media in the 1990s allowed the media to combine their traditional official role with marketized mass appeal. This encompassed expanded coverage of the legal system, including a significant volume of critical reporting on the courts. The Internet has facilitated such coverage, with news on major cases spreading rapidly online and courts finding it more difficult to block critical reporting.[27]

The media are playing an important role in exposing injustice and in pressuring courts to behave fairly. At the same time, media coverage reinforces Party oversight of the courts. Media efforts to stir up and claim to represent popular opinion can lead officials to intervene in cases. Judges complain that there is little they can do to resist media pressure, even when media views are inconsistent with substantive or procedural law.

When media and court views diverge, party-state leaders appear to continue to trust the media more than they do the courts. In a system in which intervention in individual cases by Party officials remains legitimate, even the threat of intervention can be sufficient to affect cases. Deference to media views is accentuated by concern for social stability: the fact that a case is attracting significant media and popular attention is often sufficient reason to justify intervention, regardless of the underlying dispute. The media's ability to influence the courts, and to do so by stirring up popular sentiment online, reflects the degree to which assuaging popular demands for justice remains more important than deciding cases according to legal and procedural norms.

Petitions and protests

Courts have also increasingly come under pressure from petitioners and protestors. As Table 19.1 shows, courts reported handling just under four million letters and visits in 2005. The figure includes only letters and visits to the courts—and thus excludes complaints about the courts raised with other party-state actors or institutions.

Judges say that pressure from letters and visits has increased in recent years and that courts are often under pressure from court and Party superiors to resolve petitioners' grievances. This is the case even when, according to judges, such complaints lack legal merit. In some local courts the annual evaluation of judges' performance and bonuses are based in part on the volume of letters and visits resulting from their cases.[28] Court officials and academics have noted that dealing with petitions and visits is distracting judges from their work handling cases and that courts handle nearly as many petitions as they do cases.[29]

Much press coverage of the issue highlights how letters and visits have led courts to alter incorrect decisions or have assisted in compelling parties to implement court judgments.[30] Judges confirm that some petitions and protests do result in courts reexamining and correcting erroneous cases.[31] Other accounts, however, note that courts have paid petitioners themselves when court decisions fail to provide sufficient funds to petitioners.[32] Commentators have argued that courts are being forced to change decisions to protect social stability and that the letters and visits system is weakening judicial authority.[33] Judges comment that they sometimes alter decisions, pay parties from court funds, or pressure losing parties to pay more money than ordered by the court in order to assuage protestors.[34]

Judges know that the more they respond to protests, the more they will encourage similar actions by others. As with media influence, courts' inability to resist popular pressure reflects concern with social stability by party-state officials. Fear that popular discontent may result in unrest encourages officials to respond to such complaints. Given such concerns, persuading protestors to terminate their protests becomes more important than following legal and procedural standards.

Other problems are also undermining efforts to strengthen the judiciary. Courts continue to lack transparency, with decisions generally not publicly available.[35] They have also imposed new restrictions on the media's ability to cover court proceedings, in an apparent effort to ensure positive coverage of the courts.[36] Courts are increasingly dealing with difficult or sensitive cases by inaction—refusing to accept cases or leaving them unresolved.[37] In addition, there is growing inequality within the courts, with those in less developed areas struggling to find sufficient qualified personnel as existing judges leave to pursue higher-paying jobs as lawyers.

HORIZONTAL DEVELOPMENT AND INNOVATION

Despite these problems, significant change is occurring in China's courts. The most important recent developments are coming from lower courts. Three trends are particularly notable.

First, lower courts are increasingly looking to other courts for guidance when they encounter new or difficult legal questions.[38] In the past, courts generally had little option but to consult higher courts. In recent years, however, judges have increasingly looked horizontally, to courts of equal rank outside their jurisdictions, for guidance. They routinely consult the Internet to assist them when they encounter new questions, to learn how courts elsewhere have handled similar issues. In particular, judges in less developed areas note that they frequently look to online media reports, case summaries, and in some cases decisions posted to court websites to learn how other courts have handled cases.

Such judicial networking, and the development of informal patterns of precedent, may lead to more consistent application of the law. The growth of the Internet may also be facilitating the development of professional identity among judges, who increasingly interact online and who appear ever more aware of the challenges similarly situated judges face elsewhere in China.[39] Greater professional identity among judges is unlikely to alter how they decide sensitive cases, but it may assist them as they seek to combat interference from both within and outside the courts. The growth of horizontal relationships suggests that courts may be able to expand their own autonomy by looking to other courts for guidance rather than to party-state officials or court superiors.

Secondly, judicial networks may foster legal innovation. A small number of local courts have engaged in significant legal innovation. Courts in China have long engaged in experimentation, but in recent years some have issued decisions that appear to challenge existing legal norms directly or consciously break new legal ground. Thus, for example, a court in Henan ruled, in what became known as the *Seed Case*, that a provincial pricing regulation was "spontaneously invalid" because it conflicted with the national Seed Law. The court thus challenged norms that dictate that courts lack the power to invalidate laws or regulations. The case generated a backlash from the provincial people's congress, which ordered the judges responsible to be removed from office. The judges regained their positions after the national media reported on the case.[40]

Likewise, courts in Shanghai, Beijing, and Guangzhou have innovated by finding for the media in defamation cases brought by famous persons. The courts have directly or indirectly suggested that famous persons should withstand a higher degree of scrutiny than ordinary persons—despite the absence of any distinction between ordinary and "public persons" in Chinese defamation law.[41] And in a series of cases brought by university students, courts have held that universities may be sued under China's Administrative Litigation Law—despite the widespread presumption that the law did not apply to universities.[42] The cases have been interpreted as efforts by Chinese courts to expand their jurisdiction in administrative litigation, a notable trend given that commentators have argued that courts have been reluctant to undertake administrative cases given the often influential positions of defendants in such cases.[43]

Some judicial innovation is a consequence of the wide discretion Chinese judges have in resolving cases. Unclear legal standards mean that courts must frequently fill gaps. Nevertheless, in some recent cases they have gone further, directly challenging norms, as in the *Seed Case*, or creating legal standards that lack statutory support.

Court experimentation and innovation occurs in politically safe cases, and outcomes are usually consistent with the interests of important party-state actors. Indeed, it may be that innovation is only possible in cases in which outcomes are consistent with powerful interests or there are no strong adverse interests. Thus, for example, the first case to find a public person standard resulted in a judgment in favor of a newspaper that was a subsidiary of the official mouthpiece newspaper of the Shanghai Municipal Communist Party Committee.

The modest reach of judicial innovation in China highlights a key element of court reform. The SPC does from time to time issue judicial interpretations that go beyond the text of laws the National People's Congress has passed, but such interpretations rarely directly challenge the authority of other institutions. When courts do appear to be seeking to expand their authority, including in defamation litigation, the *Seed Case* and some aspects of administrative litigation, such steps have come from lower courts.[44] Significant institutional change is not the direct result of top-down reform.

The third trend is that, although China's courts are not fora for adjudicating public rights, they have become the place for airing a range of grievances.[45] Over the past decade, litigants have brought a widening array of what might be thought of as public grievances into the courts—including class actions, public interest lawsuits on such issues as women's and environmental rights, and constitutional claims.[46] Many such cases are being brought with the assistance of lawyers who are explicitly seeking to use litigation to bring social change; the fact that China now has more than 150,000 lawyers[47] is resulting in greater incentives for them to bring novel cases. Courts have not always been receptive to such claims. The party-state appears increasingly wary of these efforts, and has imposed new restrictions on lawyers and on public-interest litigation.[48] But the fact that these claims have been permitted and at times even encouraged is particularly notable given China's political system: the combination of class actions, contingency fees, administrative litigation, constitutional litigation, and cause lawyering is not common in authoritarian systems (or in many systems of any type outside the United States).

Such claims also highlight a characteristic of public litigation and cause lawyering in China: when they succeed it is rarely because of court decisions. The primary goal of many of these lawsuits is to generate public, and in particular media, attention sufficient to compel official action. When change does result, it is more often from the intervention of party-state officials than from a court opinion. Litigants may hope for a binding court decision, but using the courts as a forum for generating public pressure is often equally, if not more, important in cases in which claims succeed. The use of litigation to create public pressure and to compel extrajudicial action is not unique to China, but China may be distinct in its extreme reliance on extrajudicial responses to major public disputes in the courts.

RESTRICTED REFORM?

Recent developments do not suggest fundamental changes in courts' power relative to other state actors. This is not surprising: increasing power is not something courts can do on their own, and central Party leaders have not emphasized strengthening the courts' formal power. Nevertheless, despite the formal limitations on court authority, their future role may be significantly influenced by how they define their own roles and by how litigants use them.

Bottom-up developments may also be resulting in courts that are increasingly in conflict with other party-state and official institutions. This is particularly apparent in court interactions with the media, where courts have responded to media oversight by imposing limits on reporting and filing defamation lawsuits. But courts also appear to be increasingly in conflict with People's Congresses and procuratorates, both of which have attempted to strengthen their supervision of the courts, and also with administrative departments.

Explaining new roles

Recognizing the limitations of court reform in China is not meant to trivialize the changes thus far. Indeed, asking why China's courts are not more independent or more powerful may be less important than understanding why they have been permitted to develop as they have. Why have courts been permitted to hear a wider range of grievances and to take even modest steps in the direction of increased authority and autonomy?

Western writings on the roles of courts have largely focused on the question of why a democratic regime would create independent courts.[49] Theories include the desire to make political bargains credible, the usefulness of courts to politicians who wish to shift blame for unpopular policies, courts' roles in keeping administrative bureaucracies in line with government policy, and courts' attraction to political parties that may one day find themselves out of power. Such theories have limited applicability in China, where a nondemocratic regime has encouraged development of the courts, and where courts have limited powers over other administrative actors.

Another common explanation for the creation of a functional legal system is that such institutions are necessary for economic development. An interest in economic development has certainly played a role in China's legal reforms. But this explanation appears unsatisfactory, because economic development has progressed despite the absence of a legal system that provides effective guarantees of property rights. A desire to conform to international norms may play some role—but also seems a weak explanation for China's recent experiences, in particular the encouragement of class actions and cause lawyering. Three alternative theories are more plausible.

First, courts are one of a number of party-state institutions serving as a safety valve for a widening range of popular complaints. Permitting grievances to be raised through class actions, administrative litigation, or even (in a small number of cases) constitutional litigation may be preferable to such complaints not being heard at all—or being raised on the streets. The safety valve function of courts also explains why they may accept but then not decide some difficult cases: the hope may be that once cases are filed, grievances will dissipate over time. The courts are not unique, or even particularly prominent, in this role. The letters and visits system plays a broader, and arguably more significant, function as a safety valve. Courts are thus one of a number of fora for raising grievances, and courts that permit such grievances to be raised act in the interests of social stability.

Concern with social stability also helps explain inconsistent trends in court reform. The party-state has emphasized the role of the courts and has given tremendous attention to courts and law in the media. At the same time, party-state leaders continue to tolerate, and even encourage, a range of official and quasi-official actors to intervene in court decision-making. Concerns with social stability force party-state officials to strive to be even more responsive to public views regarding the courts than might be the case in a democratic system, where the political process provides a mechanism for public grievances to be aired and resolved. The legitimacy of China's leadership depends on its ability both to channel and to contain populism; concerns that popular expressions of outrage may spin out of control encourage rapid intervention in the legal system. The counter-majoritarian function of courts thus may be harder to accept in a non-democratic society, where courts lack authority and public confidence, than in a democracy. This is particularly the case in China, where the rise of social unrest makes officials particularly sensitive to public opinion and where the courts lack a history of being viewed as either authoritative or neutral.

Secondly, the evolving roles of courts, including increasing conflicts with other party-state institutions, reflect the development of institutional competition in the Chinese political system. The central party-state has encouraged a range of official actors—including courts, the media, letters and visits bureaus, the procuratorates, Party discipline authorities, and people's congresses—to play oversight roles, often over each other. Attempts by the courts to expand their autonomy and authority are consistent with similar steps being taken by other actors. This reflects an emerging characteristic of institutional relationships in China, one that appears to be a crucial part of the institutionalization of the party-state that has helped to explain its resilience.[50] The aim appears to be to encourage a range of official actors to expand their roles in resolving grievances and fighting abuses, and to serve as checks on each other. Some greater transparency is encouraged, but within the limits of Party oversight and primarily by party-state actors. Wrongdoing is addressed, and party-state legitimacy is maintained, without fostering the development of nonstate checks on official action. Thus any expansion in court roles or authority may reflect the increased attention to resolving grievances and expanding oversight in the Chinese system in general, not greater authority of the courts. China's leadership is sensitive to the possibility that allowing more prominent roles to nonstate actors may undermine central authority. In the legal system, however, allowing a widening range of grievances to be brought by individuals and organizations may also be an effective tool for asserting state control.

Thirdly, bottom-up development of the courts may be a source of judicial power. The ability of judges to network horizontally may lead to greater authority and autonomy of the courts. The trajectory of court development may not be entirely determined by top-down edicts or constitutional structure. Chinese judges themselves are increasingly looking to the roles judges play in other countries as they seek to define their own positions. Likewise, litigants' aspirations for the legal system appear to derive from both rising attention to the role of law and courts and from international norms.

Fairness without independence?

Understanding why the Chinese party-state has permitted even the level of court reform experienced thus far yields insight into a central question facing China's courts: what are the possible limits of court development in a nondemocratic society? Many in the West and in China have looked to China's courts in the hope that they may play a transformative role in the Chinese political system. But the more pertinent question may be what role courts can play within the current system. Can they serve as fair adjudicators of private disputes, and as checks on some forms of official action, without political change? And, if they do, will they legitimize Party rule, or will the development of a more professionalized judiciary inevitably lead to courts that challenge Party authority? Recent developments and debates in China have largely avoided this question.[51]

China's effort to create courts that act fairly without challenging single-party rule is not unprecedented. Other single-party states—including Spain under Franco and modern Singapore—have had courts that commentators have viewed as largely fair and independent in their handling of nonsensitive or nonpolitical cases.[52] Parallels may also be drawn with Japanese courts, which were largely independent both in the late imperial period and also, after democratization, during the long period of Liberal Democratic Party rule.[53] Similarly, research on Egypt has explored why that authoritarian regime has created an independent constitutional court.[54]

Recent Chinese experience does not fit squarely into any of these models. In contrast to Singapore and Japan, for example, the range of cases deemed to be sensitive in China is extraordinarily wide—and includes not only direct challenges to Party authority or major criminal cases but also a wide range of cases attracting public attention, as well as those involving litigants with ties to party-state officials. In contrast to Franco's Spain, where a degree of independence was possible because courts' powers were extremely limited and courts played little role in creating legal values, China's courts have become significant fora for the airing of rights-based grievances. And in contrast to Egypt, where the constitutional court was established and developed to a great extent because of its role in furthering economic development, courts in China have developed into significant fora for the airing of rights-based claims even without serving as effective guarantors of property rights.[55] Moreover, the most significant changes in Chinese courts' roles appear to be coming from lower courts.

Developing the capacity of China's courts to handle routine cases fairly would be a significant accomplishment. Doing so would also be consistent with two of the three explanations offered above for the development of the courts to date: serving as a safety valve for discontent and grievances and institutionalizing the operation of the party state. But the third explanation, that horizontal and bottom-up development may lead to greater court autonomy, suggests that further development of the courts may also give rise to increased tensions with other party-state actors. As courts continue to develop horizontally, and as judges develop professional identities, it may become increasingly difficult to constrain court development. By encouraging the development of more professional judges, the party-state may also be fostering greater challenges.

Recent developments suggest that courts' ability to serve broader aims may depend on their developing greater authority, either on their own or at the behest of the party-state. Their ability to do so will be shaped by party-state policy, but will also reflect their continued bottom-up development. The roles of courts and judges are no longer solely defined by top-down pronouncements. Judges appear to be looking to the roles judges play in other countries as they seek to define their own positions; litigants' aspirations likewise appear to derive both from rising attention to the role of judges and from international norms. Recent attempts to steer judges away from "Western rule of law theories" are a tacit acknowledgment of such trends. Continued bottom-up development may be crucial to courts' serving the Party's interests—but may also promote new challenges. The most significant development regarding China's courts is that their role in Chinese society is increasingly contested.

NOTES

1. Previously published in *The China Quarterly*, 191 (September 28, 2007): 620–38. © School of Oriental and African Studies, published by Cambridge University Press, reproduced with permission. Links to Internet references in the paper were current at the time of publication in 2007.
2. Clarke (2003: 164–92).
3. For example, see Liao Weihua, "Fayuan zuzhi fa jiang chutai zhuanjia jianyi jiang renmin fayuan gaiming fayuan" ["Court Organization Law will Come Out, Experts Suggests Changing People's Courts into Courts"], *Nanfang Chuang*, December 4, 2004, available from <http://www.southcn.com/news/china/zgkx/200412040062.htm>. Although noting that any reforms must accord with China's "national conditions," the Supreme People's Court (SPC) has acknowledged the need to look overseas in designing court reforms. SPC, "Renmin fayuan dierge wunian gaige gangyao (2004–2008)" ["The Second Five-Year Reform Plan of the People's Courts (2004–2008)"], October 26, 2005, available from <http://www.law-lib.com/law/law_view.asp?id=120832>.
4. "Beijing susong shuliang baozhashi zengzhang, qunian 76% anjian weineng jiean" ["The Number of Cases in Beijing Increases Explosively, the Percentage of Not Closed Cases Increased by 76% Last Year"], *Fazhi Wanbao* [*Beijing Legal Times*], April 27, 2005, available from <http://news.xinhuanet.com/legal/2005-04/27/content_2884636.htm>.
5. Xiao Yang, "Zuigao Renmin Fayuan gongzuo baogao (2007)" ["SPC Work Report (2007)"], March 14, 2007, available from <http://www.chinacourt.org/public/detail.php?id=239089>.
6. For analysis of the decline in caseloads, see Xin He (2007).
7. Interviews. Much of the information in this article is based on interviews with more than 200 judges, lawyers, and academics. Interviews were conducted in Beijing, Shanghai, Guangdong, Jiangxi, Hubei, Jilin, Sichuan, and Shaanxi between 2003 and 2007.
8. Interviews.
9. The number of disputes resolved through People's Mediation Committees grew in 2005, the first increase in more than a decade. The increase probably reflects renewed state emphasis on mediation as part of efforts to construct a "harmonious society."
10. Although the total number of complaints raised is not made public, the system handles an enormous volume of grievances each year (Minzner 2006).
11. Wen Jie, "2006 Niandu quanguo zhongcai anjian shouli shuju jianxi" ["Brief Analysis of Arbitration Cases Decided Nationally in 2006"], *China-arbitration.com*, March 15, 2007, available from <http://www.china-arbitration.com/readArticle.do?id=ff8081 8111440b34011153d7086a0046>.
12. Ministry of Labor and Social Security, *Zhongguo laodong tongji nianjian (2005)* [*Yearbook of China Labor Statistics (2005)*], pp. 523–4, available from <http://www.molss.gov.cn/images/2006-11/16/27110316153762520791.pdf>.

13. For example, see Jiang Zemin, Report to the 15th National Congress of the Communist Party of China, September 12, 1997 (discussing judicial reform), available from <http://dcdj.ccp.org.cn/old/ReadNews.asp?NewsID=3395>.
14. SPC, "Renmin fayuan wunian gaige gangyao" ["The Five-Year Program for Reform of the People's Courts"], October 20, 1999, available from <http://law.chinalawinfo.com/newlaw2002/SLC/slc.asp? db=chl&gid=23701>.
15. "The Second Five-Year Reform Plan of the People's Courts (2004–2008)."
16. Although the plan covers the period 2004–9, it was not made public until 2005. The delay may reflect internal division regarding its contents.
17. "Woguo faguan he jianchaguan zhengti suzhi tigao benke bili guoban" ["The Overall Quality of our Nation's Judges and Procurators is Raised, More Than Half are University Graduates"], *Renmin Ribao* [*People's Daily*], July 17, 2005, available from <http://news.xinhuanet.com/legal/2005-07/17/content_3228617.htm>. The 50% number probably includes not only graduates of four-year universities, but also those from evening classes, junior colleges, or *da zhuan*, as well as correspondence courses. These degrees are not necessarily in law.
18. "Wenping shangqu budengyu shuiping tigao, faguan peixun buneng zhi benzhe wenping qu" ["An Advanced Degree Does Not Equal Enhanced Ability, Judge Training Should Not Solely Aim at Degrees"], *Xinhua Wang* [*Xinhua Net*], March 11, 2004, available from <http://news3.xinhuanet.com/newscenter/2004-03/11/content_1360136.htm>. Obtaining such training, however, appears relatively easy.
19. The failure to reform the appointment system for court presidents continues to serve as a major impediment to strengthening the courts.
20. "Zuigao Renmin Fayuan guanyu zai quanguo fayuan minshi he xingzheng shenpan bumen kaizhan 'Guifan sifa xingwei, cujin sifa gongzheng' zhuanxiang zhenggai huodong de tongzhi" ("Notice of the SPC Regarding Implementing the 'Standardizing Judicial Acts, Enhancing Judicial Justice' Special Alteration and Correction Movement in the Civil and Administrative Divisions of Courts Nationwide"), July 15, 2005, available from <http://www.findlaw.cn/findlaw/lawdetail.asp?id=94852>.
21. Interviews.
22. "Zhongyang Zhengfawei: Dongyuan shehui liliang, qieshi jiejue zhixing nan" ("Central Political-Legal Committee: Mobilize the Resources of Society, Conscientiously Solve the Problem of Enforcing Judgments"), *Xinhua Wang*, January 23, 2006, available from <http://news.xinhuanet.com/legal/2006-01/23/content_4090238.htm>. One response of courts to problems in enforcement has been renewed stress on mediation to reduce contradictions and conflict in society. The most recent SPC work report stated that 30% of all civil cases were resolved through mediation in 2006, and that 55% of first-instance civil cases were mediated or withdrawn prior to judgment (SPC Work Report 2007). Judges cite two primary reasons for this trend: mediated decisions are more likely to be enforced than adjudicated cases, and they are less likely to result in protests and complaints.
23. Yu Zhong, "Lun Zuigao Renmin Fayuan shiji chengdan de zhengzhi gongneng: yi Zuigao Renmin Fayuan linian 'gongzuo baogao' wei yiju" ["On the Actual Political Function of the SPC: Using the Annual 'Work Report' of the SPC as a Base"], *Qinghua Faxue* [*Tsinghua Legal Studies*], 7, available from <http://law-thinker.com/show.asp?id=2829>.
24. "Ganshou sifa zunyan: chuan fapao qiao fachui xingshi beihou de yiyi hezai" ["Feeling the Honor of the Judiciary: What's the Meaning Behind the Actions of Wearing Robes and Hitting Gavels?"], *Xinhua Wang*, June 5, 2002, available from <http://news3.xinhuanet.com/newscenter/2002-06/05/content_425067.htm>.

25. "Luo Gan zai shehui zhuyi fazhi linian yantaoban shang qiangdiao: shenru kanzhan shehui zhuyi fazhi linian jiaoyu, qieshi jiaqiang zhengfa duiwu sixiang zhengzhi jianshe" ["Luo Gan Emphasizes in a Symposium on Socialist Rule of Law Theory: Deepen Education on Socialist Rule of Law Theory, Enhance the Ideological and Political Construction Among Workers in the Political-Legal System"], *Zhongguo Fayuan Wang* [*China Court Web*], April 14, 2006, available from <http://www.chinacourt.org/public/detail.php?id=201753>. In a speech in November 2006, Luo again called for strengthening Party oversight of legal institutions. He also added a more direct critique of those advocating judicial independence and Western-style legal reforms. Luo warned against underestimating the influence of such arguments, in particular arguments that deny the Party's leadership of legal and political institutions, on those working in the political-legal system. He also stated that "hostile forces" were trying to use legal institutions as an entry point for Westernizing and splitting China. Luo Gan, "Zhengfa jiguan zai goujian hexie shehui zhong danfu zhongda lishi shiming he zhengzhi zeren" ["Political and Legal Institutions Shoulder an Important Historical Mission and Political Responsibility in the Construction of a Harmonious Society"], *Qiushi* [*Seeking Truth*], 3 (2007), available at <http://www.qsjournal.com.cn/qs/20070201/GB/qs%5E448%5E0%5E1.htm>.
26. "Cao Jiaming zai shehui zhuyi fazhi linian yantaoban shang qiangdiao: renmin fayuan yao laogu shuli shehui zhuyi fazhi linian" ("Cao Jianming Emphasizes in the Symposium on Socialist Rule of Law Theory: The People's Courts must Steadily Establish Socialist Rule of Law Theory"), *Zhongguo fayuan wang* [*China Court Web*], April 14, 2006, available from <http://www.chinacourt.org/public/detail.php?id=201755>. Cao also spoke of the need to avoid "extreme 'left' thoughts" and the "remnants of feudalism." His speech appeared primarily aimed at placing the courts in line with current Party ideology, and thus perhaps designed to insulate them from criticism for excessive reliance on Western models. But such comments also reflect the SPC's move away from aggressively promoting court reform.
27. For analysis of court–media relations, see Liebman (2005).
28. For example, see "Beijing fayuan dui zhongda shesu xinfang an jiang shixing lingdao baoan zhidu" ["Beijing Courts will Implement a System Making Court Leaders Responsible for the Resolution of Major Litigation-Related Letters and Visits"], *Zhongguo Xinwen Wang* [*China News Net*], July 28, 2005, available from <http://news.qq.com/a/20050728/000926.htm>.
29. SPC Work Report 2004; Zuo Weimin and He Yongjun, "Zhengfa chuantong yu sifa lixing: yi Zuigao Fayuan xinfang zhidu wei zhongxin de yanjiu" ["Politics and Law, Tradition and Judicial Rationality: Research Centered on the SPC's Letters and Visits System"], *Sichuan Daxue Xuebao: Zheshe Ban* [*Journal of Sichuan University: Philosophy and Social Science Edition*], No. 1 (2005), available from <http://www.usc.cuhk.edu.hk/wk_wzdetails.asp?id=4523>. The SPC's 2007 Work Report did not include figures on the total number of letters and visits raised with the courts, but did note that letters and visits to local courts decreased by 11% in 2006 and that those to the SPC decreased by nearly 5%. The continued declines probably reflect the SPC's instruction that courts at all levels should work to reduce litigation-related letters and visits (SPC Work Report 2007).
30. For example, see "Jiangsu Hebei deng sheng bufen qunzhong yueji xinfang shijian diaocha" ["An Investigation of Skipping-Level Letters and Visits by Masses from Jiangsu, Hebei, and Other Provinces"], *Liaowang Xinwen Zhoukan* [*Outlook Weekly*], October 30, 2004, available from <http://news.xinhuanet.com/newscenter/2004-10/30/content_2156474.htm>.

31. Interviews.
32. "Jinhua Zhongyuan zhashi zuohao shesu xinfang gongzuo" ["Jinhua Intermediate Court Works Hard on Litigation-Related Letters and Visits"], December 27, 2005, available from <http://www.jhcourt.cn/news/news_detail.asp?id=626> (link no longer valid; copy on file with author). Courts have also created "judicial relief" funds to assist poor litigants who are unable to enforce judgments in their favor. "Zuigao fayuan tan tuidong quanguo fanwei nei jianli zhixing jiuzhu jijin" ["SPC Discusses Promoting the Establishment of an Enforcement Relief Fund Nationwide"], *Sina.com*, January 21, 2007, available at <http://news.sina.com.cn/c/2007-01-26/114912148273.shtml>.
33. "Woguo xinfang zhidu xianru sichong kunjing mianlin fazhi tiaozhan" ["Our Nation's Letters and Visits System Encounters Four Difficulties, Faces Challenges from Rule of Law"], *Xinhua Wang*, June 30, 2004, available from <http://news.sina.com.cn/c/2004-06-30/12143565398.shtml>.
34. Interviews.
35. He Weifang, "Panjueshu shangwang nan zai hechu" ["What's the Difficulty in Putting Court Decisions Online?"], *Fazhi Ribao* [*Legal Daily*], December 15, 2005, available from <http://law-thinker.com/show.asp?id=3025>.
36. Vivian Wu, "Press Quiet on Changes to Reporting Court Cases," *South China Morning Post*, September 14, 2006.
37. For one example, see "Guangxi bu shouli 13 lei ruoshi qunti an, sheng gaoyuan cheng you guoqing jueding" ["Guangxi Refuses to Accept 13 Categories of Cases Relating to Disadvantaged People, High Court Asserts it is Decided by the Situation of the Country"], *Zhongguo Qingnian Bao* [*China Youth Daily*], August 24, 2004, available from <http://news.qq.com/a/20040824/000070.htm>. Doing so is understandable: many such cases in practice involve complex or sensitive issues potentially touching on social unrest, and are disputes that courts could not resolve on their own.
38. Liebman and Wu (2007).
39. Similar observations have been made regarding the growth of transnational judicial networks (Slaughter 2004: 65–103).
40. For a discussion of the case, see Zhao Lei, "Li Huijuan: tiaozhan difang lifa" ["Li Huijuan: Challenging Local Legislation"], July 25, 2004, available at <http://www.dffy.com/fayanguancha/fangyuan/200407/20040725162155.htm>.
41. Liebman (2006).
42. For analysis of the cases, see Kellogg (forthcoming 2007).
43. For an example of such arguments, see Li Fujin, "Xingzheng shenpan de kunjing yu chulu" ("The Difficulties In and Remedies For Administrative Adjudication"), September 19, 2003, available at <http://www.dffy.com/faxuejieti/xz/200311/20031119203349.htm>.
44. One exception to this pattern was the Qi Yuling case, in which the SPC in 2001 seemed to suggest that a case could be brought directly under the PRC Constitution. The decision was both opaque and controversial, and no subsequent cases have endorsed or acknowledged the principle.
45. Liebman (2006).
46. For example, see Liebman (1998).
47. *Zhongguo falü nianjian* [*China Law Yearbook*] (2006: 1001).
48. In March 2006 the All-China Lawyers Association issued a notice requiring lawyers handling collective (defined as involving ten or more people) or sensitive disputes to report such representation to, and accept "guidance from," the local lawyers' association and justice bureau, "Zhonghua quanguo lüshi xiehui guanyu lüshi banli quntixing

anjian zhidao yijian" ["Guidance Notice of the All-China Lawyers Association Regarding Lawyers' Handling of Group Cases"], March 20, 2006, <http://www.dffy.com/faguixiazai/ssf/200606/20060620110110.htm>.

49. The list provided here is not exhaustive. For more detailed analysis, see Stephenson (2003).
50. Nathan (2003).
51. One exception is the work of "new-left" scholars such as Pan Wei, who have argued that China can and should establish rule of law without democracy. See, for example, Pan Wei, "Fazhi yu weilai de zhongguo zhengti" ["Rule of Law and China's Future Political System"], *Zhanlüe yu guanli* [*Strategy and Management*], No. 5 (1999), at pp. 30–6.
52. Toharia (1975).
53. Haley (2005) notes a long tradition of judicial independence in Japan stretching back to the nineteenth century. In contrast, Mark Ramseyer and Eric Rasmusen (2003: 122– 3) argue that courts in democratic Japan, although generally independent, have yielded to LDP interests in certain sensitive cases. Haley finds no evidence of such political influence on modern Japanese courts.
54. Moustafa (2003).
55. In Egypt, as Moustafa describes, the Constitutional Court has developed into a forum for challenging the regime. In China, in contrast, courts have neither challenged single-party rule nor served as fora for those seeking to do so.

REFERENCES

Clarke, Donald (2003), "Empirical Research into the Chinese Judicial System," in Erik Jensen and Thomas Heller (eds), *Beyond Common Knowledge: Empirical Approaches to the Rule of Law* (Stanford: Stanford University Press), 164–92.

Haley, John O. (2005), "The Japanese Judiciary: Maintaining Integrity, Autonomy and the Public Trust," Washington University in St Louis School of Law, Faculty Working Papers Series, Paper No. 05-10-01. Forthcoming in Daniel J. Foote (ed.), *Law in Japan: A Turning Point* (Seattle: University of Washington Press, 2007).

Kellogg, Tom (forthcoming 2007), "Campus and the Courts: Education Litigation and Judicial Protection of Rights in China," *Harvard Human Rights Law Journal*.

Liebman, Benjamin L. (1998), "Note, Class Action Litigation in China," *Harvard Law Review*, 111: 1523.

——(2005), "Watchdog or Demagogue? The Media in the Chinese Legal System," *Columbia Law Review*, 105/1: 1–157.

——(2006), "Innovation Through Intimidation: An Empirical Account of Defamation Litigation in China," *Harvard International Law Journal*, 47/1: 33–177.

——and Wu, Timothy (2007), "Chinese Network Justice," *Chicago Journal of International Law*, 8/1.

Luo Gan (2007), "Zhengfa jiguan zai goujian hexie shehui zhong danfu zhongda lishi shiming he zhengzhi zeren" ["Political and Legal Institutions Shoulder an Important Historical Mission and Political Responsibility in the Construction of a Harmonious Society"], *Qiushi* [*Seeking Truth*], 3, available at <http://www.qsjournal.com.cn/qs/20070201/GB/qs%5E448%5E0%5E1.htm>.

Minzner, Carl F. (2006), "Xinfang: An Alternative to the Formal Chinese Legal System," *Stanford Journal of International Law*, 42/1: 103–79.

Moustafa, Tamir (2003), "Law Versus the State: The Judicialization of Politics in Egypt," *Law and Social Inquiry*, 28: 883–930.

Nathan, Andrew J. (2003), "Authoritarian Resilience," *Journal of Democracy*, 14/1: 6–17.

Ramseyer, J. Mark and Rasmusen, Eric B. (2003), *Measuring Judicial Independence: The Political Economy of Judging in Japan* (Chicago: University of Chicago Press).

Slaughter, Anne-Marie (2004), *A New World Order* (Princeton: Princeton University Press).

Stephenson, Matthew C. (2003), "'When the Devil Turns . . .': The Political Foundations of Independent Judicial Review," *Journal of Legal Studies*, 32: 61–4.

Toharia, José J. (1975), "Judicial Independence in an Authoritarian Regime: The Case of Contemporary Spain," *Law and Society Review*, 9/3: 475–96.

Xin He (2007), "The Recent Decline in Economic Caseloads in Chinese Courts: Exploration of a Surprising Puzzle," *The China Quarterly*, 190: 352–74.

Yu Zhong, "Lun Zuigao Renmin Fayuan shiji chengdan de zhengzhi gongneng: yi Zuigao Renmin Fayuan linian 'gongzuo baogao' wei yiju" ["On the actual political function of the SPC: using the annual 'work report' of the SPC as a base"], *Qinghua Faxue* [*Tsinghua Legal Studies*], 7.

Index

Introductory Note: References such as '178–9' indicate (not necessarily continuous) discussion of a topic across a range of pages. Wherever possible in the case of topics with many references, these have been divided into sub-topics and/or only the most significant discussions of the topic are listed. Because the entire volume is about 'law', 'economics' and 'China', the use of these terms as entry points has been minimized. Information will be found under the corresponding detailed topics.